Richard Henry Cearke

Old and new Lights on Columbus

Richard Henry Cearke

Old and new Lights on Columbus

ISBN/EAN: 9783743324510

Manufactured in Europe, USA, Canada, Australia, Japa

Cover: Foto ©ninafisch / pixelio.de

Manufactured and distributed by brebook publishing software (www.brebook.com)

Richard Henry Cearke

Old and new Lights on Columbus

OLD AND NEW LIGHTS

ON

COLUMBUS.

WITH

OBSERVATIONS ON CONTROVERTED POINTS AND CRITICISMS.

BY

RICHARD H. CLARKE, LL.D.

RICHARD H. CLARKE,
NEW YORK,
1893.

TO
Our Country:
DISCOVERED BY COLUMBUS, LIBERATED BY WASHINGTON;

IN WHICH

THE LOVE OF LIBERTY IS ONLY EQUALLED BY THE LOVE OF JUSTICE;

UNION IS ENHANCED BY DIVERSITY,

AND

PERPETUATED BY THE LOVE OF COUNTRY;

IN WHICH

MAN AND RELIGION ARE FREE;

CIVILIZATION AND PROGRESS CROWNED BY THE ARTS AND SCIENCES;

AND

EQUAL LAWS PREVAIL;

THIS WORK IS AFFECTIONATELY DEDICATED

BY

The Author.

PREFACE.

MUCH as has been written of Columbus, and numerous as are the works published in regard to his great discovery, especially during the quarto-centennial celebrations, there is a widespread ignorance among the people in regard to many important points. This may be partly attributable to the want of works in one volume and of convenient size; but many and serious misconceptions of events in his life and services, of his motives, of his public and private character, and of important details, as well as of salient points in his career, have become widely circulated of late by adverse criticism and hostile methods of treatment. Not a few able pens and potent names have been enlisted in unfriendly comment, and controverted points have been handled with forensic and partisan animosity. The spirit with which many of these phases of the subject have been handled would be worthy of living controversies in which Columbus were now a living participant, or would seem appropriate to a contemporary public trial in which he were the indicted or impeached official arraigned at the bar of public justice.

On the other hand, excessive eulogy and blind advocacy, in other quarters, have seemed to invite opposition, and it has been cogently said that the undue hostility to Columbus, which has been manifested in recent publications, is the reaction which was awakened by the spirit of resistance to injudicious and indiscriminate laudation. These elements have rendered both extremes unreliable and devoid of historical calmness and judgment. A well-balanced mind and sober historical pen—that of Mr. John Fiske, of Cambridge—has pronounced this reaction more than energetic—as, in fact, violent. Hence it may be said that the works of Count Roselly de Lorgues and Justin Winsor have equally lost that recognition to which industrious research would otherwise have entitled them. Of the latter, Mr. Fiske has justly said : " No one can deny that Las Casas was a keen judge of men, and that his standard of right and wrong was quite as lofty as any one has reached in our time. He had a much more intimate knowledge of Columbus than any modern historian can ever hope to acquire, and he always speaks of him with warm admiration and respect; but how could Las Casas ever have respected the feeble, mean-spirited driveller whose portrait Mr. Winsor asks us to accept as that of the discoverer of America?" The vast importance of the discovery achieved by Columbus, the immense results and unparalleled benefits resulting from his personal services to mankind, while not sufficient to justify a travesty of history, should at least make every true man just and impartial in relating the history of that discovery and of those services. I have aimed with honest purpose to place myself with the latter in the preparation of these pages, and in handling controverted points I have followed this course; but when this method resulted in a conviction that positive wrong had been done to Columbus, as in the charge that he deserted his wife and family when he left Portugal for Spain, and in that other more received impression that Columbus was never married to Beatrix Enriquez, the mother of his son and historian, Fernando, then I have espoused the cause of truth and justice with energy and zeal. On controverted points I have endeavored to be exact and ample in detail, and in order to make the work complete, have given a full history of the personal and public life and career of Columbus. In leading up to him and his work, I have brought in the voyages of the Northmen in the tenth and succeeding centuries, and have related with greater detail the expeditions and explorations of the Portuguese on the west and southern coasts of Africa, in search of Southern Asia. I have taken pleasure in vindicating the great name of Las Casas against the common statement that he was the originator of African slavery in America, and in defending Americus Vespucius against the charge of having purposely robbed Columbus of the honor of bestowing his name upon the new world which he discovered. A vindication of Columbus seemed scarcely necessary, even after such adverse accounts as those of Harrisse and Winsor, for the latter have had little effect on the reputation and honor of Columbus, since he has now received from mankind and from the nations of the earth, and especially from our own country, such honors as have never before been paid to any man.

LIST OF THE PRINCIPAL AUTHORS CONSULTED IN THE PREPARATION OF THIS WORK.

Fernando Colombo, "Historia della Vita e dei Fatti dell' Ammiraglio Don Cristoforo Colombo, suo padre," Venezia, 1686.
Navarrete, "Colleccion Diplomatica."
Spotorno, "Della Origine e Della Patria di Cristoforo Colombo."
Las Casas, "Historia de las Indias."
Muñoz, "Historia del Nuovo Mundo."
Herrera, "General History of the Voyages and Conquests of Castilians."
Oviedo y Valdez, "Historia Nat. y gen. de las Indias."
"Letter of Christopher Columbus to their Majesties."
Malte Brun, "Géographie Universelle."
Humboldt, "Histoire de la Géographie."
Gomera, "Historia de las Indias."
Feragallo, "Cristoforo Colombo in Portogallo."
Humboldt, "Cosmos."
Irving, "The Life and Voyages of Christopher Columbus and his Companions."
Lafitare, "Conquêtes Portugais."
Oviedo, "Cronica de las Indias."
Cura de los Palacios, MS., "Hist. Ferdinand and Isabella."
Peter Martyr, "Letters and Decades of the Ocean Sea."
Charlevoix, "Histoire de St. Domingo."
De Lorgues, "Histoire de la Vie et des Voyages de C. Colomb."
De Lorgues, "L'Ambassadeur de Dieu."
Mariana, "Historia de España."
Ramusio, "Della Navigazioni e Viaggi."
Fernando Columbus, "Journal of Columbus."
Humboldt, "Examen Critique."
Barros, "Asia Portugueza."
Robertson, "History of America."
Hakluyt, "Collection de Voyages."
Herrera, "Historia des Indias."
"Letter of Dr. Chanca," "Raccolta di Viaggi."
Christopher Columbus, "Memoria del Almirante."
Fernando Colombo, "The Admiral's Narrative of his Third Voyage."
Marmocchi, "Raccolta di Viaggi," "Letter to the Governess of the Infanta Don Juan."
Christopher Columbus, "Letter from Jamaica to their Majesties."
Diego Mendez, "Narrative."
Francesco Tarducci, "The Life of Christopher Columbus." Translated by Henry F. Brownson.
Rev. Arthur George Knight, S. J., "The Life of Christopher Columbus."
General James Grant Wilson, "Memorials and Footprints of Columbus," in Bulletin of the American Geographical Society, 1884, No. 2.

Cotolendy, "La Vie de Cristophe Colomb et la Découverte."
Giralomo Benzoni, "La Historia del Nuovo Mundo."
R. H. Major's "Letters of Columbus," Hakluyt Society, 1847.
Prescott's "Ferdinand and Isabella."
"Columbus and How he Received and Transmitted the Spirit of Discovery," by Justin Winsor.
"The Discovery of America," by John Fiske.
"Have We a Portrait of Columbus?" Charles P. Daly, 1893.
The Marquis de Belloy's "Columbus and the Discovery of America." English Translation, 1878.
"Christoforo Colombo," by M. A. Lazzaroni, Milano, 1892.
"The Wife of Columbus," by Nicolau Florentino (Pereira) and Regina Maney, N. Y., 1893.

TABLE OF CONTENTS.

CHAPTER I.

Introductory—The new and the old worlds each ignorant of the existence of the other when Columbus discovered America—Views of the learned on the existence of continents and great islands beyond the western ocean prior to and at the time of the discovery—The sea of darkness—Christopher Columbus meets the prejudices and opinions of the learned world, and breaks the spell—The man of genius and achievement.. 13

CHAPTER II.

Birth of Columbus—Controversy over his birthplace—His parentage, early boyhood, education—A weaver of woollen goods—Becomes a sailor at the age of fourteen—Early voyages—Conditions of commerce and customs of warfare in the fifteenth century—The Colombos, a family of naval and maritime adventure—The naval services of Columbus—Adventures and encounters at sea—At Lisbon, Madeira, Funchal—His first marriage—Makes maps for a living—Residence at Funchal—Birth of his son Diego—Death of his first wife—His hair turns gray—Voyage to Iceland—His plan of western Atlantic discoveries—His studies.. 24

CHAPTER III.

Pioneer discoveries of the Portuguese in the fifteenth century—Prince Henry the Navigator, of Portugal, the precursor of Columbus—Character of Columbus—Residence at Lisbon—Maritime history and spirit of the age—Thirst for new discoveries—Columbus studies ancient and modern authors—The foundations upon which Columbus built his theory of western and undiscovered countries—His enthusiasm and firmness—Correspondence with Dr. Toscanelli—Columbus announces his theory and plan—Proposals to Venice, to Genoa, and their rejection—Presents them to the King of Portugal—Again rejected—Bad treatment—Columbus shakes the dust of Portugal from his feet—An accusation refuted. 49

CHAPTER IV.

Columbus in Spain—Negotiations with Spanish noblemen—Ferdinand and Isabella—Columbus at the Spanish court—Royal audiences—Presents his plan—Columbus at Salamanca—Follows the court—A soldier—Refusal—Departure from court—Columbus at the Convent of La Rabida—Visits Lisbon—Sends his brother to England—Renews his application to Spain—Delays—Departure—Recall—Renewal of Negotiations—Success—Terms of compact between Columbus and the Spanish sovereigns—Cristoval Colon—Lofty aspirations.......... 78

CHAPTER V.

Columbus at Cordova—His social position—Beatrix Enriquez—Second marriage—Birth of their son Fernando—First origin of the question raised as to the second marriage of Columbus—Nicolao Antonio—Palma y Freytas—Spotorno—Napione—Navarrete—Count Roselly de Lorgues—Cancellieri—Washington Irving—Humboldt—The Jesuit, Father Knight—The question discussed—Thirty reasons sustaining the marriage of Columbus and Beatrix—Lazzaroni's "Cristoforo Colombo" sustains the second marriage—Copious extracts therefrom—The judgment of an American woman—Constance Goddard Du Bois's "Columbus and Beatrix"—Extracts—Conclusion............................ 100

CHAPTER VI.

Preparations—First voyage—The Pinta disabled—Arrival at the Canaries—The Pinta repaired—Escape from Portuguese vessels—Fears of the sailors—Columbus discovers the line of no variations of the needle—Indications of land—Watches day and night—His devotions—Masses of seaweeds—Fears of sailors and mutiny—Columbus overcomes them—Hope revived—Columbus sees a light on the shore—The new world is discovered—The landing................ 158

CHAPTER VII.

Columbus cruises among the Bahama Islands—St. Mary of the Conception—Fernandina, now Exuma—Saometa—Island of Isabella—Columbus in search of Cipango and the kingdom of the Grand Khan—Discovery and exploration of Cuba—In search of the fabled island of Babeque—Columbus deserted by the Pinta—Discovery of tobacco and the potato—Discovery and exploration of Hispaniola—Shipwreck—Intercourse with the Indians—Guacanagari's hospitality—Fortress of La Navidad erected—Columbus sails for Spain—Meets the deserter Pinzon and the Pinta—Skirmish with the natives—Storms at sea—The Azores—At the island of St. Mary's—Lands in Portugal—At the Portuguese court—Return to Palos... 183

CHAPTER VIII.

Columbus received with joy at Palos—Triumphant entry into Barcelona—Reception at court—Honors paid to him by Ferdinand and Isabella—The pope divides the new lands of the world between Spain and Portugal—Preparations of Columbus for a second voyage—Difficulties with officials—Second voyage of Columbus... 210

CHAPTER IX.

Columbus crosses the Atlantic a second time—Discovers the Caribbee Islands—Guadeloupe Island—Cruises among the Caribbees—Cannibals—Arrival at Hispaniola—Finds the fortress and garrison of La Navidad destroyed—The Cacique Guacanagari—The city of Isabella founded—Disease among the Spaniards—Exploits of Alonzo de Ojeda—Ships sent back to Spain—Dissatisfaction and mutiny in the colony—The admiral at Cibao—The interior of the island; the natives; their character, customs, religion, and traditions—Sickness—Spanish soldiers distributed through the island—Disappointment and discontent against Columbus—Enmity of Father Boïl... 236

CONTENTS.

CHAPTER X.

The condition of Hispaniola—Columbus makes a voyage of exploration to Cuba—Discovers Jamaica—The Queen's Gardens—East and southern coast of Cuba—South side of Jamaica—Voyage along the south side of Hispaniola—Columbus falls into a deep lethargy—Return to Isabella—Bartholomew Columbus—Henry VII. might have taken the place of Spain as the patron of Columbus—Margarite, the rebel, and Father Boíl; their departure from Hispaniola—Caonabo besieges Fort St. Thomas—Arrival of ships from Spain—Indian slaves—Columbus subjugates the rebellious natives—Tribute imposed—Columbus intrigued against at court—Aguado sent out to investigate his conduct—Aguado's arrogance toward the admiral—Mines discovered at Hayna—Columbus returns to Spain with Aguado... 278

CHAPTER XI.

Columbus arrives in Spain—Awaits an invitation to court—Wears in public the habit of a Franciscan monk—His reception at Burgos—Proposes a third voyage—Refuses a principality—Establishes a mayorazgo—Makes his will—Delays suffered from the Bureau of the Indies—Third voyage—Discovers Trinidad—Sails through the Gulf of Paria—Discovers the continent—Discovers the equatorial swelling of the earth and the Gulf Stream—His theories and speculations—Reaches Hispaniola—The Adelantado—Military posts—Conspiracy and rebellion of Roldan—Treatment of the rebels—Insurrections of the chief Guarionex—The Adelantado's campaign in Ciguay—Confusion in Hispaniola—Roldan and the rebels take possession of Xaragua—Negotiations with the rebels; their treachery; Columbus compelled to accept their terms—Columbus and the Indians—Why his name was not conferred on the new world—Las Casas not the originator of African slavery in America—Americus Vespucius.. 332

CHAPTER XII.

Roldan resumes his office as alcalde mayor—His arrogance—Columbus grants lands to Roldan's followers—Indian service—Rebels returning to Spain—Roldan and Ojeda—The admiral despondent—Vision of Columbus—Improved condition of affairs—Intrigues against Columbus at the court of Spain—Bobadilla appointed to examine into the affairs of Hispaniola and the administration of Columbus—His violence—Columbus summoned before him—Arrested and placed in chains—Sent to Spain in this condition—Sensation in Spain—Appears at court—Bobadilla superseded by Ovando—Columbus proposes to redeem the Holy Sepulchre—Proposals for a fourth voyage—Departure for the new world—His precautions—Signature.. 406

CHAPTER XIII.

Fourth voyage of Columbus—Repelled by Ovando from San Domingo—Foretells an approaching storm—Escapes unharmed, while Bobadilla and Roldan are lost at sea—Discovers the continent at Honduras—Severe illness—Veragua—Exploration of the Mosquito coast—Abandons the search for a central passage to the other sea—Attempted colony at Belen River—Hostile encounters with the natives—Abandons Veragua—Loses two ships—The remaining two ships, with the admiral and his companions on board, stranded on the coast of Jamaica—

Endures disaster heroically—Heroism of Diego Mendez—Desperate condition of Columbus—Mutiny of the Porras brothers—The natives of Jamaica—Eclipse of the moon—Mendez and Fiesco carry word of his condition to Ovando—Ovando's conduct—Battle with the Porras rebels—Ovando's administration at Hispaniola—Escape from Jamaica—Visit to Hispaniola—Return to Spain..... 475

CHAPTER XIV.

Columbus enters Spain—His sickness, poverty and distress—Application to the court for justice—Death of Queen Isabella—Columbus has himself conveyed to court—His petitions for redress and the restitution of his rights unheeded—Ingratitude of King Ferdinand—The last illness of Columbus—His death—His epitaph—Removals of his remains—His family—His character and services—The quadri-centennial celebration of the discovery of America by Columbus... 554

OLD AND NEW LIGHTS ON COLUMBUS.

CHAPTER I.

> "Ocean, thou dreadful and tumultuous home
> Of dangers, at eternal war with man'
> Death's capitol, where most he dominates,
> With all his chosen terrors frowning round,
> Wide opening and loud roaring still for more,
> Too faithful mirror!"
> —ANONYMOUS.

> "Let ignorance with envy chat;
> In spite of both, thou fame shalt win."
> —HERRICK, TO BEN JONSON.

> "His was the gifted eye, which grace still touched
> As if with second nature; and his dreams,
> His childish dreams, were lit by hues of heaven—
> Those which make Genius."
> —MISS LANDON.

> "Our fortunes meet us;
> . . . if good, the act of heav'n."
> —DRYDEN.

IN spite of occasional theories of Greek or Roman philosophers as to the shape of the earth, and of dim traditions of savage tribes almost shapeless and objectless, the old world and the new were equally ignorant of the existence of each other, from remotest times down to October 12th, 1492, when Christopher Columbus, with undaunted courage, consummate skill and action, realizing his own theories and verifying traditions and prophesies, electrified the one by his discovery of the other. Now at last mankind saw their own planet, a beautiful sphere bathed in celestial light.

When the admiral and his companions approached and anchored their three vessels at the islands of the Western Hemisphere, which they had just discovered, the gentle natives either fell upon the earth on their faces and worshipped the new-comers as divine beings, or, frightened and dismayed at so sudden and marvellous an apparition, fled to the woods in terror. When they saw these noble and resplendent strangers land with pomp and pageantry, and, displaying their golden banner, take formal possession of the country, a ceremony then little understood by the natives, they exclaimed : " Turey, Turey !" " You are from Heaven !" The fierce Caribs of the Caribbean Islands, and later the warlike tribes of the mainland along the coast of Honduras, marshalled their naked warriors in battle array to repel the celestial visitors.

On the other hand, when Columbus broached his theories and presented his propositions and plans, for the discovery of new countries in the western ocean, to the civilized world, and demanded ships to sail westward across the Atlantic in search of the promised land, his suit was rejected by one sovereign after another ; he traveled from country to country, and from one royal court to another, to plead the cause of a new world, before unwilling and incredulous nations. He was derided as a needy adventurer and visionary theorist, and as he passed through the streets, which afterward he traversed in triumph, even the little children mocked and scoffed at him, and they placed their hands upon their foreheads to indicate, as they had been taught, that he was a madman. The august Council of Salamanca, composed of the most learned men of the age, to whom the propositions of Columbus were referred for investigation by Ferdinand and Isabella, the Spanish sovereigns, and before whom he elaborately and ably explained them and answered all objections, reported to their Majesties that the plan " was vain and impossible, and that it did not become such great princes to engage in an enterprise of the kind on such weak grounds as had been advanced."[*]

Whatever may have been the learning and the intelligence of the ancients in relation to the shape, size, extent, and geography of the earth, and as to the existence of other continents, all these had been swept aside and buried in oblivion by the great social, political, and moral cataclysm caused by the terrific incursions of the northern barbarians into Southern Europe. It is certain that, at the time Christopher Columbus sprang the subject upon the world toward the close of the fifteenth century, Europe and Asia knew nothing of the existence of western islands and continents in the Atlantic, and wholly rejected every such theory.

---

[*] Irving's " Life of Columbus," vol. i., p. 100.

The Atlantic Ocean, vast, unexplored, and stormy, was an object of fear and terror to all men ; even the learned and experienced navigators regarded it with awe and aversion. It was called the Sea of Darkness,* and the belief was universal, except possibly with a very few learned ones, that it was unnavigable and impassable. It was regarded by the most experienced navigators as a boundless and tempestuous expanse, without opposite shores, and they regarded the known world as already reaching to the limits of the habitable or passable globe. It was universally believed that our planet was embraced by a raging and torrid zone, subject to the unbridled, fiery, and all-consuming flames of the sun, and that this zone formed a region of impassable and impassive heat, and that the two hemispheres were forever and irretrievably separated from each other by it ; the waters of the torrid zone, under the vertical and raging fires of the sun, were a caldron of boiling and seething billows, and that sea and land were scorched to a heat in which animal and vegetable life could not be maintained.† Iceland was regarded as the *ultima Thule*, the utmost boundary of the earth ;‡ and the learned Gravier, in our own times, writes, while commenting on the space lying beyond Thule or Iceland, in passages which I translate from his profound work, thus : " According to Strabo, who quotes Polybius, Pythias should have said that beyond Thule there is no longer to be met nor earth, nor sea, nor air, but a concretion of these different elements, similar to the *marine pulmonate*, which holds in suspension and reunites by one common bond the earth, the sea, and the air, and no longer allows man to walk or to navigate.

" The learned have much discussed this *marine pulmonate*, and have successively transferred it into smoke thrown out by Mount Hekla, into polar seas, into pumice-stones proceeding from volcanoes, which seem to exist toward the seventy-fifth degree.

" A seaman, who had seen only the beautiful blue sky of the Mediterranean, who partook more or less of the ideas prevailing in his time upon the cosmography of the hyperborean regions, could believe that he had reached the extreme border of the

---

* De Costa, " Pre-Columbian Discovery of America," xii.
† " Historia Espan. Mariana," lib. ii., cap. 22.
‡ Strabo, " Polybius."

globe accessible to man, and compare the atmosphere of these regions to the *marine pulmonate*." *

Even the famous "Dialogues of Plato," preserved in their temple by the Egyptian priests, and now given to the modern world in all their details, represent the Atlantic Ocean as having been in ancient times navigable, but in consequence of the great cataclysm, which destroyed the island or continent of Atlantis, it had now become impassable by reason of the vast quantities of slimy mud resulting from the submerging of those immense regions of the earth. "But afterward there occurred violent earthquakes and floods, and in a single day and night of rain all your warlike men in a body sunk into the earth, and the island of Atlantis in like manner disappeared, and was sunk beneath the sea ;' and that is the reason why the sea in those parts is impassable and impenetrable, because there is such a quantity of shallow mud in the way ; and this was caused by the subsidence of the island." †

Considering the age of the human race and the duration of man's dominion on the earth, we can but be surprised at the slow growth of the science of geography, and how little was known in the time of Columbus concerning the planet upon which we live. While several of the wisest men of the ancients entertained most intelligent views of the shape and size of the earth, still after the overthrow of the Roman Empire scarcely more was known of the earth than the countries immediately around the Mediterranean Sea, and while scarcely anything was known of Scandinavia, Russia, and Northern Germany, the vaguest and most erroneous notions prevailed as to them and other lands known only by name ; and almost nothing was known of Siberia, Tartary, China, Japan, and of the great Asiatic archipelago. There was a strong tendency, even among the learned, to exaggerate the proportions of Europe and to underrate those of Asia. Among the egregious errors then prevailing were the belief that the Ganges flowed entirely to the east and emptied into the eastern ocean, while the Caspian Sea was believed to be the northern limit of the earth ; and what we know now to be

---

* "Decouverte de l'Amerique par les Normans au X° Siècle," xvii.

† Plato's "Dialogues," ii., 517. "Timæus," as given in Donnelly's "Atlantis," p. 11.

Siberia and Tartary were regarded as an inland sea connecting the Caspian with the eastern ocean. The Mediterranean borders of Africa alone were known, and all south of these was regarded as the torrid zone and so ravaged with the solar flames as to be uninhabitable. This view of the torrid zone toward the equator prevailed even to the time of Columbus, and was only dissipated by the bold explorations of the Portuguese along the west coast of Africa, and by Columbus himself, who visited the equator. Strabo, in the first quarter of the first Christian century, while rejecting the ancient belief that Africa was circumnavigable, intelligently adhered to the belief in an encircling ocean ; and Pomponius Mela, the earliest of the Roman geographers, in the time of the Emperor Claudius, divided the world into two hemispheres : the Northern, which embraced all of the known world, such as Europe north of the Mediterranean and west of the Tanais ; Africa, south of the Mediterranean and west of the Nile, and such parts of Western Asia as were known ; the Southern Hemisphere embraced all the rest of the earth, which was unknown. But in the middle of the second century, when the Roman Empire had acquired its greatest extent and all its provinces were known and surveyed and their census taken, the great geographer Ptolemy, who had abandoned the more intelligent notion of Strabo as to a circumambient ocean, contented himself with the theory of a vast expanse of unknown land ; but while he added much to mankind's knowledge of the geography of the earth, including slight glimpses at the Baltic countries, Russia, Scythia, and even China and India, still Africa was delineated as extending indefinitely to the south, and was continued around so as to join Eastern Asia, thus surrounding the Indian Ocean by land, like the Mediterranean. It is true and wonderful that in the ninth century the Northmen from Iceland discovered and colonized Greenland, and visited lands now known by us to be the shores and islands of our own Atlantic coast ; but these bold adventurers never understood the geographical bearing of their own discoveries, nor that they had entered a western hemisphere, nor was the knowledge of these discoveries given to mankind until recent years. Such were the circumstances and results as to deprive their achievements of the character of discoveries. Some have supposed that Columbus may have heard of the expeditions of the Northmen during his visit to Iceland in

1477; but his son, Fernando, who recorded the sources of information upon which his father acted, fails to mention this as among the varied and numerous data possessed by the great admiral; for the latter left, among his papers, the most ample memoranda of all the information he had ever obtained, bearing upon his theory of the existence of western islands and continents across the Atlantic.

But it was the progress of European advances into Eastern Asia that contributed the most important results to the progress of geography, and it was this growth of European knowledge of the vast extent of Asia in that direction that so greatly influenced the work of Christopher Columbus, who to the last aimed at discovering a Northwest passage to Asia, and lived and died in the belief, in which all the world united with him then, that the islands and lands he had discovered in the Western Hemisphere were parts of Asia. Prior to the thirteenth century Asia was but little known to Europeans, but in that century the Popes sent missionaries into the distant regions of that continent. Thus in 1246 we behold Pope Innocent IV. sending the celebrated Father John de Plano Carpini with Franciscan monks to convert the subjects of the Tartar Emperor, Kayuk Khan, and these zealous missionaries extended their apostolate to the far regions of Thibet. But even prior to this, toward the middle of the twelfth century, startling rumors were current in Europe that there reigned in Asia a powerful Christian emperor, Prester John, who had already broken the power of the Mussulmans, and was ready to come to the assistance of the Crusaders. Pope Alexander III. determined to lose no time in opening communication with this famous yet shadowy chief, who was at once both king and pontiff, and on September 27th, 1177, he sent a special embassy, headed by the heroic physician, Philip, bearing a letter and proposal for a union of this Asiatic part of the Church with the rest of Christendom. Although Dr. Philip never returned with tidings of Prester John, this effort was followed by the missions under Pope Innocent IV., in the thirteenth century, and again in 1253, when St. Louis, King of France, sent Rubruiquis and other missionaries in search of Prester John, and these penetrated into Asia far beyond all other European expeditions. In 1271 the celebrated Venetian discoverer and geographer, Marco Polo, went forth with his father and uncle to reach the far-famed court of the Tartar conqueror of China, the celebrated Kublai Khan. They traveled three years, reached the city of Yehking, which was near the present site of Peking, and Marco Polo, after a residence of twenty-four years in Asia, returned to Europe and published his great work on his travels, thus revealing to Europe the existence of the vast Empire of Japan and of many of the islands of the East Indies. Marco Polo was a favorite author of Columbus, who was confident that in his voyages to the Western Continent he would reach the countries visited and described by that great traveler and writer, and that he was destined to reach the court of the Grand Khan of Tartary, and effect the conversion of that famous potentate and the union of the Grand Khan and his vast empire, teeming with countless populations, with the Christian Church, a result which had been sought in vain for centuries by popes, kings, and apostles. On his first voyage Columbus actually carried letters from Ferdinand and Isabella addressed to, and which he expected to deliver in person to, the Grand Khan. The most enlightened view reached by the advanced cosmographers and scholars of the fifteenth century, by such men as Columbus and Dr. Toscanelli, the learned and venerable cosmographer of Florence, the friend and correspondent of the admiral, was that the eastern shores, countries, and islands of Asia lay over against the western coasts of Europe and Africa, and that they would be reached by sailing across the Atlantic, the Sea of Darkness, in a direct western course.

It was during the lifetime of Columbus, and before his great discovery, that the most gigantic strides were made in the science of navigation and in the knowledge of the earth's geography. We shall show hereafter, in this book, the brilliant and useful part he took in these enlightened and practical advances—a part which culminated in the greatest achievement in the history of our race, the discovery of America. But, in order to accomplish this great boon for mankind, he had to contradict the opinions, the traditions, and the honest convictions of men and of the world. The chaos spoken of by Washington Irving, in the following passage of his "Life of Columbus," is similar to the conglomerate of earth, air, sea, and smoke spoken of by Gravier under the name of *marine pulmonate*, as expressing the absurd views entertained concerning the Atlantic, even by the most learned in the time of Columbus. "Certain it is," says Mr.

Irving, "that at the beginning of the fifteenth century, when the most intelligent minds were seeking in every direction for the scattered lights of geographical knowledge, a profound ignorance prevailed among the learned as to the western regions of the Atlantic; its vast waters were regarded with awe and wonder, seeming to bound the world as with a chaos, into which conjecture could not penetrate and enterprise feared to venture." In pressing his great suit and pleading the cause of a new world, Columbus encountered all the supposed learning of past ages, as well that of his contemporaries, to which, I think, Mr. Justin Winsor attaches an exaggerated importance.* Rejected by the Council of Salamanca, as it had previously been pronounced by the most learned men at the court of Portugal, as an "enterprise of a wild, chimerical nature," the admiral, toward the close of the fifteenth century, had also to meet and refute the arguments mistakenly based upon passages from the Bible, and also such as could be found or deduced from the writings of the Christian Fathers. Lactantius, one of the earliest and most learned of the Fathers of the Church, had rejected and ridiculed the theory of the Antipodes, which had been broached by the ancients, in the following remarkable and sarcastic passage: "Is there any one so foolish as to believe that there are antipodes with their feet opposite to ours—people who walk with their heels upward and their heads hanging down? that there is a part of the world in which all things are topsy-turvy; where the trees grow with their branches downward, and where it rains, hails, and snows upward? The idea of the roundness of the earth was the cause of inventing this fable of the antipodes, with their heels in the air; for these philosophers, having once erred, go on in their absurdities, defending one with another." † And St. Augustine wholly rejected the fact of the antipodes "as incompatible with the historical foundations of the earth." Having no acquaintance with the geography of the polar regions and the lay of the land of Northern Asia, as we know them, he regarded the theory of the antipodes as contradicting the scriptural account of the unity of the human race; and the races of men in-

---

* "Christopher Columbus, and how he Received and Transmitted the Spirit of Discovery," by Justin Winsor, 1891.

† Firmiani Lactantiæ, "Divin. Instit.," lib. iii., cap. xxiv.

habiting the opposite side of the earth could not have been descended from Adam and Eve, since there was no land passage for them to take from the cradle lands of the old world, " and it was impossible for them to have passed the intervening ocean." *

The genius, the learning, and the convictions of Columbus arose above opposition, prejudice, and tradition. His knowledge of the subject, acquired by long years of study, his cogent, clear, and unanswerable reasoning, his bold and confident pledge to the world that, if afforded the opportunity and provided with ships, he would discover a new world—all point him out for all time, as it did to the intelligent minds of Ferdinand and Isabella, as the man that was fitted, if not destined, to achieve this splendid and unparalleled conquest. He believed in his own destiny, and being a man of profoundly religious character, he failed not to find in the sacred writings texts which pointed to him as the man of destiny—the man that was to lead the way, by his grand discoveries and achievements, to extending the realms of Christendom to vast and unknown countries. He sustained his startling propositions with scientific knowledge and facts drawn from the very nature, size, shape, and from the known geography of the earth, from the reports of experienced and veteran navigators, and the writings of the learned in all ages. While there were errors of detail in the theories and anticipations of the great discoverer, such as his expectation and belief that Asia was the land he would find, and his miscalculation of the size of the earth, arising out of the then current imperfect geographical knowledge of the world, his main proposition was correct, and he made it good by the unanswerable argument of success. All the learned men, scientists and scholars of his day, with few exceptions, derided the startling conceptions of Columbus. After the great discovery had been accomplished they also adopted the mistaken hypothesis that the countries discovered were parts of Asia. But they now rejoiced that their lives were cast in an age of such brilliant achievements ; that they had been permitted to witness the consummation of so grand an event, and to welcome discoveries pregnant with the fate of empires and of worlds. I cannot more appropriately close this introductory chapter than by quoting the language of the historian, William H. Prescott, who,

---

* St. Augustine, " De Civitate Dei," lib. xvi., c. ix.

after describing the magnificent and royal reception accorded to Columbus on his return from discovering the new world, says : " It was, indeed, the proudest moment in the life of Columbus. He had fully established the truth of his long-contested theory, in the face of argument, sophistry, sneers, scepticism, and contempt. He had achieved this not by chance, but by calculation, supported through the most adverse circumstances by consummate conduct. The honors paid him, which had hitherto been reserved only for rank or fortune or military success, purchased by the blood and tears of thousands, were, in his case, an homage to intellectual power, successfully exerted in behalf of the noblest interests of humanity." *

It seems almost impossible to study the life and character of Columbus without becoming impressed with an indulgent if not sympathetic view of the idea which the man himself entertained, that he was foreordained to become the discoverer of the new world, and to yield our admiration to the thought. Many learned, grave, and practical authors, who have written on the subject, appear to become unconsciously imbued with the idea of destiny, which Columbus entertained of himself. The good but perhaps over-zealous Count de Lorgues, in one of his spirited works on Columbus, boldly asserts that " he who does not believe in the supernatural cannot comprehend Columbus ;" and our own Bancroft, seemingly yielding to the same inspiration, says : " Poets of ancient and of more recent times had foretold that empires beyond the ocean would one day be revealed to the daring navigator. The genial country of Dante and Buonarotti gave birth to Christopher Columbus, by whom these lessons were so received and weighed that he gained the glory of fulfilling the prophecy." † And again he speaks of Columbus as one " who was still the promiser of kingdoms, holding firmly in his grasp ' the keys of the ocean sea,' claiming, as it were from Heaven, the Indies as his own, and ' dividing them as he pleased.' It was then that through the prior of the convent his holy confidence found support in Isabella, the Queen of Castile, and in 1492, with three poor vessels, of which the largest only was decked, embarking from Palos for the Indies by way of the west,

---

* Prescott's " Ferdinand and Isabella," vol. ii., p. 164.
† " History of the United States," 1883, vol. i., p. 7.

Columbus gave a new world to Castile and Leon, 'the like of which was never done by any man in ancient or in later times.' " *
And again, speaking of the predictions by ancient poets of the discovery of America, and of the belief prevalent for ages " that vast inhabited regions lay unexplored in the west," he says : " But Columbus deserved the undivided glory of having realized that belief."†

---

* Bancroft's "History of the United States," vol. i., p. 9.
† *Ib.*, 1854, vol. i., p. 6.

CHAPTER II.

> " How young Columbus seem'd to rove,
>   Yet present in his natal grove,
>   Now watching high on mountain cornice,
>   And steering, now, from purple cove ;
>
> " Now pacing mute by ocean's rim,
>   Till in a narrow street and dim,
>   I stay'd the wheels at Cogoleto,
>   And drank, and loyally drank, to him."
>
> —TENNYSON.

> " The dark blue jacket that enfolds the sailor's manly breast
>   Bears more of real honor than the star and ermine vest ;
>   The tithe of folly in his head may wake the landsman's mirth,
>   But Nature proudly owns him as her child of sterling worth."
>
> —MISS ELIZA COOK.

THE time and the place of the birth of Christopher Columbus have been, among rival cities and historians, the subjects of warm controversy and of consequent careful research. While the day of his birth has never been ascertained, and there exists a difference of many years between the earliest and the latest years assigned for his nativity, it is now considered by the far greater number of authentic historians that he was born in the year 1446, or possibly early in 1447.*

Still greater has been the diversity of claims as to his birthplace, and far more earnest the controversy. While Genoa is the foremost and most successful claimant, even the Genoese have warmly disputed among themselves for the honor, and whether Columbus was born in the city, or in some village or

---

* Mr. Irving gives 1435 as the year of his birth (" Life of Columbus," vol. i., p. 22). The Count de Lorgues adopts the same year (Dr. Barry's translation of the Count de Lorgues' " Life of Columbus," p. 48). Francesco Tarducci, a learned Italian author, prefers the year 1436, on the authority of Andres Bernaldez, known in history as the Curate of Los Palacios (Mr. Brownson's translation of Tarducci's " Life of Columbus," vol. i., p. 10). Various authors give different years for the birth of Columbus, and the time covered by these years varies from 1430 to 1456. I think, after consulting many opinions and authorities, and considering the events and course of the admiral's life, the year of his birth was most probably 1446.

other part of the Genoese territory, was long and is possibly now a question that has provoked considerable rivalry and local research. Savona, Finale, and Oneglia, western coastwise towns of Liguria, and Cogoleto (the place where Lord Tennyson drank his health in verse), Boggiasco, and several other towns and villages have claimed the great admiral as their native townsman. While Cogoleto and Savona have successively been adjudged the victors, and finally Genoa carried off the palm, other places, such as Placentia, and especially Piedmont, have laid claim to the distinction, and the controversy is still warmly and stoutly maintained. Yet the victory is now almost universally acknowledged to be with Genoa as the birthplace of Columbus.* This contest for the honor of having given birth to this illustrious man was never raised until after his death, for during his lifetime there have been few men of any distinction who have borne more disappointment, ridicule, ingratitude, and poverty than he. His fate in this respect has been similar to that of another gifted and famous personage, the earliest and greatest of Grecian poets, Homer ; for of the latter it has been said that

> "Seven cities claim great Homer dead,
> Through which the living Homer begged his bread."

Columbus was the oldest of the four children of Dominico Colombo and Susannah Fontanarossa ; three of them were sons, Bartholomew and Giacomo (written Diego in Spanish and James in English) being his brothers, and of these our history will make frequent mention ; but of his only sister, who was married to an obscure Genoese named Giacomo Bavarello, we know nothing further. Since his death efforts have been made to deduce the descent of Columbus from ancient and ennobled sources, and several illustrious and noble families have claimed him as of their

---

* At first the claimants for the honor of having been the birthplace of Columbus were six ; but in after years, as his fame increased, the number increased to fifteen—viz., Genoa, Quinto, with Terrarossa in the valley of Fontanabuona, Bogliasco, Chiavari, another Terrarossa, Cogoleto or Cugureo, Albissola, Savona, Oneglia, with a third Terrarossa—all places or lands on the Ligurian coast ; and beyond the Apennines, Casseria, Cuccaro ; in the Montferrat, Pradella, near Piacenza ; the city of Calvi, in Corsica ; a place in France ; even England. (Tarducci.)

Hon. Charles P. Daly, in an interesting pamphlet, "Have we a Portrait of Columbus?" states that the places claiming to be the birthplace of Columbus number twenty-three. From the same source we learn that there are about five hundred alleged portraits of Columbus.

lineage. However this may be, his descendants have now sensibly preferred to regard the discoverer of America as the founder of their family, and the most illustrious and proudest families of Spain have courted their alliance. It is certain, however, that at the birth and during the youth of Columbus his family was in obscure and poor circumstances; his father followed the occupation of a weaver of woollen goods, and the illustrious son assisted his parent in this humble but honest calling.

There is also a deep significance in the name of the great admiral, which in his native language was rendered Colombo and in Latin Columbus, which signifies a dove, and his son and historian, Fernando, regards this as marvellously mysterious and typical, as the very name dove was a token of his having been foreordained to " carry the olive branch and oil of baptism over the ocean, like Noah's dove, to denote the peace and union of the heathen people with the Church, after they had been shut up in the ark of darkness and confusion." * There is a further, and greater significance in the name of Christopher, which means the Christ-bearer in Latin, in token of his zeal for the conversion of the Indians to Christianity, and of his being the first Christian to salute the new world, to display the cross to its inhabitants, and to carry missionaries for their instruction and conversion.

Christopher Columbus was baptized at the Dominican Church of St. Stephen, at Genoa. Of his early boyhood we know but little. His father, from his scanty resources, found the means to send his oldest son, at the age of ten years, to the University of Pavia, a fact, as already mentioned, held in dispute, but which the stronger arguments have well sustained; and here the bright and gifted youth availed himself, to the best advantage, of the short collegiate course of two years, in acquiring some knowledge of Latin, geometry, geography, astronomy, and navigation.† The instruction he thus received gave him but a faint glimpse at sciences which, however, in after life, his energy, his intellectual powers, his ambition, and his indomitable persever-

---

* Fernando Colon, " Historia del Almirante," chaps. 1 and 2.
† The extent of the admiral's education is a much-disputed question. The University of Pavia claims him as an alumnus; has erected a monument there to commemorate that fact; and, in recognition of it, a small portion of his relics has been sent there.

ance enabled him to acquire and apply to a degree that made him quite early one of the foremost men of his age, and a leader of thought, study, and action in the most important events in the history of mankind.* At the age of twelve years, such was his poverty, he returned to the humble suburban home of his father, and assisted him at his business as weaver of woollen goods. It was greatly to the credit of the young Columbus that he steadily assisted his father in his useful avocation, but his brief yet studious education had inspired him with loftier and more important aspirations. His family was, as is alleged, of honorable descent, and he himself had acquired no inconsiderable knowledge of the practical sciences, which he wished to make the stepping-stones to his own and his family's advancement, and "in which," says Prescott, "he subsequently excelled." It is claimed by his son, Fernando, that he spent two years in study at the University of Pavia, and Las Casas repeats the statement on the authority of Fernando; but the fact is strenuously disputed by many astute historians and critics,† while others have conceded the fact.‡

He was a youth of uncommon promise. His native city of Genoa was a centre of commercial enterprise and of maritime adventure; but as it was surrounded by lofty and rugged mountains, and looked only toward the sea, it afforded no inland field for youthful adventure in the case of so gifted a boy. The Mediterranean Sea was the field for brave exploits and bold adventures. Commerce and war in those days went hand in hand together; piracy still prevailed, and was almost legalized, or at least connived at and openly practised. A state of war was the

---

* The following passage from the Dublin *Review* for April, 1893, will prove interesting as suggesting new or divergent views in regard to events in the life of Columbus which have been much discussed. It is a notice of Mariana Monteno's "Christopher Columbus." "It records the chief events in the life of the great discoverer, as we have been accustomed to understand them, and without reference to modern criticism—*e.g.*, it states that Columbus was educated at Pavia; Father Knight says Padua, and Markham maintains that he was not educated at either university, but at the weaver's school at Genoa. Again, in the matter of the marriage of Columbus, the authoress follows the older accounts, whereas some modern writers maintain that the first wife of Columbus was not Doña Perestrello, daughter of the Governor of Porto Santo, but another lady by the name of Moniz" (p. 487). We will show that she bore both names.

† Tarducci's "Life of Columbus," H. F. Brownson's translation, vol. i., p. 13.
‡ Winsor's "Columbus," etc., p. 79.

normal condition of the sea-bordering countries. What exploits could be more fascinating to a gallant and noble youth, than encounters with these reckless marauders and highwaymen of the sea!

Even religion entered into this strange and interesting belligerency, for the Mediterranean was then infested by Mohammedan corsairs. The expeditions of Christian merchantmen always went to sea with warlike armaments suited for encounters with these enemies of the cross, and the mariners were accoutred with personal arms for hand-to-hand encounters with these desperate followers of the Prophet.

The Columbuses, though perhaps of various stocks, were, in fact, mostly a seafaring family. At this time two Colombos were famous for maritime and naval exploits: the rugged and hardy old admiral, who is represented to have been a bold and adventurous seaman and warrior, ready to encounter either the enemies of his country or of his faith, and fond of fighting on the sea as a vocation; and his nephew, Colombo the younger, who was distinguished in the same field of perilous adventure. Christopher Columbus is said to have served under both of them. Such was the reputed school which was to prepare a future admiral, if much credence is to be given to uncertain details and romantic narrative, for his subsequent career of unparalleled discovery and brilliant achievement.

At an early age Columbus, influenced by the prevailing and growing tastes of the age, manifested a decided inclination for a seafaring and maritime life. His earliest studies, and especially his two years of university training, were directed and shaped so as to promote and cultivate this inclination and prepare him for the sea, for in those days the only course that led to distinction and success was one of maritime adventure. The sciences of geometry, geography, astronomy, and navigation, with which he followed up his earlier and more elementary studies, were of sufficient depth to enable him in after life to become distinguished in those sciences, and also to make a skilful practical use and application of them. The humbler yet important study of drawing was kindred to these, and possessed in his case a special significance, as it enabled him to become a map-maker of unusual skill, and thus earn a scanty subsistence during the long years of disappointment and rebuff he spent in waiting upon the courts of

Portugal and Spain ; and this assisted him in those cosmographical studies which formed a prominent part in the great work of self-education which he so eminently accomplished. These studies were enthusiastically followed by him from his youth, and such was his regard for them that, after he had achieved his great discovery, he claimed, and even so stated in one of his letters from the West Indies to the Spanish sovereigns, that his youthful and ardent love for nautical and other kindred studies, at so early an age, had marked him out from his birth as the one foreordained by Heaven to reveal to mankind the existence of the Western Continent, and the true shape and size of the earth. Inspired by the prevailing tastes of the age, and impelled by his own ardent enthusiasm, Columbus became a sailor at the age of fourteen.

Of the early voyages of Columbus we have some accounts, which, however, are too meagre and confused to satisfy our curiosity as to the first practical and earnest endeavors of our young seaman in a career, which afterward gave fame and splendor to his name, or to gratify our desires to know and study the details of those experiences and conflicts with men and floods, which formed his more advanced education for the career of usefulness and renown he was destined to accomplish. The famous admirals of that day were claimed by the admiral's son, Fernando, as relatives and as instructors of his father ; but more reliable accounts show them to have been Frenchmen. Yet even the admiral himself in after life said he was not the first admiral of his family. But while the admiral no doubt served under Colombo the younger, because Genoa and France were then in alliance, many authors suppose that he served also under the elder Colombo, who was then prominent in the maritime annals of that day as a brave and hardy commander, who sometimes led a squadron of his own and at others commanded in naval expeditions of the Genoese Government, from which he is supposed, though doubtfully, to have held an admiral's commission. The Mediterranean in those days was the scene of tumultuous adventure and perilous encounter. A voyage in those days, even in the should-be peaceful prosecution of trade, was hazardous and daring, for the sea was then frequented by roving adventurers and reckless freebooters of every kind. The commerce of Europe, Asia, and Africa was subject to constant depredations of pirates, and the ships of commerce had to protect themselves by force of arms and to fight their way. Thus they resembled warlike expeditions rather than amicable ships of trade. The navies of rival Italian States then openly depredated on the commerce of their neighbors. The States bordering on the Mediterranean made this the seat of their naval wars, which were mostly piratical. Even private noblemen and wealthy families maintained a sort of feudal sovereignty over their retainers, and not only supported military equipments on land, but also miniature navies at sea.

The rude and reckless expeditions and ships of the Catalonians also constituted a bold feature in the naval life of the times, and even private individuals fitted out ships of their own, with which they either accepted service from some belligerent or openly roved over the waters of the Mediterranean as pirates in search of plunder. But one of the most startling and interesting features in these commingling and disordered scenes was the Mohammedan expeditions by sea, which sought encounter with Christian navies or plundered the merchant ships of the Christian countries. To go in pursuit of these godless depredators and assailants of everything that was Christian was deemed an act of religious merit, and blessings and spiritual privileges accompanied the pious and zealous Christian sailors, who embarked in such holy warfare. It was amid such scenes and exploits that the character and prowess of Columbus were moulded and trained.

Of one of the early services of Columbus, supposed by some to have been performed under the old Admiral Colombo, but more probably under the younger, we have interesting but doubtful accounts. In 1459 John of Anjou, Duke of Calabria, equipped a naval expedition, which sailed from Genoa against the city of Naples, its purpose being to reconquer that kingdom for the duke's father, King Reinier, Count of Provence; and as Genoa became his ally, the old Admiral Colombo joined the expedition, and young Christopher Columbus, it is claimed, served under him with distinguished gallantry and courage. The expedition was unsuccessful, indeed, unfortunate, as few of the ships were left; but it was of great service in educating and inuring to severe service and tests of character the future discoverer. He relates of himself an incident which occurred during this naval expedition, and which is worthy of reproduction, as it throws light upon characteristic expedients which he resorted to in his first voyage of discovery to America, many years later. King Reinier gave orders to our young captain, who commanded a vessel in the expedition, to sail to Tunis and capture the galley Fernandina, which was represented to be there alone and without protection. Columbus gladly accepted the task, but when his vessel reached the island of St. Pedro, in Sardinia, he learned, to the consternation of his crew, that the Fernandina had for consorts two ships and a carrack, whereupon the frightened crew refused to proceed to the encounter, though their gallant young captain only yearned for the attack; and they insisted on returning to Marseilles for reinforcements of ships and men. Columbus, who was powerless to compel them, seemed to acquiesce in their determination, and spreading all sail, orders were issued accordingly; but Columbus secretly altered the point of the compass, and next morning, instead of finding themselves sailing for Marseilles, the crew found that he had piloted the ship within the Cape of Carthagena. When we come to relate the history of Columbus's first voyage across the Atlantic, we will have occasion to show how, by the stratagem of altering the reckoning of the log-book, he deluded his rebellious crew as to the distance they had sailed from Palos, and thus secured a continuance of that momentous voyage until the sight of land soon gladdened the hearts of all.

For several years Columbus, according to current accounts, more or less unreliable, continued to follow the sea, and to render gallant and intrepid service either in the employ of the Genoese Government or as captain of a vessel under the leadership of the renowned old captains of his name, uncle and nephew, the latter of whom also gained great notoriety as a reckless and daring corsair, whose name was a terror to the Mohammedans; and it is said that disobedient children in Moorish families were frightened by their mothers into subjection and obedience by the very mention of the name of Colombo. After Christopher Columbus became famous as the discoverer of America, and historians ransacked every annal and reports of the past for incidents of his life during this earlier and obscurer portion of his active career, some of the reckless and even questionable deeds of the elder and of the younger Colombos were, in the confusion of the annals, attributed to Christopher Columbus. Great obscurity and confusion prevail in the accounts of events and dates on the career and life of Columbus from 1450 to 1470, the period of his seafaring life. We come now to his advent and residence in Portugal, upon which we hope to throw some new light.

The circumstances or motives which led Columbus to go to Portugal have been variously assigned. Fernando, his second son, who wrote the first history of his father, with evident and recurring pleasure taken in linking his name with the adventures at sea of the two French commanders, Colombo, relates that shipwreck off the coast of Portugal was the first cause of his father's advent to Lisbon. This account would attribute to chance one of the most important steps ever taken by Columbus, but it is not well authenticated, and other more probable and reasonable causes for his going to Lisbon are not wanting. Columbus acted with a purpose in this, as in the other great events of his life.

The most usual time assigned for the advent of Christopher Columbus to Portugal is 1470. It certainly was between 1470 and 1474. If we take the former year, 1470, he evidently did not then make Lisbon or the Portuguese possessions his permanent home, since we find him at Savona with his father in 1472 and 1473. Documents published by Harrisse, in his "Christophe Colomb," * to which the name of Christopher Columbus is signed, together with those of his mother and next brother, Giovanni, relinquishing all their right to a house and lot then sold by the father, Dominico Colombo, show this.

In these documents, of which the last is dated August 7th, 1473, or at least in the earlier ones, the signature of Columbus is followed, according to the Genoese custom, with his occupation, which was stated as that of a weaver of woollen goods, which was the trade of most of the members of the Columbus family.†

The occurrence of the name of Columbus in legal documents at Genoa and Savona, during the years generally included in the

---

* Harrisse's "Christophe Colomb," tom. ii., pp. 419–26.

† "The Wife of Columbus," 1873, by M. Nicolau Florentino (whose real name is Senhor Gabriel Pereira, Director of the National Library of Lisbon) and Senhora Regina Maney, a valuable contribution to Columbian literature, and one based upon authentic archives and documents.

seafaring period of his life, would indicate that he was occasionally if not frequently at home during that period with his father; that his profession, as given, was more or less continuously during those years that of a weaver of woollen goods, and hence that probably his exploits at sea were not so constant or so long as his son Fernando had been led to believe and to relate. It is probable that Columbus commenced his visits to Portugal in 1470, and went to stay in the latter part of 1473, for it is nearly certain that he went to the island of Madeira, a leading Portuguese possession, in or prior to 1474.* The occasion of his going to Portugal was not accident or battle or shipwreck, but it was in pursuit of occupation and fortune, as many other Italians had done and were then doing. During the period of Portuguese leadership in maritime enterprise, there was a considerable immigration of French and Italians to Portugal; and as the latter now only concern us, the names of the Spinolas, Cezares, Uzadamari, Cataneos, Lomellinos, Dorias, Grimaldi, and many others will testify. But his own name and blood preceded him to Portugal, for when he went to Lisbon he found his brother Bartholomew there, and this, no doubt, had added strength to his motives for going, for the two brothers were devoted to each other throughout their eventful lives. Independently of these considerations, Lisbon, at that time especially, was the centre of maritime energy, enterprise, and adventure, and offered great attractions to one of Columbus's temperament, who had followed the sea from the age of fourteen, and whose mind was fired with the ambition for discovery and renown. The enthusiastic study of the art of navigation, the bold pursuit of discovery, and the love of adventure, had passed from Lisbon to other countries, and as Columbus, flushed with a gallant career at sea, studious of maritime sciences, emulous of rivalling the great discoveries of Portuguese mariners and captains, perhaps, even probably, then meditating on his plans for a westward voyage, was alive to the spirit of his age and country, he very naturally followed so many of his own countrymen and his own brother to that busy capital. It was greatly to his credit that after so many years of active service at sea, and after such continuous exposure to the vices so prevalent among seafaring men, Columbus escaped moral con-

---

* "The Wife of Columbus," by Nicolau Florentino and Regina Maney, pp. 43, 44.

tamination, and preserved his purity of character and a highly religious and devout demeanor. He was twenty-four years old when he first visited Portugal in 1470. It would seem that he did not linger long at Lisbon, but followed many of his countrymen to the Portuguese Islands, those advanced posts of Portuguese enterprise and discovery.

The researches made by Senhor Gabriel Pereira, Director of the National Library at Lisbon, and by his associate in the work, Senhora Regina Maney, among official and authentic archives,— the Torre de Tombo, national archives at Lisbon—the results of which they have embodied in their interesting little volume,* just published, seem to justify essential changes in the oft-repeated accounts given of the first marriage of Columbus. Up to this time historians have uniformly related that this marriage occurred at Lisbon, and that the acquaintance between Columbus and Donna Philippa Moniz de Perestrello commenced at the chapel of the Convent of All Saints, where he was in the habit of attending mass daily, and where the young lady was one of several of her age and rank who, while living in the world, were regular attendants of the convent, probably for purposes of education as well as of devotion. Senhora Maney, in her preface to " The Wife of Columbus," declares that she and the Director of the National Library of Lisbon had been able to discover among the national archives a different history of this interesting event, and I have embodied their account of it in this work. " We have established," she says, "the time and place of his marriage, along with other data, and we have found much about Columbus that is entirely new."

The families of Moniz and Perestrello were both of distinguished lineage in Portugal. The Monizes were of noble rank. Bartholomew Perestrello, the father of Donna Philippa, the first wife of Columbus, left early without a father, obtained when very young a position in the household of the Infante Dom John, who was in his earlier life united with his brother, the famous Prince Henry the Navigator. He was afterward created a knight in the household of the Infante Dom John, and still later he received a grant at his own request of the island of Porto Santo, and undertook its colonization. He does not appear to

---

* " The Wife of Columbus," by Florentino and Maney, *passim*.

have been its discoverer, or even to have been a companion in that maritime achievement of Gonçalves Zarco and Tristan Vaz in its discovery. He was married three times; his first wife was Donna Margarida Martins; his second wife was Donna Brites Furtado de Mendonça, and his third wife was Donna Isabel Moniz, daughter of Vasco Martins Moniz, who, after an active and successful career, had retired with large wealth to Machico, on the island of Madeira, where he lived in "grand style" and dispensed a liberal hospitality. Donna Isabel, when she married Bartholomew Perestrello, was only eighteen years old, and she then left the luxurious and wealthy home of her father to share the declining fortunes of a gentleman of worth, energy, and enterprise, but to whom Porto Santo had proved a fatal gift, Bartholomew Perestrello. The governorship of this island had already sunk the portions of two wives, and all the donations he could get from the crown for the purchase of fertilizers, agricultural implements, stock, equipments, and the assistance necessarily extended to his colonists. It now absorbed the portion if any of his third wife; the rabbits, which had marvellously increased on the island, destroyed its productions, and the governor's health now gave way under the losses, struggles, disappointments, and ruin of many years. He died at Baleira, in 1457, at the age of fifty, leaving his widow, at the age of twenty-five years, with a son and daughter, and in circumstances most precarious. The mother devoted her life entirely to the education of her children, Bartholomew and Philippa; but now, with the consent of King Affonso V., the fruitless governorship of Porto Santo was assigned to Pedro Corêa, who had married Donna Izeu Perestrello, a daughter of Bartholomew's second marriage, a member of the noble family of Corêa. The price paid by Corêa for the island was three hundred thousand reis in gold, and an annuity of thirty thousand reis. Donna Isabel Moniz, now relieved from anxiety, retired with her son and daughter to the sumptuous mansion of her father at Machico, and no care or expense was spared in educating the children according to their rank. Young Bartholomew embraced the military profession, and was correspondingly equipped by his good mother for the king's service in Africa with everything suited to his rank and aspirations; but in 1473 he returned to Porto Santo and disavowed his mother's disposition of the island,

and with the consent of the king annulled the sale to Corêa, and assumed the task which had cost his father so many fortunes and his life. This ungrateful and undutiful conduct of the son completely estranged him from his mother, who was now left at Machico with her father and her daughter Philippa. Although the father of Donna Isabel Moniz was very rich, he had sixteen children, and no trace can be found of any portion of this fortune received by his daughter Isabel, or by his granddaughter Philippa. The latter is represented as very beautiful, and the social and educational advantages she enjoyed must have made her quite accomplished.

It was at this time, 1474, that Christopher Columbus arrived at Machico and joined the Italian colony in the Portuguese archipelago. Through his compatriots, who were frequent visitors and guests at the hospitable mansion of Vasco Moniz, he became acquainted with the young and beautiful Philippa, or perhaps the story of his meeting her at daily mass at a convent chapel may be transferred to Machico. Although he was the son of a woollen weaver, and had followed his father's calling at home, he was hospitably received by the noble family of the Monizes, for few if any there were among the young men of Machico so handsome, accomplished, and plausible as the bold Genoese. He was then of the age of twenty-eight years. Donna Philippa was only twenty-one. The interesting little work from which these particulars are mostly derived,* which, however, places his age at thirty-eight, thus refers to Columbus at this interesting period of his checkered career: " Once landed in Madeira, the daring Genoese immediately set about getting acquainted with the important families of the archipelago, through his compatriots already established. He insinuated himself by his sympathetic manners, his fluent speech, which many took for proof of great instruction, and finally by his taking advantage of the fraternal predisposition of the Portuguese toward the Italian immigrants, who were much liked, whether in the ordinary occupations of life, acquiring the good will of the chiefs of families, or in the amorous adventures and most beautiful progeny, as far as the young female portion of the inhabitants went, who looked despairingly on the gallant Portuguese youth going off to Africa

---

* "The Wife of Columbus," by Florentino (Pereira) and Maney, p. 44.

to die unmarried, or to come back with hair whitened by the hardships of ocean and battlefield. . . . The very Donna Philippa Moniz de Mello, of whom it is said she was a very handsome young girl, demonstrated the case in the alliance of the Monizes and Perestrellos, already mixed with the blood of the Teixeiras; and this rapid sketch of Donna Philippa, made by a genealogist, reveals to us a marriage of simple affection contracted with Christopher Columbus." The character of Columbus must have been above reproach to have won such a prize.

Columbus himself was poor. It is conjectured that the sale of a house by his father at Savona, in 1473, was either the result of family reverses or was necessitated to provide an outfit and traveling expenses for his sons Christopher and Bartholomew. Married at Machico, in 1475, with the solemn rites of the Church, the young couple went immediately to live in Funchal, " a residence preferred by Columbus, because he thus remained in direct contact with the whole maritime movement."* No circumstance could have been mentioned nor any step taken which could more clearly have indicated the deep purposes and high aspirations of the future discoverer of America, than his immediate departure, after his marriage, from the luxurious mansion of his wife's grandfather, in order that he might be in constant touch with the great movement of the age toward geographical discovery, maritime enterprise, and heroic conquest. It is related that Columbus and his wife were poor. The work of Pereira and Maney† thus speaks of this event in the life of the future admiral : " On the other hand, what did Columbus bring from Genoa? If anything came to him from the product of the sale effected by his father on the eve of Christopher's departure for Portugal, little could be left, over and above the traveling expenses, for his maintenance at the first, until fortune should smile upon him or open some way or other for earning a living. The fact is. that he must have worked hard either to sustain himself while alone, or to provide, however poorly, for the indispensable exigencies of his married life. Did he draw sea-maps and charts? Where did he learn to do so? Did he open a shop or a boarding-house? Did he exercise any other branch of activity that one could conjecture or discover? This is certainly an important question for

---

* " The Wife of Columbus," p. 46.   † *Id.*, p. 45.

Christopher Columbus, the discoverer of America, but of very secondary order for Christopher Columbus, the husband of Donna Philippa Moniz de Mello." Senhor Pereira was convinced from his access to and study of the public archives, as well as from inquiries made of surviving members of the Perestrello family, that few if any marine maps or maritime traditions had been left by Bartholomew Perestrello to serve his future son-in-law in his vast schemes of discovery, for he had never been a mariner, discoverer, or a follower of the sea. Neither did Columbus obtain much information or inspiration from his brother-in-law, Pedro Corêa, who, according to these recent researches, never fixed his residence in Porto Santo during his gubernatorial incumbency, nor in Graciosa, of which island he was also the donee, nor was he a navigator or an adventurer in the maritime enterprises of the day. On the contrary, Corêa was a resident on his farm in Charneca, near Lisbon, and died there in 1485.*

The marriage of Columbus and Philippa, in 1473, was followed by the birth of their son Diego, in 1476, at Funchal. These facts, which seem well sustained, go far to upset the usual narratives of historians that Columbus was married at Lisbon, that his son Diego was born there, and that he went with his wife and mother-in-law to Porto Santo. According to the accounts, based upon such recent researches, Philippa Moniz de Perestrello, the wife of Columbus, died shortly after the birth of their son Diego, who thereupon fell to the tender care of his grandmother, Donna Isabel de Perestrello, who continued to reside at the house of her father at Machico. On this subject we shall have more to say when we come to relate the circumstances of the departure of Columbus from Portugal for Spain. In the year following the death of his wife, 1477, or possibly in the latter part of the year 1476, Columbus, most probably to assuage his grief, divert his mind, and to study further the great problem engaging his mind as affected by questions of climate and latitude, made his voyage to Iceland, of which we will speak in another place. The little volume† before us, to which reference has been made, thus speaks of his departure upon this important expedition: "The father, profoundly wounded in his passionate attachment to his

---

* "The Wife of Columbus," p. 42.   † *Id.*, p. 47.

wife, took one of those extreme resolutions in which great moral sufferings sometimes end."

The circumstance mentioned by Las Casas and other contemporaries of Columbus—that of his having had his hair turn gray prematurely—now becomes a thread of testimony in connection with the charge of Harrisse and Winsor that he deserted his wife when he left Portugal for Spain. At the time of his wife's death he was thirty years old, and the time assigned by his contemporary historians for his hair turning gray was precisely at that age. It is, therefore, but a natural conclusion that so sudden and violent a grief, one which forced him to seek mental relief in a trip then regarded as heroic even among veteran mariners—the voyage to Iceland—was the cause of his hair turning gray. Sudden grief or excitement has frequently been known to produce that result. The death of his wife and the change in the color of his hair occurred at the same time. The ardent temperament of Columbus lends strength to the conclusion.

The period of time from 1470, when Columbus first visited Portugal, to 1484, when it is generally agreed that he left Portugal, is one in which the greatest confusion exists as to the exact dates of events in his life. The whole period agrees with the time which Columbus, in 1505, in a letter to King Ferdinand, wrote that he had spent in Portugal, in which he says that " God must have directed him into the service of Spain by a kind of miracle, since he had already been in Portugal, whose king was more interested than any other sovereign in making discoveries, and yet God closed his eyes, his ears, and all his senses to such a degree that in fourteen years Columbus could not prevail on him to lend aid to his scheme." This eventful but confused period covered many events which are no doubt true, but without correct dates. He landed in Portugal in 1470, visited his father at Savona in 1472 and 1473, took part in engagements at sea under the French Colombos, corresponded with Dr. Toscanelli in 1474, went to Madeira in 1474, was married to Donna Philippa de Perestrello in 1475, witnessed the birth of his son Diego and the death of the mother in 1476, went to Iceland in 1477, and on his return therefrom made one or more expeditions to the Portuguese islands or stations on the mainland of Africa, and during the remainder of the time was engaged in unceasing and wearisome negotiations with the King of Portugal for the adoption of his plans for a westward voyage across the Atlantic. Owing to the uncertainty of the dates of this period, we have treated the various subjects without strict adherence to the supposed dates, aiming rather at presenting the character, studies, efforts, struggles, and aspirations of Columbus as essential events in themselves, rather than attempting, as so many others have tried in vain, to reconcile dates or arrive at correctness. Hence our accounts of his studies, inquiries, investigations, self-preparations, and the formulation of his plans, may relate to periods of sojourn either in Lisbon or at Funchal, for it seems probable, if not certain, that he may have gone back to Lisbon several times between 1474 and 1477.

It was in the heated atmosphere of nautical and scientific studies, of naval adventure, and of pioneer discovery, at Lisbon or at Funchal, that the mind of Columbus caught fire with the prevailing fever. While it is not known at what precise time his theories and convictions, as to the existence of western lands and continents, were conceived and matured, or his ambition to become the discoverer of a new world was awakened, such were the attractions and influences of the scene and of the times, and such his opportunity of comparative repose and studious inclination, in the intervals between his voyages, that this period of his residence at Lisbon would seem to have been the crucial time, which developed the grand schemes he afterward accomplished for the glory and benefit of mankind. This view is strengthened by authentic facts. His wife's mother, accustomed as she had been to scenes and narratives of adventure and discovery in her married life, and finding in her son-in-law an enthusiastic listener and ardent student of such subjects, took pleasure in relating to him all she had heard from her deceased husband concerning current voyages, expeditions, colonization, and discoveries. Thus, too, Columbus was afforded ample opportunity and time for inspecting and studying the papers, charts, journals, and memoranda of the old and experienced navigators and mariners he must have met at Funchal, which proved to him a rich mine of nautical and maritime treasures and information. His residence and marriage in Portugal and the Portuguese possessions made him a resident subject of the king of that country, and, as Portugal was then the leading nation in discovery and colonization, thus acquiring the islands in the Atlantic and along the west coast of Africa.

Columbus served occasionally in the Portuguese expeditions to and along the coast of Guinea. These studies and voyages, and, still more, the deeper researches which he made in the practical sciences, especially the science of navigation and its kindred sciences, raised him to a foremost rank among enlightened and learned men of his day. Indeed, as the sequel will show, he was centuries in advance of the times in which he lived. Cosmography became a leading study and favorite science of his, and in his straitened circumstances he turned it to good and fruitful account, during the intervals between his voyages, by making maps and charts for a livelihood. We have already related how slight had been the advances made by the scientific world in cosmography since the days of Ptolemy, who prepared his famous map of the known world at Alexandria about the middle of the second century of the Christian era; and this map, considered the most perfect, like all the other maps produced then, was, in the light of our present knowledge, a tissue of errors and absurdities. Such, too, was the map brought by Marco Polo from Cathay, and such the celebrated map of Mauro, the Italian friar, scarcely more than an improved copy of the former, which, however, gained for him from the Venetians the title of the "incomparable cosmographer," and the distinction of a medal struck in his honor. Yet during all this period, and throughout the fifteenth century, the most perfect maps, by the most learned cosmographers, were absurdly incorrect and ludicrously quaint. The studies and voyages of then recent times, and the explorations of the Portuguese and Spaniards along the western coast of Africa and around the islands adjacent thereto, had tended to lift the science of geography out of the chaos and darkness of centuries. Even yet, in the days of Columbus, the map of Ptolemy was among the foremost authorities of the time. In many of the maps conjecture boldly supplied the place of knowledge, and popular fables of the most incongruous character were handed down and accepted in an age of advancing intelligence. Learning and ignorance were here strangely and grotesquely commingled. Able disquisitions on astronomy and navigation were set off with the fables of monsters, such as men with the bodies of lions and women with the faces of dogs, salamanders, giants, pigmies, and sea monsters so large as to kill and devour large stags and able to cross the ocean. Here we have the origin of the sea monster, which figures even in our day in the stories and yarns of mariners and seamen. The study of drawing, which Columbus had pursued at the University of Pavia, though slight, now came to his aid, and enabled him, with his thorough and advanced knowledge of cosmography, to produce the best maps and charts. Another fact which added greatly to his knowledge of this subject, the most engrossing study of that age of nautical adventure and geographical discovery, was his correspondence with Dr. Paulo Toscanelli, of Florence, who was one of the foremost scientists of his age, and the most accomplished cosmographer. And here we might cite this remarkable correspondence, which commenced in the early part of his visits and sojourns at Lisbon after 1470, as further proof of our view that it was during this early period of the life of Columbus that he conceived and developed his grand and learned propositions and plans, which led him to the discovery of our continent. Thus it was that during his sojourn at Lisbon, Columbus, rich in learning, science, religion, and exalted purposes, but poor in worldly goods, was compelled to practise the most unsparing economy; and it was during this period that he supported himself by preparing and disposing of maps and charts of the earth. Such was the avidity with which good and accurate maps were sought in those days, that Columbus made this his entire source of revenue and support. Such was his honorable and generous nature that, from his scanty and pinching income, he spared the means to relieve the necessities of his venerable parent at Genoa, and to educate his younger brother, Diego, in whose subsequent love, loyalty, and service, and to a greater extent in those of Bartholomew, he found consolation amid the calumnies of men and the ingratitude of sovereigns.

Columbus won position among the learned and scientific men of his day by his admirable maps, to the production of which he brought the most advanced cosmographical study and the skill of an accomplished draughtsman. His labors in this congenial, and to him then most useful and necessary avocation, were greatly aided and stimulated by numerous and important voyages which he made during this time. The whole circle of Columbus's acquaintance was thoroughly imbued with the spirit of the age. The Portuguese court and nation were foremost. The Portuguese islands in the Eastern Pacific were recent instances of progress in discovery and geography, for they lay on the very frontiers of the then known world. They were on the ocean highway of the frequent and important voyages between the coast of Guinea and the ports of Portugal. Columbus and all his connections and associates were seafaring people, and hence they unavoidably, and indeed from choice, fell in with the experienced and veteran sea captains and navigators, who constantly touched at Funchal or Machico in their cruises to the western coast of Africa. These circumstances and others of a similar character, which we will relate hereafter, are most important facts, for it was such surroundings at Lisbon that gave confirmation in the mind of Columbus to the great thought of western continental discovery, and fostered that exalted conception until it culminated in the noblest achievement of man. They formed the more immediate education which prepared the man for his mission, and are second only to the great conception itself and its realization in the final triumph. They also go far to point out the period of his life, a question regarded by great historians as involved in doubt, when his mind opened to the possibility and progressed to certainty as to the existence of vast countries across the Atlantic. In a future chapter we will give an account of the great strides made by maritime nations, especially by Portugal, in exploring the western coast of Africa, discovering and settling islands in the Atlantic, and in expanding the sphere of human knowledge as to the geography of the earth. The writings of the ancients and of classical authors, which referred in unmistakable terms and with inspiring grandeur of thought to distant continents, were brought into prominent reference, and were studied with enchanting delight. The Carthaginians and their great island of Antilla in the western ocean, now, after the rest of centuries, came forth to inflame the public enthusiasm and to fan the flame of maritime adventure and exploration. The "Dialogues of Plato," containing the account of the great island or continent of Atlantis, and of its submersion in the western ocean, were studied, and their authenticity found then, as now, many earnest and learned advocates. Then, as in our own day, there were many among advanced scholars, who adopted and advocated the theory that the islands then known to the world—the Canaries and the Azores—were remnants of the submerged Atlantis, and that other and vaster insular remains of

that vast continent or island existed in far distant regions of the
Atlantic, all of them being more elevated and mountainous limits
of the lost country.* While there was much of reason and fact
to rest such theories upon, the feverish state of the public mind
gave rise to other and imaginary islands and lands of vast extent,
which mariners, driven westward from their course, had seen or
dreamed of as lying clearly in sight on the western horizon; and
many a voyager related to willing ears the exciting and fascinating stories of discoveries of lands lying far out in the ocean,
which subsequent knowledge of the Atlantic showed to have
been mere clouds or clusters of clouds, which are commonly seen
at sea, resting low and flat on the horizon on summer afternoons,
and closely resembling islands. The thirst for such exciting
accounts and wonders invited exaggeration and even wilful invention, and many a tale of western land was fabricated to feed
the popular tastes and fancies. We know that a noted story of
this kind was told to Columbus by one Antonio Leone, who resided at Madeira, and who assured our hero that he had distinctly seen three islands lying in the western distance while he
was sailing westward from the island of Madeira. Such imaginary islands were not seen alone by the inhabitants of Madeira,
for the people of the Canaries labored under a similar imagination, and optical delusion became a chronic disease with them.
When the skies were clear and the weather warm, they could
distinctly see an immense island lying to the westward, and
its majestic mountains broke forth high above the horizon;
while they admitted that the island was seen only at intervals, it
was always seen in the same place, though frequently not visible
in the clearest weather. Anxious to nurse their belief, the credulous islanders thought that the fact of the distant island always
presenting the same shape and same outline of mountains was
sufficient to prove it a reality. Authorities from the literature
of the past were not wanting to show the existence of islands or
lands lying westward, with which this new discovery might be
identified. There were also advocates for the claim that this
was the famous Antilla which Aristotle mentioned. This island
apparition also gave revival to the old Spanish legend of the
island of the Seven Cities, which were founded by the seven

---

* Donnelly's "Atlantis," *passim*.

bishops who are said to have abandoned their country at the time of its conquest by the Moors, and who, under the special protection and pilotage of Heaven, sailed to this beautiful island with their flocks, and there built the seven famous cities. Other zealous believers in the newly discovered island believed it to be the far-famed island of St. Brandon, which, according to ancient tradition, was discovered by this celebrated priest of Scotland in the sixth century. So universal was the belief in St. Brandon's Island, that it passed into the domain of history, is alluded to in the current literature and histories of our day, and it was actually located on the maps of the fifteenth century as lying in the very direction in which the people of the Canaries now saw it. The new island was also identified by others with the Antilla of the Carthaginians. Such was the faith of the people in this wonderful island, that they actually petitioned the King of Portugal to grant them permission to fit out expeditions for its exploration and conquest, and expeditions actually went in search of it; but it ever eluded their grasp. Such was the atmosphere in which Columbus, in the prime of his life, ardent and ambitious, lived for years, and as he carefully recorded accounts of all these things among his notes and memoranda, it is reasonable to suppose that they exerted some influence in generating his earliest thoughts of discovery, and led him through and from the field of the imagination to those severer and deeper studies, which subsequently enabled him to expound his theories before the most learned bodies of Europe, and to refute all their misconceived objections.

It was also during this period of his life, as supposed by historians, though probably erroneously, in the light of recently discovered facts, that Columbus may have taken part in other expeditions which extended through the Mediterranean and to the Levant, some of which were in the prosecution of commercial enterprises for Venetian merchants, others in taking a gallant part in naval wars and engagements, in which the rival States of Italy then unfortunately engaged against each other, and others still were undertaken with religious zeal against the Mohammedan rovers and pirates, enemies of his faith and his Church. In several of these adventures Columbus commanded a ship either under his uncle, Admiral Colombo, or under Colombo the Younger. In one of these singular and characteristic adventures, under the latter, Columbus, as usual, commanded a vessel, and took a conspicuous part in so eventful and perilous an encounter that it was only his own presence of mind, endurance, and good swimming that warded off the catastrophe that, by his death, would have left America undiscovered perhaps for centuries. It is related by his son and historian, Fernando, that the commander of the expedition, Colombo the Younger, went with all his ships to the coast of Portugal and lay in wait for four Venetian galleys returning from Flanders and laden with rich cargoes. The engagement which ensued at the meeting of the two fleets was desperate and frantic. The attacking ships and the merchantmen, which were no less well armed and prepared for war, grappled each other in deadly contest, and the officers and crews, as was the custom of the age, fought their antagonists hand-to-hand from their respective ships, each endeavoring always to board the enemy. The struggle, which was marked with extraordinary carnage on both sides, lasted all day, and fierce was the encounter. Columbus with his ship engaged a powerful Venetian galley; the vessels were fastened to each other by chains and grappling-irons, for they fought in those days after the manner of pirates, and one or other of the vessels and its crew, if not both, was sure to be destroyed. Both vessels were toward evening enveloped in flames from the hand-grenades and other burning projectiles, and were involved together in certain destruction from fire. The officers and crews of each vessel had to take refuge from the fire by throwing themselves into the water. While many perished, if not most of them, Columbus calmly seized an oar and swam the distance of six miles to the shore. Fernando Columbus states that, after recovering from his exhaustion, his father proceeded to Lisbon, and finding many of his countrymen, Genoese, there, he readily consented to make it his place of residence. But as this engagement took place several years later than 1470, and it seems well established that it was in that year that he went to Lisbon first, it is more probable, as Mr. Irving concludes, that this disaster merely led to his return then to his former residence at the capital of Portugal. Tarducci discredits almost entirely the accuracy and truthfulness of Fernando's account.*

As it seems clear that Columbus went to Madeira in 1474, and

---

* Mr. Brownson's translation of Tarducci's "Columbus," vol. i., pp. 20, 21.

after his marriage there in 1475 went to Funchal to reside with his wife in 1476, and thence on his voyage to Iceland in the latter part of 1476 or early in 1477, there is but little probability of his having been in any such engagements during this period. His correspondence with Dr. Toscanelli took place about the year 1474, and then and ever afterward his mind was absorbed in the grander field of oceanic and western voyages and discoveries. In 1477, while residing at Funchal, and after the death of his wife, and after leaving his son Diego with his grandmother at Machico, Columbus made that voyage, to which allusion has already been made, not the least remarkable of his many adventures on the sea; this was his visit to Iceland, then regarded as the *ultima Thule*, the utmost boundary of the earth. Subsequent historical discussions in relation to the voyages of the Northmen to Greenland and our own northern coasts have developed the conjecture that Columbus might have learned of the voyages and discoveries of lands west of Iceland, of Greenland, and even of our own country, from Icelanders, in 1477, during his visit to their country. But Columbus kept such ample notes and memoranda of all he saw and heard bearing upon the geography of the earth, that, had he heard of the western discoveries of the Northmen at Iceland, he would have assuredly mentioned it in his writings, and in the letter he wrote to his son, Fernando, on his voyage to Iceland. The following extract from that letter tends to exclude, upon the laws of evidence, the presumption that he had heard of the Norse voyages and colonies in the Western Hemisphere, which had then ceased. "In the year 1477, in February, I navigated one hundred leagues beyond Thule (Iceland), the southern part of which is seventy-three degrees distant from the equator, and not sixty-three, as some pretend; neither is it situated within the line which includes the west of Ptolemy, but is much more westerly. The English, principally those of Bristol, go with their merchandise to this island, which is as large as England. When I was there the sea was not frozen, and the tides were so great as to rise and fall twenty-six fathoms."* But doubtless his observations of the earth and sea at that point strengthened the grounds, upon which Columbus founded his firm conviction and confident assurance, that extensive lands and countries would be found by sailing due

---

* Fernando Columbus, "Historia del Almirante," cap. 4.

west across the Atlantic. After his Icelandic voyage Columbus is reported to have visited the Portuguese settlement of San Jorge de Mina, on the coast of Guinea. During this period of his life which we are now considering, he acquired great stores of knowledge in relation to the progress and results of modern discoveries, the location of regions and islands discovered and explored on or along the western coasts of Europe, and especially of Africa, and in the practical sciences of cosmography, geography, astronomy, and navigation. His good judgment, clear perception, and varied experience enabled him to distinguish between the real and genuine information and knowledge then accessible, on the one hand, and the visionary reports and conjectures of the heated and ardent imaginations of ignorant navigators on the other; but he kept a record of all he saw and heard, and stored up, in his ripened and cultured mind and memory, all the learning and facts developed in the past and in his own times. Yet there was nothing that his vigorous mind and enterprising spirit did not utilize in evolving his grand conceptions of the earth and ocean. Believing that it was this period of his life that gave birth to his admirable and practical views and plans, we have thought it important to give at some length the history of his voyages and expeditions, of the means and opportunities he possessed, and of which he availed himself from the time of his first arrival in Portugal, soon after which he must have presented his claims and propositions to the king of that country. The following passage, from Mr. Irving's life of the admiral, will fitly conclude the review of this interesting part of his career, and of his progress from poverty and obscurity to fame and glory: " His genius having thus taken its decided bent, it is interesting to notice from what a mass of acknowledged facts, rational hypotheses, fanciful narrations, and popular rumors his grand project of discovery was wrought out by the strong workings of his vigorous mind." We should add that the memoranda and writings of Columbus, covering this extensive field of inquiry and study, were carefully preserved by him and transmitted to his son Fernando, who has given their contents to the world in his " History of the Admiral;" and though impaired by the enthusiastic and indiscreet exaggerations of the compiler and editor, the work forms a noble monument raised by a loyal son to an illustrious parent!

CHAPTER III.

> "Theirs was the tread of pioneers,
> Of nations yet to be;
> The first low wash of waves where soon
> Shall roll a human sea."
>
> —ANONYMOUS.

CHRISTOPHER COLUMBUS lived in an age of discovery. Spain and Portugal were the leading and pioneer nations that awakened among modern peoples the study of navigation and its kindred sciences, the spirit of discovery and the thirst for maritime adventure and conquests. The Canary Islands, now generally believed by historians and cosmographers to be the Fortunate Islands of the ancients mentioned by Pliny the Elder, by Plutarch, and by Ptolemy, visited by the Moors in the twelfth century and by Italian navigators in the thirteenth, were rediscovered by a Spanish vessel driven by a storm to that quarter in 1334. In the beginning of the fifteenth century many abortive attempts were made to bring them within the Spanish dominion, and though Spanish naval commanders landing there saw nothing of the fabled gardens of the fair daughters of Atlas and Erebus, nor of the golden apples which Terra gave to Juno as a wedding gift in the times when deities mingled in the convivialities of earth, such were the beauty and attractions of these noted islands that continued expeditions were renewed, until they were finally and effectually conquered by a joint Spanish and Norman expedition under a Norman commander, the gallant Jean de Bethencourt; and though claimed subsequently by both Spain and Portugal, they were eventually adjudged to and became a permanent possession of the former. Great interest attached to the Canary Islands on account of the ancient and mythical traditions connected with them, for not only did the poets of Greece and Rome locate here the enchanted gardens of the Hesperides—a transformed tradition of the Mosaic Garden of Eden—but it was these gardens that Ptolemy, the great Helleno-Egyptian mathematician, astronomer, and geographer, who flourished in the second century of the Christian era, the first to prove the earth to be a globe, a favorite author of Columbus, established as the point from which to compute the longitude of the earth. But they had long been lost to the world, except in dim traditions and mythical legends, until the advancing spirit of discovery in the fourteenth and fifteenth centuries added them, in fact, to the realms of the civilized world. Even in that more practical era, which still retained the traditional chivalry and romance of the Middle Ages, the most real events bore a tinge of sentiment, and some have supposed that the excitement and stimulus to adventurous discovery which this age manifested was not wholly attributable to their practical importance, but rather to a romantic story of love adventure. Sentiment was then a potent element in all public events. The discovery of Madeira was traced by some to the accounts given in the fourteenth century of the flight of two lovers, an Englishman named Macham and a beautiful lady of France, enamored with each other, who fled from the lady's home in a vessel, went to sea, were driven by storms far beyond the sight of land, and were tossed and carried long and far over dangerous waters, until they finally saw and landed on a fair and wooded island unknown and without human presence save their own, then, for the first time. This lover's retreat was afterward identified as the island of Madeira.

The Cape Verde Islands and the Azores, though dimly known, and even in the fourteenth century laid down on the maps, were only explored and taken possession of in the fifteenth by the Portuguese. These events, together with a greater familiarity with the Atlantic coasts of Africa, prepared the way for one who, like Columbus, was in advance of his time in all the studies, sciences, enterprises, and discoveries of an age eventful beyond precedent in advancing the progress of the human race over the earth. This remarkable person was Prince Henry the Navigator, of Portugal ; a prince whose career of energy, enterprise, and progress—adorned, too, as he was with scientific studies, profound and learned research, and princely liberality—have handed his name down to succeeding ages an ornament to his rank and his race. He did not leave events to drift slowly and fortuitously to their results ; he advanced at once to be a leader of his age ; he was a worthy and brilliant precursor of Columbus, who carried the work commenced by Prince Henry the Navigator to its culmination in the discovery of America.

Prince Henry was the fourth son of King John I. of Portugal, and on his mother's side he was descended from John of Gaunt, Duke of Lancaster. He was born on March 4th, 1394, and was distinguished while a youth for his courage and brilliant achievements in the wars against the Moors of Barbary. Returning from the conquest of Ceuta, in 1415, he received the order of knighthood for his chivalrous deeds, and then, going to reside at an Atlantic retreat near Cape St. Vincent, he fitted out naval expeditions against the Moors on the coast of Africa. Having served through three campaigns of naval warfare, besides the military expeditions under his father in Barbary, he acquired a vast amount of information in relation to Africa, both in the interior, south of the Mediterranean, and along the coast of Guinea. Instead of spending his life amid the allurements of the court of Portugal, he devoted himself to study and to works of utility and glory to his country. He was distinguished for his learning, especially in the sciences of mathematics, geography, and navigation. In his retreat in the Algarve, near Sagres and Cape St. Vincent, he attracted by his enterprise, learning, and munificence men of science and study around him. He became also an accomplished astronomer. He erected at Sagres a naval and astronomical observatory and nautical school, at which young noblemen and other earnest students might study all the sciences connected with navigation, and he appointed as its president the learned cosmographer and scientific navigator, James Mallorca. Prince Henry, after studying ancient and modern scholars and authors, boldly adopted the opinion that the prevailing belief that the coast of Africa ended at Cape Nun was false ; that, on the contrary, the torrid zone at the equator was not·impassable and unnavigable, on account of the stifling and destroying heats of the sun ; that Cape Bojador was not the last and only secure point of navigation ; that beyond this cape the Atlantic was navigable ; that great and valuable discoveries could be made by tracing its line to the southward ; and, finally, he adopted the view that Africa was circumnavigable, and that India, with its vast and wealthy empires and lucrative commerce, could be reached by sailing around the southern end of Africa. Prince Henry commenced sending out expeditions to solve this dreaded yet fascinating problem. The first of these, in 1418, consisting of two vessels under the command of João Gonçalves Zarco and Tristan Vaz, intended to pass Cape Nun, was driven off the coast by storms, and resulted in the accidental discovery of Porto Santo. The next year the same captains discovered and colonized the island of Madeira, under the patronage of Prince Henry and the court of Lisbon. During twelve succeeding years he continued to send expedition after expedition. Cape Nun was passed, and Cape Bojador was reached, but beyond this nothing was accomplished, except to seem, alas! to confirm the popular belief that this was the limit of the habitable world, and that whoever doubled Cape Bojador would never return. The undaunted prince persevered against these prejudices and the home clamors at the expense of these fruitless expeditions, until, in 1433, one of his expeditions doubled this dreaded cape—an era in the history of navigation which, together with the recent discovery of the Azores, produced a great sensation in Portugal and throughout maritime Europe. These expeditions were regarded now with universal favor, as tending to enlarge the domain of Christendom. In 1441, at the solicitation of Prince Henry, the Pope granted to Portugal all the countries it could conquer from Cape Bojador to India. Indeed, these expeditions were regarded as holy or as naval crusades, and the Holy See conferred upon them extraordinary spiritual favors. Having extended their discoveries to the mouth of a river nearly two hundred miles south of Cape Bojador, in 1445, the Portuguese sailed down the coast of Africa as far as Cape Verde; and now these expeditions became profitable on account of the rich returns in gold and slaves, and the glory of Portugal's having advanced in that direction farther than any other European nation. In 1447 the limit of discovery was advanced to the river Gambia, and just before the death of Prince Henry, which occurred on November 13th, 1460, one of his expeditions had reached Sierra Leone. This noble prince did not live long enough to realize his fond hope of reaching India by sailing southward and eastward around Africa; but he had seen the Portuguese flag carried beyond the limits of all other European discovery and conquest in that direction. He bequeathed his spirit and his ambition to his country. Portugal, persevering in his grand purposes, which had now become national, in 1524, under Vasco de Gama, succeeded, but after

Columbus had discovered the new world, in doubling the Cape of Storms, whose name was then changed to the Cape of Good Hope, in reaching and sailing along the southern coast of India, and in thus opening to Europe the rich Oriental markets of Asia. So noble and brilliant a man was Prince Henry, and his work was so conducive to that of Columbus, that we will give here a personal account of him by one of Portugal's oldest and most distinguished historians : " He was bulky and strong ; his complexion red and white ; his hair coarse and shaggy. His aspect produced fear in those not accustomed to him, not in those who were ; for even in the strongest current of his vexation at anything his courtesy always prevailed over his anger. He was patient in labor, bold and valorous in war, versed in arts and letters ; a skilful fencer ; in the mathematics superior to all men of his time ; generous in the extreme, and zealous in the extreme for the increase of the faith. No bad habits were known in him. He did not marry, nor was it known that he ever violated the purity of continence." *

Had not Columbus been a man of original thought and independent character, he would have assuredly followed up the unaccomplished plans of Prince Henry the Navigator, for sailing and exploring around Southern Africa, and reaching Asia by a southeastern passage around the Cape of Good Hope. Like all the leading men of his times, he was deeply interested in and thoroughly aroused by the achievements of the Prince and the great discoveries of the Portuguese. Columbus, like Prince Henry, was "full of thoughts of lofty enterprise and acts of generous spirit," and, led by these noble sentiments, we now find him, in 1470, at Lisbon, among the throng of enterprising men, navigators, mathematicians, astronomers, and cosmographers, who had been attracted thither by the excitement of discovery, of which that capital was the focus, and by the pre-eminent energy and activity in maritime undertakings and conquests, which had raised Portugal from the smallest in size to be the foremost of European nations in glory and conquest.

Columbus was the most earnest and studious man in that active and restless throng of progressive men, and in his deep thoughts was generated a new departure from the accustomed course of

---

* Favia y Sousa, "Asia Portuguesa."

navigation and discovery. From the accounts given by Fernando Columbus and Las Casas, Mr. Irving summarizes the following personal description of the man, who was then coming forward to the accomplishment of results far grander and more useful to mankind than the great achievements of Prince Henry, for these two men stand forth as the paragons of that remarkable age. "According to these accounts," Mr. Irving writes of the coming man, " he was tall, well-formed, muscular, and of an elevated and dignified demeanor. His visage was long, and neither full nor meagre ; his complexion fair and freckled and inclined to ruddy ; his nose aquiline ; his cheek-bones were rather high, his eyes light gray, and apt to enkindle ; his whole countenance had an air of authority. His hair in his youthful days was of a light color, but care and trouble, according to Las Casas, soon turned it gray, and at thirty years of age it was quite white. He was moderate and simple in diet and apparel, eloquent in discourse, engaging and affable with strangers, and his amiableness and suavity in domestic life strongly attached his household to his person. His temper was naturally irritable, but he subdued it by the magnanimity of his spirit, comporting himself with a courteous and gentle gravity, and never indulging in any intemperance of language. Throughout his life he was noted for strict attention to the offices of religion, observing rigorously the fasts and ceremonies of the Church ; nor did his piety consist in mere forms, but partook of that lofty and solemn enthusiasm with which his whole character was strongly tinctured." This account by Mr. Irving has prepared us for another description by the manly and even more admiring pen of the Count de Lorgues, which is substantially given in the next paragraph.

The personal appearance of Columbus, prepossessing and imposing as it was, gave but a faint insight into the higher qualities of his mind and soul, as reverently represented to us by the venerable Count de Lorgues. His character was embellished with rich gifts of nature and of grace, of education and study, of magnanimity and virtue. The simplicity of his attire, so far from lessening the appreciation and respect of men, seemed to accord with the grandeur of his nature and the loftiness of his mind. His modesty only gave distinction to his presence. The grace and ease of his manners and the dignity and self-consciousness of his purposes enabled him to appear to advantage before

the proudest noblemen and grandees, as well as before the most
powerful and ceremonious sovereigns. His garments were long
worn but well preserved, spotless and unrent, and his linen was
always of the finest texture and purest white. He had a refined
and delicate taste, loved nature and the beauties of nature, and
while he admired the productions of the sea, he eagerly enjoyed
and admired flowers, birds, and other productions of the land.
His long and frequent following of the sea never tainted his mind
or manners with the coarseness or vices of seamen ; his language
was refined and chaste, he never indulged in games of chance,
avoided all effeminate pleasures, used but little wine, preferred
vegetable food, was frugal on land as he was at sea, and his
favorite beverage was orange water flavored with sugar or candy.
His religious inclinations were as fresh and constant at sea and
among distant and barbarous peoples as they were in his own
family. He sought the guidance of Heaven, and whenever he
succeeded in any of his undertakings, his first impulse was to
render thanks to God.

In his temperament, I must say, he was irascible, but this
failing he is known to have controlled and subdued by the
strength of his mind and the scrupulous and religious training of
his conscience. I will have but one occasion to relate his
yielding wholly to the anger and violence which injustice and
petty persecutions so naturally aroused in men of his nature ; but
the wrong had been long endured, and the yielding was of short
duration. He was generous almost beyond question, and gave
away the scanty means he needed even for purchasing the neces-
saries of life, in order to succor and relieve the poor or shipwrecked seamen who had followed him over the seas, and to
those even who had requited his generosity with the basest ingratitude. In his intercourse with men he was patient, condescending, and affable. To the rough and profligate, the treacherous and violent, with whom he was so constantly thrown in contact, and over whom he held almost at times unlimited power,
he was mild, just, and forbearing, and his conduct, in many of
the most trying and embarrassing positions in which it were
possible for a man to be thrown, was marked by wisdom, tact,
and good sense. With all this, his nature overflowed with sentiment, and his fancy revelled in the most portentous anticipations
and achievements. In the midst of his struggles and successes

he took an exquisite pleasure in the beauties of nature, and failed not to notice and admire the smallest as well as the grandest things of creation. His enthusiasm was unbounded, his faith jubilant, his hopes inexhaustible. In the home circle he was amiable and gentle, and won the hearts of those around him; yet he was capable of the most uncompromising severity when needed, and of the most just indignation. Even royalty itself was made to feel his just abhorrence of wrong. Such is a faint outline of the character of the man to whom the world owes and now acknowledges so much.

At Lisbon, on the arrival and during the residence of Columbus in that capital, all was activity, energy, bustle, and excitement; and every pulsation of the public heart and aspiration of the popular ambition were directed toward prosecuting the great works commenced by Prince Henry in the discovery, exploration, and conquest of distant countries. The king, the court, the high dignitaries of the Church—who then usually discharged the highest and most important functions of the government—the nobility, the gentry, the middle and lower classes of the people, were all swayed by the prevailing sentiment, dominated by the popular enthusiasm, and carried along by the ambition of the day. Portugal was still prosecuting the patriotic enterprises of Prince Henry, and to reach Asia, with its vast and populous empires; to make the wealth and markets of the East tributary to European predominance, interest, and luxury; to plant the national flag on distant conquests; to find the brilliant and imperial court of the Grand Khan and the long-sought Christian empire of Prester John, and to unite vast Oriental countries, with their teeming populations, to the Latin Church and to the spiritual sway of the successors of St. Peter, were the aspirations of the maritime European nations, and especially of little Portugal, in the fifteenth century. From time to time Lisbon was agitated over the successes of the national expeditions sent to explore the coast of Africa and to open the passage to Asia; by the return of fleets that had extended the field of discovery and enterprise, and by the departure of new expeditions—all which gave constant food to the excitement of the public mind.

The public events of the day, the new discoveries of the Portuguese, and the expansion of the boundaries of human knowledge and of human civilization, went far to educate the mind of

Columbus up to the great work for which he seemed destined ; but his intelligent, active, and enterprising intellect did not stop at this point of educational and mental development, which was attained by others, his contemporaries. He studiously delved into the writings of ancient and modern authors on cosmography, and studied all the existing maps of the earth. Though comparatively an obscure man, he became, in actual merit though not in reputation, one of the foremost men of his age in such learning ; and, though destitute of prestige, he became a man far in advance of his age and times; and prepared to meet and refute the opposition of most learned bodies that could then be assembled in any country. He evidently became self-conscious of a high and irrepressible destiny.

It is believed that Columbus, after studying the subject for years, had about the year 1474 arrived at a definite and positive belief that, by sailing westward across the Atlantic, the unknown lands, islands, and continents of the western ocean would be discovered. He did not follow the theory of Prince Henry of Portugal, that the only route to Asia by sea was that which led around the continent of Africa and by doubling the Cape of Good Hope. He believed that the most direct route to Asia was a western passage across the Atlantic ; and while this latter part of the theory of Columbus was an error of detail, the theory upon which he based it was correct, for the lands were there ; they lay in the very direction in which he sailed ; and by sailing westward he found them ! It is singular that neither Prince Henry the Navigator nor Christopher Columbus lived to realize the real value of the services which they had rendered to mankind. It was in the last year we have named above that Columbus is known to have mentioned for the first time his great theory to others. Heretofore his thoughts lay buried in his mind, but in his mind they constituted a real discovery.

Early in 1474 Columbus opened a correspondence with Dr. Paul Toscanelli, the learned physician, cosmographer, and geographer, of Florence, one of the most advanced scientists of the age, and one not only known and honored at Rome, but appealed to and consulted by the explorers and cosmographers of the time, who had already been in correspondence with King Affonso V., through the Canon Fernando Martinez, on the subject of the Portuguese voyages to Guinea. To this learned doctor Columbus wrote, and announced his theory and intention of testing the whole question, by making in person a voyage westward across the ocean, and his desire to find the opportunity of thus demonstrating the true shape and formation of the earth by sailing around it ; and he sent to the doctor a small globe explaining his views. Dr. Toscanelli's answer to Columbus is dated June 25th, 1474, in which he applauds in enthusiastic terms the latter's intention of sailing westward, imparts to him much new and quaint information on the subject, assures him of success in such unmeasured terms as to assume the result as an actual fact, and praises his zeal for the extension of the area of Christendom. Believing, as he did, in the practicability of reaching India by the western route, as proposed by Columbus, Dr. Toscanelli sent to the former, with his noble letter of encouragement and commendation, and as a return for the globe he had received from him, a map then of great value, which was prepared and made up of information and suggestions partly obtained from the celebrated map of Ptolemy and partly from the writings of Marco Polo. This celebrated map, which was carried by Columbus on his first voyage—the one which resulted in the discovery of America—confirmed the previous impressions of Columbus, for it located the eastern coasts of Asia in front of the western coasts of Europe and Africa ; the intervening ocean was regarded as the great highway leading from Europe to Asia, and while it seems to us singular how the width of the Atlantic could have been so greatly underestimated, this must be understood as a mistake caused partly by the imperfect knowledge of the earth possessed at that day, and by the corresponding exaggeration by Marco Polo and other authors of the size and width of the continent of Asia, and its supposed vast unknown empires. On this early and pioneer map are delineated and located, at convenient but conjectural distances apart, the great continental islands of Cipango, Antilla, and other islands of Eastern Asia. This noted map, with all its errors and misconceptions, was far in advance of the geographical knowledge of the age in which it was produced, and withal contained the pregnant and fruitful germs of many truths. Columbus was wonderfully encouraged and animated by this assuring and sympathetic letter of Dr. Toscanelli, and his mind became immovably bent on the great enterprise upon which it had been so long meditating. He procured a copy of the work of Marco Polo, in whose learned and fascinating pages he read of the vast and great empires of Cathay and Mangi, of their boundless riches and inexhaustible resources, and upon whose shores a navigator, sailing directly westward from Europe, according to Dr. Toscanelli, would be certain to land. In these richly laden pages Columbus read of the boundless empire of the Grand Khan of Tartary, of his wealth, grandeur, and power, the magnificence and splendor of the metropolitan cities of Cambalu and Quinsai, and the vastness and astounding details of the immense island of Cipango or Zipangi, which last is located in the ocean five hundred leagues from and opposite Cathay. Cipango abounded in gold, spices, precious stones, and the choicest articles of Oriental wealth and commerce, and the sovereign of the Imperial Island lived in palaces of immeasurable brilliancy, splendor, and luxury, the very roofs of which were of solid gold. While Marco Polo's narratives were exaggerated in their details, they contained much that was substantially true, and we now know that Cathay and Mangi were Northern and Southern China, and Cipango is now identified with Japan. The map and letter of Toscanelli and the work of Marco Polo had an unbounded influence upon the mind and faith of Columbus. They fired up to the highest pitch the already enkindled and enthusiastic imagination of that bold and ardent sailor, and they form a most important part of our history, by reason of the untiring and active influence they ever afterward exerted on the opinions, theories, actions, and career of the future admiral. During the whole remaining course of his checkered and eventful life, and to the hour of his death, the views interchanged between himself and Dr. Toscanelli remained among his firm convictions. As he presented his cause to one nation after another, he depicted the grandeur and wealth of the great Asiatic empires he expected to reach and bring into relations with the European world, and, in his deep religious feelings and zealous propagandism, he hoped to bring those empires, their sovereigns and peoples to embrace the Christian faith. Even when success crowned his efforts, he saw in the islands and lands he discovered the outposts of the great Oriental empires depicted on the map of Dr. Toscanelli and portrayed in the graphic pages of Marco Polo. The errors as to the size of Asia and the width of the earth, east and west, were fortunate errors; for had the reality been known,

Columbus could never have obtained recognition, nor ships, nor a crew of sailors, to undertake the voyage.

Columbus, as we are informed by his son and biographer, Fernando Columbus, as the great scheme for discovering the remaining unknown portions of our globe developed in his well-stored mind, arranged the grounds upon which he built his propositions and plans under three distinct heads. He relied in support of his theories on three sources of information: First, upon the very nature of things; second, upon the authority of learned writers; and, third, upon the reports of navigators. And Columbus, with great method and consummate skill, had arranged his arguments and facts under these respective heads; and this classification well represented the studies of his subject through which he had passed.

First: He contended that the earth was a globe or terraqueous sphere; that the circuit of this earth could be made by a traveler going either east or west, and that he could return to the spot from which he had started; he boldly announced his belief in the antipodes, and then, following Ptolemy, he divided the circumference of the earth from east to west into twenty-four hours, each hour containing fifteen degrees, or three hundred and sixty degrees in all. While he believed that the ancients had known of fifteen hours, extending from the Canary Islands to the Asiatic city of Thinæ, which was supposed to be the most eastern limit of the known world, the Portuguese had carried the western limits an hour farther west by discovering the Azores and Cape Verde Islands; and he computed that his proposed discoveries would disclose to mankind the remaining eight hours—one third—being the balance or unknown portion of the earth's circumference. This space was occupied by the Atlantic Ocean and the eastern portions of Asia, and, though as estimated by him less than the actual circumference of the earth as now known, he thought might be even reduced by the computation of Alfraganus, the Arabian astronomer, who had diminished the size of the degrees. With this data, drawn from the nature of the earth, correct in the main theory and erroneous only in detail, he contended that it was evident that a vessel sailing from east to west was certain to reach Asia, and whatever islands or lands rested in the intervening space of the ocean would thus be discovered.

Second: Under the second head Columbus manifested his usual research and learning. The classic authors of ancient Greece and Rome afforded him far greater authority for his theory even than modern authors, though his citations were well supported by the latter. Such writers as Aristotle, Seneca, and Strabo had believed that a ship might sail in a few days from Cadiz to the Indies. Strabo, too, had contended that it would be quite possible for a vessel to navigate on the same parallel, due west from the coast of Africa or Spain to the Indies, and that the ocean surrounds the earth, washing the shores of India on the east and those of Spain and Mauritania on the west. A passage from Aristotle is too remarkable to be omitted, and may be translated thus: " The whole inhabitable world consists of an island, surrounded by an ocean called the Atlantic. It is probable, however, that many other lands exist, opposite to this, across the ocean, some less, some greater than this; but all, except this, invisible to us." * Plato's "Dialogues" have already been alluded to, and here we have a direct allusion to a great island or continent called Atlantis, which had been the seat of a vast population, of powerful kingdoms, and of an advanced civilization; but that a great cataclysm had involved this vast island in ruin and had engulfed it in the ocean, leaving the Atlantic unnavigable by reason of the mud and slime that prevailed in its waters.† So, too, in Ælian mention is made of "Europe, Asia, and Africa composing one island, around which flows the ocean, the boundary of the world, and that only is continent which exists beyond the ocean." ‡ There is also another work published among the writings of Aristotle, but which some authors attribute to one of his disciples, entitled " De Mirabilibus," in which it is related that, in the days of Carthage's ascendency, certain Carthaginian merchants sailed over the Atlantic Ocean, and after many days arrived at a large island, which was at a great distance from any continent, was well wooded, watered with great rivers, and possessed a fertile soil. The voyagers made a settlement on the island, had their families brought thither, and the colony grew in power and population. The magistrate of Carthage, when he became aware of this new em-

---

* Aristotle, " De Mondo," cap. iii.   † Donnelly's " Atlantis."
‡ " Var. Hist.," lib. iii., cap. xviii.

pire springing up in the ocean, and saw the mother country depleted of its population, feared that the new nation might grow powerful enough to endanger the independence of Carthage herself, and issued his edicts forbidding the emigration of Carthaginians for this new settlement under penalty of death. Pomponius Mela* relates that when Quintus Metellus Celer was proconsul of Gaul, the King of Sweden presented him with Indians, who had been driven by a storm upon the shores of Germany; and although the Indian Ocean is mentioned as the medium over which they had been carried to Germany, the absolute absence of any such water communication between India and Germany or Sweden would leave the inference complete that they must have been borne across the Atlantic. Cornelius Nepos and Pliny mention this same circumstance. It is also related by Hugo Grotius that, in the time of the Emperor Frederick Barbarossa, Indians had been driven by a storm on the ocean upon the shores of Germany, as will be seen by reference to his treatise on the origin of the American tribes.

The remarkable lines of the learned Seneca, written in the first half of the first Christian century, are regarded as wonderfully prophetic of the discovery of America:

> "Venient annis,
> Sæcula seris, quibus Oceanus
> Vincula rerum laxet, et ingens
> Pateat Tellus, Typhisque novos
> Detegat Orbes, nec sit terris
> Ultima Thule."†

Mr. Joshua Toulman Smith, in his "Northmen in America," thus freely translates this passage, now nearly nineteen centuries old, as follows:

> "Naught now its ancient place retains;
> Araxes' banks the Indian gains;
> The Persian, Elbe and Rhine hath found,
> Far from his country's ancient bound.
> And ages yet to come shall see
> Old Ocean's limits passed and free,
> Where lands, wide-stretched, beyond our view lie
> Remoter than remotest Thule."

The Latin professor in one of our classical colleges has furnished me with the following more literal and graceful translation:

---

* "De Situ Orbis," lib. iii., cap. v.   † Seneca's "Medea."

> "An age in the dim distant future
> Shall the bonds of the ocean unbind;
> Shall open up earth to its limits,
> And continents new shall it find,
> When ultima Thule has left
>   But a name or a record behind."

In more modern times, about two centuries before Columbus announced his intention of revealing to the world the undiscovered lands of the western ocean, Dante had announced in divine verses his belief in such a fact :

> " De' vostri sensi, ch' è del rimanente,
> Non vogliate negar l'esperienza,
> Diretro al sol, del mondo senza gente."*

This beautiful passage has been admirably rendered by Carey, as follows :

> "'O brothers,' I began, 'who to the West
> Through perils without number now have reach'd,
> To this the short remaining match, that yet
> Our senses have to wake, refuse not proof
> Of the unpeopled world, following the track
> Of Phœbus.'"

And Longfellow, our own illustrious countryman, has rendered the same inspired words of the divine Dante into the following expressive English verses :

> "'O brothers, who amid a hundred thousand
> Perils,' I said, 'have come unto the west,
> To this so inconsiderable vigil
> Which is remaining of your senses still,
> Be ye unwilling to deny the knowledge,
> Following the sun, of the unpeopled world.'"

The "Cosmographia" of Cardinal Aliaco, who was born in 1340 and died in 1425, was a favorite work with Columbus, and while the text and the map accompanying the same partake greatly of the marvellous, for myths go hand in hand with facts and history, it gave valuable information on the subjects of Columbus's deep and constant thought and study.

But the most remarkable passage, that occurs in any work published before Columbus had achieved his great discovery, is one in the "Morgante Maggiore" of the Florentine poet Pulci, who makes the devil answer his companion Rinaldo, in allusion to the

---

* Dante's "Inferno," cant. 26, v. 115.

common superstition respecting the end of the earth being located at the Pillars of Hercules, our modern Gibraltar, thus:

> "Know that this theory is false; his bark
> The daring mariner shall urge far o'er
> The western wave, a smooth and level plain,
> Albeit the earth is fashioned like a wheel.
> Man was in ancient days of grosser mould,
> And Hercules might blush to learn how far
> Beyond the limits he had vainly set,
> The dullest sea-boat soon shall wing her way.
> Men shall descry another hemisphere,
> Since to one common centre all things tend;
> So earth, by curious mystery divine
> Well balanced, hangs amid the starry spheres.
> At our antipodes are cities, states,
> And thronged empires, ne'er divined of yore;
> But see, the Sun speeds on his western path
> To glad the nations with expected light."*

The author of these enlightened verses, showing a knowledge of scientific facts not fully demonstrated until more than a century afterward, was a contemporary of Columbus. He was born at Florence in 1431, and died, before the admiral had succeeded in getting any recognition of his theories, 1487. The "Morgante Maggiore" of Pulci was first published at Florence in 1481.

We have already alluded to the work of Marco Polo, who had traveled through many parts of Asia in the thirteenth century, and the influence it exerted upon the mind, theories, and subsequent career of Columbus He also attached great importance to the work of Sir John Mandeville, an English traveler, who in the fourteenth century proceeded to the East, visited the holy places in Palestine, and by the favor of the Sultan of Egypt acquired facilities for traveling through Armenia, Persia, India, Tartary, and Northern China, which last-named country was then called in the books Cathay. It is curious and interesting to notice in the life and writings of Columbus how his strong mind, while appropriating all the solid learning and verified facts related by these learned and enterprising authors and travelers, was, like their own minds, swayed by the mixture of fact and fable which characterized theirs and all the other cosmographi-

---

* Pulci, "Morgante Maggiore," cant. 25, st. 230. I have given Mr. Prescott's translation of these verses. See his "Ferdinand and Isabella," vol. ii., p. 117.

cal works of that and of previous ages. It was from such sources that Columbus derived his idea of the vastness of the Continent of Asia, which he believed filled the greater part of the unexplored space of the earth's surface, and left the width of the ocean to be crossed only about four thousand miles from Lisbon to the province of Mangi, near Cathay, now known to be Northern China. Columbus concluded that a voyage of no long duration would carry him to the eastern provinces of Asia and the vast and opulent adjacent islands. Dr. Toscanelli, the learned Florentine correspondent of Columbus, had also transmitted to him a letter he had previously written to Fernando Martinez, the learned canon of Lisbon already mentioned, giving a magnificent description of those wealthy Asiatic regions, taken from the work of Marco Polo, maintaining the practicability of the western Atlantic route to Asia, and mapping out the voyage as laying in the route of the opulent and favored islands of Antilla and Cipango, at whose safe harbors the ships of such an expedition could touch, replenish their supplies, rest their crews, and open those rich and productive markets to the commerce of Europe. It was even undertaken to show the distance between Antilla and Cipango, which was stated at two hundred and twenty-five leagues. The previously conceived views and plans of Columbus were greatly confirmed by such cogent and respectable authorities, and his alert mind expanded to the vast achievements which it had originated.

Third : The reports of navigators concerning their voyages, and the indications of unexplored lands which they had observed, also made a deep impression on the mind of Columbus. In that active age of discovery every circumstance, however trifling in itself, was seized upon to confirm the aspirations of ambitious explorers and discoverers. Columbus allowed nothing of this sort to escape his vigilant eye. His theories were confirmed by numerous objects which had floated ashore in Europe from the ocean, as so many indications of the existence of western lands ; shreds of knowledge derived from the veteran navigators of the coast of Africa ; the statements and rumors current among the inhabitants of the newly discovered islands along the African coasts ; the statement of an old Portuguese pilot named Martin Vincenti, that he had taken from the ocean a piece of carved wood, evidently wrought with an iron tool, at a distance of four hundred and fifty leagues west of Cape St. Vincent; the reported sight of a similar piece of wood by his brother-in-law, Pedro Corêa, on the island of Porto Santo; the narration by the King of Portugal concerning the reeds of immense size, which had floated to the shores of some of the Portuguese islands in the Atlantic from the west, and which Columbus recognized as answering the description of the mighty reeds which Ptolemy describes as growing in India—all these, and other similar reports, brought the theories of Columbus to a certain conviction of fact. Following up this line of inquiry, his notes show that he received also information from the inhabitants of the Azores of large trunks of great pine-trees, such as never grew on these islands, which were floated to their shores from the western ocean. Still more important and startling, he was informed of the floating ashore, on the island of Flores, of the bodies of two dead men, whose features were not similar to those of any of the then known races of men. A mariner of the port of St. Mary reported that, in a recent voyage to Ireland, he and his crew had seen lands to the west, which they believed were the remote eastern lands of Tartary. The traditions and fables of the past centuries were revived in a maritime age like that, such as those relating to St. Brandon's Island, the islands of the Seven Cities, and other similar mythical colonies of less enlightened times. It is interesting to observe from his notes, referred to by his son Fernando, how the practical mind of Columbus, though now worked up to a degree of wonderful enthusiasm, distinguished between fable and fact. He saw, however, from all these things, that an unbroken tradition—such, no doubt, as Mr. Winsor builds his whole work on Columbus upon—showed the belief of ages that many undiscovered lands existed, and that the field of enterprise was open to him, and that the time had come.

The authors to whom I have referred show, not the current and ordinary belief of the age in which Columbus lived, but they are wholly the examples of the most advanced and exceptional thought in preceding times and in his own. We have shown in our first chapter how the Atlantic was regarded as the Sea of Darkness, and the hearts of the most experienced navigators recoiled with fear from its terrors. Asia was then unexplored; the size and shape of the earth were unknown; the ocean was a sealed mystery and a seething vortex of death; the laws of specific

gravity and of central gravitation had not been discovered ; and
it was natural under these circumstances that astonishment and
opposition should be provoked by so daring a project as that of
Columbus. These facts, however, also show how Columbus,
availing himself of rare works and studies, had advanced to a
conviction far beyond the development of knowledge and science
in his age. It is an unchallenged fact that to Columbus alone is
due the merit of this great discovery, the revelation of one half
the world's surface to the inhabitants of the other half. The
achievement proves the fact. His studies and struggles, so far
in advance of his age and so much in conflict with the prevailing convictions of the civilized world, present a most interesting
phase in the history of the human mind—it was the effort of
man, led by one master mind, to assert dominion over the whole
earth ; it was the movement of human intellect to cast off the
inherited ignorance and prejudices of ages ; it was a vast stride
of civilization, of science, of thought, of conquest. Such was
the mental and moral movement, with all its train of social,
political, and commercial results, in which the world was led by
Christopher Columbus. Truly did he say of himself : " I have
been seeking out the secrets of nature for forty years, and wherever ship has sailed, there have I voyaged."

We have already related how the bold plans of Columbus for
discovering the remaining undiscovered portions of the earth,
and for exploring the space of ocean between Europe and Asia,
had matured in his mind as early as the year 1474. Between
that time and the period of his final career of success, which we
are now approaching, it would seem that he actually proposed
his plans first to his native city of Genoa and then to Venice,
"the city by the sea." The times and circumstances of these
negotiations are not precisely known, and some obscurity rests
upon this part of the admiral's career. It is thought that, from
motives of patriotism and love for his native place, he proposed
to Genoa first to take up his scheme and supply him with ships
to carry it into execution. Not only was his proposal refused by
the Senate of Genoa, but, after pleading the depleted condition
of the public treasury, they even threw doubts upon his being
the originator of the theory and plan. They alleged that the
records of their city showed that, two hundred years before, two
noble Genoese captains had sailed westward over the Atlantic,

and had never returned or been heard of. Turning next to Venice, he met with a courteous but firm refusal. It is probable that these events occurred prior to 1476, as it is asserted that from Venice he returned to visit his aged and venerable father at Savona, whom he found bent under his seventy years and his lifelong embarrassments, and that he assisted his good parent from his own scanty means. He returned to Lisbon, which was then and for many years the central point of nautical and geographical enterprise.*

At length the time seemed to have arrived for Columbus to advance upon his great mission. The epoch seemed propitious. The late King Alphonso had been too much occupied with dynastic and political ambitions to embark in other and more beneficent, though expensive undertakings. Yet it is thought that Columbus proposed his plans to him before the death of that king. Though the expeditions commenced along the coast of Africa by Prince Henry the Navigator had produced great results for Portugal, and though the mariner's compass had grown into more extensive application, the mind of the king and the sentiments of the people had not thrown off the timidity and fear of the ocean, which had been transmitted to the Europe of the fifteenth century from past ages. But now, in 1481, a young, more intelligent, and ambitious monarch had reached the throne of Portugal in the person of John II.; the invention of printing had given great impetus to all kinds of study and research, and the secrets of knowledge were now an open book to all. The young king seemed to have succeeded to the energy and enterprise of Prince Henry. He erected a fort at St. George de la Mina, on the coast of Africa, for the protection of Portuguese commerce, and looked with pride upon the maritime achievements of his country. The publication of the geographical works of Marco Polo, Sir John Mandeville, and other great travelers and geographers had deeply interested all, and now the narratives of Benjamin ben Jonah, of Tudela, in Spain, intensified the already deep interest felt in the study of the earth and the remote nations, empires, and countries thereof. Rabbi Benjamin had started from Saragossa in 1173, with the view of

---

* On these points the reader can consult with interest the pages of Irving and Tarducci.

reaching the remnants of the scattered tribes of Israel, wandered
over almost the entire Oriental countries, advanced into China,
and reached the extreme southern Asiatic islands.* So popular
and instructive was this work, that after its translation into
Western European languages, it had sixteen editions. To this
publication was added the works of travel by the two friars,
Carpini and Ascelin, whom Pope Innocent IV. had sent as apostolic envoys, respectively in 1246 and 1247, to announce the
Gospel to the Grand Khan of Tartary. So also was read with
avidity the journal of William Rubruquis, a Franciscan monk of
the Cordelier branch of that order, whom St. Louis, King of
France, had dispatched on a like pious errand, and who went
forth from the French crusade at Palestine, in 1253. The publication of these great works in print in the fifteenth century, and
their influence on the learned mind of Europe and their promotion of the spirit of maritime enterprise and inland continental
exploration, form an interesting guide in estimating how greatly
the invention of printing was influential in hastening the discovery of America. So prominently did the famous and long-sought-for Christian monarch of the East, Prester John, figure
in most of these narratives, that, as late as the times of which
I am now writing, King John II. of Portugal sent pious missionaries in search of this mythical and renowned personage, with the
desire of reuniting him and his supposed Christian subjects to
the one fold of Christ. He determined to revive the efforts of
Prince Henry, and he expended both energy, study, and treasure
in the most active prosecution of nautical and astronomical
studies and improvements, and in increasing the means and appliances of maritime development. In his efforts to secure greater
certainty of results and security to ships and crews, as well as
more accurate guides and means of navigation, he brought together the three most learned astronomers and cosmographers
of Portugal, his own physicians, Drs. Joseph and Roderigo, and
the distinguished navigator, Martin Behaim ; and the grand result of their joint studies, researches, and experiments was the
application of the astrolabe to navigation, by whose aid mariners
were able to ascertain at sea at any point the distance from the

---

* Irving's "Life of Columbus," vol. i., p. 62 ; Bergeron, "Voyages en Asie," tom.
l. ; Andres, "Hist. B. Let.," ii., cap. 6.

equator. The effect of this great discovery on navigation was
magical. The learned saw in it the loosing of the shackles which
bound the gallant ship to the timid limits of the coastwise navigation, and the unlearned sailor needed only to experience its
unerring guidance at sea to inspire him with courage to brave
the terrors of the ocean. Yet all these influences were principally confined for the time to the learned few, and to the advanced thinkers of the age; but there was no living navigator,
whose quick and experienced mind saw the value of this great
step, and appreciated it more or as much, as that of Christopher
Columbus. He saw that the age predicted by Seneca had
arrived, when the bonds of the ocean should be loosed, when the
earth's limits should be reached, and when a man of skill and of
courage should discover continents. He saw at once from the
astrolabe that

"the sky
Spreads like an ocean hung on high."

It seemed at first like a providence that had led his steps to
Lisbon, whose king and court were such enthusiastic patrons of
maritime science and discoveries. His mind did not rely upon
common report or popular rumor and conjecture; with him it
was an immovable conviction resting upon scientific data. At
the same time, being of a sanguine temperament, his enthusiasm
rose to the highest elevation, and he felt himself justified in meeting kings and courts, and claiming the trial and the inevitable
and just reward of his labors and researches. So exalted was
his perception of the truth, that he felt that he could dictate his
own terms to those who would reap the fruits of his bold conceptions. At the same time, he regarded even a hearing as a
boon. In his intercourse with men he was courteous, simple,
and gracious, and used both the persuasiveness of his eloquence
and the cogency of his arguments. He knew that King John of
Portugal was most anxious to find the route to India, for which
Prince Henry had sought so many years, and this he thought
opened to him his opportunity. He sought an audience with the
king, which, after some delay and hesitation, was granted. He
now presented his plan of a shorter, more direct, and safer route
to the coveted regions of India, and proposed that, if the king
would supply him with the necessary vessels, he would accomplish the voyage to India, not by sailing around Africa, as the

Portuguese had been for years endeavoring to do, but by sailing directly westward across the Atlantic Ocean. He supported his proposals by arguments and facts drawn from the nature, size, and shape of the earth, from the writings of learned authors, and from the reports of veteran navigators. While he dwelt eloquently on the vastness and wealth of the Asiatic empires he would find, he expressed the conviction that Cipango, the great island of unbounded opulence, would be the first land he would reach on his route.

Fernando Columbus,* no doubt deriving his information from the note-books of his father, represents King John as receiving favorably these startling proposals, but that he declined them at first on account of the vast expenditure already incurred in endeavoring to reach Asia by the African coastwise route; that Columbus sustained his proposals with such facts and reasons, enforced them with such eloquence, that the king consented to the proposals; but, when it came to the adjustment of the terms, as Columbus demanded concessions of such titles and substantial rewards, commensurate with the magnificent results he felt sure of accomplishing, that the negotiation fell through. The Portuguese historians, however, represent the king as regarding Columbus as overconfident and vainly presumptuous, and treated him merely with royal condescension. In fact, the king's credulity in Oriental fables far exceeded the enthusiasm of Columbus in behalf of a rational, but then regarded as a new and rash enterprise. The proposals were referred by the king to three learned men, Roderigo and Joseph, two expert cosmographers, and Diego Ortiz de Cazadilla, Bishop of Ceuta, a man of great reputed learning; but this learned Junto, regarding the plan as unfounded and chimerical, reported against it. But as King John was not content with this summary method of disposing of the subject, he convened a council composed of the savans of the kingdom, and requested their views on the subject. Though this learned body rejected the proposition of Columbus, it is evident from the speeches of the Bishop of Ceuta and of the Count of Villa Real, Don Pedro de Mereses, that Columbus must have gained some ground with the council, since his proposals were

---

* "Historie," etc., cap. xii.; Mr. Brownson's translation of Tarducci's "Columbus," vol. i., p. 66.

now apparently not rejected on account of their visionary and impracticable nature, but on account of the depleted exchequer and the preference of the Portuguese, through national pride, for the route proposed by Prince Henry, the route around the Cape of Good Hope, which had already, in its prosecution, led to such glorious results for Portugal, and had made her the foremost of maritime countries, though the smallest. Even this result did not satisfy the inclinations of the king toward an effort to accomplish what, if successful, would crown Portugal and his own reign with imperishable glory. It was at this juncture that Portugal made choice of a course, in respect to Columbus and his noble propositions, as disgraceful as the opposite course would have been wise and honorable. Yielding to the dishonorable suggestions of one of his council, King John, after mendaciously procuring, as if for the council, from Columbus, a minute plan of his proposed voyage and the maps and charts illustrative thereof, secretly and treacherously dispatched an expedition of his own, designed to rob Columbus of his glory and appropriate it for himself. Thus a caravel was sent out to cross the ocean in search of the promised land of Columbus, under the false and deceptive pretext of carrying provisions to the Cape Verde Islands. The captain had instructions to pursue the route westward indicated by Columbus. After the departure from the Cape Verde Islands, and pursuing the westward route for some days, the first severe weather, accompanied with storms, brought back to the imaginations and faint hearts of the crew the traditional terrors of the Sea of Darkness. They quailed before the task, and disgracefully returned to the land they had disgracefully left. To shield themselves, they had recourse to open ridicule and raillery against Columbus and his project, representing his plans as impossible, vain, and absurd.*

The lofty spirit of Columbus rose with indignation at this treachery when he heard of it, more especially when practised by a king and his council. He proudly rejected every offer of the king to enter into new treaties. Portugal had not only rejected his offers, but had attempted to rob him of his glory. He resolved to leave the treacherous land. The loss of his wife in

---

* Mr. Brownson's translation of Tarducci's "Columbus," vol. i.; Irving's "Columbus," vol. i.

1476 had long ago broken the last social link that bound him to the country.

Mr. Irving justly writes of the difficulties Columbus experienced in getting recognition of his grand projects : " To such men the project of a voyage directly westward, into the midst of that boundless waste, to seek some visionary land, appeared as extravagant as it would be at the present day to launch forth in a balloon into the regions of space in quest of some distant star."

Taking his departure from Portugal, in the autumn of 1484, Columbus, accompanied by his young son Diego, turned his course toward Spain. His departure from Lisbon was a secret one, as is supposed for the double purpose of avoiding forcible detention by the treacherous yet envious king, or by his creditors, for the former was desirous of reopening negotiations with him ; and such was the poverty of this most aspiring man of the age, that he was probably compelled to beg his bread, or purchase it on credit, while on the eve of bestowing continents on mankind.*

The dignity and justice of history, the conservative caution and necessity for substantial material as the basis of a statement or conjecture, which ought to characterize historical criticism of an acceptable standard, should have prevented historians or critics, such as Harrisse and Winsor, from uttering another calumny against the name and fame of so eminent and historical a personage as Christopher Columbus, or even a mere sinister insinuation —for such only is it—such as the intimation that he deserted his first wife and other children when he left Portugal in the latter part of 1484. Winsor, unreasonably following Harrisse, to whom he himself attributes habitual scepticism, gives expression to this, among his many calumnies against the great discoverer, in the following illogical and unhistorical passage : " Irving and the biographers in general find in the death of Columbus's wife a severing of the ties which bound him to Portugal ; but if there is any truth in the tumultuous letter which Columbus wrote to Donna Juana de la Torre, in 1500, he left behind him in Portugal, when he fled into Spain, a wife and children. If there is the necessary veracity in the ' Historie,' this wife had died before

---

* Irving's "Columbus," vol. i., p. 69 ; Mr. Brownson's translation of Tarducci's "Life of Columbus," vol. i., pp. 70, 71. See also the Count de Lorgues' "Columbus." and the general list of authors herein given, bearing on the subject of Columbus, etc.

he abandoned the country. That he had other children at this time than Diego is only known through this sad, ejaculatory epistle. If he left a wife in Portugal, as his own words aver, Harrisse seems justified in saying that he deserted her, and in the same letter Columbus says that he never saw her again."

Now the letter in question had no reference whatever to his leaving Portugal or to his first wife, whom he married in Madeira. It was written in 1500, when he was returning to Spain in chains, and with his manacled hands. It was addressed to a friend whom he had at court, and who, he knew, would communicate it to Queen Isabella, Donna Juana de la Torre; and she, in fact, did communicate the letter to the queen. This letter is one of complaint over the wrongs he was then suffering from the hands of Bobadilla, in the name of the sovereigns, and was an appeal to them for justice, to which end he recounted what he had done and suffered in their service. Portugal had passed far away from his daily memories, at that dread moment especially, and he had no regrets for having fifteen years before abandoned a country where he had met with nothing but delay, deception, treachery, and wrong. The wife and children to whom he alluded in this letter were Donna Beatrix Enriquez and his two children, Diego and Fernando, all of whom he had left living together at Cordova, in order to embark in the perilous and momentous service of the Spanish king and queen; his family was never reunited again, and it was true, as stated by Columbus in this important letter, he never had the happiness of living with his family again. Such was the treatment which Columbus had received in Portugal, that it would be a violent interpretation to put upon a letter written at any after period by him, that he expressed regrets at leaving that country, or that he regarded it, as in any sense, a sacrifice to have exchanged it for Spain.

This letter serves the double purpose of refuting two calumnies, which Mr. Winsor repeats after other writers, against the character of Columbus: first, that he deserted his wife and children in Portugal, and second, that he was never married to the mother of his second son, Fernando. It was, in fact, his son Fernando who accompanied his father on his fourth and last voyage, and received from the admiral's lips the details of his eventful life. These sacred communications between the father and son were, after the admiral's death, used as the materials for the "Historia del Almirante," written by this devoted son; and in this important work Fernando states expressly that the admiral's first wife died before he left Portugal. Could there be a better witness than this, who repeated the very account he received from the admiral himself? Is it possible that Columbus should, in this very same voyage, in a letter to Donna Juana de la Torre, have contradicted what he had just told Fernando? But Mr. Winsor, in order to maintain his accusation against Columbus, found it necessary to deny the veracity of his son and historian, Fernando Columbus. It is the uniform voice of history that the character of Fernando Columbus was above reproach. In a Spanish work giving the history of the eminent families of the very city in which Fernando was born, he is spoken of as "a gentleman of great intelligence, bravery, virtue, and a great scholar."

The letter of Columbus to Donna Juana de la Torre, which Mr. Winsor uses so uncandidly as the basis of his assertion that Columbus, in 1484, deserted his first wife and children in Portugal, was, on the contrary, relied upon by other writers as proof of the opposite conclusion, and they applied it to his leaving his second wife, Beatrix Enriquez, and his two sons at Cordova, in order to find a new world for Spain. Count Roselly de Lorgues, in his "Life of Columbus," writes of this very point as follows: "Finally, these assurances (as to the legitimacy of Columbus's relations with Beatrix) received their last irrefragable guarantee from the very hand of Columbus himself. In a letter to persons whose duty he considered it was to support his reclamations at the court of Spain, he reminds them that for the service of the crown he quitted all—wife and children—and never enjoyed the sweetness of living with his family."* Mr. Fiske, with the same misconception of the allusions in the letter, draws quite a different conclusion—one, on the contrary, honorable to Columbus. He says: "My own notion is that Columbus may have left his wife with an infant and perhaps one older child, relieving her of the care of Diego by taking him to his aunt" (in Spain), "and intending as soon as practicable to reunite

---

* Winsor's "Columbus," etc., p. 154; Count Roselly de Lorgues' "Life of Columbus," by Dr. Barry, p. 43.

the family. He clearly did not know at the outset whether he should stay in Spain or not." *

But now we have the result of the researches of Senhor Pereira, Director of the National Library at Lisbon, and of Senhora Regina Maney, among the national archives of Portugal —results bearing directly and powerfully on this point. For the information they thus give on the subject we are indirectly indebted to Mr. Winsor himself, for in her preface Senhora Maney states that when she applied to the Director of the National Library at Lisbon to join her in her researches, " he opened our Winsor's book on Columbus at the page where that author intimates that much that was new could probably be learned about Columbus from documents not yet examined in the Torre de Tombo (the national archives)." They accordingly looked where Mr. Winsor pointed the way, and most of their conclusions are based upon those very archives. " In 1476 Diego Columbus was born, the only fruit of this union, the little fecundity of which has been to us an object of some reflection, when we consider the healthy stock both Donna Philippa and Columbus sprang from, as well as a few facts several writers hint at with regard to the epoch of that lady's death.

" In Pira Loureiro's genealogical work, whose twenty-eight volumes have been most useful to us, we see the confirmation of our suspicion that the death of Columbus's wife must have followed quite close upon the birth of her son. Before the name of Donna Philippa is to be read the summary notice, ' that she did not live long after the birth of her son.' Did she die in child-bed ? Did she enjoy only a few days or weeks of the ineffable happiness of being a mother ?

" This species of revelation, which by itself cannot define an epoch, contains a fact in the life of Columbus that has a certain logical value in turning that life less vague, which has much impressed us. This fact consists in the departure of the daring navigator for the Arctic regions in 1477.

" We observe Columbus got married in 1475, had a son born to him in 1476, and left for a most dangerous voyage in 1477, there existing no known engagement of any kind or plans conceived and matured beforehand. The rapid succession of the

---

* Fiske's " Discovery of America," vol. i., p. 399, *note*.

three facts has a something of mystery about it, on account of the precipitation of the latter. Reason and heart alike refuse to believe that the peaceful life of Columbus and Donna Philippa, who saw their union blessed and their poor home gladdened by the birth of a son, should in the very year following this event be rudely disturbed by a long separation without a sudden and powerful motive.

"The above transcribed phrase, and the fact of this rather violent separation, concur in perfect harmony in fixing the epoch of Donna Philippa's death as between the birth of the son and the voyage of her husband to the northern seas.

"The grandmother of the little boy-child was to take the place of the mother, substituting her love and care for that of which death deprived the poor infant all too soon. The father, profoundly wounded in his passionate attachment to his wife, took one of those extreme resolutions in which great moral sufferings sometimes end." *

The important facts thus arrayed by these accomplished Portuguese scholars, as I am credibly informed they are, already confirmed by the explicit statement in Loureiro's genealogical works, receive further confirmation from Columbus's voyages among the islands and main stations in Portuguese Africa immediately after his return from Iceland, from his abandonment of Funchal and Machico as a residence, his return to Lisbon, his long and ultimate stay in that capital, and the fact that during the remaining seven years of his sojourn in Portugal no mention is made of Philippa or of his having a wife. Repeating the cogent language of the authors of "The Wife of Columbus," "heart and reason alike refuse to believe" that it was possible that Columbus under such circumstances and facts could have "deserted" her, who had married him in poverty at Funchal, and shared his sorrows.

---

* "The Wife of Columbus," Pereira and Maney, pp. 46, 47.

CHAPTER IV.

> " Ay, nerve thy spirit to the proof,
>   And blench not at thy chosen lot ;
> The timid good may stand aloof,
>   The sage may frown—yet faint thou not !
> Nor heed the shaft too surely cast,
>   The hissing, stinging bolt of scorn ;
> For with thy side will dwell at last
>   The victory of endurance borne."
>
> —Bryant.

Though Columbus left Lisbon in the autumn of 1484, we have no traces of his immediate movements or presence until the following year. Some have supposed that it was during this uncertain interval that he made propositions to Genoa and Venice. Such was his filial piety, such his love for home, that he now, no doubt, visited and assisted his venerable father, carrying with him his son Diego. It is quite probable, as asserted by some authors upon tradition only and without any authentic proofs of the fact, that from Portugal he again proceeded to Genoa, in 1484, and for the second time earnestly pressed his application upon the Senate of his native city. It is further stated that the vessels of the little republic were all needed and were then actively in service at home, and not a ship could be spared for a service which would have reflected much greater profit and honor upon the Genoese.

The first information we have of Columbus's arrival in Spain, according to Mr. Irving,* was in the year 1485. According to others it was in January, 1486. The chivalrous spirit of that noble nation, its zeal for the ancient faith and for its extension to heathen peoples, the union of the crowns of Aragon and Castile under Ferdinand and Isabella, and the intelligence and energy of those two young and accomplished sovereigns, induced him to go, discouraged but not disheartened, to that gallant people.

---

* Irving's " Columbus," vol. i., p. 72.

Tired, however, of the delays and disappointments he had experienced at the various governments to which he had applied, we find him first in the south of Spain negotiating with opulent and powerful noblemen, such as the Dukes of Medina Sidonia and Medina Celi, who possessed immense estates, who even maintained armies of their own, and were more like allies than vassals of the crown. The Duke of Medina Celi received Columbus as his guest, and was so thoroughly convinced of the practicability of his plans, that he was on the point of placing at his disposal a fleet of three or four caravels then ready for sea in his own harbor of Port St. Mary, near Cadiz ; but the consideration that such an undertaking was more fitting for the king and queen, and that he might thereby provoke the animosity of the crown, deterred him from the undertaking. The apprehension that Columbus would go to France caused the duke to give him a letter to Queen Isabella, in which he recommended him and his project to her Majesty, and requested, in case the expedition was undertaken, that himself might be permitted to share in it. Columbus repaired at once to the Spanish sovereigns, then holding their court at Cordova.

There is a singular difference in the account given of this part of the life of Columbus by Mr. Irving and by Senor Tarducci. The latter does not find any trace of him in Spain until the spring of 1486, when he states that his first visit to the Convent of La Rabida, accompanied by his son Diego, took place. Columbus is represented as leaving his little son with the prior of the convent, while he, supplied with money for his journey, a letter of introduction to the Father Prior of the Monastery of El Prado, and fortified with the blessing and encouragement of Father Juan Perez de Marchena, started in the spring of 1486 for Cordova to lay his proposals before the sovereigns. Mr. Irving makes Columbus pay but one visit to the convent before the signing of the capitulations with the Spanish sovereigns, while Tarducci relates two such visits, the second one being in 1491 or 1492, when Columbus, after exhausting all his efforts with the crown, was on the eve of departing from Spain for France.

The Count de Lorgues states that Columbus went from Portugal to Genoa and Venice, there in succession had his proposal declined, and that he returned to Spain in 1485, when his first visit to the Convent of La Rabida took place. He also states that in 1491 or 1492 Columbus, despairing of aid from Spain, was about to go to France, but paid a second visit to the Convent of La Rabida. Yet the still later account of Justin Winsor, in 1891, shows that author unable to determine whether Columbus visited the Convent of La Rabida once or twice. In one place he writes : " Ever since a physician of Palos, Garcia Fernandez, gave his testimony in the lawsuit through which, after Columbus's death, his son defended his titles against the crown, the picturesque story of the Convent of Rabida, and the appearance at its gate of a forlorn traveller accompanied by a little boy, and the supplication for bread and water for the child, has stood in the lives of Columbus as the opening scene of his career in Spain." * And again he says : " This story has almost always been placed in the opening of the career of Columbus in Spain. It has often in sympathizing hands pointed a moral in contrasting the abject condition of those days with the proud expectancy under which, some years later, he sailed out of the neighboring harbor of Palos, within eyeshot of the monks of Rabida. Irving, however, analyzed the reports of the famous trial already referred to, and was quite sure that the events of two visits to Rabida had been unwittingly run into one in testimony given after so long an interval of years. It does, indeed, seem that we must either apply this evidence of 1513 and 1515 to a later visit, or else we must determine that there was great similarity in some of the incidents of the two visits."† But subsequently, narrating the events of 1491, the same writer says : " A consultation which now took place at the Convent of Rabida affords particulars which the historians have found difficult, as already stated, in keeping distinct from those of an earlier visit, if there were such." ‡

Mr. John Fiske, however, with historical acumen and decisiveness, but with less pretension to expert criticism, was able to arrive at a definite and positive opinion on the subject. He makes Columbus go into the service of Ferdinand and Isabella in January, 1486, after an interval of over a year of unascertained engagements, possibly in Genoa and Venice, and he places the only visit of Columbus to the Convent of La Rabida in 1491, when he was about to abandon Spain in hopelessness. In this

---

* Winsor's "Columbus," etc., p. 154. † *Id.*, p. 156. ‡ *Id.*, p. 173.

account he says: "For some reason or other—tradition says to ask for some bread and water for his boy—he stopped at the Franciscan Monastery of La Rabida, about half a league from Palos. The prior, Juan Perez, who had never seen Columbus before, became greatly interested in him, and listened with earnest attention to his story." * And in another place he says: "It is pretty clear that Columbus never visited La Rabida before the autumn of 1491."

Ferdinand and Isabella were two of the most remarkable, successful, and promising sovereigns in Europe. As two prominent figures in the history of the discovery of America, they seem to stand in parallel yet contrasting attitudes with Prince Henry the Navigator and Christopher Columbus the discoverer. Their reign was in many respects the most glorious and the most remarkable in the history of Spain. Their crowns were only united by marriage, each retaining a separate and yet a co-ordinate sovereignty. They could act for their respective kingdoms independently of each other; each had a separate exchequer and a separate council; and yet all the acts of sovereignty were their joint acts; they both joined in signing royal documents; the coin of the country bore the images of both; and the arms of Aragon and Castile were united on the royal seal. Such, however, was the independence of the one from the other, that it was almost entirely the separate glory of Isabella that Columbus was enabled to discover the new world. Ferdinand was rather an impediment, and even when a new world was placed at his feet he was not grateful.

Ferdinand's character was set off by many lights and shadows, and it seems strange how so many good and bad qualities could be united in the same person. He was fortunate to a marvellous degree, inheriting Aragon, acquiring Castile by marriage, seizing Navarre on the excommunication of its sovereigns, taking Granada and Naples by conquest, reducing by his arms Tunis, Tripoli, Algiers, and most of the Barbary States, and making them vassals of his throne. His extraordinary fortunes were crowned by having a beautiful and accomplished queen for his wife, and in having a new world placed at his command with little effort, sympathy, or expenditure on his part. He was a

---

* Fiske's "Discovery of America," vol. i., pp. 399, 410.

man of deep and uniform, though perhaps not always consistent religious faith and zeal; he prosecuted with success the conquest of the Moors in Spain and added their country to his crown, and expelled the Jews from his dominions. He was rewarded by Pope Innocent VIII. with the title of Most Catholic Majesty. But Ferdinand was selfish, intolerant, grasping, wily, ungrateful, and, when his interests were involved, unscrupulous.

The character of Isabella was a model of moral, intellectual, religious, and queenly symmetry. Beautiful in person, graceful in movement, and benignant in every expression, she possessed a tender heart, a quick and expansive intellect, a generous nature, and a pure and upright conscience. She surpassed in judgment and intellect her more astute consort; she had more genius than he, and on many occasions exhibited greater firmness and intrepidity. He was subtle and calculating; she was gifted with higher genius and with a truer and more noble nature. Saintly in her life and devotions, she was wholly free from intolerance. She opposed the expulsion of the Jews, tempered the treatment of the subjugated Moors with mercy, hated slavery and oppression of every kind, was simple and frugal in her private life while regal in her public administration; she was fond of liberal and learned studies, and promoted the highest forms of education in her realm. While Ferdinand possessed the traits of a successful politician, Isabella possessed many of the masculine and sterner qualities that fitted her for a ruler and a conqueror, without losing an iota of the graceful and tender virtues that adorn preeminently the character of woman. While her reign would have been even more glorious without a Ferdinand, his career would have been less commendable without an Isabella. It was fortunate for Columbus, for the cause of human development and civilization, and for the sake of the teeming nations now inhabiting the new world, that by the duke's letter of commendation the cause of Columbus was placed under the generous and enlightened patronage of the illustrious Isabella, rather than subjected to the cold and selfish scrutiny of Ferdinand. As it was, the cause was lost so far as his calculating and short-sighted policy could crush it, as it was only saved by the personal generosity of the noble queen.

On his arrival at Cordova, Columbus found the sovereigns, the court, the army and the nation all absorbed in the war against the Moors. It was a turning-point in the war. The two rival Moorish kings of Granada, Muley Boabdil, the uncle, and Mohammed Boabdil, the nephew, had become reconciled, and had united their strength for a last struggle against the combined forces of Aragon and Castile. The court, resembling more a military encampment, the nobles and grandees of Spain, the chivalry of Aragon and Castile, and all the military forces of the nation were assembled, and the busy and ceaseless din of war resounded on all sides. The king and queen prosecuted the war in person, and moved from one point to another to meet the exigencies of the campaign. At one moment siege had to be laid to the Moorish city of Loxa ; the siege of Moclin followed ; and scarcely had the sovereigns time to make their thanksgiving for these victories at Cordova, when they had to hasten to Galicia to quell the rebellion of the Count de Lemos. In the mean time, Columbus at Cordova was the guest of Alonzo de Quintanilla, the comptroller of the Treasury of Castile. In the winter of 1484-85, the court having temporarily established itself at Salamanca, Columbus followed thither. He had not yet had an audience. During his tedious sojourn at Cordova he had made earnest converts to his cause of his generous host, Quintanilla, and of the Papal Nuncio, Antonio Geraldini, and of his brother Alexander, the latter being tutor to the royal children.

At Salamanca Columbus, through the influence of his friend, Quintanilla, was introduced to His Eminence Cardinal Pedro Gonzales de Mendoza, Archbishop of Toledo, who occupied so important and influential a position at court that Peter Martyr used to call him "the third King of Spain." This learned and noble-hearted ecclesiastic at first hesitated about countenancing one whose theories as to the form of the earth seemed to him to contradict the accounts of the sacred Scriptures ; explanations of the theory of Columbus followed, and the intelligent mind of the cardinal soon perceived and acknowledged that no truths of science or of actual discovery could militate against the truths of religion, for all truth is one and harmonious. He received Columbus, who, knowing the importance of such an audience, exerted his best abilities and most thorough efforts to convince his illustrious hearer of the truth of his theories, and he succeeded. Admiring the learning, the simplicity, and frankness of

Columbus, as well as his great and self-conscious dignity and lofty bearing, the cardinal secured for him an audience at court. Appearing before the astute and discriminating Ferdinand, for it seems in doubt and improbable that the queen was present, Columbus with modesty, self-possession, eloquence, and zeal stated and explained his propositions to the king, who was evidently impressed by his scientific and practical views, by the immense advantages he would gain over other nations by such an enterprise crowned with success, and especially over his rival, Portugal. Ferdinand, however, was too cautious to commit himself; but the first step was gained by the king's ordering Fernando de Talavera, Prior of the Monastery of Prado, a man of great learning, but one who had no special knowledge of the scientific studies connected with the enterprise of Columbus, to call together the most accomplished and learned astronomers and cosmographers of the kingdom, with the intention of sifting the matter, and more especially of interrogating Columbus on the foundations and reasons for his theories and plans. This learned Junto was to report to the king. Columbus repaired to Salamanca, by the professors of whose famous university his theories, proofs, and propositions were to be examined. At Salamanca he became the guest of the Dominican Convent of St. Stephen, a part of the university. The Junto was composed of professors of astronomy, geography, mathematics, and of other sciences, besides whom there were present as members of the council several high ecclesiastics and erudite friars. The time when this famous conference was held was probably the winter of 1486-87. It is difficult for us, after four hundred years, and under such different circumstances of time, place, country, institutions, and ideas, to comprehend the almost appalling difficulties under which Columbus appeared before this august body to plead the cause of a new world. Confirmed prejudices against all that was new, the pedantry of learning, the power of place, the timidity of conscientious pastors, confessors, and theologians lest some danger of disturbing the faith of the flock or of the schools might occur, the national distrust of foreigners, the disposition of placemen to regard a man in his poor circumstances and with his startling propositions as a visionary, an adventurer, a mendicant, if not even a lunatic—all these and many other disturbing and disheartening sentiments and influences stood in the way of Columbus. Under such adverse circumstances Columbus appeared before the learned Junto at Salamanca with a calm and confident mien; his manner and address were courteous and reverential, his mind was clear and full of conviction, the resources of argument, science, learned tradition, and many years of study were ready at his command; his bearing was dignified, lofty, and conscious of truth and justice; he felt and expressed the inspiration of his vocation. He felt that he had carried his appeal from ignorant and capricious public opinion to the candor and discrimination of a learned and dignified body; from the rabble, that had jeered at and had ridiculed him, to the erudite and responsible representatives of the Spanish crown and of the educated and devout world. Yet this learned assembly piteously fell below the standard of their own fame and pretensions. With the exception of the good and learned friars of St. Stephen's Convent, the most learned body in the far-famed University of Salamanca, who paid deep attention to Columbus from the beginning, these dignified officials and shallow scholars prejudged his cause and his scientific problems and propositions. It seemed absurd that an obscure mariner should know and be able to do more than all the world beside had known and done for so many centuries. Passages from the sacred Scriptures and from the Fathers of the Church were quoted and wrested to the refutation of purely scientific propositions. Then, entering upon the discussion on scientific grounds, the ignorance and errors of ages were adhered to, rather than the new light of advancing knowledge and science; the existence of the antipodes was regarded as absurd; the earth was argued to be flat and not round; even if an opposite and habitable hemisphere existed, it would be impossible to reach it or return, in consequence of the unendurable heats of the torrid zone; or if this were not so, the circumference of the earth must be so great as to require three years at least to reach the other hemisphere, and all attempting it must perish of hunger and cold; that only the Northern Hemisphere was habitable, and the heavens did not extend beyond it; that all else was chaos; and that, even if vessels should succeed in sailing down the route to India, it would be impossible for them to sail up again to Europe, as the rotundity of the earth would present a mountain-like barrier, which the most favorable winds would never enable them to surmount.

Columbus, in face of such unexpected methods of considering a scientific proposition, rose to the full strength and dignity of his mission. The contrast between traditional and learned ignorance, on the one hand, and the advanced theories of modern and awakening science, on the other, was presented. There was an immense gulf between them. Columbus broke down the barriers, and the human intellect expanded to receive the new results of actual demonstration. The attitude, the bearing, and the answer of Columbus to his opponents in the council are described by his contemporaries as having been impressive. With remarkable clearness he argued that the passages from the sacred writings did not profess to use scientific or technical language, but rather aimed at reaching the human mind by the figurative language of the current age and country; the Fathers of the Church, also, he demonstrated, were writing devout commentaries, and in illustrating them merely used such scientific views and facts as then prevailed or were possessed by the world. But even here he was superior to his opponents in their own field of scriptural inquiry and sacred lore, for, taking them on their own grounds, he quoted those renowned and startling passages of the Scriptures, those mystic prophecies of the inspired prophets of old, which he, in his devout zeal, construed as prophetic and typical of the grand results he aimed at, and of the man himself, who, as he believed himself to be, was destined to accomplish them. In appealing to the writings of the ancient philosophers of Greece and Rome, the opponents of his problems and plans found in Columbus an over-match, for he was familiar with them, and he was able to show a wonderful consensus of ancient authors in favor of his views as to the size, contour, and shape of the earth and the ocean. As to the torrid zone being impassable, he assured them, from what he saw in his voyage to St. George la Mina, in Guinea, which was near the equator, that the torrid zone was inhabitable and traversable; that it possessed a teeming population, and was rich in the productions of the animal and vegetable kingdoms. As to a ship's inability to overcome the rotundity of the earth, his own voyage to Iceland and back, and the expeditions of the Spanish and Portuguese navigators between the ports of Spain and Portugal and the islands far south on the African coast, demonstrated the absurdity of the objection. In this contest of the intellect Columbus stood

forth inevitably victorious on all points in reality, for scientific
and actual truth were on his side. His answers made a profound
impression on many of his hearers. Among those convinced of
the truth of his propositions and converted to his cause was
Diego de Deza, a good and learned friar of St. Stephen, afterward Archbishop of Seville ; but Fernando de Talavera, who
was charged with conducting the investigation, was indifferent,
too much absorbed in pressing public interests, in the war against
the Moors, or other official cares, to give much countenance to
what seemed an abstract and visionary scheme. The learned
Junto, with some few illustrious exceptions, was still uncon-
vinced. The majority was against the plan. Some further conferences were held, but no result was attained. Mr. Winsor,
with his usual scepticism, attributes but little importance to the
conference at Salamanca, alleging that it was held with Talavera
and a few councillors, and that it was in no way associated with
the prestige of the University of Salamanca.*

In the mean time, the Moorish war was prosecuted with great
activity. In the spring of 1487 the court returned from Salamanca to Cordova ; the campaign against Malaga followed ; the
war was conducted in a rugged and mountainous country, and
through various vicissitudes the city of Malaga was forced to
surrender on August 18th, 1487. Columbus followed the court
and army, and was several times summoned before the sovereigns
in intervals of warlike struggle, or during the comparative leisure
of a long siege, to explain again and again his plans ; but each
time disappointment and postponement awaited him. Returning
to Cordova after the surrender of Malaga, the hopes of Columbus
for a more patient hearing were again blasted, for the court and
its retinues were almost immediately driven away from the city
by the outbreak of a pestilence, and from Cordova to Saragossa ;
then in another campaign in Murcia, then at Valladolid, and next
at Medino del Campo. Nearly a year thus passed—a year of
cruel delays and disappointments to Columbus. During its shifting scenes, arduous marches, and many perils, Columbus followed up his suit at this ever-migratory court with zeal and perseverance, and thus encountered the hardships of war in the
pursuit of a scientific enterprise. His patience, however, was

---

* Winsor's " Columbus," pp. 161, 162.

severely tried. While expounding his proposals in Spain, he had been cautious in not imparting enough of his plans to enable any treacherous adversary, if there should be one at hand, to attempt to defraud him of his glory, as was done in Portugal.

While Columbus was baffled in Spain by the delays and the uncandid pretensions of King Ferdinand, Portugal had made a noted and proud advance toward discovering the African route to Asia. Ferdinand did not yet trust in the Atlantic or western route, and yet he kept the inventor of it fruitlessly hanging around the wandering and warlike court. It is a singular fact that Bartholomew, the brother of Columbus, had taken part in the Portuguese expedition, which resulted in the discovery of the Cape of Good Hope, under Diaz, and in December, 1487, he had returned to Lisbon with the electrifying news. It is supposed by some that Columbus had now become so disgusted with Spanish delays, that early in 1488 he thought of again opening negotiations with the King of Portugal, John II., and went to Lisbon for that purpose; he had asked for and obtained a safe conduct from that sovereign, and left Spain. Other accounts represent him as going to Lisbon toward the last of the summer, for the purpose of meeting Bartholomew and of sending him to England to open negotiations with Henry VII. He went to Lisbon, however, at this time under King John's safe conduct, which was dated March 20th, 1488. Probably the Portuguese king, in giving him so full a protection, which it is supposed was also intended as an assurance against the interference of creditors with Columbus, who had been so absorbed in his great project as to neglect his private affairs, had in view the renewal of negotiations for an arrangement with Columbus for his proposed westward voyage of discovery. But this was not practicable; or at least Columbus did not entertain such proposals for his once rejected and attempted-to-be-stolen plans, or did not tarry for them, for he was back again in Spain in May, 1489.

Bartholomew Columbus, the ever-faithful brother and supporter of the admiral, a man of no mean ability, whether with the pen or the sword, for he was at once a good map-drawer, sailor, and soldier, was sent out to open negotiations with England and France. Directing his course first to Bristol, where he had many acquaintances of his seafaring life, and captured on the way by pirates, he finally arrived at London undaunted and well equipped for his brother's cause. At the court of Henry VII. he made a deep impression by his arguments and facts upon the mind of the king, especially with the assistance of a map of his own skilful workmanship. While the English monarch fully appreciated the scheme, he did not feel inclined hastily to embark in so remote an enterprise, and Bartholomew went to France. At the court of Charles VIII. he had an influential friend in Madame de Bourbon, a sister of the king; but now again his cause was slow of success, and he resorted to his occupation of Lisbon in making geographical maps, chiefly for the members of the court. In the mean time, Henry VII., probably stimulated by the advancing prospects of Columbus in Spain, came to a favorable conclusion in the spring of 1492. The next meeting between the two brothers, Christopher and Bartholomew, as to the circumstances of time, place, and results, as I shall mention hereafter, was interesting and historically dramatic.*

Mr. Irving, in relating this portion of Columbus's life, states that, wearied and discouraged by delays in Spain, he was thinking of looking elsewhere for the aid he had sought in vain from Ferdinand, and that he applied to John II. of Portugal, and received in reply encouragement and the safe conduct. He also states that Columbus received a letter from Henry VII. of England, inviting him to that country, and holding out promises of encouragement.† Though he does not give the source of this information, this correspondence may have quickened his efforts and those of Bartholomew in the direction of England and France. It also stimulated the wary and selfish Ferdinand, who summoned him again to court and provided him with means for his journey through Gonzalez, the royal treasurer. But he again resorted to his former system of delays, and it was not until Bartholomew's departure for England and Columbus's return from Portugal, in the spring of 1489, that he summoned Columbus to appear before another learned council at Seville, and again made royal provision for his travel; his expenses on the way and his entertainment at Seville were provided for him out of the public treasury. He repaired to the beautiful city flushed with hope; but, alas! another disappointment followed, another campaign

---

* "The Discovery of America," by John Fiske, vol. i., pp. 401-408.
† Washington Irving's "Life of Columbus," vol. i., pp. 95, 96.

commenced. The court and army departed to invade Granada, besiege the city of Baza, and crush the Moors in their stronghold. Columbus, however, was not inactive. He served in this eventful campaign as a soldier " with distinguished valor," and on December 22d, 1489, he was present on that august occasion when Boabdil the Elder surrendered his own crown and his remaining possessions to Ferdinand and Isabella.* It was also during this campaign that the devout mind of Columbus conceived the thought and made the resolution—a vow registered in his own soul and openly declared—of devoting the profits of his projected discoveries, in case of success, to the expenses of another crusade for the rescue of the Holy Land and the sacred places from the hands of the infidels. This occurred during the siege of Baza, in Granada, and during the campaign of 1489, in which Columbus fought in the army of Ferdinand and Isabella with such intrepid personal valor as to have won the meed of a distinguished mention in the history of the war. Two venerable monks from the convent at the Holy Sepulchre at Jerusalem arrived, bringing a message from the Grand Soldan of Egypt that he had resolved to massacre the Christians of Palestine, destroy the Holy Sepulchre, and devastate their convents and churches unless Ferdinand and Isabella discontinued the war against the Moors. The holy friars received immediate audience with the Catholic sovereigns; the court and the army and all Spain were deeply excited at the threat; the war was prosecuted with renewed vigor, until the last inch of Moorish territory in Spain was surrendered. Isabella granted a perpetual annuity of one thousand ducats, equal to $4269 of our currency, for the support of the convent at the Holy Sepulchre, and sent an embroidered veil, the work of her own hands, to be suspended before the sacred shrine. The big heart and munificent soul of Columbus then consecrated to a new crusade he would inaugurate for the rescue of the holy places the profits of the princedom he felt sure of winning, and which he afterward won, but which the ingratitude of princes rendered barren in his hands and those of his family.

But the suit of Columbus was again postponed in the interests

---

* Irving's " Life of Columbus," vol. i., p. 97 ;. Diego Ortiz de Zuniga, " Ann. de Sevilla," lib. xii., anno 1489, p. 404.

of the Moorish war. The victorious sovereigns, returning from the surrender of Baza, entered Seville in triumph and with extraordinary pomp and grandeur in February, 1490. The national rejoicings ensued, and then came the preparations for the nuptials, and their celebration in April, of the Princess Isabella with Prince Don Alonzo, heir-apparent of Portugal. The stirring and exciting events of battles, triumphs, and wedding rejoicings stood in the way of Columbus now, and while the discoverer stood ready to reveal the reality of his long-dreamed plans, and followed the court as a member of the royal suite, his heart felt at every moment the pangs of bitter disappointment. What next? Then came the campaign for the conquest of the Vega of Granada, and it was announced that neither sovereign nor soldier would rest from battle until Granada was theirs. Columbus saw his life waning with the passing years of toil, delay, broken promises, disappointment, and neglect. He resolved to brook no further postponement of his cause ; he insisted upon a decision of his suit. Bishop Fernando de Talavera was directed by the sovereigns to hold a decisive consultation of the sages of Salamanca, and after some further delay the answer was given that this learned Junto regarded the project as " vain, impracticable, and resting on grounds too weak to merit the support of the government." * Columbus was informed through the bishop that, in consequence of the engrossing prosecution of the war and its great expense, the sovereigns could not then entertain his propositions, but that when the war was successfully ended they would feel disposed, with more time at their disposal, to negotiate with him. In the mean time, at court, in the army, and in the cities where he tarried, he was mocked and jeered at by the ignorant and the giddy, and when he passed through the streets the children meeting him sneeringly pointed to their foreheads to indicate that he was regarded as a man of unsound mind. During portions of this time he provided for his support by making maps. Six years were thus lost in fruitless petitions to the Spanish court. While he had assurances from individual members of the Junto of Salamanca—Diego de Deza, tutor of Prince Juan, and others—of their confidence and support, he not-

---

* Fernando Colon, " Historia del Almirante," cap. 2 ; Prescott's " Ferdinand and Isabella," vol. iii., p. 121 ; Irving's " Life of Columbus," vol. i., p. 100.

withstanding regarded the answer of the sovereigns as final, and he indignantly left Seville and turned his face toward France, from which country he had received a letter from King Charles VIII. inviting him to come to France and lay his project before that monarch.

We next find the illustrious discoverer standing at the gates of the Franciscan Convent of La Rabida. According to Mr. Irving, this was Columbus's first and only visit to La Rabida; according to Tarducci, it was his second visit, before the signing of the capitulations. Traveling on foot, holding his young son Diego by the hand, he asked the porter at the lodge for a little bread and water for the exhausted child. With the great man the heart alone was weary. He had traveled thus from Seville; the stranger was poorly but genteelly dressed, but there was something noble and exalted in his aspect and demeanor. According to the account of Tarducci, his son Diego was left at Columbus's first visit as a guest of the convent, and his intention now was to take him to Cordova and leave him there with his second son, Fernando, in the care of Beatrix Enriquez. He regarded it as a providence that directed his steps to the enlightened prior of the convent, Juan Perez de Marchena, for the good monk immediately entered into conversation with the strangers, and although Columbus was on his way to the neighboring town of Huelva, to visit his sister-in-law, and, according to other accounts, leave with her his young son Diego during his proposed visit to France, the good prior succeeded in inducing him to tarry at the convent and become its guest. The intelligent prior and friars of La Rabida had never received at their hospitable board so remarkable and extraordinary a guest. They became intensely interested in his theories and projects, for Columbus spoke of nothing else, and as their proximity to the seaport of Palos had given the monks some familiarity with maritime subjects, they stood astonished at the magnificence and grandeur of the proposals of the Genoese stranger. They became still more surprised if not convinced by the arguments and facts, scientific data and traditional learning by which he sustained his propositions. They were edified by the deep religious convictions and boundless zeal for the faith manifested by their guest. The physician of the convent, Garcia Fernandez, one of the most scientific men of the neighboring maritime town of

Palos, was sent for, and a number of conferences were held at the convent, and these were also attended by several "ancient mariners" of Palos, among whom was Martin Alonzo Pinzon—the Pinzons being a prominent, wealthy, and nautical family of standing and experience. The plans and arguments of Columbus had more effect among the well-informed and practical mariners and scientific men of Palos than among the sages of Salamanca's famed university. Pinzon was so especially impressed with the plan that he tendered his means and his personal services in such an expedition as Columbus proposed, and offered to bear the cost of another effort to engage the co-operation of the court of Spain. There was no dissenting voice in the councils of La Rabida.

The good prior, Juan Perez, who had formerly been confessor to Queen Isabella, resolved to make a direct appeal to her, for she had from the beginning been favorable to the plans of Columbus, and he immediately sent to her Majesty a letter by a trusty and shrewd messenger, Sebastian Rodriguez, a pilot of Lepe, a man of intelligence and of importance in the neighborhood. In fourteen days Rodriguez returned with the queen's answer, in which she expressed her thanks for the prior's opportune exertions, and requested him to give hope to Columbus, and that the prior would immediately visit her at court. Juan Perez without delay saddled his mule, started before midnight, and, having traversed the conquered territories of the Moors and arrived at the new city of Santa Fé, where the king and queen were pressing the siege of Granada, he found no difficulty in obtaining a prompt audience. He now pleaded the cause of Columbus with zeal, eloquence, and learning, and he gave his personal assurances of the integrity, skill, and knowledge of Columbus, and of his capacity to fulfil his every engagement; he also gave an intelligent exposition of the grounds upon which the propositions were based, and depicted in glowing words the advantages and glory which Spain would gain by such an enterprise, of the success of which he felt confident. The Marchioness de Moya, a favorite of the queen, united her gentle and persuasive eloquence to the strong appeal of the prior, and the result was that Isabella requested Columbus again to repair to her presence, and forwarded to him a sum of money, equal to $216 of our currency, to bear the expenses of the journey and enable him to make a suitable appearance at court. Columbus replaced his worn garments with a court suit, and, having purchased a mule, journeyed at once to the royal camp before the besieged city of Granada.

Amid the triumphs and rejoicings of the Spanish arms before the ill-fated city of Granada, the last stronghold of the Moors, Columbus arrived at court. In his former applications he was put off by the press of warlike preparations and active operations in field or siege; now at least the war was over. He had witnessed the surrender by Boabdil, the last of the Moorish kings, of the keys of the Alhambra to Ferdinand and Isabella, and the crusade of eight centuries was triumphantly brought to an end. In the midst of national rejoicings, wherein the court, the army and the people abandoned themselves to unbounded jubilation; amid the songs of minstrels, the shouts of victory, the hymns of thanksgiving, military and religious pageants, the frequent appearance of king and queen in public surrounded by more than imperial magnificence, the throngs of grandees, warriors, and ecclesiastics of dignity and station, the glitter of arms, and the sounds of music and clangor of arms—all tended to thrust aside the long-seeking and long-waiting discoverer of worlds. Columbus counted among his friends and the advocates of his cause the good prior of La Rabida, Juan Perez, Alonzo de Quintanilla, the accountant-general, the Marchioness de Moya, and Luis de Santangel, the receiver of ecclesiastical revenues. Now again he had to wait until a moment of comparative quiet enabled him to gain an audience. Clemencin, a contemporary writer, and one who saw him now at court, no doubt reflected the general sentiment of the community when he described Columbus as an obscure and unknown man following the court, one of numerous importunate applicants brooding in antechambers over the vainglorious project of discovering a world, melancholy and indifferent in the midst of the national and universal rejoicings, contemptuous of all glory except his own anticipated triumphs, dejected yet puffed up. To the few friends I have named he appeared as the seer, the scientist, the deliverer of nations, the benefactor of Spain and of the world, the hero of hemispheres. The sovereigns now appointed several persons of rank and influence to negotiate with Columbus, and among them was Fernando de Talavera, then promoted as Archbishop of Granada. Columbus entered upon the negotiations of the terms with the air of

one confident of success; but when these dignitaries of Church
and State, noblemen and officials, heard the obscure stranger
demand as the price of his success terms that were princely—a
viceroyalty of all the lands he discovered and a tenth of the
gains, whether from trade or conquest—they were filled with
indignation mingled with contempt. Columbus was unmoved,
and when sneered at for his spirit of self-aggrandizement, he
boldly offered, relying on Pinzon's proposition, to defray one
eighth of the expense on his being guaranteed one eighth of the
profits. Notwithstanding this confident and liberal offer, the
terms insisted on by Columbus were regarded as extravagant,
presumptuous, and vainglorious. The report of Fernando de
Talavera to the queen represented the terms as exorbitant, and
that it would be beneath the dignity of the crown to bestow such
dignities, powers, and emoluments upon any one, but especially
upon a stranger without means, titles, or prestige, one who, it
was well known, was regarded as a dreamer and an adventurer.
Isabella had commenced to feel great inclination to favor the
proposals of Columbus, but this report of so important a personage as the Archbishop of Granada, her confessor and spiritual
adviser, the one who had been from the beginning entrusted
with the conduct of the affair, caused her to hesitate. Lesser
terms were proposed to Columbus, but he remained immovable,
even with the prospect of utter failure or of undergoing at other
courts the delays, neglects, ridicule, and disappointments he had
already experienced for eighteen years, the best portion of his
life and manhood. His lofty and confident spirit should now
have inspired more respect if not admiration, but he was permitted to depart from Santa Fé, and he now turned his face
toward France. Well might Mr. Irving exclaim, while alluding
to the long years of solicitation and denial he had spent at European courts, " What poverty, neglect, ridicule, contumely, and
disappointment had he not suffered!" It was in February, 1492,
that this illustrious man, after having taken leave of his few
friends at court, mounted his mule and wended his weary way
toward Cordova. The noble Luis de Santangel and other
friends of Columbus, actuated by the loftiest and most patriotic
sentiments, resolved to make a final effort to prevent France
from wresting from Spain the glory of the impending discovery.
He and Alonzo de Quintanilla hastened to the queen and obtained

an immediate audience. They appealed to her by every consideration of patriotism, glory, interest, and justice not to let Columbus carry to France the honor of discovering new worlds, which had been so unwisely rejected by Spain, and in their ardor for the cause they mingled the highest eulogies on Columbus, with almost reproaches on their own sovereigns. The expedition would only require two vessels and about three thousand crowns, and the great discoverer had generously proposed to bear one eighth of the cost. The Marchioness de Moya was present at this momentous interview, and warmly and eloquently supported the fervid appeals of Santangel and of Quintanilla. The mind of Isabella had been so engrossed with the Moorish war and other cares of State, that the proposals of Columbus seemed now for the first time to dawn upon her generous spirit in all their grandeur and glory, and with characteristic spirit and judgment she resolved to embark in so exalted a work. The king was still indifferent and sat coldly by, his thoughts grovelling over his depleted treasury. Was Isabella now to displease her royal consort and subject the public treasury to a further drain, when he was opposed to it? Her mind hesitated between the two views—a cold and calculating State policy, on the one hand, and the noblest of human undertakings, on the other. All present felt the crisis of the moment, but Isabella rose now to the full elevation of her exalted character, and with an inspired ardor she exclaimed: " I undertake the enterprise for my own crown of Castile, and will pledge my jewels to raise the necessary funds!" The boundless joy of Santangel, Quintanilla, and the Marchioness de Moya broke forth in expressions of gratitude and honor for the queen, whose illustrious career she had now crowned with the noblest act of her life. She seemed like the angel of intercession, whose wings extended over two hemispheres, to unite them in a common humanity and in one common faith.

Columbus must be sent for at once and brought back to Santa Fé; but in his generous zeal Santangel assured her Majesty that there was no need of pledging her jewels, as he would advance the requisite money. It was arranged, therefore, that San Angel, the receiver of ecclesiastical revenues, should advance the necessary funds, which were taken, in fact, from the treasury of Aragon, to the amount of seventeen thousand florins.

This sum the king took care afterward to have reimbursed to him from a part of the first gold brought by Columbus from the islands he discovered in the West Indies, by having it applied to gilding the vaults and ceilings of his own royal saloon in the grand palace of Saragossa, in Aragon. In the mean time, Columbus was pursuing his lonely and dejected journey from the court; had crossed the Vega of Granada and reached the bridge of Pinos. He had traveled about two leagues from Granada; the lofty mountains of Elvira were before him, and every spot was rendered historical by Spanish triumphs over the Moors; but they were associated in his mind with the causes of the delays and disappointments he had sustained for so many years. Here he was overtaken by a royal messenger at full speed, who requested his return to the court at Santa Fé, and assured him of the pledge the queen had made, and of her ardor in the cause he had so long pleaded in vain. Columbus hesitated; he was reassured by the messenger; and then, feeling unbounded confidence in the word of the noble Isabella, his heart filled with an unaccustomed joy. He hastened back to Santa Fé. When two such minds and souls as those of Columbus and Isabella came to understand each other and to act in accord, the civilized world had at once advanced more than it had done before for centuries. Man was now to become the master and ruler of the whole earth; the shackles of ignorance, prejudice, and cowardice were to fall from the human race; it was the proudest moment in the life of Isabella, the most hopeful in that of Columbus, the most auspicious in the progress of the world!

Isabella received Columbus most graciously on his return to Santa Fé. Ferdinand was unable to resist longer the generous resolve of the queen, and he concurred in what he had failed to prevent; but Isabella was the inspiring mover and supporter of this magnificent enterprise. The views of Columbus as to terms were already understood; his terms were accepted and reduced to writing by the secretary of the queen, Juan de Coloma, and were substantially as follows. Talavera had said that " a beggar made conditions like a king to monarchs." Now the parties stood on more equal terms. All was now understood and stipulated between the contracting parties. First: Columbus was to be the admiral of the seas and countries he should discover during his own life, and the office should be hereditary in his family, with dignities and honors equal to those enjoyed in his district by the high admiral of Castile. Second: He was to be viceroy and governor-general over the countries and islands, and invested with power of nominating three persons for the governorship of each island or province, from whose number the sovereigns were to select the incumbent. Third: He was to receive a share of all the pearls, precious stones, gold, silver, spices, and of all other articles and merchandise that might be found, gained, brought, or exported from the discovered countries. Fourth: He in his quality as admiral, or his representative, was to be the sole judge in all mercantile matters, causes, and disputes arising between those countries and Spain, provided the high admiral of Spain possessed the like power in his district. Fifth: He should have the privilege of contributing one eighth of the cost of fitting out all ships to be engaged in the undertaking, and receiving one eighth of the profits in return. These terms were embodied in a written contract or capitulation signed by both Ferdinand and Isabella, written out by Almazon, and countersigned by Coloma, the secretary, on April 17th, 1492, and they were also set forth in a letter of privilege signed by the sovereigns, April 30th. In the latter document, not only were the titles and offices aforesaid made hereditary in his family, but also Columbus and his heirs were privileged to affix the title of Don to their names, which was in those days a rare distinction.

It has already been observed that the Italian name of Columbus was rendered Colombo, while the French, if it be true that he had French relatives, was Colomb, or Coloup. In Spain his name underwent decided changes. The Duke of Medina Celi called him Colomo, which was changed into Colom, which Tarducci supposes was changed into Colon for the sake of euphony; but the admiral's son Fernando argued that as the Roman name was Colonus, that could easily be transformed into Colon. The signature to the contract with the Spanish sovereigns was quite Spanish, Cristoval Colon. Fernando says the admiral's object in changing his name in Spain was to distinguish his own immediate family and descendants from the collateral stock of the Italian Colombos. Oviedo calls him Colom.

While Mr. Winsor thinks that Columbus failed in Portugal and again in Spain by his arrogant spirit and demands, and thus also disgusted Talavera by demanding in his poverty and ob-

scurity what could only be conceded to proved success, the
answer is very complete with less unfriendly critics of the discoverer, that he finally succeeded in obtaining the concession of
those very terms which at first seemed so arrogant ; and when
made in the manner so distasteful to Mr. Winsor, they were
always accompanied by solid and true arguments, based on his
scientific data, and were never urged except in terms and manner
of Columbus's acknowledged and uniform courtesy, forbearance,
and precatory demeanor. His success justifies his conduct in
this respect. Far more admirable than such criticism is the view
which Columbus took, that he was the instrument of Providence
for the achievement of a great mission. Such a spirit of criticism is never found united with that magnanimity of spirit which,
in Columbus, before he unfurled a sail at Palos, had dedicated
the expenditure of fortunes in the restoration of a Saviour's tomb
to Christendom.

CHAPTER V.

> "Love is life's end; an end, but never ending;
> All joys, all sweets, all happiness, awarding."
> —Spenser's "Britain's Ida."

> "Nothing shall assuage
> Your love but marriage; for such is
> The tying of two in wedlock."
> —Lilly's "Sappho and Phaon."

> "For know, Iago,
> But that I love the gentle Desdemona,
> I would not my unhoused free condition
> Put into circumscription and confine
> For the sea's worth."
> —Shakespeare's "Othello."

WE have accompanied Columbus in his journeys in pursuit of the Spanish court, and of audiences with King Ferdinand; in his services as a soldier and his return, in the spring of 1487, with the court to Cordova. During his several sojourns at this beautiful and ancient city he had mingled in its social life. He had made influential friends in Spain, and among them were the powerful Dukes Medina Celi and Medina Sidonia; Diego de Deza, the noble Dominican friar; Alonzo de Quintanilla, who was comptroller of the treasury of Castile; Antonio Geraldini, the papal nuncio, and his brother, Alexander Geraldini, who was tutor to the royal infants; and, above all, Pedro Gonzales de Mendoza, Archbishop of Toledo and Grand Cardinal of Spain. He had been the guest of several of these illustrious Spaniards. It was, no doubt, through such powerful social influences, as well as by his own engaging manners, eloquence of speech, courtly appearance and address, his religious devotion and constancy in attendance at the solemn services of the Church in the venerable Cathedral of Cordova, his learning on rare and attractive subjects, the very mystery and attraction that attaches always, with the refined and cultivated of every land and age, to aspiring thoughts and noble purposes, that gained for him the *entrée* into the best society of Cordova, so noted for its nobility and aristocracy. Many of his friends were noted ecclesiastics, who, besides at that time holding the most important and influential offices in the State, were mostly themselves members of the noblest families of Spain. It is no small tribute to the worth, purity, reputation, and ability of Columbus that he, a foreigner and a stranger, coming into Spain unintroduced and without a friend or acquaintance to start with, without means, but actually destitute and threadbare, either accepting the hospitality of some of his friends or making a scanty and precarious living by drawing maps, should have won the friendship of such powerful friends and should have won recognition both in aristocratic circles and at court; but such was undeniably the fact. His acquaintance with and reception by the noble and ancient family of the De Aranas, of Cordova, is proof of this.

The Spanish court had come to Cordova in the spring of 1487, and after the most stirring and determined preparations, had departed thence for a fearful campaign and siege of the impregnable Moorish stronghold at Malaga; but Spanish prowess had already carried many a Moorish city of equal strength, and the doomed city of Malaga surrendered to Ferdinand and Isabella on August 18th, 1487. The court then returned in triumph to Cordova. Columbus followed the court back to that famous city. This brings us to the consideration of the question of his marriage to Beatrix Enriquez, which has become the subject of so much criticism and difference of opinion. I have investigated this controverted point with impartiality and research. My judgment at first was balanced; but persevering study has solved the question for me, and now, having a conviction, I shall advocate that conviction with my best efforts.

It was during his second or third sojourn at Cordova, in the autumn of 1487, that the second marriage of Columbus took place, his second wife being Donna Beatrix Enriquez, a lady of surpassing beauty, most amiable disposition, and a member of one of the oldest and most influential of the noblest and most aristocratic families of Spain. Few Spanish families had a higher prestige than that of the de Aranas, to which Beatrix Enriquez belonged, though their wealth at this time did not correspond with their distinguished lineage and station. The marriage of Columbus to Beatrix Enriquez took place at Cordova toward the end of November, 1487, and Fernando Columbus, the only child of this union, was born on August 29th, or, as others state, August 15th, 1488. According to the customs of the country, as the Count de Lorgues informs us, and as she had brothers who alone could inherit the family estates and titles, her marriage portion must have been limited to the usual *legitime;* but he thinks it was such as to insure her an independent living.

Little is known of this lady or of the influence she exerted on the admiral's fortunes, or of the part she took in his future struggles, successes, triumphs, and misfortunes. Her life was spent modestly at Cordova, and she is not known ever to have left that city. During his lifetime no man ever had more enemies, or such bitter and untiring maligners of his conduct and motives, or such industrious inquisitors into every act or step of his eventful career. The enemies who had carefully and maliciously brought forward every accusation against him which hatred and revenge could suggest, never once attacked the purity and integrity of his moral character; never was the legality of his connection with Beatrix Enriquez questioned; never was his marriage to her doubted; never was the legitimacy of his second son, Fernando, challenged. On the contrary, during his residence in Cordova the associations of Columbus were of the most unexceptionable—nay, more, of the most distinguished character. He was a guest in the house of one of the queen's most trusted and honored officers, Alonzo de Quintanilla, the royal treasurer, and he was an associate of such distinguished prelates as Antonio Geraldini, the papal nuncio, and of his brother Alexander, whom the queen had selected as the tutor of her children. Columbus recognized on all occasions Fernando, the son of this marriage, as equal in all respects to his first son, Diego, and in his will, which is based upon the express principle that legitimacy of birth should be a prerequisite for inheriting his entailed estate, the Mayorazgo, the only preference given to his son Diego over his son Fernando is that in which the customs and laws of the State were followed, the right of primogeniture. This universal recognition of the validity of his second marriage, and of the legitimacy of Fernando, was followed by historians and by an uninterrupted concurrence and acquiescence of one hundred and thirty years after the death of the admiral.

It was not until 1672 that the question was raised for the first time, and this was a trivial and unauthorized one, as to the second marriage of Columbus or the legitimacy of his second son, Fernando. This question arose apparently in the most casual manner, and without thought or investigation on the part of the doubter. Nicolao Antonio, whose functions were rather those of a librarian than of an historian or critic, came across a copy of the admiral's will, in which a pension was provided for Beatrix Enriquez, " mother of his second son, Fernando." This clause of the will reads as follows : " And I desire him (Don Diego) to devise unto Beatrix Enriquez, mother of Don Fernando, my son, a sum which shall enable her to live in a suitable manner, as being one to whom I am much indebted. And let this be done for the relief of my conscience, for it weighs heavily on my soul. The reason of this it is not right to insert here." While Nicolao Antonio held the rather high-sounding title of Procurator-General of Spanish Affairs at the court of Rome, he is not known to history as either a jurist or lawyer or historian, and in his capacity of librarian he was more accustomed to handling the manufactured book than passing on its merits ; more versed in arranging, cataloguing, and billeting volumes than digesting or weighing their contents. The rashness and precipitancy of his action in this case have shown him to be a man of little prudence, discretion, or discrimination. Noticing in the above passage, in the admiral's will, the absence of the word wife in the allusion to Beatrix Enriquez, and the reference to some undisclosed circumstance in his past course of action toward her, the librarian rashly, yet perhaps artlessly and almost unconsciously, wrote down in the copy of the will Don Fernando Columbus was an illegitimate son of the admiral.

This obscure note, made without comment, reason, or proof of any kind, and without any inquiry or research after the truth, made no impression upon the general belief that Columbus and Beatrix were lawfully married, nor upon the minds of historians and biographers, nor upon the fame and reputation of Columbus and his wife. It was too obscure and unauthentic an act to attract any notice. Its insignificance consigned it to oblivion. Revived now by modern authors, I have carefully and impartially examined the accusation, and have been forced to the conclusion that it is not sustained.

One hundred and twenty years after the penning of this rash

thought of the librarian Nicolao Antonio—that is, about the year 1794—in order to promote his success in conducting a lawsuit in behalf of one Diego Colon y Larriategui, in which he was interested, the licentiate Luiz de la Palma y Freytas, true to the most inferior instincts and training of his profession as a lawyer, and knowing nothing of the merits of the question as one affecting an illustrious name, and not caring, availed himself of the assertion made by Antonio; but his plea, based upon the illegitimacy of Fernando Columbus, was thrown out of court. Numerous lawsuits arose from time to time over the succession to the estates and titles of Columbus, and remote kindred in Italy attempted to win the prize, even at the expense of historic truth. The parentage of Columbus, the place of his birth, and every circumstance bearing upon the question of the succession, became the subject of bitter contention and of contradictory testimony. What these cavilling and hair-splitting attorneys, who could not rise to the height of an honorable profession, were unable to accomplish was next attempted by a learned critic from motives of vanity and ambition. In 1805 Galeani Napione, a vain and frivolous writer, of some repute for learning, but unsuccessful as a historian, sought, in the mass of the documents brought into existence by the voluminous and conflicting lawsuits which had been prosecuted in Spain over the succession to the titles and estates of Columbus, for an opportunity of enhancing his reputation as a commentator and critic. His eager eye fell upon the point forensically made by the lawyer, Palma y Freytas, in behalf of his client, and with equal astuteness he amplified the point by a series of keen and critical arguments, and thus gained some credit to himself as an original and discriminating critic. But what can be thought of the assumption of a writer who, contrary to all testimonies bearing upon the parentage and birth of Columbus, had insisted that the admiral was born at the Château of Cuccaro, in Montferrat? Thus, too, in 1809, François Cancellieri, a French antiquarian and bibliographer, gave some circulation to Napione's arguments, by accepting the fact of Fernando Columbus's illegitimate birth, and reasserted it; but although Cancellieri had won some repute for skill in collecting and classifying facts, he is known not to have made any examination into the charge, thus confirming the general opinion of his contemporaries that he was a man destitute of philosophic acumen.

It is singular how much bitter feeling has been generated by the disputes over questions relating to Columbus. None of these controversies have equalled in bitterness the disputes over the questions of his birthplace and of his second marriage. An old Barnabite father, Spotorno, a Genoese, who felt a special pride in having Genoa recognized as the birthplace of Columbus, took offence, however, at the supposed effort of Fernando Columbus, in his history of the admiral, to cast doubt on the subject of his father's birthplace. He was unsparing in his denunciation of Fernando for daring to cast a doubt on the claim of Genoa. The imputation of Napione was eagerly seized upon by the enthusiastic Genoese for accusing Fernando of being a bastard. His resentment was aided by his vanity as a claimant to repute as a scholar, and it was his vanity which led him to ignore Napione, and trace his authority for the assertion back to Cancellieri, the French critic. Such was the heat of his passion and resentment for Fernando Columbus, that it led him to asperse the reputation of Columbus himself, whom he was proud to claim as a native countryman of his own. "His dislike of the son," writes Father Knight, "seems to have outweighed his respect for the father."* For his zeal in behalf of his own Genoa as the birthplace of Columbus that city rewarded him with honors. He was appointed by the city to write a preface to a collection of documents relative to Columbus.† This afforded him an opportunity of repeating in his preface, in 1823, the calumny against Fernando Columbus, and through him against his father, of the same unauthorized and unauthenticated libel which had, in 1819, been uttered in his book, "Of the Origin and of the Country of Columbus," and subsequently repeated in his "Literary History of Liguria." The Count de Lorgues accuses the learned Barnabite of plagiarism, in claiming as his own an accusation which he had found in the pages of Napione and Cancellieri.

One of the bitterest posthumous enemies of Columbus was Martin Fernandez de Navarrete. His hatred for Columbus arose out of his being the hired and paid advocate of the Spanish dynasty in defending King Ferdinand against the universally accepted charge of ingratitude to Columbus. Navarrete, fired

---

* "The Life of Christopher Columbus," by Rev. Arthur George Knight, S. J.
† "Codice Columbo Americano."

by the resentment of a Spaniard and stimulated by official patronage, undertook to defend Ferdinand from the charge of ingratitude toward Columbus, which had then been recently but briefly repeated by Bossi and his French translator. Nearly about the same time that Spotorno was accusing Columbus in Genoa, in the pay of the Genoese Government, 1823, Navarrete was engaged in the lucrative service of the Spanish Government in a similar unworthy crusade against the good name of Columbus. If Columbus was blameless, then King Ferdinand was guilty of ingratitude ; if Ferdinand was capable of defence, it could only be by casting odium on Columbus. Navarrete accepted his unworthy task. The public purse was at his back. He was continuing that great work, the " Collection of the Maritime Voyages of the Spaniards," which the learned Bautista Muñoz had commenced in the time and by order of Charles V. He was also employed by the Spanish crown to edit and compile the "Coleccion Diplomatica." Rewarded, or rather subsidized by the government, and loaded with many offices, honors, and emoluments, he became an enthusiastic eulogist of his royal client in the person of King Ferdinand. Yet in his unworthy task, " he undertook," as the Count de Lorgues so earnestly says, " the task of exculpating the most ungrateful by calumniating the most generous of men. Vengeance armed his pen. Yet in the whole course of his researches Navarrete could find nothing that could cast the least suspicion on the relations of Columbus with Beatrix Enriquez. All his annotations showed Fernando as the legitimate son of the admiral of the ocean." It was under such circumstances as these that Navarrete revamped the often-made and as often-refuted charges of the contemporaneous enemies of Columbus, commencing with the accusation that he had left Portugal secretly in order to defraud his creditors, down to the charges of cruelty, avarice, and disloyalty. Navarrete thus ranges himself on the side of such desperate and unscrupulous men as Roldan and his fellow-rebels, and of the host of wild, vicious, desperate, criminal, and outlawed men who in his lifetime united with Ferdinand in sending this most loyal and useful man to a death-bed of poverty, disease, misery, and injustice. With a mockery of historical style and dignity he undertakes to praise King Ferdinand for his clemency, graciousness, and kindness to Columbus. It is not surprising, then, that Navarrete should have appropriated the calumny of Spotorno with avidity, in order to increase the already swollen sum of his unjust charges against Columbus. "The calumny of Spotorno," writes the Count de Lorgues, "came to give him a new arm." The fact that Navarrete's work is, with all its learning and research, an unmanly and ungenerous indictment of the moral character of Columbus, a repetition of refuted charges made by his avowed enemies, overflowing with undisguised prejudice, and inspired by lucrative governmental patronage, deprives it of all authenticity when treating on the life, character, and merits of Columbus.

It was unfortunate for the cause of truth and justice that our distinguished and learned countryman, Washington Irving, who, on being informed while at Bordeaux that Navarrete's work was in press, went to Madrid with the intention of translating it into English, and while at Madrid saw its issue from the press, should have mainly followed that author in preparing his own beautiful life of Columbus, in so far as to express the opinion that the relations of Columbus with Donna Beatrix Enriquez were not sanctioned by marriage. Differing on many important subjects from Spotorno and Navarrete, it seems to be a subject of regret that Mr. Irving, while rejecting parts of their accusations, mitigating others, and accepting still others with evident repugnance, should not have given himself ample time to investigate the charge of illicit relation with this lady, the mother of his second son, who in her own native city and for nearly two centuries stood without reproach, and would stand so to-day, but for the overwrought criticism of a passage in the will of Columbus, thus casting a blemish upon the good names of two such persons at once, and a blot upon the birth of a third. Spotórno, emboldened by the admission of Mr. Irving, subsequently repeats the charge, while reproaching him with timidity in not admitting more; and Humboldt, whose researches were in quite a different field from that to which the investigation of such a charge belongs, and without investigation of his own, follows Mr. Irving in accepting the accusation of illicit relations between Columbus and Beatrix.

It must be admitted, however, that this investigation rests solely upon the original rash and inconsiderate note made by the librarian, Nicolao Antonio, on a copy of the will of Columbus. None of the writers who have followed this view have added any testimony or evidence in support of it. In fact, the note of Antonio is solely his own conclusion or argument deduced from the obscure but not mysterious language of the will. The clause in question is in truth the only data upon which we have to consider the charge. The list of authors who have inconsiderately accepted the charge as true, or rather as probable, constitute by derivation but one accuser, the librarian Antonio. The Count de Lorgues pithily presents the list, showing no increase or accumulation of authority or strength in the following climax, disclosing the genesis, so to speak, of this charge against a distinguished name. That author says: "Here is the bibliographic filiation of this calumny: Humboldt derived it from Washington Irving; Washington Irving derived it from Navarrete; Navarrete derived it from Spotorno; Spotorno derived it from Cancellieri; Cancellieri derived it from Napione; Napione derived it from the Attorney Freytas; Freytas derived it from the bibliographer Nicolao; Nicolao derived it from his own dull brain."*

As the accusation originated with the librarian Nicolao, and he rests it solely upon the circumstance and language of the will of Columbus, the question must be regarded as one depending solely upon these data and upon the construction to be given to the words. Upon these data we must determine whether his opinion, accepted by these authors, is warranted. The assertion of the librarian, made one hundred and sixty years after the admiral's death, gives no authority to the charge, which he was the first to make; neither does the concurrence of the same writers, following his lead and having no additional data or evidence, give any authority to the charge as an historical question.

Does the language of that quoted clause in the will establish or justify the fabrication of such a charge, or prove the fact charged? Does a mere obscurity of language, intimating at most that Columbus felt that he had fallen short of his obligations to Beatrix, and should in some measure make a tardy reparation, justify a charge or prove a fact so utterly at variance with all the evidences tending to prove the contrary to be the case? Would not the fact that Columbus, though lawfully married to Beatrix, had, under the pressure of his engrossing cares, labors,

---

* De Lorgues, "Ambassadeur de Dieu," p. 382; "Christophe Colomb," vol. i., p. 44; "The Life of Columbus," by Father Arthur George Knight, p. 45.

and misfortunes, neglected to provide adequately for her since
their marriage, or had not made her the partner of his successes
and triumphs, have naturally called forth the same language and
expressions in his will? Would not any other grievance, which
he might have felt he had inflicted on her, have naturally called
forth the same expressions? Is this interpretation, so hastily and
rashly put upon the will of Columbus by the librarian, the only
one of which the will is susceptible? Is it consistent with the
canons of interpretation or with the fair use of reason, one hundred and sixty years after the date of it and after the events, to
place upon these obscure words in a will a construction which
is wholly contradicted by the entire life, character, professions,
conduct, and principles of the person using the language, and of
the person of whom it is written? As the admiral expressly
states that he withholds the reason for his inserting this clause
in his will, was it reasonable, just, or fair in Antonio to attempt
to supply what he purposely withheld, and that upon mere conjecture, and at a distance of over a century and a half from his
death? Was it not the positively expressed effort of Columbus,
in so wording his will, to withhold his reasons? Then how
could a man of such varied and educational experience in life, of
such acknowledged intellect, of such lively sentiments and sensibilities, of such acute observation, of such eloquence and accuracy
of language and expression from his youth, have so glaringly
defeated his own purpose? Would it not have obviously been
more natural and sensible for Columbus to have declared the
reasons? If a blundering and dull librarian saw the meaning of
the language so plainly and so readily, could not the superior
intellect of Columbus have perceived the same, at least after it
was written? Is it not more probable to find in the separation
of Columbus from his wife, during his roving, adventurous and
checkered career since their marriage, the reason for his language, rather than in the theory that two persons, known as they
were to be devoted to each other and the parents of an honorable
and noble son, were not married? If, in his ambitious projects
and struggles for glory, he had left the woman he loved, his
wife, and the mother of his son in solitude, neglect, and obscurity, what more natural or appropriate language could he
have used to give expression to his sorrow, and then to do her a
tardy justice? Is it probable, if the charge were true, that so

sensitive a nature would have thus divulged it, even when designing to withhold it? Is it possible that so capable a pen as that of Columbus would have so blundered as to express what it was designed to suppress? In order to fasten so grave a charge upon Columbus, is it not necessary that the language he used should be utterly inconsistent with any other theory than the one contended for? Is it not a principle of justice, common sense, and of law, in a doubtful case, based on circumstantial evidence, that in order to justify conviction of an offence, the facts proved, or the data relied upon, should be inconsistent with any other theory than that of guilt? Surely the man, who suffered so much from the calumny of his enemies during his lifetime, should be reasonably spared from the breath of voluntary censure after the lapse of centuries. Would the man so slandered and libelled by his enemies during his life have become his own accuser, and that, too, of a crime of which his worst enemies had never dared to accuse him?

Mr. Irving's opinion on this subject, as well as that of the other writers with whom he agrees in part, seems to have been influenced by the impressions that this clause was the fruit of remorse experienced by him at the approach of death, and he was laboring under the belief that the will itself, or rather the codicil in question, was drawn up during the admiral's last illness. Such, however, is not the case. The codicil containing this language, on the contrary, was drawn up and signed by him four years previously, when his health was comparatively good, and the career of glory was yet before him. Indeed, these authors plainly assert the compunction of Columbus to have arisen at his last end, and that his provision for Beatrix was then made; but such is not the case. The codicil in question was made and dated on April 1st, 1498, prior to his departure on his third voyage. On August 25th, 1505, he reproduced it in his own hand, thus reaffirming it, and on May 19th, 1506, he deposited his whole testamentary depositions in the hands of the notary of the court, Pedro de Hinojedo, and then, too, he named his executors, his son Diego, his brother Bartholomew, and Juan de Porras, the Treasurer-General of Biscay.

While this accusation against Columbus must fall to the ground for want of proper foundation, either in fact, in reason, or in law, to sustain it, I will state *seriatim* some positive grounds for its utter refutation.

First: Columbus was a man of deep and sincere religious convictions, and by his faith an illicit love was anathematized, and would, in his own opinion and faith, consign his soul to eternal punishment if he should die in such a sin. In this belief and conviction he frequently resorted to the confessional.

Second: The practice and observance of his whole life were marked by purity, continence, and chastity. He was pre-eminently pure in his life, as was demonstrated in Hispaniola, in contrast with his Spanish followers.

Third: He was not an inexperienced man, nor one unaccustomed to encounter temptations, and thus liable to succumb to them when suddenly assailed. He had been a follower of the sea from the age of fourteen, and was at the time he met Beatrix approaching fifty years of age, thirty-six of which he had spent either at sea, in many strange lands, or otherwise exposed to temptations of every kind. She was less than half his own age. It was the habit of his life to resist and conquer such temptations. In the Indies, where Spaniards of high and low degree had given themselves up to the most unbridled licentiousness and indulgence with the Indian women of the country, the life of Columbus was chaste, continent, and pure. Of this sin he was never accused. He is known to have resisted every temptation to commit it while in the Indies, when to commit it was leniently condoned toward men separated from home, and freed from the restraints of religion and social ties. In an atmosphere of impurity he was pure.

Fourth: The family of Arana, to which Beatrix belonged, was a proud and noble family, as well as a pious and religious one. The rigid social safeguards, then as now, observed in Spanish families, would prove a sure preservative against the fall of a member of such a family into such a fault. As with Columbus, so with Beatrix: her religion would prove a powerful preservative against such a fall. Her pride of family would have alone preserved her. As she had brothers, proud, influential, aristocratic and chivalrous, the sentiments and practices of the age would have compelled them to avenge their sister's dishonor in the blood of her betrayer. Had there existed at any time an illicit love between Columbus and Beatrix, the proud members of the Arana family would never have associated with Columbus; whereas, on the contrary, there were always some members of this distinguished family accompanying Columbus in his expeditions. A brother of Beatrix, Rodrigo de Arana, a distinguished nobleman of Cordova, one whom Oviedo, the royal historiographer, calls "the virtuous gentleman," would surely not have permitted his and Beatrix's younger brother, Pedro de Arana, to accompany Columbus on his third voyage, nor would he have permitted his and her nephew, Diego de Arana, whom Ramusio calls "a good gentleman of Cordova," to have accompanied him on his first voyage, had this fact thus charged been true. Nor would Columbus, after he had become the discoverer of the new world, the grand admiral of the ocean seas and viceroy, have dared to appoint the former, a brother of his mistress, to the command of one of his vessels on the third voyage, thus placing under the command of a member of a disgraced family members of proud and noble families, and gentlemen of Spain. Nor would the admiral have placed in command of Fort Navidad, as we shall see hereafter he did, the nephew of his mistress, thereby placing under his orders two honorable officers of the crown. Spotorno destroys his own credit as a critic by denying even the noble birth and blood of Beatrix; but in this he is contradicted by such a writer as Navarrete himself, who could not refrain from declaring her noble, and her family to be the principal house of Cordova. Even after the death of Columbus and of his son and successor, we have evidence that Diego de Arana, a member of Beatrix's family, was a member of the household of Donna Maria de Toledo, the vice-queen of the Indies, the widow of Don Diego Columbus, where his rank, as well as his alliance with the family of Columbus through Beatrix Enriquez, gave him precedence over the officers of the household of the vice-queen. Donna Maria de Toledo was the widow of the second admiral, Don Diego Columbus, the first son of Columbus, and she was a niece of the Duke of Alva. It is not possible that the proud and punctilious family of the Toledos would have tolerated the presence of a relative of Beatrix had her relations to Columbus been other than the most honorable.

Fifth: During the voyages of Columbus the members of the family of his first and of the family of his second wife were brought together in social and official intercourse, which the former would never have permitted or submitted to had the relations of Columbus and Beatrix Enriquez been tainted with dishonor.

Sixth: From 1487 to 1494 Columbus left both his sons, Diego, the son of his first wife, and Fernando, the son of Beatrix, with his second wife, Donna Beatrix Enriquez, at Cordova, and there the education of these two sons of Columbus was superintended by that lady. If his alliance with her was of the scandalous character represented by the authors we have named, would Columbus, after he had broken away from the influence of her charms, have voluntarily added one scandal to another, by putting his young son Diego, his heir and successor, with a woman destitute of virtue? Would he have so deliberately braved the odium of public opinion and the proprieties of social and Christian life? Would he have done so gross an injustice to his son and successor, whose legitimacy is unquestioned, as to place him for education with his mistress? Would Columbus have maintained a household at Cordova during so many years, with Beatrix Enriquez at its head and his two sons in her charge, subject to her authority, recognizing her position, and associating with each other upon terms of perfect equality? If it be alleged that the second son belonged to her, then what can be said of his sending his first son to her care for his education? Would he have sent the son of his wife to the care of an adulteress? Would he have sent on such a mission that worthy priest, Father Martin Sanchez, when the latter carried Diego to Beatrix?

Seventh: On the return of Bartholomew Columbus, the noble brother of the admiral, from England and France, about 1494, he went to Cordova to visit his sister-in-law, Beatrix Enriquez, who was there engaged in rearing and educating the two sons of the admiral. Would that stern, inflexible, proud, and conscientious man have thus recognized this lady as his brother's wife and his own sister-in-law, had the admiral's relations with her been illicit and immoral? Would he not have struggled to bury his brother's shame, his nephew's disgrace, and his family's embarrassment, rather than have thus given publicity to them?

Eighth: Bartholomew Columbus carried his two nephews, Diego and Fernando, from the guardianship of Beatrix to Queen Isabella, and presented them at court; and the latter immediately received them with respect and honor, and appointed both of them pages at court. Would so pious, devout, and scrupulous a Christian as Isabella have received into her royal household either the illegitimate son or his associate, both just from the house of such a person as these modern authors have represented Beatrix to have been?

Ninth: Queen Isabella expressed great admiration at the manner in which the two sons of Columbus had been reared at Cordova under Beatrix Enriquez, by her open acts and consequently by corresponding words praised their deportment, and herself proposed and decided to receive them from the household of Beatrix into her own household and make them members thereof, and provide for the continuance and completion of their education. She appointed both Diego and Fernando pages to her son the infante, Prince Juan; and to their uncle the queen issued letters of nobility, and gave him the command of three ships to proceed to the relief of the admiral. Are such acts on the part of such a religious and scrupulous woman consistent with the alleged disrepute attributed to this part of the private life of Columbus and his family? Would she have given a bastard to her son, the prince and infante, Don Juan, as his page and companion?

Tenth: It was during the very period of his relations and marriage with Beatrix at Cordova and of the birth of his second son, Fernando, at that city, and the following years, that Columbus enjoyed the friendship and patronage of the prelates and hierarchy of the Church, and of such high ecclesiastics as the queen's confessor, of the Archbishop of Toledo, of the prior of Prado, of members of the venerable Council of Salamanca, of the prior of the Franciscan Convent of La Rabida, and other devout and irreproachable members of the hierarchy. His son Fernando was born at Cordova on August 29th, 1487. No secrecy was thrown around the event.* On the contrary, he was the recognized son of the admiral and of Beatrix. Would such recognition have followed an alliance of such a character, especially when it was accompanied by the birth of an illegitimate son? Would Columbus have been received at all, much less befriended, in such exclusive, religious, and punctilious circles under such circumstances? Would he have been received at court?

---

* Dr. Barry's translation of Count de Lorgues' "Life of Columbus," p. 39.

Eleventh : It was at this very time that Columbus was making the most earnest efforts to secure the patronage of the king and queen to his urgent proposals. It was the most critical period of his long struggle. Is it possible that a man whose all depended upon every and the least, as well as the most important act and event of his imperilled career, would have risked the loss of all his highest and dearest aspirations by the commission of such an indiscretion as is now charged against him? His own age would have made the act more offensive to a Christian court; more hazardous to himself and his dearest hopes.

Twelfth : It was during this period of his life also, that the religious and devout character and every-day life of Columbus was marked with the features of a conscientious and devoted Christian. How could a man, who was a daily worshipper at the altars at Cordova, a constant frequenter of the confessional and of the Lord's table, have been at the same time a seducer of female virtue and the recognized father of an illegitimate son? Of all the crimes imputed to him by his enemies, religious and moral hypocrisy was never one of them.

Thirteenth : The subsequent reception at court of Columbus himself by Isabella, the relations of respect, confidence, affection, admiration, and honor, which sprang up between these two remarkable persons, both deeply imbued with religion, would seem to contradict in the most emphatic manner the charge of immorality from which we are now obliged to defend him.

Fourteenth : During the long and disastrous struggle of Columbus with his countless enemies, when all Hispaniola and all Spain resounded with accusations of every kind against him; when it was a virtue to malign and libel his character, and a service to the State and to humanity; when falsehoods of every kind were invented against him, if such an unfortunate and unworthy event as this now under consideration had existed in any part of his life, it would, without the possibility of its omission, have been brought out against him. The atmosphere would have become sonorous with so available an accusation against the man, whose enemies were active incessantly in bringing forward every possible charge against his character. It would have proved an irresistible weapon in the hands of his countless enemies. The silence of such foes, at such a time and under such circumstances, is the virtual acquittal of the admiral.

Fifteenth : During the whole lifetime of Columbus, and for nearly a century and a half after his second marriage, not the least suspicion was cast on the nature of his connection with Beatrix Enriquez ; no trace of it can be found ; no Spanish author ever alluded to such a charge ; its origin is foreign to Spain, where his life was spent and well known. It is traced to an unfair advantage taken of his own words at so great a distance of time from his death and of space from the scenes of his life. Its author was obscure and irresponsible. His first follower in the charge was prejudiced. He had a motive for his charge against Columbus. On the contrary, Spanish historians speak of his second marriage. The gravest of his historians, Tiraboschi, asserts his marriage with Beatrix Enriquez, as do all historians near the time of Columbus.

Sixteenth : From the columns of *L'Univers*, the leading Catholic paper of France, for January 11th, 1877, we have obtained a copy of a valuable document, a manuscript history, written only one hundred years after the death of Columbus, which is as follows :

" Rev. Father Marcellino da Civezza has addressed to the *El Siglo futuro* the following letter :

" ' MR. EDITOR : I have the pleasure of informing you that I have discovered a new and decisive document on the subject of the legitimate marriage of Columbus with Beatrix Enriquez, of Cordova, in the Library of the Royal Historical Academy of Madrid. This valuable document is to be found in the " General History of Cordova and of its Noble Families," by Dr. André Moralés of that city, a manuscript which is preserved in the above-named library.

" ' The Bibliographical Dictionary of Thomas Munoz de Romero, 1858, expresses itself as follows in speaking of this manuscript :

" ' " Manuscript in two large volumes. This extensive work treats of the history of Cordova as well as of the patrician families who have their origin there, whence some call it ' Nobiliary History of Cordova.' The author, as we learn from a note in the manuscript, is Father Alphonse Garcia, of the Company of Jesus, brother of Dr. André Moralés. Concerning Father Garcia, Father Ribadedeira, in the ' Biblioteca Scriptorum Societatis Jesu,' speaks of him as follows :

"'"'Alphonse Garcia, Spaniard, native of Cordova, entered at an early age in the Society; having professed the four solemn vows, he evangelized the Canary Islands, from whence he came to Ossuna, where he was appointed rector of the college, and died there soon after in the year 1618.'"

"'Now we come to the valuable document.

"'"'Christopher Columbus, Grand Admiral of the West Indies, married twice: the first time in Portugal with Donna Philippa Moniz de Perestrello, who gave him his eldest son, Don Diego; the second time in Cordova, with a young lady of that city named Beatrix Enriquez de Arana, of high lineage, a descendant of the Viscaya, and from her he had Don Fernand Columbus, a knight of great intelligence, bravery, virtue, and a great scholar, after leaving the service of the Prince Don Juan, whose page he had been."

"'This document is of superlative importance, agreeing in every respect with the one discovered at Valencia by the Rev. Raymond Buldée.

"'I take the opportunity, Mr. Editor, etc.,
"'BROTHER MARCELLINO DA CIVEZZA,
"'*Historiographer of the Order of St. Francis.*'"

The other works alluded to in connection with this subject, both *pro* and *con*, have been general histories; but the work above quoted, and containing the valuable document on the legitimacy of the second marriage of Columbus, is specially devoted to the history of Cordova and of its noble families. It is also written by a Cordovan. Such a work is the most authentic and reliable authority on all questions relating to the local history of that city and its noble families, and its positive assertion of the legitimacy of the second marriage of Columbus is the traditional voice and testimony of the entire community of Cordova, in which the second wife of Columbus was born, lived and died, and the language of Father Alphonse Garcia is equivalent to the contemporary voice of that community at the very time of the second marriage itself continued down to his time. It will also be noticed that reference is made to another and similar document, affirming the legitimacy of the second marriage of Columbus, which had also been found at Valencia by the Rev. Father Raymond Buldée. A copy of this last work I have not been able to obtain. This first work has been found by the learned compiler of Lazzaroni's "Cristophoro Colombo," published at Milan in 1892, and from the latter work I shall hereafter make ample quotations, which will cover this and other points discussed in relation to the second marriage of Columbus.

Seventeenth : Spotorno, in order to support his accusation, alleges that Beatrix was poor, and that she was of plebeian origin. Both these statements are shown to have been untrue. The Aranas were one of the oldest and proudest families in Spain, and the pension provided for her by Columbus was never demanded by her, and when provided by his will, only paid for a time and then discontinued after a few years. She never made any complaint. Had Fernando been an illegitimate son of Beatrix, her nobility of birth would never have been referred to by the annalist of Seville in the necrological notice of her son. In later times her purity of descent was actually pleaded by the descendants of Columbus through his first marriage. In 1671 Don Pedro Columbus, in pleading the cause of the Dukes of Veragua, reminded the Queen of Spain that the two sons of the admiral were descended from mothers of noble birth.* Antonio de Herrera, the royal historiographer of Spain, records the second marriage of Columbus in the following words : " After the death of his first wife he espoused a second, named Beatrix Enriquez, of the city of Cordova, by whom he had Fernando, a virtuous gentleman, well versed in the seience of sound learning." So also such eminent writers as Charlevoix, Tiraboschi, and Robertson state that Columbus was married also in Spain, and the eminent Alvarez de Colmenar speaks of his having been twice married. The Marquis de Belloy refers to the marriage of Columbus and Beatrix Enriquez in the following terms : " While he was at Cordova, Columbus took up again for a living his art of map-drawing, all the while, however, enlisting partisans for his project and making numerous and powerful friends. The merit of the man shone through his humble circumstances, and obtained for him the hand of a girl of noble birth, Beatrix Enriquez, by whom he had a son named Fernando or Ferdinand. This marriage is related by the Historiographer Royal of Spain, Antonio de Herrera. It encountered some opposition from the

---

* Dr. Barry's translation of Count de Lorgues' " Life of Columbus," pp. 35. 36.

Enriquez family, but the extent of that opposition has been grossly exaggerated, for on his very first voyage, when his greatness was yet a question for the future to decide, Columbus took with him a nephew of Donna Beatrix, and at a later date a young brother of hers commanded one of the ships of the third expedition."*

Eighteenth : The objection raised by Navarrete to the legitimacy of the admiral's marriage to Beatrix, that no registry of his marriage with her can be found or produced, is answered by the facts that no record of his birth or of his death can be found, and at the time of his marriage, in 1486, neither registry nor witnesses were required either by the laws of the Church or of Spain in order to validate a marriage. See this point more fully treated in thirtieth reason, *postea*.

Nineteenth : The authors who deny the marriage of Columbus to Beatrix, from Nicolao to Navarrete himself, allege as a reason for their denial that Columbus, in alluding to and providing for her in his will, does not call her his wife; and yet he does not say she was not his wife, nor does he there allude to her in any other light. But this objection is utterly refuted, and the fact that she was his wife is wholly proven by the testimony of Columbus himself, and this, too, in a letter printed and published by Navarrete; for in a letter he addressed to persons whose duty it was to support his claim at the court of Spain, he states that he had "quitted all—wife and children—and never enjoyed the sweetness of living with them." " Y deje mucher y fijos que jamas vi por ello."† A grandson of Navarrete virtually recognizes the legitimacy of Fernando in speaking of the two brothers, Diego and Fernando, in the same sentence and as being on equal terms; he says that Fernando, equally with his brother Diego, was one of the greatest favorites of the Prince Royal of Spain.‡

Twentieth : It will be seen that Columbus in his will recognizes both his sons as on a perfect equality in all respects, except

---

* Herrera, "General History of the Voyages and Conquests of Castilians," 1st dec., b. i., c. 7.

† Barry's De Lorgues' "Columbus" p. 43; Navarrete, "Coleccion Diplomatica," num. cxxxvii.

‡ Eustaquio, "Coleccion ineditos para la Historia de España," por D. Miguel Salva. t. xvi., p. 291.

in the necessary and indispensable respect of the primogeniture of his elder son, Don Diego. This same and only distinction between them would have occurred had both been the sons of the same mother. The priority of the birth of Don Diego was simply a fact, and Columbus recognized it. In all other respects he places them on a perfect equality.

Twenty-first : So also in his correspondence, both private and official, he refers to his two sons in equal terms. His manner of referring to Fernando is free, natural, and unrestrained ; and in his letters to the Spanish sovereigns he refers constantly to Fernando without reserve, and with paternal pride he praises his precocious talents and his youthful but faithful services. If he had been illegitimate, would he have thus constantly recalled his own shame and his son's dishonor by praising him, and would he have so often recalled the embarrassing fact to such august and important personages? In fact, the alleged irregularity of the admiral's connection with Beatrix and the alleged illegitimacy of Fernando, if true, would cause him embarrassment in his lifetime, but it did not do so.

Twenty-second : Mr. Irving, following Navarrete and Humboldt, assigns the attractions of Beatrix's charms and the pregnancy of that lady as the cause for the admiral's refusal to leave Cordova on the request of King John II. of Portugal, that he would return to Lisbon. This is a fair illustration of the inventions which enter into supposed history ; for the fact is that the letter of the Portuguese king came to Columbus toward the last of August, 1488, whereas the accouchement of Beatrix and the birth of Fernando had already taken place eight months before, and Columbus, in the year he received King John's letter—1488 —was following the court at Seville and Valladolid. His great mission had already carried him away from Cordova.

Twenty-third : In the solemn conventions between Columbus and the Spanish sovereigns, dated April 17th, 1492, the prologue of the journal of Columbus, the royal decree of May 20th, 1493, and all other documents in which reference could be made to them, the two sons of Columbus are uniformly referred to ; and where Diego is to be distinguished from Fernando, it is only as the elder of his sons. The Count de Lorgues states that the language of the Mayorazgo or entailment of Columbus's estate implies evidently that Columbus was then married, in foreseeing that he might have other children than the two sons he therein named, and yet excluded the possibility of a third marriage.

Twenty-fourth : The fact that Columbus regarded Cordova, the residence of Beatrix, as his own residence, is proved by the official document awarding him the premium for first seeing the land of the new world, and the award was made payable at Cordova. This was the city where his family resided. He was then leading a wandering life of discovery. He had no other residence than that of his wife and family. His family consisted of his wife and two sons. This fact is inconsistent with any other theory than that of legal marriage. What but legitimate marriage and offspring could give him a legal residence at Cordova after he had left that city?

Twenty-fifth : His two sons associated together on terms of perfect equality before the world. They were introduced at court and in society together. They were universally recognized by their contemporaries as equally legitimate. When Columbus sent to congratulate the Portuguese governor of Arcilla, who had among his officers near relations of his first wife, he sent his very son Fernando on the embassy. Would he have sent a bastard son of a mistress to meet and associate with a near relative of his first wife? Would not this have been an insult to the officer himself and to the memory of his first wife? How could Fernando himself, a man of refined education, have recalled afterward in his history of his father a circumstance so humiliating to himself?

Twenty-sixth : In the genealogical trees of the Columbus family, the two sons of the admiral are always regarded as equally legitimate. Such evidence is of the highest weight. The Italian members of the Colombo family, at the trials for the succession in the Spanish tribunals, presented genealogies in which Fernando was placed on the same branch with his brother Diego. The senator, John Peter Sordi, the solicitor or advocate for Balthazar Colombo, in consultations in behalf of his clients, always recognized the legitimacy of Fernando. An eminent jurisconsult, Don Perez de Castro, of Madrid, in his memorial to the Court of Appeals, dated July 15th, 1792, indignantly rejected the insinuation of the attorney de la Palma y Freytas, as to the illegitimacy of Fernando, and declared that no portion of the proceedings cast the least doubt on the legitimacy of Fernando. The genealogical tree of the Cucarro branch of the Colombos places Diego and Fernando side by side and on the same branch, and this family always recognized the legitimacy of Fernando. Luigi Colombo, in express terms, recognizes the legitimacy of Fernando. Family trees and family recognitions constitute the highest evidences on all questions of marriage, legitimacy, and descent.

Twenty-seventh: While some obscure words in the will of Columbus, though capable of being construed quite differently, are relied upon for the charge that Columbus was never married to Beatrix Enriquez, so by another and clearly expressed portion of the same document we are able to prove the legitimacy of Fernando Columbus, and consequently the legality of the second marriage of the admiral. In this remarkable document legitimacy of birth is expressly declared to be the test of succession to his inheritance or entailed estate, and illegitimacy is made an insuperable obstacle to the succession. In the same instrument he makes his son Fernando, the son of Beatrix Enriquez, his heir and successor in the event of his eldest son Diego dying without children. Such provisions of the will are equivalent to an express declaration by the admiral himself, and that, too, in the most solemn document he ever executed, that Fernando Columbus was his legitimate son, and that Beatrix Enriquez was his lawful wife. It would not seem possible that a man of the great intellect of Columbus, so clear and logical, so consistent and uniform in every act, could have perpetrated such a blunder or could have been guilty of such an inconsistency as this would prove to be if Fernando Columbus be declared a bastard. So important is this evidence, that I will give the clause in question as it is written in the admiral's will.

"In the first place, I am to be succeeded by Don Diego, my son, who, in case of death without children, is to be succeeded by my other son, Fernando. . . . And should it please the Lord that the estate, after continuing for some time in the line of any of the above successors, should stand in need of an immediate and lawful male heir, the succession shall then devolve to the nearest relative, being a man of legitimate birth. . . . This entailed estate shall in nowise be inherited by a woman, except in case that no male is to be found, either in this or any other quarter of the world, of my real lineage, whose name, as well as that of his ancestors, shall have always been that of Columbus. In such an event (which may God forfend), then the female of legitimate birth most nearly related to the preceding possessor of the estate shall succeed to it."*

Twenty-eighth: While it would not be fair or just or consistent with the canons of correct construction to put upon the clause of the will relating to Beatrix Enriquez a construction which would make Columbus assign himself and her, whom he loved so well, to obloquy or disgrace, such a construction would be still less to be tolerated if any other rational construction can be placed upon it, or any other state of facts established which would harmonize with the language of the will. This can be done.

Shortly after his marriage to Beatrix he was compelled to leave her and the city of Cordova, to follow the court from place to place, and to prosecute his great mission. The remainder of the year of his marriage—1486—he was seeking an audience at court. In 1487 he was before the Scientific Congress or Junto of Salamanca. He was absent from Cordova when his son Fernando was born, and the end of this year finds him at Saragossa. In 1488 we find him at Seville and afterward at Valladolid, and it was in this year that he went to Lisbon to meet his brother Bartholomew. In 1489 we find him again at Seville, following up the court. The remainder of that year he spent in the field as a volunteer in the campaign of Baza. During this year he paid a flying visit to Cordova and to Beatrix and his sons. In 1490 he was the guest of the Duke of Medina Sidonia and of the Duke of Medina Celi. He was the guest of the Duke of Medina Celi through the year 1491 and a part of 1492. In this latter year he had secured the confidence of the sovereigns, negotiated his solemn conventions or treaties with them, went on his first voyage, and discovered the new world. From that time to the day of his death, a period of alternate labor, trials, successes and misfortunes, and of incessant toil and application to his assumed and recognized mission, we have no account of his having visited or seen Beatrix, except at intervals stolen from his engrossing duties. When his sons were taken from Cordova he was in the

---

* Dr. Barry's translation of Count de Lorgues' " Life of Columbus," pp. 619, 620 ; Irving's " Columbus," vol. iii., p. 444.

Indies, and his brother Bartholomew had to go to that city for them. During these years of feverish excitement and incessant travels, the wife shared none of his solicitude and participated not in his triumphs, and yet she performed the duties of a mother and guardian to both his sons. She also maintained his legal domicile at Cordova. She was evidently ever submissive, uncomplaining, faithful, maternal, domestic, and loving.

Was it not true, then, that Columbus was greatly indebted to her? Was it not true that so long a separation from his wife, the head of his household at Cordova, the guardian and educator of his children, the silent and uncomplaining partner of his love, a neglect and forgetfulness of her which we have not sufficient facts to explain, except in the overwhelming engrossment of the husband, should weigh heavily on his soul and on his conscience? Was not this tardy provision made to enable her to live suitably —that is, in a manner suitable to his wife—when once made, a relief to his conscience? Why should he be so solicitous for the suitable living of one whom he had neglected, if she were not his wife? Having established a house in Cordova, was it not proper and just that he should suitably maintain and support the long-neglected wife therein? And why should so sensitive a nature as Columbus's disclose to the world the causes or reasons for his action? Had there been anything cruel in the conduct of Columbus toward Beatrix, his countless enemies would certainly have accused him of it. From this it would seem that his long absences from Beatrix assumed in his just mind exaggerated proportions, and he repentantly endeavored to satisfy the suggestions of his conscience. There was no occasion for his publishing such a matter to the world. Had the facts for which he thus showed such regret been culpable or criminal, as charged against him, involving also the inculpation of one loved by him and the dishonor of one he loved with a father's love, Columbus would never have made the slightest allusion to them. This theory, I think, fully accounts for and explains the clause in the will, and sets the conduct of Columbus above all reproach.

Twenty-ninth: While, of course, there is nothing authentic known to the public in relation to the process for the canonization at Rome of Christopher Columbus, the fact that there is a widespread desire among learned and devout members of his Church, including eminent ecclesiastics and authors, for his receiving the honors of the altar, go far to remove and discredit the accusation of an illicit connection between him and Beatrix Enriquez. Tradition and general reputation, and the fame of religion which has always clung to his life, acquit him of every such stain. There has been printed by the American newspress during the centennial year a statement, purporting to come from Rome, that the process for his canonization had been arrested on account of the charge that his relations with Beatrix Enriquez were not sanctioned by marriage. But the present writer has good authority for stating that no such statement as this has ever emanated from the Sacred Congregation of Rites at Rome, which has charge of the process of canonization. In no instance are such statements permitted to issue or receive countenance from that holy commission. Mention has already been made in these pages of important documents said to have been found within recent years in Spain, which it is thought will go far to authenticate a legal marriage, and I have good reason for the belief that private documents have also been found and presented which establish that fact.

Thirtieth: There is another view of this subject which seems not to have been presented in other works relating to Columbus. Taking the facts as they are known to us and are undisputed, it is clear and indisputable that, according to the ecclesiastical law of the time, Columbus and Beatrix Enriquez were lawfully married. That ecclesiastical law, at the time of the marriage, not only determines its validity, but as the law of Spain and the continental law generally conformed thereto, their marriage was valid under the civil law. The law of the Catholic Church on this subject is clearly set forth in the following passages from a recent work, which bears the *imprimaturs* of the Rev. Edward S. Keogh, Deputy Censor of the Congregation of the Oratory, of His Eminence Cardinal Manning, Archbishop of Westminster, and of His Eminence Cardinal McCloskey, Archbishop of New York.

" The conditions for the validity of marriage are mostly identical with the conditions which determine the validity of contracts in general. The consent to the union must be mutual, voluntary, deliberate, and manifested by external signs. The signs of consent need not be verbal in order to make the marriage valid, though the rubric of the ritual requires the consent to be expressed in that manner. The consent must be to actual marriage, then and there, not at some future time."*

"The validity of clandestine marriages was fully recognized by the Church, and the common opinion of the mediæval doctors made the essence of marriage consist in the free consent of the contracting parties. The Council of Trent introduced a new condition for the validity of the contract, and therefore of the sacrament. It declared all marriages null unless contracted before the parish priest or another priest approved by him for the purpose, and two or three witnesses."†

Now, as I have already stated, the marriage of Columbus and Beatrix Enriquez took place in the latter part of November, 1486, and the first session of the Council of Trent did not take place until December 10th, 1545, so that at the time of the marriage in question—1487—the consent of the parties manifested by words or other signs of consent, *in presenti*, constituted a valid marriage, and so the law remained for nearly sixty years thereafter, when the Council of Trent, in 1546, for the first time required the presence of a priest and of two or more witnesses.

There is no question in this case as to the affection and consent between Columbus and Beatrix, for all authorities testify to this, nor is there anything even to exclude the additional fact of a ceremony in the presence of priest and witnesses, even though these features were not requisite. A registry was neither required nor, as it seems, customary. The subsequent birth of a son, at the wife's residence at Cordova, the recognition of that son by the most frequent and solemn acts, the establishment of a house and residence at Cordova for his wife and his children by the two marriages, his return to that house and residence from time to time, the education of his children there by the wife, his acquisition and claim of a legal domicile at the place where he had established the residence and domicile of his family— Cordova—over which Beatrix presided as wife and mother, are facts and circumstances which bring the case clearly within the requirements both of the laws of the Church and of the State.

---

* "A Catholic Dictionary," etc., by William E. Addis, secular priest, sometime Fellow of the Royal University of Ireland, and Thomas Arnold, M.A., Fellow of the same university. New York: The Catholic Publication Society, 1884, p. 548.
† *Id.*, p. 435.

Such a state of facts would, at common law, prove a valid marriage both in England and America at the present day.

The following instructive and interesting passage from Shelford's "Law of Marriage and Divorce," on the Council of Trent and its action on the subject of marriage, will be read with interest by our readers.*

"This celebrated council was held in the bishopric of Trent, a province of Germany, in the circle of Austria, situated upon the Alps. It sat with some intermissions from the year 1545 to 1563, when the doctrine of the Pope's infallibility, transubstantiation, etc., were confirmed. The council was first opened under Paul III., on December 13th, 1545, continued under Julius III., interrupted under Marcellus II. and Paul IV. by the wars and troubles of the continent, and terminated about the year 1563, and was confirmed by a bull signed by a legate of the Holy See, who, according to the practice of all ages, presided at the assembly. (Halkerstone's Dig., 69, note. See History of this Council, by Father Paul, fol., London, 1676, and Pallavicino.)

" 'There is, among the true believers, nothing more certain and undoubted than that the marriage contract has been elevated to the dignity of a sacrament; this is a truth inherent to the Roman Catholic tenets, established by the sovereign pontiff, Eugene IV., in his decree instituted for the Armenians, section 7, repeated by the Holy Council of Trent, in section 24, "Of the Reform of Marriage," chapter 1, and learnedly upheld and illustrated by Bellarmino, in his book entitled " Of Holy Marriage," against the attacks of Luther, Calvin, and other heretics. In order, therefore, that the faithful should celebrate the marriage most religiously, which the apostle, in his Epistle to the Ephesians, chapter 5, denominates " a great sacrament in Christ," and in the Church, from the earliest times of the Church itself, it has been instituted and held that the marriage ought to be celebrated before the priest, by whom it was validated with his benediction. However, whatever may have been the ancient discipline respecting the validity of those marriages which had been celebrated without the assistance of the rector, it is now beyond all doubt that no marriage can at present be validly celebrated unless with

---

* See "Canones et Decreta Concilii Trident." sess. 24, c. 1.

observance of the forms prescribed by the Holy Council of Trent. That doctrine appears to be strictly established by the said council in section 24, "Of the Reform of Marriage," chapter 1, in which we find the following passage: "Qui aliter, quam præsente parocho, vel alio sacerdote, de ipsius parochi seu ordanarii licentia, et duobus vel tribus testibus matrimonium contrahare attentabunt, eos sancta Synodus ad sic contrahendum omnino inhabiles reddet et hujusmodi contractus irritos et nullos esse decernit, prout eos præsenti decreto irritos facit et annullat" ("Concilii Trident. Canones et Decreta," p. 250, ed. 1615). "If any person shall presume to contract marriage otherwise than in the presence of the parish rector, or of another priest delegated by the said parish rector or the ordinary, and in the presence of two or three witnesses, the holy synod renders them unapt for so contracting; and it declares such contracts as null and void, as by this present decree it renders void and annuls the same. And it is hereby declared that the marriage benediction shall be given by the proper parish rector, and that the license for so giving the said benediction cannot be granted to another priest by any other person than the rector himself or the ordinary." It is therefore quite clear that in Rome, and in all other places where the Council of Trent is received, the marriage must be celebrated before the proper parish rector, and in the presence of two witnesses. By "proper rector" is to be understood the rector in whose parish the contracting parties have their residence; and as it may happen that the two contracting parties are residents in two different parishes, it will then be sufficient for the validity of the marriage that the act be performed with the intervention of the parish rector of either of the parties. And this principle is so far a matter of strict rule, that even foreigners and travelers, who may happen to be making but a temporary sojourn in some place where the Council of Trent is received, cannot validly contract marriage without observing that formality, as among other matters is laid down and explained by Pirking in the Decretal, Book IV., title 3, section 2, No. 10, in which is contained the following (from the Latin): "Foreigners who are merely passing through a place in which a decree of the Council of Trent is received cannot validly contract marriage, unless it be done with the assistance of the parish rector and before witnesses, even should the said decree not be received at the place in which they make their residence, because they are bound to observe the laws of the place through which they are then passing. In addition to this, neither the parish rector nor the ordinary himself, or any other superior authority, could grant faculty for uniting in marriage two persons who were not Roman Catholics, because it is an absurdity that those who are disunited from the Church should be made participators of a sacrament of that same Church." From the deposition of Belloni, Doctor of Civil and Canon Law, stated in joint appendix to the case of Swift *vs.* Kelly, before the judgment committee of the Privy Council, pp. 138, 139.'"

It was not until after the foregoing pages had been written that I saw and read a new book, a noble monument to Christopher Columbus, a work recently published at Milan, and entitled "Cristoforo Colombo. Osservazioni Critiche sui punti pui rilevanti e controversi della sua vita, publicata per cura di M. A. Lazzaroni." The learned and accomplished author of this work devotes a considerable space to the consideration of the question of the marriage of Columbus and Beatrix Enriquez, regarding it as one of the most salient and controverted points in the life of the admiral. He handles the subject with research, with impartiality, with learning, with eloquence, and with consummate ability. He intelligently and cogently espouses the cause of the legitimacy of the second marriage, and his arguments seem unanswerable. The logic of his facts is most convincing. He has found in the valuable and important work of Dondero, on "The Morality of Columbus," quotations from two important works: the one written by the Jesuit Father Alphonso Garcia, in 1618, and the other written by Father Pietro Simon di Parillas, in 1627 —works which show the voice of authentic history during those one hundred and sixty years prior to the invention of the librarian, Nicolao Antonio, that the relations of Columbus and Beatrix were not sanctioned by marriage. And these quotations he gives us. He also gives the full title of the manuscript or document first mentioned in this chapter in the sixteenth reason for sustaining the marriage of Columbus and Beatrix. He also gives us important testimony from the pen of Columbus himself, taken from an authentic copy of an autograph letter of Columbus, dated April 23d, 1497. The treatment of the subject in Signor Lazzaroni's fine work is so unique and so cogent that I have deemed it but just to the learned author to introduce it here in full, which I have done in a translation made of the following pages:

"Want! yes, Columbus had felt it that first year of his sojourn in Spain, and, perhaps, afterward, but did not allow himself to be cast down by it, as happens with weak minds, and never listened to its dangerous counsels. He was so absorbed in the idea, become now the absolute master of his spirit, as not to advert to the sad contingencies of life; so compassed by the loftiness of his conceptions as to carry his head erect amid trials, and wear gracefully and with dignity his torn cloak. A gravity tempered by modesty, a cheerful comeliness, facile eloquence, goodness and authority, breathing from his whole air, are the lines that prevail in the portraits left us of him by contemporary writers.

"Although these notes portray the discoverer at the zenith of his renown, they all the same attest that which he would be under adverse fortune, granting that happy successes and propitious fortune deteriorate rather than better the character's good qualities. A precocious old age, that from thirty years bleached his blond locks, made more striking the vivid bloom of his cheeks, above which his clear eyes benignantly shone, and outlined with imperative evidence his aquiline nose.

"With these manners and appearance, Columbus presented himself to the sovereigns of Spain, and placed at their feet a new world, and knew how to make his poverty light for himself and respected by others. We were about to say that he knew how to make it lovable; for not only admiration and friendship were drawn to him, but love, too, discerning the excellence of his spirit under his modest garb, was there to console him with its sweetness. This brings us to touch another very ticklish point of Columbus's life, and seriously controverted in our day. Columbus had, when dying, a sad souvenir of her who, when he was poor and almost unknown, had yielded up to him her affections, and made bud forth some roses on the thorns of his first residence in Cordova. However, the secret grief that tempers those memorable words seemed the ill-disguised expression of a remorse, the mysterious hinting at a fault, and that testamentary disposition became the gauge of battle and controversy. But to return. Columbus had in manners and mien all that best pleases, but his rare loftiness of soul, that vibrated in his warm and eloquent speech, was the bait by which were taken all who had relations with him. He was, withal, a very simple man, but the simplicity that rarely dissociates itself from true greatness flowed in him from a special fountain—from his singular piety. One would give an imperfect and disfigured portrait of the great navigator, who would be silent with regard to his sincere and almost mystical piety, his living faith, which, blending itself with genuine spiritualism, uplifted to the height of mysterious revelations the offspring of his own intellect. That such religious fervor, which characterizes Columbus, was not borne by him from Italy, a country republican, commercial, greedy of riches, as Humboldt affirmed, but learned in Andalusia, at Granada, and in conversation with the friars of La Rabida, seems to us the assertion best founded of the celebrated German writer.*

"Without diffusiveness, let us say in passing that to souls of the temper of Columbus certain qualities do not attach themselves ; they are born and develop with the individual, and constitute rather, at times, the secret of his singularity and greatness. Had not Humboldt written of Columbus : ' In effect, all that seems to belong but to the narrow circle of the material interests of life rise in the occult mind of this extraordinary man to a nobler sphere, to a mysterious spiritualism ' ? † Why, then, take back one's word ?

"Republican and commercial Italy had also her religious or theological fervor, as Humboldt calls it. It will suffice, among many examples, to remember that in the country of Macchiavelli, Savonarola arose, and that from the hearing of thirty votive masses of the Holy Ghost, Cola di Rienza, who professed to be His envoy, mounted the capitol to then awaken pagan echoes and fantasies of the republic and the tribune's office. Would it not be more likely to say that in Columbus, believing like a man of his time, as a mariner, as a good Genoese, religious fervor mounted to the height of his other stupendous qualities ?

"To affirm that he acquired it in Spain, besides being improper to us, seems dangerous to the reputation of Columbus ; the glare of the funeral pyres, the fierce san benitos, and the

---

* "Hist. de la Geograph.," etc., vol. iii., p. 258, Paris, 1837.
† *Id.*, vol. i., p. 109. Paris, 1837.

fearful figures of the D'Arhues and the Torquemadas might cross athwart the reader's mind.

"Columbus was pious by temperament and by conviction; was a theologian from tireless reading of the Bible and the Fathers, and because, as Humboldt well wrote, his ardent mind was upborne to a mysterious spiritualism; however, as in him practical sense was not unaccompanied by profound idealism, so to sublime religious theories he knew how to adopt the minute practices of worship.

"On this it behooves us to cite some words of Fernando, his son and historiographer :* 'Of religious things he was so observant that, in fact, in saying the entire canonical office, he might be deemed a professed religious, and was such an enemy of oaths that I never heard him swear; and when he found himself most angry, his reproof was to say, "I give you to God; why have you done or said this?" and if anything were to be written, he did not begin without first writing these words: "*Jesus cum Maria sit nobis in via*" ("May Jesus with Mary be with us in the way").' And this, we repeat, was indispensable to the representation of the entire moral physiognomy of Columbus, of which the religious spirit constitutes a typically profound feature. If to some it may seem that we have too much insisted on this, we invite them to kindly join us in judging men according to the age they live in, not according to current prejudices. Nowadays greatness and devoutness may, perhaps, seem incompatible; but 'twas not so in the past, and the example of Columbus may stand for a hundred other luminous proofs of it.

"To us the having discoursed somewhat at length of it seems also as a substratum for what we are about to say of that affection, which relieved the enforced idleness of Columbus, and rendering less bitter for him the awaiting, contributed, indirectly, to retain him in Spain.

"History is silent about the particulars which we should most wish to know of this love episode, and only hands down to us the name of the maiden. She was called Beatrix, of the family Enriquez de Arana, nobles of the city, and descended from an illustrious Biscay lineage, but, as it appears, no longer with a large rental. Columbus and Beatrix loved one another, and of

---

* "Historia dell' Almirante," cap. iii.

this love was born Fernando Columbus, the historian of his father's deeds—learned, noble, virtuous hidalgo—to whom history has been lavish of praise.

"So we now come upon, as is easily seen, another of the controverted moments in Columbus's history, a point most hotly disputed, now that they wish to make a saint of Columbus, despite the deductions realistically pessimistic of modern criticism. There is question of nothing less than establishing the character of the bond that united Columbus to Beatrix—was it concubinage or marriage? Of this last opinion the Count Roselly de Lorgues has been, and very partially, one of the hottest and most dramatic narrators of the life of Columbus. His great error, so much cast up to him by his contradictors, is that of having a wish to maintain, with drawn sword, the all-around moral perfection of his hero. And we Italians ought to know how to be grateful to him for the same, because holiness and greatness do not absolutely exclude one another; but the contrary happens, and it is beautiful to see among the most bitter those who by country and temperament ought at least to have kept themselves in a certain reserve. Count Roselly de Lorgues, whose excellent ability as a writer in no way yields to the exquisite courtesy he displays in his rich and peaceful Parisian home, knew how to gather together and weigh so many arguments in favor of the lawfulness of the love of Columbus and Beatrix, as to make one despair of attempting the work again. We, who are not invested with the spirit of the illustrious Frenchman, cannot go down into the arena with him, not through fear of being laughed at, nor to withhold ourselves from the defence of truth, but because it frightens us to think of pitching headlong into another conjectural question. We shall, however, bring forth testimony and considerations gathered here and there on the battle-field, or drawn from our own sentiments, leaving the verdict to the reader.

"Before all, this new love-throb of Columbus, amid the grave preoccupations of his intellect and the trials of life, seems to us a proof of the gentleness and exhaustless exuberance of his soul. The mind absorbed in arduous speculations renders unfruitful and inert all the other faculties of the spirit, and love seldom knocks where intellect reigns supreme. Only to a few privileged because in well-formed minds, like that of Columbus, and in contingencies like to his, the youth of a woman has a special effect, a sweetly irresistible charm, and, besides, a love late in coming, or that is renewed at the age less favorable to love, never comes without great usury.

"How came Columbus to see near at hand, and speak to Beatrix, and be heard in her own home ; because, even in the worst hypothesis, he must have been received willingly. This is not known, as even the epoch is uncertain, which, however, in our opinion may be believed to be toward the end of his first year of residence in Spain, when the public voice had already become familiar with his name, and some presaged favorably of the successes and the future of this singular foreigner. With such recommendations Columbus addressed himself to the respectable family of the young lady ; saw himself shortly admitted to their confidence. The fact that one of the Enriquez de Arana, Beatrix's nephew, followed Columbus in a certain rank in his first voyage of discovery, is a proof that the De Arana believed and hoped from the first in their guest, and wished most cordially to strengthen these hopes by the bond of relationship.

"There is thus far nothing unlikely in the ideal reconstruction we are making of this obscure passage in the life of Columbus, who, either that his growing reputation or a mutual friend he met recommended him in that home, has suddenly shown himself better than his reputation. His commanding beauty of mien, graceful manners, and jovial conversation, which rose at times to eloquence even, were calculated to win ; but in his favorite theme his speech flashed from his lips ; his movement, look—all were in him those of a prophet. We delight to represent him to ourselves, then, in the home of De Arana, in the attentive family circle, coloring his plan of transatlantic navigation, foretelling the wonders of another sea, another sky, other regions vast, fertile, rich, leaving his little audience dazed. With these phantasmagoric revelations of another hemisphere, which already seemed present realities, to the assurance of tone on the part of him who evoked them, Columbus perhaps mingled the recital of an intrepid youth passed upon the seas in bold explorations, in perilous deeds ; and this part of his discourse, wherein there was so much to cause admiration and enthusiasm, made perhaps a special impression on the timorous Beatrix. Out of pity and sympathy for the intrepid seafarer, so young of heart despite the premature bleaching of his locks, her mind yielded to the fascination of this strange promiser of kingdoms, and a vague presage of greatness and glory thrilled her.

"These fancies of ours with regard to the second and last love of Columbus recall to us, without our wishing it, the admirable recital in which Othello recounts to the venerable, grave, and reverend signors of Venice how he learned to love Desdemona, and was loved by her in return. Should Columbus have ever needed to vindicate his power over the mind of Beatrix Enriquez, and to declare by what arts he had caught the maiden in the toils of love, the words of Othello would have supplied him with a most touching defence.

"*Othello.* Most potent, grave, and reverend seigniors,
My very noble and approved good masters,
That I have ta'en away this old man's daughter
It is most true ; true, I have married her ;
The very head and front of my offending
Hath this extent, no more. Rude am I in my speech,
And little blessed with the set phrase of peace ;
For since these arms of mine had seven years' pith,
Till now some nine moons wasted, they have used
Their dearest action in the tented field ;
And little of this great world can I speak,
More than pertains to feats of broil and battle,
And therefore little shall I grace my cause,
In speaking for myself. Yet, by your gracious patience,
I will a round, unvarnished tale deliver
Of my whole course of love ; what drugs, what charms,
What conjuration, and what mighty magic,
(For such proceeding I am charged withal)
I won his daughter with.
* * * * * *
I do confess the vices of my blood,
So justly to your grave ears I'll present
How I did thrive in this fair lady's love,
And she in mine.

"*Duke.* Say it, Othello.

"*Othello.* Her father loved me ; oft invited me ;
Still questioned me the story of my life,
From year to year ; the battles, sieges, fortunes,
That I have passed.
I ran it through, even from my boyish days,
To the very moment that he bade me tell it.
Wherein I spoke of most disastrous chances,
Of moving accidents, by flood and field ;

> Of hair-breadth 'scapes i' the imminent deadly breach;
> Of being taken by the insolent foe,
> And sold to slavery; of my redemption thence,
> And portance in my travel's history,
> Wherein of antres vast, and deserts wild,
> Rough quarries, rocks, and hills whose heads touch heaven,
> It was my hint to speak, such was the process;
> And of the Cannibals that each other eat,
> The anthropophagi, and men whose heads
> Do grow beneath their shoulders. These things to hear,
> Would Desdemona seriously incline:
> But still the house affairs would draw her thence;
> Which ever as she could with haste dispatch,
> She'd come again, and with a greedy ear,
> Devour up my discourse: which I observing,
> Took once a pliant hour, and found good means
> To draw from her a prayer of earnest heart,
> That I would all my pilgrimage dilate,
> Whereof by parcels she had something heard
> But not intentively: I did consent;
> And often did beguile her of her tears,
> When I did speak of some distressful stroke,
> That my youth suffered. My story being done
> She gave me for my pains a world of sighs:
> She swore: In faith, 'twas strange, 'twas passing strange;
> 'Twas pitiful, 'twas wondrous pitiful:
> She wished she had not heard it; yet she wished
> That Heaven had made her such a man; she thanked me;
> And bade me, if I had a friend that loved her,
> I should but teach him how to tell my story,
> And that would woo her. Upon this hint, I spake;
> She loved me for the dangers I had passed;
> And I loved her, that she did pity them.
> This only is the witchcraft I have used.*

"It did not occur to the mind of Shakespeare to bring upon the scene the loves of Columbus and Beatrix, otherwise who knows what new melodies he would have known how to draw thence; in what manner the threads of this love would have entwined themselves in his master hand. The disentangling of them proves very difficult to us, who are not aided by the expedients of the renowned poet; to us, the slaves of systematic

---

* Shakespeare's "Othello," act i., scene 3. I have not confined myself strictly to the quotation as contained in Signor Lazzaroni's "Cristoforo Colombo," but, on account of the aptness of the quotation, I have given it with slightly increased length and fulness.

prejudices or lawless enthusiasm, and placed in the straits of historical contradictions.

"Count Roselly transfuses, as we have said, the lifeblood into such a question, and makes the debated point shine with dazzling light; and with him a squad of proselytes, quickened by the spirit of such a master, gave itself to the ransacking of libraries and archives in search of an explicit and decisive word, of an unquestionable document, which would put a seal on the world of shrewd, splendid, and reasonable induction evoked by them. But archives and libraries have thus far obstinately refused the so greatly desired answer. It has not been proven that Columbus legalized his love for Beatrix, nor has it been established peremptorily that it was concubinage.

"Oviedo, Herrera, Ortiz de Zuniga, contemporary and non-contemporary historians, beset by those who impugn the lawfulness of this union, assert nothing *pro* or *contra*, pass over it, and, with expressions far from definite, leave the field open to controversy.

"However, the not affirming is very different from denying, as one of Roselly's* most active followers shrewdly observes; besides, one ought when in doubt keep the safer course, conformably to the legal axiom : the doubtfulness of a witness is to be interpreted in favor of the lawfulness of the cause, and reticence with regard to special circumstances is an indication of the publicity and notoriety of the fact. Even they who incline to believe this tie unlawful find their side weak, and strive to find a solution of the controversy in the existence of certain forms of marital relations that we may call civil, admitted and tolerated by the laws and customs of that time. Signor Pinilla treats this matter very precisely, and it will serve to cite here a translation of his words. He begins by saying that the defenders of the ecclesiastical marriage of Columbus and Beatrix 'have persisted in discussing a thing that does not belittle or throw the least shadow upon the life, honor, lustre, and halo of Columbus.' He, however, omits mention of his devoutness, which is the war-horse of his opponents.

"Putting aside thus the real question, one understands that they do not succeed, nor will they ever succeed, in understanding

---

* Avv. A. Dondero, "L'Onestà di Colombo," ecc., Genova, 1877.

each other; but he (Pinilla) goes on : 'Count Roselly is a man of very great genius and vast knowledge, but in this contest he forgets what was, at least in Spain, the society of the fifteenth century in the matter of morals, inasmuch as they relate to marriage and to the constitution of the family. With regard to this point, let us hear a priest of irreproachable morals and great knowledge.'*

" ' The ideas of our predecessors by no means resemble our own, and they would surely have been scandalized and deemed us barbarians did they know them. To have a son, even if not born in wedlock or not recognized by the law, was for the common weal, and so the laws did not consider him of condition inferior to them that were born by a lawful wife (before the Church), nor did they degrade him, or repute him unworthy of public office, or to succeed to the property of his father. They merely required that the sonship be certified, and this was wont to be done by the sponsors on the day of baptism, or publicly in the junto, according to the formalities prescribed by the statutes. The father, instead of being ashamed of them, treated them with regard equal to that shown the legitimate, and counted on them as useful members of domestic society. The laws imposed upon mothers the burden of feeding and educating both one and the other.' †

" All this goes to prove, from the condition (not despised) of the offspring, the relative morality of the parents, and the bond, though unblessed and not perfectly legitimate, that united them. Hear him (Pinilla) further : 'Let Count Roselly and his supporters, then, see how Beatrix suffered nothing in her character or nobility in not being before the Church‡ the wife of Christopher Columbus ; and that despite this he might fitly call her his wife, as he a hundred times over called Fernando his son.'

" ' Wherefore Count Roselly cannot be ignorant that concubinage was a perfectly legitimate act, not only because tolerated, but even authorized in explicit dispositions of our forensic legislation. It was not a vague, indeterminate, arbitrary bond, says

---

* Pinilla here quotes Martinez Marina, "Ensayo historico, critico, sobre l'antiqua legislacion," etc., de Leon y Castilla, sez. 206.

† Pinilla, "Colon en España," cap. viii.

‡ The wife who received the blessing was veiled, and observed all the rites of the Church.

the above-quoted author, but was founded in a contract of friendship and companionship, the principal conditions of which were permanency and fidelity. In our juridical history, according to the statutes and customs, three kinds of bond between man and woman were known and authorized by law: marriage *in facie ecclesiæ* (solemnized during mass), "the marriage by promise, and concubinage. Whether the marriage of the Genoese navigator and Beatrix Enriquez was of this last class, or was a marriage by promise—*i.e.*, a marriage of conscience—we shall not stop to discuss." "The words of the will lend themselves to one and the other opinion. However, whichsoever of the two kinds of union was that of which Don Fernando was the fruit, it does not lessen the merit, the honorableness, the fame or good name of Christopher Columbus; none of them would belittle his glory, nor the nobleness of Beatrix Enriquez, nor the estimation, preeminence, and esteem which his son Fernando enjoyed and deserved."' *

NOTE.—This view of the subject is confirmed by Leonard Shelford, of the Middle Temple, Barrister at Law, in his able work on the "Law of Marriage and Divorce," already quoted, in which he traces this form of marriage to the civil law, and after speaking of its qualities of permanency and fidelity, says: "Those characters show how widely mistaken we should be if we annexed the idea of immodesty or contempt to the name of concubine among the ancients, as we do in modern times" (pp. 10; 33 Law Library, p. 31). In a foot-note of that work is given an extract from Gibbon's History, vol. v., pp. 399, 400, in which this form of marriage as existing among the Romans is described, and it is stated that it prevailed from the age of Augustus to the tenth century both in the West and the East, and states "that this companionship was often preferred to the pomp and insolence of a noble matron." The Christian Church struggled to abolish this form of marriage, but did not wholly succeed until the enactments of the Council of Trent from 1545 to 1563. It must not be supposed, however, that the author of Lazzaroni's work, or any of the advocates of the regularity and legitimacy of the marriage of Columbus and Beatrix, classify their marriage under this head. On the contrary, they contend that the marriage of Columbus and Beatrix belonged to that class of marriages which is denominated as marriage *in facie ecclesiæ*. The trend of this argument in Lazzaroni's quoted authorities is simply that the alliance of Columbus and Beatrix at worst was lawful, customary and honorable. But with Columbus's firm adherence to the strictest methods of the Church, no marriage less than marriage *in facie ecclesiæ* would ever have satisfied him. Beatrix must have been no less rigid in so sacred a rite.

"In all this defence they very properly are silent concerning that upon which their adversaries insist—namely, the piety of Columbus. This, shouted from one side of the field, suffices to

---

* Pinilla, above cited.

dismount the batteries on the other. Notwithstanding this, Count Roselly and his companions on their part do not decline the combat upon any field; putting aside the holy water stoup and aspersorium, all arms are good even for them to repel the assault.

"Apropos, it would be useful and pleasant to put side by side some of the reasons of Pinilla and of the others of his school, and those taken from every department of knowledge by the lawyer Dondero, who, with all the resources of his profession, combines much critical acumen, culture, and great convincing powers. But besides going to too great length, it would prove difficult to choose and to separate, considering the copiousness and the concatenation of his arguments.

"He proves, and to us it seems without doubt, that none of the contemporary or quasi-contemporary historians of Columbus explicitly declare against the legitimacy of his union with Beatrix Enriquez, and among the conjectural and positive proofs in favor of the same produces some historical testimonies of great weight. These are, it is true, of dates a hundred years or more subsequent to the times of the admiral, but the less credence which they would seem on that account to deserve is compensated for by the authority and the competence of the writers. It is, then, a 'principle of truth,' as the same Dondero writes,* 'and every-day experience confirms it, that a just cause acquires steadily, as time goes on, new arguments and data, or helps that demonstrate its perfect justness; whereas, on the contrary, a false cause, although masked at first under some appearance of truth, loses ground with the lapse of time, just as happens with genuine and counterfeit money.' So the union of Columbus and Beatrix since it began to be considered and discussed seems ever to put on a better face. The following testimonies could not be more favorable. One is of the Jesuit Alphoriso Garcia, who died rector of the College of Ossuna, in 1618, and who consequently lived at the epoch of the famous litigation for the succession to the entailed estates of Christopher Columbus, and who ought therefore to be better informed than any other of that which occurred in it, and of the status of Columbus and his sons.

---

* "L'Onesta di Colombo," ecc., p. 109.

"'Don Christopher Columbus,' he writes, 'first conqueror and discoverer of the Indies, was High Admiral of the same, Duke of Veragua, and Marquis of Jamaica. He married twice: first in Portugal, where he lived in his youth, Donna Philippa Moniz de Perestrello, by whom he had his elder son, Don Diego; secondly, he married in Cordova, where he resided six years, a lady of that city called Donna Beatrix Enriquez de Arana, of the lineage of the nobles of this city, in the province of Biscay, and by her had Don Fernando Colombo, a chevalier of great understanding, valor, virtue, and literary attainments, after he left the service of the Prince Don Juan, whose page he was.'[*]

"Not less conclusive is this other testimony drawn from the history of Father Pietro Simon di Parillas, printed at Cuenca in the year 1627, and dedicated to Philip IV., which is found in the library of Valencia.

"In the fourteenth chapter is the following: 'Don Christopher Columbus came to Portugal, where he married, firstly, Donna Philippa Moniz de Perestrello, by whom he had Don Diego Colombo. Left a widower, he married a second time, in the city of Cordova, Donna Beatrix Enriquez, a native of that city, who gave birth to Don Fernando Colombo, who made himself so famous by his virtue as well as by his erudition.'[†] The just-quoted testimony, which, though being that of sixteenth-century historians, might not merit too much credence, yet it assumes from circumstances a special value. Let it be borne in mind that it was published during the celebrated litigation of the above-mentioned succession, which, reviving the memory of the glorious discoverer, caused the acts and the words and all the events, public and private, of his life to be by all spoken of and discussed; genealogical trees were prepared, relationships and whatever else could be connected with the burning question of legitimate descent were examined. But let the reader make what account of it he may. We ourselves are merely readers in this controversy, and we prefer not to go beyond the limits of a simple statement.

---

[*] "There exists in the Library of the Royal Historical Academy of Madrid, chapter xxxviii., a manuscript entitled 'General History of the very Illustrious and Loyal City of Cordova, and of its Noblest Families,' by Dr. André de Moralés (this title is in Spanish), and which treats of the lineage and descent of the Admiral Christopher Columbus. See Dondero, pp. iii., 111, 112."

[†] Dondero, *loc. cit.*, pp. 113, 114.

"Among the many things that we have happened to read apropos of this matter, we shall never forget a phrase that escaped Columbus, in one of those moments in which the fulness of his sorrow and bitterness encumbered his style. Returning from his third voyage to the new world, his soul full of anguish, in irons, almost ready to succumb under the weight of so many misfortunes, persecutions, and accusations, worse than which they would not be able to invent in hell, he drafts a letter to influential and friendly persons, as it would appear, who still remained to him at the court. Having called to mind the years of his trying and loyal service, their stupendous results and unworthy recompense, he touches upon the hardest sacrifice that can be demanded of the human heart—to wit, that of husband and father at the same time, and adds that to serve Spain, or rather their Highnesses, he had forsaken wife and children, and had never lived for them; or, in other words, besides fatherly affection and domestic joys, he had sacrificed their most sacred interests to those of Spain (' Y deje muyer y hijos que jamas vi por ellos ').*

"Wife? Not certainly Donna Philippa Moniz de Perestrello, who had died in Portugal twenty years before. Sons? Not certainly Diego, the only one born to him by his first wife. How is it possible not to recognize in these expressions Beatrix Enriquez and his sons Diego and Fernando? True, *muyer*, in Castilian, means also woman simply; but that it would have been used by Columbus in that sense seems so absurd as not to merit confutation. In fine, whatever may be the attenuating circumstances taken from the different kinds of marital union tolerated then and even recognized by the laws, which were unable to prevent them, considering the great relaxation of morals, it would have been, it seems to us, a very bad recommendation in a proud and bigoted court to appeal to a love-tie unblessed and not really legitimate. It will be, perhaps, difficult to persuade the contrary of all that to good sense, even though

---

* "The autograph exists in the archives of the Duke of Veragua, and is a fragment of a letter in bad copy, and for that some give little weight to its expressions, as if Columbus would lend himself to the invention and coloring of lies in the drafts of his letters! It begins, 'Gentlemen;' but it is not known to what persons in authority it may have been addressed. It was published by Navarrete, with Diploma II., Document 87, Torre, 'Writings of Columbus,' p. 293."

it appear refined gold to criticism. To leave his woman and young sons is equivalent, even among us, to leaving one's own lawful wife and children, as also the actual usage in speech is that where to woman is added the possessives, mine, thine, his, it is understood to mean the lawful wife.

"And of this *muyer*, his abandonment of whom, in order to expose himself to the dangers and to the hardships of the boldest of marine explorations, he cast up to Spain and to the court, he writes with tenderness to Diego, his firstborn, during one of his many periods of absence: 'Let Beatrix Enriquez be recommended to thee by the love of me, absent from thee, and regard her as thy mother; let her have from thee ten thousand maravedis yearly besides those which she already holds from the butchers' shops of Cordova.' These words, full of respect and affection, were found in an ancient manuscript by Father Marcellino da Civezza, General Historiographer of the Franciscan Order, and another champion of the morality of Columbus.* You would say that these reappear to ratify, after about three hundred years, the genuine and specific meaning given by Columbus to the word *muyer* in the above extract, and to warn us that personal and epistolary accounts, direct or indirect, must exist, covering the period of his public life, between the admiral and Beatrix Enriquez, though history affords no indication of them. The words of this letter throw a new ray of light on a passage in the will of the great discoverer, which has and will be always a stumbling-block, and as the battering-ram of those who impugn the lawfulness of his second marriage.

"In this last will, drawn up by him in Segovia, August 25th, 1505, and probated in Valladolid, March 19th, 1506 (the eve of his death), the admiral returns to recommend his Beatrix to his firstborn, Diego.

"Having enjoined upon him to pay certain debts, of which he

---

* "The manuscript belongs to the Collection Vargas Ponce, of the Library of the Royal Historical Academy of Madrid, in two volumes, with the title 'Columbus and his Sons, Memorandum of Documents.' Its discoverer maintains that the document in question is the authentic copy of an autograph letter of Christopher Columbus, under date. City of Burgos, April 23d, 1497, which contains certain other dispositions and reminders for Don Diego, and is referable, according to the date, to the year passed by Columbus in Spain between his second and third voyages to the New World."

will find the memorandum attached, he goes on: 'And I order him that he have care of Beatrix Enriquez, mother of Don Fernando, my son; that he see that she may be able to live becomingly, as one to whom I owe so much. And let this be for the unburdening of my conscience, as this weighs heavily on my heart. The reason of this it is not allowed to write here.'*

"It is a sad puzzle, nor is it easy to solve it. This perplexity of broken and ambiguous phrases, lending themselves to so many interpretations, is not unique in history. 'I pass into eternity, and I know why,' the dying Clement XIV. said; nothing more was required to believe him the victim of poison, and that it was administered to him by the Jesuits. How much wrangling has there not been and now is among interpreters upon the first canto of the 'Divina Commedia'! A like bequest in the context of a legal document, which prescribes the payment of certain pecuniary debts, seems *prima facie* to refer to property interests.

"We point out in another chapter the persistent and serious anxiety of Christopher Columbus, already great and renowned; from all his glorious labors, there was not left to him, as he wrote the king, a roof to cover him; and there was even wanting to him wherewith to pay his host and innkeeper. These were not certainly the greatness and comforts implicitly promised by him to the Enriquez de Arana, who trustingly confided to him, a poor and obscure man, their daughter, and—who knows?— perhaps a dower, which he was to have returned to them a hundred-fold. And to what were reduced these seducing phantasms of prosperity and glory, so dear to the heart of woman, that he had awakened in his Beatrix? Into persecution and poverty. Columbus, returned gloriously from his first voyage, had perhaps scarcely time, amid official receptions and the preparations for the second expedition (from March 15th until September 25th, 1493), to see again his Beatrix, and share with her and family the first moral fruits of his wonderful discovery. He had already done so much for them, that the De Arana and the wife had reason to be flattered in his naming, as his own lieutenant in that new world just discovered, Diego de Arana.

"In the embryonic fortress which first arose upon the virgin shores of Hispaniola, at the head of the first nucleus of a Euro-

---

* Navarrete, Col. Dipl., II., doc. 158; Torre, "Scritti di Colombo," p. 369.

pean colony planted in the new world, the young Diego of the De Arana remained champion and guardian of the new possessions, with full powers. Such a beautiful prelude was to be followed by a sad catastrophe; and when, after the second arrival of the admiral in the island, there came to Spain the dreadful news of the destroyed fortress and butchered garrison, the grief, the sorrow, and the fury of the Arana family can well be imagined. Was it not improvidence to abandon there, upon those unknown shores, a prey to faithless savages, amid the unwonted temptations of climate and demoralizing manners, a handful of men ill defended within and from without? and upon Columbus the tremendous responsibility of it fell. As the reader can see, we are walking in a path hitherto untrod, in the hope of succeeding, if not in solving, the enigma of the will—at least, in simplifying it. Meanwhile, it appears to us that to make heavier still the heart of that glorious testator, the remembrance of the slaughter of Diego de Arana, and the sad consequences that thence followed for the sister, conspired.

"A feud, after the style of the Middle Ages and like to Cordovan fierceness, would have sprung up among the De Arana against him who, in exchange for so many hopes, had brought back to them not even the body of their relative, done to death by the hands of savages! The effects of this feud could well interpose between Beatrix and Columbus one of those barriers which are accustomed to arise between two loves, two allegiances, by reason of mediæval party strife and family rancor. Behold, in our opinion, the probable cause of certain reticences in the admiral's writings, and of that strange silence observed with regard to his marital relations with Donna Beatrix Enriquez.

"But we have only made conjectures, desiring to leave to the kind reader the verdict, and to deduce thence the consequences. Resuming, with regard to the ambiguous sense that involves the testamentary provisions of the dying man, we believe that nothing can be definitively asserted that would exclude more or less specious objections on one side or the other.

"Without arraying ourselves with those who would represent Columbus as impeccable, although forced in the case by a hundred favorable appearances to believe him such, we advise the not trusting too much for his condemnation to the ambiguousness of the wording of his will. Given that as a man he might have sinned, his devout and honorable character, but, above all, his extraordinary piety, would have led him, it appears to us, to make timely atonement for his fault rather than to wait to repent him of it till the last moment of his life. If he did not believe it such, nor deem that he ought to make amends for it in twenty years, to what purpose express sorrow for it then, in a public act, to the disgrace of his own sons and the scandal of all who had perhaps forgotten it or never known it, and to the discredit of the beloved woman he left behind, and of him who was born of her? To what purpose, we say, such ill-advised, useless, cruel publicity? If upon this enigmatical testamentary document, by which the impugners of the legitimacy of the second marriage of Columbus strengthen themselves, the question were proposed to the courts, it would not be a lost cause."

The brilliant and captivating effect with which Lazzaroni has introduced those quoted passages from Shakespeare's "Othello," to show how Columbus may have wooed and won Beatrix, from the example of the Moor winning the love of Desdemona and marrying her, has suggested to me the introduction here of some passages from a historical novel, entitled "Columbus and Beatrix," by Constance Goddard Du Bois, a niece of Mrs. Admiral Dahlgren, to whom she has dedicated her book. This is a practical demonstration of the parallel between the marriages of Othello to Desdemona and of Columbus to Beatrix. But, first of all, the author tells us, in her preface, in graceful yet forcible language, what she thinks of the denial of the marriage of Columbus and Beatrix. Her judgment is the natural, instinctive, and almost inspired decree of refined and cultured womanhood that Columbus and Beatrix were innocent—that they were man and wife.

"The object of this work is to attempt the reparation of an injustice which history has done to a noble and long-suffering woman. Beatrix Enriquez has been denied her lawful position as the wife of Columbus by writers from Humboldt and Irving to the tourist, who publishes his impressions of a few weeks' sojourn in Spain; and the illicit connection of Columbus with a beautiful lady of Cordova has been expatiated upon in every tone of impartial narrative and jesting allusion. The slander is, however, of modern origin. Although Columbus was loaded with calumny during his lifetime, no one dreamed of denying his connection by marriage with the noble house of Arana, or of questioning the legitimacy of his son Fernando.

"It was not till an obscure lawyer at a later time raised a legal quibble about the matter, for the purpose of gaining a suit for a client, that the idea was suggested; and that it was repugnant to the facts of history is evident, since the unscrupulous attorney lost his case and the affair remained forgotten until 1805. Napione, followed by Spotorno and Navarrete, revived the unwarranted assumption with eagerness, as throwing a new light upon the character of Columbus.

"The only apparent support to this theory of an illicit connection is the fact that Columbus in his will mentions Beatrix Enriquez by name, without adding the title of wife, and adds that in recommending her to the care of his heir he eases his conscience, since he is under great obligation to her, ' the reason of which,' as he says, ' it is not expedient to mention here.'

"Out of this weak material the web of falsehood has been spun. Without following the discussion in its full extent, the argument of common sense may be applied in Beatrix's justification. It is known that her two brothers (some say a nephew and a brother) sailed with Columbus upon two of his voyages in a distinguished position of trust under the admiral. Would the sons of a noble house thus condone their sister's dishonor?

"The mystery involved in Columbus's allusion to Beatrix, without giving her the title of wife, is supplemented by the singular fact that in the most important crises of his life she was absent from his side or unmentioned. The theory, upon which the following story is constructed, offers an explanation which is maintained to be more deserving of credence than that of Spotorno, since it fits every subsequent event in the life of Columbus with the congruity of a historical fact. It is not the reputation of Columbus that is at stake. History, while accepting his offence, has readily excused it—' He was a man of his times,' forsooth; but the beautiful young Beatrix Enriquez, whose life, linked to his, was undoubtedly a sad one, should be delivered from unmerited reproach; and the open-minded student of history, as well as the enthusiastic champion of slandered innocence, should unite in rendering a tardy justice to her memory."

As was to have been expected, the authoress relates how Columbus had been introduced to the family of the Aranas by

Geraldini. The wealth of the family had been squandered by its present head, the father of Beatrix, in vain efforts to acquire immense wealth by the discovery of the philosopher's stone. Columbus had met Beatrix, both in prayer, before altar and shrines of the Cathedral of Cordova. It was well known in the city that he had a petition to the sovereigns which had long been deferred. Don Fernando Enriquez had been prostrated with grief at the sudden death of an aged and wealthy suitor for the hand of Beatrix, and by the rejection of another by the maiden. Beatrix lived a secluded life, but she had learned to venerate the devout and prayerful stranger whom she saw so often in the cathedral, and concerning whose mysterious aspirations so many conjectures were indulged in. Geraldini had interested, but had failed to convince his friends of the truth of Columbus's theories. Columbus informs the careworn father, this dreamer after the philosopher's stone, through his young son, Don Pedro, to whom he had been introduced by Geraldini, of his own skill. 'Will you not tell him for me that Cristoval Colon, a Genoese, desires to make his acquaintance? I have no intimate knowledge of alchemy, yet I am versed in astrology as well as cosmography and astronomy, and I could tell him much that he would be glad to hear.' An interview takes place between the aged father of Beatrix and Columbus, in which the former eagerly asks, 'Have you found it? Do you know, and will you impart the secret of the philosopher's stone?'

"Colon shook his head. 'I hardly believe that nature will yield that secret to our most ardent search,' he answered; 'but I know a greater one, from which will flow results still more surprising. After years of research as laborious as your own, but guided by divine inspiration, I have reached with absolute certainty the conclusion that across the western sea there lies a path, easy enough to the adventurous mariner, which leads direct to Manghay and Cathay, the kingdoms of the Khan, and the land of Zipanga, famous for its wealth of gold and precious stones.'

"'I have heard of that,' said Enriquez, impatiently. 'Rodrigo and Geraldini have wearied me with this talk of yours about cities of gold and temples of ivory. If the king grants your petition for ships and men, and you go forth and possess it in his name, what is that to me? Will it further my discovery, which is of greater worth to me than the realms of the Kha

"'Yes,' answered Colon, 'I care little for the wealth I shall win, except for the purpose to which I shall apply it—the purchase of the Holy Sepulchre from the hands of the infidels. This lies as near my heart as your precious discovery does to yours; but I hope to possess more than enough to equip an army to ransom the Sepulchre at the highest price the Soldan may put upon it. The surplus shall overflow to meet every demand of duty and friendship—to you first, if close relationship shall warrant it. Señor Don Enriquez, I ask you to bestow upon me your daughter Beatrix in marriage.'

"Enriquez was astonished beyond measure. His mind quickly reviewed the words of the Italian, and all that he had heard of him and of his pretensions since his coming to Cordova. He was disposed to believe in his theory, and he was impressed, as the scholarly Geraldini had been, with the grandeur of his views. The proposed connection with himself placed the matter in a new light. It was through his daughter's marriage alone that Enriquez had hopes of acquiring the fortune he coveted. Since Don Francisco's death he had looked in vain for the suitor who should unite wealth and generosity with a sympathy for the views and pursuits of the alchemist. Garcia de Silva would inherit a competence which his extravagant tastes would spend on every object rather than the purchase of chemicals and costly books for his father-in-law. Placing himself first, as he always did in such considerations, Enriquez did not consult the probable wishes of his daughter, or consider that the younger man would be more likely to win her heart.

"'I will not refuse you, Señor Colon,' he said; 'neither can I give you much encouragement. Our family is one of the most ancient in Cordova. My sons would look higher for a husband for their sister, but other things than rank are to be considered. Wealth is a necessity, a generous spirit, such as you have already manifested, being combined with the power to give, for I will not deny that my fortune has been spent, worthily but as yet in vain, and I need money. Fill my hands with the golden treasures you promise, and my daughter shall be yours.'

"Colon smiled with a lofty pity for his impatient greed. 'Years as well as floods may roll between me and the distant shore, which I behold with the eye of faith,' he said. 'The maiden would not wait for me. A younger suitor would claim her. You would part us, who are destined for each other, and to what purpose, and to what purpose? Only to oppose yourself to the greatest good that fortune has ever offered to you—connection with the discoverer of more than the philosopher's stone—one whose name, as the instrument of Heaven, is to resound through all the centuries to the utmost limit of time.'"

Columbus meets Beatrix under the friendly invitation of her father to visit the Enriquez mansion as a friend who is always welcome. She stands in awe of him, while venerating him. Even a suspicion, a temporary suspicion passes through her mind that he might have been the cause of the death of Don Francisco Hernandez; but her respect, her growing interest in the stranger, who had now become a friend of her family, and her sympathy in his deep religious sentiments and in his vast aspirations, enable her to cast it off.

"'Why did you flee from me?' asked Colon, in a tone of tender reproach, as he joined her.

"'I do not know,' answered Beatrix, her heart beating quickly. 'It seemed to me that you were changed. In the cathedral I was not afraid, though I saw you for the first time. It must be that I feel my guilt in having suspected you of a dreadful crime.'

"'Let us not speak of that,' interrupted Colon; 'that may well be forgotten. Let no suspicion henceforth come between us. I am changed only because a breath of happiness has blown over me, reviving hopes and feelings which I thought were long since dead, as a spring shower revives the flowers in your garden. Do you think, Beatrix, that a woman of youth and beauty could learn to love me? What would she answer me should I ask her to be my wife?'

"Beatrix attempted no reply.

"'You are the only woman I could wish to wed,' continued Colon. 'You are free from frivolity and selfishness, you are gentle and patient, religious, and capable of noble emotion. Heaven has led me to you as the footsteps of a wanderer are directed in the desert to the one spot of verdure and fertility where he may rest, before he leaves it for a further weary march over burning sands beneath a sky of brass. Your tender heart will not refuse this solace to one who needs your companionship and love. You will not say me nay.'

"This was not the impassioned wooing of a youthful lover, but it appealed to Beatrix's lifelong habit of self-sacrificing devotion to interests other than her own. Pedro (her brother) had told her in a few words the story of the Italian's life, and she had been thrilled with pity and admiration. Where others derided, she was ready to believe and uphold.

"'Tell me about yourself, Señor,' said Beatrix, making no direct reply. 'How can I help you?'

"Colon took a seat beside her in the shadow of a pomegranate-tree, where a nightingale was singing. The moon cast arabesques of shade through the leaves upon the sand at their feet and the whitewashed wall of the house before them. The brooding silence of the summer night was full of peace.

"'Let me enjoy these halcyon days while they last,' exclaimed Colon. 'It is a moment's calm for a shipwrecked mariner, a truce from misfortune, which Heaven grants. Ah, Beatrix, the Virgin blessed her worshipper when she led his steps to thee!'

"Then he began the story of his great ambition, which was to be fulfilled, like a Delphic prophecy, both more and less completely than he hoped. It was not of a new world that he was dreaming, nor did he imagine that the purpose which inspired the enterprise with the sacredness of a crusade—the conversion of the heathen and the final crowning of the whole by the rescue of the Holy Sepulchre with the treasures of the Indies—should fail of fulfilment and remain a forgotten dream. As he unfolded it to her, it seemed to Beatrix the grandest project a mortal could conceive. She did not discredit the element of the supernatural which Colon everywhere recognized in the leadings of his life. When he again referred to their meeting as ordained by the divine will, Beatrix's heart was filled with a conviction that he spoke the truth. What higher fortune could there be than an alliance with this messenger of Heaven? Her eyes shone with tears of sympathy for the man who had been despised and misunderstood, derided and neglected. She could console him for the past and inspire him with strength for the future. When Colon ceased speaking, Beatrix gave him her hand.

"'It is yours,' she said, with a smile which was a benediction."

In a subsequent chapter the marriage ceremony is related.

"The marriage service took place in the cathedral, attended by priests and acolytes, and by a throng of the friends and acquaintances of the bride, although her father and younger brother alone represented the family. It was a grief to Beatrix that her husband should be thus slighted by her relatives, but Colon was unconscious of the intended affront, or indifferent to it. The two Geraldinis were at his side, and many young nobles of the court were present, who had been drawn to the wedding by curiosity and the fame of the bride's beauty."

There are so many periods in the life of Columbus in regard to which the facts are meagre, that historians, biographers, and even the writers of historical novels have indulged largely in conjectural explanations of those periods thus involved in uncertainty. Constance Goddard Du Bois, while stating that the *motif* of her book* was gained from Roselly de Lorgues' "Life of Columbus," accounts for the separation of Columbus from Beatrix for a considerable portion of time after their marriage, and especially during his last years, his final illness and death, by conjectured religious vows and a monastic alliance, in aid of his great religious mission as the Christ-bearer, that had intervened. Such instances have occurred in the lives of married persons by their mutual consent and embracing a religious vocation, and with proper ecclesiastical sanction. Columbus, according to this theory, became a Franciscan monk. There are not wanting authentic facts tending to support this view. His well-known partiality for the Franciscans during his entire life; his intimacy with the prior, Juan Perez de Marchena, and monks of the Franciscan Convent of La Rabida, and the immense obligations under which he stood to them, and still more with that other Franciscan monk, Antonio de Marchena, who had befriended Columbus from his first arrival in Spain and sailed with him as astronomer on his second expedition; his coming from his ship, on return from the second voyage, wearing the habit of the Franciscans, a fact which shows that he carried that monastic dress with him on his voyages and wore it in his private quarters; his publicly wearing the Franciscan habit, cowl, and girdle in the streets of Seville, where Las Casas relates that he met him thus dressed, and his wearing the same during his entire visit at the house of the worthy curate of Los Palacios;

---

* "Columbus and Beatrix," p. ix.

his being attended in his last illness and death alone by the Franciscans; his burial by them in their convent vaults at Valladolid; his being again interred in their convent on the removal of his remains to Seville—these and other circumstances go far to give probability to the theory. The secluded life of Beatrix, who is never known to have left Cordova or to have taken any part in public affairs, even in the triumph of Columbus at Barcelona, and the traditions concerning her piety, are in unison with the same, and tend more or less to suggest that by mutual consent and with ecclesiastical sanction Columbus and Beatrix embraced a form of monastic affiliation. Fernando, their only son, spent his life in study, was never married, and may have united with his father and mother in some similar affiliation, for he is always spoken of in the early histories as a man of great learning and piety.

As I have stated, similar instances of religious dedication by married people have taken place and been sanctioned in the Church, even to our own day. Among several instances of that kind may be mentioned those of Lord and Lady Warner, in England, and of the Rev. Virgil Horace Barber and his wife, in America, all of whom were distinguished converts to the Catholic Church. Lord and Lady Warner, having been born and educated as Protestants, both embraced the Catholic faith; afterward the husband became a priest in the Society of Jesus, and the wife became a nun in a convent on the Continent. Ample provision was made for their children, two daughters, who received the whole estate of their parents, were thoroughly educated, and they, too, entered a convent at Dunkirk. In the case of the Barber family, the husband was an Episcopal minister of learning and reputation. He and his wife and all their family became Catholics. He became a priest in the Society of Jesus, and the wife became a nun. Their only son became also a Jesuit priest, and their four daughters became nuns.* It is not indispensable that the children should become members of religious organizations, provided a suitable provision is made for their support. This was done in the case of Fernando Columbus, who maintained a residence for himself at Seville, and erected therein a valuable library.†

---

* "Catholic Memoirs of Vermont and New Hampshire," by Bishop de Goesbriand, pp. 62-163.

† Winsor's "Columbus," etc., p. 603.

The marriage contract, as manifested by the ceremony in the Cathedral of Cordova, between Columbus and Beatrix, described in the book of Constance Goddard Du Bois, is not a mere fiction, it is a fact arising under the presumptions and proofs of circumstantial evidence. Under the known and admitted facts in the case of Columbus and Beatrix, there arises a presumption of law that a marriage contract had been regularly entered into between them, and at the time it occurred neither the laws of Spain nor those of the Church required more. Such a marriage is good now by the common law, and is valid under the laws of the States of this Union. Let us refer to some New York legal authorities on this subject: "Marriage is a civil contract, and may be entered in any manner which evinces the intention of the parties. Solemnization by a magistrate or clergyman is not necessary." (Court of Appeals, 1862, Hayes *vs.* People, 15 Abbott's Practice Reports, 163.) "It is a sufficient actual marriage, . . . that the parties agree to be husband and wife, and cohabit and recognize each other as such." (Same case, 7 Abbott's New York Digest, 438.) In the case of Clayton and Wife *vs.* Wardell, decided in the New York Court of Appeals, Harris, Justice, said: "It is not pretended that there is any proof of such prior marriage, nor is such proof necessary. A valid marriage may exist without any formal solemnization. . . . Like every other contract, all that is necessary for its validity is the deliberate consent of competent parties entering into a present agreement to take each other for husband and wife. . . . But in this State the common law exists; and whatever may be thought of its wisdom, the existence of the marriage contract is a fact which may be proved, like any other fact, either by positive evidence of the agreement, or by evidence from which it may be inferred. . . . In the case before us, it is not claimed that there is any direct evidence of actual marriage. For the want of such proof recourse has been had to secondary and presumptive evidence. It is attempted to establish the marriage . . . by evidence of cohabitation, of acknowledgment of a marriage, of the reception of the parties as husband and wife by their relatives and friends, and by proof of their common reputation." The principle upon which these decisions are based is, that while a marriage agreement is essential, such an agreement may be legally inferred and presumed to have been entered into from the circumstantial evidence alluded to. There are few cases, however, so strong as that of Columbus and Beatrix, which, in addition to the ordinary circumstantial evidence adduced in these pages, and reinforced by the extracts from Lazzaroni's work, possesses the notoriety, as an actual marriage, of having been recorded in current publications and histories for a long period following the event.

CHAPTER VI.

"And farewell goes out sighing."
—SHAKESPEARE.

"Had I miscarried, I had been a villain;
For men judge actions always by events:
But when we manage by a just foresight,
Success is prudence, and possession right."
—HIGGONS'S "GENEROUS CONQUEROR."

"Applause
Waits on success; the fickle multitude,
Like the light straw that floats along the stream,
Glide with the current still, and follow fortune."
—FRANKLIN'S "EARL OF WARWICK."

THE long and dreary years of delay and disappointment are now succeeded by fleeting days, hours, minutes of cogent preparation. It was originally intended that the expedition should consist of two vessels, but Columbus, in repelling a taunt of a Spanish nobleman that he was seeking the accomplishment at the expense of others, had agreed to bear one eighth of the cost, so that he now added a third vessel by the aid of the Pinzons of Palos and of the worthy prior of La Rabida. While it was apparently the joint expedition of Ferdinand and Isabella, the queen was the real patroness of the enterprise. The expenses of it were defrayed out of the treasury of Castile, and during her life few but Castilians were able to gain establishments in the new world.

It is difficult at this day and under such altered circumstances to ascertain or record the exact thoughts that now arose in the mind of Columbus. But his past history, his belief in his divine destiny and mission, his highly wrought and sensitive nature, his close observation of all that concerned or affected his great undertaking, his quick and lively versatility of sensations and conclusions, might assure us of their unique and soaring character. Dreams had become realities. The theories of a lifetime now greatly spent were to be at last realized; opinions were to become demonstrations; the opulent empires of the Grand Khan, of Prester John, and other Oriental regions were to be united to the Church; countless populations of benighted heathens were to see the light of the Gospel; new worlds were to be brought to light and colonized; boundless wealth and honors were to be his and those of his posterity; the Holy Sepulchre was to be wrested from the hands of the infidels; the prophecies of sacred and profane writers were to be fulfilled. The stranger, the visionary, and the adventurer now became the most noted and rising man in Spain. King and queen united in honoring and trusting him. The resources of the kingdom were placed at his use. Columbus felicitated the sovereigns on the grand results now almost within their grasp. And while Ferdinand looked with complacent but cool acquiescence on what would redound to his interest and glory if successful, and if disastrous could be disowned by him as not his measure, the noble Isabella felt that she was performing the will of Heaven, and earnestly desired the conversion of nations buried in darkness, and the extension of the area of Christendom. She manifested to Columbus all sympathy and honor. Of her own motion, she appointed his son Diego a page to Prince Juan, heir-apparent to the throne, an office only bestowed upon the sons of the most distinguished families, and she added the generous salary of 9400 maravedis for his support.* She lavished upon the father every mark of respect and confidence. The title of Don was bestowed upon him and his heirs, and those of viceroy and governor made hereditary in his family.

It seemed at first fortunate that Palos should have been selected as the port of departure for this momentous expedition. That town had, for some delinquency, become liable to supply the crown with two vessels; there the voyage was to commence; there the Pinzons, the good prior of La Rabida, Juan Perez, and other good friends of Columbus resided; and thither he joyously sped his way, after taking a respectful and grateful leave of his royal friends at Santa Fé on May 12th. He was received with great joy at the Convent of La Rabida, and was an honored guest of the sympathizing and generous prior and his devout monks. On the morning of the 23d Columbus and the prior of the convent repaired to the Church of St. George at Palos, and here, meeting the summoned alcalde, the regidors and other

---

* Mr. Brownson's translation of Tarducci's " Life of Columbus," vol. i., p. 115.

principal citizens, a notary read the royal command that the authorities of Palos should prepare two caravels in readiness for sea within ten days, and that the vessels and their crews should be delivered to Columbus, who was also authorized on his own account to add a third vessel for the expedition. The ships and sailors were placed under the immediate and plenary authority of the admiral, and the crews were to obey his commands, and go where he directed. But the admiral was cautioned to avoid, however, the Portuguese possessions on the coast of Africa. The crews were to receive the same wages as sailors in the Spanish naval service, to receive four months' pay in advance, and the admiral alone could discharge them. Royal commands were also issued to the local authorities and inhabitants of the seaport towns of Andalusia to supply provisions of every kind at fair prices. The outfits and provisions were declared free of export duties, and the officers and crews were exempted from criminal process during the voyage and for two months after the return. The royal commands met with a ready compliance, until it was discovered that the expedition was to sail into and across the Atlantic Ocean, and in quest of unknown lands. Heretofore the proposals of Columbus had been submitted to learned and thinking men, who were at least amenable to reason, facts, and demonstration. But now the common people—sailors, noted for their superstition, shipowners and purveyors, men of every class—were called upon to accomplish what so many of the learned had pronounced impracticable and fatally dangerous. They felt like victims led to the slaughter. The ships were refused, and no crews could be obtained. The air rang with reports, traditions, and stories of the dreaded ocean, now more than ever regarded as the Sea of Darkness. Many weeks were lost in fruitless efforts to procure ships and crews. The government had to be again appealed to, and orders again were issued for the impressment of ships and sailors for the expedition. Even the presence of an official, Juan de Peñasola, an officer of the royal household, clothed with full powers, failed to secure success.

The Pinzons now most fortunately came to the relief of the admiral, and Martin Alonzo and Vicente Yañez Pinzon, veteran mariners and citizens of wealth, standing, and influence, volunteered to embark in the expedition with themselves, their ships and their crews.* Two other ships were impressed by Peñasola, but the owners of one of them, the Pinta—Gomez Rascon and Cristoval Quintero—resisted the impressment, and fomented the prevailing tumults as much as possible. The towns of Palos and Moguer were agitated beyond description, disturbances resulted, and nothing could be accomplished. The impressed ships made no progress in getting ready for sea. The mechanics employed on the ships, when compelled to work, slighted their tasks, and finally abandoned them clandestinely. The sailors recanted their enlistments, deserted, and hid away. The opposition and obstacles now encountered were more difficult to overcome than the delays and arguments of learned Juntos and courts; now everything had to be done by main force, for the whole community was aroused to a state of frantic tumult. The favorable action of the Pinzons went far to allay the excitement and diminish the resistance. Columbus greatly reduced his demands, and by dint of force, persuasion, inducements, and the influence and example of the Pinzons, three small ships were procured, two of which were mere caravels or undecked vessels, having high prows and sterns, forecastles and cabins for the crews. The third vessel had decks and was named the Santa Maria, in honor of the patroness of the expedition, its previous name having been the Gallego. This was the admiral's vessel. It had been prepared expressly for the voyage, and bore the admiral's pennant. One of the caravels, the Pinta, was placed under the command of Martin Alonzo Pinzon, who was accompanied by his brother, a good pilot, Francisco Martin Pinzon. The third, also a caravel, was placed under the command of Vicente Yañez Pinzon. Each vessel had additional pilots, men who became noted in the future history of the discoveries—Sancho Ruiz, Pedro Alonzo Niño, and Bartolomeo Roldan. Many friends and relatives of the three brothers, Pinzon, embarked in various capacities in the expedition. There was also an inspector-general of the armament, Roderigo Sanchez, a chief alguacil; Diego de Arana, a near relative of his second wife, Beatrix Enriquez, and a royal notary, Roderigo de Escobar; also a phy-

---

* It was claimed afterward, in behalf of Martin Alonzo Pinzon, that he had some previous knowledge of a western route to Asia, derived from an ancient book at Rome, and had thought of following it up. But this statement, coming from his son, is not credited. (Tarducci.)

sician, a surgeon, some private adventurers, servants, and ninety sailors—in all one hundred and twenty persons. But the prejudices, fears, and opposition of the two communities of Palos and Moguer were not allayed; they looked with amazement on these rash and foolhardy people, thus, some of them, voluntarily offering themselves as victims of a forlorn and desperate adventure, and others submitting to impressment in an expedition already doomed to ruin and death. Sad were the hearts of those who had relatives or friends embarked in this mad attempt to brave the terrors and dangers of the unbounded ocean.

Quite different were the sentiments of Columbus. He regarded this expedition as undertaken by the inspiration of Heaven, as a mission of religion and of Christianity, and, in a human aspect, as the highest effort of national patriotism. He realized more than ever the grandeur and solemnity of this crowning event. With sentiments of the deepest devotion he made his sacramental confession to the good prior, Juan Perez, and received the holy communion with profound piety; and in this solemn act of religion he felt deep consolation in being joined by the officers and sailors of the expedition.

But the whole community of Palos was cast down in the most profound sorrow, and the gloomiest forebodings were felt and expressed by the people and families of the town as to the fate of the adventurers. Officers and mariners had been taken from every family, and these regarded the uncertain and dread fate of relatives and friends as more afflicting than if they saw them die at home of natural deaths. The gloom experienced by the sailors was intensified by the tears and lamentations of their friends and relatives. Amid this universal consternation Columbus was calm, hopeful, confident, and prophetically triumphant. He saw his destiny now about to be fulfilled. He took his son Diego from the Convent of La Rabida and placed him with Juan Rodriguez Cabezuda and Martin Sanchez, of Moguer.* The expedition, with the Santa Maria, the Pinta, and the Nina (the last name signifying the baby), under the command of the admiral of the ocean seas, sailed forth from Palos on Friday, August 3d, 1492.

Though Columbus kept a journal at sea and recorded much

---

* Tarducci's "Life of Columbus," Brownson's translation, vol. i., p. 123

that he saw and felt, yet the world would wish now to know more of this crucial voyage, which resulted in the discovery of America. With a formality in keeping with the loftiness of his conceptions, he opened his journal, "In the name of our Lord, Jesus Christ." He reminds his sovereigns, as if writing a testamentary paper, of the glory and success of the Moorish war now ended, which he had witnessed; of his revelation to them of the ocean path to India; of the Empire of the Grand Khan; of the desire of Christendom to unite the Oriental empires to the Church; of his new proposal to attempt this great work by a western voyage across the Atlantic rather than an eastern journey over land; recounts his commission from the Spanish sovereigns, his patent of nobility, and his powers received from them; his departure from Palos; his purpose to devote his powers to the great task, to forget sleep in his close attention to the navigation of his ships until India was reached; his purpose of making a correct map of the new countries discovered, and of writing each day the history of his progress. It is an interesting fact that Columbus prepared for his guidance on the voyage a map similar to but greatly improved upon that of Dr. Toscanelli, and that he located the land he expected to discover, which he supposed was Marco Polo's Cipango, about in the same meridian where Florida was afterward found.*

The first course taken by the little fleet was southwest toward the Canary Islands, and thence it was the intention to sail due west; but, before reaching the Canaries, the first exultation and triumphant joy with which he found himself the admiral of an expedition, with armament and equipment for discovering the western world, were changed into distress and indignation at finding the Pinta, on the third day's sail, in a disabled condition. The vessel gave signal of distress; her rudder was broken and unhung. Columbus conjectured that this was treacherously contrived by the owners of the vessel, Gomez Rascon and Cristoval Quintero, whose vessel as well as themselves had been, against their will, impressed into the service. It was the experience and seamanship of the skilful captain of the Pinta, Martin Alonzo Pinzon, that prevented the susceptible and anxious crews

---

* Mr. Brownson's translation of Tarducci's "Life of Columbus," vol. i., p. 126, Irving, and other authors on our list of authorities.

of all three vessels from becoming panic-stricken at this untoward accident. The rudder was secured with cords, and again secured the following day on the fastenings giving away. The ship was leaking. The fleet made direct for the Canaries, where they arrived on August 9th. After three weeks' delay it was found impossible to secure another vessel to replace the Pinta. A new rudder was made for her, she was repaired generally, and her lateen sails were altered into square ones. The crews were easily cast down and disheartened at every circumstance. The eruption of Teneriffe, now in full view, was regarded as an evil omen, and then a vessel arriving from Ferro reported three Portuguese caravels cruising among the neighboring islands. Columbus, by his cheerful words and manner, had to parry the approaches of panic and disaffection among his crews, and this he succeeded in doing with remarkable skill and success. But the presence of Portuguese vessels in the vicinity was looked upon seriously even by himself. He distrusted the Portuguese. He succeeded, however, in getting his fleet again under sail from the island of Gomera, on the morning of September 6th. Here again he met with a check, for a calm of several days detained him near land; and when he again got under weigh, he found himself near Ferro, and in dangerous vicinity of the spot where the Portuguese caravels had been reported as sailing. On Sunday, September 9th, a favorable wind arose, and before night the last land of the Eastern Hemisphere was to his joy, but to the consternation of the sailors, out of sight, and the boundless, open ocean, the dread Atlantic, the fabled Sea of Darkness, was all before them,

> " in all time
> Calm or convuls'd—in breeze, or gale, or storm,
> Icing the pole, or in the torrid clime
> Dark heaving—boundless, endless, and sublime,
> The image of eternity!"
> —BYRON'S " CHILDE HAROLD."

Such was now the reality of sight and feeling with the sailors who first braved the western ocean. All seemed lost to them— their country, their friends, their families, their homes had been given up for a boundless waste of waters and of storms. Tears and lamentations broke forth on all sides, which the cheerful mien, the confident assurances, the brave and sincere exaltation of the admiral could scarcely assuage. He stood like a man of self-assured destiny amid the cowering forms of weaker men.

Columbus now gave his orders for the conduct of the voyage. In case of separation the ships were to continue on the direct western route, and after making seven hundred leagues, the distance within which he expected to reach land, they were to lay by for the night; and, in order to lessen the growing fears of the mariners as they advanced farther and farther from their homes, he kept, besides the correct reckoning intended for the government and for history, another and an incorrect one, showing the distance traversed much less than it was in fact; and this latter was open to the inspection of all. The Spanish sailors were thus by stratagem kept in ignorance of the distance they had sailed from home. On September 11th, being then one hundred and fifty leagues from Ferro, a part of a large mast was seen floating, and this fact, while it inspired Columbus with hope, added to the fears of the sailors, who apprehended at once that in that vast and stormy ocean shipwreck was inevitably awaiting them. He exerted consummate skill in calming the blind apprehensions of even the oldest sailors.

Columbus, true to his mission and his promises, had vigilantly watched the course of the voyage and every circumstance, however trifling, and continued to do so. By day and during much of the night he was at stern or compass box, taking in the progress of the ships and the signs of the heavens and the ocean. A crisis seemed approaching. For some days prior to September 13th the keen eye of Columbus observed that the deflections of the magnetic needle increased every day as he boldly sped his way westward, and on the 13th, while observing that the ships were encountering adverse currents and their location was now three degrees west of Flores, the variations seemed to reach a climax where they ceased, and the magnet pointed to the true north, such as it had never before pointed. In fact, the magnetic north and the north-star stood in conjunction. With quick and unerring perception Columbus had discovered the line of no variations in the magnetic needle. Keeping his observations to himself, as his superstitious and frightened crews seized on everything unusual to increase their fears, he boldly and calmly but thoughtfully passed the mysterious line, and pressed his course still westwardly. But as he moved farther and still farther to the west, again he saw the magnet point farther and still farther away from the pole, as it had done prior to the eventful 13th. Then the variations moved from the northeast more and still more westerly toward the pole. On the 13th the magnet had pointed directly north—

> "So turns the faithful needle to the pole,
> Though mountains rise between and oceans roll."
>
> —Darwin.

But now he discovered that deflections were reversed, and the magnetic line was moving farther and still farther away from the pole and from the true north. Though reticent and thoughtful, it was impossible to conceal the astonishing change in the deflections of the magnet from the intelligent pilots or from the eager and fearful crews, who were ever on the alert for new alarms. Panic, already prevailing, now became universal. The fearful question was asked, What does this mean? Were the laws of nature reversed in those remote and desolate regions of the earth and in the midst of this boundless and trackless ocean? Had the forces of nature lost their power? Were the stars no longer a guide, the needle no longer an index to fateful mariners on the deep? What unknown influences were to decide the destiny of the ships and crews in that vast waste of waters? Were they thus blindly to continue this ill-fated voyage in search of unknown lands, in an unknown ocean beset with such fearful phenomena? Had the compass refused to the mariner its friendly and unerring aid? How was their commander, this foreigner to Spain and Spaniards, who professed to converse with Nature and to know all her secrets, to explain this dread phenomenon?

The most unfriendly and reluctant historians have here acknowledged that Columbus made an important and startling discovery. Justin Winsor, the theory of whose book on Columbus and how he received and imparted the spirit of discovery, is based, as its title shows, on the assumption that there was nothing new in his great career, has admitted that "his observation of this fact marks a significant point in the history of navigation." And again he says: "But it was a revelation when he came to a position where the magnetic north and the north-star stood in conjunction." Not only must it be acknowledged that Columbus had now brought to light one of the unknown secrets of nature, but also that he, by the force of his ready genius, struck upon and revealed the true theory and use of the discovery. Pressed by his panic-stricken crews, Columbus showed his familiarity with nautical science and a ready application of its principles. He explained the line of no deflections of the magnet to be a meridian of longitude, a crucial or test line, and deflections from this meridian line might be found to possess sufficient regularity to furnish a method and means of ascertaining longitude—a method more certain than longitudinal tables, water clocks, or other methods. This view of Columbus was confirmed by another distinguished navigator, Sebastian Cabot, a few years later, when he crossed the line of no variations in approaching the northern Atlantic coasts of our Continent. It was at first supposed that Cabot was the first to discover this new phenomenon, but the subsequent publication of the journal of Columbus gave that honor to the admiral. Various theories have since been started to explain the line on some other theory. Columbus endeavored to demonstrate his theory on his return voyage to Spain from his second expedition. He and Sebastian did not know of each other's observations of the line of no variations. But Cabot kept his observations to himself as a supposed or claimed secret, and Humboldt, as Winsor remarks, conjectured "that the possibility of such a method of ascertaining longitude was that uncommunicable secret which Sebastian Cabot many years later hinted at on his death-bed." Columbus freely communicated the secret to his officers, pilots, and crews, when the prevailing panic gave way to renewed belief in the wonderful learning of the admiral, or, as Fiske remarks, "their faith in the profundity of his knowledge prevailed over their terrors." The permanency which Columbus attributed to the line of no variations in 1492 has been studied now for four centuries, and science has discovered that the lines of deflection are not parallel, neither are they straight, though sometimes nearly so, and more or less inconstant. The line as then discovered by Columbus, at three degrees west of Flores, has shifted farther to the west since his day, and now the line of no variations is almost a straight line from Carolina to Guiana. The line, however, is now known to be sufficiently permanent to constitute for several years at a time a safe guide, when delineated on magnetic maps, for determining the longitude in any latitude. The quick and offhand explanation, which Columbus gave at a crisis in his first voyage to quiet the fears of his men, has thus been confirmed by the subsequent scientific observations of four hundred years. "So science has come round," as Justin Winsor says, "in some measure to the dreams of Columbus and Cabot," though it is difficult to say that Cabot had any such theory that is known, or was ever divulged by him. Columbus was called a dreamer in his early years of seeking and delay, but it is hardly correct to apply the term dream to his method of applying the line of no deflections as a method of determining longitude, now verified in modern science, as it would not be to apply it now to his proposals, in 1492, to discover a new world. The causes of those variations of the needle, and of the shifting westward of the line, are as much a mystery now as they were in the days of Columbus, in the face of modern scientific investigations. Columbus adhered to the last to what he had said to his sailors. He was mistaken in details then too wholly unknown to all the world. And even though he may have supposed the pole-star to be a moving star, and have attributed the deflections to that cause rather than to the needle itself, just as he supposed the lands he discovered to be a part of Asia rather than the land portions of another hemisphere, or may not have succeeded in determining the exact shape and size of the earth, such theories on his part are far from making a dreamer of the man, who opened the path to the rest of mankind which has led to more and greater discoveries both in geography and applied sciences generally than the achievements of any other man. It was on the same 13th of September that he thought he observed evidences of a great change of climate from signs around him, but this conjecture he exploded as he advanced, the first of men, across that unexplored ocean. His critics have yet to learn from the lives of Copernicus, Newton, and the Herschels that life is too short to achieve all things at once, and that

"Life is short, and art is long."

As the voyage progressed various indications of land were witnessed; and always occasioned great joy among the officers and men. Now a water wagtail, a bird of the land, hovered over the vessels. A meteor now flits across their path and plunges in the sea. Green weeds floating around the ships he thought indicated the vicinity of islands. They next encounter the trade-winds and the ships make fine progress with their assistance; yet no one but Columbus knew the actual distance they had sailed westward. Now the temperature becomes more mild, the air more soft, the skies clear, and the fragrance of the groves and flowers of the lands they are approaching seems to them all to be quite perceptible. Other indications of land which they observed were the quantities of herbs and weeds, increasing as they advanced, some withered and others quite green, such, too, as grew in rivers and in fresh water. A live crab was found on one of the clumps of weeds. They saw a white bird such as grow in the tropics, and never sleep upon the sea; also tunny fish. The sea water seemed to become less salty, the air purer and sweeter, great numbers of birds were seen, and the appearance of the northern horizon was thought to indicate the proximity of land. Columbus found that he had not traversed more than three hundred and sixty leagues, and his calculations placed Asia at a much greater distance. Great animation prevailed among the crews of the three ships, each one being ambitious of seeing land first, for the sovereigns had promised a pension of ten thousand maravedis to the man who first should descry the land. The Pinta was the fastest sailer, and was generally ahead. The sailors were frequently deceived by the apparent looming up of lands and islands, but this was caused by the peculiar appearance of the clouds on the horizon of that tropical region, though such conjectures have been partly confirmed by charts showing that breakers were seen in that part of the ocean in 1802. Drizzling showers without wind were regarded by Columbus a favorable sign, but the soundings made did not reach bottom. He resolved to pursue the direct westward line, though he supposed he might be sailing between lands or islands which were not in sight. Why should he not turn from his westward course and seek them? The hopes inspired by so many supposed indications of land were turned into disappointment, fear, discontent, murmurings. But as Columbus had from the beginning declared that land would be found by sailing due west, he firmly refused to deviate from that course. His religious faith in the guidance of Heaven was in all these difficulties an unfailing source of confidence and firmness. The only times when he was not at the poop or watching the compass were the stated hours at which he retired and locked himself up to make his appeals to Heaven, recite his office of devotion, and fortify his soul. As the vesper-time approached the ocean breezes wafted to heaven the notes of the "Salve Regina" and "Ave Maris Stella," devotional hymns, which he and his crews addressed to the Virgin Mother. His confidence, his firmness, and his untiring watchings, day and night, might under less appalling dangers have either inspired his crews with courage or at least have won their confidence. But the great length of the voyage, the repeated failures of the signs of land, the favorable winds from the east which they regarded as the evil means by which they were carried each moment farther from home and farther into the vast wastes of ocean—all led the crews to the verge of mutiny. They did not disguise their discontent; they applied the most disloyal epithets to the admiral; his arguments ceased to have effect on them, his authority was fast waning. They thought that the winds never blew from any other quarter than the east, so that when the winds veered to the southwest, on September 20th, the panic-stricken seamen felt some relief. The vast expanse of surface covered with floating sea-weeds, an area stated by Humboldt to be seven times larger than the whole of France— for they were ploughing through that vast prairie of sea-weeds, Saragosso Sea—still filled their minds with apprehensions, and what was at first regarded as a sign of nearing land was looked upon now as a forerunner of disaster. They thought the sea-weeds were getting thicker and more matted together, and that soon the ships would not be able to pass through them. The superstitious sailors feared they could never return; that the surface weeds concealed the immense sea monsters that would devour them and their ships; submarine giants, the heroes of early nursery tales and sailors' yarns, were revived, to seize and feast upon them, and the mild winds suggested their becoming becalmed in mid-ocean. Stories of whirlpools that would suddenly draw the ships into their vortex and hurl them to the bottom, and even the fabled winged roc of the Arabians, the giant bird of the air, might seize, with its huge bill, not only seamen, but entire ships, and, ascending with them to the clouds, tear them to pieces and drop the fragments into the ocean.

The fears of the sailors made them mutineers. Columbus acted with consummate courage and wisdom in such an unprecedented crisis; his calmness was admirable, his ingenuity in pointing out new signs of land was inexhaustible. While the men were stimulating their own imaginations to evil, some imagining that the water was growing shallow in mid-ocean and the ships might be stranded, others reviving the stories of ships becoming frozen up in the ice, and others speaking of quicksands, of hidden rocks, of a dead calm, and of the rotting of the ships and the perishing of the crews, he pointed out to them that the calmness of the ocean was an indication of the vicinity of land. On September 25th his arguments were aided by a heavy sea-swell, which dispelled at least their apprehensions of becoming becalmed and perishing from hunger. This he regarded as an intervention of Providence, and felt that, like another Moses, he was delivered with his people from the dangers of the sea. But his assurances to the men had but a temporary effect. They were getting farther every day from home, and handed over to the most cruel of fates, which might overtake them at any moment. The murmurs of the mariners grew louder with every league they made; they began to cluster together in little knots about the ships, and vent against the admiral their discontent and anger.

The admiral was, in fact, at their mercy. They could have murdered him or have compelled him to return to Spain, and this, too, perhaps just as he was on the point of realizing all his hopes. The rough sea of September 25th was followed by fine weather, and the ships were making good progress. Columbus had been studying his charts most anxiously in the endeavor to determine where they were. He sent one of his charts to the captain of the Pinta, Martin Alonzo Pinzon. They had much consultation together, and both Columbus and Pinzon thought that the great island Cipango could not be far off, though the former conjectured that the ships may have been carried out of the direct course by the currents. The Pinta and the Santa Maria were near together; the chart had been returned to Columbus, who, with his pilot and several other old seamen, was endeavoring to discover their location, when suddenly they heard from the Pinta the cries of land! They saw Martin Alonzo Pinzon standing on the poop of the Pinta, crying with a loud voice, "Land! land! Señor, I claim my reward!" To the southwest, about twenty-five leagues away, all thought they saw the land. Columbus, falling upon his knees, rendered thanksgiving to God, and he and Pinzon and their entire crews united in chanting the "Gloria in Excelsis." Many seamen at the masthead or from the rigging saw the same object, which all took for the land, and Columbus turned his course in that direction; but, alas! on the arrival of morning the hoped-for land had disappeared. The cloud had disappeared during the night. The hopes of the crews now sank more than ever. But the admiral, with unfailing confidence, again resumed the direct western course. From day to day new signs of land revived their fading hopes. The reckoning showed they had voyaged five hundred and eighty leagues from the Canaries, while, in fact, the true reckoning, which Columbus kept, showed seven hundred and seven leagues. The former number was enough to frighten the crews, while the latter did not discourage Columbus. But as the signs of land disappeared, and the course of the floating weeds was from east to west, and the visiting birds had all departed, gloom again took possession of the minds of the sailors.

All thought they had passed the lands which the signs had indicated, and even Columbus considered this quite probable. But in order to calm the minds of the now eager sailors, who were constantly and on the slightest appearance crying out land, he announced that any one who should thus erroneously announce the sight of land should forfeit the reward; and when Martin Alonzo Pinzon, on October 6th, proposed that the course of the voyage should now be changed to the southward, he still persisted in the direct west course. He also ordered the caravels to keep the west course in case of separation, that they should rejoin him as soon as possible, and at sunset and sunrise the whole fleet should endeavor to be near together, for those hours were most favorable for descrying land. It was another severe trial to Columbus when Martin Alonzo Pinzon began to lose confidence in the direct course pursued. The island of Cipango had not been found, though its estimated distance had been traversed. In deference for Pinzon's opinion, he slightly altered his course to the southwest on October 7th, thus yielding to the sailors' partiality for following the flight of birds; and for three days on that course the encouraging indications of land increased.* Small birds and fish made their appearance; a heron, a pelican,

---

* It is estimated that if Columbus had not thus altered his course, he would have landed on the North American continent, probably on the Florida coast.

and a duck were seen, and all bound in the one direction ; fresh and green herbage floated on the tranquil sea, and the air was sweet and fragrant. But while the distance between the ships and home increased, the land did not appear ; all appearances were disheartening delusions ; the crews openly expressed their discontent, and turbulently clamored to return to Spain. The conspiracy had been forming for some time—nearly every man in the three crews had joined it. The three Pinzons were well aware of this, and while haughty and dictatorial in their bearing toward Columbus, and not perhaps absolutely disloyal, preserved silence. The officers of the crown, Arana, his wife's nephew, his own crew and pilots, were all in the plot. Columbus stood alone in mid-ocean ; alone loyal to sovereigns, to himself, to his mission. This part of his history is distinguished for consummate action and conduct. He had frequently exhausted all arguments and persuasions. He now asserted the full measure of his authority. He informed them that he had sailed across the ocean for the Indies, and the Indies he could and would reach ; that neither man nor devil could change his course, and as their complaints were vain, submission was their only course. At the same time he assured them of the assistance of Heaven in reaching the promised land. The effect of his deliberate courage was magical ; revolt hid its head before such personal virtues, and overpowering numbers yielded to a single will.

The story that within a day or two before land was discovered, Columbus had promised the sailors to return to Spain unless land was found within three days, is rejected by historians ; it rests solely on the unreliable statement of Oviedo, and is not found in the admiral's journal nor in Las Casas' or other works ; it is wholly at variance from the dignified character of Columbus.

In this crisis of discontent and mutiny the perilous and desperate situation of the admiral was somewhat relieved by the increasing indications of land. His course was now due west. Fresh river weeds, then a green fish, such as frequent the rocks, then a fresh thorny branch or twig having berries, then a reed, a board, a carved staff—all in succession appeared to cheer up and exert a good effect upon the hopes of all. So deeply was Columbus impressed, even under such desperate circumstances and in such an appalling crisis, in which all was staked and all seemed lost to others, that when on the memorable evening of

October 11th he assembled his crew on the deck of the Santa Maria, to recite the vesper hymn of "Salve Regina," he followed the services with an address most characteristic of the man and most impressive upon his wayward and dejected hearers. Gratitude to God for their preservation through such perils and travels, and for the frequent signs of land which had been given them, was his first sentiment. The promised land was near! He renewed the orders given at the beginning of this momentous voyage, that after sailing seven hundred leagues the ships should not sail after midnight, as he regarded this more important now than ever; he expressed his faith that land would be discovered that very night; he ordered a most unceasing watch to be kept up at the forecastle, reminded them of the reward promised by the sovereigns to the one who should first see the land, and he promised to add to it himself a doublet of velvet.* Great animation prevailed among the officers and crews. It was the courage of Columbus that had held them together; but for him they would have reversed their course and returned to Spain. He alone was the moral motive power that carried the ships westward. The vessels were making rapid progress under favorable winds, and the Pinta was ahead. Such was the effect of the speech the admiral had made to them, that not a man slept that night. He stood as usual on the roof of the cabin of the high poop of the Santa Maria; his watch was that of a prophet, a seer, a man who felt his destiny accomplishing itself,

> ". . . the spirit . . .
> Undaunted . . . looks,
> With steadfast eye."
>
> —Mrs. Stoddard.

His ever-watchful eye was the first to rest upon the land of the new world. It was about ten o'clock in the evening when he saw the glimmer of a light far distant. Calling Pedro Gutierrez, he inquired of him if he saw the light, and he answered that he did. Then, calling Rodrigo Sanchez, of Segovia, he asked him the same question, but the light had vanished. Again and again during this brave vigil the light appeared, and again disappeared. It seemed like a torch or lantern in a canoe, or carried in the human hand, for its motion was undulating. While he thought

---

* Fernando Colombo, "Historia del Almirante," cap. 21.

modestly of the circumstance, Columbus felt that his task was accomplished. Hour after hour passed away, when at two o'clock on the morning of October 12th, 1492, a gun from the Pinta announced the same land in sight. Well has this historic night been commemorated with a noble statue of Columbus by Samartin, erected in the Spanish Senate Chamber at Madrid, and bearing the inscription,

"*A las Diez de la noche en* 11 *October* 1492
Tierra !"

A sailor named Rodrigo de Triana* was the first to see the land ; it was in the very direction where Columbus had seen the light on the land. All now saw the land distinctly ; it was two leagues distant. At the report of the gun on the Pinta, Columbus fell upon his knees, and with tears of gratitude thanked God for sustaining him to the end, and for enabling him to accomplish his mission. He sang with joyous heart the hymn of thanksgiving, "Te Deum Laudamus," in which he was joined by the officers and crews of all three vessels. In the midst of his exultation, he preserved his prudence and good judgment. By his orders the vessels lay to, all the sails were furled except the lugsail, and the ships were put in a state of defence ; the arms were cleaned and polished, and whatever might be the development of events in the morning, whether of conflict or welcome, all was readiness. The entire crew of the Santa Maria came forward to offer their congratulations to the chief, and to do him homage. Columbus retired to his cabin and awaited the arrival of the dawn with sentiments of devotion, gratitude, and joy. With these were mingled intense and tumultuous feelings, which are usually inspired by sudden even though expected success, by uncertainty as to the developments of the coming day, and by the brilliant hopes inspired by a great and unprecedented event.

---

* I have given the name here as rendered by Mr. Irving. The Count de Lorgues and Dr. Barry state that the name of the mariner who saw the land first was Juan Rodrigo de Bermejo. Triana claimed the reward promised to the one who should first see the land, but it was adjudged by King Ferdinand to Columbus, as he had first seen the light on the land. Oviedo relates, but without authority, that Triana was so offended at being deprived of the reward, which he regarded as justly his, that he renounced his country and his faith, went to Africa, and became a Mohammedan. Mr. Irving discredits the story. De Lorgues and Barry do not mention it (Oviedo, "Cronico de las Indias," lib. ii., cap. 2 ; Irving's "Columbus," vol. i., p. 274).

He noticed before retiring every minute sign—the fragrance of the groves on this virgin land, the vegetables floating from its shores, and the indications of its fertility. The morning light showed the newly found land to be the residence of man, just as the light he had seen on the shore the previous evening had indicated ; but what manner of men were its inhabitants : were they savages, cannibals, civilized men, or perhaps monsters, or some such strange race of beings as the maps of the Middle Ages portrayed ? was this a part of the Continent of Asia, the outposts of the great empire of the Grand Khan, or the approaches to the dominions of the long-sought Christian prince, the Prester John ? or was this the famous island of Cipango, so abounding in riches and grandeur ? Such and many other similar thoughts rushed tumultuously through the mind of Columbus as he gazed toward this promised land, now found, but still buried in dimness and mist.

It was Friday morning, October 12th, 1492, when an auspicious dawn revealed to the eyes of Europeans this beautiful island in the Western Hemisphere, which so many labors, sacrifices, and struggles had been made to discover. It was a land of majestic forests, reaching as far as the horizon ; a land of natural flowers, which perfumed the air, and of purest lakes, reflecting the landscape and the heavens. A vast extent of level country was spread before eager eyes that had never seen this land before. But there is no feature of a new-found land so important, so significant, so startling, so full of past and future history, and so instinct with present and future consequences as the presence of man ! Columbus saw with eager eye human forms issuing from the woods in all directions and flocking to the shores ; they were perfectly naked, well formed, and even majestic in stature and carriage. They were overpowered with awe at the sight of the mighty canoes before them, the apparitions of a night.

Columbus, followed by his staff officers, the captains of the other ships, and by the armed men of the crews, landed with due ceremony. He was clad in the scarlet mantle and other insignia of his high office of admiral of the seas and lands, and bore in his hand the royal standard of Spain as he descended into his boat. The two Pinzons, each with a banner emblazoned with a green cross, and bearing the initials of Ferdinand and Isabella and the crowns of the sovereigns, followed. All the officers and men were perfectly armed. It seemed like a moment only when all stood on the land. Columbus immediately fell upon his knees, and prostrating himself before the Almighty, kissed the land he had just discovered. Three times with bending form he kissed the earth. Then rising, and drawing his sword, Columbus displayed the royal standard, and calling around him the royal notary, the commissioner of marine, and the captains of the ships, took possession of the country in the name of the Saviour for the Spanish sovereigns. The notary by his order drew up the official proceedings in due form, and all present joyously and loyally took the oath of obedience to him as admiral and viceroy, and as the representative of the Spanish sovereigns. He named the country San Salvador, or Holy Saviour, in token of his gratitude to God, who had guided him to the new world.*

> " The dashing,
> Silver flashing
> Surges of San Salvador !" †

The words of the prayer so fervently uttered by Columbus on this historic occasion have been preserved, and are as follows : " Lord ! Eternal and Almighty God ! who, by Thy sacred word, hast created the heavens, the earth, and the seas, may Thy name be blessed and glorified everywhere ! May Thy Majesty be exalted, who hast deigned to permit that, by Thy humble servant, Thy sacred name should be made known and preached in this other part of the world." This prayer, by order of the Castilian sovereigns, was repeated by other discoverers in the new world, by such men as Fernando Cortez, Vasco Nuñez de Balboa, Pizarro, and other Spanish founders of empires.‡

By direction of the viceroy, grand admiral, and governor-general, for now his well-earned titles and powers were vindi-

---

* De Lorgues' and Barry's " Columbus," p. 159 ; Irving's " Columbus," p. 156 ; Ramusio, vol. ii., folio 1 ; Robertson's " History of America," t. i., Book II., p. 120 ; Oviedo, lib. i., cap. 6 ; Las Casas, " Historia Ind.," lib. i., cap. 40.

† The precise spot and indeed the very island upon which Columbus first landed has always been and now is more than ever a question involved in doubt, and hence too in controversy. While Humboldt, Irving, Tarducci, and authors generally give the honor to San Salvador, or Cat Island, Navarrete espouses the cause of one of the Turk Islands, named Grande Salina ; Varnhagen, that of Marignano ; Fox, that of Samana, and Munoz, that of Watling Island. This last contention is supported by Beecher, of the London Hydrographic Office.

‡ Barry's translation of De Lorgues' "Columbus," p. 159.

cated and acknowledged, the carpenters cut down with their axes two large trees, which, having been joined in the form of the cross, they lifted and planted in the soil. The island thus first discovered was called by the natives Guanahani, and was in the centre of the first line of the Lucayas Islands, occupying the middle of the lengthened group forming the Bahaman archipelago. The officers and crews crowded around Columbus and went as far in their expressions and protestations of admiration, devotion, and loyalty, as they had so recently gone in their insubordination, distrust, and mutiny. Their assurances of future and perpetual submission were unbounded.

The most important feature in this great drama was the coming together of different races of men, heretofore strangers to each other. The immediate event affected the Europeans and aboriginal Americans quite differently. The former had regarded themselves, up to the moment of the discovery, as victims of the chimerical aspirations of an adventurer and desperate man, who had staked all on a new theory, a dream of his own; and they were hurrying on to a certain and inexorable fate. Now that the theory was established and the dream realized, their feelings and the open expression of them went to the other extreme of joy, gratitude, and exultation. The simple natives, on the other hand, when they beheld the great ships of the Spaniards, were struck with amazement and awe; they flocked to the shore, and saw with astonishment the easy and graceful movements of the ships, which seemed to obey the commands of the captain. At first they thought them huge monsters that had come up from the deep during the night, but the opinion that the great ships had descended from the clouds, using their great wings for that purpose—for such they took the sails to be—or coming down upon the clouds themselves, was universally adopted by the natives until they became better acquainted with Europeans. Every minute detail of these huge canoes, of their movements, and of the celestial beings on board was watched with simple wonder and close attention. Their astonishment was increased when they saw the smaller boats let down into the water and manned by these extraordinary visitors, clad in metal and splendid trappings, and bearing in their hands brilliant banners and powerful weapons of polished metal. As the boats approached the shore the natives fled precipitately to the woods, and from their concealment eagerly watched the astounding and to them, then, unintelligible ceremony of taking possession of their country. They trembled with fear, and yet were attracted, even riveted, to the scene by curiosity. They gazed with awe and admiration at these wonderful beings, at their fair complexions, their beards, and their gaudy dresses. While the royal notary was reducing the proceedings to writing, the simple natives began gradually to show themselves at the edge of the woods, and seeing no harm in the celestial strangers, but, on the contrary, as they smiled and received them with gentleness, they approached nearer and nearer, while Columbus and the others, following his example, permitted themselves to be touched by the curious and awe-stricken Indians, their beards to be felt by them, and their armor and clothes examined. They readily recognized Columbus as the chief by his tall and commanding appearance, and by the homage rendered to him by the others. He won their confidence by his benignity and kindness.*

Columbus and his companions scanned the natives with intense and intelligent interest. He observed that they were all young, that they differed from the natives of Asia and Africa, and from all other races of men known to Europeans in color, stature, features, and shape of the head. He saw no human habitations, nor signs of wealth or civilization; they were perfectly naked, and their bodies were painted in various colors, some being painted over their whole bodies, others on their faces or around the eyes alone. Their natural color was tawny or copper, somewhat resembling the natives of the Canaries, and they wore no beards. They had large heads, straight and coarse hair, which they cut about the ears but preserved in long locks, hanging from their crowns down their backs. They had lofty foreheads, prominent cheek-bones, were of medium stature, and, so far as they could be seen from the grotesque and fantastic manner of painting them, their features were rather agreeable. Some painted only their noses. All were males, with the exception of a single female, young, perfectly naked, and handsomely shaped. Their arms consisted of clubs hardened by fire, and pointed with sharp flints or the teeth of sharks. Their appearance was wild,

---

* Las Casas, "Hist. Ind.," lib. i., cap. 40; Oviedo, lib. i., cap. 6; Barry's De Lorgues' "Columbus," p. 161; Irving's "Columbus," vol. i., p. 158.

but gentle. They were so unacquainted with metals that, when handed a sword, they handled it by the edge until they felt it cutting their flesh.

Columbus made presents to the natives of colored caps, glass beads, hawks' bells, and other small articles, which they eagerly accepted, and regarded as of inestimable value. They proudly placed the caps on their heads and the beads around their necks, and the sound of the bells was wonderfully charming. They respectfully and generously offered to the Spaniards everything they possessed. Columbus was delighted with the gentleness of the natives, which he regarded as a promising sign of their easy conversion to Christianity. His zealous mind rejoiced in the prospect of bringing countless souls to the joys of heaven. The Spaniards spent the remainder of the day in rest and recreation on the shore and in the woods, and in the evening all returned on board their ships.

While the Spaniards were delighted with the grand and dazzling result of their expedition, and spent a night of joyful rest, the natives were busily engaged in spreading the news of the arrival of the great ships and noble men from the clouds far and near. Early next morning the ships were surrounded by canoes made from a single log of wood, and crowded with natives. They brought their offerings to the mighty strangers, such as large balls of spun cotton, darts, domesticated parrots, and other native productions. They handled their canoes with perfect ease, some of which were large enough to hold fifty men. They also brought cakes of cassava bread, their principal article of food, and though at first it was insipid to the taste of the Spaniards, it afterward became one of their most important articles of food. The natives were called by Columbus Indians, because he still thought, and continued to his death to regard these people as natives of India; and this singular name became the universal appellation of the American aborigines. The Indians sought with eagerness to exchange their parrots and large rolls of cotton, weighing twenty-five pounds, for the merest trifles received from the Spaniards, regarding such things as possessing a supernatural virtue, because they came, as they believed, from heaven. Columbus from the beginning treated them with the utmost justice and generosity, and he would not permit the men to take the large rolls of spun cotton without giving an equivalent there-for. Their cassava bread was made of the yuca root, but they had another kind of yuca, of which they ate the roots cooked in different ways. They esteemed their own goods of little value when compared to the wonderful trinkets of the marvellous strangers, which they eagerly sought, even the fragments and pieces of broken china and glass.

But now a new element, developing, in fact, the sordid aspirations of civilized avarice, appeared in the dealings between the Europeans and the Indians, for the former had caught the sight of some small gold ornaments worn by the latter in their noses. Well have poets in all ages lamented in man the accursed thirst for gold! These gold ornaments were gladly exchanged by the natives for glass beads or hawks' bells, and the Spaniards with even greater eagerness embarked in the traffic. The sight of gold roused the avarice of the Spaniards to a fearful extent. Columbus was compelled to forbid all traffic in gold, as this was an article reserved to the crown, and so with regard to cotton brought in in any large quantities. He felt anxious to meet the expectations of the Spanish sovereigns in pushing his search for the gold-bearing regions, and he inquired minutely of the natives concerning the location of the countries from which it was procured. The answers he received of the existence of other islands and lands, some lying to the south, others to the southwest, and others to the northwest, deeply interested him, for the natives represented the lands to the south as so abounding in gold that the tribes from the northwest made predatory expeditions thither, remorselessly plundering those countries of their gold and carrying off the islanders as slaves. Columbus accepted these answers as confirming his belief that he had reached the famous countries described by Marco Polo as lying opposite Cathay, in the Chinese sea, and the marauding expeditions mentioned by the natives he took to be from the mainland of Asia, the Empire of the Grand Khan, whose inhabitants were warlike and dealers in slaves. He took the southern countries, from which the gold of the natives was procured, to be the famed island of Cipango, for Marco Polo had related that its king was served from vessels of gold, and his palace was roofed with the same precious metal.

Some historians have regarded the triumphant entry of Columbus into Barcelona as the discoverer of America the proudest moment of his life ; but what could exceed the glory and triumph of that supreme moment when he stood upon the virgin soil of the new world itself, its discoverer, planting the standard of Christianity and unfurling the banners of Spain !

CHAPTER VII.

> "Attempt the end, and never stand to doubt;
> Nothing's so hard but search will find it out."
> —Herrick.

> "But he who labors firm, and gains his point,
> Be what it will, which crowns him with success,
> He is the son of fortune and of fame;
> By those admir'd, those specious villains most,
> That else had bellowed out reproach against him."
> —Thomson's "Agamemnon."

> "Columbia, Columbia, to glory arise,
> The queen of the world and the child of the skies."
> —Timothy Dwight.

Columbus, having rested and refreshed his crews for two days, commenced now the work of exploring this unknown region of the world, which he had discovered after unprecedented opposition, sufferings, hardships, and labors. He who was so lately the object of ridicule, of mutiny and threats, was now regarded by his sailors and officers as the greatest of discoverers and navigators; they who so recently plotted his death at sea, with the intention of returning to Spain and falsely accounting for his death by accident, were now his enthusiastic and united supporters, ready at a word and a moment to obey his orders, and to follow him loyally wherever he should lead.* On the morning of October 14th, with the Santa Maria and the boats of the caravels he set out to explore San Salvador and the neighboring islands, for the natives had told him of the existence of many adjacent islands. The islanders everywhere had heard of the arrival of the visitors from the clouds, and they ran in great crowds to welcome him, and to see the marvellous strangers and their great canoes. So eager were they to see their new acquaintances, that they called in loud voices to those remaining at home in the villages to "Come and see the men who came down from heaven, and bring them meat and drink." They ardently thanked the great deities for directing these wonderful

---

* Irving's "Columbus," vol. i., p. 164; Tarducci's "Life of Columbus," Brownson's translation, vol. i., p. 154.

beings to their shores. Columbus consoled himself with the
prospect of making Christians of these benighted people, even
at that early and critical moment noticing the presence of stone
in the country suited for building churches. He also observed
their homes, implements, kitchen gardens and their orchards,
and saw as he advanced the rich forests and undulating hills of
this and of a succession of other beautiful islands. The new
world looked beautiful to his eyes. The coast of San Salvador
was surrounded by a reef of rocks within whose shelter were
deep waters and secure harbors. He selected a place for a fort,
a small peninsula, which could be easily separated by water
from the rest of the island. Six Indian cabins were standing on
this point, and the admiral thought the gardens surrounding
them equal to those of Castile ; but he was now in search of the
opulent island of Cipango. He took on board seven natives,
with the intention of carrying them to Spain, in order that, by
learning the Spanish language, they might serve as interpreters
for converting their countrymen to Christianity. He took also
a supply of wood and water, and sailed the same evening in
search of Cipango and its fabled riches.

The 15th was spent in approaching the largest of the numerous
and attractive islands, which he reached that evening, and named
it St. Mary of the Conception. Here also he found the natives
amiable, gentle, and generous with all their goods, naked, like
those of San Salvador, cordial in their welcome and in their
simple hospitality. The Indians on board the admiral's ship had
represented to him the existence of numerous other islands of
great wealth and abounding in gold, which he eagerly thought
he identified as the seven or eight thousand islands described by
Marco Polo as located in the Chinese sea, and as abounding in
gold and silver, spices, and precious goods. Every incident
was now of deep interest to him. Just as the ships were about
to sail, one of the seven Indian captives, already tired of his new
and celestial companions, suddenly plunged into the sea, and,
swimming swiftly to a large canoe near the shore, made his
escape to the woods with the Indians who had been in the boat.
A party of sailors from the Nina pursued, but only succeeded in
capturing the Indian canoe after the fugitives had escaped.
Soon afterward an Indian in a canoe approached and offered his
ball of cotton from a distance, being afraid to come nearer,

whereupon he was captured by the sailors. Columbus had the captive brought to him, and having refused the proffered cotton and decked his prisoner with a colored cap on his head, beads around his neck, and hawks' bells in his ears, sent him ashore to his great delight, and at the same time restored the captured canoe. On the following day, while sailing for another island, he extended similar kindnesses to another native taken up by one of the ships with his canoe, and returned him to his friends with many presents. Such repeated acts of kindness completely won the hearts of the natives, who flocked in great crowds to the ships, and they also received presents and refreshments from the admiral. Nothing could have been more generous and humane than the treatment which he extended to the Indians, which was in marked contrast to the cruelty and rapacity which so many of his companions and succeeding discoverers practised toward them from the beginning. Had Columbus been invested with ample powers and supported with loyal Spanish soldiers, his whole administration would have been marked by the same just and kind treatment of the Indians.

Columbus was so enraptured with the beauty of the lands and sea, forming such a succession of delightful surprises, that he was embarrassed to determine in which direction to turn his ships first. "I know not," he said, in one of his letters, "where to go first, nor are my eyes ever weary of gazing on the beautiful verdure. The singing of the birds is such that it seems one would never desire to depart hence. There are flocks of parrots that obscure the sun, and other birds of many kinds, large and small, entirely different from ours. Trees also of a thousand species, each having its particular fruit."

Columbus found the inhabitants of Fernandina similar to those of the other islands, but they were more intelligent and ingenious in their domestic comforts, or, as he expressed it, "more sociable, more civilized, and even more cunning." Their cabins were neat and clean, constructed in the form of a pavilion, with branches of trees, reeds, and palm leaves, and located in the groves. The hammock was in general use for sleeping. The natives here as elsewhere regarded the Spaniards as celestial beings; they gave plentifully of their fruits and foods, and filled the casks of the ships with the purest spring waters; they made propitiatory offerings to these superhuman beings. In sailing around this island they found a fine harbor two leagues from the northwest cape. Columbus wrote that "the country was as fresh and green as in the month of May in Andalusia; the trees, the fruits, the herbs, the flowers, the very stones, for the most part, as different from those of Spain as night from day."* On the island of Saometa, called by Columbus Isabella, he remarked the superiority of the natives, but he did not find the king of the island clothed in rich garments decked with gold, nor the abundance of gold, nor the mines of gold, which he was told by the other islanders he would encounter there. As he approached this island he thought, in his usually enthusiastic frame of mind, that he perceived the aromatic odors of Oriental spices and herbs; but though he found the island the most beautiful one he had visited, his hopes were never realized; but he was always directed by the natives to other lands of promise. Having, after several days' hovering about the island, failed to discover the opulent king or the mines of gold, his hopes were next directed to another great island to the south, which the natives represented as abounding in wealth, and rich in gold, pearls, spices, and fine merchandise. Still impressed with the writings of Marco Polo, and intent on verifying his statements, he sailed for this great island, which he persuaded himself was Cipango. The great vessels of trade described by the Indians must be the ships of the Grand Khan; the great island of Bohio, the natives said, was not far distant, and opposite to these and about ten leagues distant he thought must lie the Empire of the Grand Khan himself, with its magnificent capital of Quinsai. Thus, taking leave of the Bahamas, he sailed for these fabled regions of the East, carrying with him the letter which Ferdinand and Isabella had entrusted to him to deliver to the Grand Khan with his own hands. Columbus, with his mind filled with the fairy legends and mythical geographical traditions of the Middle Ages, and at the same time unfolding the true map of the world to mankind, with the aid of advanced science, stands forth in history as the connecting link between the ancient and the modern world. It was with such splendid dreams that he gayly and joyously sailed from the Bahamas to the Antilles.

---

* Irving's "Columbus," vol. i., p. 168; Navarrete, "Primer Viage," lib. i.; Mr. Brownson's translation of Tarducci's "Columbus," vol. i.

After several days' delay from adverse winds, the admiral was under sail October 14th, and after passing a small group of islands which he named Islas de Arena, now the Mucaras, and crossing the Bahama, on October 28th, he sighted the queen of the Antilles, and was astonished and delighted at its size, its magnificent scenery of mountains, valleys, plains, noble rivers, majestic forests, promontories, and headlands. He approached the island on the coast west of Nuevitas del Principe; he landed on the banks of a beautiful river, which he called San Salvador, and taking possession of the island, he called it Juana, as a compliment to Prince Juan. This majestic island broke upon the sight of Columbus like the realization of a golden dream. As he sailed up the beautiful river and observed with rapture its fruits and flowers, its ever-changing scenery, its noble trees, its green pastures and lawns, its grand mountains, the variety and luxury of its vegetation, its birds of many-colored plumage, its balmy air, its clear sky, the fragrance of the woods and plains, he felt convinced that he had found the long-sought island of Cipango.* Continuing his voyage, he occasionally landed, visited the villages, gave names to them and to the rivers, and here, as elsewhere, he allowed none of his men to take the goods or properties of the affrighted and flying inhabitants. He saw an improvement in the architecture of the houses, saw the cleanliness of the cabins, the rude statues of their idols, ingeniously carved wooden masks, and from the indications of a semi-civilization he concluded that he was in the approaches to a great, wealthy, and civilized empire. Seeing in every hut quantities of fishing tackle, he concluded that this was the fishing coast of the empire they were approaching. The Indians taken from the island of Guanahani, or San Salvador, and on board the Pinta, told the captain, Martin Alonzo Pinzon, that beyond the cape and on a river lay, at four days' journey, the golden region of Cubanacan, abounding in precious metals. Pinzon communicated the information to Columbus; the map of Dr. Toscanelli was consulted; the belief that this island was Cipango was abandoned, and it was concluded that they had actually landed on the mainland of Asia; that Cubanacan was no less than a part of Asia described

---

* Charlevoix, "Hist. St. Domingo," lib. i., p. 20; Irving; Barry's De Lorgues' "Columbus;" Robertson's "Hist. America," etc.

by Marco Polo; that it had for its ruler the Tartar sovereign Kublai Khan, who was at war with the Grand Khan, and that the empire of the latter would soon be reached; that they could not be far from Mangi and Cathay. He accordingly doubled the cape, which he had named the Palms, with the intention of visiting Kublai Khan and delivering to him one of his letters of recommendation from the Spanish sovereigns, and then proceeding to visit the Grand Khan himself at his capital at Cathay, the great object of his mission.

So complete was the delusion under which Columbus and his companions labored, led thereto by the works of Marco Polo and other mediæval authors and by the map of Toscanelli, that he actually sent a deputation, consisting of Rodrigo de Jeres and Luis de Torres, the Hebrew, Chaldaic, and Arabic linguist, and two Indian interpreters, with Indian guides to the court of Kublai Khan, with messages of friendship and peace, and to announce that the admiral would come in person with letters from his sovereigns and a present for the Asiatic king. It adds a pleasant tinge of romance to the momentous history of the discovery of America, that in the fifteenth century an embassy was sent in the name of the Spanish sovereigns, predecessors of the present enlightened ruler of Cuba, across the plains and mountains of that island to a fabulous prince of an Asiatic kingdom, who was then and there at war with the Grand Khan of Tartary.

The ambassadors returned on November 6th to the ships, and no one in the eager crowd that gathered around to hear their report was as truly anxious to receive with credulity the expected tidings of the Tartar king as the admiral. They had penetrated twelve leagues across the country; the great Oriental ruler was a naked Indian chief; his capital was a village of fifty cabins and one thousand inhabitants, equally naked as himself, with the exception of a covering of netted cotton around the middle of the body. They saw no gold or other valuable articles, no spices or precious stones. They were treated with the utmost deference by the chief and his people, and many of the latter desired to accompany them back in their journey to the skies. While this unexpected report shattered many of the admiral's cherished dreams, so firm was his belief in the theories he had formed, that one temporary delusion followed another.

This expedition into the interior of Cuba, though it may seem

almost grotesque to the people of the present day, formed one
of the processes whereby, step by step, Columbus and the first
discoverers felt their way in an unknown world. But there were
two articles discovered by the Europeans in this strange embassy which give a practical importance of the highest order to
it, one of which has done more to affect the question of human
food throughout the world ever since than any other event that
could have happened ; and the other has given to all the nations
of the world a luxury of universal indulgence, so much prized
that its abolition, if attempted, would revolutionize the governments. These events were the first discovery of the potato and
of tobacco by Europeans. While Mr. Irving refers the former
to the more immediate researches of Columbus and his men
during their exploration of the resources and products of Cuba,
other authors attribute the discovery to the embassy we are now
describing. Thus while Columbus was in search of gold and
spices, he discovered, without knowing its value, an article of
human food more useful than the most precious metals, and
more valuable to mankind than all the aromatic products of the
East. But it was, without doubt, these ambassadors of the
admiral who first discovered tobacco. Passing through the
country they saw many of the natives, both men and women,
carrying large rolls of a dried herb or plant, which were lighted
at one end, while the other end was held in the mouth, and they
sucked the smoke into their mouths and then expelled it with
their lips. Astonished at so singular a custom, they inquired of
the natives the meaning of such strange movements, and were
told that the large roll, in shape like a flageolet, was called a
tobago (tobacco), a name which has ever since been given to the
plant itself.*

While waiting for the return of the ambassadors, Columbus was
busy in having his ships careened and repaired, and still more
in seeking information from the natives. The latter, in their
endeavors to enlighten him, frequently led him astray for want
of a common language, or by the use of terms susceptible of
different meanings. He had, however, gathered from the natives
the impression that to the southeast lay a great island, but

---
* Barry's De Lorgues' " Columbus," p. 171 ; Irving's " Columbus," vol. l., p. 182 ;
Murray's " Lives of the Catholic Heroes and Heroines of America," p. 74.

whether it was named Babeque or Bohio he could not tell; but the great capital city they mentioned, Quisquay, he thought must be Quinsai (the celestial city), which Marco Polo had so frequently mentioned. He gave the name of Rio de Mares to the river he had discovered, and sailed on. He took on board several natives of both sexes, to be carried to Spain and to be instructed in the tenets of Christianity and in the Spanish language, in order to return them as interpreters, to aid in the conversion of their people, and on November 12th he turned his course to the southeast in quest of the populous and opulent island of Babeque.*

In all his intercourse with the islanders, it is to be observed that the admiral made the most earnest inquiries for gold. This was prompted by no sordid motive of his own, but, as the Count de Lorgues justly observes, his motive and his necessity were to meet the expectations of his sovereigns, to interest them and all Spain in continuing his voyages by such evidences of promised recompense, and he was also anxious to collect gold in great quantities, in order to build up that princely fund with which he intended to equip and sustain the new crusade, that was destined to redeem the Holy Land from the hands of the infidels. He stated that Cuba must contain the land of unbounded gold and wealth, Cipango. "According to the globes I have seen and the delineations in atlases, it must be situated in this region." Again he writes: "I wish to discover and see as many countries as I can." † He wrote the most urgent appeals to Ferdinand and Isabella to excite their zeal and efforts for the conversion of the Indians to Christianity. This aspiration was uppermost in his thoughts; his journal and letters exhibit his character in this respect in the most striking light. On November 6th he entered in his journal also, "I go this day to the southeast to search for gold, spices, and unknown lands."

Columbus directed his course away from Babeque for fear the Indians from that island whom he had on board might desert. But he found them quite contented with their new mode of life.

---

* Brownson's Tarducci, vol. i., p. 173.
† "Journal of Columbus;" Irving's "Life of Columbus;" Barry's De Lorgues' "Life of Columbus," p. 166.

They had learned a number of Spanish words, made the sign of the cross, knelt before the crucifix, showed great devotion at their prayers, which they recited with hands lifted up to heaven, and chanted the "Salve Regina" and the "Ave Maria." A circumstance occurred, while sailing for Babeque, which deeply impressed the religious feelings of Columbus. He observed a large cluster of islands, countless in number and forming quite an archipelago, and as he was proceeding to take possession of the first in the name of all, he saw a huge cross on an eminence formed by two falling trunks of trees, the arm of the cross having fallen across the larger trunk. He fell upon his knees; he thanked God for this sign of His mercy, and having had the cross fitted together by his carpenters, on the following Sunday he and his staff officers and others made a solemn procession, and erected the cross firmly in the soil.

But Columbus found some of his own followers less manageable than the barbarians on board the ships, for he already noticed that the Pinzons did not punctually obey his orders, and occasionally let expressions drop which were inconsiderate or insubordinate. On November 20th the Pinta paid no attention to his signals; at night he shortened sail and signalled to the Pinta to join him, but at dawn, to his great disappointment, the Pinta was not to be seen. Martin Alonzo Pinzon, with his ship, had deserted the admiral! The latter was deeply affected by this ignoble act; he was in doubt as to the designs of Pinzon; he could not overtake the Pinta, with her superior speed; he therefore returned to continue the exploration of the coast of Cuba. He reached the point of Cuba on November 24th, anchored in a magnificent harbor formed by the mouth of a river, which he named St. Catherine. In the bed of the river he discovered stones veined with gold. He made note of the various vegetable products of the country, especially of its gigantic trees, and while thus coasting and landing from time to time, he discovered a cake of wax in one of the Indian cabins, though this was subsequently believed to have been brought from Yucatan. From one of the great fir-trees he caused a mast to be made for the Nina. In the midst of his sorrow at the desertion of the Pinta, his journal is full of expressions of gratitude to God, such as the following: "It pleased our Lord to show him every day something better than that of the preceding day; and that he went from good to better in all his discoveries."* Having reached the eastern extremity of the island of Cuba on December 5th, the admiral concluded this must be the eastern limit of Asia, and he called it the Alpha and Omega.

Laboring under this impression, still embarrassed by the desertion of the Pinta, and undecided whether to continue the navigation of the Cuban coast until he should reach the rich regions of farther India or pursue the search for the golden island of Babeque, he was sailing almost without an immediate aim, when he discovered an island which he took at first for a gold-bearing island mentioned by the Indians under the name of Bohio, but which turned out to be Hayti, to which he gave the name of Hispaniola. This majestic island, with its grand scenery, its lofty and rocky mountains, its expanding verdure, all seen through a clear atmosphere, reanimated the spirits of the admiral. He entered a fine harbor at the western end, and called it St. Nicholas. There were many signs of the island being quite populous. It abounded in fish, and possessed beautiful rivers and harbors. While detained in his exploration of the coast, he named another harbor Conception, and entering it, they took solemn possession of the island on December 12th, erecting a cross in token of that event. The natives at first fled from beings whom they took for messengers from heaven, but the kindness and generosity of Columbus soon won their confidence. His descriptions of this beautiful island, written at the time, represented it as closely resembling the most favored parts of Spain. The first of the natives with whom the Spaniards came in contact was a young female, captured after the ceremony of taking possession of the country. She was brought, trembling with fear, before the admiral, who treated her with even more than his usual kindness. He caused her to be clad in European garments, and bestowed upon her the usual presents of beads, brass rings, hawks' bells, and other trifles. He then returned her to her people, even against her will, as she was well pleased with the finery and kindness she received. On the following day nine robust Spanish soldiers were sent to find the Indian village, and soon the best relations were established between the Haytians

---

* Barry's De Lorgues' "Columbus," p. 175; "Hist. del Almirante," cap. 29; Las Casas," Journal of Columbus, 25 de Noviembre;" Irving's "Columbus," vol. i., p. 191.

and their celestial visitors. While at the village the Spaniards saw the good effect the kindness shown to the Indian woman on the previous day had produced, for she was brought in triumph on the shoulders of the men into the village, and her husband expressed unbounded happiness at the honors and favors shown to her.

The natives of Hayti were in a state of primitive simplicity; the spontaneous soil and serene climate yielded them abundant food without labor; clothing was unknown; and they had no wants beyond those simple needs which nature supplied. The accounts written by Columbus and by contemporary authors represent Hispaniola, which was the name he bestowed upon the island of Hayti, as an earthly paradise. While enjoying a superfluity of good things, they gave lavishly of all they had; there was no distinction of mine and thine; no code of laws or officers of the law were necessary, but, as Peter Martyr wrote, " They deal truly with one another, without laws, without books, and without judges." Columbus wrote of the inhabitants, " Men and women were as naked as when they came from the bosoms of their mothers," and, as De Lorgues writes, Columbus " ordered the greatest decency to be observed toward these simple children of nature." It was related that while the ordinary members of the tribe were contented with one wife, the chief was allowed twenty. When once acquainted with the Spaniards, they immediately placed unbounded faith in them. Columbus rejoiced at the prospect of making these innocent people Christians.

The admiral made another effort between December 14th and 16th to discover the fabled island of Babeque, but, like other visions created by the mistaken information of the natives, it eluded his search. He resumed the exploration of the coast of Hispaniola. At a beautiful harbor, which he named the Port of Peace, he liberated another Indian whom he had taken up with his canoe from the waters during his cruise, and sent him with presents to his people. Here he received a visit from a young cacique, carried in a litter by four of his subjects, and attended by two hundred others. Presents were exchanged. Columbus entertained the chief at dinner, and in the evening sent him ashore with great ceremony and a salute from the cannons of the ships. Great ceremony was observed in the chief's return to his village, and the presents he had received were carried at the head of the long royal procession. While on board the admiral showed him all the parts of the ship, Spanish coins, and a crucifix, and was lavish in his presents, avowing to his officers his hopes thus, and by setting them an example of Christian virtues, to predispose the chief favorably for the Christian faith. He wrote to the sovereigns, " They are the best people in the world, and I have great hope in our Lord that your Highnesses will make them all Christians." * He caused a large cross to be erected in the village of his visitor, the cacique, around which the Indians assembled and prayed after the manner of the Spaniards, and Columbus "hoped in our Lord that all these islands would become Christian." Continuing his examination of the coast of Hispaniola on December 19th and 20th, he anchored in a fine harbor, which he called St. Thomas, supposed to be now the Bay of Acul, and here the natives flocked to the anchorage in great numbers and offered as presents to the celestials small pieces of gold, calabashes of fresh water, yam bread, and whatever they possessed, with unbounded generosity. The admiral ordered that in every case presents should be given in return. Several neighboring caciques visited the ships, invited the Spaniards to their villages, and entertained them with unbounded hospitality. On December 22d Columbus received an embassy from the great cacique of the country, Guacanagari, who sent presents of gold, beads, and other Indian articles, and requested a visit from the august strangers from the clouds. The fleet was immediately sailed to the eastward, and at the town built on the river called by the Spaniards Punta Santa was the capital of this great cacique, the largest and finest village they had seen. A deputation, consisting of the notary and several mariners, was sent to the chief, who received them with every honor, and he and his people loaded them with presents. Though asking nothing in return, they received the presents of the Spaniards with great joy and superstitious veneration. The cacique sent presents of parrots and gold to the admiral, and the delegates were escorted to their boats by a large crowd of Indians eager to do them every service. In the mean time, lesser caciques and great numbers of their subjects visited the ships, and

---

* "Journal of Columbus," Sunday, December 16th.

these, as usual, assured the admiral of the existence of rich regions in the interior, and especially of one named Cibao, which he persuaded himself could be no other than Marco Polo's opulent island of Cipango. And yet, with his accustomed submission of all things to the heavenly guidance, he wrote in his journal the inmost sentiments of his soul: "May our Lord, who holds all things in His hands, be pleased to vouchsafe to me what is most for His service." While at this anchorage five caciques and several thousand people visited the admiral, mostly in canoes, yet five hundred swam to the ships for want of canoes, all bringing presents and receiving them in return. The scene was one of unequalled novelty and interest. Caciques and subjects all assured him of the gold-bearing region in the interior and of other districts rich in gold, so that he felt assured of meeting the views of the sovereigns and of redeeming the Holy Land; and he audibly exclaimed in his ardor, "May our Lord in His great mercy aid me in finding that gold." *

The fleet set sail on the morning of December 24th from Port St. Thomas for the harbor of the great cacique, Guacanagari, and had reached within a league and a half of the place when Columbus, who had seldom slept and had kept incessant watch almost all the day and night, was forced by exhaustion to retire to his cabin and throw himself with his clothes on upon his bed for a short sleep. A steersman was left in charge of the helm, and the admiral felt perfectly secure, as the weather and sea were calm. The visitors to Guacanagari had reported to him there were no rocks nor shoals in or near the harbor. "For two consecutive days and the preceding night," says De Lorgues, "the concourse of the natives, the presents to be given and received, the exchanges to be watched over, the questions to be put to interpreters, and their answers, the classifying and preservation of the different productions of these countries, which he wished to take to Castile, his religious exercises, and the multiplied cares of the command, did not yield him a single minute for rest." Throughout the voyage he had ordered that the helm should never be entrusted to boys or novices, and on this occasion he left a steersman at the helm. Scarcely had the admiral retired to his room when the steersman abandoned his

---

* Barry's De Lorgues' "Columbus," p. 192.

post to a boy, and he and the other mariners who had the watch all retired to sleep. The boy left at the helm also fell asleep. The Santa Maria, the admiral's own ship, thus left to herself, was drifted by the currents against a sand-bank. Though the roaring of the breakers was heard a league off, it failed to awake the sleeping crew. The cabin boy gave the alarm. The admiral was the first to reach deck. A boat was let down by his orders to carry out an anchor astern and warp the ship, but instead of executing his order, the master and men of the boat deserted, and went to the Nina for shelter. Refused admission on the Nina, these deserters had to return to the caravel; but the boat of the Nina reached her first. The admiral, seeing himself deserted, ordered his mast cut down in order to lighten his ship, but he had not men enough to execute the order. The ship had swung across the stream, was leaning on one side, and the water gaining upon her. He and his remaining crew had to abandon the Santa Maria and take shelter on the Nina. The sea broke over the former, her seams opened, and though she did not sink, she was a wreck. At daybreak the admiral sent word of his disaster to the chief, Guacanagari, who was moved to tears by the disaster to his new friends, and immediately sent all his people with their canoes to aid in saving the provisions and property on board the stranded ship. In a few hours she was unloaded, and the chief gave the admiral three large buildings for the storage of his effects. During the progress of the work he sent repeated messages of sympathy to the admiral. Indian guards were placed about the buildings, and, to the credit of these untaught children of nature, not a thing was lost or stolen. Columbus consoled himself with the thought that it was the will of God he should remain here. The sympathy and hospitality he and his men received from the cacique and his tribe were most generous, and they were delicately bestowed. Columbus was moved to admiration for their goodness, for the cacique had placed all he possessed at his disposal. Well has Mr. Irving said: " Never, in a civilized country, were the vaunted rites of hospitality more scrupulously observed than by this uncultivated savage." Guacanagari and his people were delighted to have the Spaniards settle in their dominions. Columbus wrote in his journal, " There is not in the world a better nation nor a better land."

The good and amiable cacique visited Columbus on the Nina on December 26th, and was moved to tears when he saw the great admiral looking dejected. He offered more houses for the accommodation of his goods and his men, and indeed offered everything he possessed. The stream of visitors still poured in from all the country, and considerable quantities of gold were acquired by barter and presents. When the cacique saw the pleasure the gold gave the admiral, he renewed the assurances that great quantities of gold could be procured at Cibao, in the interior, and the admiral, delighted at the quantities of gold reported by his men as constantly coming in from the natives, and at the assurances of the cacique, felt confident that he should soon find the much-sought Cipango. The natives freely exchanged their trinkets of gold for trifles, and nothing could exceed their delight when they found the hawks' bells resounding to the measure of their dances. The Indian king and the admiral entertained each other with generous hospitality, and their friendship strengthened every day. The feast given by the cacique was worthy of a prince in its abundance and the choiceness of the varied foods, for it consisted of utias or coneys, fish, roots, and a variety of fruits. The prince delighted the admiral also by his courtly and royal manners. The entertainment was followed by the national games and dances, performed by a thousand naked Indians in the beautiful groves surrounding the cacique's residence. These were succeeded in turn, by the orders of the admiral, with the exercises of the Moorish bow and arrow, performed by the Spaniards, which greatly delighted the chief and his people; but when Columbus had the Lombard cannon and arquebus discharged, the Indians fell upon their faces with fear, and were dismayed at the havoc the balls made with the trees they struck and shivered. Columbus assured the Indians and their chief that he would use these weapons for defending them against the attacks of their dreaded enemies, the Caribs, and they were transported with delight at being thus taken under the protection of these children of heaven. The chief distributed presents among the Spaniards with princely grace and generosity, and the Indians received the trifles the admiral gave them in return with a delight which showed that they regarded them as gifts from heaven. The life of these Indians was simple and happy beyond description. In that mild climate clothing was unnecessary, and Las Casas describes them as living in a state of primitive innocence. Labor was unnecessary, as the bountiful earth yielded them spontaneously the most unstinted abundance of all they needed. Above all, they were contented and happy. Even the great admiral of the seas drew consolation in his disaster from the sympathy of the barbarian chief. The Spaniards mingled freely with the natives, were charmed with the relaxations and indulgences now enjoyed by them, and many petitioned the admiral to allow them to remain behind when he should return to Spain. In his own personal intercourse with the cacique and his subjects, Columbus was a model of propriety and honor.

The scientific attainments of the admiral were now successfully called into requisition in the planning and erection of a fort or fortlet with the wreck of the Santa Maria. It was a small, square castle, with bastions at the angles, and its erection was the joint work of the Spanish mariners and of the Indians under the personal direction of Columbus. Guacanagari and his subjects were delighted at the prospect of having this work of defence against the Caribs, of having it manned with the ironclad soldiers from heaven, and at looking forward to future visits of the admiral with new ships and fresh supplies of beads and hawks' bells. They worked on the fortress with a hearty goodwill, "little dreaming," says Irving, "that they were assisting to place on their necks the galling yoke of perpetual and toilsome slavery."

Columbus was now forced to decide upon his immediate future course. A vessel like the Nina was reported to have been seen off the eastern end of the island by the Indians. The ever-sanguine admiral was sure this was the Pinta, and he sent a large canoe manned by Indian oarsmen and commanded by a Spanish seaman to find the erring Pinzon and deliver to him a letter, which was couched in terms of mildness and conciliation, and urging him to join his command immediately. A three-days' search resulted in finding no such ship, and the admiral saw himself and all his men, his specimens from the new world, the Indians on board, destined to be carried to Spain, his gold and other treasures, and the very record of his great discovery, all subjected to the risk of utter loss on a return trip to Spain with

a single ship. The desertion of Pinzon and the wrecking of
the Santa Maria compelled him to abandon his plans for prosecuting his explorations and discoveries of the new countries lying
within his very grasp. He resolved to return to Spain. While
building the fort, streams of visitors came to the site, including
Guacanagari, the chief cacique, several of his tributary caciques
and their tribes in great numbers. The great cacique never
wearied of entertaining and honoring the admiral, treating him
and his companions with unbounded hospitality and honor, and
among the many delicate attentions which he paid the celestial
chief, one was on the occasion when Guacanagari, attended by
five inferior caciques, all wearing coronets of gold, received the
admiral with distinguished honor, and, seating him in a chair of
state, took the coronet of gold from his own head and placed it
on that of Columbus. Little did he suspect that this courteous
act was emblematic of the transfer of dominion over the new
world from its aboriginal rulers and owners to the European
race. Streams of gold poured in, and Columbus felt consoled at
the prospect of meeting the expectations of his royal patrons at
home. Indeed, it was with the hope of establishing a trade in
gold that he determined to leave a Spanish colony behind him.
Already he had, by traffic with the natives, amassed a good
quantity of the precious metal for the home government and for
his own share, the latter of which was to be appropriated to the
recovery of the holy sepulchre.

To the fortress, which was now finished, he gave the name of
La Navidad, in honor of the Saviour's birth, and from the many
volunteers who offered themselves, he selected nine of the stout-
est and best men in his service, including a physician, ship-car-
penter, calker, cooper, tailor, and gunner, and placed the garrison under the command of Diego de Arana, of Cordova, a near
relative of his wife, who was also the notary and alguacil of the
expedition. He gave the colony, or rather the garrison, the
long boat of the Santa Maria, to be used for fishing; also medicines, seeds for planting, and a large quantity of merchandise for
traffic with the natives in exchange for gold. He also left with
them utensils of every kind, a year's supply of biscuits, some
wine, and a supply of arms and artillery. He established thorough discipline in the garrison, and he endeavored to inspire

them with his own noble and lofty sentiments. Truly was this the advance-guard of European civilization in the new world! Would that they had proved worthy of such a rank!

In the mean time, all things were set in order on board the Nina for the return voyage—a voyage scarcely less momentous, considering that the outfit had now been reduced from three ships to a single caravel, than the first outward voyage of discovery. Might not the garrison perish on land, and the admiral and all his men and his only ship perish at sea, and the world become convinced that the Western Hemisphere was an empty vision and a delusive dream!

Before taking leave of his colony, this first hope of their country and race, he provided most amply and even tenderly for them and for their every want. They had a fort capable of resisting any attack of the Caribs, however numerous, ample provisions, were surrounded by a friendly and admiring people, and under the protection of a noble and generous cacique. They could not have been in better condition for continuing the great and exalted work of Columbus, until his return with reinforcements of men, ships, colonists, and all the appliances of European colonization. The fortress of La Navidad is supposed to have been located near Haut de Cap; the capital of Guacanagari, called Guarico, was where the village of Petite Anse now stands. Columbus assembled his garrison and made them an address, which was a model of great thoughts eloquently expressed, of high aims, of noble purposes, of wise forethought, profound sagacity, and of honorable and conscientious principles and conduct. He impressed upon them the glorious object of the discovery, the propagation of the Christian faith, and he besought them, by studying the Indian language, to qualify themselves to instruct the natives in Christian doctrine. In the name and by the authority of the sovereigns he commanded the men to obey their officers, to maintain the utmost respect for Guacanagari, their best friend, and maintain good and honorable relations with him, his tributary chiefs, and all his subjects, and, above all, to observe the most rigorous continence in regard to the Indian women; to maintain friendly relations with all the Indians, to remain within Guacanagari's domains, not to scatter, but to sleep always at night in the castle; to explore the mineral and other resources of the country, to look out for another and better place of settlement by the time of his return, and in general to maintain the honor of their nation and their faith.*

Columbus went on shore from his ship on January 2d, 1493, and took a deeply felt and impressive farewell of his generous friend, Guacanagari, his chieftains, and his people. He invited them to a parting feast, which was served at one of the houses occupied by the Spaniards ; he gave the great chief presents, which he prized above all others, a new shirt, put a collar of gems on his neck, a scarlet mantle on his shoulders, red buskins on his feet, a ring of silver on his finger, and embraced him with such deep and generous good-will that the noble cacique was bathed in his own tears. He commended to the cacique's generous friendship the Spaniards he was about to leave behind, particularly Diego de Arana, Pedro Gutierrez, and Rodrigo de Escobedo, his lieutenants. The admiral assured the cacique that he would, on his return to Hispaniola, bring him presents worthy of his rank and virtues. The cacique exceeded all the admiral's wishes in the extent of his generous promises of provisions and services to the garrison, and expressed the utmost sorrow at his departure. Columbus then caused his men to give a fine display of skirmishes and mock fights in order to impress the minds of the Indians with the military skill and power of the Spaniards. The Indians were overwhelmed with terror mingled with admiration, and would have shrunk from such destructive engines but for the thought that they were to be used for their protection. After the parting between Columbus and the cacique, the separation between the departing Spaniards and those who were to remain behind followed, and was truly affecting ; but the hope of soon meeting again inspired the hearts of all. Columbus sailed from La Navidad on his first return voyage from the new world to Spain, on January 4th, 1493. He had most assiduously secured and stored away on the Nina specimens of all the productions of the countries he had discovered, including a considerable quantity of gold and a number of the natives, the latter being destined to return to their people as Christian interpreters and instructors.

After two days' sailing in an easterly direction toward a lofty

---

* Herrera ; Munos ; Navarrete ; " Hist. del Almirante ;" Irving's " Life of Columbus ;" Barry's De Lorgues, " Columbus."

promontory, which Columbus named Monte Christi, the Pinta was discerned in the distance, and soon the deserter came bearing down toward the Nina, and on joining company Martin Alonzo Pinzon came on board the Nina and made many excuses to the admiral for his conduct, which, however, were either contradictory or purely false. Columbus prudently refrained from reproaches, as the two remaining vessels were still commanded by the Pinzon brothers, and many of their relatives and friends were in the crews; he was, in fact, somewhat in their power still. Pinzon had availed himself of the superior speed of his ship, though delayed some time among the entanglements of the Caicos Islands, and had reached the gold-bearing regions of Hispaniola, where he had collected much gold, retaining half for himself as captain and dividing the other half among his men to secure their support and secrecy. But Columbus succeeded, notwithstanding, in getting these particulars, and, as he distrusted the Pinzons on account of their unworthy conduct, he abandoned his wish to continue a while longer with the two ships to explore the islands and countries of the new world, and resolved to return to Spain immediately.

Though Pinzon had concealed the details of his conduct, Columbus learned of them. His misconduct in appropriating the gold to his own and the use of his crew was a flagrant violation of the orders of the sovereigns and of the fundamental law of the expedition. De Lorgues, in speaking of his wise suppression of his indignation at the conduct of Pinzon, says: "He became resigned, and sacrificed his self-love, his sense of justice, his personal dignity to a duty which was of still greater importance than his rights."

The admiral sent to a large and neighboring river for wood and water, and the stream, from the particles of gold seen in its sands, he called Rio del Oro, or River of Gold. He also mentions having seen in this vicinity large turtles, and goes on in his journal to state that here also he saw three mermaids, which elevated themselves above the water, and resembled those he had seen on the coast of Africa; but though retaining traces of the human features, they were by no means "the beautiful beings they had been represented to be."* Continuing his

---

* Barry's De Lorgues' "Columbus," p. 199; Irving's "Columbus," p. 231; "Journal of Columbus."

course, he reached, on the evening of January 9th, "the river where Pinzon had been trading, and here, on the complaint of the natives, he released with presents four Indian men and two girls, whom Pinzon had seized and had concealed in his ship with the intention of carrying them to Spain and selling them as slaves. Pinzon submitted unwillingly to this act of justice, but was outspoken in his language to the admiral. The river he called Rio de Gracia, but it retained its name of Martin Alonzo, after its discoverer. With a favorable wind Columbus reached a beautiful and elevated headland, which he called Capo del Enamorado, or Lover's Cape, now Cape Cabron, and still further on he found the natives warlike and hostile, well armed with a powerful and hard wooden sword and other formidable weapons, and treacherous. Columbus sent a party of armed Spaniards on shore, after he had feasted one of these warriors and sent him back delighted to his people, but this warlike people treacherously attacked the Spaniards, who immediately formed and advanced upon their assailants, killing two and putting the remainder to flight. Columbus deeply lamented this first contest with the natives and first shedding of native blood by Europeans in the new world; but on the following day these warlike natives and their chief made amicable approaches, which the admiral encouraged, and which resulted in a friendly visit to the caravel, an entertainment, the bestowal of presents, and the establishment of friendly relations between the new world and the old once more. The native warriors seemed to have admired the superior prowess of their antagonists, and treasured no resentment for the defeat of the day before.

Having resolved to return immediately to Spain and forego his desire for further explorations and discoveries, the remainder of January was lost in waiting daily for a favorable wind. It was not until the early part of February that he could avail himself of a breeze on which to sail directly for Spain. In the mean time, he had endeavored to find and visit the Caribs and carry one or two of them to Spain, and to remove his doubts as to the existence of such beings as cannibals; but he did not succeed in finding them. He had no better success in finding another island mentioned to him by the natives and called "Matinino," and which was represented to be inhabited by armed women alone, without any men, and which reminded him of the fabulous Amazons of old. Now finally the prows were turned to the east and to home. The homeward voyage was overtaken by the most violent storms, which tested the utmost skill of the admiral and his mariners to keep the ships from sinking. At his suggestion all on board the ships promised that three pilgrimages should be vowed to heaven for their safe deliverance: one, to be performed by the person drawing the lot, to be made to the shrine of Our Lady of Guadalupe, bearing a wax taper weighing five pounds. This was drawn by the admiral. As the storm continued, another lot was drawn to determine who should make a pilgrimage to the chapel of Our Lady of Loretto, in the Pontifical States, and this fell to a sailor named Pedro Villa; but as he was too poor to bear the expense of the journey, the admiral agreed to bear his expenses. Now again, as the storm grew still fiercer, a third lot was drawn to determine who should make a pilgrimage to the church of Santa Clara, at Moguer, and again the lot fell to Columbus. He religiously and devoutly performed his vows on reaching Spain. But, notwithstanding their prayers and vows, the storm grew so violent as to cause all to despair; not only the sailors, but even the admiral, that man of faith, gave up all for lost, though he accepted all things as the will of God. The Pinta had disappeared, and was believed to have foundered in the storm. His hopes gave way. A prey to the most tumultuous thoughts, he felt that all was gone; that he would never reach Spain to report his discovery, the knowledge of which would be buried with himself and his men in the ocean; that he would never see his two sons again; that they would be taunted with the wild adventure and failure of their father, and that sacrifices and sufferings such as no man had suffered would all go for naught. With faltering step he reached his cabin, and with a hand yet firm he wrote a brief account of his discoveries on parchment; this he sealed and directed to Ferdinand and Isabella, and promised a thousand ducats to the person who should deliver it to the sovereigns unopened; he then wrapped it in a waxed cloth, placed it in the centre of a cake of wax, and enclosing the whole in a barrel, threw it into the sea, leaving the crews to suppose he was making another vow for the safety of the return voyage. A duplicate was made and placed upon the poop, so that, in case the vessel sunk, the barrel would float on the sea and reach the shores of Europe.*

His mind was now more at rest. If he perished, his discovery and his fame might survive; but on February 14th the skies brightened; on the 15th, though the sea was rough, the skies were brighter, and, to the joy of all, land was descried. " The transports of the crew," says Mr. Irving, " at once more gaining sight of the old world, were almost equal to those experienced at first beholding the new." The pilots thought they were off the coast of Castile, but the superior skill of Columbus enabled him more correctly to say they were approaching the Azores. The admiral was almost wrecked in health. Though nearly paralyzed with gout, he had remained four days and nights on deck amid the storm, drenched with rains and tossed by the waves; now, almost disabled and inactive, he was compelled to retire to his bed for rest. It was not until February 17th that he reached the land at Santa Maria, the most southern of the Azores, one of the possessions of Portugal. The astonishment of the inhabitants was great, but it was beyond bounds when they were told whence the strangers had come—that they had reached Asia across the Atlantic, and had discovered the Indies. Remembering the vow to be performed at the first landing-place they should reach, the admiral sent one half the men on shore, who procured a priest to say mass for them at the chapel of the Blessed Virgin near by, while the pilgrims walked from the shore to the shrine in procession, barefooted and in their shirts; the admiral and the remainder of the men stayed in the ships, intending to make their pilgrimage in like manner next day. Castañeda, the Portuguese governor, treacherously surrounded the chapel and made all the pilgrims prisoners. His object was to seize the admiral, acting under the orders of the Portuguese Government, and it was fortunate that his pilgrimage was set for the following day. Finding himself foiled in the attempt to get possession of Columbus, he returned the prisoners to their ships, while the admiral from his deck reproached the treacherous official for his base conduct. It was thus, as we have seen in these pages, that the first of Europeans were received with joy and hospitality by the

---

* Barry's De Lorgues' "Columbus," p. 206; "Hist. del Almirante," cap. 36; Irving's "Life of Columbus," vol. i., p. 243.

far-off and heathen natives of an unknown world on reaching the Western Hemisphere, while on returning to their own, the Eastern Hemisphere, from which they had sailed, conquerors, discoverers, and missionaries of Christianity, and while lifting up their voices in praise and thanks to God for their safety, they were treacherously betrayed by a kindred race, their fellow-Christians. While few men ever reaped such glory as did Columbus, history discloses no one who ever experienced more of the baseness of his fellow-men than he. Thus does the history of the world seem to vibrate between glory and shame!

Columbus rejoiced on February 24th at being once more at sea, and with thanksgiving he turned his ship toward the coveted shores of Spain; but the little fleet was again overtaken with a violent storm, and on the 27th they seemed at the very point of shipwreck. Even the fortitude of Columbus was scarcely equal to such repeated misfortunes. Again the crews resorted to vows in securing the intervention of Heaven for their safety, and every man on board promised to fast on bread and water on the first Saturday after their arrival in port. Again the storm seemed to redouble its fury, and at midnight on Saturday, March 2d, the caravel was struck by a storm with overpowering violence, tearing her sails to pieces and compelling her to scud under bare poles, and threatening her with immediate destruction. Now again their only hope was an appeal to Heaven, and a lot was cast for the performance of a pilgrimage, with bare feet, to the shrine of Santa Maria de la Cueva, in Huelva. The lot was again drawn by the admiral, for he was ever a willing pilgrim; though Las Casas, commenting on the singular frequency with which the lot fell to him, suggests that Providence intended these frequent disasters to humble the admiral's pride and to prevent him from arrogating to himself the glory of discoveries which belonged to God, and of which he was only the instrument. Columbus was himself religiously well inclined to apply to his own soul so wholesome and chastening a counsel. Though there were now indications of land, the storm was increasing in fury; they knew not where they were, and they feared they would be dashed to pieces on the rocks. On the morning of March 4th, at daybreak, they were off the rock Cintra, in the mouth of the Tagus, again within the domains of the rival sovereign, the treacherous John II., King of Portugal, who had so recently from envy ordered the Governor of St. Mary's Island, Azores, to seize and detain the returning discoverers of a new world. But the storm was still raging, and though he distrusted the Portuguese Government, Columbus had no alternative but to enter the port for safety. He and his crew were congratulated on their safe arrival by the inhabitants, who, when they saw the peril of the caravel, had flocked to the church with lighted tapers and prayed for their safe deliverance. Their escape was regarded as miraculous. The oldest mariners of the place told Columbus they had never known so stormy a winter. He ardently contrasted the mild weather and placid waters of Hispaniola with the storms of the Eastern Hemisphere.

Having despatched a messenger to Spain with tidings of his discovery, he wrote a letter to the King of Portugal requesting permission to go with his vessel to Lisbon for its safety, for the report was circulated that she was richly freighted with gold and other treasure, and he felt unsafe from attack on the Tagus, assuring the king that he had not been to the coast of Guinea or other Portuguese colonies, but that he had discovered, by a western voyage, and just returned from, Cipango and the extreme provinces of India. The marvellous news now spread far and near, and the Nina was visited by throngs of people of every grade, cavaliers and officers of the crown, as well as the common people, all eager to listen to the startling accounts of the admiral. Varied effects were produced on his different visitors by the marvellous words of Columbus—admiration, envy, cupidity, curiosity, enthusiasm, and distrust. The king invited him to court, then being held at Valparaiso, nine leagues from Lisbon, and though he distrusted his good faith, Columbus thought it best to go and conceal his distrust, as he was already in the king's dominions. He was received by king and cavaliers with every honor, and though he congratulated the admiral, the king expressed his apprehensions that the discovery belonged to Portugal agreeably to the capitulations of 1479 with the Castilian monarchs, and thought Columbus may have found a short route to the very countries he was himself endeavoring to find, and which the Papal bull had conceded to Portugal. The Portuguese councillors, who, twenty years before, had scoffed at Columbus and his proposals to the crown of Portugal, endeavored to confirm the king's suggestions; they suggested that Columbus was insulting Portugal by entering it as if in triumph; that he had encroached upon the conceded discoveries and claims of Portugal; that he was haughty, boastful, and actually revenging himself upon the king for rejecting his proposals. They went so far as to propose his assassination! They counselled the king that a pretext could be found for drawing him into a quarrel; that he could thus be despatched as if killed in an honorable and justifiable contest. Such baseness and perfidy seem incredible; but they came from the same councillors who ten years before had advised the King of Portugal to secretly and treacherously rob Columbus of the glory of his discovery by sending out a secret expedition, guided by his maps, charts, and information, for the discovery of the promised western lands. The king was more honorable than his unworthy councillors, and refused to listen to their treacherous advice. He feignedly gave due credit and honor to Columbus. The council next suggested his being permitted to return to Spain, and before he could make another voyage to the lands he had discovered, that Portugal should send out a powerful armament, under the guidance of two Portuguese mariners, who had sailed with Columbus, and seize the lands he had discovered, and maintain their ill-gotten possession by force.* That John II. should have consented and agreed to this nefarious proposal seems scarcely consistent with a record not undistinguished for uprightness; but, to the discredit of royalty, he assented to it, resolved to put it secretly and promptly into execution, and he decided to appoint for this dishonest expedition a distinguished sea captain, Don Francisco de Almeida. Columbus, after receiving distinguished honors at the court of Portugal, prepared to sail for Palos in his own caravel, preferring this to the trip by land, which was proposed to him by King John, with offers to escort him honorably to the frontier. On his way to the caravel, at the mouth of the Tagus, escorted by Don Martin de Noroña and a large retinue of cavaliers, himself and pilot mounted on mules provided by the king, he stopped at the monastery of San Antonio, at Villa Zanca, at her request to visit the Portuguese queen, and was received by her and her ladies of honor with the most distinguished honors. The king presented

---

* Barry's De Lorgues' "Columbus," p. 215; Las Casas, "Hist. Ind.," lib. i., cap 74, M S.; Irving's "Life of Columbus," vol i., p. 257.

the admiral's pilot with twenty gold ducats, and in offering to escort himself to the frontier, ordered that horses, lodgings, and all things necessary to the journey be provided at the royal expense. But Columbus availed himself of the prevailing fair weather, sailed from the Tagus on March 13th, arrived at Saltes at sunrise on the 15th, and at mid-day sailed into the harbor of Palos. He had sailed from this ancient port the year preceding, on August 3d, the inventor of a great theory, the hope of Spain and of the race, the scoffed-at dreamer of new worlds. Now how changed, how advanced, was the condition of the man himself, of the nation and sovereigns that had befriended him, and of the civilized world! For by his genius and prowess Europe and Asia were about to embrace each other across the oceans, and midway lay the newly discovered continents of a new world. The last eight months had been the most momentous era in the history of mankind. Prophecy and theory had now become demonstration and history.

CHAPTER VIII.

> "Crown the brave! Crown the brave!
> As through your streets they ride."
> —HEMANS.

> "A thousand trumpets ring within old Barcelona's walls,
> A thousand gallant nobles throng in Barcelona's halls;
> All meet to gaze on him who wrought a pathway for mankind,
> Through seas as broad, to worlds as rich as his triumphant mind;
> And king and queen will grace forsooth the mariner's array—
> The lonely seaman scorned and scoffed in Palos town one day!
> He comes—he comes! the gates swing wide, and through the streets advance
> His cavalcade in proud parade, with plume and pennoned lance,
> And natives of those new-found worlds, and treasures all untold,
> And in the midst the admiral, his charger trapped with gold;
> And all are wild with joy, and blithe the gladsome clarions swell,
> And dames and princes meet to greet, and loud the myriads yell;
> They cheer, that mob, they wildly cheer—Columbus checks his rein,
> And bends him to the beaüteous dames and cavaliers of Spain."
> —G. H. SUPPLE.

IF the civilized world was electrified at the announcement that Columbus had returned from discovering the Western continents, how much more must not the little maritime port of Palos have been moved with joy and exultation when the great discoverer and his veteran mariners returned from their glorious achievements to that historic place! Palos had sent forth the little fleet that was to unite the unknown parts of the earth; it was her privilege now to receive back again the triumphant admiral and his crews, discoverers of a world! For eight long months and more no tidings had been received of the forlorn hope, and the people of Palos had abandoned all expectation of seeing their brave friends and relatives again—no doubt all had been engulfed in the Sea of Darkness or devoured by the monsters of the deep. Their joy exceeded all bounds when, at mid-day, on Friday, August 3d, 1493, they recognized the Nina returning in triumph, with the flags of Castile floating from her masts. The Santa Maria, it is true, was gone, and the Pinta had not been heard from; but the admiral was there, the discoverer in fact of what Plato and Aristotle had only dreamed of. Spain was now the foremost of maritime nations, and Palos was the historic port! The whole town broke forth in transports of joy and exultation; the bells rang forth their merriest notes, the cannons were fired, the shops were closed, the houses were festooned in gayest drapery, business was suspended, and the whole population turned out to welcome the greatest of discoverers returning in triumph. Scarcely had the admiral and his men landed, when the entire population formed in procession and marched with the returning heroes to the nearest church to thank God for the success of so momentous a voyage. If Columbus had been a noted king, says Robertson, he could not have received greater honors.

In the midst of this universal joy, in which the people of the neighboring towns and villages were pouring in to participate, the Pinta entered the port from sea. Martin Alonzo Pinzon, who had enjoyed the opportunity of ranking almost next to Columbus, was disloyal to his chief, and lost all in grasping for what was not his own. Having taken shelter in the Bay of Biscay, Pinzon, thinking that the Nina with the admiral and all on board had perished in the storm, had addressed a letter to the sovereigns giving an account of the discovery, and claiming it as his own. He asked permission to go to court, coveting, no doubt, the ovation which belonged to Columbus, and which was then preparing for him. When he entered the harbor at Palos, and saw the Nina riding at anchor, and heard the sounds of triumph accorded to Columbus, his heart sank within him; he stealthily landed from his yawl, avoiding the admiral for fear of arrest, and concealed himself at his home; but when a reproachful letter from the court arrived, upbraiding him with his treachery and falsehood, and forbidding his appearance at court, he sickened with chagrin, and died a few days afterward of a broken heart. It is vain for Harrisse or Winsor to attempt any palliation of Pinzon's conduct; there are too many evidences of misconduct on his part to leave a doubt of his disloyalty.

Columbus, on the other hand, in the midst of his triumph, did not forget the vows he had made to his heavenly patroness. Many of his crew asked leave to go at once to their homes to receive the continued and joyous felicitations of their families and friends, but the admiral refused their petitions until they and he had fulfilled their vow of making a pilgrimage of thanksgiving at the nearest church of Our Lady on landing—a fulfilment which had been commenced at Santa Maria, and had been treacherously interrupted by the governor of the island. The shrine in which they now performed their grateful vow, according to all current history, was none other than that of Our Lady of La Rabida, and the generous monk, Juan Perez de Marchena, who had sustained Columbus in his darkest hour, and had offered up at Palos the mass of supplication for the departing fleet, had now the happiness of celebrating the mass of thanksgiving on its triumphant return. The scene that ensued, when those two tried friends met again at Palos, after the vicissitudes and successes which had involved the highest and grandest interests of mankind, must have been one of the most interesting and significant in the pages of history. Columbus and Juan Perez again prayed together!

It was in one of the cells of the shrine of La Rabida that Columbus, according to the Count de Lorgues, though without historical support, secluded from the rest of the world and sanctified with unceasing prayer, elaborated and meditated on that important project for the peace of the world—that a geographical and natural line of separation and partition should be drawn and established between the newly discovered countries of Portugal and Spain. It was there, too, in devout prayer and consecrated cell, that he conceived the nobler thought of recommending those rival maritime nations to refer the whole question of dividing the new lands between them to the Holy See, then the common tribunal of arbitration for the Christian world. On this subject the Count de Lorgues has broken forth in the following enraptured though extravagant language:

" So, full of confidence as if he held the whole space of the globe beneath his eyes, although two thirds of it were as yet unknown, with a sublime boldness, or rather an angelic quietness, he makes the section of the equator which nobody had yet traversed, traces across immensity a vast demarcation, draws from one pole to the other an ideal line which will divide the earth, in passing at a main distance of a hundred leagues to the west of the islands of Cape Verd and those of the Azores. To accomplish this astonishing geographical division, he chose precisely the only point of our planet which science would choose in our day: the singular region of the line without magnetic declination, where the transparency of the waters, the balminess of the air, the clearness of the atmosphere, the abundance of the submarine vegetation, the tropical resplendency of the nights, and the phosphorescence of the waves indicated in the unsteady empire of the billows a mysterious demarcation made by the omnipotent Creator.

"This vast calculation was the boldest conception that ever issued from the human intellect. Still, Columbus, without being astonished, without hesitating, without perhaps being aware of the vastness of his operation, calmly takes his calculations of demarcation, and simply demands that they be sent to Rome."

As might well be supposed, the letter of Columbus to the Spanish sovereigns produced intense sensation at court. The event was regarded as the most extraordinary and important one of their eventful reigns; the small territories of the Moors had been acquired after eight centuries of war, and with immense loss of human life and expenditure of treasure. Here, on the other hand, vast empires and boundless continents were acquired by the voyage of a small caravel! Besides all this, the glory acquired by Spain was imperishable. Columbus had proceeded as far as Seville. Here he received the sovereigns' letter, addressed "To Don Christopher Columbus, our Admiral of the Ocean Sea, Viceroy and Governor of the Islands discovered in the Indies," expressing their unbounded pleasure, inviting him to court, and suggesting preparations for another and more extensive expedition to the Indies. In obedience to their request, he made a memorandum of the ships, men, and supplies needed for another expedition, commenced the necessary preliminaries of preparation for the second undertaking, and started for the court at Barcelona, carrying with him the companions of his voyage, the six Indians he had brought from the Indies, and the many and interesting specimens of the productions, curiosities, and articles he had brought home with him. His journey from Seville to Barcelona was one continual triumphant procession. The people on the route turned out in mass to honor the great discoverer and to see the wonders he had brought back with him from the new world. His progress was impeded by the throngs of people, all pressing forward to see himself, the Indians, and the other wonders he displayed. The streets were crowded, the windows and balconies filled with eager and admiring spectators, the air was rent with applause, and ovation after ovation awaited the hero of the age as he passed from city to city. The wonders which the people saw only excited their imaginations to fill the newly discovered lands with other and more startling marvels. The court resolved to give him a triumphal reception at Barcelona, and here he arrived by the middle of April. As he approached a cavalcade of youthful courtiers, gayly dressed hidalgos, and the people of the city advanced to receive him. No Roman conqueror ever returned to the imperial city with more renown or honor. The arrangement of his suite was admirable—preceded by mariners of the Nina under arms, the royal standard borne by a pilot, and others bearing branches of unknown trees and shrubs, enormous calabashes, specimens of raw cotton, pimento, cocoas, ginger, and other products. The Indians, bearing ornaments of barbaric gold on their persons, and painted according to their native customs, advanced behind them; next were carried a great variety of living parrots, with their gorgeous plumage, and stuffed birds of rich and many colors, animals of unknown kinds, and plants of rare qualities and brilliant foliage; also Indian coronets, bracelets, and other barbarous decorations of gold. Then came the admiral, mounted on a splendid Castilian horse, and surrounded by a brilliant cavalcade of Spanish chivalry and aristocracy. The grand old city was in all its brightest attire; the streets, windows, balconies, and even the roofs were crowded with people to see these wonders of a new world, and the great and wonderful man who had discovered another hemisphere, with its islands and empires. The gold of the new world especially made a bright and fascinating show. The royal throne was erected in public, under a rich canopy of gold brocade, in a spacious saloon of regal splendor, and here Ferdinand and Isabella received the admiral in state, attended by the young Prince Juan, and by the grandees, dignitaries, and nobility of Spain. Though surrounded by the noblest of the Spanish chivalry, Columbus towered above all, and won admiration by his tall and dignified stature and carriage, the smile of conscious yet modest triumph, and the dignified expression of acknowledged worth. He was received by the sovereigns with the highest honors a subject could receive. They lifted him from his knees when he knelt to kiss their hands, and ordered him to be seated in their presence, a richly deco-

rated arm-chair having been provided for him. He now related, at their request, the great events he had achieved, described the various islands and lands he had discovered, and displayed the birds, animals, specimens of gold in the dust or in crude masses or in savage ornaments, and especially the living natives of the countries he had visited. The king and queen were moved to tears, and sinking upon their knees, all present following their example, the *Te Deum* was chanted with intense devotion and gratitude. Such was the grandeur, unity, enthusiasm, and devotion manifested by the entire assemblage—sovereigns, nobility, and people—on this memorable occasion, that Las Casas speaks of them all as " Christian souls enjoying a foretaste of the joys of Paradise." The discourse of Columbus on his discovery, on the new countries and peoples found, and on the productions of the new world, was marked with learning, scientific arrangement, rare and beautiful thoughts and illustrations, and with consummate wisdom. He seemed like one rarely and richly gifted. Dismissed with the highest honors, he was escorted to the lodgings prepared for him by the lords of the court, and by the populace.*
The city was given over to universal and unrestrained delight and exultation.

The news of the discovery of the western islands and countries produced a profound sensation throughout Europe. The illustrious Sebastian Cabot, first explorer or discoverer of our own coasts, then at the court of Henry VII. of England, acknowledged that the discovery was rather a divine than a human work.† Great cosmographers and mariners everywhere rejoiced. Rome was especially delighted with this great triumph of science, the opening of so vast and new a field of Christian zeal ; and the sovereign Pontiff, with the College of Cardinals and dignitaries of the Church and the ambassadors of all the nations there assembled, united in public manifestations of joy and services of thanksgiving. The delight of the learned world was well represented and expressed by the joyful tears shed at this great event by the learned Pomponius Lœtus.‡

---

* Las Casas, " Hist. Ind.," lib. i., cap. lxxvii. ; Helps, " Life of Christopher Columbus," ch. v. ; Muñoz, " Hist. del N. Mundo," t. i., liv. ; Barry's De Lorgues' " Columbus," p. 231 ; Tarducci's " Columbus," vol. i., pp. 233–36 ; Fernando Colombo, cap. xii.

† Hackluyt, " Collection of Voyages," p. 7.

‡ " Letters of Peter Martyr," lib. 153 ; Irving's " Columbus," vol. i., p. 273.

A great and representative historian and geographer of that time, a contemporary of Columbus, who had communicated the discovery to Pomponius Lœtus, the celebrated Peter Martyr, thus addresses that eminent scholar : " You tell me, my amiable Pomponius, that you leaped for joy, and that your delight was mingled with tears, when you read my epistle certifying to you the hitherto hidden world of the antipodes. You have felt and acted as became a man eminent for learning, for I can conceive no aliment more delicious than such tidings to a cultivated and ingenuous mind. I feel a wonderful exultation of spirits when I converse with intelligent men, who have returned from those regions. It is like an accession of wealth to a miser. Our minds, soiled and debased by the common concerns of life and the vices of society, become elevated and ameliorated by contemplating such glorious events." The event thus alluded to by the great and shining intellects of that age is also mentioned in many contemporaneous chronicles ; and yet, owing to the fact that the discovery was announced to the world, even by the great discoverer himself, as merely a discovery of the extreme and unknown parts of Asia, these allusions are brief and casual. Neither Columbus nor his most learned contemporaries knew the vastness and actual importance of the discovery ; much less did mankind in general. Had it been known that new continents, surrounded by oceans and similar in their relations to the earth to the Eastern continents, had been discovered ; had it been known that these continents would become the seats of great and free republics and empires, realizing the highest developments of civilization, of free government, and of civil and religious liberty, as we now enjoy them, the impression would have been far different ; the joy of mankind would have been more exultant and unbounded.

It was natural for the Count de Lorgues to take the religious rather than the scientific view of the subject, as he more particularly represents that phase of these events and of the life and work of Columbus, and yet, like the admiral himself, he recognizes the union of science and religion in the achievement. Thus he, while extolling the learning, science, and experience of Columbus, and especially his great common sense, yet attributes a supernatural character to the enterprise : " The superiority of Columbus, of his genius and of his grandeur, was owing to his religious faith." And again he says: "He who does not believe in the supernatural cannot comprehend Columbus." The great admiral himself attributes his success to the favor of Heaven. Scarcely had he retired from the presence of the sovereigns and from the public triumphs he received at Barcelona to his own private apartments, when, falling upon his knees, he made a vow to redeem the Holy Land from the hands of the infidels, and for this purpose to furnish from the immense incomes he expected to receive from the new world, within seven years, an army of four thousand horse and fifty thousand foot, and a similar force within the five following years. This vow was not only recorded in one of his letters to Ferdinand and Isabella, but was also communicated in a letter to Pope Alexander VI., to whom, in 1502, he gives the reasons for his inability up to that time to fulfil it. There is surely no trait more conspicuous in the character of Columbus than his acknowledged magnanimity.

The fame of Columbus was thus spread throughout the learned and civilized world. In Spain he stood at the highest point of honor a subject could attain. Admiral of the ocean, viceroy and governor-general, he stood as a man in the world almost without a peer. He received in public and in private the most unusual honors. Admitted freely to the royal presences, consulted by the king and queen on every detail of the second expedition, and on the general affairs of the Western lands; while the king took him for his companion in his trips on horseback in the city and country, having Columbus on one side and Prince Juan on the other, the queen created new armorial bearings for him, combining the royal arms of Castile and Aragon, the castle and the lion, with his own bearings, which were a group of islands surrounded by the waves of the ocean. The pension promised by the sovereigns to the one who should first discover land was awarded to him, because he had first seen the light on the shore. The highest dignitaries of the Church and the proudest of the Spanish nobility vied with each other in honoring the great discoverer, and many were the banquets and entertainments given in his honor. The Grand Cardinal of Spain, Mendoza, gave a great banquet in his honor, and it was on this occasion that the well-known anecdote of the egg is alleged to have occurred. Columbus was assigned the highest place at the banquet, seated under a raised dais, and served with covered dishes, like a monarch, each dish presented to him being tasted before him, according to royal etiquette. He received on all occasions the ceremonious honors due to a viceroy. While the distinguished company were at dinner, a courtier with more tongue than brains is said to have asked Columbus somewhat abruptly, and with envy toward a foreigner, whether he did not think that if he had not succeeded in discovering the Indies there was not in Spain some other person who would have been capable of doing so; Columbus, without making any other reply, according to this oft-repeated but unauthentic story, called for an egg, and when it was brought he asked any one of the company that could do so, to make it stand on end. Each one tried it, but failed, amid the laughter of the guests; then Columbus took the egg, and striking it gently on one end, so as to break it slightly, thus caused it to stand on one end. It was in this way that he showed how easy it seemed for any one to discover the new world after another had shown the way. This anecdote has been questioned. While Mr. Irving and other historians cite it as characteristic of the admiral's practical sagacity and readiness of expedients, others, such as the Count de Lorgues, while relating it, reject it as frivolous, and as a story of a mere juggler's trick, unworthy of and unlike the gravity and dignity of Columbus. Tarducci discredits the story entirely. Yet the anecdote is of universal popularity. Lamartine goes so far as to relate it as occurring at the table of King Ferdinand.

In keeping with the envious disposition of ungenerous minds to disparage the great discovery of Columbus, after it had been accomplished, various attempts were made to deprive him of the glory of his achievement. One of these unworthy efforts was an idle tale to the effect that Columbus received information of the existence of land in the western parts of the ocean from an old tempest-tossed pilot, who had been driven by violent easterly winds westwardly across the Atlantic, and on his return he and his companions were hospitably received by Columbus as guests in his house at Porto Santo; that one after another of the survivors of this expedition died, until only one, the pilot, whose name was afterward asserted to be Alonzo Sanchez de Huelva, survived; and he finally, like his companions, all exhausted by their recent hardships at sea, also died in the house of Columbus, bequeathing to him his written accounts of an unknown land in the West. Although a number of authors either accepted or repeated the story, as happened also with the invention that Columbus was never married a second time, it is now quite generally if not universally rejected as an invention of the envious to deprive Columbus of the well-merited glory of having discovered the new world. It has no greater foundation in fact than the fabulous island of St. Brandan, or the island of the seven cities, or the landing of Martin Behem, in the course of an African expedition, accidentally on the coast of South America. While a tempest-tossed and shipwrecked sailor, who, on being cast on shore, sickened and died, could hardly be believed to have been able to write out an account of his wanderings at sea, it must be remembered that the indigent condition of Columbus at Funchal, for thither we must transfer the story from Porto Santo, precludes the idea of his being able to entertain so many guests, or of his having a house of his own at all. Benzoni states that the story was expressly invented " to diminish the immortal fame of Christopher Columbus, as there were many (in Spain) who could not endure that a foreigner and an Italian should have acquired so much honor and so much glory, not only for the Spanish kingdom, but also for the other nations of the world."

The startling discovery by Columbus of a new route, as it was believed to be, to the Indies, was singularly made known first to Portugal, the rival of Spain in maritime discoveries and conquests, by the accident of his being driven by storm into a Portuguese port. The relations of Spain and Portugal became now more than ever strained. It was under such circumstances that Christian nations, fortunately, acknowledged a common head, an impartial arbitrator between nations, a recognized preserver of the peace of Christendom. Such were the sovereign Pontiffs in those days. There never was a case in the history of the nations when the peaceful intervention of arbitration was more necessary to prevent the outbreak of war, which would have been a war greatly detrimental to the prosecution of the most important geographical discoveries. Alexander VI. was now Pope. His predecessors, as early as 1438, had permitted the Spaniards to sail west and the Portuguese to sail south, as witnessed by the bulls of Popes Martin V. and Eugenius IV. Nicholas V. had subsequently confirmed these papal concessions, and, in 1479, the two rival maritime powers had agreed to respect each other's rights under these decisions. How far the Portuguese king had now kept the spirit of his agreement, when he permitted with impunity proposals to be made to him for the murder of Columbus, and basely accepted proposals for sending out a secret expedition to seize the western lands he had discovered and taken possession of for Spain, does not seem to be a question admitting of much doubt. In the mean time, Spain was hurrying its preparations to send out a second expedition under Columbus to secure and follow up its western discoveries. When Columbus landed in Portugal after discovering the supposed Indies, the king of that country plainly intimated to him that the lands he had taken possession of for Spain lay within the previous papal concessions made to Portugal, and was assured by Columbus to the contrary. Negotiations now followed between the two competing powers. Ferdinand was prompt in appealing to Rome for a confirmation of his possessions taken by Columbus, as Portugal had done under the predecessors of Alexander VI.

The part which Columbus may have taken in the matter of establishing the famous line of demarcation is one of the controverted points in his remarkable career. Roselly de Lorgues and other authors most partial to Columbus have contended that in his cell at the Convent of La Rabida, where he is believed to have rested in waiting for a summons to court from the sovereigns, after his return from his first voyage, Columbus was the first to conceive the thought of establishing a line of demarcation between the new countries of the earth that should belong respectively to Spain and Portugal,* and that he was the first to suggest the selection for this purpose of the line of no variation of the needle, which on his first outward voyage he had discovered at the distance of a hundred leagues west of the Cape Verd and the Azores islands. At this mysterious line there seemed to be a sudden change in the sky and stars, in the temperature of the air and sea; and the needle, which in approaching it had deviated to the east, here stood still, and on passing it commenced to deviate to the west, as if crossing a ridge of the earth, and the polar star described a daily circle of five degrees.† John Fiske simply relates the selection of the

---

* Dr. Barry's translation of Count de Lorgues' "Columbus," p. 221.
† Tarducci's "Life of Columbus," vol. ii., p. 76.

line of no deflection as an historical fact, giving rise to no controversy for him to enter upon; but Justin Winsor rather scoffs at the claim that Columbus had anything to do with the selection or suggestion of this line for the line of demarcation. His general style of handling controverted subjects in the career of Columbus, and he controverts many, is exemplified in the following passage on this subject: "To make a physical limit serve a political one was an obvious recourse at a time when the line of no variation was thought to be unique, and of a true north and south direction; but within a century the observers found three other lines, as Acosta tells us in his 'Historia Natural de las Indias,' in 1589; and there proved to be a persistent migration of these lines, all little suited to terrestrial demarcations. Roselly de Lorgues and the canonizers, however, having given to Columbus the planning of the line in his cell at Rabida, think, with a surprising prescience on his part, and with a very convenient obliviousness on their part, that he had chosen 'precisely the only point of our planet which science would choose in our day —a mysterious demarcation made by its omnipotent Creator,' in sovereign disregard, unfortunately, of the laws of His own universe!"*

It seems scarcely just or logical to dispose of the subject in this way. There are some uncontroverted facts which seem to throw light upon the claim thus made in behalf of Columbus. We do not know historically that he wrote a letter from his cell at La Rabida to Ferdinand and Isabella, suggesting the line of no variations as the line of demarcation between the possessions of Spain and Portugal. But we do know that immediately after the arrival of Columbus at Barcelona and his interviews there with the Spanish sovereigns, an ambassador was despatched to Rome to ask, and he obtained, from the Pope, Alexander VI., the establishment of a line of demarcation which would secure to Spain the exclusive right to the lands discovered by Columbus. The most important of all the facts bearing on the subject is that Columbus had recently discovered the line of no variation, and had necessarily taken a lively and leading interest in its nature, effects, and future possibilities of utility. One of the severest injunctions imposed on him was that he should steer

---

* Winsor's "Columbus," etc., p. 254.

clear of the dominions and discoveries of the Portuguese, and the rival claims of those two competing powers constituted one of the foremost and burning questions of the day. Columbus is known to have felt an intense interest in everything connected with or flowing from his own great achievement. The attendant circumstances would rationally point him out, in this remarkable event, as a figure scarcely less if not more important in fact and indirectly than either the King of Spain or the King of Portugal, or even the Pope. But for his services and achievements there would have been no need of a line of demarcation, nor would there have been known so ready a mode of solving the difficulty as the line of no variation. It was not to be supposed that so fervent a Catholic, and so prominent and indispensable an actor in the crucial events leading up to it, could have been a silent or indifferent witness of this remarkable exercise of the papal power and jurisdiction. It is far more probable that so ardent a supporter of the universal jurisdiction of the Popes as then exercised, as the arbitrators of Christendom—that one who was then contemplating his own proposal to the Holy See for another crusade to recover the Holy Sepulchre—should have been second to any one in suggesting this obviously necessary appeal to and recognition of the papal power. The heart and the face of Columbus were always turned to Rome.

Much speculation has been indulged in by theologians, publicists, and historians as to the origin of the power exercised by the Popes in disposing of temporal empires and kingdoms, and especially in partitioning among Christian princes the heathen and unconverted countries of the earth. The most extraordinary instance of the exercise of this power, the one which affected the right and ownership of an entire hemisphere or half of the earth, and which was most far-reaching in its scope and effects, was this very bull of Pope Alexander VI., the bull *Inter Cetera*, by which the famous line of demarcation was established between the two great maritime and discovering nations, Spain and Portugal. It is doubtful whether this power was ever traceable or was ever traced to the fictitious "Donation of Constantine." It was not of sudden creation; it was rather the offspring of the gradual growth of ages, of the exigencies of the kingdoms of the world, and the consent of princes. Popes Gregory VII., in the eleventh century, and Innocent IV., in the thirteenth, seem to have claimed such authority as inherent in the papacy, and Alvaro Pelayo, the Franciscan monk, and Agostino Trionfi, in the fourteenth century, also maintained it in its fullest extent, and maintained that the Popes were suzerains of the whole earth, and had absolute power to dispose not only of all Christian kingdoms, but also of all heathen lands and powers.* The Church has never defined such a power as among the powers conferred on the Popes by divine right. The only correct method of viewing the subject from the historical point of view, which recognizes the fact that such power was, indeed, exercised by the Popes in those centuries, is that its actual origin is historically traced to the consent of reigning sovereigns, and that, having served its purposes in those ages, wherein it was recognized, it has now ceased to exist or to be claimed The following passage from the recognized authority of the Most Rev. Francis Patrick Kenrick, Archbishop of Baltimore from 1851–63, will be read with conclusive effect upon all candid minds :†

" The bull of Alexander VI., fixing limits for the discoveries of the kings of Spain and Portugal, is frequently represented as the most extravagant instance of papal pretensions ; yet learned men, Protestant as well as Catholic, regard it only as a solemn sanction of rights already acquired according to the laws of nations, and as a measure directed to prevent war between Christian princes. It is certain, as Washington Irving‡ well observes, that Ferdinand and Isabella conceived, and in their application to the Pontiff stated, that their title to the newly discovered lands was, in the opinion of many learned men, sufficiently established by the formal possession taken of them by Columbus, in the name of the Spanish crown ; but they desired a public recognition of their right, lest others should profit by the discovery who had not shared in the enterprise. From the position which the Popes long occupied as fathers of princes and highest expounders of law and of the principles of justice, his act was the most solemn confirmation of the title, and the greatest safeguard against encroachment. The terms of ' giving, grant-

---

* Baronius, " Annales," tom. xvii., p. 430 ; Alvaro Pelayo, " De Planctu Ecclesiæ," 1350 ; Venice, 1560. See also a note on this subject in John Fiske's " Discovery of America," vol. i , pp. 455–58.

† " The Primacy of the Apostolic See Vindicated," Baltimore, 1855, pp. 314, 315.

‡ " Life and Writings of Christopher Columbus," l. v. c. viii., p. 186.

ing, and bestowing of the plenitude of authority,' are only designed to express in the fullest and strongest manner the pontifical sanction and confirmation. 'The Roman Pontiffs,' says Cardinal Baluffi, 'as universal fathers, not because they imagined themselves to be the lords of the whole earth, but in order to prevent the effusion of Christian blood, found themselves, at the epoch of the discovery of America, in circumstances which rendered it desirable that they should divide the countries, and mark mutual limits to the conquests of the nations that took arms against unknown nations.' * Wheaton, in his great work on international law, observes : ' As between the Christian nations, the Sovereign Pontiff was the supreme arbiter of conflicting claims; hence the famous bull issued by Pope Alexander VI. in 1493.' † 'This bold stretch of papal authority,' says Prescott,‡ ' was in a measure justified by the event, since it did, in fact, determine the principles on which the vast extent of unappropriated empire in the Eastern and Western hemispheres was ultimately divided between two petty States of Europe.' It should not surprise us that the right to give, as it were, a charter for the discovery of unknown lands to a national corporation in a Christian confederacy should be recognized in him whose office imposed on him the duty of spreading the Gospel throughout all nations. This temporal attribution might easily attach itself, by general consent, to his spiritual supremacy, the exercise of which, in the diffusion of religion, it facilitated, by the support and protection given in return by the princes whose enterprise was favored. The personal character of the Pontiff did not disqualify him, in their minds, from discharging the high function of arbiter between them; and Divine Providence gave to the world this sublime instance of the salutary influence of the papacy in directing an enterprise which has resulted in the discovery of the new world."

Mr. Fiske has well said : " As between the two rival powers, the Pontiff's arrangement was made in a spirit of even-handed justice." And again : " It was a substantial reward for the monarchs who had completed the overthrow of Mohammedan rule in Spain, and it afforded them opportunities for further good

---

* " L'America un tempo Spagnuola," da Gaetano Baluffi, Ancona, 1844.
† " Elements of International Law," Part II., chap. iv., p. 240.
‡ " Ferdinand and Isabella," vol. ii., chap. xviii.

work in converting the heathen inhabitants of the islands and mainland of Asia."*

In confirmation of the view that Columbus must have taken an important part in the selection of the papal line of demarcation in 1493, it may be mentioned that the question of this line was again raised in 1494, and the readjustment of it was under consideration at the urgent demand of Portugal, which was dissatisfied with the line as established by Pope Alexander VI., and then the Spanish sovereigns made a special and pressing communication to Columbus, who was then in Hispaniola, on the subject. While they informed him that the principles of an adjustment between Spain and Portugal had been agreed upon, informed him what they were, and requested him to respect them in the course of his discoveries, yet, as the adjustment of the same and the drawing of the proposed new line was so important as to render his presence in Spain and counsel at the convention desirable, he was requested to return to Spain and take part in this adjustment; and in case it was not in his power to leave the new world at that juncture, he was requested to send his brother Bartholomew, or any other competent person he should select for this service, and to send by such person the maps, charts, and designs, such as he might consider as of service in such a negotiation.† As neither Columbus nor Bartholomew could leave Hispaniola at that time, the admiral's brother Diego was fully instructed and sent to Spain to represent the admiral at this important conference.

After considering this subject, the able publicist, Francesco Tarducci, gives his clear judgment of the part taken by Columbus in this affair, as follows : " No doubt the idea of placing the line at that distance was suggested to the Pope by Columbus himself, who had derived it from the observation of various strange phenomena at that place."‡ Alexander VI. acted with extraordinary promptness in this affair—a promptness which indicated that the crisis between Spain and Portugal was urgent. Thus on May 3d, 1493, he issued his celebrated Bull of Demarcation, conferring upon Spain all lands already discovered or thereafter to be discovered in the western ocean, with jurisdic-

---

* "The Discovery of America," vol. I., pp. 454, 455.
† Irving's " Life of Columbus," vol. ii., p. 39.
‡ Tarducci's " Life of Columbus," Brownson's translation, vol. i., p. 246, note.

tion and privileges in all respects similar to those formerly bestowed upon Portugal; but, in further proof of the urgency of the case, Alexander VI. on the following day issued his second bull, whereby, in order to prevent any occasion of misunderstanding between the rival nations, he decreed that all lands discovered or to be discovered to the west of a meridian one hundred leagues west of the Azores and Cape Verd Islands should belong to Spain. It does not redound much to the credit of John II. of Portugal that he remained unsatisfied with the decision of the very tribunal he had on several previous occasions invoked in his own behalf. In the present concession to Spain, as in previous ones to Portugal, the favorable action of the Holy See was always based upon the condition that Portugal and Spain should send out missionaries for the conversion of the heathen nations to Christianity. Even now we find in the pages of Justin Winsor's book a reluctant admission that Columbus had exerted some influence in the selection of the line of demarcation, for he says: " It will be observed that in the placing of this line the magnetic phenomena which Columbus had observed on his recent voyage were not forgotten, if the coincidence can be so regarded. Humboldt suggests that it can." *

Amid the honors and dignities heaped upon Columbus from sovereigns, princes, nations, and pontiffs; amid the distractions and festivities of the rejoicing court; amid the engrossing labors and duties he sustained in preparing for his second voyage across the Atlantic, it is greatly to the honor of Columbus that his thoughts reverently turned to his venerable father, who was still surviving at Genoa, and who had lived to see and rejoice at the brilliant successes of his son. Columbus sent to his father a trusty messenger bearing the evidences of his filial love and devotion. At the same time, he requested his father to permit his younger brother, Diego Columbus, who was till then assisting his father at the trade of wool-combing, to come to him in Spain and enter the service of the sovereigns, under the admiral's command. The venerable father now willingly parted with his last remaining son. We shall subsequently see Giacomo, whose name in Spanish was Diego Colon, serving as aide-de-camp to the great admiral, and as governor *ad interim.*

---

* Winsor's " Columbus," p. 254.

Shortly after his arrival at Barcelona, Diego Columbus took a prominent part in a novel and truly interesting and important ceremony. The seven Indians whom Columbus had brought to Spain from the islands in the western ocean had been sedulously instructed in the Christian faith, and now all of them, of their own motion, asked for the privilege of receiving Christian baptism. They were found, upon examination, worthy of this grace, and the sovereigns resolved that the event should be celebrated with solemn religious pomp and grandeur. At the baptismal ceremony the king, Prince Juan, Don Diego Columbus, and several of the first grandees of the court were the sponsors or godfathers. The reason assigned, according to the Count de Lorgues, for Columbus not becoming one of the sponsors was, that he was the father of all the Indians, and the Church did not permit the father to become the godfather for his own children.*

During the diplomatic game which, as we have stated, was carried on between Ferdinand and his royal cousin and rival, John II. of Portugal, each sovereign was secretly struggling to be the first to dispatch a fleet to secure the islands and countries which Columbus had discovered as supposed parts of India. But Ferdinand was more crafty than his wily competitor, and he succeeded in being the first to send out his fleet; so that Portugal for a while was content to continue her explorations along the coast of Africa, until the Cape was doubled and the southern route to India accomplished. These expeditions engrossed the attention of Portugal for some years, and achieved success and honor for that kingdom.

Ferdinand and Isabella now bent all their energies to forward the sailing of the second expedition under Columbus, in order to secure to themselves the full measure of success in respect to the lands already discovered, and those which were yet to be reached. But in order that all the affairs of state relating to the Indies and the future prosecution of the great enterprises involved in the recent discoveries should be adequately promoted and administered, the sovereigns now commenced the foundation of that official and powerful organization which was afterward

---

* Tarducci's "Life of Columbus," vol. i., p. 243; Irving's "Columbus," vol. i., p. 285; De Lorgues' "Columbus," translated by Dr. Barry, p. 250.

so prominent as the Council of Indies. The selection of the officials to fill these important offices was not the most happy. Columbus was desirous of going to Rome in order to give the Sovereign Pontiff in person an account of his discoveries and of the discovered countries, and to receive the blessing of the Holy See; but the pressing duties which now occupied all his time prevented him from doing so, and he was compelled to meet and co-operate with the newly appointed officials presiding over the affairs of the Indies. The sovereigns had appointed as Director-General of the Marine one whom the Count de Lorgues, following Las Casas and other authors, justly described as a " worldly-minded ecclesiastic, Don Juan de Fonseca, Archdeacon of Seville, but a bureaucrat by instinct, and a brother to men in high credit with King Ferdinand ;" an appointment which was afterward the source of much of the vexations and injustices which Columbus had to endure, and an obstacle in the way of the western enterprises. Juan de Soria, a man who resembled Fonseca in his instincts and methods, was appointed Comptroller-General, and Francisco Pinelo was appointed Paymaster. All historians represent Fonseca as a man of great ability for business, for he not only retained his offices during life, but was successively promoted to the Sees of Bajadoz, Cordova, Palencia, and Burgos, and finally to the patriarchate of the Indies. Mr. Irving but expresses the general sentiment of history when he says that "he was malignant and vindictive ; and, in the gratification of his private resentments, not only heaped wrongs and sorrows upon the most illustrious of the early discoverers, but frequently impeded the progress of their enterprises." *

The offices of the Director-General of the Indies and of his officials was located at Seville; a custom-house was established at Cadiz for the trade of the Indies, and a correspondent office was directed to be founded in Hispaniola under the direction of Columbus. The strictest regulations were promulgated for the management of Indian affairs. Columbus now prepared to take his leave of the sovereigns; he received by their orders from Francisco Pinelo a thousand doubloons of gold for his expenses; an order was issued for supplying him and his five domestics gratuitously with all necessary entertainment wherever he

---

* Barry's De Lorgues' "Columbus," p. 251 ; Irving's "Columbus," vol. i., p. 282.

arrived; he was named Captain-General of the Fleet of the Indies, was authorized to make all appointments to office in the new government, the royal seal was confided to him to be affixed to such documents as he might issue in their names; and by a solemn act the sovereigns ratified and confirmed to him all the titles and privileges stipulated for by the compact entered into at Santa Fé. When he took his final leave of the king and queen he was conducted to his lodgings by the entire court with great pomp and honor. Thus loaded with honors, dignities, and power, Columbus repaired again to the active scenes of maritime preparation. The instructions he received for the government of the Indies were all based upon his own suggestions, and the prevalence of a zealous and devout impress is observable through all of them, which reflected the pious sentiments, characters, and aspirations of Isabella and Columbus. The conversion of the heathens was the great feature in the plans and instructions stamped upon the new government. Twelve apostolic men were appointed missionaries for the new spiritual vineyard to be cultivated in the western world, and a brief from Rome appointed Father Boïl, a religious of the Benedictine Order, to be Vicar-Apostolic of the Indies. This apostolic band was furnished with a complete ecclesiastical equipment for all religious services and functions, and the queen gave from her own royal chapel the ornaments and vestments for the most solemn ceremonies of the Church. This noble lady, like the admiral, had an earnest desire for the conversion of the natives, and from their gentleness and amiability of character it was hoped that a rich harvest of souls would be gained for the Lord. The strictest injunctions were given for the punishment of any acts of injustice or wrong which Spaniards might inflict on these innocent people. It would have been well if adequate power and means had been given to Columbus to enforce this order.

When Ferdinand heard, through his secret dispatches from Lisbon, of the designs of the Portuguese King to hasten an expedition intended to appropriate by an early possession the new countries in the western ocean to the crown of Portugal, orders were issued to Columbus and all the officers of the Spanish crown concerned in the Indian service that the second voyage to the Indies should be expedited, and for the sailing of the fleet as soon as possible. In order to defray the expenses of this noted expedition, two thirds of the church tithes were placed in the hands of Pinelo, the funds realized from the sale of the confiscated jewels and properties of the banished Jews, and in case these funds proved inadequate, Pinelo was authorized by a loan to raise the necessary amounts. The military stores and arms left from the war with the Moors were drawn into the service of the ships, provisions of all kinds were provided under requisitions of the crown, and artillery, powder, muskets, lances, corselets, cross-bows, and other arms and warlike articles provided. Columbus was clothed with fuller powers of appointment to office, and with unlimited powers for the government and management of the crews, of the ships, and all the establishments connected with the Indian countries. Rumors arriving from time to time that John II. was endeavoring to anticipate the sailing of the fleet by one of his own, though it was always treacherously announced that the Portuguese ships were merely destined for the African coast, there was a feverish anxiety in Spain to get the new fleet under sail, and all the energies and resources of the kingdom were bent to this object. Columbus having left the court at Barcelona on May 23d, he and Fonseca and Soria joined all their energies at Seville to expedite the embarcation of the new fleet of seventeen vessels. Pilots were engaged, and expert husbandmen, miners, carpenters, and mechanics of every trade were enlisted ; and horses for military service and for agricultural work were purchased, and cattle and animals of all kinds, seeds and implements for all purposes provided. Living plants, vines, sugar-canes, grafts, saplings were to be transplanted to the virgin soil of the new world. Great quantities of every kind of merchandise, besides trinkets, beads, hawks' bells, looking-glasses, munitions of war, medicines, wines and liquors, and hospital supplies for the sick.

The fame of this great expedition spread throughout Spain, and was bruited throughout the world. The greatest enthusiasm prevailed among all classes in Spain to join it, and the high and the low were led to seek admission to the opportunity of realizing the golden dreams which had been awakened by the glowing accounts of Columbus and his companions of the new countries in the west. While on the first voyage men had to be impressed and forced into the service of a forlorn yet brilliant hope, now it was impossible to answer the numerous applicants seeking acceptance or permission to embark. Some were led by the specimens of Indian gold exhibited in the admiral's triumphant entry into Barcelona to go, in the hope of soon returning with boundless wealth from the transatlantic mines; others would embark in the trade of Oriental spices, perfumes, pearls, and gems. The heroes of the Moorish war sought new fields for military prowess in the vast Indian empires, and many others sought official position, consequence, and emolument in the government of the Indies. Spanish hidalgos, cavaliers, and officers now pressed for permission to go to the new world along with laborers, mechanics, and tradesmen. To others the conquest and conversion of the heathens gave the new expedition the grandeur and chivalry of a new crusade. What glory might not be won on those distant shores by measuring strength, valor, and arms with the most famous cohorts of the Grand Khan! Several personages of distinction joined the expedition. Among these one of the most prominent and gallant was Don Alonzo de Ojeda, a nobleman distinguished for his personal beauty, agility, strength, fearlessness and undaunted prowess, who in the new world was to add to the laurels already won in the old.

There was another person of note in this second expedition, the good and learned friar, Antonio de Marchena, who, in the similarity of names and the confusion of data, has been singularly confounded by such writers as Navarrete, Humboldt, Irving, Tarducci, and De Lorgues, with that other noted personage in the history of Columbus and his discovery, Juan Perez de Marchena, the prior of the Convent of La Rabida.* But more modern and recent researches, aided by the publication of Las Casas's great work, have clearly shown that they were two different persons, the two friars de Marchena.† Deeply interested as she was in every detail of this second expedition, Queen Isabella wrote to Columbus, on September 5th, recommending him to rely not entirely on his own great knowledge, but to take

---

* Navarrete, "Col. Dipl.," No. lxxi.; Humboldt, "Cosmos," ii., p. 255, note xiv.; Tarducci's "Life of Columbus," Brownson's translation, vol. i., p. 255; De Lorgues' "Columbus," Barry's translation, p. 252.

† Las Casas, "Hist. Ind.," lib. i., cap. xxix., xxxi.; Harrisse, "Christophe Colomb," tom. i., pp. 341-72; tom. ii., pp. 227-231; Fiske's "Discovery of America," vol. i., p. 412; Winsor's "Columbus," p. 259.

with him the eminent astronomer, Fray Antonio de Marchena. This learned monk is the one of whom Columbus said that he was the only person who, from his first arrival in Spain, had always befriended him and never mocked at him. Of the learned men in Spain, Fray Antonio was probably the most accomplished astronomer, and he is supposed to have steadfastly upheld and supported Columbus from the beginning from scientific considerations, no less than from personal regard.

Still another famous personage, whose name is connected with the second expedition of Columbus to the new world, one who acquired unbounded fame from the discovery of the Indies by the admiral, and, by an almost unaccountable stroke of fortune, won a distinction which was due only to Columbus—that of giving his name to the new World. This was Amerigo Vespucci, whose name as Latinized was Americus Vespucius. He did not, however, as erroneously stated by Count de Lorgues and Dr. Barry, accompany the second expedition; his connection with it consisted in assisting his employer, Juanoto Berardi, a Florentine merchant then settled in Seville, who took part in the business preparations and contracts for the outfit of the voyage, and Americus was his clerk. He was then regarded as a man of arithmetical, cosmographical, and polite learning. Americus was at this time forty-two years of age, and it was during these busy days of preparation for the second voyage that Columbus saw for the first time and perhaps frequently the man, whose very name was destined to exert a potent influence on the fortunes and fame of the great discoverer.

Among the noted persons who sailed on this important expedition should be mentioned Giacomo Colombo, the younger brother of the admiral, who now assumed the corresponding Spanish name of Diego Colon, and who had remained with the father at Genoa until a summons from the successful discoverer of the Indies brought him to Spain; also Pedro Margarite, a gentleman from Aragon and favorite of King Ferdinand, whose name has not come down to us with honorable renown, as it might have done; the celebrated Juan Ponce de Leon, the hero and namer of Florida; Francisco de Las Casas, the father of the illustrious Bartolomé de Las Casas, historian, bishop and philanthropist, and the famous pilot, Juan de La Cosa, so noted for his maps and charts. It is no compliment to the above to name with them the notorious Roldan, the rebel, who afterward embittered the life and efforts of Columbus.

While the number of persons who were to be permitted to join the expedition was limited to one thousand, so great was the pressure for admission and participation in the expected glories, profits, and renown to be reaped from it, that the Spanish sovereigns yielded to the general importunity and increased the number of the fortunate ones, as it seemed at the time, to twelve hundred. The officers, missionaries, and men of various occupations in the pay of the crown amounted to five hundred; the others, persons of every grade and class, and of every age and condition, amounted to seven hundred. Even then many had to endure the disappointment of refusal; but at the last moment as many as three hundred more succeeded in surreptitiously getting on board the ships and secreting themselves until the fleet had sailed, thus increasing the entire number to fifteen hundred. Columbus, in his great zeal for the prestige and success of the important expedition, spared no effort and no expense to add to its efficiency and results. Thus the expenses of the preparations necessarily exceeded the estimates, and who could then estimate for so unexampled an enterprise? Fonseca and Soria complained much at this, and hesitated, and even refused to pass the admiral's accounts. Thus commenced the first outward manifestations of the jealousy and ill-will cherished by these officials against him. They went so far as to come into unpleasant conflict with him, and on several occasions to treat him with discourtesy and rudeness. Repeated reprimands from Ferdinand and Isabella only served to suppress the outward exhibition of a hatred now more than ever secretly cherished. When it came to passing the personal accounts and requisitions of the admiral, their malice could not be disguised. They demurred to his requisitions for footmen and other domestics for his personal and immediate service, his household and retinue, pretending to regard these requisitions as superfluous, and alleging that he had at his service and command the whole *personnel* of the fleet. The sovereigns gravely reprimanded these officious placemen for their unworthy treatment of so eminent a person. Columbus, on his part, insisted now, as he had done in his negotiations with the sovereigns, upon the full measure of his terms and rights. Orders from Barcelona now settled the dispute by fixing his domestic retinue at ten squires afoot bearing swords,* and his other domestics at twenty; and Fonseca was cautioned against interfering with the wishes or comforts of the admiral, or opposing his requisitions. He and his subordinates obeyed, but these transactions only added to the rancor of the admiral's enemies, and it was reserved for Fonseca and his abettors to vent their malignant hatred against the man in various petty ways in the future prosecution of the enterprises in the new world. As long as he lived they contrived to throw impediments in his way, while pretending or not seeming to do so.

Again, while the expedition was on the eve of sailing, the Spanish sovereigns received secret advices of preparations made in Portugal for the sailing of a ship, ostensibly to the African coast, but with concealed orders to sail westward, and circumvent the prosecution of Spanish discoveries under Columbus. The latter now received the most urgent requests from the sovereigns not to delay the sailing of his fleet another hour. The expedition consisted of three large ships of heavy burden and fourteen caravels. The admiral's ship was the Gracious Mary, and in addition to and including some of the remarkable personages I have mentioned as going on the expedition, there were on board the admiral's ship, besides himself, Gil Garcia, alcalde-mayor; Bernal Diaz de Pisa, lieutenant of the Comptroller-General; Sebastian da Olano, receiver of the crown taxes; Dr. Chanca, the chief physician; a number of Spanish hidalgos; Melchior Maldonada, cousin of the cosmographer of that name; two of the baptized Indians now returning to their homes, one of whom had for his godfather Diego Columbus, and was named after him Diego Colon, and Diego Columbus himself, the younger brother of the admiral. At the moment of sailing the city of Cadiz and its beautiful harbor were alive with excitement, with bustle, immediate preparation, the hurrying to and fro of members of the expedition and their friends, and many were the sympathetic and heart-felt adieus then fervently exchanged. The scene was gay and joyous, and the old city and its harbor had never looked so brilliant, so active, so enchanting. There were seen the cavalier, the navigator, the adventurer and

---

* Tarducci's "Life of Columbus," Brownson's translation, vol. i., p. 254; Navarrete, "Col. Dipl.," vol. i., p. 225; Irving's "Life of Columbus," vol. i., p. 298.

speculator, the sailor, the artisan, the husbandman, the pilot, and, last but not least, the zealous and venerable missionary; while others were seeking worldly honors or wealth, the last was intent on gaining souls for heaven, the imperishable treasures of immortality.

In the midst of this scene of hurrying preparation and of ardent sensations, Columbus was the object of universal interest, admiration, and veneration. Every one pressed forward to see and honor the discoverer of continents. His lofty stature, his commanding presence, and his noble and engaging expression of countenance attracted every eye, and made every tongue eloquent in his praise. He was attended by his two sons, Diego and Fernando, who had come to spend the last moments with their illustrious parent, and to bid him farewell. The admiral had been for several days quite unwell in consequence of the great labors of mind and body which he had undergone in the preparations made for hastening the urgent voyage. But when a favorable wind decided the selection of the day for sailing, his mind rallied under the excitement of duty and hope, and he sailed with his fine fleet from the ancient and renowned port of Cadiz on the morning of September 25th, 1493.

CHAPTER IX.

> "There is a traveler, sir ; knowns men,
> Mariners, and has plough'd the sea so far
> Till both the polls have knock'd ; he has seen the sun
> Take coach, and can distinguish the color
> Of his horses, and their kinds."
> —BEAUMONT AND FLETCHER'S "SCORNFUL LADY."

THE crucial line had been drawn by Pope Alexander VI., by which the demarcation between the east and west was established. Spain and Portugal had separate fields assigned to them for discovering and taking possession of the unknown lands and waters of the earth's surface, and for extending the realms of Christendom. Columbus, on his second voyage, steered clear of the islands within the realms assigned to Portugal, and of all her possessions. The line of demarcation was his own discovery. It proved the solution of the question of peace or war. Making for the Canaries, he touched at the Grand Canary on October 1st, and, departing the next day, he anchored at Gomera, where he took in wood and water, and procured, for stocking the new countries, calves, goats, and sheep, which he thought could be more easily acclimated there than animals taken from Spain. He also purchased eight hogs, which formed the parent stock for nearly all the abounding swine of the islands and of the new continent, and which now supply Europe and other parts of the earth with American pork. So also with the domestic fowls and the seeds of oranges, lemons, melons, bergamots, and various orchard seeds, all which were thus introduced by the discoverer of the new world himself.

After sailing from Gomera, the admiral handed to the commander of each ship a sealed letter, to be opened only in case of separation, and by which they were instructed to steer for Hispaniola and for the residence of Guacanagari. It is said that he purposely kept his exact course somewhat in doubt, in order to prevent the Portuguese from becoming acquainted with it. Becalmed among the Canaries, it was not until October 13th that he could get under weigh with a favorable wind. He directed his course to the southwest with the view of reaching first the Caribbean Islands, of which he had received such strange accounts from his Hispaniola Indians. No seaweeds were encountered on the voyage, but the appearance of a swallow on one day and on others the prevalence of sudden showers of rain convinced the admiral that land was not far off. Toward the end of October a severe thunder-storm, which lasted four hours, greatly alarmed the sailors, but their confidence was restored at seeing the play of the wavering flames of lightning among the masts and rigging of the ships, which was regarded as a sign of good omen. They saw in them the apparition of St. Elmo, whom they would usually, and according to ancient marine traditions, salute with reverence, and whose appearance was not infrequently received by mariners with tears of joy. The admiral felt calmly confident of safely reaching his destination, because he had from the beginning of the voyage placed it under the protection of the patroness in whose honor he had named his ship, the Gracious Mary, and he had promised to give her name to islands he would discover. Such was his experience and good judgment as a sailor, that he announced his belief that land was near on Saturday, November 2d. On the following day the land appeared, and a hymn of thanksgiving, the " Salve Regina," was joyously chanted by all the crews. As the ships speeded on, one island after another came in sight. He named the first island Dominica, in honor of the Sunday on which it was discovered, and the second island he called Maria Galanta ; and here he landed, bearing the royal banner, and took possession for the Spanish sovereigns. The largest island of the group he called Guadaloupe, in honor of Our Lady of Guadaloupe, in Spain. Columbus, with his usual sagacity, had struck the very centre of the Caribbean Islands, as he had desired, and on landing at the island of Guadaloupe, which the natives called Turuguiera, and visiting the cabins, which they had just abandoned on his approach, he saw the evidences that the natives were cannibals. In the cabins were also found provisions, cotton spun and unspun, hammocks, utensils of earthenware, bows and arrows and domesticated geese, and parrots of many-colored plumage. But the sight of human bones, the remnants of their shocking repasts, and human skulls, which were apparently used as vases for domestic purposes, greatly agitated the Spaniards. The natives fled on the approach of the visitors, who, having continued their course about two leagues and anchored in a convenient harbor, and having landed, saw a number of deserted villages on the shores, and finally succeeded in capturing a boy and several women. From their captives they learned that the natives of this and two adjoining islands were in league against the others, and in warlike expeditions supplied themselves with human food by capturing and feasting upon their enemies. Not only did they kill and consume their captives, they even fattened them for their cannibal feasts. Their principal weapons were bows and arrows, the latter being pointed with poisoned shells or bones of fishes.

At evening Diego Marque, captain of one of the caravels, and eight men, who had gone into the country, had not returned to their ship, and the admiral and his companions concluded that they had been killed and eaten by the natives. Next day scouting parties well armed were sent to scour the island in search of the missing Spaniards; trumpets were sounded and guns discharged, but these guides did not bring back the wanderers. The scouting parties visited many towns, and had their feelings much disturbed by seeing human limbs suspended to the beams of houses, and they saw the suspended head of a young man still bleeding, portions of his body roasting before the fire, and other portions being boiled together with the flesh of parrots and geese. The cannibal warriors were absent on one of their inhuman expeditions, the women, who were expert archers and almost as masculine as the men, remaining at home to defend the country from invasion and the villages from plunder. Columbus allowed nothing to be taken which belonged to them. As the missing party had not been found or heard from, Alonzo de Ojeda was sent out in search of them with forty men, and, after penetrating far into the interior, returned without them. In the mean time, Columbus, who was anxious to reach Hispaniola, had caused the ships to take in wood and water, and was preparing to sail, though unwilling to do so without recovering the lost part of his crews. Eight days had elapsed, the fleet was about to sail, when at last, to the great joy of all, Diego Marque and his companions made their appearance at the shore, and were received on the fleet now ready to sail. They brought with them ten Indian women and boys. They had not throughout their wanderings met with a single man; they had lost their way in the dark and trackless forest, had suffered with hunger, fatigue and fear, and returned to the fleet with haggard and exhausted aspects, and felt like men just rescued from a certain death. Columbus, while commiserating their sufferings, regarded their conduct as a serious breach of discipline, and from a sense of duty he put the captain under arrest, and stopped a part of the rations of the men. As the fleet was ready to weigh anchor when the wanderers reappeared, no further time was lost, and the fleet sailed on November 10th, steering to the northwest.

While steering through this beautiful archipelago, the admiral discovered island after island. The first, a high and picturesque island, was wholly depopulated by the Caribs in their predatory expeditions in search of human food. This he called Montserrat, in honor of the celebrated sanctuary of the Virgin Mother of the hermitage of Montserrat in Spain. He wrote: "The Caribs have devoured all the inhabitants." The next island was named Santa Maria del Rotunda, and the third Santa Maria la Antigua, now known by the abbreviated name of Antigua. The third day brought the Spaniards in contact with the Caribs. Landing on an island which showed some signs of habitation and civilization, a party was sent on shore for wood and water, and to obtain information. They entered a village, which was deserted by the men, and secured several women and boys, who were captives from other islands. As the boat was returning, the men saw a canoe turn a point of the island and come in view of the ships; it was occupied by four men and two women, all of whom were so amazed and so intently gazing at the ships that they did not observe the movement of the Spaniards' boat, which came in between them and the shore, until to their amazement their retreat was cut off. As soon as they saw this they all seized their bows and arrows and furiously attacked the Spaniards, who covered themselves with their bucklers, but not until two of them had been wounded. The women fought as furiously as the men, handled the weapons with equal strength and skill, and one of them discharged an arrow with such force as to penetrate through and through a stout buckler. The Carib canoe was overturned by the boat of the Spaniards by running against it; the men and women in the water were expert swimmers; they discharged their arrows as well from the water as from the boat. They all escaped except one, and such was the ferocity of this savage, that even when bound in chains and in the hands of the Spaniards he was as fierce and defiant as ever. The natives used poisoned arrows, and one of the Spaniards died a few days afterward from a poisoned arrow with which he had been wounded by one of the Carib women. The Carib prisoner also died of a wound he received in the struggle with the Spaniards.

Continuing his course, the admiral discovered many more islands. To one he gave the name of Holy Cross; to another, St. John Baptist; and to another, St. Ursula; and a group of islands he named the Eleven Thousand Virgins, in honor of those who were the companions of St. Ursula in martyrdom, according to one of the most interesting traditions of the Middle Ages. Some of these islands were well inhabited by people, who lived in neat cottages, showed ingenuity in their houses and gardens, and defended themselves from the Caribs by the use of bows and arrows and the war club. To this island had fled the entire remaining population of the other islands ravaged by the Caribs, and here they were all united under one cacique. The admiral wrote most minute and accurate accounts of these cannibals, which deeply interested the scholars of Europe. The learned had doubted the stories of human flesh-eaters, which they regarded as myths of former times, but now the accounts of the Lestrigonians and of Polyphemus had become authenticated by the description given by Columbus of the Caribs in the fifteenth century, and their repasts on human flesh. The existence of this fierce tribe, in the midst of the other and neighboring islands inhabited by gentle, peaceful, and unwarlike people, was a singular historical, social, and ethnological fact. While prejudice and fear have, no doubt, tended to exaggerate their cruel ferocity and shocking love for human flesh for their food, there can be no question of their existence as a distinct tribe and of their being cannibals, of their warlike habits and merciless inroads upon their weaker and more peaceful neighbors. Inquiries by the learned have led to the general adoption of the view that they were a colony of the warlike people inhabiting the deep valleys of the Appalachian Mountains; that they had fought their way across the northern continent until they reached the end of the Florida peninsula, and thence made their way, from island to island, until they had founded their permanent home in the group of islands of which Guadaloupe was the centre. Traces of this fierce tribe are found in the South American Continent and through its interior, and even as far as the southern ocean, for among the aborigines of Brazil were found Indians calling themselves Caribs. Wherever their descendants have thus been traced they formed a contrast with the other populations or tribes by their greater strength, endurance, and fearlessness.*

The admiral now took leave of his fierce acquaintances, the Caribs, and with a sagacity and memory for which he was remarkable, he steered almost directly for Hispaniola, though he had never traversed this route before, and none of his former companions recognized the island when his superior discernment confidently pointed it out to them. On November 22d the fleet arrived off the eastern extremity of Hispaniola, the Hayti of the natives, and while the others were eager to land after a long voyage and enjoy the delights of this favored land, as described to them by those who had accompanied the admiral on the first voyage, the latter was painfully anxious to revisit the colony and garrison of La Navidad and learn the results of the effort to engraft European civilization on the new world. Having had occasion to send a party ashore to bury a young Biscayan, who had died on board one of the ships from a wound received in the conflict with the Caribs, the news of the arrival of the great fleet of ships from the clouds was soon spread among the inhabitants, and many visited the fleet with invitations to the admiral and his companions to land, and with promises of much gold. One of the converted Indians who had been brought back from Spain was liberated by the admiral, after being handsomely dressed in fine clothes and well provided with presents, in the hope that his accounts would predispose the natives favorably. But this Indian is supposed to have been murdered by his countrymen, envious of his wealth in raiment, for no tidings were afterward received of him. There still remained on board another converted Indian, the godson and namesake of Diego Columbus, who continued to the end true to his new faith and to his new friends. The admiral declined all invitations to visit this part of

---

* Irving's " Life of Columbus," vol. i., p. 318 ; "Hist. Nat. des Iles Antilles," Rochefort ; Barry's De Lorgues' " Columbus," p. 267.

the island, and hastened on toward La Navidad. On November 25th he anchored off Monte Christi, and was observant of the country in hopes of finding a more suitable place for a permanent settlement. Here, while some of the sailors were wandering along the shore, they descried the dead bodies of a man and boy, so far decomposed as to baffle all conjecture as to whether they were Indians or Spaniards ; but the man had a cord of Spanish grass around his neck, and his arms were tied to a stake in the form of a cross. This discovery produced a deep gloom in the mind of Columbus and of all his followers, and sad apprehensions as to the fate of the garrison of La Navidad. On the following day a party of Spaniards visited the shore, and to their dismay they found, in a spot some distance from the place where they had seen the dead bodies the day before, two other dead bodies, and now there was no doubt as to their being Spaniards, for one of them had a long beard. The dread apprehensions thus awakened were not wholly allayed by the confidence and frankness with which the natives visited the ships, and yet the admiral could but hope that his colony might yet be found in safety and health.

The admiral and his fleet reached the harbor of La Navidad on the evening of November 27th, and, as it was too late to land, he anchored a league from the shore ; but he could not wait till morning to ascertain the fate of his colonists. He accordingly had two cannons fired, but the only response was their own echo along the shore ; no light appeared on land to show there was life in the colony, no shout of welcome greeted their ears ; silence and darkness reigned where the first European colony had been planted. At midnight an Indian canoe approached the admiral's ship, and the occupants, calling out, asked to see him. Seeing and recognizing him, they entered his ship. One of the Indians was a cousin of the friendly cacique, Guacanagari ; and, on being questioned, the Indians told the admiral that some of the Spaniards had been carried off by disease, others had fallen victims to others in a quarrel among themselves, and others had gone into the country and taken Indian wives ; that Guacanagari had been attacked by Caonabo, the savage chief of Cibao, had been wounded and defeated in the engagement, his village was burned, and the good cacique lay wounded in a neighboring hamlet. As he could not come in person to welcome the admiral, he had sent these envoys. Sad as the news was, the admiral was relieved by the thought that the garrison had not been murdered by the natives, and he hoped soon to recall those who had gone into the country. His kindly nature led him to take the most favorable view of the situation, and all the officers and sailors enjoyed a feeling of relief and a ray of hope. But on the following day Guacanagari did not come to the admiral, as he had promised by his deputies, and instead of seeing the harbor and the shores swarming with Indians, eager to welcome him and to give and receive presents, the scene was one vast wilderness, buried in silence and gloom. After a day's weary delay and sad disappointment, Columbus sent a boat's crew on shore to look for the Spaniards and the garrison; but alas! these returned with dejected looks that told the sad story before they had spoken a word. They found the fortress a ruin, with its palisades beaten down, and it had evidently been sacked and burned. Chests broken open, decaying food and shreds of tattered garments were all that remained. Neither Spaniard nor Indian was there, but they saw at a distance one or two natives watching them from the woods, and disappearing on perceiving that they were seen. With thoughts most gloomy and sad the admiral went ashore next day in person, and having gone directly to the site of the fort, not only saw the desolation and ruin of all, but also visited the site of the burned village of Guacanagari. Both Spaniards and Indian allies had met with one sad and similar fate. A slight relief was experienced in the thought and hope that Guacanagari had not proved a traitor.

Recalling his instructions to Arana, he ordered his men to search for the spots in which he might have buried the gold he gathered, and to look into the wells to see if it was hidden there. He went in his boats to explore the coasts and neighboring country, but all he found was a deserted village containing such articles as stockings, European cloth, a new Moorish robe, and other articles that the Spaniards could not be supposed to have willingly parted with. The treasure was not found in pit or well, but they discovered the graves of eleven Spaniards, so long buried that the grass had grown over them. A few Indians timidly showed themselves. By finally assuring them they became confidential and communicative, and Columbus learned gradually from them the appalling story of the awful fate which had destroyed, in its first effort, the transplanting of the European race and its civilization to the new world.

Had the garrison of European intruders been overpowered by the swarming hordes of natives and destroyed by brute force or vastly preponderating numbers, or had their Indian friend and ally, Guacanagari, turned traitor and betrayed to their destruction those to whom he pledged his protection and offered his hospitality, the case would not have been so discouraging. Time, repeated efforts, and the certainty of European success and power in the end, would have reassured the minds and hearts of the admiral, of the Spanish sovereigns, of the Christian Church and missionaries of the faith, and of the great and good and learned friends of human progress, the leading men of the times. But that this first footprint of European society should have been obliterated by the baseness and sordidness of European crimes and vices; that this first germ of Christianity, transplanted to the virgin soil of the Western Hemisphere, should have perished by the misdeeds of the very Christians that were its heralds, were facts most humiliating, at once to our civilization and to our religion. In history and in all human efforts results are greatly dependent upon the agents selected to accomplish them. Withering was the contrast between the virtues, wisdom, and patriotism of Columbus, of the Spanish Queen, and of the Christian scholars and apostles of Europe, on the one hand, and the vices, the recklessness, and the sordid avarice of the first European colonists, who were selected to found the Christian faith and Caucasian civilization among the heathen and savage nations of the western world. With the exception of Arana, their commander, they were mostly men of the lowest grades of society, and were steeped in the worst vices and passions of the most degraded classes of human society, without possessing the virtues which are common to all.

During the admiral's visit to the desolated site of the ruined fort other Indians gradually came thither, and among them came a brother of Guacanagari, escorted with guards, who saluted Columbus in Spanish, and related to him the same distressing and humiliating history he had already learned from the natives; and yet more forcibly from the desolation he saw around him than from the decaying corpses of the Spaniards exhumed, he learned the history of this sad result. Oviedo* relates in detail this story, at once a disgrace to civilization and a betrayal of religion. Nothing had been left undone or unspoken by Columbus, when he confided the cause of mankind in its advance from the Eastern to the Western Continent, that might secure its safety and its success. The men he selected for this all-important task were the best his limited resources would afford; but, with the exception of Don Diego de Arana and one or two others, they proved unfit for the noble work they undertook, and faithless to the exalted mission they had to perform. His wise and far-seeing counsels and admonitions to these men vanished from their minds with the disappearance of his ship on its homeward course from their sight. Ordinary regard for their own safety, and for the restraints which their position as a handful of strangers in a far distant world and surrounded by strange and heathen tribes of savages imposed upon them, should have been sufficient to guide them in paths of order, discipline, self-restraint, and honor. That they should have yielded, almost immediately, to every excess in their conduct toward the natives, and to the worst impulses in their dealings and intercourse with each other, are facts which illustrate the depths of depravity to which human nature may sink. While a portion of the Spanish garrison avariciously sought to despoil the natives of every piece of gold they possessed, even the ornaments attached to their persons, by the most rapacious and unjust means, or to wrest from them everything of value; others, to whom Guacanagari had already allowed two or three female companions, yielded to such gross sensuality as to seduce the wives and daughters of the natives. They quarrelled over the dishonest booty they had wrested from the Indians, as well as in their struggles for the companionship of the Indian women. Avarice and lust were the characteristic vices exhibited by the men, whom the Indians received with veneration as guests from heaven. The authority of Don Diego de Arana was set at defiance. The two lieutenants whom Columbus had named to Arana to succeed him in the command, in case of his death, showed their unfitness by their insubordination to their own commander, and went so far as to assert in

---

* "Hist. Ind.," lib. ii., cap. 12; Barry's De Lorgues' "Columbus," p. 270; Irving's "Life of Christopher Columbus," vol. i., p. 326.

themselves an authority equal or superior to his. Finally, having killed a man named Jacomo in their broils and struggles for command, and not having succeeded in supplanting Arana, they revolted with nine others, and marching forth with these and with a number of their women, they wended their way to the famed regions of the notorious Caonabo, where rumor had located unbounded treasures of gold. But Caonabo, a prince of Caribbean origin and birth, himself an intruder and conqueror in this once peaceful island, had no sooner secured these formidable visitors within his power, than he slaughtered them all with savage ferocity. Other revolting parties deserted the fortress and went in small bands to different parts of the island in search of gold. And again there were other parties of three or four who deserted the garrison and marched and marauded through the country, forcing themselves upon the Indians, consuming their provisions, carrying off their wives and daughters, and cruelly treating the men with wantonness and dishonor. The protection of the good Guacanagari scarcely sufficed to protect the Spaniards from native vengeance in their crimes and vices.

The brave and loyal Arana remained, like a true soldier, at his fortress, true to his honor, to his country and his race, and loyal to his relative Columbus, the husband of Beatrix Enriquez de Arana. But there were only ten Spaniards with him, constituting the garrison. The others were quartered in houses outside the fort. Confiding in the protection of Guacanagari and the friendship of his subjects, in whose dominions the fortress stood, the Spaniards at the fort relaxed their discipline by omitting to keep up a strict guard at night, little supposing that a more distant enemy would take advantage of their confidence. The wily and fierce Caonabo had no sooner massacred the Spaniards who had entered his own dominions, than he conceived a plan for slaughtering the remainder of the Spaniards in the fort. He ascertained that no guard was kept at the post. It was at the dead of night that this savage chieftain, at the head of his warriors, rushed with savage yells and imprecations upon the garrison and gained possession of the fort before the Spaniards could recover from sleep or defend themselves. The houses outside, in which other Spaniards were living, were surrounded and set on fire. All the Spaniards were slaughtered in cold blood, except eight, who escaped, and rushing into the water, were drowned. This cruel massacre was not alone the work of Caonabo and his tribe; other caciques and their tribes, who had suffered from the pillage and outrages of the Spaniards, joined to make up a numerous army bent upon revenge. The faithful Guacanagari and his subjects rushed to the defence of their friends and allies, but his unwarlike followers could not stand up against the fierce attacks of Caonabo's warriors; they were badly defeated and dispersed; Guacanagari was wounded by a stone thrown by the hand of Caonabo; his village was burned, and he was forced to seek shelter and concealment in the woods.

It was thus that the Spaniards by their misconduct and vices brought not only ruin upon themselves, but also disaster and destruction to their innocent native allies. The prestige of civilized man was lost in the eyes of the savage; the cause of Christianity was lowered by the crimes of Christians themselves below the level of paganism; the civilization of the Caucasian suffered in comparison with primitive and heathen barbarism.

While Christopher Columbus, that explorer and discoverer of continents, that herald of civilization, that Christian gentleman, had done all that his wonderful foresight could do to prevent the calamities he now realized, his sanguine nature drew new energy from disaster. His thoughts now were bent on the selection of another and more suitable spot for the European settlement, and a commission was appointed, under the presidency of Melchior Maldonado, to explore the country for this purpose. While coasting to the eastward on this duty, Maldonado encountered a canoe containing two Indians on their way to visit the caravel. One of these Indians was recognized as the brother of Guacanagari, who, on boarding the ship, entreated the captain to visit the cacique, who was then confined at the village, suffering from his wound. On complying with this request Maldonado found the cacique resting in his hammock, and attended by seven women, in a village of about fifty houses. Guacanagari manifested his sorrow at not being able to visit the admiral, related how the Spaniards had been massacred by Caonabo and other hostile caciques, how the fortress and houses of the Spaniards had been burned, and how he and his subjects had suffered in their efforts to succor the Christians. Believing the accounts of the cacique, the Spaniards carried his invitation to the admiral to visit him, and they were accompanied on their return by the brother of Guacanagari, who was sent to urge its acceptance.

The admiral accepted the invitation of the cacique. On the following day he landed in state, accompanied by his staff officers and the seventeen captains of the caravels, all dressed in their richest attire and glittering with arms and armor. Guacanagari received this august and brilliant party with great emotion, and in his hammock extended to them every honor and hospitality. He again related in detail the recent disasters, not omitting the part he and his subjects had taken in defence of the Spaniards, pointing to the destruction of his own residence and the wounds received by himself and many of his followers as evidences of their sincerity. Columbus was moved by the narrative and by the tears of the prince, and gave full faith to his words. He requested Dr. Chanca and the skilful surgeon of the expedition to examine and treat the cacique's wound; the latter readily submitted his leg to examination, and while the doctors could discover no contusion or bruise, even on a second examination in the open light, the cacique expressed a great sense of pain, and shrank with suffering when the injured part was handled. Columbus gave generous presents to the prince and his attendants, and the latter was munificent, according to his means, and gave in return eight hundred beads of the ciba stone, which were esteemed of great value, one hundred beads of gold, and three small calabashes of gold dust. With royal refinement he regarded his generosity as greatly outdone by the admiral's presents of glass beads, hawks' bells, knives, pins, needles, small mirrors, and copper ornaments. The cacique expressed great joy at the admiral's announcement of his intention to settle in his vicinity, though he informed the latter that the spot was unhealthy. Columbus addressed the prince in zealous appeals that he would accept the Christian faith, and requested him to receive and wear around his neck a medal of the Virgin Mother until he should be baptized. The cacique was anxious to do whatever the admiral requested, but he was not prepared to receive the faith which had been so dishonored by those who had professed it, and if the medal was an emblem of the religion which did not restrain the gross licentiousness of the garrison, he shrank from wearing it. Even after the kind words of the admiral and the friendship he bore him had induced him to wear the medal, the king seemed uneasy with this token of the religion professed by the garrison.

Companions of Columbus, who had not witnessed the unbounded kindness and princely bearing of Guacanagari at the first visit of the Europeans to his shore, now distrusted the sincerity of the chief and the truthfulness of his statements about the recent disasters. Father Boïl, the spiritual superior or vicar apostolic, united with these, and he was convinced of the heathen's bad faith when he saw the bandage removed from his leg showing no exterior appearance of a wound, and more especially when he saw his reluctance to receive the blessed medal. He accordingly urged the admiral to arrest and deal with him in the most summary manner; but the milder nature of Columbus led him to do justice to his friend, to wait for undoubted proofs of his treachery, and even then to act with moderation, and with a desire to maintain as long as possible peaceful relations with the natives. Most of the colonists sustained the wiser and humane view of Columbus toward the native chief, but the over-zealous vicar apostolic and some others not only differed from him, but even entertained resentment at the just decision of the admiral.

The friendly chief accompanied the admiral to his ships notwithstanding his lameness, and on boarding the flag-ship, although he had seen the caravel on the first voyage, he was exceedingly astonished at all he saw, especially at the numerous and powerful fleet and its equipment, at the great ship of the admiral, at the goods and implements brought out, at the cattle, asses, sheep, swine, and goats, and, more than all, at the Andalusian horses. His amazement was unbounded.

But the tender-hearted chief was not wholly engrossed with his celestial visitors, but was also deeply interested in some of the passengers, especially in the ten female native women, whom the ships' crews had rescued from the Caribs, and whom he saw on the Gracious Mary. But his sensitive feelings in their regard became immediately centred in one of their number, a young and handsome female, who had already been named by the Spaniards Donna Catalina, who was lofty and queenly in her appearance and bearing. The susceptible cacique was seen to speak to her with special interest and with marked expressions, and, though their dialects were different, a new-born sentiment, mutual and effective, made them perfectly comprehend each other. It was thus that Guacanagari and Donna Catalina, in the presence of all and without being suspected by any, entered into an engagement with each other, and they would certainly meet again. The admiral entertained the king at collation, and mutual interchanges of friendship were made. The intelligent native, while realizing the ever-true and unchanging cordiality of Columbus, with native keenness and observation could not but observe that Father Boïl and others exhibited by their cold reserve a certain lack of confidence in him. It was this fact, no doubt, that caused him to request to be sent ashore before sunset. On the following day large numbers of natives were seen along the shore. A messenger came from the cacique to inquire when the fleet would sail, and was informed that it would the following day. The brother of the cacique visited the Gracious Mary, and while on board, under the pretext of bartering some gold, he was seen to avoid most studiously the presence of the interpreter, Diego Colon; but in his absence he spoke to the Indian women, and especially to Donna Catalina, and to the latter he delivered a message from his brother, the amorous cacique. The plot soon matured. At midnight a beacon light on shore gave love's signal to the captives. Catalina conveyed the intelligence to her companions, and the ten Indian women, following her example and leadership, noiselessly let themselves down into the sea by the side of the vessel, and all swam bravely for the shore, a distance of three miles. But their escape, notwithstanding it was managed so quietly, was detected by the watch, the alarm was given, the boats were let down, and immediate chase was given. The fugitives had already gained some distance; they all reached the shore before the boats, and though four were recaptured, the comely and high-spirited Catalina and four of her companions succeeded in effecting their escape. At the dawn of day Columbus sent to demand the return of the fugitives from Guacanagari, but when reached the late royal residence was silent and deserted; the cacique and all his subjects had departed to unknown parts, carrying with them all their effects and properties, together with the stately female beauty and her four companions in flight. This singular occurrence seemed to confirm the suspicions of Father Boïl and the others as to the disloyalty of Guacanagari, and it was the prevailing opinion of the Spaniards now that it was he who had destroyed the fort and massacred the garrison, and that he was at heart and in secret deed a traitor and deceiver. The admiral, however, who felt the burden of responsibility for the expeditions and for the future relations of the two races, and who saw more deeply into the importance of every event in these early stages of intercourse between the two hemispheres, and who was full of human kindness, refused to credit the charge or to consent to a rupture of the friendly relations existing between his countrymen and their nearest neighbors. Upon every principle of natural justice it must be admitted that the conduct of this chief and his people, though somewhat irregular on this last occasion, contrasted favorably, even up to this time, with that of the Spaniards, with the exception of Columbus himself and a few others who participated in his more moderate counsels. The true principles of statesmanship and administration would certainly prefer a postponement of any rupture with the natives as long as possible.

The topographical commission sent out under Melchior Maldonado had not only proceeded to the eastward farther than any Spaniards had done, but they also obtained from the Indians of other tribes, which they had encountered, accounts confirmatory of the statements of Guacanagari and his subjects, and exculpating that prince from the charge of having destroyed the fortress and garrison. All accounts pointed out Caonabo as the author of the disaster. Convinced that a change of the site for the proposed settlement, on the score of health and for many other reasons, was necessary, the admiral caused all the ships to sail on December 7th, with the intention of seeking out the port of La Plata; but after they had proceeded about ten leagues east of Monte Christi they entered a spacious harbor, commanded by a point of land bounded on one side by rocks and protected on the other side by an impenetrable forest, and adjudged by Dr. Chanca and by the general opinion as the best place for the settlement. It was thought that Providence had sent them the recent bad weather, which induced them to enter this favored harbor at first for safety, and now as their permanent home. To an excellent harbor and a choice spot for a fort was added the important circumstance that the climate was delightful and the soil inexhaustibly fertile. The admiral had scarcely given the word of command when man and beast rejoiced in being released from the confinement of the ships, and in the enjoyment of the delights of the woods, the verdure of the fields, the refreshing water of the springs, and they felt an inexpressible pleasure in the perennial springtime, the songs of birds, the fragrance of flowers, the freshness of the grass, and the delights of fruits and fountains.

The scene presented now was most active, picturesque, and inspiring. The crews, artificers, and laborers were landed, and these laboriously assisted in landing the provisions, guns, ammunition, implements, cattle, and live stock of every kind. The animals themselves, so long confined in the vessels, seemed to take delight in the refreshing change from the prison life of the ships to that enchanting and open region. Buildings were immediately erected to receive the property of the Spaniards, and an encampment was established on the side of a plain and near a beautiful sheet of fresh water. Such was the foundation of the city of Isabella, the first permanent settlement of Europeans in the new world.

The three public buildings—the church, the storehouse, and the admiral's residence—were constructed of stone, while all the other houses were built of wood. As every man aspired to the possession of a house for himself, the greatest activity and enthusiasm were manifested by all in hastening the erection of the three stone houses, and each then was soon building for himself a private residence. Primitive in style and construction, however, were these structures. Such energy was exerted as to secure the completion of the church and the celebration of solemn high mass therein by January 6th, which was the anniversary of the entrance of the Spanish sovereigns into Granada. This imposing and significant ceremony was performed with all possible pomp and grandeur, under the circumstances, by Father Boïl, the vicar apostolic, assisted by Father Antonio de Marchena and the twelve religious monks who had come out with the expedition. The new city of Isabella was regularly planned and laid out in projected squares and streets, after the usual style of Spanish towns. There were near the place a large river and a smaller one, which presented several sites favorable for mills, and on the banks of one of the rivers was an Indian village. So rich was the soil and so genial the climate that in January the admiral was presented with ripe ears of corn from seeds sown in the December previous. This certainly seemed like an earthly paradise. To add inestimably to its advantages, it was related by the Indians of the neighboring village that at no great distance in the interior lay the famous gold-bearing mountains of Cibao, and the harbor of Isabella, as the admiral thought, would become the outlet for those boundless treasures.

But, alas! a reaction was at hand. The long confinement on shipboard, the rations of salted meat and fish and mouldy biscuit, had impaired the health of many unaccustomed to the sea, and now the fatigues of building up the new city and the effects of the new climate, subject to rapid successions of hot and humid weather, completed their prostration, and many fell ill of ravaging fevers. Disappointments soon followed, for the expectations of vast and sudden wealth had been the chief inducement with many to join in the expedition; and now it was discovered that the golden regions of Cipango and Cathay were not at their feet, and treasures were not acquired without labor or care. Instead of a region of Oriental luxury they found themselves within a limited area of wilderness, surrounded by impassable forests; and instead of a brilliant career of noble adventure and captivating exploits amid powerful and wealthy heathen nations, they had to struggle with the primeval wilderness, overcome unparalleled obstacles, and labor, in an enervating climate, for a bare subsistence. Sickness and disease, aggravated by mental care and disappointment, now settled like a pall over the infant colony.

Columbus suffered in common with his followers from the prevailing fever; but his sufferings of body and mind were greatly intensified and increased by the personal and individual surroundings, responsibilities, and duties of the man. At the time of embarkation at Cadiz, his health was so bad that he could not attend in person to the selection or inspection of the provisions, animals, and munitions of war procured and shipped for the colony by the comptroller-general and the administration of the marine. On landing everything at Isabella it was found that the greater part of the provisions were damaged or of inferior quality, the wine had leaked from badly bound casks, the medicines fell short of the quantity ordered by the chief physician, the magnificent Andalusian chargers, which the admiral had reviewed at Seville, had been replaced by inferior animals, and in every department of preparation the colony had suffered by the fraud, corruption, and peculation of placemen and office-holders at home. The history of the world is not wanting in such features. The nineteenth century is not the first to indulge in such official misconduct. The politicians and office-holders of our times have had their instruction in the history of every nation and of every century since cities and States and governments were founded by mankind; but where are the lessons which history should teach?

Added to these causes of the admiral's illness should be mentioned the difficulties and engrossing cares of his great undertaking, his great responsibilities, which were not limited to his crews, or to the natives, or to his country and his sovereigns, but extended to the interest which all mankind had in the great results of his splendid enterprise. The labors growing out of his extensive command, his loss of rest, his watchings, his sorrows at the fate of his garrison, his uncertainties as to the relations he might maintain with the aborigines, the mixed and unreliable character of the materials composing his followers, his recent cares and labors in founding and building the new city of Isabella, the circumspection, study, and forethought required in establishing and conducting his future government under such unprecedented circumstances—all contributed to bring upon him mental and physical exhaustion. His illness confined him to his bed for some weeks; but from his sick couch, with characteristic clearness of mind and energy of character, he governed and managed his new colony and fleet, and he directed all things with vigor, promptness, and success. The frauds of the bureau at Seville made his task more appalling, and the colony suffered from the beginning by its misdeeds. Yet, such was the energy of this man, and such the zeal with which he inspired others, that by the end of January a large number of houses had been erected and completed, and the new city was encircled by a stone wall.*

The city having been built and the goods and effects brought out, landed, and stored, the admiral knew that some report was expected from him and the garrison by his sovereigns. The

---

* Barry's De Lorgues' "Columbus," pp. 278, 280; "Hist. del Almirante," cap. 50; Irving's "Columbus," vol. l., p. 341; Peter Martyr, decad. i., lib. ii., etc.

gold and valuables which it was expected the garrison would have collected he could not send, but in their stead must be despatched the appalling accounts of disaster, ruin, and death. Before sending the fleet on the homeward voyage with the sad tidings of the ruin of La Navidad and the destruction of the colony, with his usual fruitfulness of expedient he sent an expedition under Alonzo de Ojeda into the interior of the island, to visit and explore the country of Caonabo, whose name, signifying "the lord of the golden house," gave promise of rich returns of the precious metal, and hopes for a valuable return cargo to the Spanish sovereigns for their great outlay. The very tidings of the discovery of a country so rich in precious metals would of itself make some compensation for the disasters and disappointments of the past. Ojeda rejoiced at this opportunity for exercising his prowess and displaying his courage. Accompanied by a small but selected and gallant command, including several high-spirited cavaliers scarcely inferior in daring and love of adventure to himself, he marched out of the city of Isabella in the early part of January, 1494, and proceeded southward toward the rich and storied Cibao. By several days of arduous marching, climbing lofty and rocky mountains, fording rivers, and keeping up an untiring struggle with natural obstacles, they penetrated a region of indescribable beauty, grandeur, and richness, where they were received with unbounded hospitality by the natives, who were peaceful and friendly. Caonabo, the fierce and warlike king of the country, was absent in some other part of his dominions, and no one appeared to dispute the Spanish progress. Though the natives were naked, lived in simplicity and frugality, had no large or wealthy cities, still the Spaniards saw with delight evidences of the precious metal in the sands of gold in the mountain streams, large pieces of gold ore in the beds of the torrents, and stones richly streaked with gold. The natives gave these treasures freely to the Spaniards. Ojeda himself is said to have found in one of the brooks a single piece of gold weighing nine ounces, which was seen by Peter Martyr before it was sent to Spain. The expedition returned to Isabella with the most enthusiastic accounts of the country, and especially of the mineral treasures of Cibao. Columbus was convinced that a development of the mines of this favored region would bring ample returns of the precious metals to satisfy the expectations of his countrymen and of his sovereigns. He wrote a full account of the discovery of this rich country in the interior to Spain, and sent back the fleet of twelve vessels under the command of Antonio de Torres, who sailed in the admiral's ship, the Gracious Mary, on February 2d, together with rich specimens of the gold brought from Cibao, fruits and plants of the country, and the men, women, and children he had captured from the Caribbean Islands. He wrote a letter to the sovereigns, in which he described in enthusiastic terms the rich mineral regions of Cibao, gave the particulars of the expedition of Ojeda, whom he highly commended, and whose companion, Gorvalan, returned to Spain in the fleet, and he commended to the favor of the sovereigns a number of his followers, among whom were Pedro Margarite and Juan Aguado, who were also to return in the fleet, from both of whom he ever afterward received the basest and most disheartening ingratitude. He also requested fresh supplies from Spain, as the crops would not mature in time to afford sustenance to the colony, and as the provisions brought out from Spain were inferior or spoiled, and the wine had leaked from the casks on board the ships. The colonists were suffering for proper diet. He also requested a supply of other articles of pressing necessity, particularly such as clothing, medicines, and arms. Great stress was laid on the importance of sending horses, both for the military service and the government works, and mention was made of the wonderful effect of these animals in overawing the natives. More workmen and mechanics were requested to be sent out, as well as miners and others skilled in handling the ore of the precious metals.

In sending the men, women, and children that had been taken from the Caribbean Islands, Columbus was certainly actuated by high and honorable motives, and he was in this and every other act of his affecting the welfare or destiny of the natives led by a most zealous desire for their salvation. They were familiar with or at least could use to some extent the various languages spoken by the different tribes of the West India Islands, so that he thought it was a great blessing to these benighted savages to send them to Spain in great numbers. Such as returned to their native archipelago converts to Christianity could be useful in assisting the missionaries in their apostolic labors for the conversion of the Indians; such as remained in Spain would certainly gain the faith and save their souls, even though this was accomplished as an exchange for their liberty. It is true that this noted memorial or letter contained recommendations which, while in keeping with the education and sentiments of that age, were such as the Christian and enlightened sentiment of the nineteenth century can but condemn, and which were in the end disastrous in their application to the American continents and in their effects upon the Indians for centuries to come. Desirous at once of promoting the speedy conversion of these fierce Caribs to Christianity, and to make the great enterprise in which he was embarked remunerative to his sovereigns, he proposed to establish an exchange of Carib captives for the live stock that was needed for the colony. Spanish merchants were to furnish the live stock and deliver the same at the island of Isabella, and there the Caribs would be delivered on board the ships, be carried to Spain and sold into slavery; the royal treasury would receive a considerable tax on every slave thus imported into the kingdom, by which the outlays of the government for the newly discovered countries would be returned tenfold, and the colonies would be supplied with valuable and necessary live stock without cost. While it would be unjust to judge the motives and conduct of public men and sovereigns in the fifteenth century by the more enlightened and humane sentiments prevailing in our times, there was one circumstance or fact forming a part of the history of this transaction which goes far to palliate them. The Caribbean Islanders were themselves the open and avowed enemies of human liberty, and the promoters of the most cruel forms of human slavery ; they used their superior military skill, numbers, and power for the enslavement of their peaceful and innocent neighbors. Not only did they descend, without warning or notice, upon the simple, gentle, and unwarlike communities within their reach, and seize men, women, and children and carry them off to the fiercest forms of slavery, but they practised the utmost disregard to human life ; for not only were their victims killed to make repasts for the savage appetites of their cannibal masters, but thousands of lives were wantonly and cruelly sacrificed. Such a race could not complain if another, stronger and more powerful, arrested their diabolical practices by capturing them and consigning them to a less cruel form of slavery than they inflicted upon others ; and that, too, among a people and to masters who respected and protected human life ; and, above all, in a country where the inestimable gain of the Christian faith would be theirs to accept. At the same time, while these facts have an important and ameliorating influence, the human race, in the interests of justice, humanity, and liberty, has the right to object to the transfer of any of its members from a state of liberty to one of slavery. Historians have united in doing justice to the motives of Columbus, who is recognized as " obeying the dictates of his conscience ;"* but the Spanish sovereigns have gained imperishable honor and glory in rejecting the well-meant but mistaken recommendations of the admiral, and in decreeing that the Caribs were entitled to liberty, and that their conversion to Christianity should be conducted in the same manner as that of the other Indians. Isabella is especially credited with the authorship of this benign and generous decree. This subject will be referred to again.

Retaining five ships for the use of the colony and for the prosecution of further discoveries, the admiral saw, with blended feelings of pride and shame, of hope and disappointment, the return fleet sail from the port of Isabella on February 2d, 1494, and with it went the prayers and best wishes of the man who had brought, by his genius, the two hemispheres together, face to face, and now by his wise and generous efforts was laying the foundations of new empires and of future nations. While the failure and disaster of the first colony left in the new world was discouraging to the Spanish king and queen and to all Europe, the buoyant and sanguine letter of Columbus had great weight in sustaining the advancing cause of humanity and civilization, while the specimens of gold which he sent gave promise of future wealth and of rich tribute from the new to the old world. Letters from Father Boïl, Dr. Chanca, and other prominent companions of Columbus confirmed the favorable accounts of the country and its products given by the admiral, and Gorvalan related, in person, what he had seen of the beautiful islands, the rich soil, the genial climate, the gentle natives, and the rich deposits of gold which gave value and glory to the peaceful conquests of the sovereigns and of their zealous viceroy. The sordid sentiments of selfish and pusillanimous minds were silenced

---

* Irving's "Life of Columbus," vol. i., p. 347.

by the better and higher judgment of the great and good and learned men of Europe. Scholars and philanthropists united in extolling the grandeur of the great achievement of Columbus, and in sustaining his able and exalted movements for extending the realms of trade, civilization, and Christianity.

The building of the new city of Isabella, in the mean time, had progressed; the first Christian church in the new world was so far completed as to allow the celebration of high mass within its sacred walls on the feast of the Epiphany, January 6th, 1494. This august ceremony was performed with imposing pomp and inspiring grandeur by Father Boïl, assisted by Friar Antonio de Marchena and the twelve ecclesiastics who had accompanied the former. Columbus did all in his power to hasten the completion of the city, and the Indians, whose fears were allayed by the benignity of the admiral, gave their labor with cheerfulness, and deemed themselves more than repaid by the European trifles they received in return. He gave his personal attention to every work with untiring energy and activity; but now the sad reaction continued its dread work. The miserable provisions which had been shipped from Cadiz, and others which had spoiled on the voyage, as already mentioned, had begun to spread disease in the colony. The men had become fatigued with the unaccustomed labor of building a city, or with disappointment at not realizing immediate fortunes from exhaustless mines of gold, or chagrined at seeing the homeward fleet return without them; others were affrighted at every calamity or horror; the wilderness looked silent, gloomy, and endless. The result of all these gloomy experiences was a widespread feeling of discontent. The admiral, exhausted in mind and body by his labors, cares, anxieties, the apprehension of a general disaffection in the colony, and suffering himself from bad food, was seized by the prevailing epidemic. Yet from his sick-bed he administered all things with clearness, vigor, and ability. Having inquired from the natives concerning the interior of the island, and having sent a caravel to explore it, his sanguine mind became convinced that the new city was well located, and that the wealth of Cibao, which he estimated as distant only three days' journey, must naturally pour itself into its lap. While he was seeking out the means of making the colony successful and prosperous, the fell spirit of discontent increased and was tending to mutiny. Firmin

Cado, the colony's metallurgist, one of the discontented spirits, added much to the prevailing despondency by asserting that the country was destitute of gold; that the shining particles which the admiral took for the precious metal were merely grains of mica or other substance resembling gold, and that the trinkets of wrought gold worn by the natives were the rare and old products of now exhausted sources. Such was the discontent that a leader was all that was needed in order to turn it into open mutiny or rebellion. One Bernal Diaz de Pisa, a man of some consequence, a former official of the court, who had secured for himself the appointment of comptroller of the expedition, having already had some differences with Columbus, presented himself at the head of the mutineers as leader. His plan was to seize some or all of the vessels and return with the mutineers to Spain; but as preliminary to this, and to justify it, he became the accuser of the admiral, presumed to inquire into his conduct, and to show, by living witnesses, that he had deceived the sovereigns by the recent letter he had sent them, giving false accounts of the country. Just as this lawless gang were about to seize the buildings at night Columbus suddenly recovered his health, and having information of the plot, he had the ringleader arrested, and thus discovered on his person the evidences of his treason in his own handwriting. Here again the wisdom and magnanimity of the admiral were manifested. Instead of having De Pisa tried and condemned to death, as he might have done on the spot, he generously spared him, and sent him back to Spain with an account of his treachery and misdeeds, thus referring the case to the decision of the sovereigns. Several of the co-conspirators were mildly punished in different degrees, but with marked leniency. Many historians have justly extolled the moderation of Columbus on this and many similar occasions. Perhaps the severest punishment permitted by the law would have served as a warning for future miscreants, for he had to encounter many such in his checkered and eventful career. But his generosity sustained his sympathy for his race; it never allowed the most appalling disasters, resulting from the baseness and ingratitude of men, to sour the amiability and gentleness of his nature. The admiral endeavored to preserve the infant colony free from the recurrence of any similar treason, by having the guns and naval munitions removed from four of the vessels and stored on board the principal ship, and the latter was placed in the care of true and trusty men. The five ships were now placed under the command of his brother, Don Diego Columbus. The mildness of his treatment to these malcontents had the usual effect upon unworthy souls; it seemed only to exasperate their hatred and intensify their malice against him, who, in this and in many similar and more serious trials of his life, felt the disadvantage of being a foreigner, holding authority over native Spaniards; and he was hated and despised for his alien birth, as if his services to Spain did not entitle him to the highest and most privileged form of citizenship. While reviled as unworthy to rule over Spaniards, scholars and philanthropists of all countries claimed him as a common benefactor.

From his sick-bed Columbus, with characteristic energy of mind, had planned the expedition to the golden regions of Cibao, the dominion of the famous chief, the " Lord of the Golden House."

> " Ours is the land and age of gold,
> And ours the hallow'd time."
> —GRENVILLE MELLEN.

Aroused from his illness by the plotting of Bernal Diaz, Firmin Cado, and their confederates, the admiral had given his accustomed energy and skill in organizing the march to the country of Caonabo, had made preparations for his immediate departure, and given the command of the ships and of the city, as stated, to his trusty brother. He now appointed for him a council of good and experienced men. Gold was one of the chief objects of this expedition, in order to secure a revenue for Spain. It was, therefore, the admiral's intention to erect a fort in the mountains, as the centre of permanent mining operations, and as a protection to his men and miners; and he desired to impress the interlying tribes of Indians, and especially the renowned Caonabo and his people, with an abiding conception of the power, grandeur, and prowess of the Spaniards, and to deter all the inhabitants of the island from future attempts at opposition, hostility, or warfare. Thus, not only did he choose his best men and horses, but, in fact, all the able-bodied men that could be safely allowed to leave the ships and settlement were selected; and the cavalry, so feared by the natives, constituted a prominent feature of the march. As the little army, consisting of about four hundred men, went forth, their array was enlivened with bright helmets and corselets; arquebuses, lances, swords, and cross-bows gave the impress of irresistible force to their ranks; the gay and beautiful banners added picturesqueness to the pageant; the music of drum and trumpet heralded their advance and progress; and the crowds of gaping and awe-stricken Indians showed how successfully the desired effect had been produced on the minds of the natives.

Their armament and equipment were complete. March 12th was the day of their departure; by nightfall they had traversed the low country between the sea and the mountains, and they found at dusk a delightful field for their encampment in a rich and beautiful country. Wild and rugged was the mountain-pass through which the high-spirited cavaliers opened at once a way for the troops, and, in honor of these young and aristocratic heroes of Moorish campaigns, who had rendered similar service in the mountains of Granada, the pass was called "El Puerto de los Hidalgos," or the Gentlemen's Pass. Early the following morning the gallant army struggled up the steep defile, and on reaching the gore at the top of the mountain, they looked toward the interior of the island, and beheld a landscape of surpassing grandeur and beauty. Imagination was surpassed by the grand reality; a country lay at their feet which was like an enchanted paradise, so grand were the forests, so majestic the rivers, so dim and towering the mountains, so luxuriant the pastures, so fresh and fragrant the verdure, so picturesque the villages and hamlets, so bountiful and luscious the fruits and herbs. Columbus called it the Royal Plain, or Vega, and raised his voice in thanksgiving to heaven.

But, on the other hand, the simple inhabitants of this beautiful country were struck with awe or fear or admiration at the display of arms, uniforms, and discipline. While some were terrified and ran to the woods, or hid behind their fragile barricades of reeds, others came to gaze at the wonderful strangers and to offer them the fruits of the land. Surely these were visitors from heaven! The Spaniards, by command of their chief, refrained from interfering with the natives. Having crossed the beautiful plain, forded the Golden River, or Yagui, whose mouth he had seen in his first voyage, and, through another pass which they opened, reaching the top of the second chain of mountains, the troops of Ferdinand and Isabella stood and gazed with admiration upon the country of Cibao, the dominion of the famed Caonabo. In approaching the native villages the cavalry entered first, so as to inspire awe in the simple Indians, who thought the horse and the rider were one being, "a circumstance," says Mr. Irving, "which shows that the alleged origin of the ancient fable of the Centaurs is at least founded in nature."* While the barricades of reeds behind which the Indians hid were of no avail in fact, Columbus regarded them as such, and allowed no Spaniard to pass behind them or enter their houses. Kindness gradually won their confidence. As the abundance of nature made all food a common property, the Indians accompanying the army freely with welcome entered the houses of the tribes they now passed through, and took all they needed. It was a rude contrast between nature and civilization, when afterward these children of the forest found themselves repulsed, for the first time in the history of their tribes, when they in like manner innocently attempted to enter the abodes of the Spaniards for food, which they themselves had mostly supplied to their visitors without stint.

Not only was every variety of food which the country produced brought freely by the natives to the Spaniards—they had previously been visited by Ojeda's exploring party—but they also brought the shining grains and particles of gold which they had picked up in torrent or brook. These, as they knew, the Spaniards valued more than food. Columbus and his followers saw in the beds of rivers and streams the glittering gold dust, and he readily convinced himself that the country abounded in mines of the precious metal. He also saw pieces of amber and lapis lazuli. He persuaded himself that copper also abounded. Were not these riches enough to detain them in the golden land? He decided to continue his journey no farther; he was already far from the city of Isabella; the access was arduous and difficult. On an eminence on the river Yanique, well suited for defence, he erected Fort St. Thomas, thus named after the doubting apostle, in allusion to Firmin Cado and his abettors, in reproof of their denial of the treasures in the country until they

---

* Irving's "Columbus," vol. i., p. 359; other references are Barry's De Lorgues' "Columbus;" Las Casas, "Hist. Ind.," and "Historia del Almirante."

saw them with their eyes and felt them with their hands. It was thus strangely that moral and religious sentiments were mingled with the most lucrative aspirations of men. The natives from near and distant tribes flocked in great numbers to visit the Spaniards, and entreated for the coveted trinkets in exchange for gold. They brought in all the gold dust and glittering particles they could gather. One old man, from a distance, brought in two pieces of purest ore weighing an ounce. He was enraptured at receiving a hawk's bell in exchange for these. When Columbus wondered at their great size, he gave signs that they were trifling in comparison with the pieces of gold found in his own country, which was distant only half a day's journey. This story was surpassed by that of others, who, having brought in pieces weighing ten and twelve drams, informed the admiral that in their country it was common to find pieces of virgin ore as large as a child's head. The admiral shrewdly noticed that in every instance the fabulous quantities of gold were located in some other region than the one he was then visiting. In order to test these shifting legends, Columbus sent a young and valiant cavalier of Madrid, Juan de Luxan, on an expedition, with a picked party of armed men, to explore the country of Cibao, which, as he judged from the descriptions of the natives, must be equal in size to the Kingdom of Portugal; and thus he obtained valuable information. While the general aspect of the province of Cibao resembled that of the country he had just traversed, it was equally productive, abounded in fruits, among which was the native grape, remarkable for its ready flow of juice and pleasant flavor; and every stream bore the golden particles in greater or less quantities. There was other information which Juan de Luxan only communicated to the admiral, and this was supposed to embody the secrets which he obtained from the Indians indicating the locations of the most favored gold-bearing spots in the mountains.*

Fort St. Thomas, planned and built under the sound judgment of Columbus, when completed was garrisoned with fifty-six chosen men and some horses, and placed under the command of Pedro Margarite, a citizen and gentleman of Madrid, whom

---

* Irving's "Columbus," vol. i., pp. 364, 365 ; Barry's De Lorgues' "Columbus;" Peter Martyr, decad. i., lib. iii.

Columbus, on account of his large family and poverty, had recommended to the Spanish sovereigns, but who, like many others accepting his aid, proved most ungrateful to their best friend, and disloyal to duty and country.

On his return to Isabella, Columbus rested with his followers in the Indian villages, in order to accustom the Spaniards and Indians to each other's society and to each other's methods, and to accustom the former to the use of the Indian foods. On the banks of the Rio Verde he met a party of Spaniards on their way to provide the fortress with food, and here he remained a few days and permanently fixed the route of communication between city and fort. With characteristic application he closely studied the manners, customs, traditions, religion, and native government of his new subjects, and in this he was much assisted by the intelligent observations and reports of Juan de Luxan, and by the experiences and studies of a zealous and pious hermit named Roman Pane, of the Order of St. Jerome, and commonly called " the poor hermit," who labored with apostolic zeal among the natives, studied their language, or rather the Marcorix dialect, which was the one most generally understood throughout the island, and had done good missionary service in the Royal Vega. From these studies and sources the admiral learned many things at variance with his first impressions. The natives were not so pacific as he had at first supposed, for it was found that the different tribes were sometimes at war with each other, and all of them had become somewhat inured to arms from the necessity of defending themselves against the hostile attacks of the Caribs. Though naturally of simple and gentle natures, Caonabo had introduced a more military sentiment among them. Nor were the natives destitute of religious traditions, as Columbus at first supposed, for he now found that they believed in one Supreme Being, whose kingdom was in the skies, who had a mother, but no father, and who was immortal, omnipotent, and invisible. In its minor details the religion of the natives bore some resemblance to that of the Greeks and Romans, for they seemed to have inferior or tutelar deities intermediate between man and the supreme God, and who were also the divinities of the home, the weather, the storms, the seas, forests, springs, fountains, and elements. They had their priests, the latter being also their medicine-men. They also worshipped idols, which they hid from the Spaniards, in order to prevent them from destroying them in their zeal for the Christian faith. The practice of painting or tattooing their bodies prevailed, and the images of their deities were thus painted and exhibited on their persons. Of their religious ceremonies, a principal one alone has been handed down to us, which consisted of solemn processions, offerings of cakes and flowers, dances by the females, invocations, house-blessing, and similar rites. Their idols represented beings that assisted the crops and harvests, aided women in child-birth, or invoked abundant rains and sunshine. Columbus sent to Spain some of these idols. Their traditions of the origin of man were crude and absurd, but they had a tradition of the great flood, had a funeral service for the dead, conceived the idea of soul as distinct from body, believed in a future place of happiness, and, like most barbarous nations, their dances had a superstitious or devotional character. Hospitality was a natural virtue of these simple tribes; they received from a bountiful soil all they needed for food, and they toiled not; neither did they spin, for the mildness of the climate rendered clothing unnecessary, and they were innocent of shame. Truly the Royal Vega seemed like an earthly paradise. Had the mild and just spirit of Columbus prevailed, such it might have continued to the present time, with all the ennobling and purifying elements of the Christian religion and civilization added; but, alas! the vices of Christians rather than their virtues have dominated over the native races of the new world.

The return of the admiral to the city of Isabella did not bring him rest of mind or body. Scarcely had he reached his new residence and inspected the ships, houses, fort, and colony, when he received tidings from Pedro Margarite, the commander of Fort St. Thomas, that the friendly deportment of the natives had been changed to preparations for war, as seen from their ceasing to hold intercourse with the Spaniards and from their leaving their homes and villages to assemble in some place of rendezvous. The warlike Caonabo was assembling an army to attack the fortress; but the Spanish commander omitted to relate the causes of these changes in the feelings of the Indians toward their visitors. The latter, in fact, had, almost immediately after the departure of the admiral, given way to their worst passions, the lust for gold and for women; the Indians were robbed of their property and outraged in their homes and affections. Caonabo did not recognize the right of even a Christian and civilized race to intrude upon their country and appropriate it to themselves; he deemed the title which his people derived from nature and possession as a good title, which they also possessed the natural right to defend. Columbus, above all men, abhorred and denounced the vices and crimes of Europeans toward the natives of the Western Hemisphere; he regarded his advent among them as the mission of Christianity, civilization, and justice; and while he advanced the right of Christian nations to discover and appropriate the countries of the heathens, he tempered this high prerogative with justice, truth, and equity. Knowing the weakness of the people he had just visited, he contented himself with sending to Fort St. Thomas a reinforcement of twenty men, together with provisions and ammunitions. He also improved the communication between fortress and city by sending out a party of thirty men to open and improve the road between them.

While he felt that his late expedition into the interior of the island had greatly advanced his enterprise by the acquisition of new knowledge of the country and of its inhabitants, and had secured him a fortified foothold in the mountains, he now also observed with pleasure the wonderful productiveness of the climate and soil, and the development of the agricultural interests of the colony. Having distributed the plants and seeds he brought from Europe among the colonists, he saw with satisfaction how they flourished in the new world, and how forward and rapid everything germinated and grew in this favored land. The sugar-cane was an important success, the native vine improved under skilful pruning, and the vines of Spain flourished in the virgin soil, as did every fruit and vegetable, plant and tree he had introduced. The country began to assume the aspect of culture; orchards, gardens, and farms in some instances began to rival or surpass those of older countries. He saw toward the end of March ears of wheat which had been sown with seed toward the end of January. Such was the fecundity of the soil, such the genial heat and moisture of the climate, that, while the smaller garden vegetables and herbs ripened in sixteen days, the larger ones, such as melons, cucumbers, gourds, and such like adorned the tables of the colonists within a month from the planting of the seeds.

But the beautiful harmony of nature, the co-operation of soil and climate, to produce the bountiful fruits which Providence thus provided for man, contrasted more disastrously with the discord, avarice, and bad passions of man himself. Time has shown that, under the superior knowledge which civilized man possesses of the laws of health and of acclimatization, the Spaniards could have lived in health and prosperity in the new countries they had so much coveted ; but the vices of the men themselves developed the prevalence of a disease hitherto unknown to the Indians, and, if traceable to an European origin, of probably recent origin, and not generally understood ; which would seem like a divine judgment on the lust of the Spaniards were it not for the fact that it became communicated to the helpless and untutored savages, the victims of European passions. The heat and humidity of the climate, the undrained marshes, and the uncultivated soil added the evil of malaria ; and fevers prevailed to an alarming degree among the colonists and soldiers. The sickness was aggravated by discontent and despair ; and proper food was wanting for the nourishment of the sick and suffering. While the productive soil would yield two crops in the year, the present season was marked by scarcity of food. The meats were spoiled, the medicines were exhausted almost, and the wine was scarce. But these sufferings did not allay the passions of men, and retribution soon followed. The laboring men had been overworked perhaps, but the hidalgos, wrapped in the mantle of pride and punctilio, became the drones of a society struggling for existence and life. All united, however, in denouncing and cursing the most meritorious and self-sacrificing man in the colony, its best friend, the father of all, the watchful and provident viceroy and admiral ; for had they heeded the injunctions of Columbus, a different result would have followed.

His own followers gave more anxiety and trouble to Columbus, though only a handful of men, than the whole Indian population of the islands he discovered in the new world ; but for the former, their vices and their passions, he could have probably proceeded on to discover, and could have governed the new countries, with their aboriginal populations, with comparative ease and peace. It was the misconduct of the Europeans that caused the Indians, in almost every instance except that of the Caribs, to become hostile toward the advance of European civilization in America ; but now arms had been drawn and blood had been shed.

In the trying position in which he was now placed, Columbus found it necessary to take prompt and decided measures. As a means of relieving the impoverished and hungry city from the duty of feeding so many mouths, as well as of keeping the now disquieted and offended Indians at peace, he decided to distribute the military forces at his command, consisting of four hundred infantry and sixteen cavalry, through the interior of the island, leaving only the workmen and the sick at the city. The entire population of Isabella, high and low, was placed on short allowance, and, with his usual consistency, Columbus was the first to practise his own rule of abstinencne. Wheat was almost the only food left, and this was in the grain ; so that for want of mills each one was compelled to grind his own wheat with a handmill. The viceroy determined to erect a public mill and to complete the canal that was to pass through the city, and as a measure of justice he compelled the laborer and the hidalgo to work together, and enforced this rule under severe penalties. Compulsory labor is always an unwelcome task, but to highspirited young cavaliers, many of whom had not even come out for wealth or gain, but to seek adventures worthy of their names, it was indescribably offensive. But the stern admiral enforced his orders unrelentingly. This measure drew upon him the hatred and denunciations of this class, and, on account of sons or relatives in Hispaniola, the hostility of some of the proudest and most powerful of the old Spanish families at home. So many of these proud and undisciplined young men fell victims to the condition of things prevailing at Isabella, that in after years, when Isabella had ceased to be a city and was abandoned to owls, bats, and wild beasts, a popular superstition peopled it with the living ghosts of the departed hidalgos who had been buried there.

Las Casas, Herrera, Washington Irving,[*] and other authors relate the superstitious legend ; and the following passage from

---

[*] Las Casas, " Hist. Ind.," lib. i., cap. 92 ; MS. Herrerá, " Hist. Ind.," decad. i., lib. ii., cap. 12.

Mr. Irving is as graphic and ghastly as the most morbid taste could desire: " Like all decayed and deserted places, it [the city of Isabella] soon became an object of awe and superstition to the common people, and no one ventured to enter its gates. Those who passed near it, or hunted the wild swine which abounded in the neighborhood, declared they heard appalling voices issue from within its walls by night and day. The laborers became fearful, therefore, of cultivating the adjacent fields. The story went, says Las Casas, that two Spaniards happened one day to wander among the ruined edifices of the place. On entering one of the solitary streets, they beheld two rows of men, evidently, from their stately demeanor, hidalgos of noble blood and cavaliers of the court. They were richly attired in the old Castilian mode, with rapiers by their side, and broad traveling hats, such as were worn at the time. The two men were astonished to behold persons of their rank and appearance apparently inhabiting that desolate place, unknown to the people of the island. They saluted them, and inquired whence they came and when they had arrived. The cavaliers maintained a gloomy silence, but courteously returned the salutation by raising their hands to their sombreros or hats, in taking off which their heads came off also, and their bodies stood decapitated. The whole phantom assemblage then vanished. So great was the astonishment and horror of the beholders, that they had nearly fallen dead, and remained stupefied for several days." *

In spite of every opposition and of the ill-will of the cavaliers and other unwilling workers in the colony, Columbus succeeded in pushing on the public mill, the canal, and other public works to completion, and the result showed the wisdom and necessity of his course. While the Count de Lorgues earnestly sustains his stern justice and impartiality, Mr. Irving seems affected with sympathy for the unfortunate hidalgos thus compelled to manual labor. In old and established communities, where rank and position form a part of the order and economy of the State, such measures would be justly regarded as arbitrary and despotic in the extreme. But in an infant colony, planted recently, thousands of miles away from the civilized world, stricken with sickness and famine, all men, members of such a society, are relegated

---

* Irving's " Columbus," vol. i., p. 385.

back to their natural rights and duties and to their primitive equality ; and as all needed food, and all clung to life, the law of nature would require all equally to labor and to sacrifice. But men never recede from an advantage once gained, even though it be one of mere honor or rank, if they can help it ; and the stern discipline of the admiral gave an ineffaceable insult and sense of wrong to the Spanish cavaliers.

He ordered the garrison at Isabella to the interior of the island, thus relieving the sick and hungry residents of the city, inspiring the natives with awe and fear of the Spanish power, exploring the island, gaining knowledge of its strategic points, and of the mines of gold it contained. The men thus sent out, also from necessity became accustomed to the diet of the natives. The troops were sent to Pedro Margarite, who remained in command of the Fort St. Thomas, and Alonzo de Ojeda, who conducted the expedition from Isabella to Fort St. Thomas, remained in command of the entire military force of the island. Such is the account of Count de Lorgues ; but Mr. Irving states that Ojeda superseded Margarite as commander of the fort, and the latter was placed in command of the whole army. Every able-bodied man that could be spared was placed in the army, which, when all were mustered, contained two hundred and fifty cross-bow men, one hundred and ten arquebusiers, sixteen horsemen, and twenty officers. From the fact that it was Margarite who made the military exploration of the island, it is more probable that it was he who retained, by orders of the admiral, the command of the army, while Ojeda became commander at Fort St. Thomas.

The discontent which arose from the measures of the admiral grew in extent and violence. Not only did the cavaliers take umbrage at the edict requiring all to labor, but as the admiral made the rule of short rations universal, and himself submitted to the general necessity and regulation, the rule included some who, while they should have supported the measure and have given a good example to others, inconsiderately opposed it. Among these was Father Boïl, the vicar apostolic. The charge of cruelty having been made, this ecclesiastic conferred a semblance of truth to the accusation by sustaining it. He did not submit meekly to the reduction in the allowances of food. Originally he had been an admirer of Columbus, but from the moment the admiral decided to trust in the truth and loyalty of the native chief, Guacanagari, against the severer counsels of the vicar apostolic, the latter evidently nursed a resentment born rather of wounded pride than of discreet zeal. His sentiments now found open expression. He sustained the charge of cruelty which the misguided people made so unjustly against Columbus, thus giving plausibility to it, and the course he adopted had a direct tendency and effect of fomenting disaffection and of finally leading to revolt. Father Boíl had been accustomed rather to diplomatic than missionary services, and the apostolate, which he might have honored, illy suited his tastes. Many of the twelve missionaries of various religious orders participated in his lack of zeal and self-sacrifice, and spent their time mostly in untimely regrets for the homes they had left and in criticising the actions of the admiral. There were some honorable exceptions, however, to this state of things, and the good brother, Juan Bergognon, and "the pious hermit," as he was called, Roman Pane, are entitled to be named with reverence. It is to be hoped that few of the missionaries fully participated in Father Boíl's sentiments expressed in his letter to the sovereigns, acknowledging the difficulties of the Indian language, the inutility of his remaining, and requesting his recall.

Recent researches among the Vatican secret archives have disclosed the singular fact that Father Bernard Boíl, whose name has been tortured into a dozen different forms, such as Buil, by Winsor, and Boyle, by Fiske, "which," the latter remarks, "strongly suggests an Irish origin," was not, in fact, the person appointed by the Holy See to the high office of Vicar Apostolic of the Indies ; and that the person appointed, in fact, was Father Bernard Boyle, the Provincial of the Franciscan Order in Spain.*
It was the wily Ferdinand who availed himself of the similarity in the names, and substituted a favorite of his own, Father Boíl or Buïl, a Benedictine monk of Catalonia. Both the Count de Lorgues and the Italian historian and publicist, Francesco Tar-

---

* It is not at all surprising that between Rome and Spain a mistake was made in the appointment of Father Boïl as vicar apostolic for another of a similar name, since his name was rendered in so many different forms—viz., Boïl, Buïl, Buyl, Buyll, Buill, Bueill, Buillius, Bueillus, Buelius, Buellius, Bucillus, Bucillius, and finally Boyle.

ducci, circumstantially mention this fact.* The latter says: "Father Boïl was a learned Benedictine, an accomplished diplomatist, and the king and queen had repeatedly made use of his ability, employing him with profit in the negotiations with France for the restitution of Roussillon. Now, when Columbus came back telling of his discovery, and every one believed that he had reached the extreme eastern limits of Asia, near the empire of the Grand Khan and the states of the other powerful monarchs of the East, as it was necessary to send some one to preside over the new church they were sure of establishing in those countries, the prudent Ferdinand set his eyes on this man as one who, at the same time that he was fulfilling the duties of his ecclesiastical dignity, would be of great use to him as an able diplomatist in his relations with those distant courts, and proposed his name to Rome. The consequence was that instead of a priest full of the spirit of the Gospel and of self-denial, fitted to sustain worthily and fruitfully the office of apostle, there was sent out to those naked savages a 'friar with his head filled with subtleties, cabals, and the wisdom that rules the art of politics. There has lately been discovered, in the secret archives of the Vatican, the original bull instituting the vicariate apostolic of the new regions discovered by Columbus. The date is July 7th, 1493, but the person there named for that dignity is not Father Bernard Boïl, of the Order of St. Benedict, but Father Bernard Boyle, Provincial of the Order of St. Francis in Spain; and as it is certain that it was the Benedictine who received and executed that duty in the new world, it is suspected that the Pope had nominated the Franciscan before he had received the proposal of King Ferdinand in favor of the Benedictine monk. But when the bulls were received in Spain, finding that the person named by the Pope responded perfectly in name and surname (no account being taken of the *y* instead of the *i*, both being pronounced alike), the only difference being the designation of the religious order to which he belonged, it was easily believed, or pretended to be believed, that this designation was a mistake, and the bulls were given effect in favor of Father Bernard Boïl, the Benedictine." †

---

* Tarducci's "Life of Columbus," vol. i., p. 358, Brownson's translation; Count de Lorgues' "Columbus," p. 320, Dr. Barry's translation.

† Munoz, lib. iv., § xxii.; Navarrete, Doc. No. xlv.; Brownson's translation

It must be admitted, however, that when Father Boïl accepted the appointment of vicar apostolic, he and his friend, King Ferdinand, in common with all the rest of the world, supposed that he was only to exchange the regal surroundings of the court of Spain for those of the Grand Khan and other Oriental potentates. Little did he suppose that instead of practising the subtleties of Machiavelli with brilliancy among Oriental scholars and diplomats, his mission would turn out to be the simpler yet in our eyes the more holy and exalted one of instructing the simple savages of Hispaniola in the sublime doctrines of Christ from the Catechism, the humblest yet profoundest of books. Expectation yielded to disappointment and disgust at his position, which became galling to the distinguished ecclesiastic; this was increased when he found himself less influential in the government and councils of the Indies, even though he was appointed one of the council to assist Don Diego in the administration during the admiral's absence in the expedition to explore Cuba and Jamaica; he found his influence less in Hispaniola than in Spain, under Columbus than under Ferdinand; and the ill-will he conceived at the refusal of Columbus to follow his harsh measures recommended toward the cacique, Guacanagari, culminated when the friar was put on short rations with the rest of the colony when it was threatened with starvation. Such was the resentful conduct of Father Boïl, that Tarducci says he had his food entirely cut off by the admiral; but this was not done until the culminating act of the vicar apostolic, which I will now relate.

'Father Boïl went to the extremity of using his ecclesiastical functions as a weapon in a purely secular and personal quarrel of his own. He pronounced sentence of excommunication against the admiral. It does not seem that Columbus paid any regard to this manifestly unjust proceeding, or ever sought its reversal, nor did it ever seem to affect his actual relations with the Church. The whole matter is thus mentioned and expounded by the Rev. Arthur George Knight, of the Society of Jesus, in his "Life of Columbus," wherein he quotes the high theological authority of Father Gury, in his "Compendium of Moral Theology." Father Knight says: "The real anxiety of Columbus lay in the new

---

of Tarducci's "Columbus," vol. i., p. 358; Barry's De Lorgues' "Columbus," p. 319.

city. Strange maladies, caused by noxious vapors and helped by vicious indulgence, spread among the Spaniards. The supply of flour failed, and hands to grind the wheat were growing scarcer every day. It was no time, the viceroy thought, for standing upon pride of caste. He ordered all the able-bodied men, gentle and simple, to take their turn at the grinding, under penalty of having their rations diminished. This was an indignity not to be borne by the ' blue blood ' of Spain, even though no other course could save the little colony from famine and pestilence. Father Boïl sympathized with the young cavaliers, and reproved Columbus for his ' cruelty ' when, according to his threat, he punished the refractory by diminution of rations. By loudly proclaiming his disapprobation of the measures adopted, he, perhaps thoughtlessly, did much to foment disaffection. When, in spite of his remonstrances, the admiral persisted in his conscientious efforts to save his people from destruction, Father Boïl committed the extravagant folly of excommunicating him for doing what he felt to be his duty. He was altogether incapable of understanding the great soul of Columbus. Either the theological course of study at La Rabida, or common sense, was enough to certify that the censures of the Church only fall upon sinful acts, and that where no fault exists excommunication only causes external annoyance, and imposes no obligation binding in conscience beyond the general duty of receiving even an unjust sentence with respectful demeanor. Under very peculiar circumstances acquiescence may be sinful. Even ecclesiastical superiors must be disobeyed if they command an injustice, and spiritual penalties in such case fall harmlessly upon the soul which in good faith disregards them at the bidding of conscience.* Father Boïl was resisting legitimate authority in a civil matter, and deserved chastisement. As he had not the spirit of a martyr, a little fasting on bread and water reduced him to silence, though of course it did not improve his temper. Many proud spirits had been offended beyond forgiveness, but a more conciliatory policy might have been even more disastrous, and probably was not feasible. The hidalgos were not open to argument where their pride was touched. To exempt them from a share in the burden was to throw it all upon a few poor

---

* "Compendium Theologicum Morale," P. Joan Gury, S. J., t. ii., §§ 932, 934, 937.

men, who, with their decreasing numbers, would have had to be literally worked to death to supply the growing wants of the invalids and privileged idlers. Columbus in this emergency showed once more that indomitable will which clings to duty at all costs, and braves popular clamor rather than commit injustice or depart from principle." * While historians uniformly condemn the conduct of Father Boil, and no doubt his brethren of the Order of St. Benedict unite with them, it must be acknowledged that the Benedictines have since and now a hundred-fold repaired the scandal his example then gave, as is well exemplified in America by the numerous Benedictine abbeys, priories, colleges, convents, and schools in our own country. Those venerable monks now have in the United States two arch abbots, seven mitred abbots, and a host of pious and learned religious conducting the Benedictine institutions in our midst.

While it was easy for persons thus necessarily subjected to distasteful privations for the common safety to accuse Columbus of cruelty even toward his Spanish followers, and some historians have unguardedly been led to this view, it has well been remarked that the progress of riper studies and more thorough researches has tended of late greatly to the vindication of Columbus, and to the exaltation of his name and character. Not only is this true in respect to the charge of arbitrary administration and cruel measures toward the colonists he brought to Hispaniola, but it is equally true in respect to the impression that he was destitute of the faculty of wise and discreet government, which is now a refuted statement.

The charges of cruelty and tyranny which his enemies made against Columbus have been often refuted. Mr. John Fiske, in his admirable work on " The Discovery of America," vol. i., p. 481, writes justly and ably on this subject, and says : " No marked effect seems to have been produced by these first complaints, but when Margarite and Boyle [Boil] were once within reach of Fonseca, we need not wonder that mischief was soon brewing. It was unfortunate for Columbus that his work of exploration was hampered by the necessity of founding a colony and governing a parcel of unruly men, let loose in the wilderness,

---

* "The Life of Columbus," by Arthur George Knight, of the Society of Jesus, pp. 119-21.

far away from the powerful restraints of civilized society. Such work required undivided attention and extraordinary talent for command. It does not appear that Columbus was lacking in such talent. On the contrary, both he and his brother Bartholomew seem to have possessed it in a high degree ; but the situation was desperately bad when the spirit of mutiny was fomented by deadly enemies at court. I do not find adequate justification for the charges of tyranny brought against Columbus. The veracity and fairness of the history of Las Casas are beyond question. In his divinely beautiful spirit one sees now and then a trace of tenderness even for Fonseca, whose conduct toward him was always as mean and malignant as toward Columbus. One gets from Las Casas the impression that the admiral's high temper was usually kept under firm control, and that he showed far less severity than most men would have done under similar provocation. Bartholomew was made of sterner stuff, but his whole career shows no instance of wanton cruelty ; toward both white men and Indians his conduct was distinguished by clemency and moderation. Under the government of these brothers a few scoundrels were hanged in Hispaniola. Many more ought to have been."

CHAPTER X.

> "Where'er thou journeyest, or whate'er thy care,
> My heart shall follow and my spirit share."
> —Mrs. Sigourney.

> "Oh, sad vicissitudes
> Of earthly things! To what untimely end
> Are all the fading glories that attend
> Upon the state of greatest monarchs brought!
> What safety can by policy be wrought,
> Or rest be found on fortune's restless wheel."
> —May's "Henry II."

BEFORE departing on his long-intended voyage of discovery among the islands of the new world, Columbus, with sagacity and forethought, placed everything in Hispaniola in the best condition then and there possible. He was habitually most painstaking in all such emergencies, and endeavored to foresee and provide in advance for them. In the first place, he wrote a detailed and admirable series of instructions for Margarite, to whom was intrusted the preservation of the peace of the island during the admiral's absence. His first injunctions charged that commander, above all things, to protect the natives from all injustice and ill-treatment at the hands of the Spaniards, and by kindness to win their good-will and friendship; he was on all occasions, however, to exact from the natives the respect due to the Spanish authority, and the observance of the rights of property; thefts from the Spaniards were to be severely punished; all purchases of food from the natives for the Spaniards were to be justly and fully paid for, and only in cases of necessity was he to compel them to part with provisions, and to then always temper compulsion with kindness. Private dealings between the Spaniards and the natives were strictly forbidden, and, even above all gold and food, the conversion of the Indians to Christianity was to be preferred, such being the wish of the Spanish sovereigns and his own; the strictest discipline in the army was to be kept up and enforced. These wise and honorable measures, if faithfully carried out by Margarite, would have assuredly preserved the peace of the island, and have won the friendship of the natives. It was true that the admiral gave instructions for the capture of the warlike and treacherous Caonabo and his brothers, for no peace could be preserved as long as they were at liberty to conspire and war against the Spaniards; and though he authorized resort, for this purpose, to force and stratagem, he considered that the necessity of the case and the treacherous character of these enemies justified it. How far Margarite obeyed the instructions of his superior the sequel will show; but alas! the viceroy's authority was like the crowns of earthly sovereigns, which are studded outside with diamonds, but inside are lined with thorns. Columbus had reached a plane of glory, honor, power, and dignity which made him the object of envy and malice among his followers, of slander and detraction among courtiers, and of the ingratitude of sovereigns.

In order also to secure the civil welfare, peace, and good administration of the colony and island, he appointed a council of eminent men to conduct affairs in his absence; these councillors were his brother, Don Diego Columbus, whom he made president of the council, and the other members were Father Boīl, Pedro Fernandez Coronel, Alonzo Sanchez Caravajal, and Juan de Luxan. In thus appointing Father Boīl, whose enmity to himself he well knew, was displayed one of those frequent acts in the life of this illustrious admiral which showed him to be always above private revenge, and magnanimous to his enemies. He determined to leave in the colony the two largest ships, which he knew were of too deep a draft of water to be used in exploring the coasts and inlets of the island, and he took with him his three caravels—the Nina, or Santa Clara, the San Juan, and the Cordera. The important island of Hispaniola, which was thus left under the civil jurisdiction of Don Diego Columbus and the council or junta, and under the military care of Ojeda and Margarite, deserves some notice at our hands as to its territorial and political distribution. This will aid in detailing and understanding our future historical narratives.

Hayti, as the natives called it, was divided into five kingdoms or lordships, each of which was ruled over by a king or principal cacique or chief, each of whom had under him a number of lesser caciques, lords or vassals. The five paramount caciques were

Guarionex, Caonabo, Behechio, Guacanagari, and Guayacoa. The northeast portion of the island was governed by Guarionex, a prince descended from the most illustrious ancestors, and in his dominions was situated the beautiful and grand plain, which the Spaniards had named the Royal Vega. In this kingdom was also erected the city of Isabella by the Spaniards, a liberty taken without condescending to ask the monarch's consent. The northeastern part was ruled over by the prince with whom we are now most familiar, the amiable but weak Guacanagari, and extended from Antibonite to beyond Monte Christo. The most eastern portions were under the rude sceptre of Guayacoa, whose tribe, accustomed to attacks by the Caribs, had become the most warlike and the best armed, skilled in war, and bravest, from the necessity they labored under of frequently defending their homes and country from their cannibal neighbors. The mountainous part of the island was reigned over by the redoubtable Caonabo, from the heights of Cibao to the southern shore. He was of Carib origin, and no one knew his pedigree, for he came a stranger and an adventurer. Thrown on the island by accident, he was there detained by a romantic love affair, and having become a soldier, and by his ability secured power, like another Napoleon, he crowned himself. He was feared by his neighbors, and his alliance sought. The remainder of the island, constituting its greater part, extending from Antibonite westward toward Cape Tiburon, and containing the famous salt lake of Xaragua, which was legendary with tales of wonder and mystery, was governed by Behechio. The natives were generally of a timid and peaceful character, with the exception of the tribes living at the east and toward the Caribbean Island, and the warlike tribes of the warrior and lover-king, Caonabo. The soil of the whole island was rich, the climate enervating; the food products were spontaneous and abundant, and before the advent of Europeans life was blissful, indolent, and free. Such was the first permanent conquest of Europeans in America, and such the dominion now temporarily left by Columbus to the regency of his brother Diego and the Council of State.

Having completed all his preparations, provided for all things with prudence and forethought, the admiral saw Don Alonzo de Ojeda march forth from Isabella on April 9th, with his gallant little army of nearly four hundred men, who soon arrived at Rio del Oro, in the Royal Vega. Here, learning that a neighboring cacique had connived at the robbery of three Spaniards, returning from Fort St. Thomas, by five Indians, whom he had sent ostensibly to assist the travelers to ford the river, Ojeda, with the promptness and impulse of a soldier of the fifteenth century —though four intervening centuries have not materially altered now a soldier's method of dealing with Indians—immediately pursued and caught one of the robbers, and caused his ears to be cut off in the public square; he arrested the cacique, his son and nephew, and sent them in chains to the admiral, and then coolly pursued his march. The admiral, generally lenient with the natives, now formed his judgment of the guilt of his prisoners from the account sent to him by Ojeda, and refusing to listen to the intercession of a neighboring cacique, who accompanied the prisoners to Isabella from sympathy, he ordered the poor and dejected natives to be marched, with their hands tied behind them, to the public square and beheaded. At the last moment he spared and released his royal prisoners at the entreaty of the friendly cacique, who went their surety that the offence should never be repeated. It is believed that the admiral did not from the beginning intend to punish the offenders with death, though theft was punished among the natives themselves by impalement. Just at this moment a Spanish horseman arrived in town from the fort, and reported that on passing the village of the captive cacique, he had found five Spaniards in the hands of his subjects; but on the sight of the horse and rider the natives, four hundred in number, had precipitately fled, and that he had pursued them, wounded several with his lance, and had recaptured and triumphantly brought back the Spanish prisoners. Such adventures were greatly to the tastes of the Spanish cavaliers, many of whom preferred such glory to the richest booty in the precious metal. This incident convinced Columbus that he had nothing to fear from the natives, and on April 24th, 1494, he sailed out of port, with his three caravels, on his westward cruise of discovery and exploration.

Columbus selected the Nina for his flag-ship, and on her deck he placed the admiral's pavilion. She was commanded by Alonzo Medel, of Palos. The Cordera was the property of Cristobal Perez Niño, of Palos, and the San Juan was commanded by a seaman from Malaga, but had a crew from Palos. It must be remembered that the Nina, the little caravel which was in the first voyage in which America was discovered, and which stanchly carried him back to Europe amid terrific storms, had now become the Santa Clara, so called by Columbus in honor of St. Clare, the seraphic daughter of the Order of St. Francis. Among the officers he carried were Father Antonio de Marchena, who was an accomplished astronomer, the physician-in-chief, Dr. Chanca, and others of eminence and ability.

In going to explore Cuba it must be borne in mind that Columbus and his companions, and all the world with them, believed that it was the Continent of Asia, and that by commencing his discoveries and explorations at the point where he had left off in the first voyage, and continuing to coast along its southern side, he would assuredly reach the opulent and luxurious countries so graphically described by Mandeville and Marco Polo, the golden and commercial regions of the famed Cathay. What we now know of the West India Islands was information first obtained by Columbus in this and other similar cruises; more minute knowledge of them and of the two continents of the Western Hemisphere followed from his and other subsequent voyages; and when we consider how many years passed before the continents were explored or known as such, and the Pacific Ocean was discovered or entered by Europeans, we can the better appreciate this expedition, its importance, its method of prosecution, and its results. So far from possessing little importance at the present day, it is full of interest and significance, showing the slow and gradual, timid and experimental manner in which mankind has been left by the Creator of the world to explore and become acquainted with the planet given them for their home. It constitutes an important chapter in the history of geography. What now could be easily accomplished by a school-boy on his yacht in a summer vacation, then required the greatest of seamen, cosmographers, and discoverers to undertake, and even then to leave unfinished. The feelings, thoughts, hopes, doubts, expedients, and bold adventures which then formed a part of the admiral's career of discovery and exploration must now become our own, and we must enter into them, adopt them, in order to do justice to his services, appreciate his achievements, and sympathize with his position. We must with him dream again his realizing dreams, for

> "Dreams are rudiments
> Of the great state to come. We dream what is
> About to happen."
>
> —BAILEY.

The fleet first stopped at Monte Christo, and on the very day of sailing reached the ill-fated harbor of La Navidad, so deeply associated with saddest events. He desired here to secure an interview with his friend, the cacique Guacanagari, still trusting in his loyalty and hoping to restore confidence on both sides by an exchange of explanations. But the weak and timid chieftain studiously avoided such a meeting, and retired to the woods with his family and simple court on seeing the ships enter the harbor; and though several of his subjects assured the admiral that the cacique was coming to visit him on his ship, the meeting never took place. The amorous chief was solicitous, as is supposed, for the possession of his fair campanion, the proud Catalina, now his queen. The other object of Columbus in visiting this spot was to arrange for supplies to his colony from the abundance of friendly neighbors, but this negotiation he was obliged to forego for want of time; and he sailed out of the harbor, leaving behind the saddest associations both of the dead and the living. The former could never be effaced; but Guacanagari proved his fidelity afterward, and became one of the most painful sacrifices to the advance of Spanish dominion, in the loss of kingdom, home, and life itself.

The winds not proving favorable, the fleet arrived on the 29th at Port St. Nicholas, and here he could see the extreme end of Cuba, previously named by the admiral Alpha and Omega, now called Point Maysi; and, after crossing the channel and coasting along the southern side of Cuba for a distance of twenty leagues, he reached and anchored at the fine harbor of Guantanamo, then called by him Puerto Grande. Entering the port through the narrow entrance, Columbus landed near and visited the cottages he saw; but the inhabitants had fled, leaving their fires expiring and a bountiful meal unconsumed. The Spaniards, who were still on short allowances of food, enjoyed the good things the natives had left behind; but the guanas they could not accept, even though hungry, regarding them as a species of serpent, though Peter Martyr relates that the Indians regarded them in so exalted a light that, like peacocks and pheasants in Spain, the common people were forbidden to eat of them. The fugitive Indians were seen afterward assembled, to the number of about seventy, on a neighboring eminence, and on the Spaniards approaching them, fled to the woods. The inhabitants of the whole neighborhood were struck with panic on seeing the ships. One of the Indians, however, lingered, and, with mingled fear and curiosity, finally was drawn by friendly signs to stay, though always on the alert. When the Lucayan interpreter from one of the ships accosted him in that dialect and with words of friendship, he lost all fear, approached and entered into conversation ; and when convinced of the friendly intentions of the Spaniards, he carried the tidings to his companions, whereupon these also gradually came forth from their retreat, and approached the strangers with awe and marked respect. The disposition of these people was pacific, like that of the Haytians ; they freely and pleasantly sanctioned the consumption of their feast by the strangers, alleging that one night's fishing would replace it, and accepted with unfeigned gratitude the European trifles which Columbus gave them in return. He never allowed their offerings to be received without a return of a full equivalent.* These natives had come to the shore to prepare a banquet of sea food for a neighboring cacique, whom their own chief was expecting as a visitor at his village, and the fish was cooked in order to save it from spoiling.

Columbus continued his cruise on May 1st to the west, and as he advanced the coasts became precipitate and mountainous ; he saw many fine harbors and rivers, and the country was more fertile and populous. Everywhere the neighbors came down in crowds to see the visitors from the skies, offering them cassava bread, fish, fruits, and calabashes of water, and being only too happy to have them accepted by such wonderful and mysterious beings. The admiral in one instance spent a night on shore, and was embarrassed by the urgent and unstinted hospitality of these innocent people. It is supposed that this spot is the present harbor of St. Jago de Cuba. As usual anxious inquiries were made by the Spaniards for gold, and as usual they were informed that it abounded farther to the south. The natives told him of

---

* Irving's "Columbus," vol. i., p. 397 ; Barry's translation of De Lorgues' "Columbus," p. 292 ; Peter Martyr, decad. i., lib. iii.

a great island in that direction, which, from its reported wealth in gold, Columbus was convinced must be the long-sought and opulent island of Babeque, of whose existence he had heard on his first voyage. He accordingly, on May 3d, turned his prows to the south, abandoning his exploration of Cuba, and across the open sea he sailed in quest of that favored land.

It was not many leagues before the majestic shores and mountains of Jamaica loomed up in grandeur before him, and, after two days' and nights' sailing, he reached and anchored in a beautiful harbor, to which he gave the name of Santa Gloria. He also gave to the vast island the name of Santiago, but it has ever been called by its original native name of Jamaica. Leaving the harbor the following day for a better one, he entered and anchored in a fine harbor, which he called Puerto Bueno. At his first approach to this vicinity the natives came out in canoes with hostile manifestations, but these by a few presents were dispelled. At his present harborage the natives in great numbers prepared for war, the shore resounded with yells and war-cries, and their javelins were hurled violently at the ships. The admiral, desiring to careen his ship, the Nina, for calking, and to send his men on shore for water, found it necessary first to teach a lesson of Spanish invincibility to these warlike savages. He sent his boats to the shore with men well armed ; a first discharge of arrows from the Spanish cross-bows wounded some and threw the whole native army into confusion, whereupon the Spaniards, springing ashore, discharged a second volley of arrows, which put the multitude to flight. A dog from one of the Spanish boats pursued the Indians with terrific fury, biting them as they fled. Irving relates that the Spaniards let loose the dog to pursue the Indians, and says : "This was the first instance of the use of dogs against the natives, which were afterward employed with such cruel effect by the Spaniards in their Indian wars." But the Count de Lorgues and Dr. Barry give a different version of the affair, as one of pure accident, and say : "A dog, which found its way into the party, seeing them flee, pursued them with fury, biting them in their hinder parts as they fled." They also state that it was this incident which first suggested to the Spaniards the idea of employing dogs against the Indians, as they afterward most shamefully did. Tarducci concurs in the latter view of the accidental presence of the dog.

Not only were the natives of Jamaica more warlike, but their food was better, the fruits of finer flavor, and the plants and herbs more aromatic. A fruitless cruise along the coast, for about twenty-five leagues, having disclosed the existence of no gold, the admiral determined to return to Cuba ; and he thought that by coasting fifty or sixty leagues he could determine the question whether it was an island or a continent. The admiral was surprised to find the Jamaicans so warlike, while their neighbors were pacific. They were also much more at home on the water ; their canoes were large, and were made of the trunks of single trees ; one of them was measured by the admiral, and was ninety-six feet long and eight feet broad. He took formal possession of the island for the Spanish sovereigns. Just as the fleet was about to sail a young native came and begged to be taken on board the departing ship ; and as his friends and relatives were clinging to him and begging him to desist from so rash a design, his feelings for a moment vibrated between love of home and relatives, on the one side, and a love of adventure, novelty, and romance on the other ; when suddenly he tore himself away violently from their embrace and hid himself in a secret part of the ship, and thus saw and felt no more the tears and heard not the lamentations of his sisters. Columbus caused this young adventurer to be treated with marked kindness, but his subsequent history and his fate have never been recorded by historians.*

Some historians have expressed surprise that, of the many natives of the new world whom the early Spaniards sent to Europe in their returning ships, we have no accounts, and little interest seems to have been felt in the result of this method of treating the Indians. In some cases, as we know, the red men, transplanted to the eastern world, have sickened and died, pining for their native forests and hunting-grounds.

Having decided to steer for the island of Cuba again, while anchored in a fine gulf near the western extremity of Jamaica, in consequence of his disappointment in finding no gold in the latter island, a favorable breeze had sprung up for sailing toward the former, and he called this gulf Buentiempo, or Fair Weather. The fleet arrived off the coast of Cuba on May 18th, and the

---

* Irving's "Columbus," vol. i., p. 402 ; "Historia del Almirante," cap. 54

great cape where they first arrived was called Cabo de la Cruz, or Cape of the Cross. Having landed and accepted the bountiful hospitality of the cacique of a large village and its inhabitants, the Spaniards learned from their generous entertainers that from the time of their former landing and coasting along the island, the news of their arrival had spread far and near, and all the inhabitants were eager to see these wonderful strangers from the clouds. The admiral questioned these Cubans closely as to whether this was an island or a continent, and so vague were their answers that he could conclude but little from them, though they described it as an island of infinite extent, which would indicate that such was the native idea of a continent.*

The fleet sailed the following day still to the west from the last point of landing, which the Indians called Macaca, and when it arrived at the part where the coast abruptly turned and extended many leagues to the northeast, they found themselves in a large gulf, and suddenly enveloped in a storm of extraordinary violence, in which would have perished the whole fleet but for its short duration. The navigation was rendered difficult and dangerous by innumerable keys and sand-banks, and from these were seen in the distance countless small islands, some of which were low and flat, others naked and sandy; some covered with verdure, and others elevated and crowned with fine forests. His judgment as a navigator would have led him to steer clear of such impassable barriers, but his geographical studies and theories induced him to recognize in this labyrinth of islands the coast of Asia, as described by Mandeville and Marco Polo, who portrayed that continent as approachable through an archipelago of countless islands. Now surely he was approaching the dominions of the Grand Khan. This theory induced him to attempt to sail in among them, but he was entangled in an impenetrable network of islands, and navigation was difficult, dangerous, and even impossible. To add to his embarrassment, the weather showed extraordinary features; but upon close observation there was method and regularity in its apparent caprices. Columbus was one of the most acute and correct observers of all the phenomena of nature, and in this instance he recorded

---

* "Historia del Almirante," cap. 54; Cura de los Palacios, cap. 126; Irving's "Columbus," vol. i., p. 404; Dr. Barry's De Lorgues' "Columbus," p. 295.

his observations, to the effect that every morning the wind came from the east and every evening from the west; on the approach of night the west was heavily clouded, the clouds increasing as they approached the zenith and sending forth sheets of lightning, with heavy peals of thunder; but when the moon appeared the skies immediately became serene and clear. Fruitful as his mind and memory were in selecting names from the calendar of saints, the martyrology of the Church, and from her history and devotions, he was at a loss to find names for such countless groups of islands, and he called them all together the Queen's Gardens.

During the month spent in efforts to explore this dangerous labyrinth of islands, Columbus made frequent descents on the island of Cuba, for this was the chief object of his study, and endeavored to solve the mystery of its geography; but the natives were confused in their accounts, and ignorant of its size and surroundings. They had never heard of its having a western terminus; a ship could not reach its extremity in forty moons; but they referred the admiral for more detailed information to a tribe living more to the west, and whose country was called Mangon. On inquiring further of the inhabitants of Mangon, he was told that they were accustomed to wear flowing garments in order to conceal the long tails with which their bodies were deformed; and here again his ready and well-stored mind recalled passages from Sir John Mandeville, giving an account of some naked tribes in the remote East, who ridiculed the practice of some more civilized Orientals, as they alleged, in wearing clothes to conceal the defects of their persons, for they could not conceive of any other use for clothing. The name of Mangon also was believed by him to be a mere corruption of Mangi, which was described by his favorite authors as the richest of the maritime provinces of the Grand Khan. He also recalled the Tartars, dressed in flowing robes. They described the cacique of Mangon as wearing a long robe, and such may have been the effect of this account on the imagination, or it may have been reality: but the archer of the expedition saw, while in the woods near one of the landings in Cuba, a man clothed in white, like the almoner of the Santa Clara; the number of the flowing robes, with the aid of the imagination, was then increased to three, and finally to thirty. An effort was made to capture some of these white-robed people, but the woods were impenetrable to one exploring expedition, and another was frightened off by the recent footprints on the shore of some huge animal with claws. It is difficult to say whether the Europeans or the Indians were more credulous, or laboring under more amusing delusions. Such was the enthusiasm of the admiral, that he thought he could double Aurea Chersonesus and the peninsula of Malacca, and might emerge into the seas navigated by the Arabians and known to the merchants of ancient Rome; he might pass Taprobana, and by pushing forward strike the shores of the Red Sea; thence travel by land to Jerusalem and the Holy Land, which his great discoveries would enable him afterward to restore by a crusade to Christendom; and then again, going on ships at Joppa, traverse the Mediterranean and return to Spain from the East. It is a familiar fact that Columbus lived and died under these impressions, errors in which all the learned world were united with him in opinion. Columbus, in the most formal manner, took possession of what he was convinced was a continent.

Humboldt, in his political history of the island of Cuba, mentions and comments upon a remarkable method of fishing which Columbus saw practised by the Indians of this region. It consisted in using a small live fish for the purpose of capturing larger ones, the former possessing a flat head filled with suckers, by means of which, when let loose on the water at the end of a long line, it attached itself to the game to be caught with such abiding tenacity as to be torn in pieces itself rather than relax its hold. It attached itself to the throat of a large fish or to the under shell of a tortoise, and thus both fishes were drawn in together by the fisherman. The Spaniards saw a large tortoise caught in this way, and on the coast of Veragua afterward a large shark was, in like manner, caught, as is related by Fernando Columbus. Other navigators have seen the same method of fishing practised by the Africans, on the eastern coast of Mozambique and at Madagascar, a fact which deeply interested Humboldt as an evidence of how savages, in different and unconnecting parts of the earth, exercised the universal dominion of man over the animal kingdom by the same and apparently uncommunicated methods.*

---

* Humboldt, "Essai Politique," etc., tom. i., p. 364; Irving's "Columbus," vol. i., p. 408.

These cruises had now exhausted the strength of the sailors; the provisions were running low, and the crews began to call out for a return to Hispaniola. The admiral himself felt more than any one else the exhausting strain. He was forced to abandon his proposal to sail around the land and return to Spain by way of the East.* It was resolved to go no further; it was considered as definitely ascertained that the continent had been discovered, and over three hundred leagues of its coasts explored. In order to make due and formal record of so important a result, the admiral sent a public notary, Fernando Perez de Luna, accompanied by four witnesses, to visit each vessel, with instructions to ask and receive the opinion of every one on board—captain, officers, seamen, and ship-boys—whether they entertained a doubt as to the country, or that they had discovered the continent embracing the Indies and affording a passage from the East to Europe and a return to Spain. Although some had of late affected to question his statements and conclusions and to undervalue his discoveries, his sagacity now brought them to the avowal, and every man in the fleet solemnly signed the documents presented to them by the notary, and their signatures were attested by the four witnesses, declaring their conviction in the reality and truth of the admiral's claim as the discoverer of the extremities of Asia. The experienced and veteran navigators on the fleet, after consulting their maps and charts, examining the journals and calculations of the voyage, and after mature deliberation, all declared under oath that this was their conviction, and that it was not susceptible of a doubt. The notary also drew up and certified a formal process, after the continental forms then in vogue, embodying the declarations and affidavits of all the men and officers. The admiral proclaimed severe punishments on such as ever afterward would have the perfidy to question or deny what they had now so solemnly asserted.

On June 13th the admiral steered to the southeast, and having soon sighted the splendid island now known as the Pines, and famous for its mahogany, he called it Evangelista. Having anchored and taken a supply of wood and water, he steered to the south, intending to seek a direct route by open sea to His-

---

* Brownson's Tarducci, vol. i., p. 328.

paniola and along the southern shores of Jamaica. But the fleet was soon landlocked in the lagoon of Siguanca, the provisions were nearly exhausted, the men dismayed; so he immediately returned and endeavored to make his way through the White Sea, which now again showed portents most alarming to the sailors, such as the abrupt changing of the color of the sea, which was at one time green, then black, and now as white as milk. After running aground and injuring his ship, which had to be dragged by the prow over the shoal, he was happy when he extricated his fleet from such dangers. Not only had the waters of this strange archipelago changed their color without apparent cause, but the animal kingdom, in the deep, clear waters of the Cuban coast, had presented most singular changes; for one day the sea was almost covered with tortoises, on another day the air was darkened by the flight of cormorants and cranes, and the next day the scene was obscured by clouds of butterflies, which an evening shower would dispel. On July 6th the fleet neared the extremity of the gulf near Cape Santa Cruz, and on the 7th they landed, and the hungry men enjoyed the unstinted hospitality of the cacique, whose subjects brought them utias, birds, cassava bread, and delicious fruits. On Sunday the admiral had a large cross planted, and mass was solemnly celebrated. Here an incident occurred which goes far to show how impressible the Indians were in their religious feelings, and how hopeful the effort to convert them to Christianity might have been had the cross rather than the sword been the weapon of the white man.

An aged cacique was so deeply impressed with the solemn mass he witnessed, that he fully entered into the devotions of these celestial worshippers, and he and his people evinced the greatest veneration for the imposing service. After the admiral had finished his thanksgiving at the end of mass, the venerable chief approached him with salutations, presented him with a basket of finest fruits, and taking a seat beside him, addressed him, through the interpreter Diego, in the following remarkable terms: "It is meet and just to render thanks to God for the blessings He vouchsafes us. It appears to be your manner, and that of your people, thus to render Him homage; this is all well. I have been informed that some time ago you came with your forces to these countries, which till then were unknown. Remember, I beseech and implore you, that the souls of men, on leaving the body, enter on two ways: one leading to a noisome and dismal place, covered with darkness, prepared for those who have been unjust and cruel to their fellow-men; the other, pleasant and delightful, for such as have loved and promoted peace among men. Beware, then, if you believe yourself to be a mortal man, of doing injury to anybody; and bear in mind that everybody will be rewarded or punished according to his works." *

This pious Indian was moved by the words of Columbus, who assured him that his mission to the west was one of peace and justice, of subjugation only for the inhuman Caribs, and to preach the Gospel of the true religion and of peace. Esteeming his visitors as messengers from heaven, the good cacique was only prevented from joining the Spaniards by the prayers and exhortations of his wife and children. The Spaniards remained on this coast several days, took in provisions, wood, and water, repaired the ship, and from the frequent offerings of the mass here the admiral called the place Rio de la Misa.

The cacique of Rio de la Misa saw with sorrow the Spaniards depart on July 16th; his counsel and advice to them, inspired as they were by the best sentiments of natural religion, were treasured by the admiral, but it seems from subsequent history that the Europeans, in their intercourse with the natives, heeded them not. The address of the venerable native chief sounds in our ears to this day like the last appeal of a doomed race to the justice and mercy of their Christian conquerors. Taking with him a young Indian from this place, and steering to the south, he avoided the Queen's Gardens, and directed his course through the open sea for Jamaica and Hispaniola. On getting clear of these dangerous islands the fleet was struck by a violent storm, but by good and prompt handling the ships were saved; but when at length they reached Cape Santa Cruz, the admiral's ship was greatly damaged. On July 22d they stood for Jamaica, and spent nearly a month in endeavoring to explore its coasts, and accepting the hospitality of the natives, who had now changed their former warlike conduct for that of peace and friendship. The declara-

---

* Barry's De Lorgues' "Life of Columbus," p. 298; Irving's "Columbus," vol. i., p. 426. Other works containing this Indian speech are Herrera, "Historia del Almirante," Peter Martyr, and Cura de los Palacios.

tions of the admiral that the Spaniards would break the power of the Caribs, and give protection to the peaceful islanders, enchained their attention and won their gratitude. The natives were lavish in their hospitality. So adverse were the winds that frequently, on anchoring under the land in the evening, the admiral found himself in the same place that he had left the same morning. So beautiful and interesting did this fine island appear, that he felt strongly inclined to devote some time to the exploration of its interior; he landed frequently, and on one occasion, at one of seven islands in a large bay, received a visit of state and ceremony from the cacique, whose people occupied numerous villages. The chief was attended by a large and imposing retinue, offered refreshments to the hungry and tired visitors, inquired minutely concerning the Spaniards and their country, and expressed special curiosity in relation to their immense ships. Columbus, through the Lucayan interpreter, impressed the chief and his people with long and interesting accounts of the power, riches, and grandeur of Spain, how many countries they had conquered, how many others they had discovered, and, what most interested the natives, how he had defied and defeated the Caribs and captured many of their fiercest warriors.

On the following morning the fleet sailed, but an unexpected detention occurred. The chief, accompanied by his queen and the princesses, his two daughters, and their retinue came out in three large and handsomely painted and carved canoes, and in great state, to visit the admiral and his fleet. In the centre was the largest canoe, bearing the chief and his family, and in its prow stood an Indian official gayly decked in mantle and helmet of feathers, with painted face, and bearing in his hands the royal banner of white; other Indian officials, similarly ornamented, played on tabors; others sounded the royal trumpets of fine black wood, and the royal family had a body-guard of six natives in large hats of white feathers. The cacique was decked in full royal dress, consisting of a band of variegated stones and jewels around his head, and tastily arranged, and containing in the centre at the forehead a large jewel of gold; his ears had two plates of gold suspended from them by rings of green stones; his neck was encircled by a necklace of rare white beads, from which hung a plate of inferior gold; and around his waist was a girdle studded with variegated stones. The queen was similarly decorated, and wore a small apron of cotton, and cotton bands around her arms. The princesses were beautiful in figure and countenance, especially the elder, who was about eighteen years old; both were naked, in accordance with their native custom, and they wore no ornaments, except the elder, who had on a girdle of small stones, from which hung a tablet studded with small stones, all tastily arranged on a cotton network. All were struck with the modest demeanor of the princesses; and when the visitors were on board the admiral's ship, the latter came forth from his devotions to receive his royal guest, and the cacique thus addressed him in terms which seemed like an invitation from the natives of the new world to all Christendom to receive them as fellow-creatures, children of a common Father, as members of one human society, and prospective Christians: " My friend, I have determined to leave my country, and to accompany thee. I have heard from these Indians who are with thee of the irresistible power of thy sovereigns, and of the many nations thou hast subdued in their name. Whoever refuses obedience to thee is sure to suffer. Thou hast destroyed the canoes and dwellings of the Caribs, slaying their warriors, and carrying into captivity their wives and children. All the islands are in dread of thee, for who can withstand thee now that thou knowest the secrets of the land and the weakness of the people? Rather, therefore, than thou shouldst take away my dominions, I will embark with all my household in thy ships, and will go to do homage to thy king and queen, and to behold their country, of which thy Indians relate such wonders." Columbus was too magnanimous to accept the proposition of the good cacique, when he thought of the snares and deceptions to which their innocence and simplicity would expose them in a Christian and civilized country—a severe but honest reflection upon the more favored portion of mankind. He soothed the disappointed feelings of his royal visitors, and succeeded in persuading them to return, though reluctantly, to their own country. It was only a question of time how soon the surrender would come!

Columbus, on leaving the eastern end of Jamaica, called it Cape Farol, though now known as Point Morant, and taking an easterly course, he next day saw in the distance the long peninsula of Hispaniola; he called it Cape San Miguel, but it is now known as Cape Tiburon. Not knowing then that he was off the island of Hayti, or Jamaica, he became aware of the fact in a most agreeable way when a cacique coming toward his ship addressed him in Spanish, " Admiral, admiral, how could you have conjectured that this cape belonged to Hispaniola?" These words were received with joy by all, for they had cruised for five long and dreary months, had encountered many violent storms, and felt the exhaustion and fatigues of incessant labor and the pangs of hunger ; for not only the men and officers had been reduced in their rations to a cracker and a small cup of wine, but, as on all other occasions, the admiral had led the way by submitting himself first of all to the same privations and sufferings that his companions had to endure. Being separated from his two ships, Columbus tried in vain to sight them from a high rock near Cape Beata, which, from its resemblance to a large ship, he called Alto Velo. After the caravels had joined him, he continued his cruise along the coast of Hayti, and from his intercourse with the natives he learned with satisfaction that all was quiet in Hispaniola. This news encouraged and justified him, though ever-cautious, after he had sailed some distance beyond the river Neyoa, to send nine men across the country on foot to Isabella to announce his arrival. After encountering another storm, witnessing a hostile demonstration from the Indians of the eastern end of the island, who were of Carib descent, spending eight days in the shelter under a small island to which he gave the name of Saona, and being separated again during the storm from his caravels, he finally, in company with the again united fleet, reached the eastern end of Hispaniola. Thence he sailed to the southeast, and such was the energy and courage of the veteran explorer and discoverer, that even now he felt inclined to prolong the voyage to the Caribbean Islands, and perhaps attempt their subjugation. But he was exhausted both in mind and body by the labors, privations, and anxieties of this protracted voyage, by alternate hopes of realizing the discovery of the Continent of Asia, and of discovering countries rich in gold and spices, and by the disappointments and comparatively small results of such brave efforts. His crews were exhausted also, and anxious to return to Isabella. He had actually reached a point on the island of Cuba whence a boy from the masthead could have distinctly seen the open sea on the other side of the island, and thus have solved the all-important question; but it was at this point that the fleet reversed its course, and all acquiesced in the theory that they had reached the extremity of Asia. Excitement and ambition had sustained the admiral through the vicissitudes of this expedition; but now, this stimulus being removed by his near approach to home, his whole being, with all its mental, moral, and physical faculties relapsed, and his mind and body fell into a singular and profound lethargy.

This remarkable phenomenon of human nature is spoken of by the eulogist of Columbus, the Count de Lorgues, in the following earnest language: " It was just five months since he had departed from Hispaniola. For a hundred and fifty consecutive days his study of nature, his examination of waters and soils, his contemplation of the wonderful works of God, his efforts to reconcile with each other the contradictory statements of the natives to attain some geographical verity, and his prolonged struggle against the elements, maintaining his soul, his intellect, his body, in triple activity, exhausted all his forces. The feeling of his responsibility, and the necessity of constantly directing the navigation in person himself, were too much for his age, his infirmities, his want of nourishment, and his privation of sleep. All his organs became simultaneously torpid. His brain, as well as his eyes and his limbs, yielded to fatigues that surpassed human endurance. There was a total suspension of all his physical and moral faculties. It was a state of complete lethargy. Were it not for the pulsation of his arteries, the flexibility of his members, one would have believed his sublime soul had returned to its Creator." *

Mr. Irving mentions the same singular event in the following language: " The very day on which he sailed from Mona he was struck with a sudden malady which deprived him of memory, of sight, and of all his faculties. He fell into a deep lethargy, resembling death itself. His crew, alarmed at this profound torpor, feared that death was really at hand. They abandoned, therefore, all further prosecution of the voyage, and spreading their sails to the east wind, so prevalent in those seas, bore Columbus back in a state of complete insensibility to the harbor of Isabella."†

---

* De Lorgues' "Columbus," by Dr. Barry, p. 302.
† Irving's "Columbus," vol i., p. 437.

The colony at Isabella saw with joy the good ship Santa Clara enter the port on September 29th, 1494. They had not heard any tidings of the fleet that sailed out five months before, under the admiral, to discover and explore regions of the earth then as unknown to civilized man as America had been before Columbus discovered it. They had feared that the admiral had fallen a victim to his great enterprising spirit and indomitable courage, and had perished in his great adventure. But now the chief, after five days and nights of a death-like lethargy, was aroused to consciousness by the once familiar and ever-affectionate voice of his brother Bartholomew. His brother Diego also was there, and from his arrival attended at his bedside with untiring care and tenderness.

Columbus had not seen or heard from Bartholomew for eight years, and these were years of unparalleled eventfulness. Having sent him to England to make proposals for a voyage of western discovery, on the occasion of his own visit to Portugal, in 1485, Columbus, in the mean time, as we have related, secured the patronage of Spain. On his voyage to England, Bartholomew Columbus fell into the hands of a corsair, and plundered of all he possessed, he was compelled, like his brother at one time, to support himself by making charts and marine maps. It has already been mentioned that he had made a voyage to the coast of Africa under Bartholomew Diaz, in 1486, in the service of the King of Portugal, and thus participated in the discovery of the Cape of Good Hope. His brother Christopher had met him in Lisbon in 1485. It was not until 1493 that he succeeded in reaching the English court and laying his brother's proposals before Henry VII. It is well worthy of note, and certainly much to the credit and honor of the English king, that he was pleased from the beginning with the plans of Columbus. It did not require long and tedious years of entreaty and waiting to bring that sovereign's mind to a conviction, as had been the case with Portugal and Spain. Bartholomew acquitted himself so well of his mission that Henry VII. actually welcomed the project, and entered into a preliminary treaty on the subject. It was while he was hurrying from England to Spain, as the bearer of these negotiations, that Bartholomew heard at Paris of the discovery of the new world by his brother, Christopher Columbus, and of his return and triumphal reception by the Spanish sovereigns.

The very name of Columbus had now already become famous throughout the world. Charles VIII., King of France, was his first informant of his brother's great achievement, and of his elevation to the position of admiral and viceroy. That sovereign paid him distinguished honor, and presented him with a hundred gold crowns for defraying his traveling expenses through France. He arrived at Seville not long after the departure of the admiral on his second voyage. He thence visited his sister-in-law, Donna Beatrix Enriquez, at Cordova, where the admiral's sons, Diego and Fernando, were at school, and brought them to court, where they were all received with kindness and distinction. The queen retained the youths at court, and had every pains taken to prepare them for their functions as pages to Prince Juan. The keen eye of King Ferdinand immediately detected the sterling qualities of Bartholomew Columbus and his experiences as a veteran navigator, and, having bestowed upon him letters of nobility, gave him the command of three ships destined to carry provisions to Hispaniola.

But on arriving at Isabella he again missed the admiral, who had not long before sailed on his expedition to Cuba. This faithful brother became an important actor in the future events and history of the western countries. He was a man of true worth. He was candid and truthful, prompt to decide and prompt to execute, capable, fearless, and resolute. While his manners and address were austere, and even at times somewhat abrupt, his generosity was unbounded; he was above malice or resentment; brave beyond fear, and accessible. His brother Diego, on the other hand, was gentle, mild, and sympathetic; as devout as a recluse, studious, retiring, and inexperienced in affairs; and even in his dress he resembled a monk rather than a man of the world. But for the wish of the admiral, who was the recognized head of the family, he would have retired to a cloister or have become a man of study and letters. The admiral having but two brothers available, regarded their personal services and counsels as necessary to his great undertakings. While Christopher and Diego were men of religious sentiments and devout lives, Bartholomew, while a good and earnest Christian, was a man of the world, and a master of men and of affairs.

The cheerful and reassuring influences of the society of his two devoted brothers soon restored Columbus to his accustomed health and spirits. Feeling the necessity of some one to share with him the onerous and unceasing cares of administration and of responsibility, he appointed Bartholomew to the high and responsible position of Adelantado, an office resembling that of lieutenant-governor. The advices from the court and the general tenor of the information brought out by his brother greatly consoled Columbus for his sacrifices and sufferings, and stimulated his zeal to continue the humane course adopted toward the Indians, his labors for the good of his sovereigns and his country, and for the success and permanence of his great enterprise.

It was not long before the admiral received further advices from the Spanish sovereigns of high importance, and of great encouragement and support to him—advices showing how fully he possessed the confidence and sympathy of the Spanish rulers. Antonio Torres arrived with four ships loaded with provisions, refreshments, medicines, clothing, and merchandise. The ships also brought out a physician and an apothecary, besides mechanics, millers, fishermen, gardeners and farmers ; and the queen did not fail to show her delicate regard for her admiral in providing especially for his comfort and for the dignity of his office. The letters which Torres brought out, and which were dated August 16th, 1494, conveyed the most satisfactory and comforting accounts of the feelings entertained by the sovereigns toward himself and his enterprise ; they assured him of their entire satisfaction with his conduct, informing him that his representations and engagements had all been fulfilled, and showing the greatest deference for him and his judgment in requesting him to come to Spain and take part in the deliberations going on between Spain and Portugal in relation to their respective discoveries and dominions, and to assist the same by his counsel ; or, in case he could not come, then to send his brother, Don Bartholomew, or some other competent and trusty person, to whom he would communicate his views and suggestions. The sovereigns expressed in their letters the highest interest in the colony, and adopting it as a permanent and favorite measure of the crown, arranged for a monthly passage or communication between Hispaniola and the mother country. All the admiral's appointments to office were confirmed, all persons in the colony were commanded to obey him and sustain his administration, and orders were given the bureaucratic Director-General of Marine to provide all that was needed for the colony. Every solicitude was shown, especially by the queen, for imparting the Christian religion to the natives, and a special letter was written to Father Boil, urging his zeal to activity, stimulating that missionary to exertion for this great end, and encouraging him to overcome the difficulties of the Indian language. A personal letter from the queen to Columbus, dated August 16th, 1494, as the Count de Lorgues writes, " was particularly calculated to console the admiral, and refresh his soul with its sweet sympathies."* As the admiral was aware that the tongue of detraction had already begun its efforts to undermine his influence and standing at court, these just and noble communications and commendations from his sovereigns went far to sustain his efforts for the glory and aggrandizement of his adopted country.

Columbus was prompt in making due acknowledgments of the royal missive which had been received in the colonies, and in defending himself and his administration from the aspersions of his enemies. He would have returned to Spain himself to make his own vindication in person, but he was in too feeble a state of health to undertake the voyage, and his brother, Don Bartholomew, was needed now more than ever in the then distracted state of the colony, which we are now about to relate, to manage and direct affairs with his strong arm and resolute will. He therefore sent his brother, Don Diego, who, besides the many other commissions he received from the admiral, was specially charged with communicating the admiral's views in relation to the geographical line which was destined to separate the dominions of Spain and Portugal from each other. It was thus that he hastened the return of the ships to Spain under Torres, bearing not only the most convincing proofs of the value of the great discovery he had made, but also carrying all the gold he could collect, besides specimens of other useful and valuable metals, of the fruits and plants of the new world, and other proofs of the riches of the western islands.

But there was one portion of the return cargo which Columbus sent to Spain which has been made the subject of animadversion on the part of some historians, and of excuse or extenuation on

---

* De Lorgues' "Columbus," by Dr. Barry, p. 313 ; "Documentos Diplomaticos," Num. lxxx. ; Muños, " Historia del Nuevo Mundo," lib. iv., § 24.

the part of others. Anxious to make as valuable and remunerative a return to his sovereigns for their great outlays in the new world as possible, he sent back in the fleet under Torres about five hundred Indian prisoners, who, in accordance with the practice of the age and country, were intended to be sold into slavery in order to reimburse the royal exchequer. Mr. Irving has justly said that " it is painful to find the brilliant renown of Columbus sullied by so foul a stain. The customs of the times, however, must be pleaded in his apology." Then, after giving instances wherein Spain or Portugal had indulged in the traffic in slaves, either in Africa or in the wars against the Moors in Spain, he says: " These circumstances are not advanced to vindicate, but to palliate the conduct of Columbus. He acted but in conformity to the customs of the times, and was sanctioned by the example of the sovereigns under whom he served."* The Count de Lorgues, however, mentions this circumstance in a different light, and says: " As the ships brought by Torres contained a large number of rebel Indian prisoners, captured with arms in their hands, Don Juan de Fonseca received orders to have them sold in the markets of Andalusia." And again: " Although an ordinance had been expedited for the sale of the prisoners, according to the custom that then prevailed in regard to infidels and idolaters, still a scruple arose in the mind of Isabella. The enterprise of the discovery having, as a prime object, the conversion of natives who did not know Christ, the queen considered within herself whether she should not treat these people as future children of the Church, and whether it was not contrary to the Gospel to enslave them? She commanded that the prisoners should be carried back to Hispaniola, and all set free, with the exception of nine, who were destined by the admiral to serve as interpreters, and who were to remain some time in Castile to learn the language." † But Las Casas, the illustrious Bishop of Chiapa, who was the defender of the natural rights of the Indians, and the untiring opponent of the unjust policy of enslaving them, also excuses or palliates the action of Columbus on this occasion. " If," says he, " those pious and learned men, whom the sovereigns took for guides and instructors, were so ignorant of the

---

* Irving's " Columbus," vol. ii., p. 40.
† Barry's De Lorgues' " Columbus," p. 330.

injustice of this practice, it is no wonder that the unlettered admiral should not be conscious of its impropriety." *

Having in a previous page mentioned that Ojeda was left in command of Fort St. Thomas, and that Margarite had set forth with the army to make an exploration and military reconnoissance of the interior of the island of Hispaniola, it now remains to relate how a Spanish soldier and gentleman by birth disgraced his profession and dishonored his birthright. So also it has been mentioned that Father Boil's lukewarmness as a missionary had demoralized the missions, and his disloyalty to his civil governor had fomented disaffection in the colony. It is sad, even at this remote day, to record in our pages how so high an ecclesiastic finally deserted the vineyard of the Lord, which he had been sent to till. These two unworthies naturally made common cause, and added to their misconduct the base crime of slander against their civil governor and commander.

The exalted and well-considered instructions which Columbus gave to Margarite on leaving Isabella for the exploration of the island of Cuba, if observed, would have sufficed to pilot the affairs of Hispaniola in peace and prosperity ; but that soldier reversed in his conduct every order he received from his commander. He did not commence by exploring the rugged mountains of Cibao, as the admiral had ordered, but he preferred to loiter and luxuriate in the generous and bountiful hospitality of the Vega. Yielding, besides, to unbridled sensuality, discipline was relaxed, debauchery and riot prevailed throughout the army, and the commander, his officers, and his soldiers, instead of holding the veneration of the natives as visitors from heaven, won and deserved their contempt and hatred as common ruffians. The provisions of the villages were wantonly consumed and wasted, supplies became scarce, and were justly withheld by the Indians. The Spaniards ruthlessly seized what they wanted, without the honesty of making compensation. The lust for gold led to countless acts of what the statutes of civilized countries call robbery, and the lust for women led to the most outrageous acts of injustice, insult, and oppression. The guests of late now became the masters and oppressors of the land. A letter of reprimand and orders to proceed in his reconnoissance of the

---

* Las Casas, " Historia Ind.," tom. i., cap. 122, MS.

island, as directed by the admiral, which he received from Don Diego Columbus and the council at Isabella, was treated by this proud outlaw as an insult to a Spanish gentleman of ancient lineage, and in this he was sustained by the proud hidalgos and cavaliers and by the adventurers of the colony. This was an unpardonable affront to a Spanish gentleman from a foreigner and an upstart. These vicious elements now combined together, not only against the authority of the lieutenant-governor and council, but also against the government of the absent viceroy. So far from restraining their excesses, when admonished by Don Diego and the council, Margarite and his soldiers, as Count de Lorgues remarks, "considered that they did the Indians much honor in taking from them their wives, their provisions and their gold, and in consuming in some days the provisions that would have sufficed for the Indians the third of a year." Margarite actually cast off all authority, and acted as though he were the superior of the lieutenant-governor and the council. He went to Isabella and departed whenever it suited him, and took no notice of Don Diego Columbus or of the council. After spreading ruin in the Royal Vega and among its inhabitants, he repaired to Isabella, and there formed a cabal, of which the dissipated and arrogant cavaliers were members. He and his confederates found a welcome colleague in Father Boïl, and they concerted together to seize the ships which Bartholomew Columbus had brought out, and return to Spain; the one deserting his post, the other abandoning his flock. Having taken possession of the ships, Margarite and Father Boïl sailed for Spain, hoping to justify their misconduct through their influence at court, and that of Bishop Fonseca, and by maligning the characters and administration of Columbus and his brothers. Margarite is supposed to have dreaded the return of the admiral from Cuba, and the punishment he so justly deserved; and he is thought also to have desired relief, through medical aid in Spain, for a loathsome disease brought on by his excessive lusts, and which was then new and comparatively unknown. That Columbus, so marked by his respect to the clergy, should have incurred, in the conscientious discharge of his duty, the unjust animosity of one so prominent and influential as Father Boïl, was a severe increment to his load of sorrows. But if, in the necessities of the colony, he was the first to impose upon himself the regimen of short rations, surely the example of the chief pastor of the colony was indispensable to the success of the rule. But unfortunately Father Boïl thought differently, and hence his resentment, already kindled by the admiral's humane treatment of the natives, now culminated in open rebellion. Their calumnies at court met with support from Fonseca and other unworthy officials and enemies of Columbus, and received reinforcement from proud and offended cavaliers and hidalgos and their relatives at home. As Mr. Irving writes, " The first general and apostle of the new world thus setting the flagrant example of unauthorized abandonment of their posts." And the Count de Lorgues says : " They thus schemed their departure, seized on some vessels that were anchored in the port, and basely fled as true deserters. Several religious, whom the attraction of novelty induced to follow Father Boïl to the Indies, not being able to become used to a mode of life for which they were not destined, followed him in his cowardly desertion." This zealous and intelligent writer attributes this sad result to the fact that Father Boïl was not, in fact, the one selected by the Church or the Pope for this mission, but by accident or intrigue, as already related, he was substituted for the Franciscan Father Boyle.

In deserting his command, Margarite did not even designate another to take his place, and the army lost all organization, became split up into bands of marauders, plunderers, and seducers, depriving the natives of their property, their homes, and their wives. Even these outrages were accompanied with unnecessary and wanton cruelties and insults. The poor Indians had submitted to every wrong from their celestial guests, but now, seeing the power of the Spaniards broken by their disorganization and divisions, and resenting the wrongs they had heaped on them, the hospitality of hosts became converted into a bitter and relentless hatred. Vengeance took the place of friendship. The fortress of La Navidad had been destroyed— why might not that of St. Thomas be wiped out?

The Carib chief, Caonabo, was the most inveterate enemy of the Spaniards, and now the Kings of Xaragua, of Higuey, and of the Vega united with the fierce chief of Maguana in a conspiracy to destroy the Spaniards and free the island from these cruel and oppressive foes. The mild and gentle Guacanagari, suspected by them to be friendly to the Spaniards, was not taken into the alliance, and he was treated as an enemy of his country. Endeavoring to supply the place of arms and skill by numbers, Caonabo appeared before Fort St. Thomas with ten thousand naked warriors, armed with bows and arrows, clubs and lances hardened with fire. Having reconnoitred the fort, he expected to take it by surprise, by a secret march through the forests ; he had, no doubt, taken a leading part in the massacre of the garrison of Fort La Navidad. But Alonzo de Ojeda was a foe such as Indian hordes and unclad warriors had never encountered. He was vigilant and wily, brave and fearless, profoundly versed and practised in all the arts and stratagems of war. He was intrepid and resistless in the open field, headlong in violent warfare ; he was subtle in feints and ambuscades, and, whenever he was engaged in hostilities with the heathen, he was inspired with extraordinary religious zeal and apparently supernatural motive and courage. A veteran in Moorish campaigns, he had never received a wound, and now it seemed to him and to his followers that he was under a special heavenly protection, and was invulnerable. His exploits had been recorded in many a marvellous chronicle of prowess, and even his personal strength, so out of all proportion to his small stature, inspired unwonted terror, and achieved prodigious feats of valor and success. So thorough a soldier could not be taken at disadvantage by barbarous foes. The cautious and wily Caonabo was surprised, after his secret march through the dense forests, on arriving at the fort, to find the Spanish chieftain at the head of his garrison drawn up in the tower, sharply watchful and ready for the fray. The fortress was by its location well fortified also by nature.

Assault by untutored savage warriors was fruitless, and Caonabo resorted to a siege in order to reduce his formidable foes by starvation. Skilfully distributing his men through the neighboring forests, and occupying every approach to the fort, the cacique and his colleagues, in a siege of thirty days, reduced the Spaniards to the point of starvation. But Ojeda and his veterans displayed prodigies of valor, and by dauntless sorties and reckless attacks, from day to day, decimated the ranks of the dusky besiegers ; and while every Spanish soldier killed his dozens, their intrepid leader slew with his own arm and trusty weapon still greater numbers of the undisciplined foes. The Indians were appalled at seeing their arrows fall harmless at the feet of the invulnerable commander of the fort. They were unused to such continued military service as they were then undergoing, and the undisciplined ranks of the cacique were thinned by daily returns of his subjects and allies to their homes. Caonabo conceived an unbounded wonder and admiration for Ojeda. He was forced to yield the struggle to so dauntless a foe. He now began to bethink him of other and more promising efforts to destroy the hated invaders of his domains.

An incident is here related in Spanish-American chronicles to illustrate the generous and heroic character of Ojeda in this noted siege. While the garrison was so severely pressed for food, a friendly Indian found a way of entering the tower, bringing with him a pair of pigeons as a present to Ojeda; but that gallant chieftain saw how his comrades eyed with languishing and hungry eyes those rare and delicious birds. He received them from the hands of the Indian only to give them flight and liberty from a window of the tower, and turning to his men, he said: "It is a pity that here is not enough to give us all a meal, but I cannot consent to feast while the rest of you are starving."

Returning with disappointment and wounded pride from his disastrous attack on Fort St. Thomas, Caonabo made a secret reconnoissance of the city of Isabella, and thought how easy it would be for the natives in countless hordes to rush upon and annihilate the feeble colony. So exasperated were the Indians throughout the island at the wrongs they had endured at the hands of Margarite, that the Kings of Xaragua, Higuey, and the Vega came readily into his proposals for a military alliance, having for its object the extirpation of the Spaniards. They were zealously supported by their respective tribes. Now was the time for Guacanagari, the suspected cacique of Marien and the trusted friend of Columbus, to prove the truth or falsehood of the charges against his loyalty and friendship for the admiral and his people. This chief was equally suspected of disloyalty to their cause by the other Indian kings, and when his alliance was now sought by them for a united attack upon the Spaniards, he refused to join them. He continued in his own dominions to resist their entreaties and threats, and though greatly impoverished, he entertained and fed one hundred Spanish soldiers quartered upon him with cheerful and unstinted hospitality. His loyalty to the Spaniards was fully vindicated, and now gave comfort to his friend, the admiral, in the midst of his cares and growing adversities. The three allied chiefs turned their resentment upon Guacanagari, and now Caonabo and his brother-in-law, Behechio, invaded his dominions, killing one of his wives, the beautiful Catalina, who had fled to his side from the Gracious Mary by casting herself into the water and swimming ashore, carrying another into captivity, and inflicting upon him many wrongs and outrages. He stood faithful to the admiral, and while his dominions presented a barrier between the Spanish settlement and its gathering foes, his friendly tribe assisted the Spaniards all in their power. The cacique Guatiguana, on the other hand, massacred ten Spaniards who were on the banks of the Grand River, and burned the hospital building, containing forty patients and convalescents, while the Spaniards were killed in other parts of the island.

The faithful Guacanagari lost no time in seeking the admiral, who was still on his bed of sickness, and who even there had received tidings of an unpleasant character in relation to the movements of the other caciques. Accounts of the misconduct of Margarite and his men, and of the consequent enmity and hostile movements and plots of the caciques, reached him from every quarter. Instead of remaining at their posts of duty, the commander of the army and the superior of the missions had deserted the scenes of danger and disorder, of which they had been instigators; had gone to court falsely to throw upon the admiral the blame of disasters which they had conspicuously caused, and to malign him whom they had already wronged, instead of remaining to repair the injuries inflicted upon the island by their own misconduct.*

The trusting nature of Columbus, more than ever conspicuous in such trials, felt consolation in the now vindicated loyalty of Guacanagari. He received that unfortunate chief to his renewed confidence and friendship, and extended to him the much-needed protection he sought against the hostility of the other caciques. A distinguished trait in the character of Columbus was, as we have seen, his ability and energy in rising from the bed of illness or from misfortunes to vigorous action. This he had already

---

* The authors consulted in this and several preceding pages have been Oviedo, "Historia del Almirante," Herrera, Irving, Count de Lorgues, as translated by Dr. Barry, Tarducci, Fiske and Winsor.

done when he saw his brothers at his side, and had dispatched the ships to Spain with his brother Diego, commissioned to represent him at court, and in following up these measures with a decided policy, and its execution toward the combined Indian conspiracy against Spanish authority in the new world. He deliberately and sternly planned the breaking of the caciques' league against him, and this he resolved to undertake by handling the members of the league separately. Having heard that Captain Luiz d'Artiaga had become closely besieged in the fortress of Magdalena by the treacherous cacique of Grand River, Guatiguana, he sent two detachments of soldiers, one of which attacked that chief suddenly, and the other simultaneously relieved the fort; and then the united forces overran the cacique's country and inflicted severe punishment upon him and his people, by defeating them in battle, killing many of his men, and capturing many others, the cacique himself barely escaping with his life. Then, remembering that Guatiguana was a tributary chief to Guarionex, the King of the Royal Vega, Columbus got the latter to come to see him, and by skilful diplomacy secured his reconciliation. Guarionex was not only pacified by the admiral, but he also allied his family to the admiral's household by the marriage of his daughter to the Indian interpreter, Diego Colon, and consented to the erection of Fort Conception within his own dominions. Little did the unsuspecting natives dream that by such concessions they were forging the instruments that were to complete their subjugation and finally their destruction.

Having thus secured the friendship, which was equivalent to the subjugation of the lord of the Royal Vega, Columbus now seriously considered how he should attempt the destruction of the native league, which consisted of Caonabo, his brother-in-law, Behechio, and the King of Higuey. Caonabo was the soul of the coalition. While pondering what should be his next step, Columbus was suddenly surprised and relieved by a bold and characteristic offer of Alonzo de Ojeda, which was nothing less than to capture that formidable chief by stratagem, and deliver him alive into the admiral's hands. Plunging into the thick forest with ten selected men, bold, fearless, and thoroughly armed, and after traversing sixty leagues of the territory of Caonabo, Ojeda and his party came upon the Lord of the Golden House in one of his largest and most populous towns, and surrounded by his warrior subjects. The wily Spaniard, no less skilled at strategy than in open warfare, approached the savage chief with a show of profound respect, paying him royal honors, and presenting messages and credentials from the admiral, whose Indian name was Guamiquina, signifying Chief of the Spaniards. In the name of the admiral he tendered the chief valuable presents, and so fascinated the savage by his gallantry, his personal strength, and his skill at all athletic exercises, that he and Caonabo became the best of friends. Ojeda was perfectly at home and at his ease in accepting the unbounded though rude hospitality of the descendants of the Caribs. The Spaniard invited and urged Caonabo to repair to Isabella for the purpose of making an alliance of friendship and mutual aid with the great Spanish chieftain. The most powerful argument he used was an offer to make the savage a present of the chapel-bell at Isabella, which the Indians thought was gifted with the power of speech, as they saw the steel-clad warriors from the skies obey its voice and repair to the chapel for prayer at its bidding.

When this wonderful present was offered to Caonabo, who had never seen but had heard the bell sounding the summons to mass and vespers while he was stealthily reconnoitring the city, the vain chief was captivated; such a peace-offering was overwhelming. Having consented to accompany Ojeda and his warriors to Isabella, he surprised them by presenting himself as ready for the march accompanied by a numerous body of armed warriors, shrewdly parrying the questions and allaying surprise of the Spaniards at such warlike preparations for a peaceful mission by answering that a chieftain of his power must travel in a manner worthy of his dignity. While the Spaniards were themselves planning treachery, they feared it at the hands of their intended victim. Ojeda was the superior of Caonabo in duplicity, as he was at open warfare. Not satisfied with alluring the brave native king by the prospective sounds of the promised bell, which were in this instance used to summon him to an inevitable fate, Ojeda now dazzled the eyes of the barbarian with a pair of polished manacles, which he treacherously represented to be innocent ornaments intended as another and immediate present for the chief. Leading the credulous Indian into a snare, the latter found himself manacled with the glittering steels, and before his warriors were aware of the treachery, or could rush to his rescue, he was hurried forward at a rapid pace on one of the swiftest Spanish horses a captive and a prisoner to the city of Isabella.

Columbus accepted the captive at the hands of Ojeda with expressions of pleasure, and though he treated him with kindness, he caused him to be kept a prisoner in chains and confined in one of the rooms of his own house. Caonabo to the last exhibited the utmost haughtiness, and a regal refusal to succumb to the viceroy. While for Ojeda, who had had the courage and strategy to come to his home and make him a prisoner, he manifested the utmost respect and admiration, for the admiral, who, as he said, had never dared to attempt in person such a feat, he manifested the utmost indifference, never even noticing his presence, or rising, as others did, on his entrance. In 1496, on the fleet which carried Columbus back to Spain, Caonabo was a passenger and a prisoner, for the admiral regarded him as too dangerous a personage to leave in Hispaniola, where his numerous subjects might at any time attempt his recapture. It is also said that he had hopes of seeing the barbarian's conversion to Christianity effected by his stay in Spain, and that he had promised liberty and their return to Hispaniola to Caonabo and his brother. On the voyage to Spain several of the Amazons inhabiting the island of Guadeloupe were taken as prisoners on board the ships, and the female cacique of these warrior women conceived a desperate attachment for the haughty and noble Caonabo, so much so that when the prisoners were returned to their homes she would not leave the famous Carib chief; but, having heard and sympathized with his history, she preferred to share his fortunes, keeping with her also her young daughter. Caonabo was proud and gloomy to the last, and died at sea before the termination of the voyage of a broken heart.*

The treacherous seizure and imprisonment of Caonabo aroused his subjects, and indeed most of the savages of the island. That chieftain had three brothers, and these united their efforts to raise throughout the land a large army, and succeeded in bringing into the field seven thousand warriors, in hopes of first cap-

---

* Las Casas, Herrera, Fernando Pizarro, Charlevoix and Peter Martyr; Oviedo, "Cronico de los Indias," lib. iii., cap. i.; "Historia del Almirante," cap. 63; Cura de los Palacios, cap. 131; Irving's "Columbus," vol. ii., pp. 37, 81; Barry's translation of Count de Lorgues' "Columbus," p. 323.

turing Fort St. Thomas and its garrison, now again under the command of Ojeda, and then exterminating the cruel intruders from Hispaniola. Manicatex, the ablest and most warlike of the chieftain's army, assumed command, and when Ojeda, at the head of his mail-clad cavaliers on horseback, rushed intrepidly to the attack, though a mere handful of men against seven thousand, the Indian general showed military skill in arranging his men in battalions, and using them at first with true generalship. But the rude warriors almost immediately became panic-stricken and fled from the field, while the Spaniards slaughtered many and captured great numbers. The brother of Caonabo fell valiantly fighting for his country and his race.*

The admiral, though still feeble from his recent illness, decided to take the field in person, at the head of his entire military force, and strike a final blow for the subjugation of the natives. The defeat of Manicatex by Ojeda had not broken the spirit of the natives, nor softened their determination to defend their homes and country, and to revenge the captivity of Caonabo. That Indian warrior, who had now succeeded to the throne of his imprisoned brother, his brothers, and the favorite wife of Caonabo, the beautiful Anacaona, the sister of Behechio, all united their influence and their efforts to raise the whole population of the island to arms. They succeeded in bringing out an army of a hundred thousand men, if such an assemblage of naked and undisciplined savages could be called an army. Yet when the scouts came in from a reconnoitring tour, they represented the small but intrepid Spanish army as resembling only a sheaf of corn, which the natives by their numbers could easily surround and destroy. Manicatex divided his immense forces into five divisions, so that the Spanish handful of men, when they marched into the Vega, would become surrounded and stifled ; but the superior forces of the Spaniards had no difficulty in overcoming this immense army of barbarians, which fell into panic and disorder before the impetuous charge of Ojeda at the head of his cavalry, and fled precipitately. The hordes of barbarians vanished before the irresistible attack of disciplined troops as mists in the air are dispelled before the advancing sun. The poor

---

* Oviedo, "Cronico de los Indias," lib. iii., cap. I. ; Charlevoix, "Historia de St. Domingo," lib. ii., p. 131 ; Irving's "Columbus," vol. ii., p. 39 ; Barry's translation of De Lorgues' "Columbus," p. 323.

Indians submissively and fearfully sued from the rocks and precipices, to which they had fled, for mercy. Many were killed and many more were wounded. The allied army was completely routed. Guarionex, the mild and pacific cacique of the Vega, whom the other chiefs had induced to join the confederacy, made his peace at once with the Spaniards, and accepted the yoke. Manicatex, himself the commander-in-chief, was compelled to sue for peace, and he, together with a nephew of Caonabo, was sent to join that chieftain in his prison at Isabella, and subsequently in his banishment from his country. Unlike him, they survived the voyage to Spain, but in this, as in many other instances, we have no record of their subsequent fate.

While Columbus was following up his victory by marching through the most accessible parts of the island, the unhappy Guacanagari, who had joined the Spanish forces against his own race, though his services were of little use, retired now to his dominions with the execrations of the other caciques and their people, who never forgave his desertion of their cause. The sequel will show that he gained little by his pliant submission. Considerable numbers of native prisoners were led to Isabella. While the caciques made their submission, Behechio, with sad but unavailing pride, retired to his more remote and inaccessible dominions, carrying with him his sister, the beautiful Anacaona, the favorite wife of Caonabo, to whom he was, in adversity as in former and better days, most devoted, and who seems to have survived the fate of her husband and the liberties of her race, to take a conspicuous and active part at a later day, though an unavailing one, to revenge the former and to restore the latter. She was a queen by nature, as well as by birth and recognition, for she won the love and obedience of her brother's subjects, and shared with him the actual government of his people.

Europeans have always, as we have seen, regarded the heathen and undiscovered lands and peoples of the earth as subject to lawful invasion and subjugation by their more civilized Christian neighbors ; and yet they found it convenient, when an object was to be attained, to apply to their relations with the heathens the very principles of public and international law which would have secured, from the beginning, to the invaded and subjugated peoples a perfect protection from such a fate. Acting upon this principle, Columbus, who regarded himself as forced into the war by the combination of the caciques and their peoples, sought now to avail himself of the rights of a conqueror, which consist not only in imposing the political yoke of the victors upon the vanquished, but also in making the latter pay the expenses of the war. It was thus that he decided to subject the whole native population of Hispaniola to the payment of tribute to their Spanish conquerors. The royal treasury had suffered much from the first expedition and in the subsequent enterprises of the admiral in founding a Spanish empire in the new world. How could he reimburse the exchequer? How could he give the lie to the malicious falsehoods of the assayist, Firmin Cado, Pedro Margarite, and Father Boïl at court, that the country was barren of precious metals? The tribute should be imposed and collected in gold itself; this was the crucial test. The admiral, therefore, in order to make returns to his country and sovereigns, and even to promote his remoter but yet cherished schemes for redeeming the Holy Land, imposed upon the natives of Hispaniola heavy and onerous tributes in gold. Every inhabitant of the Vega and of Cibao over fourteen years of age was required to pay to the receiver of the royal revenues a measure of a Flemish hawk's bell of gold-dust or grains every three months. An individual tribute, much greater in amount, was imposed upon all the caciques; but Manicatex, for his activity in the war, was compelled, in addition, to pay an amount of gold equal to one hundred and fifty pesos of Spanish coin. Where gold did not exist the individual was to pay instead a tribute of twenty-five pounds of cotton every three months. A certificate of the payment thus made into the royal treasury consisted of a copper medal, which was hung around the Indian's neck, and those not carrying the medal were liable to be arrested and thrown into prison. Thus the yoke of servitude and of tribute was consummated in the emblematic yoke which the taxpayers were compelled to wear around their necks.

The late King of the Royal Vega, for his sceptre had passed to Ferdinand and Isabella, besought the admiral to accept from his fertile country a tribute of grain for the food of the Spaniards, as the Vega possessed little gold, and his subjects were not skilled at gathering it in the river beds; but as the admiral knew that gold alone would meet the expectations of his sovereign, he refused the offer, though it would have secured the cultivation by the natives of a large belt of rich territory, stretching from sea to sea. Such was the necessity, that scanty grains of gold were preferred to the culture of nature's bountiful treasures of the soil. So great was the difficulty with the poor inhabitants in toiling for three months in unsuccessful efforts to gather the coveted and glittering particles, that Columbus became satisfied with half a hawk's bell of gold as the tribute in such cases.

The island of Hispaniola being now effectually conquered, and the natives now wearing the tribute-medal on their necks, the country became studded with fortifications to maintain the Spanish authority, keep the Indians in subjection, and enforce the collection of the tribute. Fort St. Thomas was put in a state of impregnable strength; so also was the fort at Isabella; and new fortresses were erected at Magdalena, in the Vega; another on the site of the town of Santiago and near the Estencia, on the Yaqui, called Santa Catalina; another on the banks of the river Yaqui, called Esperanza, and near the Pass of the Hidalgos, now called the Pass of the Marney; and, largest of all, Fort Conception, in the heart of the Vega; thus giving to the Spaniards the complete mastery over the dominions of Guarionex. The burdens now imposed upon the Indians, their sufferings under the Spanish yoke, and the tribute wrung from them gave voice and force to the plaint in the sympathetic heart of Las Casas, the tenderest of lamentations. The Count de Lorgues and Dr. Barry, apologetically yet justly casting the blame upon Spanish policy and necessities, exclaim: "But it was not grain that Castile wanted; King Ferdinand demanded gold, and not small grain!" *

The advent of the Spaniards had produced great changes in the condition of a peaceful population, from time immemorial securely reposing in peace in their own homes, yielding scarcely a nominal service or tribute to their own chiefs, enjoying the generous and unstinted abundance which nature, soil, and climate spontaneously yielded, and, after each day of dreamy idleness and blissful enjoyment of life, reposing sweetly at night, with no care for the morrow. The native sovereigns of Hayti exercised merely a fraternal sway over their tribes, their only

---

* Las Casas, "Historia Ind.," lib. i., cc. 105-10; Irving's "Columbus," vol. iii., p. 51; Dr. Barry's translation of De Lorgues' "Columbus," p. 326.

personal perquisites being a few brief rights of hunting and fishing, a small quantity of cassava or cotton, or, in lieu thereof, service in war. The fruits, vegetables, and grain which constituted their food made the Indians healthy, agile, and comely, but they imparted no robust strength; labor was as unsuited to their condition as it was unnecessary; Nature, in her gentle way, supplied their wants; though indolent, they were cheerful and mirthful; the daily courses of the sun and moon were followed by them with successive slumbers, feasts, games, songs, and dances; traditional stories of personal exploits and character were their only literature, and their wandering singers or rustic minstrels dimly resembled the troubadours of Provence, while their storytellers recalled the scalds and sagamen of Iceland. The time, action, and sounds of dancing feet supplied the place of the troubadour's harp; the professional newsmongers resembled in the abstract only the vocation of our modern newspapers. Anacaona, whose name beautifully signified "the Golden Flower," was their Homer, their Cid, their Ossian, or their Chaucer all combined. Carib adventures and the dark works of sorcerers formed the staple of their heroic poetry. The songs of the island, or *areytos*, were merely traditional poems which living poets recited to the music of the feet or the sound of the simplest drums. There were traditions among them which had their sources undoubtedly in the great fountains of original and Mosaic history The garden, the flood, the redemption were dimly shadowed in their racial and unwritten histories. But—ominous tradition!—they had received from their ancients and forefathers a prophecy that their peaceful and blissful land would some day be invaded by strangers clad in armor and flowing robes, bearing swords capable of cleaving a man in twain at a single stroke, and who would impose a galling yoke upon their necks. Were these the present steel-clad warriors and horse-mounted conquerors, with viceroy and priest, all clad in flowing robes, that had exacted the tribute, transported their chiefs beyond the seas, and erected frowning fortresses on every available hill, at every pass, and on the banks of once peaceful rivers? Were they from heaven? Would they ever return to their homes in the clouds? Or would they build for themselves earthly homes, covet and seize the native gold, take to themselves native wives, and make slaves of the free children of nature?

The days of Indian dreams were passed. Traditions had become history. The native *areytos* now mournfully sang the story of the Indian subjugation. It is the decree of human development, that wherever the foot of civilized man is planted barbarism must yield to civilization! Oh, how dearly purchased is this boon of civilization!

The military subjugation of the natives of Hispaniola plunged its former rulers and its people in gloom and despair. Finding it hopeless to struggle at arms with this mail-clad race, the Indians betook themselves to the expedient of starving their conquerors by refraining from cultivating the soil, or raising food even for themselves. They retreated to the most inaccessible mountains, after destroying the food and crops already produced, laying waste their own fields; and they preferred rather to drag out a miserable subsistence on roots and herbs than be the submissive slaves of the Spaniards. These measures, however, exposed the natives, accustomed to live in the open air and enjoy the abundance of a bountiful soil and climate, to the damp air of forests or the clammy atmosphere of caves, to the vicious effects of poisonous roots for their bread and the sickening consequences of scanty food, so that the native population was as effectually decimated by disease as it had been by the swords of the invaders. The Spaniards, on the other hand, showed the true mettle of a fully developed and civilized race; for it is a trait of the Spanish character to be able to bear, and even to be aggressive under hunger and thirst, marches and fatigues, whenever there is an object to be attained, whether it be national or personal, heroic or sordid. The Spaniards, too, unlike the natives, dependent as they were on their immediate local and scanty resources, and relying solely on the bounty of nature, had a powerful, proud, and prosperous other home beyond the seas to appeal to; a mother country to sustain them, and great ships to bring foods and medicines, and the implements of peace and of war; a nation ambitious and able to sound the trumpet of Spanish conquest, and sustain it.

Spanish resolution was not to be balked by any measure of Indian combination. The natives were not permitted to languish and perish in their mountain retreats. The Spanish soldiers followed them to their caves, now their homes, and compelled them at the point of the sword to return to the labors and toils imposed on them by their conquerors. The natives, thus driven from their caves in the mountains, fled to remoter and more desolate and deadly heights and caverns. Whole families fled from one place to another : mothers, burdened with their infants and a few articles of use, traversed in hunger, fear, and despair their once verdant and abundant fields, on the rocky cliffs and passes of the mountains, fleeing from Spanish swords or lances ; the old and tenderest young sank upon the way. The pursuers gave their victims no rest from labor or flight ; the fisheries and hunts were abandoned to the victors by the vanquished, and many of the latter perished for want of food in a country lately abounding with spontaneous crops and fruits. Every sound, even of the forest or rivers, startled the pursued. Finally there was scarcely a native found at large to be hunted ; a Spaniard could traverse the island without meeting an Indian from sea to sea. The few that escaped came down to the fields and accepted the inevitable yoke of toil and slavery ; while the conquerors became the lords of the land, even using the natives as their beasts of burden, and in their travels being carried on their shoulders.

Entire submission from the beginning brought no relief, as was witnessed in the case of the unfortunate Guacanagari. While his friendship for the Spaniards subjected him to the hatred and hostility of his own race and neighbors, it did not exempt him from the heavy tribute exacted from those who had resisted and warred against the Spanish rule, nor from remorseless cruelty and an agonizing death, a consummate fate. The payment of the tribute was exacted from him and his people, allies though they were, with unsparing exactness. He and they succumbed under the intolerable burdens their professed friends imposed upon them. Ojeda attempted to justify the cruelty of the Spaniards to him by the greater cruelty of slandering his name and character. The admiral, now engrossed with the cares and labors of conquest and administration, it has been suggested in his excuse, and feeling the harsh thrust of calumny and persecution from his own people at home penetrating his own heart, would, had he not been much absent in other parts of the island, have shielded one whom he always trusted and befriended when others attacked ? The hatred of neighboring caciques and tribes, the lamentations of his own impoverished subjects, and the exactions of the Spaniards, drove this amiable but doomed chief to the mountainous caves, and to an obscure and miserable death.*

We have already related events which showed how filled with thorns was the viceregal crown worn by Christopher Columbus in the new domains of his own discovery. Margarite, Father Boil, and other deserters from Hispaniola, chiefly cavaliers, on arriving in Spain had proved themselves busy slanderers and libellers against the name, reputation, and administration of their chief, whom they had abandoned in the moment of his greatest need. In order to justify their own perfidy, they represented Columbus as the real criminal, and they, his innocent and deceived victims, had sought refuge under the paternal wings of their and his sovereigns. Their chief calumnies were that he had designedly deceived the king and queen and the world in relation to the resources of the country, and especially in his statements of its riches in gold, while the country was in fact poor, destitute of the precious metals, and now groaning under the oppressions and cruelties of Columbus and his brothers; and they exhibited letters from some they left behind stating their miserable condition and their inability to return home because of their sickness and poverty; that Columbus had extortionately aggrandized himself at the expense of the sovereigns and the colony and natives. Sebastian de Olano, the receiver of the crown revenues, who had heard this charge commenced in the colony, had sent a letter by the same ship with the deserters, giving a direct contradiction to the falsehood. These malcontents further charged that the admiral had for months absented himself from Hispaniola, and had probably perished in his foolhardy adventures; that the island was in confusion and anarchy by reason of the tyranny and misgovernment of the Genoese foreigner. These accusations, supported by the vicar apostolic and the letters of other malcontents, made a deep impression upon the minds of Ferdinand and Isabella. To make the cause of the admiral more desperate, several mariners and pilots, who had accompanied him in his first voyage, such as Vincent Yañes Pinzon, and others, made offers to the crown to undertake voyages of discovery and colonization in the new world entirely at

---

* For these and further details, see the pages of Las Casas, Peter Martyr, Charlevoix, Irving, and the Count de Lorgues.

their own cost, and without expense to the government. Ferdinand, who was known to be sordid and mistrusting, accepted such offers, though his permits or commissions were in direct contravention of the rights of the admiral. The calumnies of Margarite and Father Boïl, so falsely and maliciously made, were unworthily and fraudulently sustained by Bishop Fonseca. These two ecclesiastics, real politicians clothed with sacred functions and duties by King Ferdinand, and which they shamefully neglected for the affairs of the State and of the world, have become recognized by all historians as bearing a " mortal hatred," as the Count de Lorgues expresses it, against Columbus. Fonseca supported the grant of licenses to Pinzon and others to make voyages to the new world, though he knew, as his patron, the king, knew, that they plainly violated the concessions solemnly made to Columbus. In fact, on April 10th, 1495, the Spanish sovereigns, by public proclamation, gave a general license to all subjects of the crown to prosecute on their own account voyages of discovery and colonization to the new world, and to all native-born subjects to settle in Hispaniola ; and detailed regulations were issued for the conduct of such enterprises, and for securing to the crown its share of gold and other products. Fonseca was directed to send out with a fleet, which was about to sail for Hispaniola with provisions and general supplies, under the command of one Juanoto Berardi, some discreet and trusty person, who should, in case of the admiral's absence, take upon himself the government of Hispaniola, and in case of his presence or return, to make strict investigation into the complaints of the malcontents, and to apply a remedy to all abuses discovered to exist. Diego Carillo, a commander of a military order, was selected for this delicate and important function ; but as this officer was not then ready to sail, the fleet of twelve ships was compelled to sail without him, and a trusty person was to go out in his stead, commissioned to superintend the distribution of the provisions and to redress and remedy the existing evils of the island ; and in case the admiral was at home, his administration was not to be disturbed. This officer was to return and make report of his trust to the sovereigns. These measures, taken as they were without his consent, were a severe blow to the popularity and position of the admiral.

Such was the condition of the admiral's fortunes at court,

when fortunately the fleet under Antonio de Torres arrived in Spain, with Don Diego Columbus on board. The sovereigns now heard directly from the admiral, and of his safe return to Hispaniola ; received the accounts of his voyages and explorations along the islands of Cuba and Jamaica, the documents and declarations showing that he had reached and explored the extremities of Asia, and had opened to his sovereigns and to his country Oriental regions of boundless wealth. These accounts were supported by the golden specimens sent home, and by the animals, trees, and shrubs of that new empire thus acquired for Spain. A reaction now set in favorable to the fortunes of Columbus. The queen ordered that, instead of the soldier Diego Carillo, a former companion of Columbus on his first voyage, who was under obligations to him, and whom on his return he had warmly recommended to the favor of the crown, and now a member of her own household, should be sent out on the important duty of investigation and relief to Hispaniola. This was Juan Aguado, whose appointment the queen delicately and kindly thought would prove acceptable to Columbus. Fonseca, having officiously and maliciously seized the gold brought over by Don Diego Columbus for account of his brother's share, Isabella ordered him to restore the same to Don Diego, with suitable explanations and courteous amends, and to take counsel from the passengers and others on the fleet of Torres as to how the measures of his department could be made agreeable to the admiral ; he was also ordered to send to court Bernal Diaz de Pisa, who was the first to disturb the administration of Columbus in Hispaniola.

Orders had been issued for the exposure to sale as slaves, in the markets of Andalusia, of the numerous Indians taken as prisoners in the recent encounters between the Spaniards and the natives—orders issued probably by Ferdinand, with the view of replenishing the royal exchequer, for which purpose the living cargo was sent out from Hispaniola. The queen, on discovering this, was deeply moved with pity ; for it was her prayer that the Indians should become Christians rather than be made slaves. She consulted her most confidential advisers on the subject of the lawfulness of enslaving the natives, and as their opinions varied, she decided the question according to her own pure and enlightened conscience, and in favor of liberty. She ordered

Fonseca to provide for returning the captured Indians to their own country, but excepted from this order nine of them, whom Columbus had selected to be educated to become interpreters, and thus be able to aid in the conversion of their countrymen to Christianity. Fonseca obeyed, though with reluctance, the mandates of the queen, in which she showed her regard for the admiral; but Fonseca felt them as humiliations to himself; and his hostility toward that illustrious person is said to have become so intensified, that he availed himself of every opportunity during the admiral's life—and his official opportunities were frequent—to delay and thwart his measures and enterprises, fraught as they were with the glory and pre-eminence of Spain.

The queen studiously studied to give no umbrage to Columbus by her acts, but rather to show her confidence in him; yet the sovereigns united in such measures of precaution and regulation as they thought could remedy the existing evils and prevent others. They instructed him by letter to limit the colony to five hundred persons; to discontinue the shortening or stoppage of rations, by way of punishment for offences, as detrimental to the health of the colonists. An experienced and skilful metallurgist, Pablo Belvis, was sent out in place of Firmin Cado, and the places of Father Boïl and his followers were supplied by a corps of missionaries. The Indian captives were sent back to freedom and their country, so far as country and liberty were left for the natives, and the admiral was enjoined to extend to the aborigines kindness and gentle treatment. Would that these measures had been sent out in time to do some good! Now, alas! it was too late; the passions of Europeans had thwarted the noble purposes of Isabella and Columbus.

By means of his unworthy and intentional delays and obstructions, Fonseca prevented the sailing of the ships before the end of August, when they sailed with Aguado as agent of the crown, who was accompanied by Don Diego Columbus. The admiral was absent from Isabella and busily engaged in the interior of the island on the arrival of Aguado. This official, though under heavy obligations to him, and though restricted by his commission and the verbal instructions he had received, lost sight of all prudence and justice; assumed the tone and air of power and administration; ignored the position of the Adelantado then exercised at Isabella by Bartholomew Columbus, refused him sight of his commission, and only afterward, and then with great pomp and sound of trumpets, caused it to be publicly proclaimed. This document was couched in indefinite language. Aguado was simply commissioned to speak to the colonists on the part of the sovereigns, and to receive from them in return faith and credit; and while even these words were restricted by verbal instructions, Aguado insolently amplified them by his assumption of authority, his interference in the affairs of the colony, and in the pretended redress of grievances. Proving himself to be a mere upstart, he was as destitute of forethought as he was of prudence, truth, and justice. While criminals and offenders of every kind, at his bidding, arose up to accuse and malign the admiral and his brothers and their administration, he allowed reports of the downfall of Columbus and of the appointment of a new admiral to circulate through the island, and he taunted the admiral with purposely remaining away from Isabella in order to avoid the investigation of his conduct and the punishment of his misdeeds.

On the other hand, as soon as Columbus heard of the arrival of Aguado, and of his arrogant conduct, he hastened from the interior to the city. Aguado had sufficient followers from the most degraded classes on the island, and from the disloyal of all classes, to espouse his cause, and he had the hardihood to start forth at the head of a body of cavalry to seek the so-charged fallen and derelict viceroy. Columbus arrived at Isabella in the midst of the turmoil and disorder created by Aguado. His friends were apprehensive that the meeting between the high-spirited and tenacious viceroy with this boasting and arrogant pretender would be stormy and violent, for it was well known that the admiral had every provocation, and that his cause was just. The queen had selected Aguado as an act of regard for the admiral, to whom he was under many obligations, and it was evident that some enemy of the latter had seduced him from the path of honor and duty, and inspired him with the unworthy purpose of seeking the downfall of his former friend. That Juan Rodriguez de Fonseca, aided by his equally unworthy colleagues in the Bureau of Indian Affairs, was now, as he proved himself from the beginning to the end, the instigator of the present persecutions against Columbus, is the accepted voice of history. He was a politician clothed with ecclesiastical power, titles, and insignia; he was a man of the world and a self-seeker, who had sought and found place in the Church. His name might now be known and venerated in history as the right arm of the Spanish sovereigns and of their viceroy, in the grand work of giving to mankind a new world to inhabit and ennoble with civilization and religion; he might have ranked among Christian heroes by promoting the conversion of the Indians to Christianity and their safety from annihilation; and his name might have gone down in history along with that of a more worthy bishop of the Church, the great and good Las Casas, the noble Bishop of Chiapa. He might have won renown by having his obscure name linked with the name of Columbus; but he preferred the part of meanness and dishonor, and his name is only associated with these great events and distinguished persons by the contrast which the little and the base things of earth bear to the grand and magnificent.

It was a part of Aguado's scheme to irritate Columbus by insulting him in the name of his own sovereigns, and to betray him into words and acts of indignation and rebellion against their authority and dignity. But the conduct of Columbus towered above the baseness of his enemies, for he had experienced too much of life and of affairs, had passed through severe ordeals of suffering and disappointment, and by long self-training and pious self-denial, he had become the master of a naturally impulsive disposition. Aguado struggled to do just what Isabella had studied to avoid—giving offence to the admiral; but Columbus experienced an inward satisfaction in standing superior to the vices, the crimes, the selfishness and machinations of bad and degraded men, and of the baser portion of mankind. He proved himself equal to the present trying emergency. He saw his enemies and detractors multiply in great numbers before his approach. The authority of his brother, the Adelantado, had been set at defiance or ignored, his own commission questioned, the colony demoralized and turned against him, and even the Indians came into Isabella under the impression that he was a fallen and degraded chief, and were seduced into joining the clamor and the slanders against their best friend. It was true, they had unparalleled wrongs and grievances to complain of, but it was not Columbus or his brothers; it was, on the contrary, such men as Aguado and his followers who had been the originators and perpetrators of them. It looked as though the discoverer of the new world was the most unworthy and the most unfortunate of its inhabitants.

Columbus, whose conduct under the delays he had experienced at Lisbon and in Spain, when there was question of discovering another hemisphere, has been pronounced by historians as marked by ability, now that the achievement was accomplished, showed even greater strength of character and conduct. Aguado advanced to exhibit and proclaim his commission from the sovereigns. Columbus with unruffled calmness received the puffed-up official with solemn and ceremonious courtesy and dignity, and with ostentatious display ordered a second reading of the letter with sound of trumpets before the assembled multitude, composed as it was of soldier and husbandman, cavalier and peasant, scientist and mechanic, Indian and European, loyal and disloyal, and people of many nationalities, varied histories, and indescribable appearances, the motley inhabitants of two hemispheres brought together. Whereupon the admiral, after listening to the reading of the royal letter with profound respect, in formal speech and with every show of loyalty and honor assured Aguado that he was now and at all times ready to make due obedience to his sovereigns and an ever-ready compliance with their orders. The audience, astonished at the lofty bearing of the admiral, remained in baffled silence, while Aguado, foiled in his scheme, and smarting with defeat, burst forth in arrogant and insolent language and tone to insult the admiral in public, hoping anew to provoke the latter to an altercation; but Columbus was equal to the occasion, and, as we are told, " bore his insolence with great modesty." Thus defeated in his first designs, this unworthy official resorted now to the shameful means of inciting the populace to clamor against the admiral, to impute to him and his brothers their grievances and the calamities of the island, to accumulate an immense mass of worthless and perjured testimony against him, not stopping at maligning his public administration, but invading the unsullied precincts of his private character, conduct, and motives. The Indians, wards of the generous Queen of Castile, were incited to assemble together at the house of Manicatex, and through their chiefs to prefer formal complaints and charges against Columbus. The misdeeds and vices of his enemies were even now imputed to him and his supporters. Such was the highest achievement of the ungrateful Aguado, who, having collected an immense mass of documentary testimonies, forming, as he supposed, an unanswerable indictment against Columbus, he prepared to return to Spain to consummate his ruin. Thus, in both hemispheres, was Columbus slandered and plotted against. He resolved also to return to Spain, and to meet all his enemies and all their calumnies at the royal court and imperial tribunal. The ships were ready to depart.

At this juncture, and just as the fleet was about to sail, a storm truly American in character and violence, and such as was unknown in Europe, suddenly burst upon the island and defeated every project. It was of unprecedented violence and disaster, even in the West Indies. It possessed the terror of storms preceding volcanic eruptions, bringing all the elements of air, fog, cloud, vapor, and water in violent struggle against each other and against the earth, with prevailing darkness and terrific lightning. Huge forests were prostrated, groves laid waste, mountains rent, and masses of rock hurled below to choke the rivers; and the earth seemed threatened with its primeval chaos. The inhabitants fled for shelter to the caverns. The expectant and ready fleet was struck with equal violence; the ships were tossed and whirled around, cables snapped, anchors were useless, and all but one of the ships was sunk with all on board, or wrecked. So unprecedented was the tempest, that the Indians superstitiously attributed it, as they now attributed all their misfortunes, to these new invaders of their country.*

The Nina, that stanch little caravel which had participated in the first voyage of the great discoverer, which had succored Columbus in his shipwreck at La Navidad, had carried him back to Spain through terrific and unprecedented European storms, and now, under the name of the Santa Clara, had borne him through the navigation of Cuba and the discovery of Jamaica

---

* Barry's translation of De Lorgues' "Columbus," pp. 334-336; Ramusio, tom. iii., p. 7; Herrera, "Hist. Ind.," decad. i., lib. ii., cap. 18; Peter Martyr, decad. i., lib. iv.; Irving's "Columbus," vol. i., pp. 63-69.

The Indian name for such a storm was "furicane," or "uricane," from which is derived our present English word *hurricane*. It has been adopted into the Spanish, French, Italian, German, Danish, and other European languages, as Webster relates, and he ascribes to it a Carib origin. Such tempests are also said to prevail in the East Indies.

and the Queen's Gardens, was the only unwrecked ship of the fleet. Columbus ordered this talismanic ship, the vessel of his fortunes, but now dismantled, to be repaired, and a new one, the Santa Cruz, to be built with the wrecks of the other ships.

Among the accusations made against him at court was the charge that he had falsely misrepresented as rich in gold the country which, as the accusers alleged, was destitute of precious metals. This accusation was bolstered up by the false assays of the pretended metallurgist, Firmin Cado. While his vindication was already prepared by himself and his brothers, with consummate ability, on all points, his cause seemed now suddenly and unexpectedly vindicated by the arrival of news of the discovery of the gold-mines of Hayna. Some months previously a young Aragonian, Miguel Diaz, attached to the service of the Adelantado, Don Bartholomew Columbus, had wounded his enemy in a duel, and fearing the inflexible sternness of that strict disciplinarian, had fled, with five or six of his companions or associates in the quarrel, to the remote southern portion of the island. In their wanderings the deserters came to an Indian village on the banks of the Ozema River, near where the present city of San Domingo stands. The female cacique of the village received and entertained the strangers with hospitality; they tarried; the princess became enamored of the gallant leader, and she became a Christian in order to marry him, taking the name of Catalina, though no formal ceremony could have taken place at the time in the absence of priest or missionary. In time, however, Miguel Diaz, feeling, in common with his companions, a longing desire to return to the society and civilization of his countrymen, such as they were in that corner of the western world, so remote from the mother country, became not unfrequently sad or thoughtful, notwithstanding the blandishments and charms of the fair Catalina. With the unerring intuitiveness of true love, always instinct with solicitude and ingenious in plans, whether at the most polished courts of Europe or in the ungilded Indian palace cabins of the western world, Catalina perceived the change, and beset herself to remove, by a lover's expedient, the danger she felt of losing her gallant and handsome lord, now the virtual cacique of the tribe. She knew that his love was shared by another divinity, and that was no other than the goddess of gold. She devised a plan for anchoring the lover to her royal bowers, even though it might transfer her country to the grasp of the stranger race. She communicated to Diaz the intelligence that rich mines of gold lay at Hayna, in her dominions, not over fifty leagues distant, and she even invited, through him, the whole Spanish colony of Isabella to abandon the latter spot, which she represented as unhealthy ; and she urged them, through him, to settle permanently in her country. Her country was to become his country, while his God should become her God. Diaz saw in this an opportunity to retrieve his name and fortune, and to condone his offence. After confirmation of Catalina's statements by the concurrent statements of the natives about the mines, and after observing how beautiful, fertile, and salubrious the country was, and yielding to the enticing offers of his Indian queen, he succeeded with the aid of native guides in finding his way back to the vicinity of Isabella. He learned that his antagonist in the duel was living and convalescent. Knowing that he brought with him the assurances of his own pardon, he entered the city, presented himself to the stern but politic Adelantado, communicated the grateful news, was welcomed by that official, reconciled to his enemy, and received his pardon and that of the Adelantado conditionally.

The Adelantado proceeded in person and without delay to visit the enchanted and golden region of Hayna, accompanied by Diaz himself, Francisco de Garay, the Indian guides, and an adequate number of well-armed Spanish soldiers, in order to insure the safety of the expedition. Proceeding southward, first by Magdalena, thence across the Royal Vega by the fortress of Conception, thence through a mountain defile and across a beautiful plain rivalling the Royal Vega, and called Bonao, they reached the river Hayna, upon whose western bank the glittering and coveted treasures were found in quantities and sizes sufficient to delight the eyes and ravish the hearts of the Spaniards. The golden deposits exceeded anything of the kind yet discovered, even those of Cibao. Over a space of country six miles in breadth, the precious metal so abounded that an ordinary laborer could easily collect the amount of three drams in a single day. Excavations, apparently old, in the golden region indicated that the mines had been regularly worked, a circumstance which had its natural effect in starting the Spanish mind to rush into the realms of fancy and speculation. Indian hospitality also in this favored region was as unlimited as the precious ore, and the country was blessed in soil and climate beyond the descriptions of Miguel Diaz. Love and lucre have often in history been intimate companions. Diaz was now pardoned unconditionally; he received not only signal favors, but was given employments of honor and trust, to which he proved himself as faithful as he did then and ever after to his Catalina, who was then regularly baptized and married, and whose constancy was rewarded with Christian offspring and Spanish friendship and protection.

> " 'Tis gold
> Which makes the true man kill'd, and saves the thief;
> Nay, sometimes hangs both thief and true man: What
> Can it not do, and undo?"
> —SHAKESPEARE'S "CYMBELINE."

When the Adelantado returned to Isabella with the tidings of the rich treasures of Hayna and with the valuable specimens of the golden ores, the admiral lost sight of his troubles of state and of administration in his gratitude to God for this providential and direct intervention in his favor, especially at the moment when all the world seemed turned against him. The anxieties of his mind and heart were much relieved. He thanked with generous gratitude his ever-faithful brother and the constant Miguel Diaz for their welcome tidings and services, and with prompt energy took measures for securing the advantages which should flow from this timely discovery. A fortress was ordered to be erected on the banks of the Hayna, near the mines, and the mines were directed to be worked with effective and diligent effort. The admiral, as his whole life marvellously illustrates, united to the most practical and sagacious ability for business a wonderful proneness to indulge in speculative and hopeful fancies based upon his study of the great geographical and cosmographical writers of the world. His conjecture that Hispaniola was the Ophir of Solomon, and that its treasures had built the temple of the true God at Jerusalem, were now confirmed, and the route by water from the Holy Land by the Persian Gulf to Hispaniola was made manifest, for Cuba was now demonstrated to be the extremity of Asia. The disputes of scholars over the location of Ophir were now settled; the riches of that treasure land had not been exhausted by Solomon, but now its exhaustless deposits of richest ores would reimburse his generous sovereigns. The new crusade, which would be known in history as the Columbian Crusade, would be successful in redeeming the Holy Sepulchre from Moslem desecration, and in placing it under the protection of an armed Christendom. His generous nature now exulted only in the good he could and would accomplish. No vain or sordid thoughts swelled his breast, for

> "But honor, virtue's meed,
> Doth bear the fairest flower in honorable seed."
>
> —SPENSER'S "FAERIE QUEENE."

The fortress and the mines of Hayna were called St. Christopher, after the admiral's titular saint. Don Bartholomew Columbus was invested with the powers of lieutenant-governor under the title of Adelantado, and Francisco Roldan was designated as superior magistrate of the island, for he was one of his personal suite, whom he appointed judge of the first resort. Zealous ever for the conversion of the natives, the admiral formed the mission with the best material he possessed, and appointed the Franciscan Father Juan Bergognon chief missionary, and gave him as his assistant the Poor Hermit, Friar Pane, who was now well versed in the native dialects. Such was the irritated feeling among the natives, in consequence of their harsh experiences of Spanish rule, that they had unfortunately conceived a low estimate of the religion of the Spaniards, and felt in their hearts deep though suppressed sentiments of resentment. Since their own religious faith and observance were simple, not deeply rooted, and almost wholly destitute of formal dogmas and symbols, the introduction of Christianity would have proved an easy work had proper measures and men been used to this end; but rancor was kept alive in the hearts of the natives by the recent outrages perpetrated upon them. The Poor Hermit was timorous at the dangers of his mission to the Indians of the interior, and requested the admiral to give him some Christian companions in his solitude, a request which was readily granted to his own selection, and for greater precaution a military post of infantry was established near the residence of the missionaries. Having done all in his power to provide for the temporal, political, and spiritual needs of his viceregal dominions and of his new subjects, the admiral, at the end of February, embarked on board his old and faithful caravel, the Santa Clara, while Aguado sailed in the new caravel, the Santa Cruz. March 10th, 1496, was the day the two vessels sailed out of the port of Isabella, carrying besides the crews two hundred and twenty-five sick, discontented, and disappointed hidalgos, and thirty-two Indians. Among the latter were the unfortunate but ever-proud and unbending Caonabo, his brother, a son, and a nephew. In consequence of the want of familiarity with the navigation of those waters and of unfavorable winds, Columbus, as late as April 6th, had not proceeded beyond the Caribbee Islands. His provisions were low, his men fatigued by battling with the weather, and many were sick. Touching at Margarite and landing at Guadeloupe, where he procured three weeks' supply of bread, and where the inhabitants were a race of Amazonian women, well capable of defending their homes against all save Europeans in the absence of their husbands, he sailed thence on his homeward voyage on April 20th. The Amazons resisted the landing of the Spaniards, who, however, landed and took several of them prisoners; but on sailing Columbus sent them back to their homes, with the exception of the female cacique, who had fallen in love with the captive, and preferred to share the ill fortunes of the noble Caonabo. During the voyage provisions became so scarce that all on board had to go on short rations, and, in their sufferings for food, some of the Spaniards went so far as to propose the killing and eating of their Indian captives; others, to throw them overboard. The latter unjust counsel prevailed, and the resolution to do so was formed and announced. Columbus nobly stood by the Indians, whose right to live was equal to that of the most favored nations of the earth. The resolution, which was announced, to throw these helpless captives into the sea in order to lessen the demand for food, and thus make the rations last longer, was indignantly rejected by the admiral, who ordered that all should fare alike. The death of Caonabo on the voyage has already been mentioned. The two vessels, after a voyage of three months, anchored in the Bay of Cadiz, on June 11th. The admiral, when his crews were threatened with starvation and the Indians with death, and when he saved their lives by his magnanimous decision and undaunted will against the combined crews of both ships, had promised that in three days the ships would reach the waters of Cape St. Vincent. The sailors and pilots, who had scoffed at his prediction, when it was verified were struck with awe; they had seen his prophetic words several times before verified under similar circumstances, when they knew not the source of his information. They now regarded him as either calling to his aid the secrets of magic, or as guided by an inspiration from Heaven.

CHAPTER XI.

> ' Know, smiler! at thy peril art thou pleased;
> Thy pleasure is the promise of thy pain.
> Misfortune, like a creditor severe,
> But rises in demand for her delay;
> She makes a scourge of past prosperity,
> To sting the more, and double thy distress.'
>
> —YOUNG's "NIGHT THOUGHTS."

IN the harbor of Cadiz, before landing, Columbus met three caravels under Pedro Alonzo Niño, about to sail with provisions for the colony of Hispaniola, the relief sent out in January having perished by the shipwreck of the four caravels then despatched. He also received from Niño the letters and despatches of the sovereigns, and it was fortunate that he now had an opportunity of reading them before the departure of the ships. He rewrote his instructions to his brother, dwelling chiefly on the importance of securing peace, of putting the island in a condition to meet the king's expectations of reimbursement and profits, on arresting rebellious caciques and sending them to Spain, and of working the mines of Hayna, near which a seaport should be established. This was the first conception of the future city of San Domingo. The caravels on June 17th sailed for Hispaniola, and Columbus landed, after having won the hearts of many of the sick on board his own vessel by his kind and unsparing nursing and generous attentions, for they were prejudiced against him on leaving Isabella, and heard only now of the unworthy treatment he had received from Aguado.

While the popularity of the admiral had been impaired by the calumnies of his enemies at court, the arrival of Aguado with his mass of documents hostile to his administration, and the unsightly appearance of the sick and dispirited colonists returning in disgust from the colony, many of whom were hidalgos and persons of consideration, did not improve the impressions of the populace in regard to the new world. Aguado, Fonseca, and their co-conspirators now became busy in misusing and torturing everything to the discredit of the noted discoverer. To the calumnies of Margarite and Father Boïl were now added the accusations of the commander Gallego, of Rodrigo Abarca, of Micer Girao, and of Pedro Navarro, all of whom were servitors of the royal household and persons of weight, though unjustly prejudiced against Columbus. His detractors were now multiplied by the arrival of so many sick, dejected, and unsuccessful colonists and adventurers. The air rang loudly with complaints against the one whose triumphant entry into Palos three years before as the discoverer of a new world had filled the air with salvos of joy which had scarcely yet died away. Now he could scarcely find audience for his recitals of the great progress since made in his advancing discoveries of the western world: the exploration of Cuba, which was now the supposed newly discovered continent, and the conjectured attainment of a long-cherished dream of the learned and the great—the geographical and maritime accessibility of Europe and Asia to each other by the northwestern oceanic route, the approach to the Aurea Chersonesus of antiquity, the discovery of mines which were then believed to be identical with the Ophir of Solomon. He had been the hero of a day; now he was regarded as the ruin of thousands, the deceiver of the world, the adventurer in unknown realms, the champion of a worthless and delusive theory, the Genoese dreamer. Sneers greeted him whom all Spain had so lately triumphantly honored and enthusiastically admired and revered.

Columbus announced his arrival in Spain to the sovereigns, and awaited with dignity and loyalty their orders. All Spain was aware of the difficulties of his situation, and he felt most keenly the difference between his reception then and the ovation he received on his first return as the discoverer of a new hemisphere. What effect were the machinations and slanders of his enemies, powerful in numbers, in position, and in influence to have in the minds of the court? Being a deeply devout man, he now took refuge from an unjust and ungrateful world in the consolations of religion. For one month he seems to have been lost to the world and to history, but he was not lost to himself or to his God. He retired from the public gaze, spent his time in prayer and devotion, and so deeply disgusted was he with all worldly affairs, that when he made his appearance on the streets of Seville, he was dressed in the monastic habit of St. Francis, wore the coarse cord of that order around his waist, and his beard was long and flowing, like that of the Franciscan monks. It would seem that he came from his ship in this mediæval garb, and Oviedo says that this was through his disgust for the world and mortification at his wrongs.* Washington Irving conjectures, but erroneously as is generally thought, that this strange and penitential garb was assumed in the performance of some vow he had made to Heaven on the voyage.† Las Casas himself writes that he saw the admiral in Seville dressed somewhat like a Franciscan monk, though the habit was not as long as that worn by the Franciscans.‡ The Curate of Los Palacios at this time received a visit from him, and relates that his dress, in its shape and color, and his beard in its length, resembled those of the Order of St. Francis of the Strict Observance. This author also mentions his entertaining the admiral and his Indian captives for several days in his residence, and that he had been shown and held in his hand the massive chain of gold which was afterward worn by the brother of Caonabo in the visit to the court at Burgos.§ Humboldt, on the other hand, attributes this wearing of the Franciscan dress to the characteristic and well-known pious and devout tendency of the admiral's mind.|| His fondness for the Franciscan Order is well known, and the Count de Lorgues, who especially dwells throughout his " Life of Columbus" upon his religious life and character, concurs with Humboldt, and even says that there is reason for believing that the admiral seriously meditated on following his friend, Father Juan Perez de Marchena, the Franciscan, to the Convent of La Rabida, which was celebrated as one of the consecrated cloisters of the Franciscans.

However this may be, after one month's delay we see him again assuming his historical character as the discoverer of new worlds ; for the letter of the sovereigns, bearing date at Almazan on July 12th, 1496, called him to court as soon as he was recov-

---

* Oviedo y Valdez, " Hist. Nat. y Gen.," etc., lib. ii., chap. xiii.
† Irving's " Columbus," vol. ii., p. 84.
‡ Las Casas, " La Historia de las Indias," lib. i., chap. ii., MS.
§ Cura de Los Palacios, cap. 131 ; Andres Bernaldez, " Hist. de los Reyes," cat., chap. vii., MS.
|| Humboldt, " Hist. de la Geograph. du Nouveau Continent," tom. i., p. 22.

ered from the fatigues of his late voyage, and congratulated him on his safe return. He lost no time in making his journey to Burgos, and on the way he endeavored to dispel the calumnies of his foes and the general depreciation of his achievements by displaying his Indian captives decked in collars and chains of massive gold, with bracelets, anklets, and coronets of the same precious metal; and he exhibited the masks, images of wood or cotton, and other objects of value or curiosity, trophies of his conquests over the princes and kings of the extreme regions of Asia and the eastern islands. It was thus that Roman conquerors made their triumphant entries into the Imperial City, bringing in their train the vanquished sovereigns and the booty wrung from barbaric nations then transformed into subjects of Rome. In both cases it was necessary to convince the minds of the populace of the efficacy and grandeur of the conquests, though Mr. Irving, forgetting that it was in the days of Columbus impossible for the people to foresee the rising of free and mighty nations in the west and in the route which Columbus had opened, deprecates the petty standard by which his sublime discovery was judged—a standard not rising above the transient and dazzling effect of golden trinkets and glaring trifles. It would have required a prophetic vision for the people of that or of any day to have anticipated the unparalleled spectacle of boundless progress, of empires and republics extending from ocean to ocean, and the great and marvellous achievements in civilization, arts, sciences, mechanics, material wealth, national grandeur, and human liberty now displayed by two continents at the quarto-centennial celebration of the Columbian discovery.

The sovereigns received Columbus with distinction and honor, and the gracious manner of their princely conduct lifted a heavy load from the heart of the discoverer. No allusion was made to the complaints preferred against him. Whatever transient effect the slanders of his enemies had produced on their minds was immediately removed by the exalted character, the past services, the constant loyalty, the candor, and by the very appearance of the admiral before them. As he unfolded to the sovereigns the progress of the great enterprise, the condition of the colony, the discovery of the Caribbees, of Jamaica, of the Queen's Gardens, and the exploration of Cuba; spoke of the mines of Cibao and Hayna; showed the masks, cinctures and purses decked or filled with the precious ores from them, and nuggets as large as nuts from Hayna; exhibited and presented the animals, birds, and plants of the new countries, and the sacred stones, images, arms, and instruments of the natives, both sovereigns became ravished with the interest and charm with which they invested their new dominions. They loaded him with kindnesses, and publicly honored their successful and loyal viceroy, greatly to the chagrin of his enemies. The queen, in an especial manner, thanked him for his great services and for his loyal aid and counsel at the time of the departure of the Infanta Donna Juana for Flanders, to join her husband, Archduke Philip of Austria.

Whether at this interview or subsequently is not clear, but the undertaking of further explorations and discoveries, the seeking out of the mainland or continent, and the vigorous working of the mines were measures then or soon afterward decided upon, and for these great ends Columbus proposed and the sovereigns ordered a third voyage under his command. During some delay, growing out of the queen's engrossed attention with the marriage and departure of her daughter, the Infanta Donna Juana, and the reception of the Princess Margaret, the *fiancée* of the Infante Don Juan, Columbus availed himself of his enforced residence at Burgos to cultivate the personal and professional acquaintance of the celebrated Jayme Ferrer, the lapidary, with whom he had already corresponded from Hispaniola at the queen's request. This eminent scientist of his day, in a letter to the queen, thus expresses his high and prophetic appreciation of the man that discovered America: " I believe that in its high and mysterious designs Divine Providence has chosen him as its mandatory for this work, which seems to me to be but an introduction and a preparation for things which this same Divine Providence reserves to itself to disclose to us, for its own glory and the salvation and happiness of the world." *

Though the Spanish sovereigns had promised to comply with the request of Columbus for the outfit of another voyage, his work was delayed by many unfortunate incidents—the ambitious foreign policy of Ferdinand; for not only was he involved in an adroit combination of schemes in regard to France, but he

---

* " Coleccion Diplomatica," doc. num. lxviii.; Barry's De Lorgues' " Columbus," p. 349.

had resolved on seizing the Neapolitan throne, and was negotiating that matrimonial alliance—a deeply laid scheme of parental and imperial ambition—which subsequently made his grandson, Charles V., the emperor and ruler of a great part of Europe. Armies of immense numbers had to be maintained at Naples, and on the Spanish frontier next to France large squadrons of ships had to be kept afloat to guard his interests in the Mediterranean. His dynastic ambition cost the royal exchequer immense sums of money, for at this very time he had sent that grand and costly Armada, consisting of more than one hundred vessels and containing twenty thousand of his subjects on board, and among them many of the very flower of the Spanish nobility, to escort to Flanders the Princess Juana to be married to Philip, Archduke of Austria. The same magnificent convoy was to return to Spain with the archduke's sister, Margarita, who was the *fiancée* of the Infante and Prince Royal of Spain, Prince Juan. It was thus that while Spanish dominion was being extended to embrace great empires in the new world, through the genius and loyal services of Columbus, diplomacy and arms, blended with family alliances, were concentrating in his dynasty the choicest empires of Europe. These great undertakings, both at the west and the east, had depleted the royal treasury, and Columbus had to wait. The king, one of the most calculating of men, had restrained his appreciation for Columbus within narrow and chilling bounds, in proportion to the amount of gold returned from the west; but it was the queen chiefly, who, in the midst of most anxious family and maternal solicitudes, never lost sight of the grand work he was doing for his country, and sustained the more glorious and enduring work of discovery and conquest in the new world. While the king was reserved, and the Bureau of the Indies, with Bishop Fonseca at its head, was openly hostile, Columbus was sustained by the ardent sympathy and substantial rewards of the queen. By royal edict his dignities, rights, and offices were confirmed as amply as they were first granted at Santa Fé, and a principality of fifty leagues in length by twenty-five in breadth in Hispaniola, in a quarter to be selected by himself, with the title of duke or marquis, was offered to him. But Columbus, while tenaciously adhering to his rights as previously conceded, had the good judgment and forbearance to decline a gift, magnificent as it was, but which would have made him more than ever the object of envy, malice, and misrepresentation. But he relinquished his share of the returns from the past voyages, on being relieved from his share of the expense of them, which was one eighth; but he was not released from the share of expense he had incurred for the first voyage. He was now to receive for three years one eighth of the gross results of each voyage, and, moreover, a tenth of the net profits, and after this term the first arrangement of division was to revive in force. While historians generally attribute to Columbus the motive we have assigned for his declining the principality in Hispaniola offered him by the queen, the Count de Lorgues, with forensic effort rather than historical truth, contends that this motive was beneath his exalted character and unselfish nature, and that his true motive was to leave himself free to continue his great discoveries until he had made the circuit of the whole globe, and to devote his efforts to the redemption of the Holy Land rather than divert his mind from these grand purposes by centring his thoughts and aspirations to the maintenance and care of such an estate, even though it afforded him an opportunity of founding a powerful house for his second son, while transmitting his titles and dignities of Admiral of the Ocean and Viceroy of the Indies to his elder son. "In him," says the overwrought Count de Lorgues, "the apostle got the mastery over the head of the family." *

The admiral, however, instead of the principality, was endowed now with the privilege of founding a mayorazgo, or perpetual entail of his estates, thus giving the lineal and united descent of his estates and titles to his eldest male branch, and thus, too, by the entail, perpetuating the renown of his illustrious deeds. He accordingly exercised this high prerogative by his will, which was made at Seville early in 1498, and by which he entailed his titles and estates on his male descendants; on failure of these, on his brothers and their male descendants; and, on failure of these last, then to the lineal females of his stock. Such entailed heir was to bear the coat-of-arms of the admiral, and in his official signature to use only the title of admiral, without regard to the other numerous titles he might enjoy. The views and aspirations of Columbus in respect to his dignities, honors,

---

* Barry's De Lorgues' "Columbus," p. 352.

titles, and estates not only during his lifetime, but also for his descendants and collaterals for all time, were in keeping with his own tenacious knowledge and appreciation of the grandeur and vastness of his discoveries. He united with mediæval religious devotion and piety the most worldly and ambitious plans of family and estate, of official dignity and jurisdiction. He was a striking example of earthly but honorable ambition mingled with the virtues and self-abnegation of a religious devotee. Yesterday we saw him emerging from the cloister in the humble garb and unshorn beard of a Franciscan monk; to-day we behold him wielding the power of disposal over titles, dignities, offices, jurisdictions, and estates vaster than the most ancient and most opulent houses of the Spanish aristocracy, and eclipsing the immense wealth of the greatest of modern corporations.

By the testament which he made during this interval of delay he provided for his other nearest relatives, members now of his own family, such as his second son, Fernando, his brother Bartholomew, the Adelantado, and his brother Diego, to all of whom he was devotedly attached, and whose loyalty to him was constant and honorable. In his generosity he provided that one tenth of the revenues of his estates should form a fund for the relief of all the poor relatives of his lineage, and for general pious and charitable uses, and provided dowries for his poor female relatives, present and future. He established a family domicile and residence for the Colombos in Genoa, his native city; commanded his successors in the entail, subject to the paramount interests of the Church and Spanish crown, to promote the honor, prosperity, and growth of the city of Genoa. Diego, his eldest son and heir-apparent to the entail, was enjoined to provide in good royal manner for the recovery of the Holy Sepulchre to Christendom, and for this purpose to invest all the surplus funds of the entail in stock of the Bank of St. George at Genoa, and to stand ready with these vast anticipated revenues to follow the King of Spain to the conquest of the sacred places, or otherwise himself to organize and lead the crusade at his own expense. The deep religious cast which this remarkable instrument received from his hand is intensified by the injunction given to his heirs, in case of schism or trouble in the Church, to throw themselves at the feet of the Pope, and devote person and estate to the defence of the honor and dominions of the Church; and next to the Church to render the same service and homage to the Spanish crown. He gives as an inheritance to his heir in the spiritual order, his own romantic loyalty to the Church, by commanding him, in the confessional, that he should before confessing request the ghostly father to examine the precious document, and question him closely as to his fulfilment of the duties thereby imposed. In this remarkable document the illustrious testator, in the very first sentence, declares that it was the Most Holy Trinity who inspired him with the idea of discovering the Indies by sailing to the west across the ocean, and afterward made this idea perfectly clear to him. In the codicil, which he made before his death, there were other interesting features, showing the elevation of spirit which characterized the admiral in life and in death. In the principal will now made the great religious purposes of Columbus through life, as provided for in the will, are divided by the Count de Lorgues under five principal heads: First, to pay tithes to God and His poor; second, to deliver the Holy Sepulchre; third, to secure the temporal independence of the Pope; fourth, to comfort the sick; and, fifth, to labor for the conversion of the Indians. The signature of the admiral to his will is equally remarkable for its religious and devotional character, and sets forth the title of Christ-Bearer, or Christopher, as illustrated by what the Count de Lorgues perhaps too enthusiastically calls his apostolate; and the Holy See has now lately declared that from historical data it is clear and indisputable that Columbus undertook his great discovery mainly with the view of bringing the heathen inhabitants of the countries he would discover to the knowledge of Christ and His religion.

In addition to the mayorazgo, a royal edict was made on June 2d, 1497, whereby the king and queen revoked the general license given or proclaimed in April, 1495, to make expeditions of discovery and exploration in the new world, which he had always regarded as an infraction of his privileges. The Spanish sovereigns, in their edict, expressly declared that, so far from intending to deprive him of any of his privileges, rights, favors, or conventions, it was their intention to bestow still further distinctions and favors upon him. While the act of Columbus had been regarded at first with displeasure by the king, whereby the office and title of Adelantado had been conferred on Don Bartholomew Columbus, because Ferdinand regarded the power to confer such an office as vested solely in himself, now the title and office were spontaneously conferred upon that worthy man by the sovereigns, without allusion to his previous enjoyment of them. The sovereigns also gave Columbus permission to take out on his third voyage three hundred and thirty persons whose pay was given from the royal treasury, forty of them being servants, one hundred foot soldiers, thirty sailors, thirty ship-boys, twenty miners, fifty husbandmen, ten gardeners, twenty mechanics, and thirty females, with authority to increase the whole number to five hundred, the additional ones to be paid from the yields of the colony. He was also given the right to make grants of land to such as would till them in vineyards, orchards, sugar plantations, and other agricultural or rural establishments, on condition of four years' residence in the island, and reserving all brazil-wood and precious metals to the crown. The solicitude of Isabella provided for the religious instruction of the natives and the lenient collection of the tribute. A few such measures alone indicated that little impression had been made on the minds of the sovereigns by the calumnies so industriously propagated against the admiral.

While Columbus was pressing his enterprises for the grand and limitless advancement of Spanish empire over countless tribes and peoples, islands and continents, encountering delay and discouragement at every step, he was chagrined at seeing millions expended and vast armadas put afloat for the promotion of dynastic schemes or for the acquisition of some trifling angle or corner of European soil. He asked only for a small number of little caravels for the conquest of continents. After great delays and disappointments, he at last was cheered by a royal order for the advancement of six millions of maravedis for the third voyage. So far not a ship was procured, not a sailor enlisted. At this juncture the remarkable changes in the fortunes of the admiral, which illustrate his whole life, so frequent, so sudden, so disastrous, were followed now by singular and similar experiences. When on the eve of receiving the six millions appropriated for his voyage, a letter was received at court announcing the arrival at Cadiz of the pilot Pedro Alonzo Niño, with three caravels from Hispaniola, and containing the cheering announcement that he had brought from the Antilles a great amount of gold. Though viewing the news from different standpoints, Columbus and Ferdinand were at first equally rejoiced. Disappointment followed. The boastful pilot had sent this misguiding letter to the sovereigns instead of repairing in person to court. He went immediately to visit his family at Huelva. It was found on investigation that he had carried the despatches of the Adelantado with him. He did not arrive at court until the end of December, and when the despatches were read, the gold mentioned in Niño's letter, as brought by him from Hispaniola, turned out to be a cargo of Indians. The pilot had used an ill-timed figure of speech, whereby the gold to be realized from the sale of the Indians was the gold he alluded to in his letter. The needy king, on receipt of Niño's letter in October, had ordered the six millions appropriated for the third voyage of Columbus to be used for repairing the fortress of Salza, in Roussillon, which had been dismantled by the French, and the six millions needed for the voyage to Hispaniola were ordered to be taken out of the figurative gold which Niño had brought home.

The admiral was stunned by this cruel and unexpected blow. Not only did he find himself without a dollar for his enterprise for pushing the great discovery to the continent, but his whole work, past and future, though it had given a new world to Spain, became, in the eyes of the public and in the clamor of his enemies, a reproach to him, a deception to the crown, a snare to the people. Not only were his hopes that immediate harvests of gold had been reaped from the newly discovered mines of Hayna dissipated, but he and his work became objects of scorn and malediction, the people pointing derisively to Indian prisoners and miserable Spanish colonists as the gold which came from Hispaniola. When it became known that the statements brought by Niño's crew represented the condition of the colony as miserable, and the very despatches of the Adelantado called for hasty relief in supplies, even his few friends staggered in their support of him. The whole claim of a new world discovered became invested with the garb of exaggeration and boasting.

A year's delay sickened the heart of Columbus, and, as he himself said, he was "oppressed with reproaches." So great was the decline of public faith in the verity of the first accounts of the new world, of its treasures and wealth, so apparently disastrous all its results, that neither ships nor men could now be procured for the coming voyage. A contemporary and eye-witness of the scenes then enacted in Spain said, " Because those who went with the admiral . . . returned sick, emaciated, and of so sickly a color that they appeared more dead than alive, the country of the Indies was so much decried that nobody could be found who would venture to go there." * The promises of royal pay and the reiterated prospects of gold failed to secure ships or recruits. The achievements now celebrated by the world with unparalleled grandeur were then in such odium that men sickened at the thought of embarking on the very voyage which brought to light the existence of the continent itself. Columbus, ever ready in expedients, even in the darkest extremities, suggested that the services of criminals sentenced to banishment, the galleys, or to the mines be commuted to transportation to the new settlements of Hispaniola, and to labor there in the public service. This was done. Nay, more ; proclamation was made of a general pardon of all malefactors at large who would come in and surrender themselves to the admiral, and embark with him for Hispaniola.† A scale of punishments commuted for certain specified terms of service in the new settlements was published. A colony of convicts, criminals, and malefactors, sent thousands of miles away from the mother country and brought in contact with the simple, unclad, and guileless natives of a new hemisphere, was a measure—perhaps the only one then possible—which ruined the very enterprise it was designed to sustain.

From a miscellaneous rabble of criminals of every degree of degradation and crime—pernicious poison to a noble enterprise— we turn to the more studied and refined marplots of bureaucracy. Notwithstanding the pronounced favor extended by the sovereigns to the enterprise of Columbus, Antonio de Torres, having been charged with the duty of purchasing supplies for the fleet of Columbus, the " red-tape" of the bureau exacted from design rather than necessity an infinite number of documents to be prepared for the signatures of the official head of the bureau and of the admiral. When it was discovered that he had abused his trust by exorbitant demands, Torres was removed, and to the

---

* Barry's De Lorgues' "Columbus," p. 353.
† Las Casas, "Hist. Ind.," lib. i., cap. 112, MS. ; Muñoz, lib. vi., § 19 ; Irving's " Columbus," vol. ii., p. 96.

sorrow of the admiral his inveterate but secret enemy, Juan Rodriguez de Fonseca, Bishop of Badajos, was reappointed, and new sets of documents more numerous than the first had to be prepared with all the circumlocution of Spanish ceremonial. Delay under Fonseca was the inevitable but disastrous result. Another misfortune followed. The generous queen was overwhelmed with sorrow by the death of the prince royal, Don Juan, whose nuptials had been but recently celebrated. Such were the straits of the colony that immediate relief must be sent out. The queen advanced the necessary funds from the dowry of the Princess Isabella, then betrothed to King Emanuel of Portugal. Two ships, under command of Pedro Fernandez Coronel, sailed with provisions for Hispaniola in the beginning of 1498. Fonseca and his minions covertly did all in their power to undermine the interests of Columbus, and to defeat the most urgent preparations for the voyage. They knew that his popularity was on the wane, and they resorted to all secret measures to annoy him, and became so emboldened as to extend to him at times open but ignoble arrogance. Though he bore these wrongs with prudent silence, yet with just indignation, he was so disheartened that it is said he meditated the abandonment of his great career of discovery, and probably his retirement from the world. The confidence of the queen was his moral support; his loyal regard for this peerless woman armed him with courage. After stupendous exertions and disheartening delays the six remaining ships were prepared for sailing, though the general horror of the people for the expedition made the number of enlisted men fall short; but to these were added a physician, a surgeon, and an apothecary, several musicians to sustain the drooping spirits of the colonists, and priests to take up the missionary work which Father Boïl and his sympathizing colleagues had abandoned.

Among the salaried instruments of Fonseca's malice was one Ximeno Breviesca, paymaster under him, and a ready minion of his plottings against Columbus. He was a Jew who, as De Lorgues says, had found it convenient to accept baptism after the conquest of Granada. Though assuming the name of a Christian, he was an alien to every Christian virtue. He was a genial tool of a Christian official whose conduct has been universally condemned by every Christian writer as a blemish upon the sacred character he bore. Not content with having delayed the third voyage for nearly two years, Fonseca hounded the admiral with persecution even to the day of his departure, following him up in this way to the port of San Lucar de Barrameda, and there even to the water's edge and on board his own ship as he entered it to embark. Ximeno was the useful man for this work of Fonseca, for he it was who dogged the steps of the admiral now with open abuse from place to place, from the shore to the ship. Insulted by this miscreant in the presence of his officers and crew, the long-patient admiral could no longer restrain his just anger. "His heart at such moments," says the eulogist of the admiral, the Count de Lorgues, alluding to his custom of commencing every voyage with prayer, "superabounded with Christian charity; he was, therefore, ready to pardon and consequently to bear injuries. But this day the offence was so grievous, so intolerable by its persistence and bravado, that the old man, now an admiral, remembered what he owed to his rank. Impunity this time may be attended with disastrous consequences. The offence was given in the presence of the whole squadron, of the crowd on the quay, of some bandits and other criminals who were on board; all these would take his patience for pusillanimity and cowardice. At the moment of departure it became, perhaps, necessary for the safety of the ships and the maintenance of discipline to prove on the spot that age had not reduced his vigor, and that he knew how to make his person respected as well as to have his orders executed. The patriarch of the ocean made a step toward his insulter, and with his fist dealt him a blow on his impudent face. The miserable wretch fell down, stunned. The admiral limited himself to giving a few kicks to this vile snarler, who fled in the midst of hootings, concealing under his humiliation and forced tears his secret joy, for from that moment his fortune was made."* It is impossible, however, to regard this account as historical.

A regulated temper, a forbearing disposition, when once the barriers are broken down, gives vent to the long-accumulated indignation and sense of wrong. The enemies of Columbus were adepts at such things; the snare had been laid for him,

---

* Dr. Barry's translation of De Lorgues' "Columbus," p. 362.

and he had unguardedly fallen into it. Not only had he displayed cruelty to the poor natives of Hispaniola, he had now in a Spanish port, under the very eyes of his sovereigns, brutally maltreated one of their subjects, and an officer of the crown. The accusations of Pedro Margarite, Father Boïl, of Juan de Aguado, and so many others were claimed to have been proved to be well founded by this very act of the accused. Columbus had a presentiment of the use his enemies would make of this incident. He sailed on the enterprise with this load upon his heart, accompanied by the unjust denunciations of his enemies and of the populace, and followed by cruel execrations. But the infamous Ximeno, hireling of the incumbent Fonseca, became an object of sympathy and favor, and while Columbus was insulted, his insulter received pity, consolation, and indemnity. Of this incident, so unimportant in itself, but magnified by the enemies of Columbus, Mr. Irving writes: "As Ximeno was a creature of the invidious Fonseca, the affair was represented to the sovereigns from the most odious point of view. Thus the generous intentions of princes and the exalted services of their subjects are apt to be defeated by the cold and crafty men in place. By this implacable hostility to Columbus, and the secret obstructions which he threw in the way of the most illustrious of human enterprises, Fonseca has insured perpetuity to his name, coupled with the contempt of every generous mind." *

Now all was ready; the admiral, inspired with hopes and purposes second only to those he entertained on his first voyage, sailed from the port of San Lucar de Barrameda on May 30th, 1498. The admiral resolved to give the name of the Most Holy Trinity to the first land he should discover, and he determined, with the help of the Holy Trinity, under whose patronage he placed this voyage, to pass beyond the region of islands and to set his foot upon *terra firma*, whose continental proportions his good ships would demonstrate to the world. His mind was filled with well-digested data, which induced him to steer to the south, because he had treasured up the statements of the inhabitants of the Caribbean Sea, that to the south there stood a vast land of continental proportions, and he had observed that the island of Cuba made an extended sweep to the south, by which he thought was

---

* Irving's "Columbus," vol. ii., p. 100.

indicated the lay of successive lands of which that island, as he believed, formed a part. He was confirmed in this view by the opinion of King John II. of Portugal, and by a letter he had formerly received from the learned lapidary, Jayme Ferrer, who had written to him at the request of the queen, and whose acquaintance he had since then and recently made at Burgos. He formed his theories also upon statements made by the inhabitants of Hispaniola in relation to a race of black men, who had formerly come to their country, and upon the assay made of their javelin heads, composed of a metal they called guanin, showing a combination of eighteen parts of gold, six of silver, and eight of copper. From his information and study of the subject he was convinced of the existence of a black race inhabiting vast countries near the equator, rich in the precious metals and favored in their climate, soil, and wealth. He felt quite sure that his new southern route would solve these momentous questions.

Information of a French fleet cruising off Cape St. Vincent caused Columbus to vary his course to the southwest, and on June 7th he arrived at Porto Santo, where he heard mass and took in wood and water; touching also at Madeira, he took in supplies and steered for the Canaries. Arriving at Gomera, on June 19th, he saw in port a French cruiser holding two Spanish prizes, which, alarmed at his arrival, immediately took its departure. He at first thought the prizes were merchant ships, but on learning their true character, he gave chase by sending out three of his vessels; but the fugitives had made sufficient distance to escape. But on board of one of the prizes, six Spanish prisoners, on seeing their countrymen approaching, rose up against their captors; this the Spanish caravels captured, and brought her back triumphantly to port. The prisoners were exchanged for six Spaniards carried off by the French cruiser, and the recaptured prize was returned to its captain. The fleet left Gomera on June 21st, and on arriving off the island of Ferro, in his solicitude for his colony at Isabella, Columbus sent forward three of the vessels to relieve the colonists, who were in need of supplies. These vessels were commanded respectively by Alonzo Sanchez de Caravajal, a most worthy man; Pedro de Arana de Cordova, brother of Donna Beatrix Enriquez, his second wife, the mother of Fernando Columbus, cousin of Diego de Arana, the commander of the ill-fated fortress of La Navidad; and the third ship by Juan Antonio Columbus, of Genoa, a relative of the admiral, one possessed of the capacity and virtues of the family. The three captains were given the command of the little fleet in alternation, a week at a time, receiving full instructions as to the route, and also on arriving in sight of Hispaniola to steer for the south side and the port of the new town, which he supposed had been founded in the mouth of the Ozema, agreeably to orders carried out by Coronel.

Columbus with the remaining three ships turned his course toward the torrid zone, still invoking, as he had done when he commenced the voyage, the name of the Most Holy Trinity. His own ship was decked, while the other two were only caravels of trade. A severe attack of gout assailed him as he reached the tropics, and this caused him fever and intense pain; yet he continued, with characteristic energy and mental power, to direct every progress of the voyage. He arrived at the Cape de Verde Islands on June 27th, where he made but a short stay, as he found it impossible to procure certain provisions he needed, such as goat's meat for the voyage and cattle for the colony. Still suffering greatly from the depressing effects of an insalubrious climate, and leaving the barren island of Buena Vista, on July 5th, he steered to the southwest, intending to persevere in this route, in spite of adverse currents and winds, until he crossed the equinoctial line and found the *terra firma* in the West Indies. Reaching the fifth degree of north latitude on July 13th, the admiral and all his crews suffered intensely from scorching heats in dead calms. In the midst of his agonies of pain, intensified by the torrid sun and calm, he used extraordinary vigilance in watching the currents of the winds and the ocean, and studying the phenomena of nature. In consequence of the opening of the seams of his ships by the solar heat, he resolved to change his course to the direct west in hope of reaching a port sooner, and he observed, on passing the papal line of demarcation, one hundred leagues west of the Azores, that the climate and atmosphere changed. In changing his course to west, he thus recorded his sentiments, after fervent recourse to prayer: "After that I resolved, if it should please the Lord to send me wind and a propitious time, to leave the latitudes in which I found myself, to push no farther to the south, but, without retrograding, to sail to the west, until I would find the temperature I had met in the latitude of the Canaries, and then to steer to the south."

The ships, as he anticipated, now passed out of the unfavorable atmosphere into a serene sky and favoring winds, and on reaching this region he had intended to sail south and then again west ; but he continued his westward course until he thought he was in the longitude of the Caribbee Islands, and then, in his distress, he changed his course northward in order to reach one of them as soon as possible. Not only were his vessels leaking, there was no wine, the provisions had spoiled, and each ship had on board only one cask of water.

At this perilous juncture, on July 31st, Alonzo Perez Nizzardo, one of the mariners, about midday saw in the distance the summits of three mountains, and joyously exclaimed, Land ! It seemed about fifteen leagues distant, and as the ships approached, the three mountains seemed united into one toward the base, thus recalling to the devout mind of Columbus the Holy Trinity, the three persons in one God, in whose honor he had commenced his voyage. In a transport of religious fervor he fulfilled his promise, and called the land La Trinidad. Columbus ever regarded this fortunate discovery of land as miraculous, and, as Muñoz relates, a signal favor of God.*

The admiral coasted from the eastern end of Trinidad, to which he gave the name of Punta de la Galera, from a prominent rock rising from the sea so as to resemble a galley under sail, westward in search of a safe place of landing, to obtain water. The country was fresh and verdant, and, as he wrote to the sovereigns, resembling the fine Spanish province of Valencia in early spring. Coming to a point where water was obtained, pure and abundant, he called it Punta de la Playa. Here were seen the footprints of men, who had suddenly fled, and of animals at rest, the latter supposed to be those of the deer.

An event now occurred of scarcely less importance than the discovery of the first land of the new world : it was the discovery of the continent. Looking to the south a long and low stretch of coast appeared, broken by numerous channels of water ; and,

---

* Muñoz, "Hist. del Nuevo Mundo," lib. vi., § 23 ; Irving's "Life of Columbus," vol. ii., p. 108.

supposing it to be an island, and still moved with his never-failing sense of the divine guidance, he called it, according to Irving and Tarducci, the Sacred Isle, La Isla Santa. While these authors speak of the admiral's having no conception of the continent which he then actually discovered, the Count de Lorgues, ever prone to the marvellous, writes: " Although there was no index to make him suppose that these islands were formed by the *embrouchure* of a great river, he had a feeling something uncommon, strange, and inexplicable in regard to the nature of these islands; for, far from giving a collected name to them, he designated the country by the name of Tierra de Gracia (Land of Grace), because the grace of God had alone conducted him there, and he did not speak of islands in this part of his report." But Mr. Irving admits that Columbus "now for the first time beheld that continent, that Terra Firma, which had been the object of his earnest search." * The first sight of the continent was gained on August 1st, 1798. It was, however, after passing into the Gulf farther that Columbus saw the land to which he gave the name of the Land of Grace. Conjecture was now ended. That Columbus realized then and there that he had discovered the continent is not now a matter of mere conjecture. Mr. Fiske says: " Presently, finding that the water in the Gulf was fresh to the taste, he gradually reasoned his way to the correct conclusion, that the billows which had so nearly overwhelmed him must have come out from a river greater than any he had ever known or dreamed of, and that so vast a stream of running water could be produced only on land of continental dimensions. This coast to the south of him was, therefore, the coast of a continent, with indefinite extension toward the south, a land not laid down on Toscanelli's or any other map, and of which no one had until that time known anything." Columbus, in his own language to Ferdinand and Isabella, describes the river as flowing from a land of infinite extent, and of which no previous knowledge had anywhere existed in Europe.†

The fleet continued to the southwest end of Trinidad, and on August 2d he named it Point Avenal; it stretched toward a

---

* Barry's De Lorgues' "Columbus," p. 370; Irving's "Columbus," vol. ii., p. 110, and farther on p. 114.

† Fiske's "Discovery of America," vol. i., pp. 493, 494.

similar point of Terra Firma, a narrow pass dividing them, in
the centre of which was a high rock, to which he gave the name
of El Gallo. Having anchored the ships here, as they were
nearing their anchorage a large canoe, containing twenty-five
Indians, approached within bow-shot, and hailed them in an
unknown tongue. The tempting offer of trinkets having failed
to allure them to the ships, the power of music with Spanish
dances on deck was tried, but this latter proved less successful,
for the men who had remained two hours gazing in wonder at
what they saw, with paddles in hand ready for flight, took this
for a hostile sign, and fled precipitately to a distance, discharging
their arrows at the admiral's ship, and receiving from him in
return a couple of cross-bow missiles. They were not so shy of
the caravels, however, but approached and parleyed with the
pilot, and accepted presents with delight. They invited the
pilot on shore, and on his acceptance of the invitation, they went
ashore to welcome him. But when they saw him go first to
the admiral's ship, which they took for the warship, they sprang
into the canoe and disappeared. These natives were well formed
young men, with no dress except cotton fillets around their
heads and colored cloths of cotton about their loins ; and they
were well armed with bows and with arrows feathered and tipped
with bane, and in their hands were seen the first bucklers observed in the Western Hemisphere by the Spaniards.

Columbus made, as was his custom, minute observations of
the natives, whom he was surprised to find not of the African
type, but rather fairer than those more north of the equator,
and with long hair and handsome forms ; and of the climate,
which he also to his surprise found more temperate and agreeable than that nearer the equator. Having landed, the Spaniards
found the only water obtainable was procured by sinking pits
in the sand. Columbus observed, with astonishment and fear,
the waters strangely agitated, boiling, hissing, and raging to
such an extent as to render the anchorage insecure. He called
the pass the Serpent's Mouth. At night he saw a huge and
raging surge of the sea rushing toward his ship, which was
struck by it, was lifted up to a perilous height, while another
ship was wrenched from its anchorage. He sent the boats
next morning to take the depths in the Serpent's Mouth, and
explore it far enough to learn whether the ships could pass

through, and he was rejoiced at their report of deep waters for the passage of the ships away from this dangerous anchorage. With a favorable wind now springing up, the admiral soon found himself in a tranquil gulf beyond.

What could be more striking than the spectacle we now behold, the discoverer of the new world struggling to explore more fully what he had discovered, and, for the first time, to determine its geography and delineate its map! Continuing his route to the northwest point of Trinidad, he saw two high capes opposite each other, the one on the island of Trinidad, the other on the west; and to the latter he gave the name of Land of Grace. The Count de Lorgues contends in effect that Columbus here felt an inward consciousness that this land was a continent, for the reason that the name bestowed was the Land of Grace and not the Island of Grace, and says that the admiral "did not speak of islands in this part of his report."* Yet such was the uncertainty and perplexity of the intricate maze of fact and conjecture in which the mind was involved, that it is difficult to know what Columbus felt. He certainly was in search of the continent. In fact, he had now found it.

Between the two capes another pass, with a more violent current than that of the Serpent's Mouth, gave vent to the roaring and struggling tide, and to this was given the name of the Dragon's Mouth. From this formidable navigation he turned to the north, coasting along the inner coast of the Land of Grace, intending on reaching its end to sail northward through the open sea to Hispaniola. The country was magnificent in fine harbors, in cultivated fields, lofty forests, and great streams. Having already observed the freshness of the water, this close observer of nature saw with amazement that it grew more fresh as he advanced, and the sea was remarkably quiet. Little did he seem to know or conjecture that he was before and within the delta of the mighty river Orinoco. On Sunday, August 5th, Columbus, according to the Count de Lorgues, anchored, and, having landed, solemn possession was taken of the continent, and a large cross erected on the shore. But I can find elsewhere

---

* Fiske's "Discovery of America," vol. i., pp. 490, 491; Winsor's "Columbus," etc., p. 354; "Life of Columbus," by the Count de Lorgues, translated by Dr. Barry, p. 370; Irving's "Columbus," vol. ii., p. 114.

no confirmation of this statement.* On the following day he
held his first intercourse with the natives, who had proved themselves so far timid and shy of these strange and fearful visitors.
As usual, the timidity of the Indians was overcome by kindness
and presents. Several of them were taken on board to serve as
guides. These people were tall, finely formed, and graceful of
motion. The men were armed with bows, arrows, and targets,
and wore cotton cloths around their heads and loins, which were
so elegantly wrought as to resemble silk; but the women were
entirely naked. Singularly enough, the sense of smell was the
principal or usual means by which they tested everything, such
as the presents, the ships, and the persons of the Spaniards.
They informed the admiral that the name of the country was
Paria. Proceeding farther along the coast a distance of eight
leagues, to a point which he called the Needle, his eyes were
ravished by beholding a country of unsurpassed richness and
beauty. Its cultivated fields and orchards, fruits, flowers, and
birds of brilliant plumage won for it the name of the Gardens.
Here the natives welcomed them with genuine hospitality, treating them with a reverence inspired by their supposed descent
from heaven. Gold and pearls were seen in abundance, the
former of an inferior quality; but the latter were fine. "I cast
anchor," said the admiral, "in order to have more leisure to
contemplate this verdure, this beautiful country and its inhabitants." The abundance of the pearls, which the natives wore in
strings about their persons, and to which they attached no extraordinary value, awakened the philosophic and commercial
studies of the admiral, while they stimulated the cupidity of his
followers. The former saw in them the confirmation of the
theory of Jayme Ferrer, the eminent lapidary of Burgos, and he
imagined he realized in this fair land of ideal beauty, where the
dew of the atmosphere was clear and abundant as the oysters in
the waters were unlimited, the realization of Pliny's beautiful
yet poetic fancy, that pearls were formed by the dewdrops falling
into the mouth of the oyster. But Las Casas, with blended
knowledge and fancy, dissipated the admiral's exuberant hopes

---

* There is a partial confirmation of the landing, which one of the witnesses said was
done by deputy, but this is denied by others. The condition of the admiral's health
and his desire to reach Hispaniola are sufficient to discredit any statement as to his
landing and holding religious services.

by the statement that the oysters of Paria were not the pearl-producing variety, while the peerless pearl, as if conscious of its value, with instinctive self-preservation buried itself in the deepest waters.* And yet it may be added that the exquisite rays of light and beauty from the pearl, piercing the deepest waters and seeking union with the solar rays, ever reached the surface and danced upon the rippling waves above. In contrast with the cupidity of the early European treasure-seekers of those adventurous days was the broad and noble aspirations of the admiral, who saw in these gems emblems of divine beauty, and the links that were to unite the most distant nations in the bonds of commerce; or, may we not recall the elegance of Milton's line, each word a pearl of beauty, when, following the theory of Pliny, he exclaimed,

"And those *pearls* of *dew* she wears!"

Leaving the Gardens on August 10th, the admiral directed his fleet westward; but as he advanced the water became sweeter and sweeter, and a caravel—the Correo—sent to explore returned with the report of successive gulfs, in which the water was sweet and fresh; and though the report represented these lands thus divided by small passes or gulfs of water to be an united land, the conclusion was so fixed in his mind that the immediate lands he saw seemed like islands, and he named two of them Isabella and Tramontura. In fact, the first lands and waters opposite to Trinidad which he encountered were the delta of the Orinoco, and now he stood before the delta of the river Cuparipari, now known as the Paria. Led by the information of the Indians, he called the small gulf he now sailed across the Gulf of Pearls, though the keenest eyes could not discern the dance of the pearl ray upon the waves.

So sweet was the water that the admiral said, "I never drank such." Disappointed in finding here a passage to the north, he changed his course to the east on August 11th, and on the 14th the ships were fearfully struggling to make their way through the surging waters of the Dragon's Mouth. While in the middle of this pass the winds ceased, and it was only the impetuosity of the waters that carried him through safely to the open sea,

---

* Las Casas, "Hist. Ind.," cap. 136; Pliny's Works; Irving's "Columbus," vol. ii., p. 120; Barry's De Lorgues' "Columbus," p. 372.

greatly to the relief of all on board. The urgency of his return
to Hispaniola prevented him from again visiting the Gulf of
Pearls, and from making an exploration of the fresh waters he
had just visited ; for he had wished to test the report brought
by the Correo, that the vast volume of seething fresh waters
came from the mouths of rivers, upon which subject he felt unsettled, believing it incredible that mere island streams could
produce such a vast volume of fresh water, or impart to them
such turbulent velocity. Here it is manifest that the vision of
the continent had risen and shaped itself in his vigorous and
intelligent mind. It was now reality.

Passing westward from the Dragon's Mouth, he saw numerous
islands ; named two islands he saw Assumption and Conception,
now supposed to be Tobago and Granada ; on the 15th the islands
of Margarita and Cubaqua, the last of which he approached to
obtain a supply of wood and water. Now he seemed to be in
the region of pearls, for on approaching Cubaqua he saw Indian
girls fishing for these precious gems, and on sending some of the
men ashore he procured from the natives, in exchange for broken
fragments of Valencian plates and other trifles, pearls to the
amount of three pounds' weight. Some of the pearls were very
large, and the collection, when sent to Spain, formed a grateful
specimen of the products of the new empire of Ferdinand and
Isabella.

The admiral was most anxious to continue his westward exploration of the northern shore of Paria, and to reach the regions
most abundant, according to Indian representations, in pearls,
but a long-continued and increasing attack of ophthalmia necessitated his return to Hispaniola. Turning all the prows toward
that island, and leaving from necessity all further nautical observations and reports to his pilots and seamen, he hastened thither
to recruit his suffering health, and with the intention of sending
his brother Bartholomew to continue and complete the exploration of this interesting region.

In passing away from the exterior coast of Paria the admiral
noticed in front of the cape three peaks, three islands, to which he
gave the name of The Witnesses, as the Count de Lorgues writes :
" No doubt in allusion to the three miraculous events of his third
voyage, which was undertaken in the name of the adorable
Trinity." The Conception and Assumption were named by

him in honor of the Blessed Virgin. Carried westward by the strong currents of fresh water issuing from the Dragon's Mouth, he sighted the island of Hispaniola on August 19th, at a point fifty leagues west of the point of his desire, the river Ozema, and anchored off the small island of Beata. Having sent ashore and procured as a messenger one of the natives of Hispaniola, he dispatched a letter to his brother, the Adelantado, announcing his arrival. Here having seen a native bearing a cross-bow, an arm not permitted in the trade between the Spaniards and the Indians, he feared that some calamity had befallen his colony, as the weapon must have been taken from some murdered Spaniard. Again setting sail, he arrived on August 30th in the mouth of the river Ozema, but no seaport had been founded there as he expected. On the other hand, he had the happiness of being met here in a caravel by his brother Bartholomew, and the affectionate meeting between these two brothers is one of the most interesting pictures drawn by the pen of the historians of the new world. He arrived at Isabella with shattered health. His grand discoveries during his third voyage were such that any one of them would have been enough to immortalize his name. The repose he now needed, and which he had hoped to find, was denied to him by the stirring events in the grand and unparalleled enterprise in which he was embarked, of bringing face to face the inhabitants of two worlds. The old world under his leadership was advancing to the conquest of the new. There was no repose for such a man!

The extraordinary phenomena of nature which Columbus observed and sagaciously pondered over, even while racked with pain and prostrated with illness, were wholly without precedent in the previous voyages, and were utterly new ih cosmographic physiognomy. His theories and speculations in relation to them form one of the important and interesting chapters in the history of the human mind, and in the progress of mankind in its efforts to assert its dominion over the earth. The soil of these new countries, the exuberance of spontaneous vegetation, the difference between the color of the natives and of those of Africa under the same latitude, the mildness of the climate, the variations in the heavenly constellations, the movements and directions of the waves and currents, the floods of struggling fresh waters apparently in the midst of the sea—these and all other signs and strange appearances of things in the skies, atmosphere, earth, and ocean impressed his active and studious mind with the conviction that he was now in a perfectly new and before unseen grand division of the earth, one of its principal continents, and in a part where its shape and elevation were exceptional and phenomenal. While he regarded these lands as the extreme limits of Asia, he was led to regard the vastness of the solid surface of the earth as far exceeding the surface of the waters, because Asia, as known and as then supposed to be extended by his discovery, if one solid continent, would cover a vast portion of the earth's surface. And yet, as the Count de Lorgues contends, he knew, without our being able to tell how, that beyond that continent, from which there came so large a river, there was still an ocean. He had many authors at his ready command to support his theories, and in his letter or report to the Spanish sovereigns he quotes from Aristotle and Seneca and from St. Augustine and Cardinal Pedro de Alliaco. Was it not also revealed in Esdras that of the entire surface of the earth six parts were dry land and one part was water? He had gone farther than any other discoverer to solve this problem, then new, but now so familiar.

In all the early stages of human knowledge there is much of error mingled with new and prodigious truths; in this remarkable instance, however, the world accords to Columbus the great glory of having discovered the western continent.

Advancing into the realm of cosmographic theory, deduced from the apparent features of earth, sea, and skies, Columbus gave to the world his theory of the earth's shape. While Aristotle located the highest culmination of the earth under the Antarctic Pole, and other scholars had placed it under the Arctic Pole, he argued, from all he saw and felt, that it was in fact under the equator. He alluded in cogent terms to the change he observed in the sky and stars, the temperature of the air and the calmness of the ocean, the variations of the needle from northeast to northwest, the apparent diurnal circle described by the north star, and other physical phenomena which occurred after he had passed the ideal line drawn from pole to pole one hundred leagues west of the Azores. On his third voyage, so much farther to the south, he passed from a region of intense heat to one of equable and delightful temperature; the ocean was free from winds, the weather serene, the air most pure, the soil most enriched. He saw his ships struggling to surmount an immense and continental swelling of the waters of the earth toward the heavens, and the lands, in reaching them, must also rise in the same proportion, for he saw and felt and tasted the fresh waters rushing in immense volumes upon the lower earth from above, and sweetening the ocean for many leagues. Perceiving this swell of the planet at the equator, he arrived at the conclusion that the earth is shaped like a pear, and that the elevated part of the pear, ending in the stem, represented the highest elevation and shape of the earth under the equator. He goes further, and conjectures that the culminating point of the equatorial swelling is the site of the terrestrial Paradise, the home of our first parents, the Mosaic scene of the creation of man.

However mingled with fanciful theories his conclusions may have been and are now proved to have been by much later scientific knowledge, the great historic fact remains triumphant that Christopher Columbus was the unchallenged discoverer of the equatorial swelling. While he erred only in degree in relation to the elevation of the earth, he was far in advance of the contemporaneous scientific world, for scientists have now ascertained and decided that the earth is a spheroid, slightly elevated in circumference at the equator, thus substantially verifying the fact discovered by Columbus, though not confirming his conclusions therefrom. The location of Paradise is still a subject of learned speculation.

We have already related how Columbus saw and was amazed at the rush of fresh waters through the passes and channels of the Paria Gulf, and how with warmth of temperature they made their way northward and carried onward his fleet, in its course to Hispaniola, far to the west of his reckonings. It was in these new and closely studied phenomena that the admiral became the discoverer of the oceanic current known in our times as the Gulf Stream.*

A remarkable trait in the character of Columbus was his power, physical, moral, and mental, to make any exertion, or to perform any work, however difficult to others, under the most

---

* On this subject see Irving, Tarducci, De Lorgues, Winsor, and other historians.

severe prostrations of bodily disease or of mental distress. The report or relation of this voyage, which he wrote to the sovereigns, was dictated by him to his secretary at sea, from his sickbed, while racked with the pains of gout, tortured with violent and acute ophthalmia, exhausted in body, fatigued beyond ordinary endurance by the watchings and labors of this voyage, almost blind, struggling in the service of an ungrateful king, expanding by his genius the realms of the world, and returning to the scenes of his solicitude and struggles, the first colony of Europeans in the new world, from whose past disasters he drew the sad anticipations of strife and trouble. Yet he continued to observe every sign that nature gave, every pulsation of ocean, every feature of the earth, every breath of the atmosphere, every phenomenon of the heavens; he had them all recorded. His mind, unclouded by illness or pain; his memory, stored with considerable learning and science of the past and present; his clear judgment—all these united in the preparation of that document which aroused the mind of Europe, and advanced the world beyond the achievements of past centuries. Of it the Count de Lorgues rather extravagantly writes : " This document bears the character of improvision, giving utterance to the abundance of his thoughts. The condensed erudition of Columbus would be noticed there, if it did not totally disappear before the grandeur of the syntheses, the immensity of the views, the profoundness of the revelations, and the new speculations offered by him to the reflections of his contemporaries. This document contains intrinsic proofs of its being written during the passage from Margarita to Hispaniola." *

Though on his arrival at Hispaniola he was almost blind, and pale, emaciated, and prostrated, he found the events which transpired during his absence had fanned the previous discontents into a flame. The mute prophecy of the cross-bow he saw in the hands of an Indian at the river Ozema became realized by the disorder and violence prevailing on his arrival. Wrecked in health himself, he had now to witness the wreck of all his hopes. It was on March 10th, 1496, that he had sailed for Spain, and he re-

---

* De Lorgues' "Columbus," Dr. Barry, p. 380; Irving's "Columbus," pp. 128–36; Peter Martyr, dec. i., lib. vi., "Historia del Almirante," cap. 66; Navarrete, "Colec. de Viajes," tom. i., p. 242; Muñoz, "Hist. del Nuevo Mundo," lib. vi., § 32.

turned on August 30th, 1498, a period of eighteen months and twenty days. The provisions sent out on the three caravels under Pedro Alonzo Niño, in consequence of the misconduct of the Bureau of the Indies under Fonseca, were of bad quality and had spoiled on the voyage, and fourteen months elapsed from this time to the arrival of the supplies sent by the admiral under Pedro Coronel. During this period no tidings had been received from the mother country; the colonists considered themselves forgotten and doomed to perish in this remote wilderness; their clothes, implements, tools, and utensils had worn out. The proud hidalgos and spirited young Spaniards, who had come out to amass golden fortunes, found themselves in rags, or wearing grotesque clothes made of the bark of trees or of native cotton. They all united in casting the blame of their ruin and humiliation upon their best friend, the admiral.

The Adelantado took steps immediately, on the departure of the admiral, to carry out his brother's directions for the development and working of the mines of Hayna, and here was erected Fort San Christopher, called by the workmen the Golden Tower, from the grains of gold found in the stone and earth used in its erection. On the Ozema was erected Fort Isabella, afterward changed in name to San Domingo, the foundation of the present city of that name. This was done in compliance with the orders of the admiral, received at the time of the arrival of Coronel with provisions. Having a large force under his immediate command, while Don Diego remained at Isabella with the other forces and the colonists, he found it difficult to feed his men. The Indians had ceased to extend their primitive hospitality to their celestial visitors, now their conquerors, and they themselves laid up no food in advance, but lived from hand to mouth. Having acquired many of the customs of their European conquerors, among which was that of exacting a price for all they parted with, they suffered all the time from the exactions of the tribute by their taskmasters. Having completed Fort Christopher, the Adelantado left a garrison there, and went with the remainder of his force to the Vega in order to exact the tribute from Guarionex, his tributary caciques, and his subjects, from whom also he received food until the arrival of supplies from Spain. After completing the Fort San Domingo and garrisoning it, the Adelantado repaired with his remaining soldiers to the remote western province of Xaragua, which was ruled over by Behechio, with whom resided his sister, the widow of Caonabo, the beautiful Anacaona. She was not only beautiful in person and graceful in her carriage, she was intelligent, sagacious, and gifted with prudence and forethought. She and her husband gave ample proof of the capacity of the American aborigines for receiving and developing our civilization, and their conduct and lives, on the whole, did not contrast unfavorably with those of their more favored European conquerors.

Behechio was a ruler of ability and dignity; he and his nation had neither recognized nor attacked the Castilian usurpation, and as his dominions were remote from the Spanish forts and settlements, this great cacique was content to remain inactive, especially as he had seen the combined strength of the island scattered and routed by Spanish soldiers. It was believed that "The Golden Flower" had greatly influenced her brother to a pacific policy. Why should they seek their own annihilation? Might they not be left securely alone by the conquerors of the rest of the island? Obedient to Spanish policy, the Adelantado regarded it as his duty to bring this inoffensive and independent people under Spanish subjugation. In fact, it was regarded as a necessary measure, according to the views of European statesmanship, that the Spanish soldiers must be kept busy at something, in order to prevent the spread in their ranks of still greater demoralization than already existed, and to maintain their discipline. Accordingly the Adelantado marched at the head of his forces, prepared for war, but under the pretext of going on an exploring expedition. Behechio, with a natural sense of pride and right, assembled an army of forty thousand men, divided into cohorts, for the defence of his dominions. At this juncture "The Golden Flower," as a medium of peace, induced her brother to disband his army. The Adelantado also assured the chief in an interview that his intentions were friendly. The chief thus saved his people from slaughter, but did not secure them from becoming subject and tributary to the Spaniards. The Adelantado was invited to the royal residence, received with eminent distinction, and entertained in regal style at a grand banquet, which was graced by the presence of "The Golden Flower." The skilful diplomacy of the Adelantado secured from the unsuspecting cacique the voluntary payment of tribute, which, however, as his dominions contained no gold, the Adelantado graciously consented to receive in provisions. The Spaniards were entertained with unstinted hospitality for several days, were quartered in the houses of the cacique and his people, and were amused with Indian games and exercises. One of the entertainments given in honor of the Spaniards was a mock battle between two squadrons of naked warriors armed with bows and arrows, and performed in a manner somewhat similar to a game of Moorish canes, with which the Spaniards had been familiar at home, and somewhat similar in its sanguinary results, and in the pleasure it gave to the Spaniards, to their national sport of the bull-fight. The contestants grew heated in the mock fray, four were killed, many were wounded, and greater carnage was about to follow, when the Adelantado and several of the cavaliers present requested the game to be stopped, though it is related that the brutal results had "seemed to increase the interest and pleasure of the spectators."

Before the departure of the admiral for Spain he had found it necessary to impose severe restrictions on the search for gold by the Spaniards, and on the working of the newly discovered mines of Hayna. Hosts of covetous idlers and broken-down hidalgos from Spanish cities had come out to Hispaniola on this second voyage, dazzled by the specimens of gold brought back from the first voyage, and the colony contained many lawless adventurers, who respected no rights in the Indians, and outraged them in their property, their homes, and in all their dearest affections. It was necessary to impose restraint upon such outlaws. Having observed that the Indians themselves had attributed a certain value to gold, and in order to discover the richest beds they made long voyages and journeys and performed religious fasts, observed continency for twenty days, and other rites and ceremonies, the admiral threw around the precious metal some similar restrictions, based upon the holy purposes for which the gold was intended to be used, such as the rescuing of the Holy Sepulchre. With this view, he required of these desperadoes, who had sought their fortunes by attaching themselves to his, that they should reform their lives, refrain from violence, observe continency, practise fasts, repent of their sins and approach the sacraments before they would be permitted to work the mines; and he gave this license only to such as would lead a regular life, and receive the services of the priests or missionaries of the colony. Don Bartholomew had endeavored rigidly to carry out these measures of the admiral during the latter's absence. These regulations interfered with these avaricious adventurers and malcontents, who had not been able to return to Spain with Aguado, and the discontents already existing now began to spread and assume a formidable shape.

When the Adelantado returned to Isabella from Xaragua new sources of disaffection had been at work, and he immediately saw the fruits they produced. Death, hunger, improvidence, sickness, sloth, that had prevented the raising of food by the cultivation of an almost spontaneous soil, the recoil of the Indians from feeding their oppressors, the lust for gold, had produced misery, poverty, and insubordination. The most civilized people of Europe were actually starving, while they listlessly roamed over a soil which produced luxuriant crops in three or four weeks after the sowing of the seed. What a spectacle for savages to witness! Don Bartholomew was, however, fertile in expedients. He ordered the building of two caravels; he distributed the sick and feeble through the country, where better air and food were attainable; and he prosecuted the work of erecting military posts and houses, five in number: the Esperanza, nine leagues from Isabella; Santa Catalina, six leagues farther off; Magdalena, four and a half leagues farther, and on the site of the first town of Santiago; and Fort Conception, in the Vega, and near the residence of the cacique Guarionex. The construction of the caravels and the building of the forts had the temporary effect of relieving the tedium of the idle, and of occupying the thoughts and perhaps the hopes of the discontented. The city of Isabella was relieved of its vicious or useless population, and the Adelantado, leaving a sufficient garrison there, repaired with his best soldiers to San Domingo, near the newly discovered mines of gold.

The pious missionaries who did not follow their superior, Father Boïl, to Spain, and whose names were Roman Pane and Juan Borgognon, had been zealously laboring for the conversion of the Indians in the Vega. In one instance a family of sixteen embraced the faith under the example of Juan Mateo, and even the grand cacique Guarionex seemed on the eve of doing the same, when the reproaches and ridicule of his tributary

caciques and people, and the outrages he received from the
Christian Spaniards, and especially his latest wrong in the seduction and outrage of his favorite wife by the Spaniards, repelled
him from the temple he was about to enter. The chapel at the
Vega mission was sacked and desecrated by the natives, and
though the offenders met with agonizing deaths at the stake, by
order of the Adelantado, the missionaries, with Juan Mateo,
their convert, removed to another district.

Punishments of such a cruel character did not make converts
but rather enemies of the natives. Had mercy been extended to
these poor people, much suffering and bloodshed that followed
would have been spared. But in the position in which they
stood Columbus and his brothers deemed it imperative on all
occasions to inspire the natives with an overpowering idea of
Spanish power and justice. It was thus that this vast and beautiful region was thrown into disorder, rebellion, bloodshed, and
cruel conquest. Pacific of nature, Guarionex was goaded on by
the appeals of his tributary caciques and his subjects to rebel
against the tyranny of the Spaniards. The fate of the brave and
powerful Caonabo and his people could not deter him from so
desperate an attempt, nor even a tradition in his family that a
strange nation would come among them, make him and his
people slaves and seize his country, could suppress the natural
and righteous outbreak of an injured race. The courage of
despair aroused the native tribes and their chiefs. A conspiracy
was entered into secretly to massacre the Spaniards at Fort Conception, few in number; and in order to allay suspicion at the
simultaneous assembling of so many natives, the day for the
payment of the tribute was selected for the purpose. Many
thousands of Indians were assembled in the Vega on that day,
and at a concerted signal they were to wreak vengeance on their
oppressors. If the first blow struck at the Spanish usurpation
proved successful, the insurgents would be emboldened to strike
another and another, until the aborigines recovered their natural
and pristine liberty and independence, for the first success would
call out to arms the whole native population of Hispaniola.

But the treachery of a native betrayed the conspirators. The
doomed garrison at Fort Conception received a warning. The
garrison sent a native with their letter of appeal to the
Adelantado for assistance, and as the Indians had a superstitious

fear of letters, so potent in their recent experiences to convey information, and so gifted as they believed with the power of speech, the letter was concealed in a reed or staff. The vigilant Indians intercepted the hastening courier, whose speed was his only betrayer; but he assumed the rôle of a lame and sick man hastening home so successfully that he was permitted to continue his journey. He reached the Adelantado at San Domingo, and that officer was the man for the emergency. With troops already exhausted by poor fare, hardships and long marches, he was yet on the spot just in time to save his countrymen. With characteristic skill and sagacity he divided his men into as many squads as there were caciques, and put an officer over each squad. The respective villages were quietly entered at midnight, the fourteen caciques were seized, bound, and immediately hurried off and imprisoned in the fortress before their astonished people could lift a hand for them. Devoted to their chiefs and destitute of other leaders, the natives submitted, and piteously sued for the release of their chiefs, surrounding the fortress and sorrowfully, with grievous yells and doleful lamentations, imploring their release. The Adelantado acted with consummate ability. He caused two caciques, the ringleaders of the rebellion, to be executed, and the rest he released. Guarionex, so gentle and so reluctant to rebel, though so shamefully wronged, was pardoned, and the Spaniards who had committed the heinous outrage upon his wife received severe punishment. Favors and promises of favor were bestowed upon the released chiefs as inducements to them to maintain themselves and their people in peace and subjection. Guarionex in a public address exhorted his subjects to peace, and they in turn carried him on their shoulders to his home amid joyous songs and shouts of gratitude for the kind treatment he had received from the Spaniards. Peace now reigned in the Royal Vega by the address and vigor of the Adelantado, who had himself led the squad that captured the principal cacique, Guarionex.

Revolts among his own people, growing out of the widespread discontent and the results of misconduct on the part of the colonists, were not so easily handled. With characteristic sagacity the Adelantado kept the malcontents and all the soldiers and people as busily engaged as possible. Having completed the forts and the caravels, he made an expedition to Xaragua to receive the tribute of Behechio, Anacaona, and their people, for word was received that the cotton was ready for delivery to the tax-gatherer. Received with every mark of honor by his royal hosts, who not only paid tribute in sufficient cotton to fill a house, but also volunteered to give cassava bread without stint, the Adelantado and his followers were entertained continuously with feasts and games, and this beautiful region, remote and not yet wholly desolated by the march of civilization, presented a spectacle of grandeur, peace, abundance, and native gentleness and grace that captivated the hearts of the Spaniards. The cotton and the grateful present of cassava bread were sent back in a caravel. The generous Behechio and the beautiful Anacaona lavished other presents upon their visitors from their long-treasured collections, such as beautiful and ingenious specimens of manufactured cotton, pottery of various and graceful forms, and tables, chairs, and other furniture wrought in ebony and other fine woods with skill and elegance astonishing in a barbarous people destitute of metallic tools or of the arts. When the caravel was about to sail the royal hosts and their people came down to the water in great numbers to see the great canoe and marvel at its wonderful size, shape, and motions. In turn the Adelantado entertained his native friends with music, the discharge of cannon, and the astonishing movements of the ship, which, to the amazement of the Indians, seemed perfectly under the control of the Spaniards. But the discharge of the cannon in the ship spread dismay and fear among these gentle people ; the savages seemed so frightened that they were about to rush into the sea and drown themselves, and the dismayed Anacaona, stunned with fright, fell convulsively into the arms of the Adelantado. The caravel sailed for Isabella amid the admiring exclamations of Behechio and his people, and freighted with tribute for the government and bread for the hungry citizens of Isabella. The Adelantado, after giving presents freely to his generous hosts, returned overland to the city.

The plots and conspiracies of civilized man were more deliberate, more organized, and more determined than the inconsiderate and sudden insurrections of the gentler Indians. The spirit of discontent, the disappointments of adventurers, the lust of gold, which had supplanted the works of industry and husbandry, and the machinations of enemies in both hemispheres, had sowed the seeds of trouble and disaster, of which the admiral and his brothers had now to reap the harvest. Aguado had found a congenial spirit in the very service of Columbus, in the person of Francisco Roldan, a man who from obscurity and ignorance had, by the favor and confidence of the admiral, been raised from one employment of profit and trust to another. From menial services in the admiral's household he was gradually promoted, and became alcalde or justice of the peace, and finally alcalde mayor, or chief justice. The meanness of his character would simply have escaped notice in his obscurity for want of opportunity; but in his responsible positions it overcame his honesty, his truth, his loyalty, and his cowardice. Aguado had already instigated him to revolt, and he went to work with method to develop his evil designs. Professing loyalty to the admiral, he commenced by insinuating charges and complaints against Don Bartholomew and Don Diego, who, as foreigners and men in authority, were easily assailed, however unjustly. He encouraged the murmurs of the working classes, and pandered to the vices and violence of sailors, workmen, and criminals. He had learned from the unworthy commissary Aguado that the Bureau of the Indies at Seville, under Bishop Fonseca, was deadly hostile to the admiral, and that Pedro Margarite, Father Boïl, and the malcontents already returned to Spain from Hispaniola would welcome any movement, however unjust or wicked, for his downfall and the failure of his grand enterprise. He formed his resolution to assassinate Don Bartholomew and place himself in command of the island of Hispaniola. An opportunity had presented itself, as was supposed, before the Adelantado departed for Xaragua to collect the tribute. A criminal named Berahona had been condemned to death. His crime is supposed to have been the outrage upon the wife of the chief Guarionex, and the Adelantado was to attend the execution. It would be easy to get up a disturbance or excitement of some kind on such an occasion, and in the *mêlée* the Adelantado could be assassinated as if by accident. Berahona was also a friend of Roldan and of others of the conspirators. This plot was defeated by the Adelantado's pardon of the condemned man, and his departure for Xaragua.*

---

* Herrera, decad. i., lib. iii., cap. i.; Las Casas, "Hist. Ind.," lib. i., cap. 118; "Hist. del Almirante," cap. 73; Barry's translation of De Lorgues' "Life of Columbus," p. 386 *et seq.*; Irving's "Columbus," vol. ii., p. 162.

During his absence in that province Roldan industriously prosecuted his nefarious purposes by bringing into his conspiracy all the disaffected colonists, who were numerous. The return of the caravel to Isabella with the tribute paid by Behechio was availed of to openly demand that, instead of being drawn upon the shore, it should be sent to Spain for the purpose of obtaining relief for the colony, and threats were thrown out to seize it and return to Spain with complaints against the two brothers for their oppressions of the people. A tumult was being fomented. Roldan, by virtue of his office as chief justice, was about to assume command in the interests of peace and order in the city and colony, and Don Bartholomew and Don Diego, as the guilty causes of all these evils to the island, were to be put aside, perhaps murdered. Don Diego, finding his just and truthful explanations and appeals in behalf of order and authority ineffectual, sent Roldan, at the head of forty soldiers, to the Vega, under the pretext of overawing the natives, who had refused to pay their tribute, or seemed bent on rebellion. Roldan availed himself of this opportunity for gaining adherents to his side, and even for inducing the natives to unite in his disloyal work. He persuaded the soldiers under his command to join him in his plot, and dismissing such as refused, he insolently returned to Isabella as a signal to his sympathizers there to unite with him in a demand to float the caravel and send her to Spain. The Adelantado had now returned to Isabella. Roldan was assuming great authority as chief justice, and the Adelantado, with characteristic firmness, peremptorily refused his demands, and gave Roldan and his following to understand that their designs were suspected.

Roldan, who had latterly placed but little concealment over his purposes, now broke out in open defiance, and at the head of seventy well-armed and resolute men he marched out of Isabella toward the Vega, intending to set up an independent rule of his own in another part of the island. He endeavored, with some success, to seduce the Spanish soldiers quartered in the Indian villages through which he passed to join his forces, and by alternate force and persuasion endeavored to secure possession of Fort Conception, under Miguel Ballester, and of the military post at the village of Guarionex under Garcia de Barrantes. Failing in the last two efforts, he seized the provisions of the latter post, and thence marched with his augmented forces to the attack of Fort Conception. Such was the widespread disaffection which Margarite, Father Boïl, Aguado, and Roldan had created throughout Hispaniola, conscious as they were that Fonseca at Seville was secretly if not openly sustaining them, that the Adelantado, usually so prompt, hesitated what to do. The Adelantado knew that many officials and leading men were in concert with Roldan, and he feared for the loyalty of Ballester, the commander of Fort Conception. But no sooner had he received a message from the latter, urging the sending of assistance, than he immediately sallied forth, and soon entered the fort with his reinforcements. Uncertain of the strength of Roldan and his rebels, which was steadily increasing, he deemed it prudent to try, in the first instance, the effect of an interview with the chief, and at his request Roldan repaired to Fort Conception, where the Adelantado parleyed with him from a window. His expostulations were treated with defiance, his demand for the surrender of the rebels was received with impudent assertions of his own loyalty and the outlawry of the Adelantado and his brother. He refused to resign his office or to submit to a trial except on command of the king, and stoutly repelled all orders which might bring him in the power of the Adelantado, alleging that the latter sought his life. Feigning submission to authority, he offered to retire to such part of the island as Don Bartholomew might designate; but on the latter naming the town of Diego Colon, the convert and interpreter who had been baptized in Spain, he abruptly refused, and, after insolently retiring, announced to his followers the enticing proposition of selecting for their retreat the attractive and beautiful province of Xaragua, where sloth, ease, lust, and abundance awaited their arrival. Availing himself of the absence of the Adelantado from Isabella, the rebels hastened thither and violently attempted to launch the caravel and sail to Xaragua. Don Diego, hearing the uproar, came forth with some of the loyal hidalgos, but finding himself powerless in the midst of such general disaffection, he was compelled to retire into the fortress. Several interviews led to no result, and when finally Roldan's offer to submit to his authority, provided he would renounce the Adelantado and set up an opposition, was refused with contempt, he marched out at the head of his lawless band to reach Xaragua by land. But assuming still to be himself in legitimate authority and the most loyal of all, he gave his lawless followers all they could seize from the public stores of arms, ammunition, and clothing, even carrying off or slaughtering the breeding stock of the colony. Taking the direction of the Vega, he endeavored by stratagem and fraud to get the Adelantado in his power, evidently intending to kill him; but that sagacious official was too much on his guard, and was fully conscious of his military inability to cope with so numerous a body of rebels. It even required within the garrison a great relaxation of his usual discipline, and resort to liberal promises of rewards, to preserve them in loyalty, to keep them at their posts of duty, and from becoming disaffected by the prevailing atmosphere of disloyalty and rebellion.

Roldan's efforts to gain the adherence of the garrison or to get the person of the Adelantado in his power proving unsuccessful, they were followed by the most criminal acts on his part and that of his following to destroy the government, to set up his own, and to gain the natives to his side. He denounced the Adelantado as a tyrant and oppressor, a foreigner and extortioner, and set himself up as the protector of the Indians. He took the Carib chief, Manicatex, into his alliance, bestowing upon him presents and the title of brother, while he exacted and received from the deluded natives the payment of tribute and the most generous supply of provisions. He roamed arrogantly and lawlessly through the country, revelling in abundance, and with a numerous following of Spaniards and Indians, while the Adelantado was imprisoned in the fortress with only a handful of men, and on short rations. Manicatex and his people, in addition to food and tribute, collected all the gold they could find and placed it at the feet of the rebel chief, and feeling emboldened by the dissensions of their conquerors, threw off all allegiance to the government, while they accepted willingly the more oppressive yoke of Roldan. The caciques and their tribes far and near joined in the rebellion and discontinued to send in their tribute to the lawful government. The Adelantado found his food, clothing, and ammunition becoming exhausted, his authority set at defiance, his own men wavering in loyalty and yielding to despondency, while confusion, anarchy, and crime reigned everywhere. Bold as he was, and quick to decide and to execute a gallant exploit, Don Bartholomew was compelled to remain under the protection of his walls and guns, for he had received the most certain information that his life would be taken on the first opportunity. It was at such a desperate juncture that Coronel providentially arrived at the port of San Domingo with two ships, bringing supplies, reinforcements, royal documents confirming Don Bartholomew in his title and authority as Adelantado, and tidings of the admiral's strength and favor with the sovereigns in Spain, and of his speedy arrival in Hispaniola with a large and powerful fleet containing all things necessary for the relief of the colony and for the maintenance of order and authority.

Roldan and his followers were dismayed, but not reduced to submission. The Adelantado repaired immediately to San Domingo, and, though his forces were greatly augmented, the needs of the soldiers relieved, and his authority sustained, he prudently resorted to leniency and persuasion, rather than force, to dispel the rebellion. But Roldan had gone too far to recede. He treated Coronel, whom the Adelantado had sent to parley with him, as a traitor,.and spurned all offers of pardon, protesting his readiness to acknowledge the authority of the admiral on his arrival, and thus finally drawing upon himself and his men the public proclamation of the Adelantado that they were traitors, and to be treated as such. Fearing lest his men might be influenced by the improved condition of the government and the persuasions of the loyal Spaniards about San Domingo, Roldan and his lawless partisans now commenced their bold and reckless march to their favorite and chosen rendezvous, the beautiful and voluptuous region of Xaragua, where they expected to revel in luxury and to indulge in every unholy passion.

One of the fruits of Roldan's rebellion was the second insurrection of the deluded and unfortunate Guarionex, the cacique of the Royal Vega. Seduced by Roldan's persuasions and by his promises of assistance, and emboldened by the distracted state of the country and the divisions among the Spaniards, he and his tributary cacique entered into a conspiracy to rise upon their oppressors and make a last effort to recover their freedom and redeem their country from the grasp of their conquerors. The Spanish soldiers quartered in small numbers in the villages were to be slaughtered, while Guarionex and his warriors were to attack Fort Conception. The full moon was fixed upon as the signal for the uprising ; but one of the leading caciques mistook the night, attacked prematurely the soldiers quartered in his village and was repulsed. On his flying to Guarionex for protection, that chief, in his rage and disappointment, inflicted upon him the punishment of instant death. These events disclosed the conspiracy to the Spaniards. The Adelantado, with his accustomed vigor, marched out with a strong force to the Vega to suppress every vestige of the uprising, but the unfortunate Guarionex, in despair, had fled with his family and a few faithful followers to the distant and lofty mountainous region of Ciguay, and threw himself upon the generous protection of its noble cacique, the brave Mayobanex, who received him with open heart and hand, and vowed to protect and defend him to the end, and to share his fate, whatever it might be. Thus we see, under the first advances of civilization in the new world, that beautiful and enchanting region, which, when first seen by the Spaniards, ravished all their senses with admiration and delight, now desolated and despoiled, its once happy chieftain a suppliant and an impoverished wanderer, its people destroyed, its grandeur and beauty wasted, its gardens and orchards desolated. Well has Las Casas, that steadfast friend of the Indians, taught us a moral lesson in pointing out the natural virtues of the untutored savages in the generous reception of the unfortunate Guarionex by the noble Mayobanex—a striking contrast to the crimes and vices then prevailing among the more enlightened and instructed Christian conquerors of the island ! *

The once peaceful Guarionex, feeling as he imagined secure in his mountain retreat and encouraged by his native allies, essayed to become the avenger of his own and his people's wrongs. Watching his opportunities, he made descents upon the plains to cut off straggling or exposed parties of a few Spaniards, and even attacked and burned the Indian villages which adhered to the Spaniards, destroying the inhabitants and ruining their fields and orchards. Don Bartholomew Columbus took effectual measures to promptly suppress these hostile struggles of an already conquered race. At the head of ninety soldiers, some cavalry, and a band of friendly Indians he advanced, through narrow and dangerous defiles, and having reached the summit

---

* Peter Martyr, decad. i., cap. 5 ; Las Casas, " Historia Ind.," lib. i., cap. 121, MS. ; Irving's " Columbus," vol. ii., p. 177 ; Tarducci's " Life of Columbus," translation by Henry F. Brownson, vol. ii., p. 115.

of the Ciguay Mountains, he descended to the plains beyond
without encountering an enemy ; but the latter was in ambush,
and it was only by capturing one of the Indian scouts that he
avoided a terrific slaughter. Now he cautiously proceeded, and
he possessed such advantages over his naked and undisciplined
adversaries that an Indian army of six thousand could do no
more than discharge their missiles and then fly and disperse in
the woods and ravines. A few Spaniards were wounded with
arrows or lances, and a few of the Indians were killed. Pursuit
of such a foe in their own country was of little avail. Continuing his march toward Cabron, the residence of Mayobanex,
the Adelantado demanded of that chief the surrender of Guarionex, with promises of rewards or threats of punishment. But
the noble chief replied, "Tell the Spaniards that they are bad
men, cruel and tyrannical ; usurpers of the territories of others,
and shedders of innocent blood. I desire not the friendship of
such men. Guarionex is a good man ; he is my friend, he is my
guest, he has fled to me for refuge. I have promised to protect
him ; I will keep my word."

Answers such as this, pronounced under less heroic circumstances, occurring in Greek and Roman history or even in more
modern times, have become immortalized in classic prose and
verse. This instance of barbarian heroism will compare with
the defence of Thermopylæ or any great event in Roman heroism. Well has Mr. Irving called it "magnanimous," and the
learned Francesco Tarducci calls it "the most magnanimous and
sublime answer in all history." But the stern nature of the
Adelantado regarded it as an insolent bravado and menacing
insult. He was as quick in executing his purpose as he was
prompt in forming it. He immediately destroyed with fire all
the villages in the neighborhood, and saw the inhabitants, men,
women, and children, the sick, the infirm, and the aged fleeing
from the homes which they had acquired by a good title from
the common father of the human race. This was followed with
a threat to Mayobanex that unless he gave up Guarionex he and
his people and his dominions should share the same fate by fire
and sword. But the heroic cacique stood firm before the threats
of the Spaniards, and resisted the entreaties of his panic-stricken
people. He sent for the hounded Guarionex and renewed his
promise of protection and defence, or to share his fate. Another

Spanish embassy was sent, and its two members, a Spaniard and an Indian, were put to death in sight of the Adelantado, to show him that Spaniards and Indian traitors were mortal, and that he appealed to his natural right to defend his own against such ruthless invaders. Yielding to his anger and to his stern nature, the Adelantado marched at once, at the head of his entire force, on these brave mountaineers; but the large army of Mayobanex, panic-stricken at the sight of the steel-clad and invincible Spaniards, dispersed and fled, and the noble chieftain was left with only a handful of men—a mere body-guard—for himself and his family. His cause was now desperate. With his family he was compelled to fly from his home and country to the most barren and rocky caverns in the mountains. The other doomed cacique, the unhappy Guarionex, warned of the intention of the desperate Ciguayans to murder him as the cause of their ruin, and hoping thereby to win mercy for themselves from the Spaniards, fled to the most distant and desolate retreat in that mountainous wilderness. Pursuing these two unfortunate caciques, the Adelantado and his men overcame by dint of courage, endurance, and strength the appalling difficulties of such a rocky, tangled, and precipitous pursuit, seeking in every rock, cavern, or thicket for their victims. Many of the Spanish soldiers sought pretexts for returning to their homes or gardens near Fort Conception, but the indomitable will of the Adelantado, with thirty remaining men and some Indian followers, kept up the hunt with unfaltering tenacity. Neither fatigue nor want of food dampened the ardor of the pursuers; but the whole country was abandoned by its once happy inhabitants. There were yet some desperate and fugitive natives, but few and solitary ones, who were forced out of their hiding-places in the rocks, here and there, to seek for a root or some berries to save themselves from starvation. If the Spaniards saw one of these wretched natives, he knew nothing of the hiding-places of the caciques; but two of the miserable subjects of Mayobanex were one day captured by the Spaniards while the former were looking for a little cassava bread for their chief and the latter were hunting utias. Carried before the Adelantado, these frightened and despairing children of nature were forced, as is supposed, in the absence of historic narrative, by untold cruelties, to disclose the hiding-place of their chief, and even to lead his pursuers to the spot. Twelve Spaniards disguised as Indians made their way to the hiding-place of the noble Indian chief, compelling and forcing the reluctant guides to lead the way. They found their victim in his secluded retreat, sitting on the ground, surrounded by his wife and children and a few noble and ever-faithful subjects, and playing with his little children, when suddenly rushing upon him, and drawing their swords from their palm-leaf disguises, they seized the chieftain, bound him and carried him off, together with his family and followers, before they could recover from their sudden surprise and stupor. Among the prisoners was a sister of Mayobanex, wife of a neighboring cacique, who, on learning of her brother's misfortunes, left her home and her realm, "which," as Tarducci says, "had not yet felt the weight of the white man's civilization," and spent several days with him to console her brother in his misfortunes, and to share his dangers, his poverty, his hunger, and his downfall. When her disconsolate husband heard of her capture and imprisonment, he went as a suppliant to Fort Conception and sued for the liberty of his wife, with tears and on his knees, offering in return for this mercy to subject himself, his dominions, and his people to the Spanish authority. In all the history of our race no more heroic, no gentler or more beautiful example of pure and devoted love than his can be found. Don Bartholomew, who knew well how to be merciful and politic as well as stern and severe, and esteeming the possession of the cacique's wife as of little value compared to the peaceful subjugation of an entire district, released the captured queen and a number of Indians to the unfortunate and tender-hearted cacique. This act of generosity gained the gratitude and willing service of the now happy chief and his people, who became the allies of the Spaniards, and their very slaves in cultivating fields for them, and supplying them with food from the fruits of their hard and unaccustomed labor. The subjects of the captive chief, Mayobanex, made hopeful by this clemency of the Adelantado, ventured down from their mountain recesses, bringing presents to the Spaniards, and with loyalty and affection worthy of the imitation of the conquerors, sued for the release of their beloved and brave chief and his family. Don Bartholomew, with his accustomed judgment and discernment, gave their liberty to all but the unhappy chief, whom he retained as a hostage.

The miserable Guarionex continued to be hunted until he was caught. The Ciguayans, the disconsolate subjects of the imprisoned Mayobanex, not able in their misfortunes to sustain the princely and exalted sentiments and conduct of their chief, and accusing Guarionex of being the proximate cause of their misfortunes, resolved to watch for him and betray him on the opportunity to the Spaniards. He wandered from one rock-bound cavern to another, attempting but once in several days to venture forth in quest of food. He was finally seen by some vigilant Ciguayans, his hiding-place communicated at Fort Conception, and a few days afterward, as he was timidly and cautiously going out for something to eat, he was captured by Spaniards concealed in rocks or brush, who suddenly sprang from their lair; and though almost exhausted unto death, he was hurried in chains before the Adelantado. This robust ruler spared a life now almost wasted, and retained him and his friend, Mayobanex, as prisoners or hostages for the good conduct of their people. By his vigorous action and unsparing energy, by a policy of mingled cruelty to his foes and of mercy to his victims, he had won complete dominion over the Royal Vega and the mountainous district of Ciguay, in which districts now reigned by his address the peace and quiet of a ruthless conquest. While the Count de Lorgues, the enthusiastic admirer of Columbus, passes over these lamentable details without even mentioning them, Mr. Irving remarks, in admiration for a character in which the nobler qualities predominated over the faults generated by his trying position, " Don Bartholomew, however, though stern in his policy, was neither vindictive nor cruel in his nature. . . . He has been accused of severity in his government, but no instance appears of a cruel or wanton abuse of authority." The learned and judicious Tarducci says, " With the opinion then universally held, that white men and Christians had full right to dispose at will of men of another color or religion, it is easy to imagine the effect produced on the haughty character of the Spaniard by the haughty answer of Mayobanex, . . . in which Don Bartholomew, with his mind filled with his right and duty to re-establish order in the colony and settle the authority of Spain over the savages, saw only an atrocious insult. Horrid times, when, in the name of religion and of civilization, a portion of the human race believed itself right in regar ing and treating the rest as worse than beasts." And again the same author, "So ended the magnanimous struggle of those mountaineers, which, if related by some Indian Plutarch, would claim from posterity as great admiration and glory as the most famous war ever carried on by any people." * It might be added that the administration of Don Bartholomew Columbus was a model of mildness compared with the subsequent ones of Bobadilla and Ovando, which, with sorrow, we will have to relate hereafter.

It was not long after these stirring and triumphant events in the administration of Don Bartholomew Columbus that his brother, the admiral, returned to Hispaniola. With shattered health, the admiral, so far from securing rest and peace on his return to the colony he had planted with so much generous hope, and sustained with such paternal solicitude and sacrifice, found the most disastrous and distressing period of his eventful and checkered life now before him. Between the wars and rebellions of the natives and the outbreak of his own followers, under Roldan, Columbus saw a scene of desolation and turbulence, of misery and anguish, where only four years ago he had beheld an earthly paradise, a field for civilization, a vineyard for the gospel of the Lord. Now all was changed. The poor natives were destroyed by war as by an unsparing pest, their chiefs were either slaughtered or imprisoned; the few that survived of a lately happy, contented, and hospitable race were timid stragglers and broken-hearted slaves in a land desolated, impoverished, ruined, and conquered; frowning fortresses lorded the once beautiful landscape; the mountains only seemed inhabited, and these by a skulking and despairing race; silence and desolation ruled in once happy and peaceful Indian villages; the unstinted hospitality of an innocent and generous people had become displaced by cruel oppression followed by hatred and the refusal to feed their conquerors; scarcely a cacique, scarcely a man of family, had escaped the most heinous outrages on man's dearest rights and tenderest sensibilities; once cultivated fields and orchards were now overgrown with a rank and

---

* Peter Martyr, decad. i., lib. v., vi.; Fernando Colombo, cap. lxxv.; Las Casas, "Hist. Ind.," lib. i., cap. 121; Herrera, "Hist. Ind.," decad. i., lib. iii., cap. 8, 9; Irving's "Columbus," vol. ii., pp. 178-85; Tarducci's "Life of Columbus," Brownson's translation, pp. 114-21.

poisonous growth, and where nature gave spontaneous crops, food was insufficient for the cravings of hunger; the songs of a people's joys and traditions were now the wails of misery and death; crime had stalked with barefaced effrontery through a land and a people once innocent and childlike; civilization had brought ruin, and Christianity, contrary to its precepts, had been heralded by vice, oppression, plunder, and lust. Unworthy heralds of the Cross had repelled a gentle race from its all-redeeming embraces. Even among the heralds of civilization, revolt, disloyalty, and violence had prevailed, and but for the stern and true loyalty and undaunted courage and sagacious administration of one man, a new world given by Columbus to mankind would have been lost to civilization, to science, to commerce, and to religion. Had Columbus been supported by men such as he would have selected, men of order and of conscience, his administration and that of his brother under him would have proved a redeeming blessing to the natives, instead of their destruction.

One of the first acts of Columbus on arriving at Hispaniola was to issue a proclamation approving the administration of the Adelantado and his acts, and proclaiming unqualified condemnation of Roldan and his followers. That reckless and unprincipled rebel had led his band of outlaws to the beautiful country of Xaragua, where they were received with unmerited and unrequited kindness by the natives. Yielding to every vice and passion of bad and desperate men, they exacted from the generous natives the gratification of every want, of every passion, and of their unbridled lusts; their avarice and their caprices were equally exacting; no discipline was imposed or observed, and that expansive and beautiful region imposed no bounds to their reckless and disorderly rovings.

But suddenly one day an event occurred, at first alarming, but which at length, owing to their falsehoods and seductions, replenished their squandered stores and increased their numbers. Three ships were sighted making for the island, and soon they approached and anchored near the land, striking the rebels with consternation. The bold and sagacious Roldan from the first saw in them Spanish vessels, no doubt sent out with supplies for the colony, and saw in them his opportunity. He and his men preserved profound secrecy as to their real character, and they succeeded in making the three captains recognize him as a part of the Spanish colony and of the administrative machinery of Hispaniola. These were the vessels which the admiral had sent out from the Canaries for the relief of his colony, and which had been carried out of their reckonings by the winds and currents. Believing Roldan's representations that he was stationed there by the Adelantado to maintain the province in peace and subjection to the Spanish authority, the three captains supplied him and his followers with provisions, arms, and ammunition. Some of the most capable of these rebels visited the ships without suspicion and poisoned the minds of many of the men on board, who, as already related, had been received from the worst populations of Spain for the third voyage. It was only after three days of such insidious intercourse that the most sagacious of the captains, Alonzo Sanchez de Carvajal, discovered the true character of this lawless band, but it was too late to correct the bad effects of their misleading visits; so that when Juan Antonio Colombo landed at the head of forty well-armed men to make the march across the country to the settlement, he found himself suddenly deserted by all his men except eight; the thirty-two joined the rebels to their great exultation, and no appeals of the captain could draw them away. The three captains made repeated efforts to induce Roldan to desist from his lawless career and return to his duty and his obedience to his superiors, but all in vain; the most they could accomplish was the promise of Roldan to submit as soon as he should hear of the arrival of the admiral, his resistance, as he asserted, being only to the unlawful usurpations of the Adelantado. The plans of the captains were now changed. The ships sailed for San Domingo, but Carvajal remained on shore with the intention of making further efforts to secure the return of Roldan and his men to their duty and allegiance. Failing in this, he returned to San Domingo under an escort of the rebels to protect him from the Indians, and bearing a letter from Roldan to Columbus, offering to recognize his authority and to negotiate for the settlement of all difficulties. The ships, after many disasters, arrived at San Domingo, but their provisions for the colony were either exhausted or mostly damaged.

In the mean time Columbus had arrived at San Domingo and learned all the distressing details of the past from his ever-faithful brother, the able and undaunted Adelantado. Carvajal's accounts did not quite remove his fear and distrust of the rebels, for so flagrant and treacherous had been the conduct and the falsehood of Roldan, that no confidence could be placed upon any promises or professions he might make, though accompanied by the most solemn vows and oaths. He did not see how his government as Viceroy of Hispaniola could be maintained while an organized band of armed and equipped rebels were in possession of an important section of the island, which they had seized, and where they were living riotously and defying his authority, or while the island was infested in every part with disaffected and disloyal Spaniards boasting their enmity to him and denouncing his conduct of affairs, and especially the administration of his brothers; while the Indians were in a state of sullen silence, gloomy and resentful submission, and ready at the instigation of the rebels to join them in a common movement against him, his brothers, and his loyal followers, representatives of the Spanish sovereigns. In order to rid the island of as many of the disaffected as possible, he proclaimed, on September 12th, his consent that all who wished might return to Spain in the five vessels preparing for sea, giving them a free passage and provisions for the voyage. So loud had been the clamor against the Adelantado, and so persistent the charges of cruelty and oppression, which had rung from one end of the island to the other, that the admiral found a deep impression had been made by them, even upon the minds and judgments of the loyal. These charges were never sustained, and historians have acquitted the Adelantado of them all. If his course toward the natives is regarded as inexorable and cruel, against natural right and human justice, as certainly it was, these elements in his administration are attributable rather to the ruthless system of European advancement and conquest, which he had represented in the absence of his brother, and which, while they overwhelm humanity with shame, are but the execution of the sentence which in past ages, and in that age particularly, civilization had pronounced against barbarism. The pretext that the discontent prevailing so generally was only aimed against his brother was an empty assertion, since it was manifest that the admiral then and thereafter fared no better at their hands.

As soon as Columbus heard of Roldan's purpose of advancing

toward San Domingo to treat with him on the discontents of the rebels, the former immediately sent word to Miguel Ballester, the veteran and undaunted commander of Fort Conception, to await the approach of the rebels with every preparation of vigilance and defence, and to trust him not in any professions of loyalty, but to entertain a parley with him and to offer him, in the admiral's name, pardon for the past if he would return to his duty and allegiance, and to suggest or invite his repairing to San Domingo to confer with the admiral, to the end of a permanent settlement of all difficulties, under the most solemn assurances of personal safety—a guarantee which would be put in writing if desired. Scarcely had the commander of Fort Conception received the admiral's letter, when the rebels began to make their appearance in the Vega, where the village of Bonao became their rendezvous, and where the residence of Pedro Requelme, one of their ringleaders, became their headquarters. This village was about ten leagues from Fort Conception and twenty from San Domingo. Miguel Ballester advanced to meet Roldan as a messenger of peace, and he had been well selected for the purpose, on account of his age and dignified appearance and demeanor, his mildness of character, unblemished record, and indomitable courage—qualities which the rebels themselves should have respected. The parley took place between this noble soldier and the rebel Roldan, with three of his chief co-conspirators, Pedro Requelme, Pedro de Gamez, and Adrian de Moxico. Roldan's forces from every quarter rallied at Bonao, and, feeling emboldened by his strength, he haughtily refused the proffered pardon, and declined an interview with Columbus. Assuming the air and tone of power and authority, he began to make new demands, and insisted on the release of some Indians, subjects of Guarionex, who were about to be sent to Spain as slaves, as a punishment for refusing to pay the tribute—a refusal which Roldan himself had instigated. He knew that in thus pretending to be a protector of the Indians, and by giving to his demand a pretended official character by virtue of his office of Alcalde Mayor, he wounded the administration of the admiral in one of its most unpopular methods; he even threw out hints that he held the balance of power in his hands, and that the admiral himself might be brought under his control for weal or woe; that he desired no terms of peace; that Carvajal was the only one he would treat with, as he was the only fair man ; and any terms he would accept must be most favorable to himself and his men.

The admiral knew well how to estimate his own and his enemy's strength, and he felt appalled at the general disaffection prevailing around him. A call on the inhabitants of San Domingo brought to his aid only seventy men, and of these scarcely forty could be accepted for military service, such was the predominant disloyalty poisoning the hearts of the community. So flimsy were the excuses given by the citizens for escaping military service against the rebels, that disloyalty was apparent through them all. Uniting great prudence of action with an exuberant enthusiasm, great courage guided by caution, the admiral hesitated to risk his authority, his person, his colony, his prestige of success, his reputation at home, his very enterprise itself, upon the uncertain result of an open battle with such numerous and unprincipled enemies. The ships already prepared for sailing to Spain had been delayed for eighteen days, in the hope of sending more favorable accounts to Spain as to the condition of affairs, but now the poor and miserable prisoners on board the ships, especially the Indians, had become desperate even to sickness, death, and suicide from their long confinement ; and the Spanish malcontents, whom his proclamation had induced to embark for Spain, were becoming more than ever restless. Delay now was worse than disaster, so that he sent the ships to sea on October 18th. He wrote by this opportunity a detailed account to the sovereigns of the rebellion of Roldan, the condition of the colony, and the administration of Hispaniola. In this important letter Columbus clearly traced the discontents and present misfortunes of the colony to the delays and machinations of Fonseca and his abettors in the Indian Bureau at Seville, in sending out provisions and in causing his own long delays in Spain. He urged the regular and speedy transmission of supplies from Spain, and asked that good and zealous missionaries be sent to evangelize the natives and check the unbridled passions of the Spaniards ; and that royal administrative and judicial officers be also sent to assist him in the government and regulation of the island and in administering justice, and recommended that they should be Spaniards, as the malcontents assailed him as a foreigner. Apprehending that his enemies in Spain had availed themselves of the chastisement he gave to the miserable Ximeno Breviesca, "Fonseca's impudent favorite," he appealed to the justice of the sovereigns against the slanders of his enemies, reminding them that he was "absent, envied, and a stranger." He also dwelt fully on the resources of Hispaniola, and reaffirmed and demonstrated the truth of his former accounts. Another letter of the admiral gave an account of his voyage through the Gulf of Paria, of the continent he saw, which he regarded as the finest portion of Asia and the seat of the terrestrial Paradise, and he sent the first pearls ever received in Spain from the new world, promising to renew the exploration and discovery of this vast and fertile country as soon as the tranquillity of the island would give him an opportunity. The following passage from the Count de Lorgues shows how eminently capable the admiral was to govern a colony by wise and practical measures, and how the wisest administration would be defeated by the rebels and criminals infesting the island; for having pointed out to the sovereigns the existing evils, and traced many of them to the Bureau of the Indies at Seville, he goes on in his letter to outline the policy to be followed in Hispaniola: "It would be necessary to prolong a year or two longer the power given the colonists to employ in their service the natives who had been made prisoners of war. With the exception of clothing, equipments, and wine, which it would be necessary to import from Spain, everything else necessary for life could be procured from the soil. He was preparing to raise large crops of cassava, a kind of food to which the Castilians had already become accustomed; sweet potatoes and ajis were abundant in every locality. The rivers were numerous, and abounded with fish; poultry and hogs multiplied soon and abundantly. Utias were so numerous there that a dog, led by a domestic, could catch from fifteen to twenty of them in a day. The means of subsistence were abundant, and there was nothing wanting but Christians who would be such in practice as well as in name." * In this letter he sent out a map and chart of the Gulf of Paria and the adjacent Terra

---

* Barry's translation of De Lorgues' "Life of Columbus," p. 392; Las Casas, "Hist. Ind.," lib. i., cap. 153, 157; Oviedo, "Hist. Ind.," lib. iii., cap. vi.; Herrera, "Hist. Ind.," dec. i., lib. iii.; Irving's "Life of Columbus," vol. ii., p. 194-99; Tarducci's "Life of Columbus," vol. ii., p. 130.

Firma, with directions how to reach it, and specimens of the pearls and gold of the new world.

The vessels carried out also letters from Roldan and other rebels, in which the reverse side of the picture was given, and every means were taken to represent the rebellion as caused by the misconduct, injustice, extortion, and tyranny of Columbus and his brothers. But these enemies of the admiral relied more on the hostility of Fonseca to Columbus, on his numerous other enemies in Spain, on their own friends and relatives, and on the growing unpopularity of the Genoese foreigner. The glory he had conferred upon Spain was not sufficient to naturalize him as a Spaniard!

Moderate and conciliatory in his character and measures, Columbus now made another and a most earnest effort to terminate the rebellion of Roldan and his confederates. The importance of resuming his discoveries and explorations of the mainland extending westward from the Gulf of Paria, and the indispensable necessity of quieting Hispaniola, now pressed with almost equal urgency upon his mind. He had to forego his intention of sending his brother, Don Bartholomew, to continue the former, because his military services were now so necessary for the accomplishment of the latter. Deeming it imprudent and unsafe to risk all by an open battle with the augmented forces of the rebels, he was compelled to resort to the humiliating expedient of renewing negotiations. Hoping that Roldan might yet preserve some remnant of his former gratitude, or might be moved even by the remembrance of his old friendship, he addressed to him a friendly letter, dated October 20th, 1498, and so characteristic of the admiral's sentiments, and written in as clear and simple a style as his heart was honest, that I will here introduce it at length:

"DEAR FRIEND: My first care on arriving in this capital, after having embraced my brother, was to inquire about you. You cannot doubt that, next to my family, you have for a long time occupied the first place in my affections; and I have always counted so much on yours, that there is nothing in which I would not have entirely depended on you. Judge, therefore, of my grief, when I learned that you were embroiled in a feud with persons who are the nearest to me in the world, and who ought to be the dearest. Still, I have been consoled by being informed that you ardently desired my return. I flattered myself then that your first sentiments in regard to me were not changed, and I expected that, as soon as you would hear of my arrival, you would not delay coming to see me. Not seeing you appear, and thinking that you apprehended some resentment on my part, I sent Ballester to you, to give you all the assurances that you could desire. The little success that attended that step has filled me with regret; and whence could that distrust come which you seem to have in me? At last you demanded to have Carvajal sent to you. I send him. Open your heart to him, and tell him what I can do for you to regain your confidence; but, in the name of God, remember what you owe to your country, to the kings (our sovereign lords), to God, and to yourself; take care of your reputation, and judge of things more soundly than you have done in the past. Consider with attention the abyss you are digging under your feet, and no longer persist in a desperate resolution. I have represented you to their Highnesses as a man of the colony whom they may most rely upon; it concerns my honor and yours that a testimony so advantageous should not be belied by your conduct. Hasten then to show yourself again the man I formerly knew you to be. I have detained the ships that were all ready to sail, with the hope that, by a prompt and perfect submission, you will place me at liberty to confirm all the good things I have said of you. I pray God to have you in His holy keeping."

In the distrust created by the general prevalence of disloyalty, the selection of one to bear this letter to the rebels became a grave question; for while Columbus would select Carvajal, and he was most acceptable to the rebels, strong objections were raised against him by many of the admiral's friends, for they remembered how he had received Roldan on his ship at Xaragua for two days; had furnished them with arms, ammunition and stores; neglected to arrest him on board his ship after discovering he was a rebel; had been escorted by the rebels from Xaragua to San Domingo, and had sent them refreshments at Bonao; had represented himself as a colleague of Columbus in the administration, and appointed to inspect his conduct; that he had invited the rebels to San Domingo; the very desire of the rebels to have him sent to treat with them, and other indications derived more from suspicion than facts. But Columbus remembered that his keen eye first discovered and exposed their true character at Xaragua, and that his subsequent consideration for them was based on his prudent regard for the weakness of the government and his desire to secure peace, and he showed his superior judgment in sending this faithful officer on the mission. Ballester accompanied him.

Scarcely had the ambassadors departed for Bonao, when the admiral received a letter signed by Roldan and his co-conspirators, Adrian de Moxica, Pedro de Gamez, and Diego de Escobar, dated October 17th, in which they vindicated their conduct, asserted that they had resented only the despotism of the Adelantado, and had now for a month awaited in vain some sign of conciliation from him, whose arrival they awaited; and they demanded now to be discharged from his service. The friendly letter of Columbus, supported by the cogent reasonings of Carvajal and Ballester, had the effect of inducing Roldan, Gamez, Escobar, and others to mount their horses to ride at once to the presence of the admiral; but the clamors of the insolent rabble at their backs compelled them to dismount. They demanded that written passports for the chief rebels should be sent and the terms of agreement should be reduced to writing, made public and submitted to them. Under the advice of Carvajal and Ballester, given after they had seen the strength of the rebels and its constant augmentation, the passport was sent, and Roldan now stood in the presence of his superior. Several interviews and the exchange of several letters brought them no nearer to an agreement. Roldan actually availed himself of his presence at San Domingo to gain recruits for his service. He finally departed under pretext of consulting his men, but, on the contrary, he wrote an arrogant letter to the admiral on November 6th, dictating his own terms and demanding a reply by the 11th at Conception, whither he was going on account of the scarcity of provisions at Bonao. As it was impossible for him to accede to Roldan's insolent demands, Columbus issued a proclamation of amnesty and pardon to all who would come in within thirty days and return to their allegiance to the sovereigns, a free conveyance to Spain for all who wished to return, and denouncing severe punishment on all who refused to comply. When Carvajal arrived at Conception with a copy of the proclamation for Roldan, he found that rebel and his forces actually besieging Fortress Conception under pretext of seizing a culprit, whom he demanded in his capacity as Alcalde Mayor, and cutting off all supply of water from the fort. The proclamation posted at the gate of the fortress only elicited insults and jeers from the rebels and threats of retaliation. At length the persuasions of Carvajal brought the rebels to terms, which were signed by Roldan and his followers at Fort Conception on November 16th, and by the admiral at San Domingo on the 21st, whereby it was agreed that the rebels would embark for Spain in two vessels to be provided and supplied by the admiral at the port of Xaragua within fifty days; that they receive certificates of good conduct and orders for the payment of their terms of service; that they were to receive the same number of slaves as others, with permission to carry them to Spain, though none of the slaves should be carried off forcibly, and if they wished, such as had native wives and children might carry them in place of the slaves; that confiscated property should be released; that the ships remaining in Hispaniola should not be used to molest the rebels on their return voyage; that they might dispose of their property before leaving the island, and receive indemnity for such as they might leave behind; and that they should have a safe conduct to Spain. The rebels were to account to the government for all slaves they took out, and for all government property they might hold. The admiral of his own generosity dispensed from penalties such of the rebels as wished to remain in the island in the king's service, or as cultivators of the soil, promising them land and Indians to work the same; but as they all preferred to return to Spain with Roldan, Miguel Ballester was sent with them to Xaragua to expedite their departure in the ships.

The urgency of this measure to the admiral's deep regret prevented the prosecution of the exploration of Terra Firma either by himself or the Adelantado. The ships were sent to Xaragua in February, 1499, but in consequence of the scarcity of ship's provisions and the confused and impoverished condition caused by the misconduct of the rebels, it was after the stipulated time of fifty days before they sailed from San Domingo for Xaragua; and even then one of the ships, which became disabled by a storm, had to be replaced by another. By the time both vessels met at Xaragua, probably in April, the rebels refused to embark, and they cast the blame upon the admiral, alleging that he had purposely delayed the ships, had finally sent unseaworthy ones, and that they were insufficiently victualled. Carvajal made a protest before a notary in his company, and as the ships began to suffer from the *teredo*, and the provisions were giving out, he sent them back to San Domingo, while he set out for the same place overland. Roldan accompanied him a short distance, and on the way manifested great distrust of his present situation, and expressed an anxious desire to treat again with the admiral, avowing his loyalty and asking safe conducts for himself and followers on their mission to the admiral ; but his followers, whom he seemed to distrust, were not to know of this proposal to treat with the admiral again. Columbus having returned to San Domingo from a tour of inspection through the island with the Adelantado, in which he had endeavored to restore peace to his distracted domain, he immediately forwarded the safe conducts to the rebels. But now, in the midst of his unceasing and herculean efforts to serve his sovereigns, he received from Spain an answer to his urgent representations of the preceding fall, in which he gave an account of the rebellion of Roldan, the confusion and disorder he had created throughout the island, and appealing to the crown for support in his efforts to bring order and prosperity to the country. When it is related that his inveterate enemy, Fonseca, had written the letter, its character may be preconceived, for instead of royal sympathy and approval to his efforts for the service of the crown, he was coldly informed that the sovereigns reserved the matter in their hands for future consideration and remedy. Thus discouraged and disheartened at the very moment he needed the rebels to know that his administration was sustained in Spain, he yet, with admirable and heroic constancy, bent all his efforts to secure some settlement with the rebels, and for this purpose, accompanied by many of his principal counsellors, he moved nearer to Xaragua in his two caravels, and anchored in the port of Azua. Here he was met by Roldan, accompanied by Moxica and other principal insurgents, who even now again showed the utmost insolence and arrogance in their interviews with him.

The terms now demanded by the rebels were that Roldan might send fifteen of his men to Spain by the vessels at San Domingo ; that those remaining behind should have separate tracts of land in lieu of pay ; that a proclamation should issue exculpating them from all blame and announcing that all the charges made against them were false and invented by the enemies of the crown, and that Roldan should be restored to his office of Alcalde Mayor. Humiliating as these insolent terms were, the admiral felt compelled to accept them as the lesser evil. Even now Roldan claimed the right to consult his followers, and after two days they sent to the admiral their terms of capitulation in writing, which embraced not only the clauses above mentioned, but also the provisions of the arrangement proposed at Conception ; and while the demands made were arrogant and insolent both in substance and in language, their final assumption exceeded all the others combined, that if the admiral should fail to fulfil any of these conditions, these rebels should have the right to assemble and compel their performance by force or otherwise, as they might think proper. Columbus, in the straitened and almost abandoned condition in which he was, anarchy reigning in Hispaniola and distrusts and machinations at work against him in Spain, had no other choice than to submit to these humiliating terms. Had he made a bold and public exposition to the world of the condition of things—the crimes of his enemies in Hispaniola and the ingratitude and neglect of his king—he would have drawn to himself the sympathy of all, but Spanish dominion in the new world would have received a stunning blow. He sacrificed every personal feeling and interest for the good of his country. He hoped at a future day to report in person to the sovereigns the condition of things, and obtain even tardy justice from the court ; and as for posterity, he knew it would do full justice to his character, his services, and his achievements. Having now granted all to the rebels, at the last moment with innate dignity he inserted a clause that all should obey promptly the commands of the sovereigns, of himself, and of the justices appointed by him. The straits to which the Viceroy of the Indies was reduced might be estimated from one among other facts : the very men around his person, those whom he esteemed the most loyal, seeing how powerless he was in the face of the rebels, and how they had dictated terms to him, openly talked of abandoning his cause, seizing the fine eastern province of Higuey and its gold mines, setting up a separate government, and enriching themselves in defiance of all honor and duty. It was the forbearance of Columbus that saved Hispaniola, the first Spanish dominion in America, from anarchy and self-destruction, and perhaps prevented the abandonment of the new world again to barbarism.

What greater humiliation could have been reserved for him than to find himself compelled to sign a commission appointing Roldan, the chief rebel, a criminal outlaw, to the responsible office of Alcalde Mayor, or chief justice of the island? It is related by the Count de Lorgues, though not mentioned by Irving or Tarducci, that the clause reserving obedience to the commands of the crown, of the admiral, and of his justices, was inserted in Roldan's commission, and that when that insolent usurper saw it, he violently ordered the words to be erased, and appealed to his lawless followers to sustain him, proclaiming his purpose of hanging any one that dared to contradict him. "The admiral," says De Lorgues, "had still to submit to the will of his former ungrateful and rebellious servitor." And Tarducci, speaking of the patience and wise forbearance which he practised under such humiliations, says "that the new continent his genius had foreseen . . . remained a glorious field for the labors and discoveries of those who came after him." And our own countryman, Mr. Irving, writes, "Thus critically situated, disregarding every consideration of personal pride and dignity, and determined, at any individual sacrifice, to secure the interests of an ungrateful sovereign, Columbus forced himself to sign this most humiliating capitulation." *

Columbus was a man of too great a mind and soul to be appreciated by his contemporaries. The ordeal of successes the most brilliant and of reverses the most humiliating serves only to enhance his exalted character in the eyes of posterity. But the severe humiliations to which in life he was subjected seemed then, in the eyes of the world, to hide from view the grandeur of his conduct, the exalted purity of his motives, the ennobling virtues which he practised, the consummate wisdom of his policy, and the self-sacrifice he made for his country and for the world. In fact, it seems to have required the toning influences of four hundred years and the unparalleled development of the Ameri-

---

* For the details of this narrative consult Herrera, "Hist. Ind.;" Fernando Columbus, "Hist. del Almirante;" Muñoz, "Hist. Nuevo Mundo;" Barry's translation of De Lorgues' "Life of Columbus;" Irving's "Life of Columbus," and Mr. Brownson's translation of Tarducci's "Life of Columbus."

can nations, enhanced by their present grandeur, to secure for Christopher Columbus the just admiration and the grateful appreciation of mankind. The recent work on Columbus from the pen of Justin Winsor, the Librarian of Harvard College, is so great a departure from historical fairness and judicious investigation, even from an avowed enemy of Columbus, that it is universally regarded as a mean attempt to deprive Columbus of the credit and glory of his discovery. Its violence will consign it to obscurity. It is a mere travesty of all dignified and impartial history.

Nothing could be more unjust than the attempts of some modern historians to hold Columbus responsible for the introduction of slavery into America, or for the cruel *encomiendas* which under Ovando, whom King Ferdinand appointed to supersede him, completed the enslavement of the natives to the Spaniards. I do not contend that Columbus made no mistakes or fell into no serious errors, but these were the mistakes and errors of judgment or of administration, which have also and equally checkered the careers of the best and greatest of men. Columbus was not the friend of human slavery, for one of the most prominent acts performed by him on his first voyage was the liberation of four natives captured and imprisoned by Pinzon on his ship with the intention of selling them in Spain as slaves—an act of justice which brought on him the undying hatred of that commander. No upright man in the nineteenth century can approve the deeds of any man in any age for the enslavement of mankind; nor can a just man now fairly judge the actions of Columbus, inspired by the prevailing sentiments and practices of the fifteenth century, by the standards of the nineteenth. In making prisoners of war of the cannibal Caribs taken in arms and attacking his own peaceful Indians of Hispaniola, Columbus only acted in conformity to the customs of his own and more recent times. The laws of war then sanctioned this policy. Mr. Fiske writes of this part of the admiral's history : " When Columbus came to Hispaniola on his second voyage, with seventeen ships and fifteen hundred followers, he found the relations between red men and white men already hostile ; and in order to get food for so many Spaniards foraging expeditions were undertaken, which made matters worse. This state of things led Columbus to devise a notable expedient. In some of the neighboring islands lived the voracious Caribs. In fleets of canoes they would swoop upon the coasts of Hispaniola, capture men and women by the score, and carry them off to be cooked and eaten. Now Columbus wished to win the friendship of the Indians about him by defending them against these enemies, and so he made raids against these Caribs, took some of them captive and sent them as slaves to Spain, to be taught Spanish and converted to Christianity, so that they might come back to the islands as interpreters, and thus be useful aids in missionary work. 'It was really,' said Columbus, 'a kindness to these cannibals to enslave them and send them where they could be baptized and rescued from everlasting perdition; and then again they could be received in payment for the cargoes of cattle, seeds, wine, and other provisions which must be sent from Spain for the support of the colony.' Thus quaintly did the great discoverer, like so many good men before and since, mingle considerations of religion with those of domestic economy." "Slavery, however, sprang up in Hispaniola before any one could have fully realized the meaning of what was going on. As the Indians were unfriendly and food must be had, while foraging expeditions were apt to end in plunder and bloodshed, Columbus tried to regulate matters by prohibiting such expeditions, and in lieu thereof imposing a light tribute or tax upon the entire population of Hispaniola above fourteen years of age. As this population was dense, a little from each person meant a good deal in the lump. The tribute might be a small piece of gold or of cotton, and was to be paid four times a year. Every time that an Indian paid this tax a small brass token duly stamped was to be given him to hang about his neck as a voucher. If there were Indians who felt unable to pay the tribute, they might as an alternative render a certain amount of personal service in helping to plant seed or tend cattle for the Spaniards." Again Mr. Fiske writes: "No doubt these regulations were well meant, and if the two races had been more evenly matched, perhaps they might not have so speedily developed into tyranny." * In another place the same author says this imposition of tribute by Columbus "was part of a plan for checking depredations and regulating the relations between the Spaniards and the Indians." † A close examination of the progress of

---

* "The Discovery of America," by John Fiske, vol. ii., pp. 432-34.
† *Id.*, vol. i., p. 481.

events shows that Columbus was not responsible for the subsequent introduction of the *repartimientos*, which may be styled a form of serfdom, and which was the act of the ruthless and rapacious gangs of lawless Spaniards who formed the colony of Columbus in the second expedition, against whom we have seen he was powerless, and was legalized and riveted upon the Indians under Aguado. It was the evident intention of Columbus to have limited his plan of regulating the relations of the two races to a moderate tribute, and this was intended as a check upon Spanish rapacity and tyranny. Under Ovando the *repartimientos* were deliberately developed into the more cruel *encomiendas*, the complete enslavement of the natives to their Spanish conquerors, and their final extermination by the most remorseless and hideous cruelties.

Even Peschel, the eminent German geographer and anthropologist, whose judgment of Columbus is in general harsh, even unjust, said, in relation to his treatment of the Indians, what Washington Irving and so many others have said, "When we see, however, in our own day how the rights of the weaker races are shamefully violated, we may have some indulgence for this man of the fifteenth century."

Even Winsor acknowledges the justice and the necessity of judging Columbus according to the prevailing sentiments of his own age, and not by those of our own, for he says, "No man craves more than Columbus to be judged with all the palliations demanded of a difference of his own age and ours." Yet throughout his book he signally violates the rule he recognizes.

Among the contemporaries and companions of Columbus was the great and illustrious Las Casas, afterward Bishop of Chiapa, in Mexico, who was an eye-witness and a conscientious historian of the great events of the discoverer's life. His "History of the Indies" is the great basis of our modern histories in all subsequent times, and as Mr. Fiske, quoting Washington Irving, justly says of it : "In a far truer sense than any other book it may be called the corner-stone of the history of the American Continent."* Now, if there is any one feature more prominent than others in a life replete with pre-eminent acts and labors of humane and heroic goodness—a life which is justly regarded as exhibiting

---

* John Fiske's "The Discovery of America," vol. ii., p. 481.

a character which was "the highest type of manhood"—it was that Las Casas was the best and noblest friend of the Indians, and their most illustrious and consistent liberator, the champion of human liberty. It is difficult for us, in the nineteenth century, after four hundred years of calumny and detraction, to form a perfect conception of the life, character, and deeds of the great discoverer of 1492. But Las Casas, his companion, the witness of his career, the great historian of that age, was, without question, the most competent to judge and record his true and undisguised acts, which passed under his own eye. Had Columbus been an enslaver of the Indians, Las Casas would have known it, and he certainly would have been the first to denounce him, for he denounced his successors, his own countrymen and those in the highest places, for the subsequent enslavement of the redmen. He won to the cause of liberty and the liberation of the Indians the Emperor Charles V., Cardinal Ximenes, and the Pope; and with these powerful allies he made the Indians of America free. That such a champion of freedom should have admired and praised Columbus for his administration in Hispaniola, and in respect to the very events which Mr. Winsor and others have used for their accusation—that Columbus was the enslaver of the Indians—is sufficient to refute unanswerably so unjust and false a charge. Mr. Fiske, in his preface to "The Discovery of America," p. xi., says: "The most conspicuous difference" (between himself and Justin Winsor in regard to Columbus) "is that which concerns the personal character of Columbus. Mr. Winsor writes in a spirit of energetic (not to say violent) reaction against the absurdities of Roselly de Lorgues and others who have tried to make a saint of Columbus; and under the influence of this reaction he offers us a picture of the great navigator that serves to raise a pertinent question. No man can deny that Las Casas was a keen judge of men, or that his standard of right and wrong was quite as lofty as any one has reached in our own time. He had a much more intimate knowledge of Columbus than any modern historian can ever hope to acquire, and he always speaks of him with warm admiration and respect; but how could Las Casas ever have respected the feeble, mean-spirited driveller whose portrait Mr. Winsor asks us to accept as that of the discoverer of America?"

Reference has been made to the fact that though Columbus

was the discoverer of the new world, the justice of naming it in honor of its discoverer was denied to him. It is curious to observe how universal was the belief that the newly discovered countries were a part of Asia, and how long it was before the world came to realize that they formed parts of a new world. It is true, Americus Vespucius was the first to use the expression *Novus Mundus*, but he had not the slightest idea that the lands which he had discovered at the south, and to which he applied that term, were parts of the same countries that Columbus had discovered as a part of Asia. The injustice of accusing Americus of contriving designedly and treacherously to have his own name conferred upon the new world is almost as great as that by which Columbus lost the honor of having it receive his name.

Americus Vespucius was a native of Florence, where he was born on March 18th, 1452. He was of a good family, possessed no mean attainments in Latin, astronomy, geography, and was an energetic collector of maps, charts, globes, and works on his favorite studies. He was a merchant by profession, and was taken into the great commercial house of the Medici at Florence. He was subsequently and successively in the employment of the Spanish and Portuguese governments, and he took part in fitting out under contracts Columbus's second voyage. He made four voyages to the Western Hemisphere: the first voyage in 1497–98; the second was made in company with Alonzo de Ojeda and Juan de la Cosa in 1499–1500, in which they explored the northern coast of South America, including the north coast of Brazil; his third voyage was made in the service of Portugal, occurred in 1501–1502, and embraced the Brazilian coast as far as latitude 34° S., and he thence ran as far as the island of South Georgia; the fourth voyage was in 1503–1504, also in the Portuguese service, in which he and Gonzalo Coelho endeavored to follow the Brazilian coast to its end, or until they solved the problem of the passage to the Indian Ocean.

It was his first voyage which gave rise to the accusation that Americus had claimed for himself the discovery of the continent before Columbus; but this accusation is disposed of by the fact now established that it was a bungling translation of a single word or proper name in one of his famous letters to Lorenzo de Medici and Soderini.* In these letters Vespucius describes a

---

* Mr. John Fiske's "Discovery of America," vol. ii., chap. 7.

country visited by him which bore the Indian name of *Lariab*, and the careless translator in the published copy of the *Quattro Giornate** rendered the name *Parias*. This region of Paria was a part of the continent. Columbus had discovered it in the summer of 1498, and Vespucius did not come within sight of it until one year afterward, in the summer of 1499; but the mistranslation, giving Lariab for Parias, would make Americus claim, over his own signature, the honor of first discovering the American Continent in 1497, just one year prior to its discovery by Columbus. While we recognize his character as incapable of such falsehood and meanness, it is satisfactory to be able to give the historical narrative of the truth, which gives an exact form and record to his acquittal.

This, too, seems to be an appropriate place for mentioning and giving the true history of the bestowal of the name of America to the western world, in honor of Americus Vespucius, instead of Columbia, in honor of Christopher Columbus. So great was the wrong inflicted upon the memory of Columbus by this misnomer, that many just and able historians and publicists have shown a strong disposition to resent it; and it was but natural to infer from the wrong itself that somebody with a motive must be guilty of basely bringing it about. It was the next natural step in the course of events to suspect Vespucius of the deed, or of procuring it to be done, and finally to accuse him of it. He was the man who had the motive for the act, and in the absence of historical data the supposed motive was sufficient to condemn him. Even the great and good Las Casas was among the first and most energetic in imputing this treason against truth and justice to Vespucius. Vexed at the circumstance, Las Casas reports that Americus " sinfully failed toward the admiral," and he said, " If Vespucius purposely gave currency to this belief" (of his first setting foot on the main), " it was a great wickedness; and if it was not done intentionally, it looks like it." † Americus was always on terms of friendship and good offices with Columbus, and he was a man of too much elevation of character to do, or to contribute toward doing, so base an action. He and

---

* "The Four Voyages of Americus Vespucius."
† Fiske's "Discovery of America," vol. ii., pp. 156–59; Winsor's "Columbus," p. 553.

Columbus were never rivals. They were friends. Fortunately for the truth of history and for the honor of our race, the means are now at hand to remove this stain from the memory of a great man and distinguished navigator. The perversion of names, for so it may be called, resulted almost from accident, certainly from the ignorance of the geography of the newly discovered countries which prevailed at the beginning of the sixteenth century and for a long time afterward. There was no treason or malice in the business.

The discoveries of Americus Vespucius created a great sensation in the world, and his graphic descriptions of them in his famous letters, which were afterward published, had the effect of placing him on a plane of honor second only to that of Columbus. Brazil was his great discovery. The line of demarcation as altered from that of Pope Alexander VI. gave this vast region to Portugal. It was west of that famous line drawn across the earth from pole to pole, as subsequently fixed by treaty between Spain and Portugal. Little did Americus or any one else imagine that this region was in the same part of the world with the countries discovered by Columbus. It was thought to be a part of another or fourth part of the earth, to distinguish it from the three parts known to the ancients—Europe, Asia, and Africa. Hence it was that Americus applied to it honestly and naturally the title of *Novus Mundus*. The famous letter of Vespucius containing this phrase was published in Paris by Giovanni Giocondo, of Florence, without the knowledge of the author, and while he was absent from Europe. This publication was the great cause of Vespucius's fame as the discoverer of a world wholly distinct from that new part of Asia which Columbus had discovered.

But now a powerful yet not wicked, an almost unconscious help was given to the wrong done to Columbus from an unexpected quarter and from an almost obscure personage. At a small town in the Vosges, in the realm of René II., Duke of Lorraine, named Saint Dié, was a college enthusiastically patronized by this royal friend of letters. The town traced back its history to the seventh century, when it began to grow up as a hamlet around the Benedictine monastery founded by St. Deodatus, Bishop of Nevers, and toward the end of the tenth century the monastery was transferred from the Benedictines to a secular chapter of canons, and was presided over by a bishop

under the title of Grand Provost. Under the patronage of the
college the town grew and prospered, possessed a population of
eight thousand, was a manufacturing and agricultural centre,
and with the changes of time St. Deodatus became more con-
veniently contracted to Saint Dié. Many eminent scholars had
filled the chair of Grand Provost, and under the patronage of
Walter Lud, the secretary of Duke René, a printing-press was
established at the college about the year 1500. To this remote
and obscure town many men of learning congregated, and among
its professors were many men of note and erudition. Among
the latter came the young professor of Latin, Ringmann, who
journeyed from Paris to Saint Dié in 1505, to adorn its councils
with his wit and brilliancy. In that year, too, there came to the
College of Saint Dié a young and talented professor of geography,
Martin Waldscemüller, from Freiburg. The two young professors were congenial spirits. It may well be imagined how the
news of recent marvellous discoveries had electrified the faculty
of this learned college. The discoveries of Columbus seemed
almost eclipsed by those of Vespucius. But Waldseemüller had
formed the acquaintance of Giocondo at Paris, and had caught
from him the greatest enthusiasm for Americus Vespucius, the
discoverer of *Novus Mundus*, which, as we have seen, was thought
to be the fourth quarter of the earth, and no doubt he had pored
over the letter of Vespucius to Medici, which Giocondo had
published with the title of " De Ora Antarctica." It was during
the height of this enthusiastic admiration for Americus that his
second letter, addressed to Soderini, which gave a brief account
of his four voyages, at Lisbon, September 4th, 1504, began to
become known through manuscript copies, became printed at
Florence in the first half of 1506 by Pacini, in Italian, and finally
a French copy was made by an unknown hand, and of this last
version in French the learned faculty of Saint Dié procured a
copy from Portugal through their patron, the Duke of Lorraine.
A rare and splendid edition of the great geographical work of
Ptolemy, in the mean time, and for some time previously, had
been in preparation by Walter Lud, Ringmann, and Waldseemüller, and was to be issued in Latin from the press of Saint Dié,
with important additions of modern geographical learning, bringing all down to that date, 1507. While Lud defrayed the expense of the publication, Waldseemüller performed the scientific

and Ringmann the philological part of the enterprise. Waldseemüller's map, *Tabula Terre Nove*, and a treatise by him also as an introductory to the great publication, were to form a part of the whole; and now just before the work was issued Duke René, having presented the French copy of Vespucius's Soderini letter to the learned trio, that, too, was eagerly made to form a part of the work. This last addition was the most important of all; but it was translated into Latin, and by a strange liberty Vespucius was made to address his letter to the Duke of Lorraine, René, instead of Soderini. This version of the letter contains the mistake by which Parias, a country and part of the continent discovered by Columbus, was substituted by Lariab, an Indian name by which Vespucius designated another and obscure country he had seen. This notable publication was issued from the press of Saint Dié on April 25th, 1507, under the title of "Cosmographiæ Introductio." It has become more famous since it was the first work published which contained the name *America*, and this was the name which Waldseemüller, in his introduction, suggested should be bestowed upon that fourth part of the earth which Americus Vespucius had discovered and described, and which formed the complement of the other three parts of Ptolemy, making now Europe, Asia, Africa, and America. We must bear in mind that the country thus designated by Waldseemüller as America was, in fact, the *Novus Mundus* of Vespucius, which was, in fact, none other than Brazil; and Waldseemüller had no thought whatever of bestowing that name upon countries discovered by Columbus. Mr. Fiske has given us a translation of the Latin passage from the young Professor Waldseemüller's introduction, which reads: "But now these parts have been more extensively explored, and the fourth part has been discovered by Americus Vespucius (as will appear in what follows), wherefore I do not see what is rightly to hinder us from calling it Amerige or America—*i.e.*, the land of Americus—after its discoverer, Americus, a man of sagacious mind, since both Europe and Asia have got their names from women. Its situation and the manners and customs of its people will be clearly understood from the twice two voyages of Americus which follow." *

---

* Fiske's "Discovery of America," vol. ii., chap. 7, *passim*.

From the beginning and then the countries discovered by Columbus were known as Asia, or the Indies. A copy of the edition of the Saint Dié work of 1509 was in the library of Fernando Columbus, the second son of the admiral, who was a scholar and the biographer of his illustrious father. His life of the admiral was written after this, and he took no exception to the suggestion of America by Waldseemüller as the name to be given to the *terra incognita* of Vespucius. There was never any intercourse between Vespucius and the faculty of Saint Dié, nor did he do anything himself toward the publications and translations of his letters to Medici and Soderini ; nor was he even in Portugal when Soderini made the first copy of the letter, but was then actually in Spain. Then, too, in Spain he visited Columbus, with whom his relations were always most friendly. Nor is there anything to suggest that Waldseemüller himself had any design to do Columbus an injustice, or to bestow the name of Americus upon the countries discovered by him. On the contrary, there is every reason to believe that he supposed these two newly discovered regions were in different quarters of the earth ; but the first link in the chain of practical wrong had now been wrought. It was easy for others to follow.

The first map which ever contained the name of America was that published in 1514, and attributed to the famous painter, Leonardo da Vinci, and on this map the region designated as America was drawn as a great island or continent by itself, and mostly south of the equator. It was Brazil. So also Schöner's globe in 1515 contained the same extensive region, which he calls " America or Brasilia, or Land of Paroquets." The *Novus Mundus* was, in fact, the southern continent, and in the course of time America became the name of the southern continent, and Brazil the name of a part of it designated as America. In the course of years all South America was circumnavigated and found to be a continent, and by 1550 the more northern lands discovered by Columbus had gradually become known to be separated from Asia. But now, in 1541, Gerard Mercator boldly forged the links that followed, for he then had applied the name of America to all the Western Hemisphere, and his map of that date gives a fair outline of both the northern and southern continents, all bearing the name of the Florentine navigator. It was now, but too late, that it was discovered that Columbus had been deprived of the justly earned honor of bestowing his name upon the new world he had discovered. Americus Vespucius was naturally but erroneously suspected of having brought this about. Las Casas, the historian of the Indies, as we have seen, was among the first to record his protest against the wrong thus inflicted on his friend, the admiral. Herrera, in 1601, openly accused Americus of the wrong, which he attempted to show was accomplished by fraud and falsehood, and the belief became general that Vespucius had deliberately attempted to supplant Columbus. Humboldt commenced the vindication of Vespucius, and Varnhagen made the refutation of the charge complete. Mr. John Fiske, of Cambridge, has added greatly to the proofs of his innocence, and has made his acquittal triumphant.

It would be a great oversight herein not to refer to an unjust charge that has been made against Las Casas, the illustrious Bishop of Chiapa, and still more illustrious as the friend of human liberty. It seems unaccountable how such a man should have been accused of enslaving the Africans in order to liberate the Indians. That he labored unceasingly for the amelioration of the hideous cruelties and wrongs which the Spaniards inflicted upon the Indians, and for their emancipation from the horrible condition of slavery, under the name of *encomiendas*, to which Ovando had reduced them, are facts in his glorious life of which humanity may feel proud. It is sad that under the second admiral, Diego Columbus, the condition of the Indians was no better than under Ovando. Las Casas, who had found good reason for praising the father, did not shrink from denouncing the wrongs which took place under the son. He united with Antonio Montesino and the other brave and noble Dominicans in Hispaniola in denouncing from the pulpit the enslavement of the Indians by Spanish planters and miners. He went to Spain as a missionary of liberty, and he ceased not to agitate for a change in the direful treatment of the natives until he obtained from the emperor the decree of 1542, " We order and command that henceforward for no cause whatever, whether of war, rebellion, ransom, or in any other manner, can any Indian be made a slave." Las Casas was not a mere champion of liberty ; he set the example to the Spaniards by liberating first his own slaves. I have said that he also gained as allies in his angelic work not only the Grand Cardinal of Spain, Ximenes, and the Emperor

Charles V., but also that illustrious Pope, Paul III. This great and good pontiff issued his brief, which bears date in 1537, five years before the imperial decree against Indian slavery, and thus the further enslavement of Indians was forbidden under penalty of excommunication; and any governor who should give or any planter who should receive a new *encomienda*, which was an enslavement, or who should despoil the natives of their property, should be refused the sacraments of the Church. Las Casas translated the Latin brief into Spanish, and he sent it to every part of the Indies. Abuse from cruel and selfish planters and miners, rebuffs from hardened officials, even from Fonseca, all tended only to inspire the heart of Las Casas with a profounder sense of his exalted apostolate. It was due to the labors and sacrifices of this true Christian bishop that the greater part of Spanish America was saved from the horrible taint of human slavery.

If Columbus suffered a grievous wrong in being deprived of the honor of bestowing his name upon the new world, which he had so bravely discovered, what shall we say of the cruel slander which was cast upon the name of Las Casas, the anti-slavery crusader of the sixteenth century, in the charge that he had been the means of introducing African slavery into America! The aspiration of this book will be amply rewarded if it succeeds in aiding to refute this calumny, and in removing from our histories and from the very text-books used in some of our public schools so grave an injustice. To the accomplishment of this end, a simple and brief narrative of the facts ought to suffice, even though it is perversely true that with superficial and hasty thinkers and readers even to our day, Las Casas is chiefly known as the man who introduced African slavery and the slave trade into America. Appearances, with a slight foundation of fact in some small and trifling particulars, have led to this gross historical blunder, whereas a comprehensive view of all the facts will easily set forth the truth with unerring light.

Now it is undoubtedly true that Indian slavery was already established in Hispaniola before even the most observant and most humane were aware of it. The rapacity of the early Spanish colonists, planters, and miners was truly appalling. It was against such odds that Las Casas waged his crusade of liberty. This struggle led to an earnest and widespread consideration and discussion of the inevitable labor question. If the Indians were set free, who would supply the labor necessary for the country and its enterprises? It was the planters who suggested that the Africans were a much hardier race than the Indians, and they proposed to yield to the demands for liberty for the Indians, if they should be permitted to substitute for their labor the labor of the Africans as slaves. These discussions reached the Spanish Court, and there, too, the champion of liberty was confronted with the same argument he had met in Hispaniola, that labor must be provided for the working of the plantations and mines of New Spain. The whole force of the situation presented itself to the mind of Las Casas as a choice between two evils. Neither the sentiments of his age or country nor the education of that century, both inherited from the past, had reached the point of opposition to slavery even in the concrete ; it would be scarcely just to expect the sixteenth century to have reached the stage of development which even we Americans have only now reached in the latter half of the nineteenth century. A man who in those times and circumstances was so far in advance of all around him as to oppose any form of slavery was a hero, a philanthropist, far in advance of the age. The thought that, upon universal principles applicable to all times and countries, human slavery was wrong absolutely in itself, had never become a part of the convictions or education of the best sovereigns and statesmen. Las Casas had himself been a slaveholder, just as thousands of American citizens now living have been ; but he, like them, had sacrificed his private interests on the altar of liberty. In such a crisis of Indian emancipation, the suggestion that it would be more humane to substitute the hardier race of Africa in place of the less robust Indian race for the working of the Spanish plantations and mines in the new world presented itself to the benevolent mind of Las Casas purely as a move in the direction of amelioration ; and in answer to the arguments used at court, in the heat of his advocacy of Indian liberty, recalling the suggestion of the Spanish planters, he suggested that it might solve the present difficulty by substituting African slaves for Indian slaves as the lesser evil.

But Las Casas was far advanced already on the road to universal emancipation, and it was but a step further—a step which he soon promptly and heroically took—to reach the conviction then so far in advance of his own and of even subsequent ages, that the same principles of right and wrong, the same title to freedom, which applied to one race, were equally applicable to the other. He afterward announced his advocacy of the universal right to liberty for all men. He even reproved himself for the apparent concession he had made to the planters and miners of Hispaniola. His great work, the " History of the Indies," sets forth the true, final, and unalterable convictions of his great soul. He there wrote that "if he had sufficiently considered the matter," he would not for all the world have entertained such a suggestion for a moment ; for," said he, " the negroes had been made slaves unjustly and tyrannically, and the same reason holds good of them as of the Indians." *

Fortunately this passing remark of Las Casas, on the choice of the lesser evil, had no effect whatever either in introducing or in increasing African slavery in America. On the contrary, the effect of his efforts was favorable to the restriction of African slavery and the slave trade. Long before the occurrence which I have related African slavery existed in Hispaniola, and African slaves were then working in its mines. A royal decree as early as 1501, while forbidding the enslavement of Europeans and various other races in Hispaniola, permitted the use there of negro slaves, and African slaves were imported there during the first ten years after the decree. It was many years afterward before African slavery, however, became greatly increased, and Las Casas was an irreconcilable opponent of it. He certainly saved the poor Indians from utter annihilation. But for his labors, services, and success in this great work of humanity also, the earlier or more complete extermination of the Indians would have inevitably led to an immense increase of the African slave trade. The facts on this interesting subject have been lately and greatly elucidated by Mr. John Fiske, of Cambridge, in his learned work, from which I have largely drawn in this connection, and I know of no more appropriate way of closing the subject than by quoting his strong language in defence of Las Casas. " When the work of Las Casas is deeply considered, we cannot make him anything else but an antagonist of human slavery in all its forms, and the mightiest and most effective antagonist withal that has ever lived." †

---

* Mr. John Fiske's "The Discovery of America," vol. ii., p. 456 ; Las Casas, "Historia de las Indias," vol. ii., doc. 175. † *Id.*, p. 458.

By the following passage, in concluding his chapter on Las Casas, Mr. Fiske exhibits a striking instance in which the eulogist wins exalted fame in the noble praises and vindication he bestows upon another: "In contemplating such a life as that of Las Casas, all words of eulogy seem weak and frivolous. The historian can only bow in reverent awe before a figure which is in some respects the most beautiful and sublime in the annals of Christianity since the apostolic age. When now and then in the course of the centuries God's providence brings such a life into this world, the memory of it must be cherished by mankind as one of its most precious and sacred possessions. For the thoughts, the words, the deeds of such a man there is no death. The sphere of their influence goes on widening forever. They bud, they blossom, they bear fruit, from age to age."*

---

* Fiske, "The Discovery of America," vol. ii., p. 482.

CHAPTER XII.

> "Trust reposed in noble natures
> Obliges them the more."
> —DRYDEN.

> "The purpose of an injury is to vex
> And trouble me; now nothing can do that
> To him that's truly valiant. He that is affected
> With the least injury is less than it."
> —JONSON'S "NEW INN."

> "Innocence shall make
> False accusations blush, and tyranny
> Tremble at patience."
> —SHAKESPEARE'S "WINTER'S TALE."

THE harsh strokes of fortune, the urgency and disaster of his position, the defeat of his best efforts by bad men, the coolness and ingratitude of his king, made Columbus exert himself the more for the restoration of order and good government in Hispaniola, and for the promotion of the honor and profit of his country and his sovereigns. Galling and excruciating as was his task, he bore himself with equanimity, patience, and wisdom. But his career of loyalty was beset with appalling difficulties.

Roldan was installed in his office of Alcalde Mayor on November 5th, 1499. Instead of carrying his stipulations into effect by supporting the authority of the admiral, he did all in his power to weaken his authority and insult him. Stalking through the streets of San Domingo with arrogance, and surrounded by rebels and disloyal people, he endeavored to win the loyal to his cause. He dismissed Rodrigo Perez as lieutenant to the Alcalde Mayor, because the admiral had appointed him; and he and his companions proudly asserted that they had crushed the tyranny of Columbus and his brothers, and they claimed and received from many the honors paid only to heroes. Roldan presented a petition of one hundred rebels asking for lands in their favorite province of Xaragua, and the admiral, in granting their request, had the address to persuade them to accept land in different parts of the country, thus wishing to scatter rather than concentrate the disloyal. In order to promote habits and methods of industry among them, and assist them on their farms, he liberated the Indians in their vicinities from the payment of the tribute, and arranged with the caciques in lieu thereof to give these Spaniards a certain number of Indians to till their lands for them. To deal with such worthless and reckless men required the most mature and consummate management, and even then the wisest measures are liable to be turned into the most unsuccessful by the wilfulness and crimes of the objects of one's solicitude and generosity. Such was the case in this important instance.

In his desire to scatter the late rebels, so as to prevent their concentration in case of further outbreaks, he managed to place them on lands granted to them in different parts of the island: some at Bonao, some on the Rio Verde in the Royal Vega, and others at St. Jago. With the lands given he assigned to them a liberal number of Indian prisoners of war. The original design of the admiral was to introduce in Hispaniola a paternal government, in which the Indians would be received as docile subjects of the crown, and led by zealous missionaries and the good examples of the Christians to embrace the faith; but the crimes and vices of the white men, their lusts and covetousness, their cruelties to the natives, and their disloyalty to the government frustrated all his purposes. Insurrections among the oppressed natives and rebellions among the Spaniards changed the whole policy of his administration. Forced by such unwelcome but irresistible circumstances, he fell in with the notions of the age and of the continental nations; reduced the natives to a form of subjection by force, and now regarded and handled them as a conquered race, and their country and its lands as spoils of the conquerors. Tribute had been exacted of the natives, their lands were given to the conquerors, and the prisoners of war were condemned to a service well calculated to lead to their enslavement. The enslavement of Indian prisoners of war seemed to lead to the servitude of free Indians to their Spanish conquerors. The placing of certain numbers of Indians in the service of the rebels and of other Spaniards for the purpose of tilling their lands was practically a reduction of the native race to the condition of servitude; but it was not personal slavery. Columbus was not the author of that system of slavery which was afterward introduced under Bobadilla and Ovando, under the name of *repartimientos*, and which became generally introduced throughout the Spanish colonies and conquered countries. By that system free Indians were made the slaves in fact though not in name of the Spanish colonists. In establishing his own disastrous system, so foreign to his own wishes and so alien to his own mild, just, and generous nature, Columbus endeavored to impress order and system upon it, and for this purpose he appointed an armed police force, each section being placed under a military captain, who patrolled the provinces, compelled the Indians to pay the tribute, checked the conduct of the colonists, and suppressed the first germs of rebellion or uprising.

While De Lorgues, the enthusiastic eulogist of Columbus, passes over or refers but slightly to such events in his administration, the voice of history, while condemning the system itself, has with just discrimination referred this measure rather to the necessities of his position and the prevailing methods of the age than to the voluntary action of the admiral. Mr. Irving says: "This was an arrangement widely different from his original intention of treating the natives with kindness, as peaceful subjects of the crown. But all his plans had been subverted, and his present measures forced upon him by the exigencies of the times and the violence of lawless men." And the learned and discreet Tarducci writes: "The first intention of Columbus in regard to the Indians was, as we saw, that of an affectionate father toward his children, and all his hopes and desires were directed to making of them good and peaceful subjects of the Catholic sovereigns, and fervent followers of the law of Christ. But the violent and licentious conduct of most of his companions, the revolts of the natives, the necessity of making up for. the want of hands and of victuals, and other disasters which befell him, forced his hand, and dragged him into the ideas of his time, which looked on discoveries of infidel lands in the light of conquests, and gave the conqueror absolute dominion over person and property."

Even then, as it originated from his hands, the measure was not necessarily cruel or oppressive, for he endeavored to temper it with mercy and regulate it with justice; and had it been practised by the colonists in this same spirit, it would have resulted in the civilization of the Indians by accustoming them to lives of regular and systematic industry and husbandry; whereas, in the hands of merciless and avaricious men, of inhuman and cruel masters, it became, under his successors, one of the worst forms of human slavery, and resulted in the disastrous extermination of the native race.*

But the leading rebel, Roldan himself, made more ample and extraordinary demands on the liberality of the admiral. Among the princely concessions made to this bold and reckless adventurer, the representative rather of the remorseless buccaneers of past ages than of the Christian colonist of the age of Columbus, may be mentioned valuable lands near the city of Isabella, which he pretended to claim by a title anterior to his rebellion; also a royal holding or farm, in the Vega, called La Lesperanza, an estate devoted to the raising of all kinds of poultry, the right to use the cattle on the royal or crown lands for the cultivation of his own farms, and finally the grant of extensive lands in Xaragua. In making these concessions to this grasping outlaw, the admiral subjected them to the condition of the pleasure of the crown when heard from; for he still hoped that the revelation to the crown of the circumstances under which he was forced to make such concessions to rebels would end in their punishment rather than in their reward for their misdeeds, and in the restitution of their ill-gotten wealth. Roldan, more intent on the care of his plunder than on the duties of his office as Alcalde Mayor, asked and obtained permission to visit his vast estates. His conduct on the way thither showed again the arrogant and lawless character of the man; for history furnishes many instances of ruffians who were remarkably tenacious of official forms and commissions while violating every principle of legitimate authority. On arriving at Bonao, the late rendezvous of the rebels, he appointed one of his late confederates, Pedro Requelme, local alcalde, or judge, conferring upon him full powers of arresting all offenders and sending them as prisoners to Conception, where Roldan, still exercising in mockery the

---

* Muñoz, "Hist. Nuevo Mundo," lib. vi., § 50; Fernando Columbus, "Hist. del Almirante," cap. 84; Herrera, decad. i., lib. iii., cap. xvi.; Dr. Barry's translation of De Lorgues' "Columbus," pp. 398, 399; Irving's "Life of Columbus," vol. ii., pp. 212-14; Mr. Brownson's translation of Tarducci's "Life of Columbus," vol. ii., pp. 143-45.

office of Alcalde Mayor, reserved to himself the right of judgment and sentence over them. Scarcely had the admiral expressed his indignation at this affront to his own authority, when he received from Pedro de Arana, a man of integrity and loyalty, information that Requelme, with Roldan's connivance, was erecting on a prominent site a strong building, so constructed as to serve as a fortress in case of need in any future disorders of the rebels. Columbus, on hearing the case, promptly and peremptorily prohibited Requelme from proceeding with his rebellious and well-understood designs and plans.

In the mean time, the two caravels intended for the passage to Spain were gotten ready, and all who desired to return to their country were permitted to do so by this opportunity. Many of Roldan's late confederates returned on the ships, carrying with them not only slaves, but also the unfortunate daughters of caciques, whom they had seduced to leave their homes and country, or perhaps seized by force for the most degrading purposes. While his generous feelings were outraged by these and many other such proceedings, the admiral found it prudent if not necessary to take no notice of them, for fear of bringing on a renewal of greater crimes. As it was, he felt that he was sending home recruits for the already augmented ranks of his own slanderers and revilers at court. It had been the intention of the admiral to embark for Spain in one of these vessels, together with his brother, Don Bartholomew; for his presence there seemed most important in order to refute the calumnies of his enemies and sustain at court his own cause and that of the new world. But how could he leave Hispaniola in its present perilous condition, when the government was not yet secure from the machinations of rebels; when rumors were reaching him of a threatened descent of the mountaineers of Ciguay upon the Vega to rescue the imprisoned Mayobanex, their chief, then in the fortress of Conception; when news also had just been received by him of the arrival off the western coast of the island of four unknown and suspicious-looking ships? His fate seemed to chain him to this, the first yet disastrous offspring of the colonial policy he was struggling to found for the glory and profit of his country and his sovereigns. In his place, and for the purpose of conveying to the court a true account of the past and present condition of Hispaniola, and of refuting the calumnies of his enemies, he sent out on the ships his ever-faithful and loyal aids, Miguel Ballester and Garcia de Barrantes.

The admiral also sent out by this opportunity important letters to the sovereigns, in which he gave for the second time a detailed account of the late rebellion, and contended, for his own honor and for the honor of the crown, that the late capitulations between him and the rebels were in fact and by right of no binding force. He gave his reasons for this statement in the fact that he yielded to duress in accepting and signing them; that it was done at sea, where he was admiral but not viceroy; that the rebels having been twice on due trial condemned as traitors, his pardoning power did not extend to such cases; that the terms of the capitulations embraced the disposal of matters of the royal revenue, reserved to the crown or its proper representatives, and because Roldan and his followers were outlawed by the violation of their oaths of obedience to the sovereigns and to himself. For these and many other reasons he requested the sovereigns to review the case and annul the iniquitous terms wrested from him by force and against his will. In these important dispatches Columbus renewed his former recommendations for the dispatch of a judge learned in the law to administer and enforce the law in so turbulent a community; also for the appointment of a council of discreet persons, and of officers of the revenues, cautioning the sovereigns most strenuously against any infringement of his own rights and dignities; and he requested that his son, Don Diego Columbus, should be sent to him, to assist him in the administration in his declining years and impaired health. Looking to the maintenance of his heirs forever in the important duties and honorable prerogatives of the high hereditary offices he held, this was a grave and prudent step toward the education of the first heir of his offices, titles, and estates, for the important career which he had marked out for himself and his family.

Before the departure of the ships bearing the protest of Columbus against any infringements of his privileges, dignities, and jurisdiction by the Spanish sovereigns, four suspicious-looking vessels had been seen to enter the little harbor of Jacquemel, on the western coast of Hispaniola. It soon transpired that the commander of this fleet was no other than Alonzo de Ojeda, who, as we have seen, distinguished himself in the service of

Columbus, and had received great favors and distinctions from him, now seduced from his loyalty by the patronage and temptations of Fonseca, and actually bearing a commission in direct violation of the rights and concessions made to Columbus by Ferdinand and Isabella in the most solemn manner. Ojeda had already visited the coast of Paria and the Gulf of Pearls; he had sailed through the Gulf of Paria, the Dragon's Mouth, coasted along the Cape de la Vera, visited the island of Margarita, discovered the Gulf of Venezuela, and had landed on the Caribbean Island, carrying off pearls and gold from Paria and Indians captured in battle from the Caribs, whom he intended to sell as slaves in the Spanish markets. Being in want of provisions, the fleet sailed for Hispaniola, after having made the most extensive voyage of discovery at that time accomplished in the Western Hemisphere.

There was another distinguishing feature in this expedition, for besides many prominent and skilled pilots, navigators, and adventurers on board the ships of Ojeda, there was among them the man who afterward gave his name to the American Continent, a merchant of Florence, skilled in geography and navigation, Americus Vespucius. Although Ojeda had received from the lifelong enemy of Columbus and of all great American discoverers and explorers, Bishop Fonseca, a commission granting him the privilege of making such a voyage to the new world, he was in fact nothing more than a freebooter and a pirate. Fonseca had treacherously furnished him with copies of the admiral's charts and papers, a license signed by himself alone, and so craftily worded as to allow his visiting any of the lands discovered by Columbus subsequent to 1495, thus including in his license the newly discovered regions of Paria. Ojeda was also bolstered up with information imparted to him by Fonseca as to the admiral's present embarrassments, the jealousy of the king, and the confidently expected downfall of the admiral.

Unfortunately for the latter, his stout and vigorous brother, Don Bartholomew, had departed from San Domingo with all the forces available for the distant regions of Ciguay, for the purpose of quelling a threatened revolt of the natives, for the Adelantado would have been the most trusty and the ablest leader to send to meet Ojeda. Though it was a risky measure, he now selected Roldan himself for this delicate and important task, trusting to his interests and his ambition, as well as to his love of renown, as incentives to his fidelity. His boldness, ability, and experience were well known. By reason of his large estates on the island he had become interested in the maintenance of peace and the security of property.

Roldan readily undertook the work so generously assigned to him by the admiral. The encounter between two such reckless men as Roldan and Ojeda was characteristic and interesting. Embarking in two caravels with the forces placed at his disposal by Columbus, and arriving on September 29th within two leagues of the harbor of Jacquemel, he landed at the head of twenty-five picked, experienced, and well-armed soldiers, and after a reconnoissance, and ascertaining that Ojeda with only fifteen men was on the land several leagues distant from his ship in an Indian village, making cassava bread, he threw himself between Ojeda and his ships, expecting to surprise him. But Ojeda had word of the approach from Indians, with whom the name of Roldan was opprobrious, and with his characteristic boldness and strategy, seeing his retreat to the ships intercepted, he suddenly presented himself face to face to Roldan, attended by only half a dozen of his men. Roldan adroitly opened the conversation by alluding to general subjects, and gradually brought the interview to an inquiry as to Ojeda's motives in landing thus on a remote part of the island and without giving notice to the admiral of his arrival. Ojeda, with equal coolness, replied that he had been on a voyage of discovery, and had been forced to put in at Jacquemel for want of provisions and for ship repairs. Roldan then demanded to see the commission under which he sailed, whereupon Ojeda calmly replied that his commission was on his ship, and on Roldan's accompanying him to the ships he showed him his license, with Fonseca's signature thereto. Roldan met on Ojeda's ships a number of persons whom he knew, and these also confirmed Ojeda's account of his voyage, as each one had some articles taken from the places they had visited. Ojeda gave Roldan his assurance that he would sail to San Domingo and report to the admiral. The baffled Roldan returned to his ships and sailed to San Domingo.

Although Ojeda had far exceeded his license in his voyage, he knew he could rely upon Bishop Fonseca's hatred for Columbus to secure an easy endorsement of his course. In fact, he had fitted out the expedition at his own expense, and the crown was to receive a fixed share of the profits. Isabella was then in such poor health that she was unable to give any attention to these or other public affairs ; but the wily and selfish Ferdinand, ever suspicious and unsympathetic with the admiral, either knew and favored this unlawful voyage, or connived at it. In itself the expedition possessed a practical and geographical importance, and many skilful men were members of it. Confident of his strength at home, and seeing now a field opening before him for his reckless and daring enterprise, he deceived Roldan with a false promise, which he never intended to keep, and then sailed to Xaragua, where he landed in February, 1500, and accepted the leadership of the rebels, a position which these miscreants had thought Roldan had basely deserted. Ojeda had now a cause to champion and defend ; he was to right the wrongs of these his fellow-subjects, and to strike down the despotism of Columbus, whom the rebels accused of every form of tyranny and injustice, even the non-payment of their dues.

Emboldened by his accession of strength, and announcing that he was chosen to advise or rather to watch the admiral, and that the loyal Carvajal was united with him in this trust, encouraged by the growing unpopularity of Columbus, sustained by the chicanery of Fonseca and by the jealousy of Ferdinand, Ojeda not only raised his standard against the admiral, but with his characteristic recklessness he proposed to march at once on San Domingo and compel the admiral to pay the men at once, or to expel him from Hispaniola. The proposal to march on San Domingo led to opposition from the timid, while it was received with applause by the reckless. A clash of strength and of arms among the rebels now took place, resulting in bloodshed and several deaths ; but the more desperate and brutal party triumphed. On to San Domingo was now the battle cry of the rebels.

Cognizant of the desperate character of Ojeda and of his treasonable acts at the head of the new rebellion at Xaragua, Columbus sent Roldan, who had proved faithful, at least as long as it was his interest to do so, to his new responsibilities, to watch the rebels and check them. On his way to Xaragua Roldan secured the union of the men then with Diego de Escobar, his former confederate, with his own, and marched toward the rebel camp. He narrowly escaped assassination by his former followers, now disgusted by his loyalty. Ojeda, in the face of such a force brought against him, now for the first time in his chivalrous career avoided his foe, and prudently retired to his ships. Roldan and Ojeda, each conscious of the other's skill at strategy or open war, tested each other's adroitness at deception as well as in manœuvres. Ojeda declined to treat with his wily adversary, messengers passed between them, and some became prisoners in the effort to open negotiations, and were held as hostages. When Ojeda sailed twelve leagues to the province of Cahay, to get provisions by plundering the natives, Roldan followed and forced him to his ships. A strategy of Roldan gained him an advantage over Ojeda, each trying to outwit the other, and Ojeda lost his small boat and its crew, several of whom were wounded and the others taken prisoners by Roldan. This last incident led to a parley on the water between these two cunning men, each in his own small boat, and after much adroit negotiation terms were agreed upon : the captured boat was restored to Ojeda, the hostages and prisoners were exchanged. Ojeda agreed to sail from the island, and while sailing out threatened to return again with a more powerful fleet and army. Hearing that he had again landed at a distant part of the island, Roldan again pursued Ojeda, when the latter finally sailed out to sea, and Hispaniola was freed from his dangerous machinations. It is related, however, that this unprincipled freebooter afterward landed either in some part of Hispaniola or perhaps at Porto Rico, where he ruthlessly seized large gangs of the unhappy natives and carried them to Cadiz, where he sold them as slaves.*

To have won Roldan over to the support of his administration and to the defence of law and order was a master-stroke of policy on the part of the admiral. In fact, but for the fidelity of Roldan and the success of his efforts it seems almost certain that the admiral would have wholly succumbed under his unparalleled trials and misfortunes. The present services of Roldan, rendered probably from interested motives, would go far to atone for his former atrocities and treasons.

---

* Las Casas, " Hist. Ind.," lib. i., cap. clxix. ; Fernando Columbus, " His^r. del Almirante," cap. lxxxiv. ; Irving's "Columbus," vol. ii., pp. 224-29 ; Dr. Barry's translation of De Lorgues' "Columbus," p. 401 *et seq.*; Brownson's translation of Tarducci's " Life of Columbus," vol. ii., pp. 154-58.

Just as the dawn began to appear to the troubled vision of the admiral, another storm burst with violence on the horizon of his saddened fortunes, in the unlooked-for conspiracy of Guevara and Moxica. Roldan's followers in the late struggle with Ojeda, being in a great measure his former confederates in rebellion, looked from the beginning for generous rewards for their services, and the time had now arrived for them to demand, as they clamorously did, for a division among themselves of the lands in the fertile and beautiful province of Cahay. Roldan was now a man of law and order, and rather than yield as he formerly did to such demands, he gave them lands of his own in the province of Xaragua. Though he requested permission to return to San Domingo, he readily yielded obedience to the admiral's request that he would remain in Xaragua to meet Ojeda in case of his return to the island.

Among the recent comers to Xaragua was Don Hernando de Guevara, a young nobleman as noted for his unbridled passions and manners as for his depravity and dissoluteness; and for the latter qualities he had been banished by the admiral from the island. He was a cousin of Adrian de Moxica, one of Roldan's late principal supporters in rebellion. On his arriving too late to embark on one of Ojeda's ships, Roldan had given him permission to remain in Cahay, a favorite spot with the idle and dissolute, and in consequence of Roldan's kind reception of him he had been received as a visitor at the house of Anacaona, the sister of the cacique Behechio, who commanded the respect even of the most degraded Spaniards, and who, in spite of the misconduct and self-degradation of the Spaniards, still entertained a friendship for the Spanish conquerors. The visits of Guevara to her house led to a mutual attachment between him and her young and beautiful daughter, Higuenamota. The young Spaniard had chosen Cahay as his residence because of its proximity to the neighboring province of Xaragua, the residence of his lover, and there also his Cousin Moxica had an estate, where he was training dogs and hawks for hunting. Roldan discovered the cause of Guevara's sojourn here, and, as some supposed, moved by jealousy and his own affection for the Indian beauty, he ordered the young hidalgo to depart from Xaragua to his post at Cahay. Seeking the girl in marriage, favored by the mother, and having had his intended bride baptized a Christian,

Guevara disregarded the orders of Roldan, and lingered on in the house of Anacaona in Xaragua. Upon further remonstrance and peremptory orders from Roldan, and while protesting the most honorable intentions and his design to enter into lawful wedlock, he obeyed and left Xaragua, and retired to Cahay. Three days of absence from his Indian *fiancée* was too much for Guevara. He returned to Xaragua, and with several of his friends was concealed in the house of Anacaona, but on discovery was again ordered by Roldan to depart. The young cavalier now assumed a tone of defiance and threats, but finding this did not move the stern Alcalde Mayor, he resorted to the most piteous entreaties, and thus won the desired permission to remain in Xaragua for the time.

Crossed in his love, and probably himself suspecting the motives of Roldan to be those of a disappointed rival, Guevara laid plans for revenge, made up a band of partisans from Roldan's late fellow-rebels, now his bitter haters, and their plan was to take him by surprise and suddenly kill him or put out his eyes. Roldan got word of the plot and acted with characteristic vigor and promptness by seizing Guevara in Anacaona's house in the presence of the expectant bride, arresting seven of his accomplices, and sending an account of the affair to the admiral, for he now professed to act in all things only by the admiral's orders. The latter ordered all the prisoners to be sent to the fortress of San Domingo.

The unfortunate island of Hispaniola was again fired with excitement and racked with Spanish sedition. Moxica, Requelme, and other former rebels and companions of Roldan, united in the most vehement appeals to all the rebellious elements of the island, to band together to avenge the wrongs of the gallant Guevara and of the beautiful Higuenamota. As if by magic a rebel battalion was formed, horses, weapons, ammunition, and all the means of war were soon brought together, and now nothing less than the rescue of Guevara and the deaths of Roldan and Columbus were proclaimed. The latter, trusting to the men to whom he had forgiven so much and upon whom he had bestowed such princely favors, would have fallen an easy victim to their rage but for a timely word of warning brought by a deserter from the conspirators, who seemed upon the eve of carrying out their plans, even to the seizure of the government, the assas-

sination of Columbus, and the usurpation of the chief command
in lieu of the murdered admiral. Both Columbus and Roldan
acted with extreme rapidity and rigor, for unless all were saved
at once, all would be lost. While Mr. Irving states that it was
the admiral who in person struck the blow, De Lorgues and
Tarducci relate it as having been accomplished in person by
Roldan. Taking the account of the two latter, it is related that
the ever-vigilant Roldan, taking with him a chosen and well-
armed few—seven of his own domestics and two soldiers—fell
upon the unwary conspirators suddenly at night, and captured
them all by a single stroke. On receiving Roldan's report of
the capture and a request for instructions, the admiral answered
in characteristic terms: "I had determined to hurt no one, but
his [Moxica's] ingratitude compelled me to alter this resolve;
nor would I act otherwise with my own brother if he wanted to
assassinate me and usurp the lordship which my king and queen
had given into my custody." Roldan was instructed to proceed
with rigor against these outlaws, and to enforce the law, which
he did without delay. Moxica and some of his ringleaders were
condemned to death, some were banished, and the others were
sentenced to imprisonment. Of Roldan, Tarducci remarks that
his proceedings were conducted "with the inflexible vigor of
justice peculiar to all knaves like him, after escaping from the
penalty their own crimes deserved, and putting on the garb of
an honest man;" and the Count de Lorgues states that he acted
in all things with "deference for the least desires of the viceroy."
His method of proceeding to execute the sentence, however,
was Roldan's, not the admiral's; for the latter was never deaf
to the voice of mercy, even when dealing with the most hardened
criminals.

When Moxica saw the scaffold erected on the fort for his execution he abandoned his ruffianism and bravado, lost all courage,
and was seized with pitiable fear. But with the deceitfulness of
his true self he sent for a confessor, and by designedly prolong-
ing his confession, or, as De Lorgues says, by repulsing his confessor, he lengthened his respite in hopes that his sympathizers
might rescue him. He even descended to the cowardly device
of accusing others. Finally, Roldan, incensed at his cowardice
and exasperated at his chicanery, cut short his confession, and
had him hung from the battlements of the fort. De Lorgues

states that he "ordered the wretch to be flung from the top of the fortress into the fosse." Guevara was detained as a prisoner for some time, but was sent on June 15th to the admiral at Fort Conception. While the execution of the others was delayed, the sentences pronounced were mostly executed with rigor, and the conspirators still at large were followed up by Roldan, who is said to have carried a priest with him to confess the criminals before death, and that they were executed on the very spot where they were caught. This account is supposed to have been exaggerated by Roldan's enemies, for the tower contained at one time seventeen awaiting trial, while the agents of the law were pursuing the others with unrelenting severity. The details of the execution of the sentences are not given, except in the case of Moxica; but De Lorgues states that the sentences were carried into effect by the united and vigorous action of Columbus and the then righteous Alcalde Mayor. It is said of the admiral by Mr. Irving, "We cannot wonder that he should at last let fall the sword of justice which he had hitherto held suspended." *

Order and peace now reigned temporarily in the island of Hispaniola, but it was the work of fire and sword, of the scaffold and the tower. The measures of the admiral had proved effectual, even at the gloomiest moment of his life, for the crushing out of a series of rebellions as wicked and lawless as anything related in history. Of Roldan it must be said that he proved himself now the most efficient and willing instrument of justice. The faction which had so long defied all law and justice; had despoiled and wronged the natives; had made a pandemonium of what had but lately been seen by the new-comers as an earthly paradise; had nearly crushed the first advances of civilization and Christianity in the new world; had nearly accomplished the destruction of the discoverer of the Western Hemisphere, and ruined his great enterprise, was now effectually broken, under

---

* See Herrera, who, however, attributes erroneously to the admiral the more prominent part taken by Roldan in these transactions; Fernando Columbus, "Hist. del Almirante," cap. 84. In his letter to the governess of Prince Juan, the admiral himself says: "The Alcalde seized him, [Moxica] and a part of his band, and the fact is, he did justice on them without my having ordered it." Brownson's translation of Tarducci's "Columbus," vol. ii., pp. 158-64; Irving's "Columbus," vol. ii., pp. 230-38; Barry's translation of De Lorgues' "Life of Columbus," p. 404.

the vigorous administration of Columbus. Results now began to bear their fruits. The Spanish power and the authority of the admiral were now universally recognized and obeyed. The Indians, whose outbreaks had been instigated by the basest of the white men, now became docile and submissive, gave evidences of their capacity to receive civilization by pursuing the peaceful labors of agriculture, by wearing clothes to cover their nakedness, and by willingly assisting the Spaniards in the cultivation of the soil and other industries.

During this scathing ordeal of adversity, disaster, danger, and humiliation Columbus passed through one of those mental and moral crises which, while exhibiting the weakness of a noble and brave nature, proves the faith of the man in God, and brings to light the profound religious caste of the admiral's character. In December, when his fortunes were at their lowest ebb, distrustful of the fidelity of Roldan, in whom he was compelled to trust, and consequently in whose power he was, harassed by the general prevalence of disloyalty and treason among his own colonists, alarmed at the descent of Ojeda upon Hispaniola and his union with Roldan's former confederates, constantly disturbed by reports of Indian insurrections, and in daily apprehension of assassination; when he felt that he was abandoned by fortune, alone in a wilderness, aged, infirm, and deserted by men, he sank beneath the load of his misfortunes. He could not even turn to his own sovereigns, whom he had so nobly served and honored, for Isabella was sinking in health, and Ferdinand had been cold, distrustful, and now almost malevolent, even in the midst of his chilling politeness; nor could he turn to his adopted country, for his enemies had covered his name with opprobrium and dishonor; nor could he find solace in even seeking protection with those poor Indians whom his enemies had exasperated against him and made his enemies, and who, scandalized by the vices of the Christians, had turned away from the religion which might have saved them. In his despondency this strong man sank down with a mortal fear—he seemed for the moment to loathe mankind. The instinct of self-preservation, induced by the constant fear of assassination, took possession of his mind; the brave man, who had faced every danger on land and sea, now became overcome with fear. He resolved to fly from men, to cast himself with his brothers into a caravel, and to take refuge on the ocean which he loved, from his enemies who so hated him. It is not related that any definite plan or place of destination had taken shape in his mind. It would seem that he thought only of casting himself into the arms of Providence.

The profoundly religious character of Columbus, in this perilous crisis of his life, was his only source of reviving hope, and restored his confidence. He related in his own fervid words this singular incident in his life, and in this, as in other similar and remarkable occurrences, he regarded his mental and moral resurrection as a miracle. In his letter to the governess of Prince Juan he writes: "On Christmas Day (1499), being in utter anguish from the torments caused me by the wicked Christians and the Indians, and on the point of abandoning everything to save my life, if possible, God our Lord comforted me by saying miraculously, 'Take courage, yield not to sadness or fear; I will care for everything. The seven years of the term of gold are not yet expired, and for that and all else I am able to provide.' . . . That same day I learned there were eighty leagues of the soil in which gold mines were found at every step, so that they seemed to form a single mine." After again repeating the account of his extreme dejection and miraculous relief, he explains or relates the vow he had taken, that on discovering the new world he would, within seven years, from the profits and revenues of his discoveries, fit out fifty thousand infantry and five thousand cavalry for the deliverance of the Holy Sepulchre, and the same number within the next five years. This explains the term "the seven years of the term of gold." He now, at this critical moment, also received confirmation of the trustworthiness of Roldan, and heard of the discovery of the new gold mines. Followed as these good tidings were by the favorable reports of peace and good order prevailing throughout the island, this devout Christian began to reprove himself for doubting for a moment that Providence would take care of him, even by a miracle. In the midst of his joy he felt remorse at his doubts, and he relates that he heard a voice within him saying, "O man of little faith, take heart; what dost thou fear when I am with thee!" *

---

* Fernando Columbus, "Hist. del Almirante," cap. lxxxvi.; letter to the governess of Prince Juan; Dr. Barry's translation of De Lorgues' "Columbus," p. 401; Irving's

Little did the man then anticipate that his joy would be soon followed by the most severe trials, humiliations, and wrongs of his checkered and eventful life.

While all the disloyal, turbulent, criminal, and rebellious elements in Hispaniola were struggling to overthrow his authority, to wrest the first American colonial establishment from his hands, and to destroy even his life, the envious elements in official and private life in Spain were banded together in an effort to blacken his reputation, to discredit his achievements and enterprises, to undervalue his services, and to multiply accusations against him. His enemies played upon the king's needs and his avarice by representing the admiral's accounts of the wealth of the new countries as exaggerated and false. Every vessel that returned from the newly discovered "Ophir of Solomon" brought fresh demands for money, provisions, and outfits of every kind, instead of being freighted with gold, merchandise, precious stones, and spices. The admiral and his brothers were represented as unused to govern others or administer affairs, were upstart foreigners, now elated with power and fortune. They were accused of being disloyal, and even the report was circulated that the admiral and his brothers were looking around for some powerful nation or prince as an ally, intending to discard the Spanish sovereigns and the Spanish nation, and proclaim the admiral to be the independent sovereign, in his own right, of the countries he had discovered. The charges of cruelty to the natives, of arrogance toward the Spaniards, and incompetency to rule were apparently confirmed by the distorted and prejudiced accounts of the disappointed, sick, or criminal colonists returning by every ship, and by the letters received from the same classes remaining in Hispaniola. These unfortunate creatures, who had returned to Spain bearing the curse of their own crimes, passions, and lawlessness, were encouraged by persons in higher positions and in official stations to flock to Granada, to besiege the king with their lamentations whenever he appeared in public, and even to invade the halls of the Alhambra with accusations against the admiral. They petitioned the king to pay them their just dues, withheld, as they said, by Columbus.

"Columbus," vol. ii., p. 237; Brownson's translation of Tarducci's "Life of Columbus," vol. ii., pp. 150, 151.

A band of fifty of these malcontents made their way into the inner court of the palace, and crowding under the royal apartments piteously held up in their hands bunches of grapes as the only food left to men who had crossed the ocean and returned in the service of the crown. The criminal and vicious of the population, and the worst of the late rebels under Roldan and Ojeda, were the most clamorous. Even the sons of Columbus, pages at court, as they passed one day out of the palace were followed with jeers and imprecations, and the mob greeted their ears with the exclamation: " Look at those whelps, the sons of the admiral, of him who discovered the land of vanity and delusion, the grave of Spanish gentlemen!"

It was in vain that Columbus wrote by each returning ship true and detailed accounts of the affairs of Hispaniola. In vain his frank and energetic letters traced the causes of disorder, misfortune, and distress to their true sources, the very vices, misconduct, and crimes of these miscreants now playing the *rôle* of his victims. In vain the defender of Spanish dominion in the new world pointed out the true evils existing in Hispaniola, and lucidly suggested the remedies. His letters arrived at long intervals, while his enemies were there on the spot, incessantly clamoring against him, and their ranks were constantly increasing by new arrivals of his enemies from Hispaniola. Ferdinand was only too much inclined to listen to such calumnies; for while his jealous nature failed to appreciate the great discovery, he regretted the bestowal of the title of viceroy upon Columbus, and never addressed or spoke of him otherwise than as admiral; he felt the pinching effects of the constant demands of the colony upon his exchequer, already depleted by his ambitious and selfish schemes, and did not conceal his disappointment at the small returns of gold from the new world. Nor could so skilful a dissimulator refrain from betraying his distrust, even his hostility to Columbus. The just and friendly mind of Isabella became influenced, in spite of her uprightness and generosity of character, unconsciously by the unceasing clamor and complaints against the true supporter of the honor of Spain. She never abandoned him or his cause, but she could not overcome the unfavorable influences of such universal discontents and accusations. How could so much be alleged, and by so many mouths, unless there was some foundation for it! She was as much distressed as she was disconcerted. Even the letters of Columbus himself drew a most lamentable picture of the condition of Hispaniola. Did not that of itself argue a want of success, if not a want of ability, for conducting its government and administration? The sight of the poor natives, men and women, children and young girls, some of the last the daughters of caciques, moved her noble heart to sympathy and indignation; and although these had been seduced away from their homes by the ruffians to whom Columbus was forced by prudence and necessity to give permission to return to Spain, others carried away clandestinely, and only a few had been given by him to those rebels under the terms of capitulation in order to secure peace to the distracted island, all were represented as gifts or transfers made by the admiral, and his conduct in this was colored with the most repulsive hues. And though his letters gave a true and quite different account of the affair, still the tale of betrayal, misery, suffering, and love of lost homes was too much for the tender heart of Isabella. Her noblest feelings were moved when she learned that some of these innocent and injured victims of remorseless passions and cruelty were pregnant, and others bearing newly born infants in their arms, and she indignantly and sorrowfully exclaimed, " What power has the admiral to give away my vassals?" This generous queen and noble woman instantly commanded all the poor Indians to be returned to their country and homes, both those recently as well as those formerly sent from the islands to Spain. The real enslavers of the Indians seemed not only to escape, but even to carry their measures. Fortune seemed to favor them and to frown upon Columbus. At this critical juncture, as we have seen already that tribute and labor as a measure of State policy and necessity, sanctioned by the sentiments and customs of the age and country, had been adopted in Hispaniola, so now unfortunately a letter was received from him recommending the continuance of Indian bondage for some time to come as promotive of the development of the colony. This letter, taken in conjunction with the instances of enslavement before her eyes, decided the indignant queen to unite in decreeing and carrying out the measures which the king and the enemies of the admiral were now designing. At this juncture in the sad career of the discoverer there were not wanting enemies in the higher and more enlightened walks of life to aid and abet in this unworthy warfare the malice of rebels, murderers, seducers, and conspirators. Shameful it is that history is obliged to record among these enemies and revilers of Columbus two persons whose influence should have been thrown on the side of truth, justice, and mercy, such men as Father Boïl and Bishop Fonseca. They certainly did not thus serve the good Master whose mission they professed to execute. Among all historians, whether lay or ecclesiastic, there is not a voice raised except in their condemnation.

There is no one of the distinguished characters who figured prominently in the discovery of America that had a more brilliant opportunity of inscribing his name and his fame on the choicest pages of history than King Ferdinand. But he faltered and failed, abandoned, and then betrayed the most illustrious personage in this great drama. Columbus and Isabella will ever receive the applause of the world and of posterity, but the default of Ferdinand has broken up an illustrious triumvirate. There are two peerless characters in this great event : Columbus, the discoverer, and Isabella, his generous patroness ; but others participated in their glory in various degrees.

King Ferdinand from the beginning acted from avaricious, selfish, jealous, and distrustful motives in these great events. If in the beginning he seemed to act like a prince, it was only the reflected royalty and generosity of Isabella. Columbus essayed the discovery of a new world, the redemption of the Holy Land, and the erection of a new Christendom. He stands forth an exalted character ; his misfortunes add grandeur to his career and win the sympathies of the world.

Failing to realize a replenished exchequer from the new world immediately, the selfish and crafty king resolved early in the spring of 1499 upon a measure of gross injustice to Columbus. It involved nothing less than the appointment of a commissioner to proceed to the viceregal domain, to investigate its condition and the administration of Columbus, to decide upon the most urgent matters, and to refer the rest to the crown. The commissioner appointed was Don Francisco de Bobadilla, an officer of the king's household and a commander of the noble and illustrious religious and military Order of Calatrava. The first commission, dated March 21st, 1499, was evidently aimed at the rebels, and while it empowered another to deal summarily with them, instead of strengthening the hands of the admiral for that purpose, it did not in effect otherwise vary from the repeated requests of the admiral himself for the appointment of such a commissioner to assist him in restoring peace and order in Hispaniola, especially the request he made in his letter of October 18th, 1498. His position and authority were in this letter, however, expressly recognized by the authority given by it to the commissioner, in case of necessity, to invoke the aid of the admiral and all others exercising authority on the island. Had the desired relief been extended to the admiral when he requested it, in the fall of 1498, there would have been no necessity for further measures, for he then requested the recall of Roldan to Europe to be judged by their Majesties.

The current of slander and injustice had now set in against Columbus with malignant and insatiable force. The measure adopted in the commission of March 21st, 1499, might have relieved the island and its viceroy, but the appointment of Bobadilla, whose subsequent unprovoked injustice and malice against Columbus showed how the enemies of the latter had triumphed in securing the selection of one of his bitterest though, perhaps, secret enemies. Not satisfied with this advantage gained, the admiral's enemies followed up their conspiracy with such persistent skill as finally to secure to their measures the approval of the noble and magnanimous queen.

The increase of the admiral's unpopularity may be measured by the steady progress of the injustice of the royal measures adopted against him. The sovereigns were next induced to issue another and broader commission to Bobadilla, dated May 21st, 1499, which is addressed to the counsellors, judges, magistrates, cavaliers, gentlemen, officers, and inhabitants of the colony, in which Bobadilla's appointment as Governor-General of the Indies is announced, and in which the admiral and viceroy is not even mentioned. Bobadilla is now expressly invested with full civil and criminal jurisdiction, and all cavaliers and other persons now in the islands discovered by Columbus, or arriving thereafter, were commanded to quit them if Bobadilla should deem it necessary for the benefit of the royal service, and not to return to them, but to repair to Spain; and for these purposes all necessary powers were conferred on him, and all were ordered to obey his orders on the spot, without recourse to the sovereigns and without appeal, under such penalties as Bobadilla himself might think proper to impose. So general were these powers and instructions, that they plainly placed Columbus himself and his brothers in the power of Bobadilla. Another letter of the same date commands Columbus and his brothers to surrender the forts, vessels, magazines, arms, ammunition, and everything belonging to the king into the hands of Bobadilla as governor, under the same penalties as were denounced against all such as refuse to comply with similar orders. In this letter Columbus was designated as admiral of the ocean. A fourth letter was signed only five days later, on May 26th, which was addressed to the admiral himself, and by that title only, announcing the appointment of Bobadilla, and commanding full faith and obedience to be accorded to him.

The first letter, being directed only against the rebels, apparently did not satisfy the enemies of Columbus, whose efforts were aimed directly at him. But they argued with the queen, whose reluctance to proceed against the admiral was manifest—why send out Bobadilla powerless in case his investigations prove the admiral to be the wrongdoer? Why in such case should he not be provided with ample authority to proceed against the real delinquent at once, rather than paralyze his work by suspending all proceedings until he could return to Spain, make his report to the sovereigns, and then, perhaps, when it was too late, send out another mandate to bring the admiral to justice? If the admiral should prove to be innocent, then the two letters of May 21st would be of no use, and it was consequently understood that in such case they should not be produced or made public. Specious as this argument was, it succeeded with the queen, though it is quite evident by this arrangement Columbus and his brothers were placed within the discretionary power of Bobadilla, for he was empowered to decide who was to blame. He could readily decide that Columbus was the one at fault, with the foregone conclusion that he would be proceeded against immediately. What could have been more unjust than the entrustment of such a discretion over any man in the hands of his enemy? It would be a temptation to any ambitious man, though not an enemy already.

So reluctant was the queen to proceed against one whom she so highly honored and esteemed, that these measures remained suspended long after they had assumed a definite shape. In the autumn of 1499 the returning rebels arrived in Spain, and in the fact that they brought with them slaves assigned to them by Columbus was the final argument and cogent reason which his enemies were anxiously awaiting, and which they promptly and eagerly used with success. The poor unfortunate Indian girls, whose sad condition touched the hearts of the good queen and her subjects, were not in fact assigned to these miscreants by the admiral, but had been seized or seduced by the rebels in their lawless marches through Hispaniola. But the contrary was industriously made to appear to the queen, and her generous nature was aroused by the charge that such wrongs were perpetrated under her reign. There was scarcely a voice raised on the side of truth and justice. Guided by her womanly sentiments and queenly indignation, she immediately commanded that all who had received slaves from the admiral should deliver them up, to be returned to their country and their families, under the penalty of death ; but she excepted from this decree all such Indians as had been previously brought from Hispaniola, alleging as the ground of this exception that it was known that these had been taken as prisoners in a just war. Alas ! how far short of perfection or complete justice do the most exalted of human actions fall ! Prisoners in a just war ! On which side does justice cling in a war waged on the one side by the invaders of the peaceful country and homes of an inoffensive portion of mankind, children of one common Father, and waged on the other in defence of country, home, family, property, wife, children, and of every natural right ? Has man no inherent rights, in a state of nature, which civilized man is bound to respect ? Again, why should the admiral, whose heart was as tender to the Indians as Queen Isabella's, and who had given a new world with all its inhabitants to Spain, be condemned without a hearing ? No wonder that Bobadilla, whose character and acts do not rise above those of Roldan and Ojeda, of Margarite and his confederates, of Boil and Fonseca, should have felt and seen that the cause of Columbus was prejudged, and that he had nothing in his meditated action more congenial to himself or more loudly demanded than to capture his victim and load him with every wrong and injustice !

The execution of these harsh measures against Columbus was

delayed for a year. Probably the reluctance of Isabella may have added to this delay; but it is manifest that this delay greatly added to the rigor and injustice of the intended blow. Heretofore the admiral had found in the noble and magnanimous queen an unfailing friend, a just and upright sovereign, a sympathizing patroness, and a bulwark of strength against all his enemies. When this support and consolation failed him, truly his cause was desperate, and well might he have felt a fear of the race, and have cast himself upon the ocean in despair. What must have been the poison instilled into her heart and mind on her visit to Seville, where Fonseca and his minions gained her over to the cause of the admiral's enemies! From the time of this visit Columbus had lost favor with this noble queen. Not only are his demands refused, and those even by which he requested that his eldest son, Don Diego, might be sent to him, but her signature was given to those unjust and ungrateful decrees which clouded his approach to the grave with sorrow and ingratitude.

Bobadilla's commission having been made out and delivered to him, with all the solemnity of so important a royal act, he thenceforth only delayed his departure in waiting for a favorable season for the voyage. He sailed from Spain for San Domingo about the middle of July, 1500, with two caravels, and he carried with him a military guard of twenty-five men, who had been enlisted for this purpose for a year. To this singular expedition was added a body of six missionaries or friars sent out in special charge of the Indians then returned to Hispaniola, and to labor for the conversion of the natives. As if to stamp the royal credence on the charge that Columbus had not paid the men enlisted in the royal service, without regard to the truth or justice of the act, a decree was handed to Bobadilla authorizing him to ascertain and discharge all arrears due by the crown, and to compel the admiral to pay whatever he might personally owe, in order that, as the decree alleged, "each one should receive whatever was due him, and there should be no more complaints." But the sovereigns made themselves responsible for all the acts of oppression and injustice their commissioner might commit, by confiding to him several letters in blank, bearing the royal signatures, in order that, filling them up with his own orders, he might accomplish all things necessary for his mission.

Whatever limits might have been placed on Bobadilla's powers by the commission, this license to use the royal signatures for his purposes placed every person in Hispaniola under the arbitrary will of this prejudiced, incompetent, and unworthy official. To his enmity for Columbus was added that bane of small minds and souls, the intoxication of authority.*

The two caravels, with Bobadilla and his attendants and soldiers on board, arrived on August 23, 1500, before the harbor of San Domingo. Don Diego, the admiral's brother, was then in command at that city, while the admiral was at Fort Conception, enlarging its works and regulating the affairs of the Vega, where the Indian population was most numerous. Don Bartholomew Columbus was then in Xaragua, engaged with Roldan in following up and enforcing the sentences pronounced against the fugitive rebels. Don Diego sent a boat to the vessels, which he supposed were sent out with supplies and to bring out the admiral's eldest son, Don Diego; but Bobadilla in person answered the inquiries thus made, announcing himself as in command of the ships, and informed the men in the boat of the non-arrival in the ship of Don Diego Columbus, the admiral's son. Eager to commence his bad work, he obtained from the messenger information of the recent insurrection of Moxica, his dread punishment, the execution of seven other rebels the same week, the present confinement of five others in the fort at San Domingo awaiting execution, including Pedro Requelme and Fernando de Guevara, who had been so prominent in the recent troubles; and he further ascertained that the admiral was in the Vega, Don Bartholomew in Xaragua, and Don Diego was acting governor at San Domingo. The news of the arrival of a royal commissioner created great excitement on shore, and awakened varied sentiments among the inhabitants, according to their respective relations to the authorities; but the most joyous and clamorous at the arrival of Bobadilla were those who claimed that the admiral

---

* Fernando Columbus, "Hist. del Almirante," cap. lxxxv.; Muñoz, "Hist. Nuevo Mundo," unpublished portion quoted by Mr. Irving; Las Casas, lib. i., cap. clxxix.; Oviedo, "Cronico," lib. iii., cap. vi.; Herrera, decad. i., lib. iv., cap. vii.; Girolamo Benzoni, "Storia del Nuevo Mundo," lib. i.; Navarrete, "Col. Doc. Dipl.," No. cxxvii., cxxviii.; Irving's "Columbus," vol. iii., pp. 239–47; Brownson's translation of Tarducci's "Life of Columbus," vol. iii., pp. 164–72; Dr. Barry's translation of De Lorgues' "Columbus," pp. 406, 407.

had not paid their dues. On entering the harbor, the first sight that met Bobadilla's eager eyes were the bodies of two of the late rebels hanging from the gallows. Many eager self-seekers and enemies of Columbus hastened out to the ships to greet the new commissioner and make interest with the rising powers. Remaining all day on his ships, he lent a willing ear to the tales of his numerous visitors, who were the most unworthy members of the community, and whose conduct still exposed them to the criminal law for their misdeeds. In fact, Bobadilla was already, and even before landing and taking possession of his office, conducting an *ex parte* trial of the admiral in his absence, and none but his enemies, criminals before the law, were his informants. Before the landing of the commissioner his victim was already condemned.

On the following day Bobadilla landed, with his attendants and followers, proceeded to the church, where he heard mass, and then, in front of the church, in the presence of the assembled crowd, which included Don Diego, Rodrigo Perez, and many principal officials of the island, he ordered to be read his letter of March 21st, giving him full authority over the rebels and their cases; thereupon he unceremoniously demanded of Don Diego and the alcaldes the surrender to him of Requelme, Guevara, and all the other rebels, together with the depositions taken in their cases, and publicly summoned before him their accusers and all who had participated in their arrest and prosecution. The mild but firm Don Diego declined, in the absence of the admiral, to accede to his demands, relying upon the titles and jurisdiction of the admiral and viceroy as superior to those of the commissioner, and demanded a copy of the royal letter for the admiral. Bobadilla insultingly refused this request, threatening all who refused obedience to him as commissioner with his powers as governor, and he asserted his power over the admiral himself.

On the following morning Bobadilla, after again hearing mass —such men are apt to affect great piety and religion—again appeared before the assembled population, which was only too anxious to catch the first intimation of the movements of this formidable personage. Having first taken an official oath he caused the second royal patent to be read—that which invested him with the government of the islands and even of Terra Firma, discovered by Columbus, and of which he was appointed viceroy, not by mere free selection, but by a solemn convention, based on mutual considerations. He demanded the obedience of Don Diego Columbus, Rodrigo Perez, and all the assembled subjects of the crown. He again demanded the delivery of the prisoners to him. The officials and citizens thus addressed, while deferentially protesting their respect for the letters of the sovereigns, firmly but respectfully asserted that the detention of the prisoners was by orders of the admiral and viceroy, who held under a solemn convention with the crown royal patents, titles, and jurisdictions of a superior character. Incensed at this refusal, and humbled by the evident impression it made on the assembly and the doubt it cast upon his authority, he now produced and had read his third royal mandate, by which Columbus and his brothers were ordered to deliver up to him all the fortresses, ships, and royal property of every kind, and still further, to ingratiate himself with the people, he produced and had read the remaining order of. May 30th, by which the admiral was ordered to pay all dues unpaid to persons in the service of the crown, as well as all to whom he was personally indebted. The shouts of the rabble now proved that Bobadilla had gained their sympathies. A second demand for the prisoners having met with the same response, he proceeded to the fort, where he demanded the prisoners of the commandant, Miguel Diaz, the same that had discovered the rich mines of Hayna, accompanying his demand with threats to use force in obtaining them unless they were surrendered. The commandant of the fort excused himself under plea of having received his orders from the superior authority of the admiral and viceroy, and parleyed with Bobadilla in order to gain time, for the fortress was a mere shell, destitute of any garrison, and occupied solely by the commandant, Miguel Diaz, and Don Diego de Alvarado. Bobadilla now assembled together his military guard, the sailors, and others he had brought from Spain, and the rabble whom he had won over to his side; and having approached cautiously and on several sides, he assailed the undefended fortress with quixotic valor and fury. The conquest was an easy one even for Bobadilla, as no defence was or could be made. On reaching the battlements he found there only Diaz and Alvarado with drawn swords, but offering no resistance to the motley rabble. The new commissioner took possession of the fortress with mock triumph and ceremony, and having had the prisoners brought up before him, and having gone through the empty ceremony of asking them a few questions, he gave them in charge of Juan de Espinosa, the alguacil. The official, Bobadilla, then seized the admiral's house and made it his own residence, plundering it completely, and taking possession of all the admiral's property and effects therein, including his arms, furniture, pearls, gold, plate, jewels, horses, together with even his private letters, manuscripts, and his most secret confidential papers. Among the properties seized were the admiral's mineralogical collection, curiosities, rare shells, his vegetable collection, and his religious memorials. Even the documents necessary for his defence were seized and many of them suppressed. He took no account of his seizures, but proceeded summarily to confiscate everything to the crown, and denounced the admiral in terms of condemnation, alleging that he would send him in chains to Spain, and obliterate his jurisdictions and viceroyalty, his name and his lineage. No blundering tyrant could have proceeded in greater defiance of his instructions, or have done more to invalidate his own proceedings; for his subsequent royal patents were only to be produced or used in case his first proceedings against the rebels proved ineffectual. He proceeded at once to execute the most remote, alternative and conditional powers, and this he did primarily and abruptly against the admiral. He thus proclaimed his true character— that of an outlaw. The admiral was condemned, and, in fact, sentenced to chains, imprisonment, transportation, and confiscation before he was seen or summoned, and before he was accused, heard, or defended, and in his absence—before even he had been made aware of the existence or powers of his judge or of the court. In his letter to the governess of Prince Juan, the admiral thus wrote of Bobadilla's plundering his house: "A corsair could have done no worse with a merchantman; but what grieved me most of all was the loss of my papers, of none of which I have been able to recover possession, and the most necessary for my exculpation are precisely those he has kept the best concealed." *

---

* Las Casas, "Hist. Ind.," lib. i., cap. clxxix.; Fernando Colombo, "Hist. del Almirante," cap. lxxxv.; Herrera, decad. i., lib. iv., cap. xiii.; Irving's "Columbus," vol. ii., pp. 248-54; Dr. Barry's translation of De Lorgues' "Columbus," pp. 408-10; Brownson's translation of Tarducci's "Life of Columbus," vol. ii., p. 172-77.

That such an outlaw should have been a member of the household of the King of Spain, that he should have been a commander of the once honorable and noble military and religious Order of Calatrava—an order created to celebrate the heroic capture of the city of Calatrava from the Moors—are facts which argue most unfavorably for the atmosphere of palaces and the discipline and honor of high-sounding orders. That he should have been appointed thus to such an office was a true index to the character of King Ferdinand. Among the plunder seized in the house of the admiral were those fine specimens of virgin gold, as large as a hen's egg, which he had so carefully preserved for presentation to the sovereigns, as the means both of verifying his statements and of sustaining the prosecution of his grand enterprise. Bobadilla did not think of the honesty which necessitated a measuring or weighing of the captured gold; and in order to prevent the good impressions these large samples of gold would make upon the minds of the king and queen, he paid them out at once among the people. Coveting the support and applause of the low and sordid, he proclaimed an unrestricted license to all to collect gold for twenty years, and reduced the royal quota of the gold from a third to an eleventh. Thus he effectually turned Hispaniola over to robbers and outlaws for plunder and disorder. How shameful it is that the grandest of human enterprises are clouded with such crimes and outrages!

Columbus had seen such outlaws as Roldan and Ojeda plunder the island and its natives; he had more recently heard of a squadron under Vicente Yañez Pinzon touching at the coasts, and rumors of other lawless adventurers licensed by King Ferdinand, or at least connived at by him, in the neighborhood had reached him. When he heard of Bobadilla's high-handed proceedings he thought he recognized in them the excesses of such or similar ruffians. It never occurred to him that this was a member of King Ferdinand's household, a commander of the Order of Calatrava, a new governor of Hispaniola, holding a commission signed by such illustrious sovereigns. Puzzled at the outrages and successes imputed by rumor to Bobadilla, he cautiously proceeded from Conception to Bonao, in order to be nearer to the scene and obtain more prompt information of the usurpation and proceedings of this intruder, for so far he had not received the courtesy of a letter, a message, or even a summons. He wrote, however, to Bobadilla in conciliatory terms, welcomed him to Hispaniola, cautioned him against such rash measures as the general license to collect gold, and announced his own intention of returning to Spain, leaving Bobadilla in possession of the government. He received no answer to his letter. But scarcely had he arrived at this place when an alcalde, bearing the staff and insignia of office, arrived, proclaimed the appointment of Bobadilla as governor, and bearing copies of his royal commissions. Conscious of his own innocence, relying upon the transcendent services he had rendered to the crown, and trusting to the honor of the sovereigns, to whom his relations were defined by solemn and mutual compact, he still thought that Bobadilla was merely a chief justice sent out to re-establish order and enforce the laws. He shaped his action for gaining time, in the hope that his vindication might come; and in order to lessen the damage arising from Bobadilla's license for hunting gold, he publicly and privately, by word and writing, denied his authority to issue such licenses, and appealed to his own higher powers granted by the sovereigns.

But now the truth rudely and cruelly burst upon the admiral. On September 7th there arrived at Bonao the royal treasurer, Francisco Velasquez, and a Franciscan monk, Juan de Trasierra, bringing with them the royal letter of May 26th, addressed to the admiral, announcing Bobadilla's appointment and commanding his obedience to him; and at the same time they served upon him a summons from Bobadilla to appear before him. The royal treasurer and the Franciscan monk informed the admiral of all that Bobadilla had done at San Domingo. The admiral could not believe that his sovereigns had been or could be capable of perpetrating such a wrong upon one who had contributed its greatest glory and renown to their illustrious reign; for what were then, what now are the conquest of Granada and the now broken empire secured to their grandson, Charles V., to the discovery of the new world! When the admiral saw the terse letter of the sovereigns, bearing their signatures, so familiar to him for better and nobler purposes, and countersigned by the secretary, Miguel Perez d'Almanza, the admiral bowed his head in submission to his sovereigns and in shame for them, not for himself. "The sovereigns broke the conventions made with him," says the Count de Lorgues, "violated their word, and disposed of privileges and offices which belonged to him and his descendants. They condemned him without a trial, or giving him an opportunity of justifying himself. At first, on thinking of this iniquity, which would have subverted the reason of any other mortal, Columbus was overwhelmed with sorrow, and blushed with shame for the sovereigns. But if they stifled the sense of gratitude, forgot their promises, and falsified their words, the admiral respected his oath. He resolved not to fail in his obedience, and to give in a Christian manner the example of submission to even unjust authority." The letter of the sovereigns, so cruelly brief, was couched in the following terms:

"*To Don Christopher Columbus, Our Admiral of the Ocean Sea:*

"We have ordered the commander, Francisco Bobadilla, the bearer of this, to say some things to you on our part. We therefore pray you to give him faith and credence, *and to obey him.*"

Mankind are substantially the same in all ages and countries. It was rapidly circulated throughout Hispaniola that the admiral was in disgrace, and was to be sent back to Spain in chains—a felon's chains. The people, so lately accustomed to bow to him and to obey his words, now poured forth in haste to San Domingo to worship the new governor, and gain his favor. The most potent way of doing this was to slander and accuse the admiral; and as Bobadilla eagerly sought every means of sustaining his illegal and lawless seizure of the government, and his disregard of every public and private right, he invited every vilifier and libeller to his presence, and a huge record was made of the crimes and misdeeds of Columbus and his brothers.

Columbus, by his act of submission to his sovereigns, gave evidence of his personal elevation of soul; his conduct dwarfed the sovereigns themselves and all their false servitors, such as Bobadilla, Fonseca, and his countless enemies. Bowing his head before such an injustice, he started for San Domingo, unguarded and even unattended save by his few servants, and stripped of every insignia of authority and power. On horseback, and with the girdle of St. Francis around his waist, the condemned went to meet his fate. Bobadilla, with a mockery of official necessity, made great show of military force, pretending that Columbus and his brothers intended to raise an insurrection and march upon San Domingo at the head of an army of caciques and their vassals and subjects, to resist the orders of the sovereigns. Under this empty pretext he arrested the mild and gentle Don Diego Columbus, placed him in chains, and sent him a prisoner to one of the caravels. Although he came to San Domingo in the humblest garb and without an escort, Bobadilla immediately ordered Columbus to be seized, loaded with chains, and imprisoned in the fort. Such an outrage on such a person appalled even the worst enemies of the admiral, and there was no one so degraded as to be willing to place the irons upon him, when the odious task was performed by one of the admiral's own domestics, of whom the venerable Las Casas writes: "He was an impudent and shameless cook, that riveted the irons on his master's feet with the same alacrity and readiness as if he were serving him some savory dish. I knew the wretch, and think his name was Espinosa."

"This outrage on a man so venerable and of such eminent merit seemed atrocious even to his enemies," writes the learned and just Tarducci. The Count de Lorgues also writes: "It was between prayer, the poetry of the Psalms, and the contemplation of nature in these equinoctial regions that the disciple of the Cross, fully resigning himself to the divine will, came humbly to his enemy." And our own Irving, with noble sympathy, penned these eloquent and indignant words: "Columbus conducted himself with characteristic magnanimity under the injuries heaped upon him. There is a noble scorn which swells and supports the heart and silences the tongue of the truly great when enduring the insults of the unworthy. Columbus could not stoop to deprecate the arrogance of a weak and violent man like Bobadilla. He looked beyond this shallow agent and all his petty tyranny to the sovereigns who had employed him. Thus injustice or ingratitude alone could wound his spirit; and he felt assured that when the truth came to be known, they would blush to find how greatly they had wronged him. With this proud assurance he bore all present indignities in silence." *

---

* Herrera, decad. i., lib. v., cap. ix.; Las Casas, "Hist. Ind.," lib. i., cap. 180; Oviedo, "Cronica," lib. iii., cap. vi.; the admiral's letter to the governess of Prince Juan; Fernando Columbus, "Hist. del Almirante," cap. lxxxvi.; Navarrete, "Col. Dipl. Doc.," cxxx.; Irving's "Columbus," vol. ii., pp. 255–62; Dr. Barry's translation of De Lorgues' "Life of Columbus," 408–12; Brownson's translation of Tarducci's "Life of Columbus," vol. ii., pp. 172–80.

The contrast between a great man and a despicable one was now constantly presented. With the populace at his back, and with Columbus and his brother Don Diego in prison and in chains, Bobadilla felt solicitous to get Don Bartholomew also in his power; but he feared him as a ruffian fears a brave man. He shrank from meeting him face to face, and even from sending him orders to repair to San Domingo. He knew the robust and generous nature of the Adelantado, his indomitable courage, his indignation at knavery, his resentment at outrage of every kind, his affection for his brother. He feared that when he heard of the indignities and cruelties inflicted upon the admiral and Don Diego, that the brave Adelantado might, at the head of his forces, march upon San Domingo and punish the official outlaw as he had merited. Bobadilla had the meanness to resort to the admiral and request him to write to Don Bartholomew to instruct him to repair peacefully to the city, and to refrain from executing or exasperating any of his prisoners. The admiral had the magnanimity to comply with his request through the desire to save the island from civil war, through respect for the letters of his sovereigns, and in the full confidence that these insults and wrongs would be redressed on his return to Spain and making known the truth. On receiving his brother's letter the Adelantado immediately laid down his command and proceeded peacefully to San Domingo. Here he was also arrested by Bobadilla, placed in chains, and imprisoned on board the other caravel. The three imprisoned brothers were never visited by Bobadilla, nor allowed to see other visitors or each other; they were not allowed to communicate with each other. While they were imprisoned and undergoing a mock trial with a foregone condemnation, they were never informed of the charges against them, nor confronted with their accusers, nor allowed to defend themselves. The Count de Lorgues, rather sympathetically than historically, thus describes the treatment endured by the admiral in prison: "Columbus had on only the light coat he had on at the time of his arrest, and which he used to wear in the heat of the day. Bobadilla had seized on all his other clothing, even his *sayo*, or surtout. On the stone floor of his dungeon, with the pains of his rheumatism and the twinges of his gout, he had to suffer cruelly from cold during the nights, for he was almost naked—*desnudo en cuerpo*. His fare was composed of the most wretched stuff."

Having secured his prisoners, Bobadilla then commenced the inquiry into the late troubles, which he was sent out primarily to make, and which he now made his last work instead of his first; and then, too, not with the object of proceeding against the rebels, but rather of using the rebels against Columbus and his brothers. Everything was now reversed. Requelme, Guevara, and their late associates in rebellion were set at liberty, while the admiral and his brothers were in prison and in chains. The accused now became accusers, and the rightful accusers were condemned without a hearing. The judge now made common cause with rebels, outlaws, criminals, and vagabonds of every description. San Domingo became the rendezvous of all the scoundrels of Hispaniola, and they were invited to become the accusers, the slanderers, and the libellers of their late governor. Every offence taken by these outlaws at the administration of justice in their regard now became a crime of the admiral, and it was he and not the rebels that was under investigation. Some accused him of insulting the honor of Castile by compelling Castilian gentlemen to work; others, of appropriating the pearls of Paria to his private use, and concealing the discovery of that country in order that he might first enrich himself; others, of imposing oppressive labor, restricted and insufficient food, tyrannical conduct, and cruel punishments on the Spaniards, while he waged cruel and unjust wars against the natives; and he was now even charged with treason, levying war against the Spanish sovereigns, and meditating an alliance and union with some other nation. Not one of these charges had the slightest basis of truth; but to the religious and devout nature of Columbus, the most offensive of all these odious and false accusations was that based upon his religiously and conscientiously having objected to the baptism and reception into the Church of adult Indians before they had been duly and sufficiently instructed in the faith. Upon this meritorious conduct he was accused of having prevented the conversion of the Indians, that he might reap profit by their enslavement and sale in the slave-marts of Spain. Another charge was so contrived as to appeal to the national pride and prejudices of the Spanish nation and crown: his persecution and punishment of the late rebels were cited as acts of cruelty and revenge on the part of a foreigner, and as betraying a secret hatred of Spaniards.

Bobadilla had a harvest of crime on the part of Columbus already sowed and ripened for his gathering. He was only too ready to condemn Columbus for every crime and offence that the malice of his enemies or the revenge of the offenders whom he had punished could make up against him. The rebels, now recognized as loyal and orderly subjects of the crown, were Bobadilla's friends, intimates, and favored colleagues in the preconcerted ruin of Columbus. A mock trial, and in many cases not even the forms of a trial, were sufficient to acquit and liberate the criminals and rebels of the island, and any injury done to the admiral merited rewards and honors at his hands. He took the criminal classes of Hispaniola into his confidence and favor. San Domingo became the rendezvous of criminals and miscreants. Men of truth, loyalty, and honor were silenced and intimidated. All these elements demanded the condemnation of Columbus. All kinds of lampoons, satires, scurrilous songs, libels, and slang resounded through the city, in the public places, and even under the very windows of the prison in which the admiral was incarcerated. Curses on the head of the admiral and praises of Bobadilla were the sounds prevailing in the common atmosphere of the city he had founded. The admiral wrote, " There was made against me a judicial inquiry into misdeeds the like of which was never invented in hell." Little did these unbridled conspirators, headed by Bobadilla and assisted by Roldan, Boïl, and Fonseca, calculate on the danger they ran, from the excess of their malignity, of proving the innocence of their victim.

With an accumulated mass of testimony, too voluminous to be true or consistent, Bobadilla rested, assured of his victim; he resolved to send Columbus and his brothers to Spain in chains, on board the caravels now nearly ready for sailing; and he would send private letters of his own urging his condemnation in Spain as he had been condemned and punished in Hispaniola, insisting upon his guilt, and pressing for his permanent removal from his offices and commands. He felt assured that he had secured thereby his own retention in office and in power. The admiral himself said : " I was never able to speak with Bobadilla, and no one was permitted to address me a word ; and I take my oath that I cannot imagine why I am held a prisoner." And again : " I was arrested conjointly with my two brothers, confined in the hold of a vessel, loaded with chains, nearly naked, subjected to the most infamous treatment, without undergoing interrogatories or sentence." While Roldan, Guevara, Requelme, and their associates were held up as models, loaded with honors, favors, and privileges, in spite of their crimes, Columbus was arrested, condemned, and loaded with chains in spite of his innocence and his services. It is not strange, when Columbus realized the lawless and brutal conduct of Bobadilla, that he felt his life was in danger. The caravels being now ready for sea, Bobadilla, hoping to ensure no leniency for his prisoners and to gain favor with Fonseca, appointed to command the returning vessels Alonzo de Villejo, who was a *protégé* of Fonseca's uncle in Spain, and while in the employment of Fonseca had been sent out in the service of Bobadilla. Bobadilla, a knight, a gentleman by birth and education, a commander of an honorable order, a member of the king's household, now became the degraded instrument of Fonseca, whom all describe as an unworthy bishop and unfaithful subject of the crown. It was generally believed and currently reported that Bobadilla's violent conduct, cruel treatment and injustice toward Columbus were instigated and protected by Fonseca. His selection of Villejo, and his ordering that officer on arriving at Cadiz to deliver Columbus and his brothers into the hands of Fonseca, his worst enemy, are facts going far to prove that Bobadilla and Fonseca were directly and understandingly allied together in the conspiracy to ruin and disgrace Spain's distinguished adopted citizen. Villejo, however, when tested, was less brutal than his employers.

When Villejo approached the admiral to carry him to the ship, he saw this fallen and devoted man bowed down under the weight of his chains and of his wrongs. Despairing of justice and of his life, and sorrowing over the ingratitude of his sovereigns; grieving over the afflictions and disasters now in store for his sons, who could no longer expect to remain as pages of the Prince Don Juan, or to inherit his own titles, offices, and estates, he was truly a man of afflictions. Immured in a secluded and silent prison, the clangor of arms and the tramp of soldiers startled the admiral from his sad reverie; and when he saw Villejo at the head of the soldiers he felt that his end was at hand. In anguish he asked, "Villejo, whither are you taking me?" "To the ship, my lord, on which we are to embark," respectfully answered the young officer. "To embark!" cried the admiral. "Villejo, is what you tell me the real truth?" "On my honor, my lord, it is the truth." Las Casas has recorded this colloquy, having, no doubt, obtained it from Villejo himself, with whom he was well acquainted, and of whom he said : " Alonzo de Villejo was a hidalgo of honorable character, and my particular friend." His humane treatment of Columbus showed him to have been worthy of a better service.

Of the sailing of the vessels with the admiral and viceroy of the Indies, the discoverer of the new world, a prisoner and in chains, Mr. Irving writes : " The caravels set sail early in October, bearing off Columbus shackled like the vilest of culprits, amid the scoffs and shouts of a miscreant rabble, who took a brutal joy in heaping insults on his venerable head, and sent curses after him from the shores of the island he had so recently added to the civilized world."* " The disciple of the gospel," writes characteristically the Count de Lorgues, " uttered no complaint. He remained silent, wishing to give an example of Christian submission to legitimate authority, even when it is deceived or abused." Mr. Prescott writes as follows of this shameless treatment of Columbus : " This excess of malice served, as usual, however, to defeat itself. So enormous an outrage shocked the minds of those most prejudiced against Columbus. All seemed to feel it as a national dishonor that such indignities should be heaped on the man who, whatever might be his indiscretions, had done so much for Spain and for the whole civilized world—a man who, in the honest language of an old writer, ' had he lived in the days of ancient Greece or Rome would have had statues raised and temples and divine honors dedicated to him as to a divinity.' " Mr. Hubert Howe Bancroft says he was " ever loyal, high-minded, and sincere. But were all the calumnies true, twice told, which vile, revengeful men had heaped upon him, he would not have merited the treatment that he now received at the hand of their Majesties' agent."

In the beginning of October, 1500, the two caravels commenced their homeward voyage to Spain—a voyage at which history blushes, humanity is shocked, and justice stands appalled. To

---

* Irving's "Columbus," vol. ii., p. 267; Dr. Barry's translation of De Lorgues' " Life of Columbus," p. 415 ; Prescott's " Ferdinand and Isabella," vol. ii., p. 473 ; H. H. Bancroft's " History of Central America," vol. i., p. 181.

the credit of the human race, however, it is to be related that scarcely had the ships sailed out of the harbor when Villejo and Andres Martin, the master of the ship, "another good and loyal Spaniard, who showed his horror of the unjust treatment the discoverer of the new world was subjected to," * came to the admiral, with every expression and demonstration of respect and reverence, and desired to remove his chains. "No," said Columbus; "I am grateful for your good-will; but I cannot consent to what you propose. Their Majesties have written to me to submit to everything Bobadilla might command me in their name; and it was in their name that he loaded me with these chains; and I will carry them until the king and queen give orders to take them off. And I will keep them in future as a monument of the recompense bestowed on my services." † Ferdinand Columbus, the admiral's second son and his historian, wrote afterward: "And I saw them afterward always in his chamber, and when he came to die, he wished them buried with him beside his bones." ‡

Although the weather was propitious, the voyage lasted little over a month, and the two high-minded officers, Villejo and Martin, did all in their power to soothe the outraged feelings of the admiral and to relieve his sufferings. The heart and mind of every noble and just man, even at this distant day, overlooking every minor detail, cannot but regard this voyage as one of the most unfortunate and discreditable events in history, the indignities heaped upon Columbus as humiliations to our civilization. The two caravels, with the illustrious prisoner on board the Gorda, arrived at the harbor of Cadiz on November 20th, 1500.

The sensation caused by the arrival of Columbus in chains at the port of Cadiz was intense—equal in degree to the sensations of joy and triumph caused by his return with exultation from his first voyage, the discoverer of a new world, but different in kind: it was a feeling of indignation, of sorrow, of shame, of sympathy, of reparation. Whatever may have been his faults or even his crimes—for he had been accused of almost every crime

---

* Brownson's translation of Tarducci's "Columbus," vol. ii., p. 186.
† Las Casas, "Hist. Ind.," lib. i., cap. clxxx.; Brownson's translation of Tarducci's "Columbus," vol. ii., p. 186.
‡ "Hist. del Almirante," cap. lxxxvi.

—nothing could justify in the estimation of public opinion such indignities, such wrongs to so illustrious and meritorious a personage. From Cadiz and Seville the thrill of indignation swept over Spain, and from Spain it reached and was re-echoed throughout Europe. His enemies had overdone their cruel and unjust work. Had their victim been guilty, it would have been unnecessary to resort to such excesses. Those very excesses of his enemies showed that they constituted a preconcerted conspiracy to condemn an innocent man. How could any one man have been guilty of so many and such heinous crimes! A lifetime does not suffice to accomplish so much infamy. The very rabble that so lately condemned him, without hearing him, now turned all their sympathies on the side of the illustrious victim. No government, not even the cold and selfish court of Ferdinand, could withstand such a reaction. The queen was indignant, sorrowed, and incensed. The impulses of the government, if impulse were possible with so calculating and selfish a man as Ferdinand, were swayed by the irresistible current of public sentiment. The generous heart of the queen inspired the nation with a profound sympathy for Columbus. The court was then sitting at Granada, and from the halls of the Alhambra the wail of sorrow, the stern voice of indignation, the overpowering current of sympathy went forth to meet the same sentiments surging forth from all Spain, and to greet the illustrious prisoner of the Gorda. Instinctive justice had already acquitted him of every accusation so maliciously made against him. Columbus was then, as in 1493, the idol of the hour.

During the voyage Columbus had written a letter to a noble and generous-hearted lady at the court, Donna Juana de la Torre, formerly the governess of Prince Juan, from which we have already derived and quoted many of our statements, and which was a detailed and spontaneous outpouring of the sentiments and sufferings of a magnanimous but wounded heart. While it detailed the history of the case, the events of his administration, its vindication, the cruelties, assumptions, and injustice of Bobadilla, it also gave expression to the anguish of his soul, the sufferings he had endured in the name of his sovereigns, and in return for the unparalleled services he had rendered. This admirable and remarkable epistle was a faithful and unerring mirror of a suffering soul, a word picture of his indignation and of his loyalty; and though, in the agitation of the moment, it may appear in parts to be somewhat confused and disarranged, it is the more valuable on that account, as containing intrinsic proofs of its truth and honesty. The recipient of this letter, being a favorite of the queen and a member of her household, and possessing a just and generous soul, was not slow in placing it in the hands of Isabella, and thus the king also read the story of a great man's wrongs. This letter the admiral was permitted by Andres Martin, the captain of the Gorda, to send off at once to the court by secret express. Copious extracts have been made by the biographers of the admiral from this interesting letter. We shall confine ourselves to a few leading sentences, and first of all we will give the opening sentence: "Although it is not usual for me to complain of the world, it is none the less true that its practice of ill-treating me is very ancient; it has attacked me in a thousand combats, and I have always resisted until the present moment, when arms and counsel have been unable to aid me, and it has thrown me to the bottom in an extremely cruel manner."

His hopeful trust in Heaven is thus expressed in this letter: "Hope in Him who created us sustains me; His help has been ever at hand. On another occasion, not long ago, being still more cast down, extending His divine hand, He raised me up and said to me, 'Man of little faith, be comforted; what fearest thou, when I am with thee?'"

The following passage relates to the Spanish sovereigns: "I was led to serve those princes by the strongest attachment, and have rendered them unheard-of services. God made me the messenger of the new sky and the new earth. . . . Every one was incredulous; but God gave my lady the queen the spirit of understanding, and bestowed on her the necessary courage, and endowed her, as a beloved daughter, with the inheritance of this new world. . . . And now I have reached the point that from the most exalted to the vilest of living men there is none but seeks to revile me; but the day will come when, thanks be to God, this will be told to the world, and my traducers will be held in detestation. If I had pillaged the Indies and given them to the Moors, I should not have been more hated in Spain." Further extracts from this important document will prove interesting, as giving expression in his own words against the injustice he received from the world.

"They have tried to give me so bad a name, that if I build churches and hospitals, they will call them dens of robbers.

"I could very well have prevented all that I have related that befell me since I came to the Indies, if I had attended solely to my personal interest, if that would have been becoming; but I am undone because I have always maintained justice and enlarged their Highnesses' dominions.

"Intrigues and calumny have done me more harm than all my labors have benefited me, as an example for the present and for future generations!"

He then mentions the manner in which Bobadilla had manufactured worthless and perjured testimony against him, and expresses his willingness to have had a just and honorable man sent out to investigate his administration, whereas Bobadilla was an implacable enemy. He indignantly refutes the trumped-up charge of his entertaining a design of giving over the Indies to some other nation; he speaks of the unfairness of judging him in his new and unprecedented position by the same standards that would be applicable to ordinary governors in old and settled countries, and speaks of his dominion in a newly discovered heathen and savage land without cities or treaties, and of his having changed the fortunes of Spain from one of poverty to that of "the richest empire in the world." He declares his purpose of proceeding anew in the track of his first voyage, or of what he had written of going to Arabia Felix as far as Mecca and thence to the North Pole, and concludes with the following warning sentence: "God, our Lord, retains His wisdom and power, and punishes ingratitude in a special manner."

It is generally regarded as an effect of the general public sentiment now turned in favor of Columbus, that led Ferdinand to unite with the queen in making it known that Bobadilla had not only exceeded but had disobeyed his instructions, and that they had now disavowed his cruelties to the admiral. Having read the latter's letter to Donna Juana de la Torre, they did not wait for the arrival of Bobadilla's dispatches, but sent immediately and commanded the distinguished prisoners, Columbus and his brothers, to be set free, and all deference extended to them. They also addressed a personal letter to the admiral, full of sympathy and affection for him, expressing their indignation at the indignities and cruelties inflicted upon him, inviting him to court,

and sending him two thousand ducats to enable him to maintain
the dignity and style suited to his rank when he appeared at
court. On December 20th he presented himself before the sovereigns at Granada in the brilliant and courtly dress of his exalted station, and accompanied by his brothers and a retinue corresponding to his dignities and offices. Received by the king
and queen with unbounded sympathy and honor, the queen
moved to tears at the sight of him, the admiral was overwhelmed
with his own feelings and sank upon his knees, bathed in tears
and unable to utter a word. Raised up from the ground by his
sovereigns, and reassured by their kindness and generosity,
Columbus made an eloquent, unanswerable, and convincing defence of his conduct and administration—a vindication which
brought forth the most earnest assurances of indemnification for
his wrongs, and restoration of his rights, privileges, and powers.
A few days later he had a private interview with the queen, at
which both shed copious tears, and at which he received from
this noble lady assurances which soothed his wounded heart and
went far to restore his hopeful spirits. Though greatly relieved in his mind by the earnest and ample assurances of the
sovereigns, Columbus knew well the necessity for securing his
rights by some official and written acts. Hence he addressed a
petition to the council a few days later, in which he recounted
the history of his relations with Spain and its rulers, of his compact with the sovereigns, of his great discoveries and achievements, of his administration, and of the injustice, ingratitude,
and indignities received from Bobadilla. He appealed to
the members of the council for the just performance of the
royal agreements with him. He reminded the council of his
having, after long delays in Spain, given the sovereigns the
preference in the offer of the discovery and conquest of the
Indies over other nations, just at the time when Portugal, France,
and England had become desirous of securing him to their service and of realizing the glories then possessed solely by Spain;
and then with fervent piety he says: " Then our Saviour ordained the route for me. I have placed under the power of their
Highnesses lands larger than Africa and Europe. There is
reason to hope that the Holy Church will prosper wonderfully
by it. In seven years I have, by the divine will, accomplished
this conquest. At the moment that I hoped to obtain recom-

penses and repose, I was suddenly seized and put in irons, to the detriment of my honor, and the service of their Highnesses."

It would seem scarcely necessary to defend Columbus against the charges made against him by Bobadilla and his minions. The haste, the animosity, the indecent turmoil and disorder, used and availed of by his enemies to suborn witnesses of no respectability or character ; the degraded type of the witnesses whose depositions were taken, their criminality, their hostility to Columbus on account of the stern justice he or his brothers were compelled to administer toward them ; the intrigues and conspiracies against him by officials in Spain co-operating with rebels and criminals in Hispaniola ; the prejudices which were fomented against him, and the shallow and reckless character and conduct of Bobadilla—all united in depriving his accusers and their accusations of every vestige of force or respectability. Some historians have thought that the fact of his not having been immediately returned to Hispaniola as viceroy, and with the full restoration of his rights, dignities, and powers, was evidence of his incapacity for the government and administration of the colonies he had founded, and that he was so regarded by the Spanish sovereigns ; but there are other explanations of this fact which are indisputable. While the Spanish sovereigns annulled the acts of Bobadilla, the administrative regulations of Columbus were re-enacted and again put in force even under Bobadilla's successor. They became the accepted policy of the Spanish rule in Hispaniola. It is also a significant fact that both of the admiral's immediate successors, with the power and support of the Spanish sovereigns at their backs, signally failed in their administrations, and the condition of affairs under them became worse than before. It was a marvel of success that Columbus, with his own Spanish colonists and soldiers in rebellion against his authority, instead of receiving their needed support, and with the native tribes incited by the Spaniards themselves to repeated outbreaks and revolts, and without ships or soldiers worthy of the name, yet by his prudent action maintained to the last the integrity of the Spanish Empire in the new world. Wise and necessary concessions proved the safety of the empire.

While the complaints made by Bobadilla and his confederates

were almost countless, they may be substantially classified, as the learned Tarducci has stated, under three principal heads: " 1. Inflexible harshness and cruelty ; 2. Attempts on the freedom of the Indians ; and 3. Want of administrative knowledge and capacity." * While the great majority of historians have acquitted him of all these accusations, there seems to be a tendency on the part of a few more modern authors, such as Prescott and Hubert Howe Bancroft, perhaps following some of those who in the lifetime of Ferdinand and Charles V. thought they could only defend the conduct of the king by accusing Columbus, to give some justification to the charge of incapacity for governmental administration. Still later Justin Winsor revives the charge, but does not strengthen it. But a careful study of the case must convince all just and discreet judges that in this very particular the career of Columbus stands forth as pre-eminently wise and prudent, even though the overpowering opposition against him deprived his administration of the success it so well merited. To have saved the first European colony in America, while all was done both in Europe and America to destroy it, was a triumph of Columbus's administration.

In regard to the first charge of excessive cruelty, it may be said that the facts here show results strongly in favor of and utterly vindicating the admiral. Gentleness and kindness were among the most marked features of his character. The measures of compelling the cavaliers to labor on the public works and to accept restricted allowances of food were so necessary for the preservation of their own health and lives, as well as those of the colonists in general, and so indispensable for the prevention of want and famine in the colony, that they became measures of mercy rather than of cruelty. Of their justice who can doubt, when it is considered how, in the face of common dangers, all men become equal, and the values of human life and health cannot be measured by the standards of rank or station? Privileges to a few, when all were equally menaced, would have been signal cruelties to all. Even apart from the general sufferings and dangers from the diseases of the climate and the want of food, the condition of the first colony of civilization, cast amid a savage race in a state of nature, would not permit of the

---

* Mr. Brownson's translation of Tarducci's " Life of Columbus," vol. ii., p. 198.

social and official distinctions of old, civilized communities. An infant cannot endure the advanced and artificial condition and treatment of manhood. It need only be added that Columbus, when privations were to be endured, was the first to set the example of endurance. Was it a degradation of his rank as admiral and viceroy that he kept the watches of the night on ship-board when he discovered the first land of the new world?

Other specifications under the charge of cruelty related to his treatment of Bernal Diaz, the instructions he sent to Pedro Margarite, and the execution of Adrian Moxica. To be sent to Spain for trial, as was the rebel Diaz, was surely mild treatment toward a Spaniard guilty not only of treason against the new colony and his sovereigns, but of treason against civilization itself. The execution of Moxica was the act of Roldan, not of Columbus; but what less punishment could have reached the case of a miscreant waging open war in a distant Spanish colony upon his associates, his sovereigns, and his country? The decree of death against Indians guilty of theft was but the fulfilment of the law of the Indian race itself, for it was with death they punished that crime. The very exigencies of the situation in Hispaniola demanded it, since stealing from the Spaniards had then become the prevailing occupation of the Indians. Bartholomew Columbus is universally recognized as a just man, but he was stern and inflexible in administering justice. While the admiral was unjustly censured for many of the severe acts of the Adelantado, it is no disparagement to the character of the latter to say that the admiral was characteristically mild, gentle, and even lenient compared to his stern but honest brother, the faithful, just, and honest Adelantado.

While, under the second charge of enslaving the Indians, we do not purpose defending the acts of Columbus in sending Indians as slaves to Spain upon the intrinsic merits of these acts, we know and must maintain that this was not the crime of Columbus, but that of the age and people with whom he was identified, and for whom he acted. Columbus never owned any Indian slaves himself, and while his accusers and his enemies were cruelly and unjustly seizing and enslaving Indians on their own private accounts, he was eminently known for his noble stand taken for restricting Indian slavery to such only as were taken prisoners in war or convicted of some grave crime. The slaves he sent to Spain were the property of the crown, and not his own. While he and his sons and brothers possessed no slaves, which they could have readily acquired without limit, as others were doing, his arch-enemy in Spain, Fonseca himself, was the owner of two hundred human victims of slavery. One of his bitterest enemies, Ojeda, sold in the slave markets of Spain droves of Indian slaves, whom he had ruthlessly seized in his ferocious raids. Christian and civilized nations at that time generally, if not universally, practised the nefarious custom of reducing infidels to slavery, and Spain was conspicuous in this cruel policy; for during the Moorish war thousands of Mohammedans were forced into slavery, and from a single city as many as eleven thousand men, women, and children were led into slavery. Of all the Spaniards of any note engaged in the conquest of Hispaniola, few were without their slaves, and even Isabella was a participator in human slavery; for, as Tarducci states, " only five months before Christopher Columbus landed a prisoner in Spain, the queen signed at Seville a contract with the navigator, Rodrigo de Bastides, by which she reserved to herself the fourth part of the slaves he might capture on the voyage he was going to undertake for further discoveries in the new world;"* and on October 30th, 1503, she authorized the Spanish discoverers to make slaves of all the cannibals they might seize in the Caribbean Islands, with the view of their subsequent conversion; and yet Isabella personally was an opponent of human slavery. Columbus actually prevented more Indians from being enslaved than he was instrumental in enslaving, under the policy and custom of the country and the age which he represented, and for whose faults he is charged. The names of Las Casas, Isabella, and Columbus, notwithstanding the toleration of slavery by their age and country, are distinguished as friends of the Indians, advocates of their liberty, and enemies of human slavery.

It has been asserted that Columbus opposed the conversion of the Indians to Christianity—a charge based upon his just and conscientious opposition to the baptism of certain Indians. This accusation is refuted by the fact that his opposition in this case

---

* Mr. Brownson's translation of Tarducci's " Life of Columbus," vol. ii., p. 201.

was grounded on the circumstance that the Indians themselves had received no instruction in the faith, were not prepared to receive the sacrament understandingly and with due reverence, and were liable again, consequently, to relapse into barbarism and paganism. While some of the missionaries were imprudently and over-zealously receiving such converts on their first and unstable request, Columbus, through a well-guided zeal for religion, on the contrary, opposed these wholesale, indiscriminate, and premature conversions. "His manner of treating the Indians," says Tarducci, "was always paternal. He recognized in the children of the forests his brethren in Jesus Christ. He loved them because he had discovered them in order to bring them under the sweet yoke of the gospel." *

While it has been charged that Columbus was the founder of the unjust system of Spanish *repartimientos*, and even Prescott and Irving state that this virtual enslavement of the Indians originated in the measures of Columbus growing out of his treaties with Roldan and the rebels, still it is demonstrable that it was not Columbus, but Bobadilla, that introduced the *repartimientos* in Hispaniola and in America, and that this system was not originated by any measures of Columbus, did not legitimately flow from them, but were rather the abuse and perversion of them. The grant by Columbus to Roldan and the rebels of the privilege of receiving into their service, for the cultivation of their lands, certain Indians under assignment by their caciques, though a measure forced from him by the helpless condition in which he was placed, affected only the services of the Indians, not their persons. "What he did permit," says an intelligent writer, "was, first, the forced labor of prisoners of war; and, secondly, the commutation of tribute in gold or in produce into labor, to be furnished by the caciques, who were to order their subjects to help on the public works for one or two days in the week, while remaining all the time free subjects of their own native princes; to pay in labor, instead of the produce of labor, the taxes which these princes had a right to claim. The arrangement, as it was made and understood by Columbus, constituted no infringement of personal liberty. The *repartimientos*, on the other hand, were distributions of Indians simply

---

* Dr. Barry's translation of Count de Lorgues' "Life of Columbus," p. 422.

as Indians, without any pretence of either penal servitude or feudal service, and they were the invention not of Columbus, the accused, but of Bobadilla, the accuser." * Tarducci, after reviewing the whole subject with manifest learning and impartiality, concludes with saying: " His pretended attempts, therefore, on the freedom of the Indians, considering the times and the opinions and customs then in vogue regarding the enslavement of the Indians, amount to nothing." † ·

The third principal charge made by his enemies against Columbus, and one which, no doubt, made the most impression on the selfish mind of King Ferdinand, was that he possessed no capacity for administration or government. While this charge seems to be, in more recent times, espoused or at least countenanced by authors of standing and authority, my own investigation of the facts and circumstances has led me to the conviction, sustained by the most thorough students and investigators of the history of Columbus and his times, that it is as destitute of truth and justice as the others. The admiral himself, in his letter to the governess of Prince Juan, shows that the standard by which his administration was judged and condemned by his enemies, as well as by the court historians of his day, and by their followers in our day, was not a true or fair standard. The history of the world had never presented the case of a governor or viceroy placed in circumstances of so peculiar a character as those by which Columbus was surrounded in Hispaniola. Civilization and barbarism were suddenly brought face to face; the law of the case must necessarily be the will of the governor evoked in each case by its peculiar circumstances; and yet his accusers applied to him and judged him by the laws, customs, situation, and conditions then prevailing in old, peaceful, well-regulated countries. No one saw the difficulties of Columbus more clearly than he did, nor pointed them out as he did, nor with consummate wisdom, prudence, and ability suggested the remedies. He never concealed the disasters and evils of the case, but he indicated to his sovereigns, in repeated communications and in the most

---

* " Life of Columbus," by Rev. A. G. Knight, S. J., 186; Brownson's Tarducci, vol. ii., p. 203.

† Brownson's Tarducci, vol. ii., p. 203.

earnest and urgent manner, how, and how alone, they could be remedied. Had his recommendations been acceded to, had his constant demands been granted and failure had followed, even then the want of success could only have resulted from the opposition, conspiracies, rebellions, and crimes of the people and country he was called upon to govern. Spanish administration in America was thwarted and defeated by the Spaniards themselves in America. But his recommendations in every instance and in every extreme emergency were disregarded by the Spanish crown. At the very moment when his administration needed support, he was treated with vacillation, injustice, and desertion. If, instead of sending out a Bobadilla and a well-equipped fleet at his service, the crown had sent out the same ships, soldiers, and supplies to Columbus, and had sustained by all their power his administration, he, and he alone, could have averted the disasters and misfortunes which resulted from the administrations of his successors, Bobadilla and Ovando. It is difficult to say whether he displayed greater wisdom and prudence in the concessions he made on some occasions, or in the firmness and severity he exerted at others. That he succeeded in preserving even his own life, and in preventing absolute collapse of the Spanish dominion in the new world, in the extremities to which he was reduced, seems to me like the achievement of moral and physical courage, and the triumph of will blended with management over countless evils and implacable enemies. The vindication of Columbus is strengthened by the more signal failures of those who were sent, with every preparation and with unstinted means, to remedy the state of things he was accused of causing ; by the re-enactment by the government of the very rules and remedies which he had in vain endeavored to induce it to sustain in his case. A spirited paragraph from the work of Father Knight ably sums up the result of this accusation : " He has been accused of incapacity for government, but the proofs are not satisfactory. Success and failure are not infallible indications of virtue ; and if they were, Columbus might bear even the test, for, with the same unmanageable materials, his successors failed more fatally than he. Bobadilla was carrying all things to destruction when his short reign terminated. Ovando kept the Spaniards in some kind of order, but it was by ruthlessly sacrificing the Indians. He has been blamed for choosing bad officers, as, for example, Pedro Margarite and Roldan, betraying thereby ignorance of character. What, then, shall we say of Ferdinand and Isabella, who chose Aguado, Bobadilla, Ovando, Fonseca and Soria? Even the most imprudent of all his public acts—the transportation of criminals to the colony—had large excuse in the crying necessities of the occasion. Few men, indeed, perhaps only saints, have escaped like Columbus with unwounded conscience from such tumultuous scenes." *

The great enterprise of Columbus and his relations to the new world he had discovered were seriously affected by the action of the Spanish sovereigns, in authorizing various voyages of discovery to the regions embraced in that enterprise and protected as his exclusive right to him by his chartered conventions with them. This authorization, general in its extent as it was dishonest in its principles, was issued by proclamation in 1495, though, in consequence of the admiral's strong protests, not published till June 2d, 1497. The expedition of Ojeda, in 1499, was one of those unjustly authorized voyages. It has already been noticed in these pages. It was no better than authorized piracy both on the part of Ojeda and the crown. Soon afterward Pedro Alonzo Niño crossed the Atlantic, coasted along Cuba and Paria, and returned to Europe with immense stores of pearls and gold, obtained in exchange for European trifles. So also the Pinzons crossed the ocean in December, 1499; and the squadron under Vicente Yañez Pinzon was the first to cross the equator in the western part of the Atlantic Ocean, and having discovered a region extending from the Amazon to St. Augustin in Brazil, he received a commission to colonize and govern that vast territory. The voyage of Diego de Lepe, from Palos, resulted in the discovery of a larger portion of Brazil, while in October, 1500, Rodrigo Bastides sailed from Cadiz, and explored the coasts of Santa Maria and the Rio Grande. He was forced to make for Xaragua in consequence of the worm-eaten condition of his ships, marched overland to San Domingo, was arrested by Bobadilla, and finally reached Spain in poverty and despair. But maritime England had eclipsed these early voyages made mostly but not wholly by the companions of Columbus on his first voyage; for it was in

---

* "Life of Columbus," by Rev. Arthur George Knight, p. 187.

1494 that John and Sebastian Cabot planted the English flag on the soil of North America, which they had discovered. In the mean time, Portugal carried her flag around Africa to the East Indies, under Vasco de Gama; and without knowing of the discoveries of Lepe and Pinzon, Cabral again discovered Brazil for Portugal, which, as it was east of the altered line of demarcation and division between Spain and Portugal, became the permanent conquest of the latter. It is worthy of notice that while Columbus, seeking a northwest passage to Asia, discovered America, so also Cabral, seeking the East Indies, discovered Brazil. The map of the world was thus being drawn by heroic lines under the lead of one who in younger days had delineated its then limited and defined outlines on maps prepared by his own hand.

Ferdinand, ever wary and watchful, thought of counteracting the advances of other nations in the western continent by a grand scheme of imperial colonization and government, embracing local administrations in the various countries discovered and settled, with a central and superior seat of government at San Domingo. Columbus saw in this vast plan of empire the first step toward realizing the boundless value and importance of his discovery in fraud of his chartered privileges, and with that sagacity which distinguished him he demanded now, more than ever, the full restoration of his rights, privileges, and offices. To this act of justice he was entitled, because he had made the first and actual discovery, and all others had profited by his exploits, followed his courses, copied his charts, and used his information. But to the selfish mind of Ferdinand the whole matter resolved itself into the question, why bestow on the admiral, or upon any one subject, even though he had given a new world to Spain, at an immense cost of grants and prerogatives, what so many were now seeking permission to avail themselves of without expense to the crown? There can be but little doubt that Ferdinand determined to deprive Columbus and his descendants of all he had so nobly won. The temporary suspension of his concessions and offices by the appointment of Bobadilla afforded him the opportunity, and the numerous offers of experienced navigators to make voyages of discovery and colonization at their own expense presented to him the sordid motive. In fact, his wily nature had long ago shrunk from a just recognition of the services of Columbus. He now disguised his purpose, and under the pretext of acting for the benefit of the admiral, in waiting for the subsidence of disaffection in Hispaniola, and in simply postponing his return to his viceroyal government to a more propitious moment, after the lapse of only two years, the treacherous king appointed Don Nicholas de Ovando, a commander in the Order of Alcantara, as Governor of Hispaniola, to succeed the unworthy and incompetent Bobadilla, both unworthy substitutes for the rightful governor.

In the mean time, all public and private interests in Hispaniola had been hastened to ruin by the governor. Bobadilla had proved himself at once a weak and grasping man, seizing powers he was too feeble to hold, granting licenses he was unable to restrain, conceding to all rebels and criminals the lands he did not own, permitting unlimited working and robbing of the mines, and compelling the poor Indians to toil for gold to hand over to their cruel taskmasters. The only injunction he bestowed upon his followers was the characteristic yet unnecessary one : "Make the most of your time ; there is no knowing how long it will last." The condition of the Indians became most deplorable, and Isabella, who indignantly asked, "What power has the admiral to give away my vassals?" might now well have asked her new governor and his minions to desist from the cruel persecution and relentless destruction of her subjects. Indian slavery, under the official name of *repartimientos*, was permanently established by Bobadilla, and the poor natives were reduced to the condition of beasts of burden by their remorseless tyrants. Criminals from Castilian prisons now assumed the state and retinues of grand hidalgos, while the enslaved Indians, the real owners of the country and its gold, fell sinking to the ground in their service. Indian girls, daughters or relatives of the native chiefs, became at once their domestic servants and concubines, without limit of number or discrimination of condition. When these miscreants traveled, they were carried on the shoulders of the Indians. It was a common thing to see the Indians bleeding from their backs and shoulders from carrying litters over the country upon which reposed the vilest outcasts of European prisons and dungeons. These ruffians consumed all the fruits of the hard toil of the Indians, until the latter were starving in the midst of their own crushing labors. Spanish pleasures and pastimes were acquired and enjoyed by cruelties, insults, and wantonness to the natives. A wail of distress went up from the island which was not prevented from reaching the Spanish sovereigns even by the enormous quantities of gold which Bobadilla poured at the foot of the throne. The tender soul of Isabella was melted by the agonies of her new subjects, while the avaricious heart of Ferdinand was consoled by the rich and golden treasures received into the royal exchequer.

Columbus had no choice but to accept the exile of two years from his colony and viceroyalty of Hispaniola, under the deceptive promise of their restoration by the king in that time. It is the opinion of historians that Columbus now thoroughly distrusted Ferdinand, but still there was a ray of hope in the natural and genuine justice and generosity of Isabella. What could he do but wait?

The distressing accounts of Bobadilla's misconduct, received by every arrival from Hispaniola, hastened the departure of Ovando. This official was a man of good repute and of honorable lineage, of modest demeanor, graceful manners, imposing appearance, temperate, even humble, and a hater of avarice, injustice, and wrong, as his portrait has been drawn by his contemporaries. Subsequent experiences show him to have been a man whose virtues were not unmixed with the gravest faults, for he was astute and dissembling, fond of command, and unsparing to the helpless Indians, which last was evidence of a nature remorselessly cruel; while toward Columbus he was ungenerous and even unjust, cavilling, mean, and unmanly, yet punctilious and ceremonious.

The fleet that carried Ovando to his new trust was the most magnificent that had ever crossed the Atlantic. It consisted of thirty ships, five of ninety to a hundred tons burden, twenty-four of thirty to ninety tons, and one of twenty-five tons. Twenty-five hundred persons embarked in the squadron, and they consisted of soldiers, officials, artisans, mechanics, a physician, a surgeon, an apothecary, seventy-three married men of good character and their families; and with the fleet sailed Don Alonzo Maldonado, who was appointed to supersede Roldan as chief justice. Besides the men on board there were also liberal supplies of every kind, including live stock, artillery, arms, ammunition, and implements. Sailing from Spain on February 13th, 1502, the fleet reached San Domingo on April 15th, but only after encountering a terrific storm, in which one of the ships perished, while, in order to save the other vessels and their crews and passengers, much of the valuable cargoes were thrown overboard. As the jetson from the storm-beaten fleet was cast up in quantities on the coast of Spain, a rumor spread over the kingdom that the fleet was wrecked; and so deeply were the sovereigns affected by the report and by the floating equipment cast upon the shore, that they shut themselves up for eight days in their apartments, and during that time they refused to see any one.

Columbus saw with sadness the departure of this noble fleet commanded by another. He keenly felt the wrong thus done to himself. It cannot be doubted that he was entitled to its command. It is probable that his superior seamanship might have carried the ships through the storm with safety and without loss of ship or cargoes. It is fair to judge that his administration as viceroy, under such favorable circumstances as surrounded Ovando, and with his vast and intelligent experience, would have proved successful and brilliant. His manly heart, with all his wrongs, rejoiced not at the misfortunes of others, but he grieved over the disaster to the fleet announced by the arrival of the abandoned cargoes on the shores of Spain.

Ovando was instructed to assume immediate command on his arrival at Hispaniola, to send Bobadilla back to Spain, to inquire into the disorders of the island, punish the guilty, and to expel all who were unworthy to remain; to revoke the licenses given for collecting gold, of which he was to exact one third of all that was already collected and one half of all future authorized collections; to build and charter cities, to exact military obedience and discipline. All commerce with the colonies was restricted to the mother country, and all mines, precious stones, dyewoods, and other articles of peculiar value were reserved to the crown. Foreigners, especially Jews and Moors, were prohibited from settling in Hispaniola or making voyages to the Indies. The Indians and their caciques were taken under the protection of the sovereigns. Though the Indians were only to pay tribute as other Spanish subjects, and to be treated with all possible gentleness, it was most unfortunately provided that they were compellable to labor on the public works and in the mines, a provision which was evidently liable to abuse, and which, as might have been obviously anticipated, resulted in annulling all provisions in their favor, and in their ultimate and cruel extermination. In vain was it added that especial care should be taken to convert them to Christianity, and that a body of pious Franciscans, the first formal introduction of that order into the new world, under the direction of the devout and venerable Antonio de Espinal, was sent out for that purpose; for the unwary provision subjecting them to be impressed for labor rendered these well-intended instructions nothing better practically than the most cruel edict for their enslavement and extermination. But there was another provision in these royal ordinances which makes humanity blush for the highest motives and purest conduct of the best and noblest of our race. While the Indians were to be protected by delusive injunctions for their conversion and civilization, their exemption from slavery was to be secured by the importation of slaves of another race in their stead. It is to be regretted that the Spanish sovereigns placed their names to a decree which recognized the reduction to slavery of the negroes brought from the coasts of Africa into Spain, and authorized the importation of their descendants, born in Spain of Christian parents, into Hispaniola, and their enslavement there continued. Such, alas! was the first introduction of African slavery into America! But even this inconsistent but well-intended measure did not save the Indians, while it enslaved the Africans!

The interests of Columbus were not overlooked, but Ovando was instructed to ascertain the damages he had sustained by his unjust imprisonment, the suspension of his rights, and the seizure of his property. The crown and Bobadilla were to make restitution of all his property taken by or for them, and his brothers were to be indemnified for all their losses. Alonzo Sanchez de Carvajal was appointed by the admiral, with the royal consent, his factor, to receive and collect his share of the receipts from Hispaniola, and to secure for him all his properties and revenues. In future the admiral was to receive his revenues, and all arrears were ordered now to be paid. Ovando was surrounded with all the dignities and retinues appropriate to his high office, and he was exempted from the prohibition against wearing silks, brocades, precious stones, and other sumptuous attire, which the ostentatious extravagance of the Spanish nobility had caused to be enacted. He was allowed a retinue of seventy esquires, of whom ten were horsemen.

It would be impossible to imagine a position more humiliating, more unjust, or more oppressive to a high-minded man, or more unworthy of great and powerful sovereigns, than that in which Columbus was now placed—that a stranger, who had never contributed a thought or an act to the discovery of the new world, should be heralded as the governor of the new countries, should be sent out at the head of so splendid a fleet, should be loaded with honors, dignities, and privileges, and should be backed by the power and prestige of the Spanish crown, while the discoverer of the western world and its legitimate ruler, viceroy, and admiral should be detained at home, silenced, neglected, and impoverished. Had half so much been done for him as was now done for Ovando, at the time when his own forces were in rebellion against him and he was reduced to the point of despair, he could have brought his administration to a successful result, and could have prosecuted his discoveries to the conquest of two continents and to the dominion of both oceans. He had instead been left a prey to the crimes of others; he had been brought back in chains from the scenes of his greatest services, and now he was left in disgrace and inactivity. Nine months were thus spent by Columbus in the thankless task of vindicating his honor, of restoring his fortunes, in making his appeal to Spain and to posterity. It was posterity alone that has heard his appeal.

In the fervent mind of Columbus there was an indissoluble link between the discovery of the new world and the rescue and delivery of the Holy Land to Christendom. The former was to provide the means of achieving the latter. His thoughts now reverted to the Holy Sepulchre, since he was now so unjustly debarred from continuing the discovery of the new world. The histories of the crusades to wrest Jerusalem and the Holy Land from the grasp of the Mohammedans do not exhibit to our view the length and depth, the elevation and breadth of the Christian idea which then lay at the foundation of this wonderful movement. The real contest was between all Christendom and all the powers of Mohammedanism. With Christendom it was more defensive than aggressive. Mohammedanism represented aggression. It was in this sense and with this motive that the Sovereign Pontiffs and Peter the Hermit preached the crusade. It was in a grand inspiration that the devout soul of Columbus made him the crusader-champion of Christendom. The idea born of the chivalrous ages survived those ages with Columbus, who was a historic figure standing between the Middle Ages and modern times, and possessing the faith of the one united with the enterprise of the other. Columbus assumed the aggressive; the Holy Sepulchre was to be redeemed, and the Eastern world of Asia converted to the faith. The character of Columbus, with its varied virtues and conceptions, in fact, belongs to all times and epochs, to all nations and continents. His mind would have grasped with equal intelligence the principles involved in the mediæval struggle between Christendom and Mohammedanism. His sword would have been wielded with equal vigor whether under the Lion-hearted Richard in the Crusades, or under George Washington in our own War of Independence.

The mind of Columbus was imbued with the faith and sentiments of the Middle Ages, and no religious question of past or present interest ceased to arouse his deep Christian sentiments. As the learned Tarducci has justly remarked, it is necessary to divest our minds of the utilitarian education of our age, and identify ourselves with the sentiments of past ages, in order to do justice to the life and character of Columbus. It is singular and interesting to recall the connection in the minds of Christian doctors and scholars of the past between the expected time of the end of the world and the crusades and all other grand and universal movements and enterprises. Notwithstanding the words of Christ, "It is not for you to know the times or the moments which the Father hath put in His own power," it was a subject that stirred Christendom—that of finding out the time of the destruction of the world. While Christendom awaited the end of the world on the approach of the year 1000, St. Augustine and Cardinal d'Ailly concurred in the opinion that the portents mentioned in Scripture as signs of the great last end would occur seven thousand years from the creation of the world. Columbus studied these and many other sacred writings on this subject, and advancing beyond the points reached by doctors and theologians, he boldly advanced the opinion, or rather the positive announcement, which he based upon the application of the Alphonsine tables to the theories of St. Augustine, that the world would come to an end in one hundred and fifty-five years. The words of Columbus were as follows: "St. Augustine teaches that the end of the world will be 7000 years from its creation. This is likewise the opinion of the holy theologians and of Cardinal Pierre d'Ailly. Your Highness is aware that from Adam to the birth of Christ was 5343 years and 318 days, according to the exact calculation of King Alfonso. We are now in the fifteen hundred and first year since the birth of our Lord, and consequently the world has lasted already 6845 years. It will, therefore, be only 155 years before the world is destroyed." *

Now the connection between the end of the world and the crusades, or the recovery of the Holy Land from the Mohammedans, is obvious; for before the end of the world all nations should be converted to Christianity, and become united under one shepherd in one fold. It was time, therefore, in the devout mind of Columbus, to prepare for these portentous events, and he believed himself to be the providential man that was sent to reveal the world to mankind and all its unknown nations, tribes, and peoples. The great monster of Mohammedanism was to be destroyed, the East and the West were to be brought together, and the recovery of Jerusalem and the Holy Land was the door which would open the way to the reunion of all the world in the one fold of Christ. "The wealth of the Indies," writes Father Knight, "to follow his train of thought, would ensure the recovery of the Holy Sepulchre; the recovery of the Holy Sepulchre would increase charity and send evangelists to the Indies. Distant nations must be added to the fold, and Christians must be free once more to worship Christ at Bethlehem and Calvary. The idea which filled the mind and soul of Columbus was to make a highway round the earth, and bring the nations in willing homage to the feet of Jesus Christ, reigning once more in Jerusalem of the Christians." † "In this time of evil, his vow to furnish within seven years from the time of his discovery," writes Mr. Irving, "fifty thousand foot soldiers and five thousand horse, for the recovery of the Holy Sepulchre, recurred to his memory

---

* Mr. Brownson's translation of Tarducci's "Life of Columbus," vol. ii., p. 212.
† "Life of Christopher Columbus," by Rev. A. G. Knight, S. J., p. 190.

with peculiar force. The time had elapsed, but the vow remained unfulfilled, and the means to perform it had failed him." "These ideas, so repeatedly and solemnly and artlessly expressed by a man of the fervent piety of Columbus, show how truly his discovery arose from the working of his own mind, and not from information furnished by others. He considered it a divine intimation, a light from Heaven, and a fulfilment of what had been foretold by our Saviour and the prophets. Still he regarded it but as a minor event, preparatory to the great enterprise, the recovery of the Holy Sepulchre. He pronounced it a miracle effected by Heaven to animate himself and others to that holy undertaking; and he assured the sovereigns that if they had faith in his present as in his former proposition, they would assuredly be rewarded with equally triumphant success." * The Count de Lorgues, on the same subject, in his usual extravagant strain writes: "Human glory was incapable of remunerating him. It was from the Most High that he expected a recompense. Columbus hoped that, as a crowning of his favors, the Divine Majesty designed to reserve for him the deliverance of the Holy Sepulchre, hitherto refused to the efforts of the Crusaders." † And again the same enthusiastic author: "Sometimes in the intervals of his researches, the contemplator of the world, electrified with the poetry of Israel and with the sublime hymns of the Church, tried also to render into verse the emotions prompted by his piety. A poet in sentiment, he was still more so in expression, even in the language of his adopted country. . . . The religious stanzas of Columbus unhappily are lost." ‡

Columbus was not alone in his conviction that he was the chosen one of Heaven for the spread of the gospel, in which great mission the recovery of the Holy Sepulchre and the Holy Land was an early step. The learned and gifted Jayme Ferrer, a famous scientist of that day, expressed the sentiments of many learned and pious people when he thus addressed Isabella concerning Columbus in 1495: "I believe that in its deep, mysterious designs divine Providence selected him as its agent in this

---

* Irving's "Columbus," vol. ii., p. 295.
† Dr. Barry's translation of De Lorgues' "Life of Columbus," p. 425.
‡ *Id.*, p. 426.

work, which I look upon as the introduction and preparation for things which the same divine Providence has determined to make known for its own glory and the salvation and happiness of the world." And afterward, writing to the admiral, he says: "I behold in this a great mystery; the divine and infallible Providence sent the great Thomas from the West to the East to preach our holy Catholic faith in the Indies, and has sent you, señor, by the opposite way, from the East to the West, till, by God's will, you reached the utmost limits of Upper India, in order that the inhabitants might learn those truths which their progenitors cared not to receive from the preaching of St. Thomas. . . . In your mission, señor, you seem an apostle, a messenger of God, to spread His name in unknown lands." * Such were the views of learned and good men in a less sceptical age than ours.

Devoting himself to this great purpose, Columbus employed all his leisure moments in preparing arguments and proofs to sustain his proposals to the sovereigns to undertake the rescue of the Holy Sepulchre. Although he had prepared calculations for furnishing an army of one hundred thousand men for this crusade, at a time when he scarcely possessed the means of purchasing for himself a coat, he now realized his present poverty, and appealed to the sovereigns to undertake the work. His studious labors were collected in a splendid manuscript work, which he entitled " A Collection of Prophecies on the Recovery of Jerusalem and the Discovery of the Indies," which he addressed to Ferdinand and Isabella. When submitted by him, before presentation to the sovereigns, to Father Gaspard Gorricio, a learned Carthusian monk, for his amendment and addition, the father could find little to add, expressing at the same time his wonder and admiration at its extraordinary learning, research, and cogent reasoning. This remarkable work, composed of collections and extracts from the prophecies relating to his subject, poetical stanzas by the author, quotations and references from the works of St. Augustine, St. Thomas, St. Isidore, and Gerson, has, with the exception of some fragments and allusions to it in the admiral's other writings, wholly perished. It was presented to the Spanish sovereigns accompanied by a no less interesting and remark-

---

* " Col. Diplo. Doc.," lxviii. ; Mr. Brownson's translation of Tarducci's " Life of Columbus," vol. ii., p. 217.

able letter addressed by the admiral to them, in which he earnestly and enthusiastically appealed to them not to reject his proposals, and assuring them of the same ultimate success that had attested the truth and practicability of his proposals for the discovery of the new world.

While preparing this unique and characteristic volume, Columbus was living in retirement and poverty, unable to appear in public for want of means to sustain his rank, scarcely able to provide a scanty livelihood or clothing, and, to his own sincere regret and mortification, unable to contribute to the Church and to the expenses of divine worship a *blanca*, smallest of Spanish coins. Not having received his just remittances from Hispaniola, he was without money or credit. It is well known that in his days of prosperity his charities had been unbounded. Not only had he cared for his aged and impoverished father at Genoa, but he cared for the household of Donna Beatrix Enriquez at Cordova, had assisted his brothers, and, as the Count de Lorgues suggests, not from historical data, but from the abundance of his admiration, he must have given generously to hospitals and other charities, and discharged in the most substantial manner the debt of gratitude he always entertained toward the Franciscan convent of La Rabida. Reduced to the necessity of living in an inn, even there he was frequently without the means of paying his board. Neglected by the Spanish sovereigns, when he "had given to Castile lands a hundred times larger than herself," he, at this sublime period of his life, "was without a foot of earth, a garden to walk in, or a roof to shelter his head." *
In the midst of such humiliations and sufferings the enthusiastic and mediæval mind of Columbus soared in solemn thought toward Heaven. The preparation of this earth for the coming of the Saviour to judge mankind by opening the way to the conversion of all nations to the faith, the ardent appeal to the most devout sentiments of the sovereigns and peoples of his age, the sacred yet almost mystic learning with which he enforced his arguments and conclusions, the elevation of mind with which he sought the sublime aims within the grasp of man, and the perfect earnestness and simple good faith in which he presented the predestined and glorious mission which he felt to be his office divinely in-

---

* Dr. Barry's translation of Count de Lorgues' "Life of Columbus," p. 432.

spired and ordained of Heaven, throw light upon the character and life of the man. The spirit of the crusades had not expired on earth ; in fact, Columbus himself had been a soldier fighting in the recent successful crusade of Christianity against Mohammedanism in Spain. A Spanish duke had but lately accomplished an expedition into Barbary against the infidels ; Spanish conquests were looking eastwardly, and the proposals of Columbus were not out of unison with the religious and military spirit of the times, nor of the court to which they were addressed. Even now the souls of Christians turn ardently toward the holy city of Jerusalem ; pilgrimages to the Holy Land are still the significant expressions of Christian piety ; while at the approaching quadro-centennial celebration of the great Columbian discovery there will be present American Christians who have visited Jerusalem as pilgrims in the same religious sentiments which affected the soul of Columbus. In February the admiral addressed a strong letter to Pope Alexander VI., presenting his plans for the recovery of the Holy Sepulchre and for spreading the gospel among all the heathen nations of the earth. He renewed his promise of visiting the Sovereign Pontiff in person.

But the currents of more modern thought and enterprise had set in ; a new world had been discovered but only partially revealed. Was it Asia, or a new hemisphere, with its continents? Portugal had reached Asia by the South African route, and had discovered Brazil. Spain and Portugal were looking with mundane ambition to the new world rather than with religious zeal to the Orient. Columbus, more than any other person, knew the importance and grandeur of his achievement. Having observed the directions of the coasts of Paria and Cuba, tending toward a central region, he believed that the currents of the Caribbean Sea could have no other outlet than between the mainlands of Paria and Cuba at the point of their nearest approach, and he located the conjectured strait near what we now know as the Isthmus of Darien. He proposed now, with an enthusiasm equal to that which inspired him before the Council of Salamanca, to the sovereigns to make another and fourth voyage for the discovery of this great passage, by which he would unite the new world and the old by a navigable strait, and bring the riches of both within reach of Europe. Success would crown his career as discoverer and add further splendor to his last days.

Ferdinand and Isabella overcame all the objections raised against this proposal of the admiral. Why should they wait for a report from Hispaniola as to his administration there, when he had already discovered a new world, and proposed to discover what might prove to be another, perhaps of greater vastness, wealth, and grandeur? While the admiral's plans for the crusade to the Holy Land produced the partial result of leading Ferdinand to gain, by negotiation with the Grand Soldan of Egypt, the preservation of the Holy Sepulchre and the protection of Christian pilgrimages, the admiral was invited to Seville in the fall of 1501 to arrange with the sovereigns the details of his fourth voyage of discovery.

Columbus, in the preparations for his fourth and last voyage to the Indies, encountered from Fonseca delays and provocations similar to those he had already suffered; yet it is stated that when it became known at Seville that the sovereigns were anxious to get rid of him, by engaging his thoughts in a new expedition, the preparations were hastened by Fonseca and his associates. His request for permission to land at Hispaniola was declined on the outward voyage, on account of the still unsettled condition of affairs, and chiefly as Ovando had then just arrived and Bobadilla was about to return home; but permission was given for his touching at San Domingo on his return. Permission was given for his taking with him his brother, the Adelantado, and his son Fernando, then a lad of fourteen years, while his son Diego was to remain in Spain to attend to his business interests. Two or three persons conversant with Arabic were selected to go on this expedition, in the expectation that now at least the realms of the Grand Khan would be reached. A letter was addressed to Columbus by the sovereigns, assuring him most solemnly that their treaties with him would be faithfully fulfilled by them and their successors, not only to him, but also to his sons, and expressing a disposition to bestow still further honors and rewards upon him, his brothers, and his children, and also expressing the hope that his mind would be at peace for the prosecution of his grand enterprise, as well as in relation to his rights and interests at home.

While the mind of Columbus was greatly relieved by this assurance, the last letter he received from Ferdinand and Isabella, which in its terms seemed both ample and generous, his sad experiences with princes led his practical and sagacious mind to take measures for preserving his fame, securing his rights, and perpetuating his titles, offices, and jurisdictions to his sons and descendants. He accordingly caused copies of all the royal letters, grants, and capitulations issued to him as admiral, viceroy, and governor to be prepared and certified by the alcaldes of Seville, and also letters of his own containing vindications of his administration in Hispaniola, and these documents in duplicates were sent by different messengers to his friend, Dr. Nicolo Oderigo, formerly ambassador from Genoa to the Spanish court, with the request to preserve them and to acquaint his son Diego of their existence and deposit. Another copy he left with his friends, the Franciscans in Spain, and another with the monks of St. Jerome. It was thus with a prophetic forethought he made his appeal to the world and to posterity for that justice which was then denied him by the king and nation that had reaped the whole honor and glory of his achievements. It was an appeal from King Ferdinand's subsequent, but then apprehended injustice, to the public opinion of the world. Four centuries have recorded their verdict in favor of Columbus.

The fleet destined for such services contrasted strangely with that which had just carried out a mere official, whose chief office was to supersede another similar official, who, like himself, had been clothed with authority. It consisted of four caravels, one of fifty tons, the largest of seventy tons, and the *personnel* consisted of only one hundred and fifty men. It was destined to solve the problem of a northwest passage to Asia, now conjectured and believed to be a central passage, to elucidate the problem of the circumnavigation of the earth, and to unfold to men the geography of the planet. Much of this programme was actually accomplished; under more favorable support the problems of geography would have been solved. The admiral was accompanied by his ever-faithful brother, Don Bartholomew, and by his younger son, Don Fernando, whose society greatly consoled the venerable discoverer in his sorrows and adversities. The fleet sailed from the port of Cadiz on May 9th, 1502.

> " What can we not endure,
> When pains are lessen'd by the hope of cure ?"
> —NABB'S " MICROCOSMUS."

Don Bartholomew Columbus had seen so much treachery

on the part of Spaniards, and so much selfish ingratitude on the part of the king, such lack of support from the mother country to her champions and heralds in the new world, that he desired to abandon all further participation in the prosecution of western discoveries and explorations; but at the request of his brother he nobly sacrificed every plan and wish of his own, and devoted himself to the new enterprise. The admiral's younger brother, always so gentle and so pious, now abandoned the world, and sought retirement and meditation in the sacred ministry. To young Fernando Columbus the queen gave a commission in the Spanish navy.

Columbus, now advanced in years, and weakened by severe mental and physical strain and by his increasing infirmities, seemed to contemplate constantly eternity, while yet making a last struggle to reveal the geography of the globe. The ingratitude he had experienced in Spain, his adopted country, had now an interesting effect in reviving and renewing the love of his native country, the home of his father and of his ancestors. His characteristic generosity was now again conspicuous in this critical epoch in his life. With patriotic love for his native country, he made a munificent donation to the Bank of St. George, at Genoa, for the relief of the poor of his native city. The letter announcing this gift, which now the revival of his hopes for the restoration of his rights and revenues and their transmission to his family gave him every prospect of making good, is so exact a mirror of his noble and generous soul, that I will give it to the reader.

"*To the Most Noble Lords of the Most Magnificent Office of St. George:*

"MOST NOBLE LORDS: Although in body far distant, in heart I am always near you. God our Lord has done me the greatest favor of any man since David.

"The facts of my enterprise, already widely published, would astonish you much more if you knew them all, and the government had not cautiously concealed them. I return again to the Indies, in the name of the Most Holy Trinity; but as I am mortal, and may leave this world on the way, I have disposed by will that my son, Don Diego, shall remit to you every year, in perpetuity, the tenth part of my revenues, to be used in reducing the duties on corn, wine, and other victuals consumed in your city. If this tenth will accomplish something, accept it; if not, accept my good will.

"I recommend my son to your favor. Messer Nicolò Oderigo knows much about me; he is the bearer also of a faithful copy of my privileges and rights, to be deposited in some safe place, after showing it to your lordships at your convenience.

"The king and queen, my sovereigns, love and honor me more than ever.

"May the Holy Triad preserve your noble persons, and bestow ever greater prosperity on the most magnificent Office of St. George.

"Done at Seville, on the 2nd of April, 1502.

"The Admiral-Major of the Ocean Sea, and Viceroy and Governor-General of the Islands and Mainland of Asia and India, for the King and Queen, my sovereigns, and their Captain-General of the Sea, and their Councillor.

.S.
.S.A.S.
X. M. Y.
.Xρo FERENS.

As all biographers of Columbus have given an explanation of this unique and interesting signature, so characteristic of the age to which he belonged and of the religion which inspired him with so many high thoughts and aspirations, my readers will find the explanation attractive and entertaining.

It has already been mentioned that the name of Christopher, which is composed of two Latin words, *Christus* and *Ferens*, signifies the Christ-bearer, and was devoutly interpreted by the admiral himself as prophetic of his mission in carrying the religion of Christ to unknown lands and nations. Among the ancient traditions of the Church is the legend of St. Christopher. The name Christopher seems to have been an emblematic name given to St. Jerom, who was martyred under the Emperor Decius, in Lycia; and while his festival was observed in the Western calendars on July 25th, it was kept by the Greek Christians and other Orientals on May 9th. It is stated by the learned Alban Butler that, according to the Mosarabic Breviary attributed to St. Isidore, the martyr's relics were translated to Toledo, thence into France, and are now enshrined at St. Denys, near Paris. Father Knight, the learned Jesuit, seems to think there were two St. Christophers, the Syrian and the Italian, although he regards the latter as mythical, or a creation of art. Dr. Butler mentions but one, and of him he relates the entire legend. St. Christopher is represented in the window-paintings of the cathedrals of the West as wading through the sea of tribulations, in allusion to his many struggles and sufferings by which he attained his exalted place in heaven. In this fearful passage, ending in his martyrdom, he bore the Saviour in his heart, and thus allegorically is represented as crossing a material sea, and carrying Christ upon his shoulders. This office of Christ-bearer led to his being always represented as of immense stature, an emblem of the strength required to carry in safety his precious burden. Dr. Butler, following Baronius, claims this representation of the saint as purely allegorical, and originating in the scenes depicted in the Gothic cathedrals, and cites the beautiful epigram of Vida in confirmation : *

> " Christophore, infixum quod eum usque in corde gerebas,
> Pictores Christum dant tibi ferre humeris," etc.
> —VIDA, hym. 26, t. 2, p. 150.

> " To Christopher, on shoulders strong,
> To bear the Christ o'er seas along,
> By artists' hands was given ;
> Just as the mystic Lamb he bore,
> Within his gentle heart t' adore,
> O'er seas of blood—to Heaven !"

The mystic letters in Columbus' signature are not unfamiliar to ecclesiastical scholars, and are, in fact, somewhat in use with members of religious communities in our own day and country. The admiral's son, Fernando, who wrote his father's life, informs us that whenever Columbus commenced to write he took up the pen with the devout prayer in Latin, " *Jesus cum Maria sit nobis in via*" (Jesus, with Mary, be with us° on our way). Even now the same devout custom prevails among religious persons ; and my own experience, like that of the learned Tarducci, has frequently brought to me letters having written at the top of the sheet the names in Latin, Jesus, Maria, Joseph, or J. M. J.— more frequently the initials. In interpreting the signature of

---

* Pimius, the Bollandists, t. 6, p. 125.

Columbus, the S. at the top is construed as standing for *Salva me* (save me) or *Salve* (hail). The second line, composed of the letters S. A. S., while Tarducci says they "have never been divined," are to be read, according to Spotorno, who is also concurred in by Tarducci, in connection with the letters of the third line, X. M. Y., the initial letters of the intended words being in the third line and the final letters of the same words being in the second line. Thus the third and second lines, taken together, signify *Jesus, Mary, Joseph*. The last line is composed of the Greek word *XPO* (for Christo, Christ) and the Latin word FERENS (carrying), and simply signifies Christopher, or Christ-bearer; and from the significant manner in which it is formed is evidently intended by the admiral to refer to his great mission, or apostolate, for carrying the faith of Christ to heathen nations. The first three lines of the signature, an interpretation in which Tarducci and other writers concur, may therefore be rendered thus:

$$\cdot \text{ S } \cdot \text{ (}Salve\text{.)}$$

S		A $\cdot$		S $\cdot$	
	Xristus		*Maria*		*Yoseplus*
X		M		Y	

Other signatures of Columbus, such as that to his will, the instrument by which he created the entail of his estates, contained the same letters, but was signed EL ALMIRANTE, instead of XPO FERENS. It is a common practice in Spanish countries still to use the ejaculation in Spanish, "Jesus, Maria y José." While the *North American Review* for April, 1827, suggests the substitution of Jesus for Joseph at the last letter of the third line of the signature, the name of Joseph is the necessary complement of the three sacred names in general use.*

The work of the Count de Lorgues dwells at length on the patron saint of Columbus. He represents him as a pagan, whose name was Opherus, a Syrian, and of gigantic stature. Having become a Christian on witnessing a miracle, he took the name of Christopher, or Christ-bearer. It was from his name rather

---

* Irving's "Columbus," vol. iii., pp. 452, 453; Mr. Brownson's translation of Tarducci's "Life of Columbus," vol. ii., p. 226; Count de Lorgues' "Life of Columbus," Dr. Barry's translation, pp. 579-85.

than from any mission or apostolate or labors that he performed that he is represented as bearing Christ upon his shoulders. In the application of the symbols to Columbus, they, as well as the name itself, are regarded as prophetic of the admiral's mission to discover heathen lands and nations, and to open the way for their receiving Christ and His religion, which he is credited with carrying to them. The aptness of the application is most striking and engaging. The profoundly religious character of Columbus, and his extraordinary zeal for the extension of the gospel of Christ, render the application most fitting and appropriate.

The Count de Lorgues interprets the admiral's signature differently somewhat from the above rendition, and as follows: SERVUS SUPPLEX ALTISSIMI SALVATORIS. — CHRISTUS, MARIA, JOSEPH.—CHRISTO FERENS. The translation in English runs thus: THE SUPPLIANT SERVANT OF THE MOST HIGH SAVIOUR.—JESUS, MARY, JOSEPH.—CHRIST-BEARER.*

---

* Barry's translation of De Lorgues' "Columbus," p. 357.

CHAPTER XIII.

> " Press on ! for it is godlike to unloose
> The spirit, and forget yourself in thought ;
> Bending a pinion for the deeper sky,
> And in the very fetters of your flesh,
> Mating with the pure essences of heaven !
> Press on ! for in the grave there is no work,
> And no device. Press on ! while yet you may !"
>
> —WILLIS's " POEMS."

SUSTAINED by the strong arm of his faithful brother, Don Bartholomew, and by the amiable and affectionate companionship of his second son, Don Fernando, then scarcely fourteen years old, the admiral undertook this his fourth and important expedition, with the brave spirit and enduring cheerfulness of his younger days. His health, however, was greatly impaired, and he felt the inroads upon his naturally robust constitution made by the labors, exposures, disappointments, watchings, and responsibilities of his previous expeditions, and still more by the wrongs, injustice, and humiliations he had received ; but his mind was clear, strong, and buoyant, and his spirit was ardent, energetic, and robust. Though he was not far from his sixtieth year, he undertook this arduous and adventurous voyage with an eye bright with enthusiasm, with a courage sustained by the grandeur of his conceptions and aspirations, and with the elasticity of character which had distinguished him in the prime of life. He always esteemed this expedition as one of the most important and momentous of his career.

Just as the squadron was about to sail from Cadiz, news arrived that the Portuguese fortress of Arzilla, on the coast of Morocco, was blockaded by the Moorish fleet. In accordance with the chivalrous customs of the age, by the instructions of the government, and with his own instincts as Grand Admiral of Castile, he sailed to the relief of the Christian garrison then threatened by the Mohammedans. Finding on his arrival that the siege was raised, and that the governor had received a wound in its gallant defence, he sent his brother, the Adelantado, and his son, Fernando, and the captains of the caravels on shore to visit the governor, to express his sympathy and friendship, and to tender the services of the Spanish squadron. This act of courtesy was gratefully received, and a deputation of Portuguese cavaliers was sent in return to visit the admiral and express the thanks of the governor of the fortress. Among the visitors were relatives of the admiral's first wife, Donna Felippa Moniz. After exchanging compliments, the admiral again sailed, touched at the Grand Canary on May 25th, and after a favorable voyage the fleet arrived on June 15th at Mantinino, one of the Caribbean Islands.

Necessity now compelled Columbus, contrary to his orders from the government, to sail for San Domingo, on account of the principal vessel's inability to carry her sails, thus constantly embarrassing and delaying the squadron. His plan had been to sail directly for Jamaica, and thence toward the continent near Paria, in search of the passage, which he thought he would discover farther to the west by following the coasts in that direction, and thus achieve the great solution of the connection or union between the two oceans. His reason for touching at San Domingo was for the purpose of exchanging his faulty vessel for one of the ships which had recently carried Ovando to Hispaniola, or to purchase there another ship. Although the reasons for the orders forbidding his going to San Domingo were prudently and wisely based upon the risk and imprudence of his making his appearance there in the disordered condition of affairs, and just as Ovando had arrived and Bobadilla was about to depart, the admiral's necessity and the interests of the public service, unforeseen as they were by the government, scarcely left him any other alternative.

Ovando having arrived at San Domingo on April 15th, he was received by Bobadilla and the inhabitants on the shore with all the ceremony of Spanish punctilio. Escorted to the fortress, the usual official oaths were taken, and the new governor entered upon his duties with apparently prudent energy and cool deliberation. Bobadilla's downfall had taught him at least the necessity of treating others with courtesy and respect, and now, too late, he saw his past folly. Neglected by all, deserted even by the people to whom he had given everything, and whose passions he had favored and indulged, he was now of not sufficient importance to challenge attention. The conduct of Roldan and his late confederates in rebellion was rigidly investigated by Ovando, and the chief rebel himself and most of the others were now commanded to return to Spain to answer for their conduct. It is said that they confidently expected when at home to gain immunity for their crimes and outrages under the patronage of Fonseca, and by the influence of their friends. It was a shameful sight to behold these outlaws, the unworthy representatives of civilization and Christianity, confidently returning to Spain loaded with quantities of gold, and relying upon this ill-gotten treasure for their pardon or escape from a just punishment. Bobadilla, though more from neglect or indifference escaping any formal accusations or trial, and sent back to Spain more to get rid of him than otherwise, trusted confidently to the magic power of gold. He was to embark in the principal ship of the returning fleet. He placed on board a huge quantity of gold, consisting of the revenues he had collected in gold for the crown by the hard labors of the natives, as well as his own acquisitions. Among the golden treasures placed on the ship was a celebrated treasure, a solid mass of virgin gold, which an Indian girl had accidentally found in the mines while carelessly moving her rake to and fro ; and as it was found on the estates of Francisco de Garay and Miguel Diaz, a suitable compensation was made to them in order to secure it for the king. It was said to have weighed thirty-six hundred castellanos and to be worth 1,350,000 maravedis, or nearly $2080 of our money. The finding of this valuable deposit was celebrated at San Domingo in a manner peculiar to the times and situation. A grand dinner was given in honor of the treasure, at which the mass of gold itself was quaintly and whimsically used as a platter for serving a roasted pig, and it was jocosely remarked by the guests that never had Castilian king eaten from so valuable a service. While Bishop Las Casas slyly questions whether the poor Indian girl received any part of the treasure or its price, Tarducci wittily remarks that history has not recorded her receiving a taste of the pig.

Roldan and his chief confederates in rebellion embarked on the same ship with Bobadilla, and each of these was to carry home immense treasures in gold, and these, together with the royal portions, gave to the flagship the richest cargo of gold which had ever been collected. It is also to be related that on this vessel, and in such unworthy company, was placed the sad and unfortunate native chief Guarionex, loaded with chains, which should have been more appropriately worn by his Spanish masters on board. On another vessel was embarked the admiral's representative, Alonzo Sanchez de Carvajal, who had recovered from Bobadilla a portion of the admiral's revenues and secured other portions of it, so that the restored property amounted to four thousand pieces of gold.

It was at this juncture of readiness to sail that the little fleet of Columbus appeared off San Domingo on June 29th. The admiral, with that close and unequalled observation and knowledge of natural phenomena for which he was pre-eminently distinguished, had detected an approaching storm when no one else could see the slightest sign of one. He now sent on shore Pedro di Tereros, one of his captains, to request permission to exchange for a good ship in port his own ship, which was unfit for the service, or to purchase one, and asking permission to take shelter with his ships in the harbor from the violent hurricane he saw approaching. While it was known that Columbus had instructions not to stop at San Domingo, and probably Ovando had been so advised, and possibly had received instructions not to admit him to enter in case he came there—an arrangement, no doubt, rendered advisable by the distracted state of the colony and the presence there of so many of his enemies—yet the stress under which Columbus found himself, in order to save the ships of the government in his fleet, and to promote the public interests in the prosecution of the voyage undertaken for the glory and profit of Spain, fully justifies his request. A stranger, even a public enemy would have been permitted to take shelter from a storm ; but even this courtesy of a common humanity was denied to Columbus. It is alleged, in extenuation of Ovando's refusal, that he might have justly regarded the reasons assigned by Columbus for entering the port as mere pretexts and ridiculous inventions ; because, as he might have asked, how could a ship only two months at sea be now unseaworthy ? and how could a storm be given as a reason when no one could detect the slightest sign of one approaching ? These excuses fell to the ground soon afterward by the established facts in each case ; and the well-known reputation of Columbus as a navigator, his acknowledged truthfulness of character, and his exalted personal and official position, all entitled him to the credit of good faith. It was but natural that the admiral should feel deeply wounded and insulted at this refusal. In his letter soon afterward written to the sovereigns, he thus expresses himself: " Who, not even excepting Job, would not have died of despair to see, when my safety and that of my son, my brother, and my other friends, was at stake, under these circumstances access forbidden me to that land and shelter in that port which, by the will of God and at the price of my blood, I had won for Spain."

Even under such an indignity Columbus's magnanimity prevailed over his anger, and he immediately sent the officer, Tereros, back to beseech the governor at least not to permit the fleet to depart for Spain or go to sea, as a fearful storm was surely approaching, and almost certain destruction would await the ships exposed to the coming hurricane. But as no other person or seaman or pilot could observe the slightest indications of a storm, and all were impatient to sail for home, the predictions of Columbus were treated with laughter and scorn, and the fleet immediately put to sea. The effect of this disdainful refusal to their commander to enter a port of their own country, or even to take shelter from a storm, so sadly and even superstitiously impressed the minds of the admiral's crews, that they murmured against the ill-treated admiral himself as if he were the cause of their exclusion, and they anticipated nothing but disaster under a commander who was thus denied the common offices of humanity. The fact alone, without reference to its injustice, was in their morbid imaginations an ill omen; but soon the portents were reversed. They almost immediately afterward acknowledged that they owed their preservation to the very presence in some way, perhaps even miraculously, as the Count de Lorgues contends, of Columbus on their fleet.

While Columbus took a partial shelter from the predicted storm in one of the harbors of this wild coast, the magnificent fleet of Bobadilla, consisting of twenty-eight vessels, with gayest music and joyous songs of home, put to sea, leaving behind them the harbor of safety. Scarcely had they reached the eastern end of Hispaniola before the storm signs gathered, and so rapidly did the tempest burst upon the fleet, that no time was given them for any measures of safety. Accustomed as was this latitude to violent storms, this was one of the most violent ever experienced. The first ship to sustain the shock of the hurricane was the flagship, having on board Bobadilla, Roldan, and the other most inveterate enemies of Columbus. Driven violently on a rock, she sank with all on board. Immense treasure went to the bottom with them. All the other ships were broken to pieces, and all were engulfed and perished with their crews except four. Of these four three, with great difficulty and in a miserable state, reached San Domingo ; but the fourth, the very ship on which was Carvajal with the admiral's gold and other property, the smallest of the fleet, rode the storm triumphantly and in the midst of universal wreck. This gallant little craft crossed the Atlantic in safety, and landed in Spain with every man and every ounce of gold. In the mean time, the four vessels of the admiral, all verging on unseaworthiness, survived the storm in safety, and while three of them—those that stood out to sea for safety from the rocks—sustained some injury, that in which the admiral was came forth totally uninjured. The four ships were separated during the storm, and the crew of each gave the other three up for lost. The ship which suffered most was the large caravel, which the admiral had desired to exchange at San Domingo, and which was saved solely by the consummate seamanship of the Adelantado. What was not the joy of all on board when, on the following Sunday, the three ships at sea joined the admiral's in the harbor of Azua, just west of San Domingo.

Columbus was now regarded as a seer by his crews, who so lately bemoaned their sad fate in sailing with him. His enemies regarded these extraordinary occurrences as grounds for fresh accusations, for he had, according to their malignant and superstitious clamor, raised the storm by magic for the destruction of his enemies and their property, while he and his ships and crews escaped ; and even the ship which contained his property, though belonging to the lost fleet, escaped in safety with its treasures to Spain. The admiral himself, in his usual impulse of devotion and gratitude, referring all things to God, pronounced his preservation and the safety of his ships and property as a great public miracle. In Spain such a calamity, so general, so national, was regarded with consternation, and was followed by general mourning. The sovereigns reproved Ovando for refusing permission to Columbus to enter the port, and for not detaining the fleet as he had advised. How would it have been if the storm had not occurred? Ovando would have been praised, while Columbus would have received the censure of both sovereigns and people. It seemed, not unfairly and justly, to require a miracle to sustain in such a crisis the cause of Columbus—which was, in fact, the cause of civilization and human progress—against the elements of selfishness and jealousy, malice and hatred, which exist against the good and great in all ages and countries—an element so ignorant and narrow as not to see and to know that human progress and civilization are carried forward in the world by the energy and genius of great leaders of thought and of men. There were few of his contemporaries who recognized such a man in Christopher Columbus. Now the fact is historical, and of general recognition.

After spending several days in the harbor of Azua, resting his crews, and in refreshing them on the savory food they found in the flesh of a large fish harpooned and caught in the bay, the squadron sailed on July 14th, and after spending some days at the small islands near Jamaica, which he named the Pozas or Puddles, in a calm, and again at the Queen's Gardens, near Cuba, they sailed again on the 27th to the southwest, toward the continent. On July 30th, having come upon a small island, now known as Guanaja, the Adelantado, at the admiral's request, landed and found the soil fertile and green and the inhabitants similar to those of Hispaniola, except that their foreheads were more narrow. While thus engaged in examining the island, a very large Indian canoe approached the shore from the west, and was captured with its occupants and carried to the admiral. It was found to be hollowed, like others they had seen, from the trunk of a single tree, as long as a galley, eight feet wide; it carried twenty-five rowers, and had erected in the centre an awning or tent made of palm leaves, under whose shelter reposed the cacique with his wives and children. Columbus was deeply interested in examining the men, the arrows, and other articles of manufacture or production, all clearly indicating his approach to countries of some civilization. He was particularly struck at finding among these people hatchets made of brass and other admirably constructed tools, which resembled those afterward found in Mexico, and formed either of clay, hard wood or marble. These natives were not in the least afraid of the Spaniards or their large ships; both the men and the women were modestly clad, and among their articles of food were bread made of maize, a beverage made of the same, quantities of cacao, which the Spaniards had never before seen, and which the Indians so highly prized that they used it both for food and money. The women not only wore a jacket, which was colored and embroidered, but also a large sheet or blanket, which enveloped their persons, and with which they covered their heads and part of the face. No doubt these Indians came from Yucatan, for they informed the admiral that they came from a very rich country lying to the west, where wealth abounded, and which was possessed of a fertile soil. They urged the admiral to sail thither. But he, ever intent on discovering the strait between the two oceans, preferred to sail to the south and to the mainland, expecting to follow and explore the coast from Paria eastwardly until he should discover the desired passage. He dismissed the Indians with the exception of an old man, named Jumbe, who proved to be an intelligent guide and interpreter, and by exchanges obtained some of the implements and products of the country. He intended to visit these Indians and their country later, as he believed he would reach them by following the coast of Cuba, which he still thought was the mainland, and whose shores must extend to those regions. Yucatan was, in fact, only forty leagues distant, and had he immediately accepted the invitation of the natives, what changes would have occurred in the history and fortunes of Columbus!

During all this time the squadron had experienced nothing but rough and tempestuous weather. The sailors had struggled day and night with the elements, were exhausted and sickened; the miserable ships seemed at every moment about to founder. 'In the midst of such continued dangers and hardships for eighty-eight days, many of the sailors religiously prepared for death by confessing to each other, or endeavored to propitiate Heaven by vows to make pilgrimages on escaping safely their ever-threatened fate. It was impossible to enter a harbor in the midst of such storms; the sun and stars could not be seen, the thunder and lightning were terrific, the ships leaked on every side, the sails were rent, anchors and tackle were lost, the cables, small boats, and even the provisions were not saved. It was under such difficulties that this great discoverer, though ill and discouraged, sought to solve the problem of the earth. To add to his extreme peril, his illness brought him to the point of death, while his ever-vigilant mind was most anxious for the safety of his young son and for that of his brother, who had accompanied him against his will and purely through love and affection. "Another thought that tore my heart," wrote the admiral, "was the remembrance of my son Diego, left an orphan in Spain, and deprived of my honors and emoluments." Carried by wind and weather to the Pozas Islands, near Jamaica, and even near to Cuba, the admiral persevered in his struggle with elements and storms, and without waiting for good weather or favorable winds, he had reached Guanaja on August 14th, and Cape Caxinas, now known as Cape Honduras, on the 16th. It is certainly an evidence of indomitable will, a proof of the characteristic courage and tenacity of his character, that under such circumstances he took possession of the country on August 17th, in the name of the Spanish sovereigns, at a spot about fifteen leagues from Cape Caxinas, on the banks of a river which he called the River of Possession. Had Columbus yielded to the advice of the Indians in the large canoe at Guanaja, and pushed westward to the continent, he would have reached Yucatan in one or two days, and, as Mr. Irving remarks, "The discovery of Mexico and other opulent countries of New Spain would have necessarily followed ; the Southern Ocean would have been disclosed to him, and a succession of splendid discoveries would have shed fresh glory on his declining age, instead of its sinking amid gloom, neglect, and disappointment."

Continuing his course to the east, and hugging the coast as far as possible in order to find the expected strait, the great object of his expedition, they reached the eastern end of Honduras, where the coast bends suddenly to the south. Here, for the first time since their departure from Hispaniola, the winds blew in their favor, and for so unusual a favor the sailors burst forth in hymns of gratitude to God. The admiral, ever devout and religious in his character and life, gratefully called the cape Gracias á Dios. As the geographical knowledge of the old Indian guide Jumbe did not extend beyond this point, he was kindly discharged and sent home. At the River of Possession, near Cape Caxinas, the natives appeared in numbers, were friendly and hospitable, and brought to their visitors abundant supplies of bread and maize, fish and fowl, vegetables and fruits. After presenting these gifts by laying them before the Spaniards, they silently retired to a distance ; received presents in return with marked pleasure, and returned next day in greater numbers and with more generous supplies of food. Composed probably of different tribes, the natives, as the Spaniards progressed, spoke different dialects, and differed from each other in dress, decorations, and customs. While they resembled the Indians seen in the islands, they had lower foreheads, and were most careful in covering their persons. As the Spaniards progressed along the coast, this modesty disappeared ; the natives were entirely naked. They painted parts of their bodies black, and had their ears pierced with such large holes—as large as a hen's egg—that their visitors called their country Coast of the Ear. Some were said by Jumbe to be cannibals, though the Spaniards saw them do no worse than eat raw fish. In another part of the coast the natives marked their bodies with the figures of various animals, using fire for that purpose. Some wore long tufts of hair on their foreheads as ornaments, and on feast days some of the tribes painted their bodies red or black, or made stripes on their bodies and faces and circles around their eyes. Young Fernando Columbus was astonished at such grotesque tastes, and thirty years later, when he wrote his father's life, he recalled their hideous appearance, and said : " They all believe that in these different states they are perfectly beautiful, whereas they are frightful as the very devils." *

It was September 14th, 1502, when Columbus turned his prows southward from Cape Gracias á Dios, and explored the Mosquito Coast, which presented many varieties of rock, meadow, and fresh rivers, with abundance of fish and tortoises, rank vegetation, and great quantities of large alligators basking in the sun. With a smooth sea and favorable wind the squadron reached on the 15th a fine river with a good harbor, where wood and water

---

* Dr. Barry's translation of De Lorgues' "Columbus," pp. 441–59 ; Irving's "Columbus," vol. ii., pp. 305–20 ; Mr. Brownson's translation of Tarducci's "Columbus," vol. ii., pp. 227–40.

were procured ; but just as the ships were about to leave the harbor, the sea suddenly rose and then rushed back with great violence into the mouth of the river, capsizing one of the ships, and carrying all on board to the bottom. Naming the place Rio del Desastre, or Disaster River, in token of their having encountered a renewal of their sad experiences, and now again continuing their course with a favorable wind, they reached, on Sunday, September 25th, a secure spot between a small island and the mainland. The admiral now rested his men from the fatigues and labors of the past three months, and repaired his ships. So beautiful was the landscape, so delightful the country on every side, that the admiral called the place the Orchard. The native name was Quiribiri, and a beautiful village on the banks of a charming river was called Cariay. At first the natives came forth with arms to defend their country, but as the Spaniards remained quietly at work on their ships, hostility was succeeded by curiosity, then by visits and the exchange of presents. But when the Spaniards gave them presents and refused to receive any from the natives, the latter with wounded pride gathered up all they had received from their visitors and left them in a bundle on the shore. Finally the Indians sent two girls to the ships as hostages for the safety of the Spaniards, who might come ashore, and these girls the admiral entertained hospitably, gave them fine dresses and presents, and sent them ashore, where they were received with great delight. But the Indians, after holding a consultation among themselves, insisted on returning all the presents received by the girls, because their visitors in turn would receive none. It is interesting and almost unaccountable thus to behold savages, utterly destitute of civilization and social culture, practising a refined reserve and artificial etiquette not always observed in the most fastidious and refined communities.

The admiral was anxious to learn more of this interesting people and their country. He sent the Adelantado with companions ashore ; and as he approached the natives came forward in the water to meet him, and two of them took him from his boat and carried him in their arms to the beach, and seated him with ceremony, in the midst of the assembled natives, on a bed of verdure on the bank. With only signs and gestures, and the play of the features of the face, little could be ascertained, and when the natives saw the notary take out his pens and ink and commence to take down the conjectured responses to the Adelantado's inquiries, by drawing his hand regularly across the paper and leaving on it mystic signs, they suddenly, as if terror-stricken, all at once arose and fled with fright and precipitation. They regarded this mysterious proceeding as necromancy and magic. What is more singular in this event, is that the Indians returned afterward and endeavored to dispel the effect of the dark art as practised on them by the Spaniards, and to exorcise the Spaniards themselves, by casting on them powder and smoke of their own contrivance; and that in turn the Spaniards, with a superstition perhaps equal to that of the Indians, became alarmed at the sorcery practised on them by the Indians. While the Indians, steeped in sorcery, suspected every act of the Spaniards which they could not understand to belong to their own dark art, the Spaniards attributed their delays and hardships on that coast to the magic arts of the natives. Even the admiral regarded the inhabitants of these coasts as dangerous enchanters, and he suspected the two Indian girls, who had been sent on board his vessel, of having the magic powder hidden under their clothes. He gave an account of these singular impressions, on both sides, in a letter he wrote to the sovereigns from Jamaica.

During several days' delay in this spot the ships were repaired, and the crews were permitted to enjoy the much-needed rest and recreation they desired, while the energetic and untiring Adelantado made an armed expedition of observation and investigation into the country. He found no pure gold, but ornaments of the baser guaniri; but as usual the natives assured him that gold would be found in abundance as the fleet proceeded farther down the coast. One custom prevailing among these people was that of taking special care of the remains of the dead, and paying a marked veneration to them. A large house was seen containing a number of sepulchres, in which were found a dead body embalmed, others wrapped in cotton, so as to prevent any disagreeable odor. The bodies of the dead were decked in ornaments more valuable than those worn by the living, and their graves were embellished with rude paintings or carvings, or with portraits of the deceased. Before sailing Columbus seized seven of the natives for guides, but their countrymen were exceedingly distressed or incensed at this act, and they sent four of their principal men with presents to the ships, to entreat the admiral to release them. Neither the presents he gave in return nor the assurances of his intention soon to restore them safely to their homes succeeded in removing the fear and grief of these people at seeing some of their companions carried away by these fearful and mysterious people.*

Columbus sailed with his squadron from Cariay on October 5th. Having coasted along a region of great verdure and beauty, he came to another, which the natives of Cariay on board called Caribaro, and which they assured the Spaniards abounded in gold. As the ships proceeded near the shores the men were astonished to find that between a multitude of small islands the boats passed through deep channels free from obstructions as securely as if they were artificial canals, while the hanging spray of trees and vines swept the rigging and masts of the ships. It was a scene of unsurpassed beauty. On arriving here the boats were sent to one of the islands, where the Spaniards saw twenty canoes, whose late occupants had timidly hid themselves in the woods; they were perfectly naked, but ornamented with gold plates. They exchanged for small trifles a plate of gold which was worth ten ducats. The boats were sent ashore again the day after their arrival at Caribao. A number of canoes were seen on the shore of the mainland filled with Indians, whose heads were garlanded with flowers and crowns constructed of animals and birds' feathers, and with plates of pure gold around their necks; but they could not be induced to part with their golden ornaments. When two of these natives were seized and carried before the admiral, one of them was found to wear a plate of gold worth fifteen ducats, and another an eagle of gold, which was worth twenty-two ducats. The captured Indians informed the admiral that there were places in the interior, and only one or two days' journey distant, where gold abounded in great quantities. They mentioned a place with unbounded treasure, which they called Veragua, a name which afterward became the ducal title of the descendants of Columbus. Veragua was twenty-five leagues distant, and was represented as particu-

---

* Mr. Brownson's translation of Tarducci's "Life of Columbus," vol. ii., pp. 241–45; Irving's "Columbus," vol. ii., pp. 321–27; Dr. Barry's translation of De Lorgues' "Columbus," p. 462.

larly rich in gold. This coast, on account of its abundance of mines of gold and silver, was afterward called and is now known as Costa Rica.

While the cupidity of his companions was greatly aroused by the sight of so much gold, Columbus, after obtaining only specimens of the precious metal, and all the information the natives could impart, was unwilling to sacrifice to any temporary gain in treasure the great object of his enterprise—the discovery of the passage he was seeking between the Atlantic and Pacific oceans. It was thus with Columbus on all occasions: his ambition and his personal glory, his fortunes and every hope of wealth, were subordinated to the great and paramount interests and welfare of his enterprise and country. On October 17th the admiral commenced the exploration of the coast of the country of great reputed wealth, to which was afterward given the name of Veragua, a name now indissolubly associated with his fame and family. He proceeded twelve leagues, and then the boats went ashore for wood and water; but the natives assembled under arms and with every indication of hostility to dispute the approach of these strangers, even advancing out into the water to their waists, yelling, brandishing their weapons, and spitting at the Spaniards a certain herb they were chewing. Signs of peace from the Spanish vessels placated the warlike savages, and when the Spaniards landed they obtained readily in exchange for bells and other trifles the plates of gold which the natives wore around their necks. Sixteen plates of gold of the value of one hundred and fifty ducats were thus obtained at little cost. On the 28th the Spaniards again went to renew the traffic in gold, but the fickle Indians had become hostile again, and prepared to rush from their concealment and attempt the massacre of their visitors. Seeing the Spaniards in their boats and on their guard, the savages, more like angry children than warriors, rushed forth into the sea, as they had done the day before, threatening the Spaniards at the water's edge, while the forests resounded with their war-whoops. The arrow discharged from a Spanish cross-bow, which wounded a native, and the discharge of a gun from a ship, terrified the warlike savages, and put them to flight; but again the Spanish sailors and soldiers, by calling to them, soon pacified them, and secured more plates of gold in exchange for European trifles. At another place farther along the coast, and called Catiba, the same scenes occurred: the warlike demonstrations of the naked natives disappeared before the friendly advances of the visitors; visits were exchanged, and a trade in plates of gold and hawks' bells ensued. At this place nineteen plates of gold were procured, and here for the first time were seen signs of permanent building; and Columbus, persuaded that he was approaching a region of greater civilization, took a sample from a large piece of stucco composed apparently of stone and lime.

The admiral continued his voyage, and availed himself of every opportunity of obtaining specimens of the products of the country, and all possible information of a geographical character from the natives. After encountering another terrific storm, which caused him to forego his intention of visiting the various rivers and their vicinities, he pushed on and passed five large villages, one of which was Veragua, from which the neighboring district was named. Veragua was also said to be the region richest in gold, and here most of the plates of gold worn by the inhabitants of the Mosquito Coast were made. Cubiga was said to be the last of the villages in this golden region, which commenced at Cerabora and ended here. Rejecting all temptations to land and explore the golden region of Veragua, Columbus continued his search for the expected passage with unwavering constancy and perseverance. His action here was justly mentioned by Mr. Irving as actuated by a "generous ambition," seeking rather the benefit of mankind than wealth, and resting satisfied for his own part with "the glory of the discovery."*

During this interesting and important voyage, the investigations and inquiries, the information and suggestions obtained by Columbus were momentous and significant; for although he did not discover with his eyes the other sea, he gathered information which unmistakably showed to his intelligent judgment and, when revealed by him, to the minds of the world, the existence of the other ocean beyond the land. Convinced that he was still in the remote parts of Asia, as all the world believed with him, and, in common with the other learned men of his age, mistaken as to the size of the earth, he concluded that the great and opulous nation called by the natives Ciguare, whose

---

* Irving's "Columbus," vol. ii., p. 333.

inhabitants wore crowns as well as bracelets and anklets of gold, used the precious metal for domestic purposes and even for ornamenting their seats and tables, carried on an immense commerce, had opulent and busy seaports, used large ships armed with cannon, rode on horseback, and were armed very much like Europeans, must be on the other sea, and was one of the domains of the Grand Khan. This view was confirmed in his mind also by the pepper and spices shown him, which he knew well were among the products of Asia, by the warlike character of the natives of Ciguare, as represented by the Indians, and, while the sea continued round to that country, the great river ten days' travel beyond must be the Ganges. We now know, from the subsequent discovery and conquest of the rich countries of Mexico and Peru, abounding in wealth of every kind, that these latter were the countries of whose existence Columbus was the first European to obtain the least and the earliest knowledge. Had he been furnished with suitable squadrons and with ample military and naval means and outfits, his enterprising career would unquestionably have been crowned by the discovery of Mexico and Peru, of the two Continents of America, and of the Pacific Ocean.

Continuing his cruise, Columbus, on November 2d, arrived at a large and beautiful bay, to which he gave the name of Puerto Bello, to commemorate its beauty. Here he saw the houses of the natives scattered through a beautiful grove, with plantations of maize, vegetables, and fruits. The natives were friendly and hospitable, generous with their provisions and fruits, possessed no gold except small ornaments of it, which the cacique and his seven chief officers wore in their nostrils. All were naked, and the people were painted red, while the cacique was painted black. As the squadron proceeded they visited a place fruitful in spontaneous products, and to which Columbus gave the name of Port of Provisions. The natives were so much afraid of the strange visitors that, when some of them in a canoe were pursued by a boat from the ship, they sprang into the water and made good their escape, swimming when necessary under water. On November 23d the admiral, deceived as to its safety by the sailors, who were anxious to land and trade with the natives, entered another small harbor, which proved dangerous, and to which he gave the name of El Retrete, the Closet. Here the inhabitants were tall, slender, well formed and handsome in face and movement, and were friendly and hospitable. The shores abounded in alligators, and so numerous as to infect the air with a musky odor. The Indians freely exchanged their provisions for European trifles, but their friendly intercourse was interrupted by the avarice and licentiousness of the sailors, who found it easy to escape from the ships at night and visit the villages on shore, outraging the natives, and bringing on nightly brawls and bloody fights, and finally causing the Indians to assemble in numbers to take revenge and drive the intruders from their country. A shot from the guns loaded with a blank cartridge failed to produce more than a temporary fright. The vices of the Spaniards had proved them, to the Indians, to be even less than human in their morals; surely they could not be invulnerable. When the Indians renewed with increased rage their preparations for attack, a cannon-ball, which struck on a little cliff in the midst of a group of them, put them all to flight. Unfavorable winds and long confinement in El Retrete, the belief that the Indians were using sorcery to influence the weather against them, and the miserable condition of the ships, were unanswerable arguments against remaining here longer. The result finally arrived at by Columbus, though with great reluctance, was that the strait which he had so studiously conjectured and meditated upon in the halls of the Alhambra, and had now so earnestly and persistently sought, must be either much farther to the south and through the great continent he had previously discovered, or not in existence. However, he found it impossible to follow up the exploration at this time, and leaving it for a future effort, he announced to the glad sailors his intention of returning to seek out the rich mines of Veragua, of which he had heard so much.

The observant mind of Columbus had been guided by the peculiar configuration of the lands to the conclusion that the interoceanic passage must here be found; for here Nature seemed to have struggled to open for herself a passage, and for the severance of the two great American continents. It is remarkable that here, too, in our times man, induced by the necessities of commerce, the formation of the continents, and the narrowness of the land dividing the oceans, has selected this very place for accomplishing by human labor and science the very thing which nature seems to have attempted, but desisted from accomplishing. They were then on the coast of Chagres, near Panama; and here it is that an artificial passage, the Panama Canal, will accomplish the union of the oceans. Mr. Irving says: "Here, then, ended the lofty anticipations which had elevated Columbus above all mercenary interests; which had made him regardless of hardships and perils, and given an heroic character to the early part of this voyage. It is true, he had been in pursuit of a mere chimera, but it was the chimera of a splendid imagination and a penetrating judgment. If he was disappointed in his expectation of finding a strait through the Isthmus of Darien, it was because Nature herself had been disappointed, for she appears to have attempted to make one, but to have attempted it in vain." Tarducci also writes: "In our days, just where Columbus looked for his strait, human genius and activity are repairing nature's fault, and opening the passage between the two oceans which Columbus had judged must exist." And the Count de Lorgues writes: "He searched for it [the passage] wherever a particular configuration seems to have prepared for the severance of the two great parts of the American Continent. One would say that Nature was suddenly arrested in her work by the Most High, who, no doubt, reserves for the genius of man the opening of this grand passage. Columbus came to designate its locality." *

For three months Columbus had encountered almost constant storms, and those of the greatest violence. His crews were exhausted. While sailing southwest, Columbus had anxiously desired a wind from the west; now when he was sailing west he encountered powerful winds from the west, driving him to the east; and unable to reach Veragua, he was compelled to return to Puerto Bello; and here the storm grew fiercest. Columbus himself describes it in his letter from Jamaica: "Never was the sea so high, so frightful, so foamy. The wind did not permit me to advance, but held me in that sea, which seemed all blood, and boiled like a caldron over a hot fire; never was the aspect of the sky seen so fearful, burning like a fiery furnace day and

---

* Mr. Brownson's translation of Tarducci's "Columbus," vol. ii., pp. 241-54; Irving's "Columbus," vol. ii., pp. 328-38; Dr. Barry's translation of Count de Lorgues' "Columbus," p. 463.

night, and thundering so that I looked every instant to see if my masts were still standing. The lightning was so dreadful that every one believed the vessels would be destroyed. During all this time the water never ceased to pour from the heavens ; nor could it be said to rain, for it was rather another deluge. The crews were reduced to such a state that they wished for death to free them from such misery."

The violence of the storm seemed to culminate in its greatest violence on December 13th, and such was the fright which prevailed among all on board, that the sudden and short peals of thunder sounded, to the crews of each ship, like signals of distress from the other imperilled ships. Then, too, the ocean became strangely agitated, while the water rose suddenly and vertically in the air, drawing in the foaming waves, and rising cone-shaped to the clouds ; and at the same moment the livid clouds came down to meet the rising waters, and joining themselves together, and whirling and advancing with great violence and noise, approached the ships. Columbus had for several days been suffering so intensely from one of his old attacks of illness that his life was despaired of ; and the pious Franciscan, Father Alexander, had already yielded up his own life on board one of the ships, the first martyr-death on that western ocean. But now the extreme peril aroused the admiral to his accustomed energy, and he arose from his bed to cheer his men and meet the emergency. He, and his sailors, following his example, in this great danger resorted to Heaven, since no human science could avail them. They all recited passages from the Gospel of St. John, to which then, as now, was attributed a miraculous efficacy, and the admiral made the sign of the cross with his sword and drew a circle as if to cut off the approach of the storm-monster. Tarducci says, " The effect corresponded to his faith ;" for the dreadful waterspout, seething and hissing, passed between the ships, tossing them about most fearfully, but finally subsiding in the immensity of the ocean with frightful noise. To the astonishment of all, and to the delight of the grateful sailors, the ships were safe. The resort to the Gospel of St. John is now a well-known custom in time of peril, both at sea and on land ; but Tarducci says it is uncertain whether Columbus followed a then prevailing devotion or was the first to commence it, which from his remarkable example and from its accorded efficacy has since become traditional and general. On the following night the Vizcaina, one of the caravels, was missing, but on the third day it rejoined the other ships, having only sustained the loss of her small boat and an anchor. The crews were now exhausted and prostrated. A strange sight presented itself to their view : the ships were surrounded by sharks, which were believed by the sailors to possess an instinctive anticipation of shipwreck and a scent of human victims for their rapacious appetites and to surround and pursue with voraciousness a ship in danger, and be ready for the coming feast. But, as it resulted, some of the sharks were themselves captured, and the keen hunger of the sailors found in their usually unsavory flesh an acceptable repast. The provisions of fish and flesh on the ships had become exhausted, and the biscuit had become so ruined by moisture and heat that it was swarming with worms. Fernando Columbus thus describes the sailors eating their biscuit-rations : " So help me God, as I saw many of them wait till night to consume their rations, so as not to see the worms they were eating ; others got so accustomed to them, that they would not cast them off when they did see them, because they would reduce the ration too much." * It is not at all surprising, then, that from such rations as these the sailors did full honor to the feast on the shark's flesh, though there was a sailors' superstition against eating it. In the stomach of one of the sharks was found a live tortoise, which afterward became a pet with the sailors on the ship ; and in that of another was found the entire head of one of his companions, which had lately been cut off and thrown into the sea. It is difficult to tell whether the appetite of the sharks or that of the sailors was most voracious.

On December 17th the vessels entered the harbor of Puerto Bello. The Spaniards visited the village of Huiva, and rested there three days. The houses of the natives were built in the trees, like the nests of birds, and poles were stretched for this purpose from tree to tree to support the houses. Whether this was resorted to as a protection from wild beasts or their no less savage and murderous human neighbors could not be ascertained. In their state of nature, and on this coast, man and beast were equally ferocious, and man was constantly at war with

---

* " Historia del Almirante," cap. xciv.

man. Owing to repeated storms and adverse winds, the fleet was nearly thirty days in reaching Veragua from Puerto Bello, a distance of thirty leagues. As they arrived at Veragua on the Epiphany, and celebrated the visit of the wise men from the East visiting the Infant Saviour at Bethlehem, the admiral named the river Belen, the Spanish name for Bethlehem. The coast which he had passed with so much difficulty and suffering was named the Coast of Oppositions.

On the river Belen, as well as on the river Veragua, the inhabitants, though at first hostile and belligerent, were addressed in their own language by the Indian guide on the ships, and were easily pacified with presents, and soon entered into trade with the Spaniards. Columbus ordered both rivers to be sounded. The natives of both places confirmed the accounts already received as to the abundance and richness of the gold-mines of Veragua. The Veraguans informed the admiral that these mines of gold lay in the distant mountains. It would seem that the Indians attributed something of a sacred character to the precious metal, for they informed the admiral that they observed strict continence and fasted twenty days before going to the mountains for gold. He made an earnest appeal to his own followers, as they were Christians and trained to render to God prayers and works of self-denial in gratitude for the gifts they received from Heaven, that they would prove themselves not inferior to the heathen natives, who, without a vestige of religious training, were accustomed to purify themselves by continence and fasting for receiving the gifts which God had bestowed upon their country. It was, however, in vain that Columbus exhorted the demoralized Spanish sailors and men to prepare themselves for the search for gold, according to Christian methods, by continence, fasting, and confession. Their avarice and their lusts found ready answers and excuses for declining his wholesome advice. For a few European trifles the Spaniards had already obtained in exchange twenty plates of gold, with a number of pipes of gold and crude pieces of ore. These treasures added stimulus to the already inflamed avarice of the Spaniards. Human passions seem ever ready in these early advances of Europeans in America to degrade Christians below the standard of their faith, and to give them no advantage in contrast with the pagans in their conduct. The impression

that they came from Heaven was soon rudely dispelled, and the
Indians learned from European vices, of which they had been
ignorant, lessons of depravity and degradation.

Columbus entered the Belen River with his ships as a secure
place of anchor, though he would have preferred the Veragua
River had it been of sufficient depth of water, as it communicated with gold regions of that name. The natives received
their visitors with apparent joy, and brought every kind of food
in which the country abounded. They also brought various
ornaments of gold, which they said came from Veragua, and
which they observed were more coveted by the Spaniards than
even food itself. They gladly accepted European trifles in exchange. Every account confirmed the reports of the golden
treasures at Veragua. The Adelantado accordingly ascended
the river Veragua in the boats, which were well manned and
armed, visited the Quibian, the principal cacique, at his residence,
about a league and a half off, was met by him on the way in his
canoes, and attended by many of his subjects. This friendly
interview was followed by a visit of the cacique to the admiral
and the fleet, where he was entertained with regal hospitality.
On both occasions the cacique was apparently well pleased to
part with his jewels of gold for trifling returns. He was a fine
specimen of Indian manhood and beauty, tall and powerful in
frame, warlike in demeanor, taciturn and cautious in his intercourse. Though his visit to the admiral was outwardly cordial,
it was significantly short.

While Columbus was thus securely resting with his ships in
the river Belen, and contrasting its quiet waters with the stormy
ocean without, a peril suddenly came upon the fleet from within.
The waters of the river came rushing from the interior in a great
torrent—no doubt a freshet from the mountains, caused by heavy
rains, and the ships were in danger of immediate wreck, as the
storm then prevailing at sea prevented them from seeking safety
without. Having escaped this unexpected peril with little more
damage than the loss of the mainmast of his own ship, the admiral and his crews found the weather too boisterous for moving
about until February 6th, when the waters became calmer. The
Adelantado then proceeded with sixty-eight men in the boats to
explore the Veragua River, was received by the Quibian at his
village with great courtesy, and was furnished by the chief with

three guides for visiting the mines, to which visit and expedition he gave his consent: The cacique was cautious and prudent, and when he saw his inability to resist openly these powerful intruders, he concealed his hostility as well as he could in his own breast. On arriving at the region to which the Indian guides had conducted him, the Adelantado was struck with admiration at the beauty and grandeur of the country. Gold abounded everywhere, and from the surface the Spaniards easily gathered considerable quantities of gold in two hours. While the soil was spangled with gold, the precious particles were imbedded in the roots of the trees. On ascending a high hill a country of great extent and magnificence burst upon his view. Boundless forests spread out before him; the trees were of the largest size; and the whole region was declared by the guides to abound in gold. Returning to the Belen, the Adelantado gave the admiral a glowing account of the country he had visited, and of its unbounded riches. It came to light, however, that the guides, under secret instructions from the wily cacique, had carried the Spaniards to the dominions of his enemy, a neighboring chief, with whom he was at war, and that the mines of Veragua were much nearer and richer.

The Adelantado was not discouraged, but on February 16th he went forth on another exploring expedition along the westward coast, accompanied by fifty-nine armed men, while a boat with fourteen men followed them along the shore. This new region was equally rich in gold, and abounded in cultivated maize and delicious fruits. The natives wore around their necks great plates of gold. The Indians parted readily with their golden treasures, and from them he heard the most glowing accounts of a great and opulent nation in the interior, whose inhabitants, unlike the naked Quibian and his people, wore clothes, were armed like the Spaniards, and were far advanced in civilization. On hearing these inspiring accounts the admiral congratulated himself on his near approach to the opulent regions of Asia; the mines of Veragua must be the same with those exhaustless gold deposits of the Aurea Chersonesus, from which Solomon drew the gold for ornamenting the great temple of Jerusalem, and the Ganges could not be beyond his reach. Such were the conclusions which so good a geographer and cosmographer drew from the dim allusions of the Indians of Veragua to what must have been the Peruvian Empire.

From the explorations of the country by the Adelantado, the admiral was convinced that the river Belen afforded the best port for ships, and that Veragua was the richest in gold of all the districts within his reach. The admiral's disappointment at not discovering the interoceanic passage had preyed severely upon his sanguine mind, and had contributed much toward the aggravation of the disease which for nine days had brought him to the verge of death. But now the discovery of a rich goldbearing country, from whose inexhaustible treasures the exchequer of Spain would be replenished, his own fortunes restored, the Holy Sepulchre wrested from the Moslem thraldom, and by the discovery of which his own fame would be vindicated before the world and posterity—these fortunate circumstances elevated his hopes and spirits to the highest point of his enthusiastic nature. "But there is one thing," he wrote from Jamaica, "I venture to report, for there were many eye-witnesses, and that is, that more traces of gold were seen in two days in Veragua than in the whole four years in Hispaniola; and that more fertile or better cultivated lands than those around it could not be desired. . . . At a single time there was brought to Solomon six hundred and sixty-six quintals of gold, besides what he had of the merchants and seamen, and not counting what was paid in Arabia. Of this gold were made two hundred lances and three hundred shields; the roof [of the temple] was decorated with this metal, and enamelled with precious stones; and many other things were made of it, and numerous large vases were spread over with precious stones. Josephus speaks of it in his chronicles *de antiquitatibus*. It is also spoken of in Paralipomenon and the Book of Kings. Josephus is of opinion that the gold came from the Aurea; and if so, I maintain that the mines of the Aurea are absolutely identical with those of Veragua, which, as I have already stated, extend westward more than twenty days' journey, equally distant from the pole and the line. All those things—gold, silver, and precious stones—were bought by Solomon; but here in this place all that is necessary, if gold is wanted, is to send to gather it. David in his testament left Solomon three thousand quintals of gold from the Indies to aid in building the temple; and, according to Josephus, it came from these same lands. Jerusalem and the Mount of Zion must be restored by the hands of a Christian, and God, by the mouth of the prophet, has said so in the fourteenth psalm. Abbot Joachim asserts that this Christian must come from Spain. St. Jerome pointed out to the Holy Spouse [the Church] the way to succeed. The Emperor of Cathay asked long ago for learned men to instruct him in the faith of Christ. Who will present himself for this mission? If our Lord grants me to return to Spain, I bind myself, in God's name, to carry him thither safe and sound." *

The admiral decided to found a colony on the Belen River, which should be the great mart for the wealth of the country ; this extensive realm should be taken possession of in the names of the Spanish sovereigns, and the mines of Veragua should be vigorously worked. The Adelantado was to remain in command of the colony with eighty men, and these were divided into sections of ten men each, and these began with alacrity and goodwill to build the dwellings and a large storehouse, which were built of wood and palm-leaf thatched. While a considerable part of the provisions and artillery was placed in the warehouse, the principal part was left on board the Gallego for the use of the colony. The food provisions were chiefly left on the other ships of the squadron, as the soil was rich and yielded abundant crops, while the river and sea abounded in fish. The fishing tackle consequently was left on the Gallego. The native beverages of the country, extracted from the pineapple, palm-trees, and other fruits would afford pleasant drink even for Europeans. The admiral with the other ships and crews was to return to Spain, and he expected soon to return with an abundant supply of men and provisions to give the assurance of permanency to the colony. He took great pains, as well he knew how, to conciliate the good will of the natives, and to reconcile them to the intrusion of strangers into their country. And now that the houses were sufficiently advanced to afford shelter for the colonists, the admiral prepared to leave, while the brave and resolute Adelantado calmly assumed the care and leadership of this, the second hopeful yet dangerous experiment of European colonization in

---

* Mr. Brownson's translation of Tarducci's "Life of Columbus," vol. ii., pp. 264–66.

America ; but now the ship, owing to the dry weather and low tide, could not pass out of the river, while the ocean lashed the shores most violently without.

The cacique of Veragua, who had nursed his resentment at the intrusion of the white men into his country, and now saw their preparations for a permanent settlement, prepared, as he trusted, to annihilate the strangers at one blow. While he was thus assembling his forces from all parts on the Veragua River for this fierce and resolute attack, it was given out that he was preparing for war with a neighboring tribe. It was fortunate that these measures of the proud and jealous chief were developed before the departure of the admiral and the ships. It was the faithful and intrepid Diego Mendez that penetrated the designs of the Quibian. He offered the admiral his services to discover the true state of things. He was peculiarly fitted for so bold and perilous a service. Proceeding in his boat with a few armed men along the coast to the Veragua River, he soon saw a thousand armed and provisioned Indians marching toward the Belen. He boldly sprang ashore and mingled with the native army, and when they said they were marching against the Cobrava Auriva Indians, he offered to go with them with his boat and men and fight on their side. He saw, from his services being declined, from their evident embarrassment of manner and looks, and their manifest desire to get rid of him, that they were treacherously marching on the Spanish colony. So, too, when the Indians saw him return to his boat and watch their movements, they returned the same night to Veragua. When Mendez returned and reported to the admiral his conviction that the warlike movement was directed against the Belen colony, and when the admiral hesitated to strike a blow against the conspiring natives for fear of doing them an injustice, Mendez, with characteristic intrepidity, offered to penetrate the Indian camp and visit the Quibian at his residence. As he proceeded to this perilous mission he received unerring confirmation of his suspicions, and yet he pushed on. Having with consummate strategy penetrated to the very residence of the cacique, and by his ingenuity and address escaped an almost certain death, he returned and reported to the admiral the plan of the Indians to march under cover of the night upon the Belen colony, and by fire and weapon destroy the settlement, the ships, and all the Spaniards at a blow.

The bold and desperate resolve was now made of gaining the presence of the cacique by stratagem, arresting him there by main force, and bringing him to the ships for immediate transportation as a prisoner to Spain. This accomplished, the conquest of Veragua and its inhabitants would prove an easy task. The Adelantado, accompanied by eighty armed men, among whom was the intrepid and wily Mendez, undertook this perilous duty, and under circumstances as remarkable and astonishing as they were romantic. Those brave and deliberate soldiers, the Adelantado and Mendez, accomplished their difficult mission. The Adelantado with consummate strategy reached the royal presence, captured the Quibian with his own stout hands, and though he thus encountered a desperate and powerful athletic and brave foe, he conquered him by personal strength and agility, and his own men rushing to his aid, made prisoners of the entire household of the chief—men, women, and children—to the number of fifty. The Spaniards, in the heart of the enemy's country, were in peril for their own safety; how could they also secure and send back their prisoners through the infuriated bands of Indians, the chief prisoner's devoted subjects? Don Bartholomew resolved to remain at Veragua to follow up his work, and Juan Sanchez earnestly sought the perilous honor of carrying the cacique and delivering him to the admiral on board his ship. It was a difficult task to carry so powerful a prisoner to Belen, and so eager was Sanchez to be selected for the accomplishment of the feat, that he offered to have his beard plucked out, hair by hair, if the Quibian should escape. Proceeding with the royal prisoner, not only bound hand and foot, but also tied by a cable to the boat's bench, the party had reached within half a mile of the mouth of the Veragua. The night was dark; all danger of rescue was over. So tightly was the prisoner secured, that he complained constantly of pain, and finally Sanchez, moved with pity for the cacique's sufferings, compassionately loosened the cable from the bench and held it in his hand. The prisoner feigned great sufferings, and pretended to be half dead. His eyes were never taken off Sanchez; suddenly, when the latter was looking another way, the wily Indian dropped into the water, and Sanchez would have been dragged in also by the cable and its ponderous burden had he not let go his hold. In the darkness of the night and confusion of the scene the cacique escaped, and Sanchez, "cursing himself and Heaven," returned to the fleet with his other prisoners, but overwhelmed with chagrin and mortification at his blunder and misfortune. He had been outwitted by a savage. Don Bartholomew found it impracticable to follow up the war with adequate results, so he returned to the colony with an immense booty captured in the cacique's house, such as large plates of gold and ornaments of every kind, amounting in value to three hundred ducats, one thousand two hundred and eighty-one dollars of our money. The royal fifth was set aside from the plunder, and the rest was divided among the brave men who had undertaken the enterprise. Don Bartholomew received as a trophy of his gallantry and success one of the golden coronets. It was the compassion of Sanchez toward his prisoner in relaxing his bonds that stood between the admiral and the conquest of some of the richest and most important portions and perhaps empires of the new world. But for this trifling incident Columbus would probably have advanced to the conquests which Cortez and Pizarro so brilliantly achieved in Mexico and Peru. So far-reaching was this act of clemency in its effects, that the destiny of future empires was affected by it, the public history of Spain, of Europe, and of the world was changed, the fortunes of Columbus ruined, and perhaps the possession of the Holy Land lost to Christendom. And yet our sympathies must go out to the act of clemency, while the cause of a chief seized and doomed to exile and humiliation for defending his own under the law of nature, in the light of true justice, seems to outweigh the highest aspirations and results of our own aggressive civilization. Retribution soon followed.

Columbus now considered profoundly and earnestly what next steps were to be taken in the momentous movement of European civilization upon the domains of nature, the advance of Christianity into the realms of paganism, in which he was the pioneer. It was thought probable if not certain that the Quibian had perished in the water, for how could it be otherwise with a man whose hands and feet were tied? Without their powerful, warlike, and popular leader, the Veraguans could be easily conquered, their fertile country seized, and the inexhaustible gold-mines worked with success. Even if the cacique survived, he and his people must have been terrified by the boldness, skill, and power of the Spaniards, and discouraged by the capture and imprisonment of the royal family. Surely these naked savages would not dare to encounter the champions of civilization and of the crown of Spain. The admiral regarded the prospects of his new enterprise as most favorable. In the mean time, heavy rains had fallen; the ships were relieved of their cargoes and towed, though with difficulty, out of the river, and when the cargoes were reshipped on board, as was soon accomplished, the admiral was ready to sail. It was the admiral's intention to touch at Hispaniola, and thence send provisions and reinforcements to sustain the infant colony, planted in a wilderness and surrounded by enemies smarting under their wrongs. It only needed a favorable wind for the ships to sail.

On April 6th, 1503, the admiral's boat was sent ashore. The sacrifice of its passengers proved the salvation of the rest of the Spaniards. The Indian cacique, though bound hand and foot, was so accustomed to the water, that he glided like a fish to the shore, crawled to the woods, and was soon once more at the head of his warriors, all vowing the utmost vengeance upon their white assailants. The chief stealthily reconnoitred the vessels, and saw his wives and children and his whole family carried out of the river, and on the eve of being carried into perpetual exile. Every natural and just instinct of his fierce nature was aroused. As chieftain, as husband, as father, as a man, he saw every right of his outraged, and he now devoted his whole existence to revenge, for the intruders had not all departed from the land to the ships. He assembled his warriors secretly to the number of four hundred. The colony did not, besides Don Bartholomew and Mendez, exceed seventy Spaniards on shore. The Indian army advanced, under cover of the woods, while the Spaniards, intent on the immediate preparations for the departure of the ships, and lured to carelessness by the confidence they felt in the effect of their recent exploit, were not aware of the deadly approach. The Indians reached within ten steps of the houses, and, but for their accustomed Indian war cry, which they thrice repeated, they could have surrounded every house, and after slaughtering its occupants have fired all. The terrific yells of the Indians brought the Adelantado and seven or eight others to the defence, while Indian arrows penetrated the palm-leaf roofs and wounded some of the inmates. The Adelantado, lance in hand, led his little band, and they fiercely attacked the Indians as they emerged from the woods. Soon the intrepid Mendez and others joined him, and with their swords the well-armed and shielded Spaniards made dreadful havoc among the naked warriors. At this juncture a furious dog, possessed by the Spaniards, rushed out, and, by leaping and seizing the Indians in the face, rendered greater service than the Spanish swords. The Indians had never seen such an animal, and, affrighted by such a monster, they rushed frantically back to the woods. The rest of the Spaniards now came up from their various occupations to the aid of their countrymen. The Indians lost all hope, and they were put on their defence by the intrepidity of the Spanish, and could only discharge their weapons from the woods, which resounded with their yells. Spanish courage, skill, and arms carried the day against the savage and naked warriors of Veragua. The struggle lasted three hours: The Indians left nineteen of their warriors dead on the field, while they carried off large numbers of their wounded. The Spaniards had one killed and seven wounded, and among the wounded was the brave Adelantado, who received a lance-wound in his breast.

The boat from the admiral's ship entered the river just as the fight was at its height. It was under the command of Captain Diego Tristan. He and his men took no part in the battle, remaining silent spectators of the startling scene. He gave as his motive in not going to the relief of his countrymen, when questioned and censured, the necessity of avoiding and preventing the struggling Spaniards, on seeing a boat approaching, from rushing to it to make their escape, overloading it, and thus causing the death of all by drowning; when, if left to their own desperate defence, their arms and valor would save them. And so it resulted. But Diego and his comrades on the admiral's boat were reserved for a more appalling struggle and a more consummate fate. He had been sent in the boat, with seven or eight rowers and three armed men, to obtain fresh water. The Spaniards on shore endeavored to persuade him to desist from going up the river, for if he went his fate seemed desperate; but he answered that he did not fear the Indians, and he would at all risks perform the duty confided to him by the admiral. Scarcely had the boat proceeded a league from the settlement, when it was set upon by innumerable Indian canoes filled with infuriated warriors, yelling as they came out from the wooded shores, and the boat was soon surrounded. The Spaniards, though few in number, might have put their assailants to flight by the terror of their fire-arms, if they had promptly discharged them; but the suddenness of the attack and the appalling yells and numbers of the Indians caused them to lose their presence of mind. Their Spanish shields were no protection against such swarms of assailants, and the showers of arrows at every side. It was in vain that Diego Tristan endeavored to sustain the courage of his men by word and example. He was repeatedly wounded, and finally fell dead from a lance which penetrated his eye. The rest of the Spaniards were slaughtered; every Indian warrior struggled to be the instrument of his nation's vengeance. The bodies of the Spaniards were cut to pieces. Only one man escaped, Juan de Noya, who in the confusion had fallen overboard, and by swimming under the water had made his escape and returned to the settlement to announce the disaster.

The scene at the village can scarcely be imagined, much less described. The Spanish colonists, though successful in driving off their Indian assailants, were appalled at the ferocity and numbers of their enemies. Instead of being humbled or frightened at the recent exploit of the Spaniards in seizing their chief and his family, their savage passions were intensified by revenge and hatred. How could a handful of men in a wilderness, thousands of miles away from home, subsist in the midst of countless enemies, whose country they had invaded, and whom they had goaded on to the fiercest consciousness of pride, injury, insult, and defiance? At the Belen colony all were in the most intense state of excitement and dismay, and nothing was talked of but the late assault of the Quibian and his warriors. It was in the midst of such tumult and consternation that Juan de Noya suddenly arrived in their midst and announced the appalling massacre of the Spaniards in the boat under Diego Tristan. Dismay was turned into a panic of the most frightful character. Terrific as was the account of Noya, the frightened colonists exaggerated in their dismay even this consummate disaster. A handful of men amid countless enemies, exasperated with hatred and revenge, had now within a few hours twice attacked the Spaniards. The admiral, ignorant of their disasters, was about to sail away; what but the most cruel death awaited them at every step? There was one simultaneous abandonment of the settlement, and the panic-stricken crowd rushed to the Gallego for safety from their enemies, and in the hope of putting out to sea. It was in vain that the clear voice and commanding coolness of the Adelantado endeavored to preserve order or calm the excitement. To their consternation, the men saw that it was impossible for the caravel to overcome the ever-increasing sandbar at the mouth of the river, and such was the violence of the sea without, that it was impossible to send out a boat with men to communicate their condition to the admiral. At this terrible moment a spectacle presented itself to their eyes which deprived them of every remnant of sense or thought: the bodies of Diego Tristan and his companions came floating past, and upon the mutilated masses of flesh and bones were crowded the birds of prey, fighting over the quivering limbs of the slain and piercing the air with their hideous cries, until there was little left on the water but floating clusters of bones from which the flesh was nearly all picked by the vultures.

At this pitiable moment the infuriated Indians, rejoicing at their triumph over the Spaniards in the boat, having practically shown their intruders to be mortal and vulnerable, and gloated with Spanish blood so recently shed by them, burst forth from the woods suddenly with yells, and the sounds of shells and drums gave notice of hundreds more approaching. The Spaniards desperately rushed and brought together all the tables, chests, casks, and other articles they could find, and with these they hastily formed a bulwark, in the centre of which they huddled together with their arms, and at the two openings were stationed falconets. When the Indians rushed upon the little fort so suddenly constructed, the discharge of the two falconets struck terror in the assailants, and these, panic-stricken at the balls and the havoc they made, rushed back to the woods. Here they swarmed, and watched for the opportunity of killing the Spaniards if any should venture out for food or water. The continued discharges from the falconets, cutting the trees with the balls or wounding some of their number, still kept the Indians in check.

The scene on board the admiral's ship was only different in degree. For ten days all on board had anxiously awaited the return of Diego Tristan, and each day's disappointment dismayed the admiral and his men beyond endurance. No means existed of communicating with the shore. At the end of this time, when all seemed to despair, an appalling event occurred on the ship Santiago, which made it seem that all the powers of evil were leagued against them.

The Indian prisoners on board the ship, the family of the Veraguan chief Quibian, who were held as hostages for the safety of the colony on shore, were every night shut up securely below the deck. The hatch was too high to reach with their hands from below, and as the sailors were sleeping upon it, the guards deemed it unnecessary to chain it down on the outside for security. The prisoners saw their opportunity in the carelessness of the men. They gathered together and piled under the hatch the stones used for ballast, and mounting upon these, the prisoners by one united effort forced the hatch, throwing off the sleeping sailors from it; then, quickly springing on deck, they were in an instant in the water, and concealed by it, were making their escape to the shore. An immediate alarm, vigorously sounded on the ship, brought pursuers to the rescue, and resulted in the capture of most of the fugitives. The prisoners were now secured under hatches which were chained down, and a strong guard placed on duty. These desperate savages, more than ever aggrieved at not escaping with their more fortunate companions, and goaded on to despair, all resolved to die together. The men and women collected the cords in the hold; all united in the sad tragedy, and strangled themselves. So intent were they in their desperate resolve, that while some stretched their feet and knees out on the bottom, because there was not space or height enough for them to hang, others with their own hands and feet drew and tightened the cords around their necks in order to ensure their own deaths rather than survive in exile, separation, and slavery. Columbus and his companions were appalled at such a revolting spectacle. Were such to be the fruits of his great discovery? Were such the early products of Christian civilization when brought in contact with pagan barbarism? Were not the hostages he had held for the safety of his own countrymen on shore either all dead or at liberty, by their own escape, to foment hostility against the Christians among their people? What days of anguish on board the ships were those ten days of crushing suspense, during which no tidings had been received of Diego Tristan and his companions, or of the Adelantado and his colonists at Belen! The cruelly treated cacique, the Quibian of Veragua, no longer restrained by the fear of reprisals, had the Spaniards on shore at his mercy.

The intense anxiety of the admiral and all on board the ships led several sailors to offer to swim ashore, provided the boat was sent to carry them to the edge of the surf. They felt ambitious to show that they were not inferior to the Indians, whom they had seen swim defiantly through the raging waves or under them the distance of a league, encountering deadly perils through natural love of liberty. Could not a Spaniard do as much for the safety of his countrymen? The admiral gladly accepted the generous offer, and a boat load of sailors were rowed to the edge of the billows; but the courage of these hardy sailors failed before the inevitable death that awaited their attempt to swim a league's distance through mountains of furious billows. One man, however, performed the marvellous and perilous undertaking, Pedro Ledesma, a sailor of powerful frame and surpassing courage. It was long painfully doubtful whether he or the waves would conquer. Human courage and strength conquered. Having reached the shore, the Spanish colonists, frenzied with their perils and sufferings, pressed around him, and with agony told him all that occurred, and with hands joined together as a pledge resolved at every risk to fly the greater danger, from which they apprehended death at any moment. The voice of the Adelantado and his officers fell powerless on their ears; they had found two canoes, and had a boat of their own. They desperately prepared to join the ships as soon as the violence of the sea permitted. They besought Ledesma to present their desperate petition to the admiral, that he would not in his charity abandon his countrymen and companions to their certain fate; that they would not and could not remain, as death was certain; that if the admiral should refuse to receive them, they would call on Heaven to witness his cruelty; that, in any event, they would put to sea in their own unseaworthy ship, preferring the perils of the sea to the certain revenge of man. The brave Ledesma ascertained all, and after receiving the instructions of Don Bartholomew, resolutely plunged into the sea, passed through the surging billows to the boat in waiting, reached the admiral's ship, and imparted to his chief, with hurried and confused words, the appalling intelligence of all he had seen and heard.

Columbus was bowed down to the earth with grief at such tidings. No man ever suffered such sorrows as he. The conviction that he was the chosen of God to perform the great mission of opening the way to the conversion of all heathen nations to the Christian faith was ever present and uppermost in his mind, and yet whenever he seemed on the point of accomplishment he was cast down, and seemed to himself and to mankind the most unfortunate and abandoned of men. It was truly said that " in all the trouble and distress which Columbus had undergone in his four voyages, he had never found himself in so desperate a situation as when Ledesma brought his news." * Could he go away and leave his countrymen in the jaws of death? Had those whom he had brought from home no claims upon his justice, his sympathy, or his charity? Was Don Bartholomew, the most devoted of brothers, to be abandoned to savages seeking his life? How could he ever become reconciled to the death of Diego Tristan, still less to the relinquishment of his plan for planting a colony in the midst of unbounded wealth? Knowing that it was impossible to send reinforcements to the colony, as he was already short of men and sailors; that to return to Belen himself with his ships and men would endanger all, without the world's ever knowing of his great discovery of the continent and the gold of Veragua, and with no means of obtaining succor or reinforcements from home, he could see no course open to him, direful as it was, than to abandon the settlement for the present, to receive the forlorn hope upon his ships, and return with all to Spain. In the midst of such crushing disasters his sanguine mind still clung to the hope of again returning with a numerous colony and with sufficient ships, soldiers, and outfits of every kind to found anew the colony in Veragua, maintain it, reduce to subjection to the Spanish crown the warlike people and caciques of that fertile and gold-bearing region, and perhaps the entire continent. But in such a resolve as that of returning to Spain, he saw the impossibility of a boat's reaching the shore in the violent high sea prevailing; his own ships were not seaworthy, being honeycombed by the teredo or strained by the tempests, almost ready to fall to pieces. He was also short of sailors. The dangers of these stormy seas, and of the rocks near

---

* Mr. Brownson's translation of Tarducci's "Life of Columbus," vol. ii., p. 281.

the coasts, rendered any effort to return to Spain scarcely less dangerous than the exposure on shore to massacre from the infuriated Veraguans. In whichever direction his thoughts turned, he encountered difficulties and dangers the most appalling. Yet every moment's delay increased the dangers and disasters of the situation, for at any moment his noble brother and companions might be murdered on shore. His own strength and health were exhausted by age, disease, hardships, disasters, nightly vigils and labors, and his mind and body were wasted by his anxieties, sorrows, and misfortunes. All seemed lost, where worlds had lately been the prize.

In this state of crushing perturbation of the admiral, his mind was racked with anguish and fever, despair and misfortune; he dragged himself out of his sick-bed and rushed to the wheelhouse and frantically called on the four winds to help him in his difficulties, while his officers stood by weeping for him and his cause. This state of mind was followed by a lethargic yet disturbed sleep, during which he experienced one of those visions in which he received what he regarded as a supernatural comfort and reassurance, and which he attributed to the divine intervention. His own words will convey most effectually the strange yet interesting condition of mind and body in which Columbus was plunged by his misfortunes:

"Overcome by fatigue, I fell asleep groaning, and I heard a voice saying to me, 'Oh, thou fool! slow to believe and to serve thy God, and God of all! What more did He for Moses, or for His servant David, than He has done for thee? From thy birth He has taken the greatest care of thee. When He saw thee come to a fitting age, He marvellously made thy name resound throughout the earth. The Indies, those wealthy regions of the world, He gave thee for thine own, and empowered thee to dispose of them according to thy pleasure. He delivered to thee the key of the barriers of the Ocean Sea, which was shut up with such mighty chains. Thy orders were obeyed in many countries, and among Christians thou didst acquire honorable fame. What more did He for the people of Israel, when He led them forth from Egypt? Or even for David, whom, finding a shepherd, He made King of Judea? Turn, then, to Him, and acknowledge thy error; His mercy is infinite. Thy age shall be no impediment to any great undertaking. He has many and vast inheritances yet in reserve. Abraham was above a hundred years when he begat Isaac; and was Sarah youthful? Thou urgest for succor despondingly. Answer! who hath afflicted thee so much and so many times—God, or the world? The privileges and promises which God hath made to thee, He hath never broken; neither hath He said, after having received the services, that His meaning was different, or was to be understood in a different sense; nor did He inflict pain in order to show forth His power. He performs to the very letter, He fulfils all that He promises, and with increase. Is not this His custom? See what thy Creator hath done for thee, and what He doeth for all. The present is the reward of the toils and perils thou hast endured in serving others.'

"In hearing this," writes Columbus, "I was as one almost dead, and had no power to reply to words so true; I could only bewail my errors. Whoever it was that spoke to me, finished by saying: 'Fear not! Have confidence. All these toils and tribulations are graven in marble, and it is not without cause.'"

Various views have been expressed of this remarkable occurrence in the life of Columbus; but no one can fail to acknowledge the grand simplicity and noble good faith with which the statement is made by the author of these words. While some suppose that this narrative of a dream was an illy-disguised lesson intended to be applied to the king, and to secure the restitution of his rights, Mr. Irving joins the great mass of writers in rejecting this view, saying: "He was too deeply imbued with awe of the Deity, and with reverence for his sovereign, to make use of such an artifice." And while attributing this strange yet simple and honest account to the characteristic faith of Columbus in the supernatural, to his belief that he was one divinely chosen for a great mission, and to the peculiar and perhaps unprecedented situation in which he was placed, Mr. Irving seems to enter the personality of this remarkable man, and see this dream partly from the admiral's standpoint, while yet wondering at such "striking illustrations of a character richly compounded of extraordinary and apparently contradictory elements." * He rejects the view of the supernatural origin of the vision. Tarducci

---

* Irving's "Columbus," vol. ii., p. 368; Mr. Brownson's translation of Tarducci's "Life of Columbus," vol. ii., pp. 282-83.

attributes this circumstance to the exalted views the admiral entertained of his mission, to his unfaltering and ever fresh sentiments of religion, and to his facing then a situation which seemed to terminate all his hopes.* But the Count de Lorgues enthusiastically announces his belief in the reality of the supernatural vision, and places the admiral in supernatural intercourse with the Deity.† Father Knight writes: "If visions are impossible, this was no vision. Comfort so opportune and so efficacious may easily have been something of a higher order than Irving, in his 'impatience of the supernatural,' supposes. The change produced could not have been more complete if the voice which Columbus heard was really, as he himself believed, a message from God," and spurns the thought that this was "the raving of a disordered mind." However it may be viewed, Columbus came out of his sleep full of consolation, courage, and perseverance. Humboldt says: "His description of this vision is all the more pathetic for the bitter rebuke it contains, directed with bold frankness to powerful monarchs by a man unjustly persecuted." ‡

On awakening from his sleep, though much encouraged, Columbus had for nine days longer to endure tempestuous weather. As soon as the storm subsided the provisions and other movable effects were brought off in boats from the Gallego to the fleet, but it was impossible to get the caravel across the bar of the river. Diego Mendez accomplished the onerous and difficult work of transferring the property to the ships with consummate skill and prudence. The men were also carried in boats to the ships, and when all was accomplished Diego Mendez with five men remained on shore to the last, and they then returned together to join their companions on the ships. The joy of the colonists on being rescued from that fatal shore was unbounded, and their return to the ships and their companions was hailed with delight on both sides. The admiral was so grateful to Mendez that he embraced him most affectionately again and again, and, as a token of his high appreciation of his services in great emergencies, raised him to the rank of captain, and

---

* Tarducci's "Columbus," vol. ii., p. 284.
† Dr. Barry's translation of Count de Lorgues' "Life of Columbus," p. 480; Father Knight's "Life of Columbus," p. 209.
‡ Humboldt, "Voyage," etc., vol. iii., book 9, chap. 28.

gave him the command of the ship which Diego Tristan had commanded before his cruel death at the hands of the Indians.

In the latter part of April—on Easter night, 1503—Columbus with his three ships sailed from a coast which was bright with gold, but had proved the harbor of death. The grandeur of his conceptions and of his enterprise, in attempting at that early period the circumnavigation of the earth, entitles him to our admiration. Though the attempt failed, it solved the problem of the earth's geography on this point, and his theories were, in the main, based upon the most advanced thought and study on the shape and structure of our planet. Had he been provided with ships and equipments in keeping with the power and grandeur of the Spanish nation, and of the importance of the enterprise, the flag of Spain would have floated, under Columbus, over empires, and on the waters of the Pacific Ocean. His spirit of intelligent enterprise and adventure would never have rested short of such results.

His intention was to sail for Hispaniola, repair his ships, obtain provisions, and then sail for Spain; but when his crews saw him sailing along the coast eastwardly instead of northwardly, in the direct route to Hispaniola, their surprise was great, and they murmured at his attempting so long a voyage without adequate provisions and with ships that were strained and worm-eaten. The Count de Lorgues construes the action of Columbus as another and final attempt to accomplish the discovery of the interoceanic passage and the circumnavigation of the globe; but this view is not tenable in face of his scanty provisions and the unseaworthy condition of the ships, and is not supported by his biographers or by historians generally. On the contrary, he and his brother had made so accurate a study of those waters and of their peculiar currents, that they knew it was necessary to gain a considerable distance to the east before attempting to cross the sea intervening between them and Hispaniola, in order to avoid being carried away and far below their destined port by the strong westerly currents prevailing in those waters. It is also conjectured that the admiral, after having experienced the disposition of his contemporaries to avail themselves of his discoveries and charts, and appropriate and claim for themselves results after he had discovered and pointed out the way, was determined now to foil such efforts by keeping to himself all knowledge of the route to the opulent regions and gold-mines of Veragua. Hence he disregarded the murmurs of his pilots and seamen, and kept his own course. Violent disputes arose among the pilots as to the proper route to take, and Columbus, in order to maintain his authority and decide for himself so important a question, in which opinions were so divided, seized all the marine charts in the possession of the pilots. It seems illogical for so eminent a writer as Humboldt to accuse Columbus in this of an abuse of power. How could discipline or obedience be maintained in so perilous or so important a service in which Columbus was then engaged, if the pilots were permitted to indulge in violent and wordy altercations as to the course to be followed? These very charts were the basis of the disputes, and their seizure was necessary for the maintenance of an authority essential to the safety of all. Not only this act, but also the following statement of Columbus in his report to the Spanish sovereigns, was rendered necessary by the treachery and bad faith which he had experienced. If, while his proposals were rejected by Portugal, the Portuguese King treacherously sent out an expedition to rob him of his discovery, and now, after he had achieved it, King Ferdinand had sent another governor to supersede him, and he was not permitted even to take shelter from a storm in the very harbor he had established, he was justified in protecting himself and in frankly declaring his purpose. "The pilots may tell the position of Veragua if they know it; I maintain that they can give no other description than this: 'We have been in certain countries where there is great quantity of gold,' and that they can certify to; but they are ignorant of the way to return thither; to go there again, they would have to discover it anew." Arriving at Puerto Bello, he was compelled to abandon the third caravel, the Vizcaina, on account of her sinking condition, and even here his most necessary acts, as, on all former occasions, taken for the safety of all, were criticised. The crew of the abandoned ship were distributed between the other two, and these were worm-eaten and too dangerous to sail in. Columbus continued his easterly course as far as Port Retrete, discovered the Mulata Islands, and went ten leagues beyond the entrance to the Gulf of Darien, and several leagues beyond his former course, apparently in search of the strait, thus giving color to the view of the Count de Lorgues, that even now, with such

odds against him, he was heroically seeking again the solution
of his great geographical and commercial problem, the inspiring
object of his fourth and last voyage. But here he called a council of the captains and pilots, and upon their unanimous opinion
against the further search for the strait, he turned his course on
May 1st to the north, and for Hispaniola. Here again the east
winds and currents swept the ships greatly to the west; the
admiral, with rare seamanship and against the remonstrances of
his pilots, kept close to the wind, for he assured them they would
be carried west of Hispaniola, while they asserted the contrary.
On May 10th the ships passed in sight of the Caymans, two small
islands northwest of Hispaniola, which he called Tortugas, on
account of the multitude of tortoises seen around them. On the
12th he found himself thirty leagues from that place, and among
a group of islands south of Cuba and the Queen's Gardens, and
with all his precautions the ships were eight or nine degrees
west of San Domingo.

The situation of Columbus was growing more perilous every
moment, for the sailors were kept at the pumps day and night,
while all they had to sustain their stomachs was a morsel of
musty biscuit, oil, and vinegar. It was difficult to keep the
water from gaining on the ships, and here at their first anchorage,
and at midnight, the leaking ships were assailed by so violent a storm that Columbus compared it to the end of the world.
Three of their anchors were lost, the two ships were thrown
against each other with such violence as to shatter the bow of
one and the stern of the other, and it seemed like a miracle that
the admiral's ship was not lost, with the cable of her only remaining anchor reduced to mere thread by friction on the rocks,
when the dawn enabled them to replace it with another. For
six days and nights the ships were in constant peril from the
storm, all the cables were lost, the water was pouring in through
worm-eaten holes, and the sailors were exhausted and discouraged. With great struggling against adverse winds and currents the ships reached Cape Cruz, in the island of Cuba, and
anchored near an Indian village in the province of Macaca,
where Columbus had touched on his voyage in 1494. Here they
rested and obtained some provisions. Another effort to reach
Hispaniola was defeated by adverse winds and currents, and the
tempest was renewed. It was a struggle between life and death;

it was not enough to keep the pumps working day and night; buckets, kettles, and pitchers were also brought into the same desperate service. On one of the ships the water had reached the deck. The dismal expedient of running the ships ashore, perhaps to fall victims to hostile Indians, was forced upon them, but even here a first attempt was unsuccessful at Dry Harbor, as there were neither natives to give them food nor water to refresh them. Forced again to sail, they finally reached the harbor in the island of Jamaica which in his first voyage the admiral had discovered and named Santa Gloria, and here the sinking ships were run upon the strand. This port is now known by the name of the admiral himself, the Bay of Don Cristobal. The ships were wrecks, little more than their frames remaining; like Shakespeare's "rotten carcass of a boat," they were tied together on the beach, a bow-shot from shore, thus forming a sort of refuge for the admiral and his companions. The water reached nearly to the decks of both wrecks. Without a roof or a home on the land, their skeleton ships were at once their homes and their barracks at the water's edge—in fact, prisons on a barbarous shore. The wrecks were put in a state of defence, and barracks thatched with straw were erected on deck, stern and forecastle. The strictest discipline was proclaimed and enforced, the men were kept busy, and visits to shore without permission were forbidden. Such measures were necessary, for the admiral knew too well that the men were prone to abuse and degrade the natives, even when they themselves were reduced to the lowest point of disaster, and in danger thereby of increasing their misfortunes. It was necessary now more than ever to gain the good will of the natives in order to secure food, and to avoid giving offence. They were at the mercy of the natives. A firebrand at night from hostile or offended Indians would consume their roofs and barracks to the water's edge, and what would be their helpless condition when in the power of countless enemies?

> "All—all the storm
> Devour'd ; and now, o'er his late envied fortune,
> The dolphins bound and wat'ry mountains roar,
> Triumphant in his ruin."
> —Young's "Revenge."

In the most overwhelming misfortunes mitigating circumstances are hopefully regarded as positive good. The admiral was not wholly among strangers, for he had visited this spot before; the island was populous, near by was the village of Maima, whose inhabitants hastened to bring provisions to the stranded ships, quite happy in receiving trifles in return. In order to maintain peace with his neighbors, the Indians, fairness of dealing, and a just division of the food among his famished men, Columbus established certain necessary measures and regulations, and appointed two of his officers to superintend. All was at first harmonious, but the Indians never provided much even for themselves in advance, and the provisions in their cabins soon became exhausted. Famine seemed at the very barracks of the Spaniards. In this emergency the ever-faithful Diego Mendez volunteered to seek and apply measures of relief. Setting out with three others, he visited successively the Indian chiefs. He was not only received and treated with hospitality, but with three caciques whom he visited he made the most satisfactory arrangements for supplies of food, and in each case he sent one of his three companions to apprise the admiral of the good results of his important mission. Left now alone, he continued his journey to the eastern end of the island, and made friends of several powerful caciques. From the last he purchased an excellent canoe, and with six Indians he returned along the coast to the ships, and was received with triumph and gratitude by the admiral and all his countrymen. His canoe was loaded with the provisions he had purchased. The supply was continued by the daily arrival of Indians well loaded, and the traffic was mutually satisfactory.

Columbus now became anxious for his deliverance from this helpless and dangerous situation, and still more anxious to secure to his country and the world the knowledge and the fruits of his recent discoveries. Cut off from Hispaniola by forty leagues of sea, and that sea subject to capricious currents and winds, with no boat, his ships wrecked, and without human hope of communication with the rest of the world, the possibility of perishing in this remote wilderness, deprived of the consolations of religion, with no prospect of realizing the results of his labors and sacrifices, and with still less hope of being able to secure the deliverance of the Holy Sepulchre to Christendom, he found himself in " a disheartening position, because there was no outlet from it." * " What was to become of them, and how were they to get away from the island?" asks the learned Tarducci. Trusting that God would provide him with the means of communication, Columbus, ever hopeful and fruitful in resources, wrote to the Spanish sovereigns a detailed account of his momentous voyage, the discovery of the gold regions of Veragua, and his present misfortunes, and he besought their Majesties to send a ship to his relief. This remarkable and now famous letter was dated July 7th, 1503.

The writings of Columbus, his letters, the living communications of his feelings to his sovereigns or to his friends present a candid reflection of the character of the man. This letter, or rather report to the Spanish sovereigns, written by Columbus from his stranded ships on the coast of Jamaica, is justly regarded as one of the most important documents of his career. Remaining for centuries forgotten and unnoticed, although it had been printed in Spain, it was again brought to light about the year 1822, when the historical and literary world was aroused by its publication, and the learned societies of Venice, Bassano, Pisa, Florence, Genoa, Milan, Pavia, Rome, and Paris were electrified by its contents, and the learned librarian Morelli, of Venice, published it with copious notes of his own under the title of "Littera Rarissima." Valuable on account of its geographical and scientific discoveries and thoughtful reflections, it derives a special interest from the critical and desperate circumstances under which it was written. Its significant and ringing notes rise like a voice of indignant and just appeal from the depths of the wilderness, and it has well been said that no other man could have written such a letter. Its method of transmission was most extraordinary. The classic language of our own Irving thus describes the letter of Columbus from Jamaica: "Nothing is more characteristic of Columbus than his earnest, artless, eloquent, and at times almost incoherent letters. What an instance of soaring enthusiasm and irrepressible enterprise is here exhibited! At the time that he was indulging in these visions, and proposing new and romantic enterprises, he was broken down by age and infirmities, racked by pain, confined to

---

* Count de Lorgues' "Columbus," Dr. Barry's translation, p. 486; Tarducci's "Columbus," Brownson's translation, vol. ii., p. 292.

his bed, and shut up in a wreck on the coast of a remote and savage island. No stronger picture can be given of his situation than that which follows this transient glow of excitement; when, with one of his sudden transitions of thought, he awakens, as it were, to his actual condition." Graphic as is this passage from the pen of Washington Irving, he seems to lose sight of the fact that Columbus was in his character and life always an entirety; in the most disastrous positions in which he might be placed, he never gave himself up wholly and exclusively to the sorrow of the occasion or to the saddening contemplation of his perils. These formed a part only of his thoughts and sensations, but never to the exclusion of other and brighter and more successful epochs and aspirations of his life, and more especially of the yet unaccomplished but never abandoned aspirations of his soul, and plans of future grandeur and usefulness. Hence we see mingled in the same letter a prayer for a ship to be sent for his rescue from destruction, and the announcement of his ever-cherished plan for the relief of the Holy Sepulchre. He sues at one and the same time for his life and for the restitution of his offices, titles, revenues, and estates. It is extraordinary that in such extremities the human mind was capable of grasping the grandest interests of mankind, and at the same moment detailing the most minute particulars of his own and his companions' affairs, even to the demand for the payment of the arrears of pay due to his crews.

After relating the unparalleled labors, hardships, and perils of his fourth voyage, he discloses the existence of the ocean beyond the lands he had discovered, narrates the discovery of the continent, the gold regions of Veragua, and, as if especially addressing himself to the king, he writes, "I make more of the scale and of the gold mines of this country than of all that has been done in the Indies." He makes a direct appeal for the payment of the back pay of his men, who had followed him through every peril, and would, on their return to Spain, announce the grandest results of Spanish discoveries. While those who had abandoned his great work, undertaken for the honor of Spain, and had culumniated the administration of the discoverer of the new world, were rewarded with offices, which he boldly denounces as a scandal, the discoverer and his companions are left to perish in a savage land. He recalls by a delicate but significant and unmistakable allusion the unaccomplished and not attempted delivery of the Holy Sepulchre, when he says, " The other affair, the most important one, remains where it was, calling with outstretched arms! It has been passed over as foreign, even to this hour!" Who could not see in this metaphor what Columbus saw with the eyes of his soul, the Saviour extending forth His arms from the Holy Sepulchre in supplication for deliverance from the hands of the infidels? Even when he claims, with severe justice, the restitution of his property, his honors, his dignities, his offices and estates, feeling ever present in his heart the desire to devote them to the deliverance of the Holy Sepulchre, he demands it as something due to God Himself, and he exclaims to the sovereigns, " It is just to give to God what belongs to Him." And again, " In acting thus your Highnesses will show a high degree of virtue, and will leave Spain a grand example and a glorious memory as just and grateful princes." And again he says, " Jerusalem and Mount Zion are to be rebuilt by the hand of a Christian. Who is he to be? God, by the mouth of the prophet, in the fourteenth psalm declares it. The Abbot Joachim says he is to come out of Spain." He appeals to the king and queen in behalf of the new countries he had given to Spain. " This is not a child, to be abandoned to a stepmother. I never think of Hispaniola and Paria without weeping. Their case is desperate and past cure. I hope their example may cause this region to be treated in a different manner." The admiral again alludes to the Grand Khan, whose dominions he still asserts he had approached, and reminds the Catholic sovereigns that that potentate had requested learned and zealous missionaries to be sent to instruct him and his subjects in the Christian faith.

Heretofore, in this great epic composition, the admiral had spoken mostly of other interests, or, in alluding to himself, to his public relations to the crown; but now the injustice he had sustained and the royal ingratitude, the tragic character of his misfortunes, and the very romance of his disasters, swell up in his soul, and he seems to place his cause before all posterity in placing it before his sovereigns. In language which reads like that of the weeping prophets of Judea, like the lamentations of ancient seers, he exclaims : " Hitherto I have wept for others ; but now, have pity upon me, Heaven, and weep for me, O earth !

In my temporal concerns, without a farthing to offer for a mass; cast away here in the Indies; surrounded by cruel and hostile savages; isolated, infirm, expecting each day will be my last; in spiritual concerns separated from the holy sacraments of the Church, so that my soul, if parted here from my body, must be forever lost! Weep for me, whoever has charity, truth, and justice! I came not on this voyage to gain honor or estate, that is most certain, for all hope of the kind was already dead within me. I came to serve your Majesties with a sound intention and an honest zeal, and I speak no falsehood. If it should please God to deliver me hence, I humbly supplicate your Majesties to permit me to repair to Rome and perform other pilgrimages."

Such a letter is truly, as Humboldt says, an initiation into "the inward struggles of the great soul of Columbus." * But that such a document should have been written by Columbus to the sovereigns of Spain, under circumstances which to all were acknowledged to exclude absolutely all possibility of transmitting it to Spain, is almost as wonderful a fact as the contents of the letter itself. How even would it be possible to communicate to Ovando at San Domingo his forlorn condition, and ask for transportation to Hispaniola and to Spain? But Columbus had faith. The following conversation and the result of it exhibit the character of Columbus in the direst extremities, reflected in the noble achievement of one of his faithful companions. He knew that his only chance of communication with San Domingo lay in the fruitful genius, ardent loyalty, and undaunted bravery of Diego Mendez, which had never failed him. Calling, therefore, that brave and gifted mariner and soldier to his side, the admiral made no direct allusion to Mendez; but the following conversation, as related by Mendez himself, occurred:

"Diego Mendez, my son," said Columbus, "of all that are here, only you and I understand the great peril in which we are placed. We are few in number, while these savage Indians are many, and fickle and irritable by nature. On the least provocation, on a mere suspicion or caprice, they may at any moment become enemies, and can easily throw firebrands on our ships from the shore and consume us in our straw-thatched barracks. The arrangement which you made with them for provisions, and

---

* "Histoire de la Géographie du Nouveau Continent," tom. iii., § ii.

which at present they keep so faithfully, may not satisfy them to-morrow, and they may withhold their assistance; and without the means of compelling them we shall be entirely at their pleasure. I have thought of a way of escaping from this danger, but I desire to hear your opinion first. It is that some one should venture to pass over to Hispaniola in the canoe you bought, and procure a ship to take us out of our perilous position. Now, tell me your opinion."

The bold and gallant Mendez replied: " I see clearly, sir, the danger we are in, and it is much greater than any one could imagine. As to passing from this island to Hispaniola in so small and frail a boat as this canoe, I believe is not only very difficult, but even impossible; for I do not know who would venture on such evident danger as crossing a gulf forty leagues between the islands, when the sea is so boisterous."

The dangers and difficulties of such an adventure can more readily be appreciated, when so fearless and adventurous a hero as Diego Mendez could not imagine how or by whom it was to be undertaken or accomplished. The expressive countenance, the very silence of Columbus, his noble and considerate bearing—all told the heroic Mendez that the admiral could think of no one else but himself as the man for this appalling yet not impossible task. Diego's generous ardor was equal to the admiral's trust, and, prompted by the exalted sentiment within, he electrified his superior by the following magnanimous and immediate reply:

" Sir, I have often risked my life to save you and all those who are here, and God has preserved me in a miraculous manner. There have not been wanting maligners of my conduct, who say that your lordship entrusts to me all the affairs in which honor is to be gained, while there are others among them who would execute them as successfully as I. For this reason, it seems fair, sir, that you should summon all the rest, and propose to them this enterprise, to see if any of them are willing to undertake it, which I greatly doubt. If they all decline, I will then risk my life for your service, as I have often done."

The admiral's plan was now sure of execution, and so manifestly wise and prudent was the proposal of Mendez, that it was immediately carried into effect, and with anticipated result. All the officers thus summoned to hear the admiral's proposition, with one voice declared it impossible. It was then that Diego

Mendez modestly but gallantly stepped forward, and said: "Sir, I have but one life to lose, yet I am willing to venture it for your service and for the good of all here present, and I trust that God, our Lord, viewing the intention by which I am directed, will preserve me as He has so often done before." * The admiral arose and embraced the noble and generous Diego with every manifestation and expression of gratitude and love, saying that he knew how Mendez could be depended upon for the execution of this most perilous and difficult affair, and expressed his confidence in the protection of God over him.

With the gallant Mendez it was no sooner said than executed. He prepared his Indian canoe with keel, boards along her sides and stern to guard against the sea, tarred it well, put in a mast, a sail and provisions, and hopefully and bravely departed on his miniature ship. A brave Spaniard, whose name it would be a pleasure to the historian to record if known, volunteered for the voyage, and six Indians accompanied him. It was the dangers on land that proved the defeat of this heroic attempt; for after having reached the point in Jamaica nearest Hispaniola, and having escaped capture by a flotilla of Indian canoes, he and his canoe were captured by the natives, who resolved to put him and his companions to death and divide the plunder. A quarrel among his captors and his own ready address enabled him, in the very presence of the Indians, who were playing a game of chance to decide the distribution of the booty, to escape by jumping from tree to tree until he reached the shore; and here, stepping into his canoe, he reached the admiral's barracks in safety. It is not known what became of his Spanish companion. He immediately and undauntedly offered to set out again on his perilous voyage, provided he was accompanied by a sufficient number of men to protect him from the natives until he should have put out to sea. The bravery of Diego Mendez now became contagious. Many now offered to accompany him on the expedition, which was thereupon increased to two canoes, one under the command of Diego Mendez, the other under that of Bartholomew Fiesco, who was formerly captain of the Vizcaina, a gentleman of Genoa, devoted to Columbus, and a man of high

---

* Mr. Brownson's translation of Tarducci's "Life of Columbus," vol. ii., pp. 293, 294.

character and courage. Each of these brave captains was accompanied by six Spaniards, and each had ten Indians to act as oarsmen. The two canoes were to keep company until they reached Hispaniola, when Fiesco was to repeat the perilous voyage in returning to relieve the anxiety of the admiral as to the safe arrival of Mendez, while the latter was instructed to proceed overland to San Domingo and deliver to Ovando a letter requesting that a ship be sent immediately to bring him and his companions to Hispaniola, and thence to proceed to Spain and deliver to Ferdinand and Isabella the important dispatches the admiral had addressed to them.

With good heart the bold deliverers started on their mission of humanity. The canoes were provisioned with cassava bread and the meat of utias, the men wore sword and buckler, the Adelantado escorted them to the end of the island with a sufficient force for their protection, and after waiting three days for a favorable sea, the generous captains passed out to sea amid the prayers of all for their safety. The Adelantado vigilantly and tenderly watched the receding canoes from the shore, until at evening they faded from sight, when he commenced his march back to the ships, visiting the friendly caciques on the way and arranging for continuing the supplies.

While his hopes and prayers followed his friends in their noble expedition, Columbus was most solicitous for the sick among his little colony or garrison in the wrecks, and for the supply of food for all, while he was himself prostrated on his bed of sickness, a prey to the most excruciating sufferings. Well might he now hope, however, that relief was not far distant. Yet were there ever such misfortunes, such treacheries, such splendid hopes dimmed by adversities, such unjust oppositions, such tormenting physical maladies, such betrayals, such revolts, such ingratitude as he had to meet and bear? Shipwrecked on a savage shore, in a remote and unexplored part of the new world, dependent on the caprice of the Indians for his daily food, prostrated with disease, spent with labor and vigils, enfeebled by age, and cut off from all assistance, surely nothing worse could come even to such a man of sorrows and misfortune! But a worse sorrow awaited the prostrated and sick but ever brave admiral, now the commander of two wretched and wrecked hulks, the remnants of the unseaworthy fleet with which he had been grudgingly supplied by Ferdinand and Fonseca for his fourth voyage—worse, as Mr. Irving says, " than storm or shipwreck, or bodily anguish, or the violence of savage hordes—the perfidy of those in whom he confided." Such was the mutiny of the Porras brothers.

Scarcely had the brave canoes of Mendez and Fiesco departed amid hopes and prayers, when a reaction set in among the shipwrecked colony. Recent labors, exposures, and fastings had been supplemented by the unhealthy climate and the unaccustomed vegetable diet supplied by the natives as causes of sickness, and these were soon followed by depression of spirits, gloomy forebodings, and despondency. The vain watchings for the return of Fiesco's canoe had increased the mental discontent, and this had ripened into open expressions of mutiny. While the chief, spent with their common sufferings and hardships, was doing all for their preservation and deliverance, was bearing with them the same adversities and meeting the same fate, they accused him of being the cause of their misfortunes, instead of extending to him a manly sympathy and support. In such a state of things the aimless clamor of the crowd was rendered formidable by the assumed leadership of two officers, whom the admiral had favored far beyond their deserts or capacities in order to please Morales, the royal treasurer, and who had proved themselves ungrateful and insolent. Columbus had met with many such official ruffians. These two officers were Francisco de Porras, whom he had appointed captain of one of the caravels, and his brother Diego, for whom he had obtained the appointment of notary and accountant-general of the expedition. Columbus had extended to them great leniency in simply reprimanding them for their past insolence instead of dismissal or suspension. To such weak and treacherous creatures the mild reprimand was an insult, and they became the enemies of their benefactor.

Availing themselves of the mutinous spirit of the crews, these brothers did all in their power to foment an open mutiny by mingling among them and spreading all kinds of slanders and insinuations and reports against the admiral. They represented the expedition of Mendez and Fiesco as a sham, not sent for the deliverance of the people, but for his own private advantage and purposes; it was not intended that Fiesco should return; the admiral was deceiving them with hopes of deliverance, whereas he was not at liberty himself to return to Hispaniola or Spain, for he had been banished from Spain, and refused shelter at San Domingo even from a storm; and that Jamaica, where he was content to stay, was as good a place of exile for him as any other. Fiesco had not returned because he was so instructed. Why should so many Spaniards be sacrificed on account of one man, and he a foreigner? Why should they not attempt their own deliverance by sailing in the Indian canoes for Hispaniola? Would they not be welcomed the more for leaving the hated admiral behind in his exile? Was not Ovando his enemy, as were also Fonseca and even Ferdinand his enemies? Morales, the treasurer, would favor their cause in Spain, as Fonseca had favored that of Roldan and the rebels; and had not these received pardon and emoluments, while Columbus had been deprived of his command and most of his concessions? The king and queen were at heart anxious to get rid of him, and could easily be induced to strip of every privilege the man they had already exiled.

The mutinous men rallied around these unworthy sowers of sedition; the only two whose names are known or who had any repute were Juan Sanchez, the pilot who had by his carelessness allowed the cacique, the Quibian, to escape from his grasp, and Pedro Ledesma, the sailor who had swum ashore in the storm at the river Belen to obtain tidings of the unfortunate colony. With such leaders the mutiny openly broke out, notwithstanding the kind and sympathetic words and assurances of the admiral that relief would soon arrive.

It was on January 2d, 1504, as the admiral lay on his couch writhing with the pains of gout, that Francisco de Porras rushed into his cabin, with excited look and violent voice, and scarcely could the suffering admiral lift himself on his elbows, when the mutineer coarsely exclaimed: " Sir, why are you unwilling to return to Castile, but keep us all perishing here?" Columbus possessed extraordinary self-control, and on this occasion he exerted it; for though his astonishment could not have been greater if, as he himself said, " the rays of the sun should emit darkness," he calmly and amiably assured the rebel that he, too, was most anxious to return to Castile, more so than any other, for his own sake as well as for the sake of those whom God and the sovereigns had entrusted to him. But what could be done

until the canoe had returned from Hispaniola? and as he had so
often assembled the captains and principal men of the expedition
in council on important occasions, so now, if Porras had any
proposition to make, he would summon them in council again to
consider it. To this fair and considerate statement Porras replied with arrogance, "There is no use for so many words, but
embark at once, or stay in God's name;" and turning his back
upon the admiral, he said, "For my part, I am for Castile; let
those who choose follow me." At this concerted signal all the
conspirators present, with one voice, shouted, "I! I! I!" and
springing up simultaneously, they seized possession of the forecastles and cabins. Some cried out, "To Castile! To Castile!!" while others shouted, "Kill them! Kill them!!"

At the noise and bustle of this outbreak, so open, so violent,
so flagrant, the admiral struggled from his couch to reach the
scene and quiet the insurgents by persuasion, while the Adelantado, seizing his lance, rushed to the defence of his brother and
his friends, whose lives were threatened. It was fortunate for
the whole community that the more prudent and calmer officers
induced each to retire, while they themselves persuaded the
insurgents to withdraw from the wrecks. Seizing the ten canoes
which the admiral had purchased, and which were tied to the
ships, the insurgents and others now joining them, moved at the
moment with the alluring hope of reaching home, forty-eight in
number, deserted the admiral, and collecting hastily their effects,
jumped into the canoes, elated with even the phantom hope of
reaching Castile. Those that remained were the sick and a few
faithful and loyal friends of the admiral. Moved by the misfortunes of the former and the fidelity of the latter, the admiral had
himself carried to the bedsides of the sick to comfort them, and
he embraced the others with every token of affection. He appealed to all to place their trust in God, and assured them of the
speedy arrival of relief. He, the most infirm and ill of all, visited
the sick every day. His cheering words and his sedulous attentions inspired the sick with hope and courage, and finally restored all to health, energy, and cheerfulness. It was on such
occasions as this that the admiral's qualities shone in a characteristic light.

The insurgents, led on by the two brothers Porras, coursed
with their canoes to the east, following the direction along the

shore taken by Mendez and Fiesco; arrived and landed at the end of the island and commenced robbing the Indians and casting the blame of their outrages on Columbus, by whose orders they professed to act, referring their victims to him for pay, and telling them to kill him if he did not pay them, representing him as the worst enemy of the Indians, and that he would enslave and murder them, as he had done with the natives of other islands, unless they should kill him and save themselves. These miscreants, as soon as the sea grew calmer, embarked in their canoes to cross the sea to Hispaniola, taking a number of the natives to work at the oars. They were soon driven back by the boisterous sea, having thrown all overboard except their arms and a few provisions. Even the poor Indians were forced into the sea, and when they swam back to save themselves by holding to the canoes, they were either murdered with the swords of the Spaniards or forced to relax their hold and sink to the bottom. Eighteen of these miserable natives were thus either murdered or drowned, for the best of the swimmers gave out and sank.

Returning to the shore, these outlaws were divided as to what course to pursue. They robbed the Indians unmercifully, and filled the land with terrors. Three times they attempted to cross the sea in their canoes, and were each time driven back. Finally, abandoning all further attempts, they overran the land with rapine and outrage. The task of feeding the admiral's companions having become onerous to the Indians, the European trinkets given in return having lost their novelty, the desertion of so many of the admiral's men, and the malicious instigations of the rebels, resulted in the indifference or refusal of the Indians to bring in sufficient food for the Spaniards at the wrecks. To use force with them was now out of the question, and starvation stared the admiral and his friends in the face. Though wracked with bodily pain and crushed with repeated misfortunes, Columbus on his sick-bed devised an ingenious method of inducing the Indians to renew their supplies—one characteristic of himself, and fortunately successful. Remembering there would be an eclipse of the moon on the third day, and knowing how the Indians regarded all the phenomena of nature with superstitious awe, he availed himself of the opportunity by inviting the Indians to assemble at a feast. He then spoke to the assembled chiefs and natives of the God of the Christians, of His power, His friendship for good Christians, as manifested by His letting Mendez and Fiesco reach Hispaniola in frail canoes, and His anger against bad men, as manifested by His not permitting the Porras brothers and their guilty followers to do the same; that He was angry, too, at the Indians for refusing to bring provisions to the good Spaniards, as they had promised, and would punish them with famine and pestilence; and as proof of His just intention to punish them, He would show them an evident proof in the heavens, so that they might know that the punishment came from God. That this portentous sign would be seen by them all and by all the world, and consist in the appearance of the moon that night, which would come forth angry and inflamed, in proof of the anger of God and the truth of what he, the admiral, now said to them.

While some of the Indians were moved to fear, others treated the threat as idle; but when the predictions of the admiral were fulfilled that night by the eclipse of the moon, the Indians were terrified, and in order to ward off the anger of the Christians' God, they ran in crowds to the wrecks loaded with provisions, begging the admiral's intercession for their pardon, and promising in return to supply him and his companions with all the food they needed. The eclipse was now progressing; the admiral, in answer to their prayers and promises, announced his intention to retire into his cabin and intercede with God for them; and when the eclipse had reached its greatest he reappeared and assured them that God had heard his prayer, and in proof of this announced that the moon would become pacified and would set aside all appearances of anger. Just then the Indians saw the wane of the eclipse, as the admiral had assured them it would occur, and as it gradually disappeared, the Indians returned thanks to the admiral and rendered praise to God. Thenceforth they were most faithful in bringing in the supplies of food for the Christians, whose chief thus had direct communication and influence with the God of the universe.*

While most historians relate this anecdote as an evidence of

---

* "Hist. del Almirante," by Fernando Columbus, cap. 104; Mr. Brownson's translation of Tarducci's "Life of Columbus," vol. ii., pp. 305-307; Irving's "Columbus," vol. ii., pp. 396-400.

the clever and ever-ready resources of Columbus in times of extreme danger, the Count de Lorgues takes a more serious and reverential yet rather extravagant view of the subject, as shown by the following paragraph : " In place of aiding him with a material miracle, as He would have done for a patriarch or prophet of the old law, and of sending him some manna or some quails, the Most High assisted him with an idea. He succored His servant with a notion derived from the scientific order dependent on the architecture of the heavens. He inspired him with a means that had never been employed since the commencement of certain history, and of which the admiral would never have thought. God reminded him that in three days there would be an eclipse of the moon. Thus the moon, that sign by which Diego Mendez was preserved from a horrible death from thirst, was to save Christopher Columbus from famine. In his perplexities, every time the messenger of the Cross went to pray, the idea of the eclipse came into his mind. Columbus inferred from this circumstance that he must derive his safety from the eclipse. God simply indicated to him the subject; his genius furnished him with the mode of rendering it efficacious." * And Father Knight says, while inclining to support the count's views, that "those who feel sure that Columbus a short time before mistook a flight of delirious fancy for a vision sent by God, might save him from the charge of impiety by consistently supposing that on this occasion he mistook a ' happy thought ' for a divine inspiration. Perhaps the poor natives were under no great delusion after all, when they drew the inference that the prayers of the persecuted just man were powerful with God." † Other historians regard the affair as purely the result of a clever device of the ever-ingenious mind of Columbus in times of necessity.

The contrasts presented by history are more remarkable and extreme than the finest drawn scenes of fiction. While Columbus was now venerated by the Indians as one holding communication with Heaven and controlling the very luminaries of the skies, his heart was racked with the most painful anxieties for the safety and return of the messenger sent to Hispaniola for

---

* Dr. Barry's translation of the Count de Lorgues' "Life of Columbus," vol. ii., pp. 501, 502.
† Rev. Arthur George Knight's "Life of Columbus," p. 215.

relief. The long expectations and delays had now again brought discontent among his remaining companions, and endangered the very life of the man so powerful with God at the hands of his own followers. The growing despair of the Spaniards at the failure of Fiesco to return was now intensified and full, in consequence of reports brought in by the Indians of a wrecked vessel so near Jamaica that fragments of the wreck had floated to the shore. All concluded that this was the vessel sent by Ovando to take the Spaniards from their wrecks to a place of safety and to their homes. Although it subsequently turned out that these reports of floating fragments coming ashore were maliciously invented by the rebels under Porras, the effect of the fraud had nearly proved fatal to their chief and their countrymen, whom they had so disloyally abandoned and defied. So disastrous were these reports and the disappointment at Fiesco's failure to return, that all hope of relief died in their hearts, and the Spaniards in their despair cast the blame for their misfortunes upon the admiral, entered into a conspiracy to take his life, and by seizing other canoes lately obtained from the Indians, to attempt the passage to Hispaniola. This second conspiracy was headed by Valencia, the apothecary, supported by Alonzo de Zamora, an esquire, and Pedro de Villatoro. Just as the conspiracy was about to break out and carry its criminal purposes into effect, Providence came to the relief of the admiral and his companions.

It was at night, and the conspirators were about to commit the worst of crimes, when a little sail was seen at sea toward the northeast; but it soon approached, and though standing off, sent its boat to the wrecks on the strand. All the Spaniards hailed the apparition with joy; the hour of deliverance was at hand. As the boat approached, rejoiced as all were to see the faces of Christians turned to them from the ocean, the appearance on board of Diego de Escobar, one of Roldan's most hardened rebels, a man who had been condemned to death during the admiral's administration and pardoned by Bobadilla, checked their hopes. Having delivered to the admiral a letter from Ovando, the governor of Hispaniola, together with a barrel of wine and a side of bacon sent by Ovando as presents, he drew off and talked with the admiral from a distance. He told the admiral that Ovando expressed great concern for his misfortunes, and regret at not having in port a ship of sufficient size to receive him and his people, but that he would send one as soon as possible, and assured the admiral that his affairs in Hispaniola were receiving proper attention. Escobar offered to carry back any letter Columbus might wish to send to Ovando.

Though stunned at the strange character of this cold and unsympathetic mission, and chagrined at the meagre relief brought to relieve even the hunger of famishing countrymen stranded on a wild shore, Columbus immediately wrote to Ovando and described his forlorn situation, the rebellion of Porras, and expressed his trust in the promise of speedy relief. He recommended Mendez and Fiesco to the confidence of the governor. Having received the admiral's letter, Escobar speedily returned to his ship, and the men's hopes of relief vanished with the ship's disappearance in the sea and the return of the darkness of night. The admiral did all in his power to dispel the inevitable and obvious gloom among his people, assuring them that he was quite satisfied with the interview with Escobar, and had urged his speedy return to Hispaniola in order to expedite the vessel which was to be sent to their relief; and he added that he had himself declined to sail back to Hispaniola with Escobar, preferring to share the fortunes of his men. When the Spaniards saw the bright countenance and heard the firm voice of the admiral, giving these assurances, confidence was restored and the mutiny dissolved.

Calm and assured as was the countenance of Columbus in this heart-rending endeavor to give hope to his companions, he felt within his heart a storm of just indignation at the meanness of Ovando. Had not the governor received at the hands of the brave and faithful Mendez the letter written in his own hand, conveying the information of his desperate condition and of the danger he and his men were in from famine, the treachery of Spanish rebels, or from hostile natives? That a Spanish governor should rest with cool indifference at so short a distance when his countrymen were in such peril, and when the very man who had revealed the new world to Spain was almost in the jaws of death on a savage shore, where he had suffered and waited in his sufferings for eight months, was something unworthy of savages, and yet we see it in this case practised by a Christian toward Christians, by a Spaniard toward Spaniards. With ample means at his disposal, he sends the unfortunate admiral a condemned criminal with empty messages. With well-filled storehouses he sends to a hundred and thirty starving men a little wine and a morsel of bacon. With ships at his disposal, he sends to the shipwrecked colony the promise of a ship. The mind of Columbus was clear in its judgment of Ovando's unworthy conduct. Knowing from the admiral's letter delivered by Mendez of the desperate situation of the admiral, Ovando had sent not even a friendly messenger to devise the means or obtain information to be used for his relief, but a spy who, like himself, would have rejoiced at finding Columbus and all his men starved to death or murdered by the Indians. If Columbus should return to Spain, the grandeur of his recent discoveries would restore his fortunes and secure his return to the administration. Ovando did not desire such results. Plainly expressed as this view is in the writings of the admiral's son, inspired no doubt by himself, the venerable Bishop Las Casas adopts the same opinion.*

While some efforts have been made to excuse the unworthy conduct of Ovando toward Columbus, based upon supposed prudential considerations connected with the governor's administration at San Domingo, or the absurd rumor that Columbus, disgusted with his treatment by Spain, was desirous of transferring the countries he had discovered either to his native Genoa or some other country, or upon some other equally unreal pretext, the strength of reasoning—nay, the whole weight of the evidences and arguments—is adverse to the conduct of Ovando. Had his motives been honest or honorable, his excuses true, he would not have sent as his messenger to Columbus the disgraced and condemned Escobar, who was his enemy. He would not have pointedly insulted Columbus while uttering empty words of sympathy for his misfortunes.

The voyage of Mendez and Fiesco from Jamaica to Hispaniola was a test of human endurance, courage, and perseverance scarcely if at all equalled or surpassed by any similar feat in history or fiction. Sailing all the first day over a calm sea without wind, the heat of the sun and the labor at the oars exhausted the poor Indians; plunges into the sea relieved the sufferings of

---

* "Hist. del Almirante," Fernando Columbus, cap. civ. ; Las Casas, lib. ii., cap. xxxii.

the oarsmen; even at night the oarsmen never rested. The Spaniards kept the watch with weapons in hand to guard against treachery or attack on the part of the Indians at the oars. The sun arose from a night of toil as sultry as the day. To the exhaustion of labor was added the sufferings of thirst, for such was the heat that the Indians had resorted to the supply of water so eagerly that none was left. At noon on the second day the oarsmen, courage and strength exhausted, could not hold their oars, when Mendez and Fiesco found two casks of water, which they had prudently pretended were overlooked, and, with this doled out more for moistening the lips than for drinking, they succeeded in rowing another day. The night came before land was sighted, and the night was spent in labor, watching, thirst, discouragement, and agonies of mind and body. The Indians resorted to salt water to refresh their burning palates, but this transient relief was followed with greater suffering. The strain upon the eyes and nerves, from constant gazing toward the horizon for land, added to their agonies. One Indian died of exhaustion and thirst. Another night was spent in increased and increasing sufferings. The strong-hearted Mendez was on the verge of despair, when standing up at dusk in his canoe and straining his eyes to their utmost power, he dimly saw and exultingly exclaimed, "Land! Land!" Another night at the oars, but now at least with hope, the dying seemed revived sufficiently to row; at daybreak they reached the land and sprang ashore with ardent thanks to God for saving them from imminent and cruel death. They had landed on Navasa, a mere mass of rocks, and here they obtained rain water from hollows in the rocks, fish from the sea, which they cooked, and rest. In the cool of the evening they rowed with renewed energy and strength, and after another night at the oars they reached next morning Cape Tiburon, the nearest point of Hispaniola. This was the fourth day after leaving Jamaica. The first great peril at least was now passed. Heroic as was this achievement, what shall be said to adequately commemorate the grandeur of Fiesco's fidelity, when he proposed to return in his canoe to relieve the anxious mind of the admiral? But so intense had been the sufferings of the Spaniards and Indians, that none were willing to return with him in the canoe. Mendez, with a valor not surpassed in the most heroic lands and ages, rested not, either from oar or foot, until he had found Ovando, then at Xaragua, and delivered to him the letter of the admiral. Tarducci characterizes this chivalrous adventure as "one of the most perilous expeditions ever undertaken by a devoted follower for the safety of his commander."

In contrast with the exalted and self-sacrificing act of Mendez in risking his own life for that of his commander and companions, stands forth the selfish, insincere, and heartless conduct of Ovando. His sordid actions leave no doubt as to the motives of Ovando in his refusal to Columbus of permission to take shelter at San Domingo from the storm, and in now doing nothing worthy of the name for his relief in such a peril. Receiving Mendez with great kindness and with expressions of great concern for the admiral's misfortunes, he made every promise, but he did not fulfil any. Days, weeks, and even months elapsed, and Mendez kept insisting all the time. Excuses and pretexts were substituted for fulfilment. Mendez asked permission to go to San Domingo, and out of the admiral's revenues there to make provision for his safety at his own expense. Not only did he refuse this permission, but insinuations that the shipwreck of Columbus was fraudulently contrived to give him an excuse for getting into San Domingo, and making a move for overturning Ovando's administration and seizing the reins for himself, were most mendaciously put out. It is more justly suspected that Ovando waited and procrastinated in the daily hope that Columbus might perish from hunger or rebel's sword or Indian's lance. The arduous efforts of Mendez to do something for the admiral's deliverance were little successful, but rather thwarted by the meanness of sending a message instead of a ship, a little wine and pork for feeding one hundred and thirty men, and selecting an avowed enemy of the admiral on this cruel mission.

Columbus, on the other hand, generously trusted Ovando's promises of relief, as expressed by Escobar. He sent to the rebels a paternal message of his intention to carry them with him to a place of safety when Ovando should send a ship, as he hoped he would, and he even divided with them the scanty measure of wine and bacon sent to him by Ovando. He promised them pardon if they would return to the wrecks, and an equal participation with the loyal ones if they would return to their allegiance. In return for these generous offers Porras returned the most insolent demands, and, on their rejection by him, fearing that his men would desert him in the hope of securing through the admiral a safe return to Spain, he threatened the admiral with violence. He told his men that these pretended offers were seductive baits intended to allure them into the admiral's power; that the story of the ship of Escobar was an invention of the admiral to deceive them; and, relying on the superstitious dread entertained of his knowledge of the elements and his power as a sorcerer, the ship of Escobar was represented as a mere phantom ship conjured up by the admiral's mystic power in the dark sciences. By his insidious falsehoods and specious eloquence and appeals, he rallied the rebels and led them toward the wrecks to seize the barracks and make a prisoner of the admiral. The latter on his bed of sickness got information of their cowardly movement only when they had reached the village of Maima, a quarter of a league off; and being himself unable to move, he sent the Adelantado with fifty men—armed, it is true, but recently invalids, and even yet pale, weak, and emaciated—as ambassadors of peace. The offers of peace and invitations to a conference were insolently rejected, and the rebels, at the instigation of Porras and under his leadership, made a sudden and treacherous rush upon the Adelantado and his men, hoping by a preconcerted plan to kill the Adelantado first, and thus, having taken the soul out of this band of sickly and emaciated soldiers, to easily vanquish the men and march upon and seize the admiral in his bed. Their battle-cry, thus suddenly raised, was "Slay! Slay!" In the assault six picked men, led by Francisco Porras, rushed at the Adelantado at the first onslaught, intending to dispatch him. That bold and fearless hero met the assault with characteristic coolness and valor, and not only made good his defence, but had in the thickest of the fray killed or wounded several of his personal assailants, when Francisco Porras rushed upon him, and the sword intended for Don Bartholomew's heart was met with his shield, which it clove in two, and wounded the hand that carried it. Before Porras could withdraw his sword from the Adelantado's shield, the latter was upon him, grappling him, and finally, after a desperate struggle, with the assistance of others took him prisoner. Inspired by the undaunted conduct and personal courage of the Adelantado, his enfeebled followers did well their part, and proved themselves more than the mere fancy soldiers Porras had represented them. Seeing their chief a prisoner in the Adelantado's hands, the rebels fled before the men they had so much despised as convalescent patients of the wrecks. The Adelantado, who at first desired to follow up his victory, was persuaded by his officers that it was more prudent to allow them to escape immediate punishment and pursuit, as an attack from the Indians, whom Porras had disaffected, was greatly to be avoided ; for, in fact, the Indians in numbers, and with their arms, were silent spectators of this disgraceful struggle between Spaniards and Christians.

Returning in triumph to the wrecks with Francisco Porras and the other prisoners, the Adelantado and his victorious companions were received with great joy by the admiral, and all united with the latter in returning their grateful thanks to God. On the field of this unworthy battle lay some of the most powerful and undaunted men that a life of active adventure and an age of war could produce, either killed or wounded. It was a commentary on our civilization, when the Indians immediately after the struggle visited the scene, and from curiosity examined the wounds inflicted on the bodies of the slain with the arms used by the Christians. It was, no doubt, a double study to them : first, the manner in which the most skilfully manufactured arms in Europe were made, and how they could be used ; and, secondly, how well and effectively the Christians knew how to slaughter each other. In their deeply interesting investigation they came upon a figure of gigantic size and herculean strength, which had fallen into a ditch, literally covered with wounds : his skull was split open, so as to expose the brain ; a second wound in the arm left that member hanging and nearly cut off ; a third wound was in the side, showing the ribs cut asunder ; a fourth opened the foot from heel to toe, and had the appearance of a sandal on the foot ; and though any one of them seemed enough to have caused the death of even such a man, other lesser wounds seemed to have left him a disfigured mass. With stoical yet eager curiosity the Indians turned his mangled and apparently dead body over and over, and opened the wounds anew in order to see how the European weapons could cut. Suddenly from the lacerated body proceeded a voice of thunder, saying, " Let me be ! If I get up, I will—" Such was the effect of this stentorian and threatening voice, proceeding from the supposed corpse of the dead soldier, that the Indians fled in dismay, believing themselves followed and chased by all the dead bodies on the field. They had supposed the Spaniards to be immortal and not subject to death, and now, having seen the field was strewn with the dead, they again believed the dead returning to life; but, alas! experience had dispelled all their delusions. The hero of this adventure was no other than Pedro Ledesma, the same that had braved the fury of the storm and the danger of the rocks at Veragua, in order to obtain information for the admiral as to the fate of his brother and companions on shore. Learning thus from the Indians of the survival of Ledesma, who was supposed to have been killed, the Spaniards from the wrecks took him from the field to a near-by thatched cottage and dressed his wounds with oil, as they had no medicines; and though, as Fernando Columbus says, "the insects and dampness of the cottage were enough to finish him," he recovered and returned to Spain. Las Casas, the venerable bishop and historian, afterward saw and conversed with this unconquerable soldier, and received from him an account of the battle. Tarducci relates that "this singular man was afterward killed in Seville by the dagger of an assassin." *

The Adelantado and Pedro Terreros were the only two wounded among the loyal Spaniards, and the latter died of his wound a few days afterward, greatly regretted. This singular battle between Christians in the wilderness of America within a few years after its discovery, and in the presence of the savages, occurred on the very day of religious rest and prayer, Sunday, May 19th, 1503. It had the effect, however, of making loyal Spaniards of the rebels. The next day the fugitive rebels sent their unanimous and humble petition to the admiral, begging for his mercy and pardon, assuring him of their repentance and desire to return to their duty, and filled with ample promises of future good conduct. In this singular document they swore by the Cross and the gospel that they were sincere, and "they hoped, if they broke their oath, that no priest or Christian should ever confess them; that no penance should help them; that they should be deprived of the Church's sacraments; that their souls, after death, should receive no relief from bulls or indulgences;

---

* Mr. Brownson's translation of Tarducci's "Life of Columbus," vol. ii., p. 321.

that, instead of being buried in consecrated ground, their bodies should be thrown in the open field, like those of renegades and heretics ; and that no pope, cardinal, archbishop, bishop, or Christian priest should give them absolution." * While Mr. Irving says, in reference to this overflowing manifestation of repentance, that " the worthlessness of a man's word may always be known by the extravagant means he uses to enforce it," the admiral, trusting to the utter abjectness of these now repentant rebels, but moved chiefly by his own accustomed magnanimity, granted their prayer. Francisco Porras, however, was to remain a prisoner.

Columbus, though already well strained to provide food for his loyal companions, now found it no small undertaking to feed his community, now swelled in numbers by the return of the rebels. His generosity, however, knew no distinction, and his discreet judgment set a value upon the union of his followers above all other considerations. Confining his prisoner, Francisco Porras, on one of the wrecks, he placed the late rebels under the command of a discreet and loyal officer, and cantoned them on the island in order to avoid too great crowding of the wrecks, and in order to lessen the danger of fresh quarrels, where so many were crowded together in such contracted quarters. Supplying the officer in command of the late insurgents with European articles to barter with the Indians in exchange for food, they were directed to look for food in this way.

The untiring efforts of the faithful Diego Mendez at San Domingo finally succeeded in securing a ship for the deliverance of the admiral ; but in the absence of all attempts to this end by the unworthy and selfish Ovando, the ship was purchased and equipped at the admiral's own expense. Such was the indignation in Hispaniola against Ovando for his open and undisguised abandonment of the discoverer of America to his terrible fate—a feeling which found expression from the pulpits and in public prayers announced for the safety of the admiral and his men—that Ovando, when he saw that Mendez had fitted out a ship, also now found it at last in his power to do the same. He

---

* Las Casas, "Hist. Ind.," lib, ii., cap. xxv. ; "Hist. del Almirante," Fernando Columbo, cap. cvii. ; Irving's " Columbus," vol. ii., p. 420 ; Dr. Barry's translation of De Lorgues' "Columbus," p. 508 ; Mr. Brownson's translation of Tarducci's " Life of Columbus," vol. ii., p. 322.

selected and equipped a second ship, and placed it under the command of Diego de Salcedo, to whom Mendez had confided the first ship, a true friend of Columbus and his agent at San Domingo. But before relating the facts connected with the deliverance of Columbus and his companions from their long and cruel exile on the savage coast of Jamaica, I will briefly relate the history of Ovando's administration in Hispaniola—an administration as damaging to his character and record in history as is his mean and ungenerous treatment of Columbus in his misfortunes.

While Columbus, in making up his third voyage, had been compelled to take with him the convicts and criminals of Spain, on account of the disgust created in the public mind at seeing so many sick and disappointed people returning from the new world, now under Ovando the tide was reversed, and thousands eagerly sought for permission to go. The craze for gold carried hosts of adventurers thither, and no sooner had the vessels landed at San Domingo than the roads leading to the mines were crowded with gold-seekers, speculators, dreamers, spendthrifts, and adventurers seeking to repair their broken fortunes. The scene resembled the rush for the California mines in our own times and country, when the gold of California crazed our own people. While hidalgos had refused to work under Columbus on the public works and for the general safety, now these gentlemen traveled on foot, with a pack containing biscuit and miner's tools on their backs, from San Domingo to the mines, jostling each other and the humblest members of society, and crowding the road in company with people of every class. Stunned, on arriving at their Eldorado, on finding that it was necessary to dig and toil to reach Nature's treasures, which she had so guarded as to render them worth laboring for if worth acquiring, a terrible reaction soon came, and the miners found their provisions consumed, themselves exhausted with toil and hunger, and many were so impoverished that they were compelled to sell the clothes on their backs in order to get something to eat. The road over which the most brilliant hopes had lately hurried them was now crowded with a reversed current of sick, disappointed, hungry, dusty, ragged, fainting, and dejected adventurers. Employment on farms by old settlers relieved some, charity relieved others, while many more died of consumption, fevers, and various diseases to the number of a thousand and more.

Ovando, while he is not recorded as having warned his colonists against such evils, as he should have done, was generally regarded in his time as a prudent and capable governor for the Spaniards; but to the poor and innocent natives his administration was an exterminating scourge. Columbus when in power, driven by the powerless condition in which the home government had left him in Hispaniola, had given lands to Roldan's rebels in 1499, and had arranged with the caciques for sending a certain number of their subjects to work upon the lands in commutation for tribute—an arrangement which, as the tribute was an inevitable result of Spanish rule, is generally regarded by historians as involving no hardship on the natives, if carried into effect with justice and fairness, and as well calculated to accustom the natives gradually to labor and to lead to the general cultivation of the land. Ovando, however, followed up most unjustly the unwise and oppressive system of *repartimientos* which Bobadilla had introduced, whereby that special agreement of Columbus was developed into a governmental system, and the caciques were compelled to assign a certain number of Indians to every Spaniard to work upon the mines, and in the end all the natives were divided into classes and distributed among the farmers. No system of human slavery could be more complete than this. Indeed, Ovando, instead of restoring liberty to the natives, as commanded by the Spanish sovereigns, and using every effort by gentleness and justice to win them to Christianity, availed himself of a clause in the royal instructions by which he was permitted to impose moderate work on the natives for their own good, in order and with the effect of completely enslaving them, free men by nature, to their Spanish masters. Instead of protecting them in the moderation of the tasks imposed on them, he allotted to every Spaniard a certain number of Indians, according to his rank or his own caprice, and the caciques were compelled to furnish them. While nominally providing for their being paid and instructed in the Christian religion, the former was a deception, and the latter was limited to the bestowal of baptism upon a miserable and abused race, who had never seen or experienced the benign principles of Christianity practised by their Christian masters.

The cruelty practised on the Indians by the Spaniards under this system was most brutal. The venerable Bishop Las Casas, himself a Spaniard and an eye-witness of what he relates, saw the Indians constantly sent on long and painful journeys to work, separated for days from their wives and children, driven with the lash most inhumanly to get up and resume work whenever they fell or sat down to rest, and treated generally worse than beasts of burden. Cassava bread, which might suffice for the life of ease and indolence they formerly led, was not enough to sustain their present life of toil, travel, and hardship, and occasionally a morsel of bacon was added in such mean measure as to suggest its want rather than its enjoyment. The bishop actually relates that he saw the Spanish overseers at their comfortable meals, while the exhausted and famishing Indians crouched like dogs under the tables, and scrambled eagerly for the smallest bone that fell to the ground; and when a morsel of bone was thus obtained, the poor Indians would gnaw it, suck it, and finally, when they could get nothing more from it by gnawing or sucking, they would grind it between stones and spread the savory but miserable bone dust on their cassava bread. Field laborers never received flesh or fish to eat, but were confined to cassava bread. While thus half-starved they were worked most inhumanly, and such as fled to the mountains for freedom and to escape inevitable death were hunted like beasts, punished most cruelly, and ironed to prevent a second escape. Many died before their terms of labor expired, usually six or eight months in the year; others expired on the roads returning to their homes, some forty, sixty, or eighty leagues off. Las Casas saw many dead or expiring on the roads, and the latter, when approached by him, could only say faintly, "I am hungry! I am hungry!" Their own homes were desolate, their lands uncultivated and overrun with weeds; they often found their wives or children dead or scattered, and many, on reaching home, sank down on the sills of once happy but now silent and deserted cabins to die. Many killed themselves in despair. Mothers destroyed their children at their breasts to save them from lives of torture. In twelve years from the discovery of the island several hundred thousands of natives had perished, the victims of the white man's ambition or avarice; and the race, as Mr. Irving says, was actually "dissolving, as it were, from the face of the earth." * How recently had the Spaniards seen this beautiful country for the first time beaming like an earthly paradise!

Turning from the sickening picture of Ovando's civil administration in Hispaniola, his military record is not less heart-rending and revolting. The kingdom of Xaragua, on the death of Behechio, its cacique, without a son, had descended to his sister, the noble, beautiful, and generous Anacaona, the firm friend of the Spaniards. It took much to shake her friendship for them, but she saw more than sufficient in the cruelties of the white men toward her race, the miseries she saw them suffer, her own distresses growing out of the love affair between the young Spaniard, Fernando de Guevara, and her beautiful daughter, Higuenamota, the excesses of Roldan's rebels in her neighborhood, and the tortures and ruin resulting from the *repartimientos*. No act of hostility, no secret intrigue, no unfriendly word, no disloyal thought could justly be imputed to Anacaona. The condition of the country was such that frequent disputes arose between persecuted Indians and tyrannical Spaniards, and where an excuse was desired, a ready one was now found in the slanderous reports brought to Ovando of a general conspiracy in Xaragua among the Indians to rise on their persecutors and slaughter them. Without investigating the matter he marched into that province with three hundred men on foot armed with swords, arquebuses, and bows, and seventy mounted men armed with cuirasses, shields, and lances. No efforts to discover the truth, no explanations asked, no declaration of war was necessary; but war lurked under professions of friendship.

What excuse can be made for his treacherous announcement that he was going on a friendly visit to the queen, Anacaona? When received by the friendly queen with gracious and queenly welcome and hospitality, and treated with every honor, in pretended return for the Indian games and national performances with which he and his army had been entertained, he falsely and dishonorably drew that noble woman and the neighboring caciques, her vassals and their people, into a snare, under the

---

* Las Casas, "Hist. Ind.," lib. ii., cap. xiv.; Irving's "Columbus," vol. ii., pp. 423-28; Mr. Brownson's translation of Tarducci's "Life of Columbus," vol. ii., pp. 323-27.

pretext of entertaining them with Spanish games and exercises. On a concerted signal given by Ovando himself a massacre, scarcely paralleled in history for its wantonness and cruelty, followed. If the Indians had risen on the Spaniards, or even designed to do so, this could have been discovered and punished by the imprisonment of the caciques; but no proof of this was taken or existed. The Spanish army suddenly rushed upon the crowd of naked, unarmed, and trusting Indians; men, women, and children, old and young, were slaughtered, trampled under foot of man and horse, while indiscriminate death was inflicted. The house containing the queen and the caciques was surrounded and seized. Anacaona was put in chains, the caciques were tied to the posts supporting the roof and burned to death beneath the fired building. Torture, horribly administered, had in this house extracted a worthless admission of the alleged conspiracy from a poor cacique. The fugitives from this wholesale carnage were overtaken and subjected to the slow death of slavery. The noble Anacaona, the white man's friend, was afterward ignominiously hanged at San Domingo in the presence of many who should have returned her friendship by at least defending her or saving her. Ovando, with unmanly perfidy, had endeavored to palliate his crime by falsely befouling the reputation of Anacaona, but history has acquitted her, while his meanness, perfidy, and cruelty stand forever against him. Eighty-four caciques were burned to death by Ovando, and, to add to the infamy of his conduct, it is related, by undoubted authority, that just before this wanton massacre Ovando had played a game of battledore with his officers!

> "Cruel of heart and strong of arm,
> Loud in his sport and keen of spoil,
> He little reck'd of good or harm,
> Fierce both in mirth and toil;
> Yet like a dog could fawn, if need there were;
> Speak mildly when he would, or look in fear."
> —DANA's "BUCCANEER."

The pretended fear of Ovando for an Indian conspiracy which never existed, his acceptance of the hospitality of the Xaraguans and their noble queen, his game of pleasure when thirst for blood consumed his heart, his treachery to the confiding Indians, his dishonorable abuse of the rites of hospitality, his violation of every precept of Christianity, his wanton cruelty, his levity in the midst of the fiercest slaughter he contemplated, his cold-blooded judicial murders, his unrelenting destruction of women and children, his remorseless and continued persecution and ruin of an already subject race, are parts only of the unworthy record of a man who had won the decorations of chivalrous and Christian orders! He was commander of Larez, of the Order of Alcantara! Well has Tarducci exclaimed, "For the sake of humanity we wish we could discredit this atrocious infamy of Ovando and his followers."

The massacre of the Xaraguans continued for six months, for the Spaniards seemed not contented with subjugation, but to aim at absolute annihilation under the pretext of suppressing the insurrection which never occurred. How could so ruined a people, absolutely flying from their homes to the mountains to escape destruction, be said to be in insurrection? And when the fugitives fled to the caves of the mountains they were said to be plotting insurrection. Their deserted houses and villages were fired; the fugitives were captured and killed; the more the affrighted natives fled from the wrath of their masters, the more the latter pursued and slaughtered them. Their retreats in the caverns became their tombs; villages were destroyed and inhabitants murdered to such an extent that there remained but little to burn and few to murder—surely none to make an insurrection! Finally the Spaniards considered order restored in Xaragua, where it had never been disturbed except by Spaniards. With an inconsistency as strange as it was blasphemous, Ovando erected on the shore of a beautiful lake a new city in commemoration of his triumph over the unresisting Xaraguans, and called it *Santa Maria de la Verdadera Paz* (St. Mary of True Peace), giving to it for its arms the olive branch, the iris, and the cross. No wonder that Tarducci, in recording this brazen mockery, exclaimed, "I know of no bloody hypocrisy that can compare with this." Sacrilege was thus added to an endless list of crimes.

There only remained now the fine province of Higuey to be conquered in order to complete the Spanish conquest and subjugation of all Hispaniola. A pretext, however slight, was only needed to draw upon the Higueyans the exterminating wrath of the Spaniards. Ovando regarded such conquests as glorious triumphs, to be commemorated with devotional shrines. But to conquerors so accustomed to acts of cruelty and suppression a pretext was not long wanting, and the pretext of course arose out of some wanton act of cruelty from themselves. Some Spaniards cruelly set a fierce dog on a cacique of the province; he was horribly bitten, and soon died of his wounds. Instead of surrendering the criminals—an utterly unheard-of thing for conquerors to do—or at least punishing the miscreants for murder, the demands for justice on the part of the Higueyans were not noticed. Ovando decided to let time and neglect allay their just indignation. But the wronged savages acted upon the natural law of retaliation, and made reprisals by seizing and putting to death a boatload of Spaniards, eight in number, near the little island of Saona, in Higuey. Now the law of justice was reversed, and the Spaniards sent four hundred armed men to punish the whole nation. The chief cacique of the district was the noble and gigantic Cotabanama, the tallest man in the country, and the best proportioned. The Spanish forces, under the command of Esquibel, pretended at first to desire to right the matter by peaceful negotiation; but the cacique, remembering the slaughter of the Xaraguans under the guise of a friendly entertainment, justly distrusted the good faith of the invaders. Strong in numbers, thoroughly conversant with the country, brave as the bravest, and conscious of the justice of their cause, the Indians appealed to the dread arbitration of arms, and in the conflict they showed the most wonderful evidences of valor, constancy, and national pride. The military skill, the discipline, the arms of the Europeans, however, gave to inferior numbers the advantage over undisciplined numbers. The brave Higueyans were defeated at every point and dispersed; they fled to mountain and forest. The Spaniards pursued them unmercifully, hounded them out of their hiding-places, slaughtered men, women, and children, burned the chiefs alive, and repeated with increased fury and in greater detail the horrors of Xaragua. The little island of Saona, where the boatload of Spaniards had been killed, received the worst punishment, showing that revenge, not protection or defence, was the object of the assailants. The land was scoured with relentless fury, and the inhabitants remorselessly murdered. Finding in one place of retreat seven hundred affrighted Indians of every age, sex, and condition, the Spanish soldiers rushed upon them and slaughtered them at the sword's point, and the enclosure of death was flowing with blood.

A few only of the inhabitants escaped a cruel death, and these were made slaves. The whole province was turned into a vast scene of desolation. The trained European soldiers, who could treacherously abuse the hospitality of a woman and wage war on her, without justice, pretext, or mercy, now had no mercy for a nation of brave men. The Indians who survived this massacre sued for peace, were reduced to slavery, and were given their lives on condition of cultivating a large tract of land for furnishing to their masters an immense quantity of cassava bread as tribute. Peace, if such annihilation be peace, having been conquered, the brave Cotabanama visited the Spanish camp to make his submission, and according to the Indian custom, took the name of the conquering chief, Juan de Esquibel, and gave his own name to the conqueror. Even in this exchange the loss was on the side of the honest Indian chief. A fort was erected on the soil of the vanquished, under Martin de Villaman, with a garrison of nine men. It was a humiliating spectacle, when the Spanish soldiers marched away, to see each one of the conquerors carrying off a number of slaves, assigned to him as the rich spoils of war.

Villaman, the commander of the fort, was a worthy representative of such humane chieftains as Ovando and Esquibel. The agreement of submission was violated even by those who had gained all by it. The Indians were compelled to carry the harvested grain on their backs to San Domingo, and on their showing the least resistance were treated with unmeasured brutality. The Spaniards were allowed unbridled license, and the Indian women, girls and wives, were subjected to the unchecked lust of these unworthy Christian conquerors. To yield to the oppression of the conquerors brought no relief to the Higueyans; and finally, when the last instincts of manhood showed themselves in a righteous revolt of the persecuted natives, the whole of Higuey was, by Ovando's orders, given over to fire and sword. The few inhabitants left alive from the late Spanish scourge, while showing unsurpassed personal courage and patriotism, were treated with the utmost brutality, and the Indians fell in the most heroic struggle for their liberty and homes rather than live to be Spanish slaves. Some, who had not found a chance to die in defending their own, were forced to act as guides to their enemies, and with ropes tied around their necks they were driven forward to show the spots wherever a few fugitives had retreated. While the Indians sought death in preference to slavery, the Spanish blades "never stopped striking or slaying as long as life remained."* In the last stronghold of the poor inhabitants, the capital of Cotabanama, strategy brought into the power of the Spaniards parties of Indians assembled or hidden to defend their country; and they were given over to merciless slaughter. One slaughter was followed by another; blood flowed like water; the Indians showed heroic bravery—the courage of desperation—and finally, when Spanish arms prevailed over their splendid heroism, they fled to the most inaccessible mountains, followed by their unsparing conquerors. The Spaniards called this "the hunt of the Indians," and so it was, for the gentle and noble Las Casas sent up a cry of horror at the atrocities of his countrymen ; and it is consoling to find one voice at least to cast infamy upon the authors of such horrors. It is no palliation of their crimes to allege that the Spaniards were made up of the lowest dregs of society and the refuse of prisons and galleys, when under the eyes of the commanders and by their orders the poor Indians caught had their hands cut off, and were thus sent to their flying countrymen to procure their submission. This was a common cruelty, and resulted in many excruciating deaths on the open roads. Other Indians were swung upon gibbets hung so low that the feet of the victims touched the ground, and thus prolonged and increased their sufferings. To add blasphemy to the atrocities of these unworthy representatives of a Christian civilization, the Spaniards hung thirteen Indians at one time, saying it was in memory of Christ and the twelve apostles. While the tortured victims were thus hanging, the Spaniards wantonly tested the strength and qualities of their swords by mangling and mincing their bodies, and ended the atrocious tragedy by gayly lighting a bonfire of their victims, thus consuming the dead and dying together. Caciques and other more important prisoners were broiled alive on gridirons by slow fires. Las Casas says that he once saw five caciques thus burned, each on a separate gridiron, and his generous heart was racked by their piteous screams. These same screams, long continued by the slowness of the fires, disturbed the sleep of the captain,

---

* Mr. Brownson's translation of Tarducci's "Life of Columbus," vol. ii., p. 336.

who sent an order to strangle the victims; but the executioner stopped their cries by stuffing chips in their mouths, while their tortures were prolonged. He continued during the night to poke the fires, that he might the longer enjoy their tortures and sufferings. Las Casas recorded such horrors of Spanish desolation in Hispaniola that, while he states that he witnessed them with his own eyes, he could scarcely believe them afterward when his pen recorded them, and they seemed like a dream.

To end this abhorrent narrative, it must be stated that the final retreat of the brave and unfortunate Cotabanama, on the island of Saona, was ferreted out by the Spaniards by means of tortures and cruelties inflicted upon the natives, his subjects, who kept his secret and guarded the way. The chief was wounded, and dragged, all bleeding from his wounds, like a wild beast to the nearest village and ironed. The wife and children of the chief escaped from the hiding-place where he was seized to another. The Spaniards who seized Cotabanama at first thought of amusing themselves by broiling him alive, but this was regarded as too selfish a sport for a few to enjoy, and he was carried in chains to San Domingo. Such was his wounded and bloody appearance that no one could recognize the once handsome chief; but neither his sufferings, his helpless condition, his approaching death from loss of blood and from his tortures, could find an honest or humane cord in the heart of Ovando to touch. By the governor's orders this noble chief was ignominiously hanged in the public square at San Domingo. He was the last of the native sovereigns of Hispaniola. With him expired all effort of the Indians to defend their homes or country, or to assert their natural independence. This once peaceful and happy race possessed a country a few years before, at the time they were first visited by the white men, which ravished the eyes of the intruders. Now this land of beauty, plenty, and of peace was a vast scene of desolation. Of the innocent and contented native race that held their country by a title derived from the God of all and from the law of nature, scarcely one-sixth part had escaped or survived the sword, the fagot, or the gibbet of their Spanish conquerors. Upon this unhappy remnant of a noble and generous race the Spanish yoke rested most cruelly, and death from the slower tortures of the mines, the fields, the lash, the rope, and the prison, and from fatigue, ill-treatment, cruel labor and

oppression came upon them as surely as it had more speedily
overtaken their slaughtered countrymen. Despair was not resignation. Death was not submission. When the brave Cotabanama claimed the protection of honor and friendship arising
from the exchange of names, and exclaimed beneath the Spanish
swords, "I am Juan de Esquibel," he was treated with scorn,
tortures, and an ignominious death. What quarter could these
poor Indians expect from the hands of men who disgraced the
very name of Christian, to which they so tenaciously clung, and
which they had hypocritically professed to desire to share with
the Indians? The generous heart of the noble Bishop Las Casas,
who witnessed the atrocities here related, and which are here
narrated on the authority of his writings, bled for the Indians.
We know of no other humane voice then and there to join har-
moniously with him in the protest against such atrocities. But
there was one other heart—a suffering one not far distant—a
heart which, though Christian, had felt the cruelties of Ovando
in the midst of his own wrongs, which bled with the heart of Las
Casas for the slaughtered Indians: this was the heart of Christopher Columbus!

The two ships fitted out at San Domingo, after a year's heartless delay and cruel sufferings on the part of Columbus and his
followers, sailed from that port. The faithful Mendez, having
witnessed their departure, availed himself of the first opportunity
of sailing for Spain to execute the important mission intrusted to
him by Columbus. Fiesco also, now that the admiral was to be
released, returned to Spain. The two ships under the command
of Diego de Salcedo, when they arrived at Santa Gloria, the
port of the admiral's shipwreck and exile in Jamaica, brought joy
for the first time to the hearts of all. On one of the vessels the
admiral embarked with such of his companions as had proved
faithful; he sent the rebels on board the other. Leaving his
loathsome wrecks and embarking on the caravel, the admiral
raised his flag, and, as Mr. Irving says, "he felt as if the career
of enterprise and glory were once more open to him." The
Porras brothers and their unworthy confederates felt anxious
about the treatment they should receive from the man whom
they had so grossly slandered and treacherously treated; but
Columbus was most generous in moments of prosperity. Not

only did he take them on board one of the caravels, but he provided for their relief and comfort out of his own purse, and after their arrival in Spain he continued to plead with the sovereigns in their behalf. Francisco Porras, while Ovando deemed it best not to investigate the affair, was sent by him to Spain for examination by the Bureau of the Indies. The admiral with the two caravels sailed from the Bay of Santa Gloria on June 28th, but he was detained by contrary winds, and it took a month for the caravels to accomplish a voyage performed by Mendez and Fiesco in Indian canoes in four days. Reaching the little island of Beata on August 3d, Columbus, distrusting the variable winds of that region, sent overland a letter to Ovando announcing his arrival. This letter he deemed necessary to remove the unjust suspicions which the governor entertained and had expressed as to his motives; but favorable winds enabled him to resume his voyage on August 13th, and he soon entered the port of San Domingo.

Columbus now received welcome and sympathy at the place where not long before he was execrated and reviled, and even refused a shelter from the storm. Not only did the people turn out and receive him with looks and expressions of sympathy, but Ovando, accompanied by the principal persons of the place, advanced to meet him, gave him a distinguished reception, and claimed the privilege of making him his guest. Fernando Columbus characterizes the change in Ovando's conduct as " the peace of the scorpion." While pretending the utmost friendship and regard for the admiral, he claimed that Jamaica was within his jurisdiction, and that he was the judge in all matters occurring there under Columbus. Hence he released Porras and sent him to Spain with his own instructions as to his disposal, and even talked of punishing such of the admiral's companions as had taken up arms in his defence and had killed in battle the rebels who were Spanish subjects. An argument of considerable warmth took place over the question of jurisdiction, Ovando claiming power over all persons and things within the islands and Terra Firma, while the admiral asserted, by virtue of his royal letters, which he produced, authority over all persons sailing with him on this expedition, from its departure to its return to Spain. Each claimant punctiliously contended for his view. Ovando, while he relinquished the idea of trying the followers of Columbus, assumed authority to dispose of the case of Porras and his rebels.

The heart of Columbus bled for the miseries and wrongs of the poor natives of Hispaniola, and he was anxious to return to Spain and plead their cause before the queen, who united with him in a sincere desire to save them and convert them to the Christian faith. Columbus also saw through the exterior courtesy of Ovando his hypocritical heart, for self-interest made a selfish and grasping man like him feel and act upon the fact that the admiral's interests were adverse to his own. It had been announced that the admiral's suspension from command in Hispaniola was only temporary ; Ovando's commission was for two years ; and at the end of this time, when it was anticipated that things would have quieted down, Columbus expected to resume his authority over the island. He found that his every movement and word were watched, as were those of his faithful followers. It was evident that, while Ovando professed a certain ceremonious friendship for him, he was at heart his bitter enemy. He determined to shorten his stay at San Domingo, and having fitted up and repaired the vessel which Mendez had sent to convey him from Jamaica to Hispaniola, and chartered another, he prepared to sail. Most of his companions on the fourth voyage preferred to remain at Hispaniola, and as they were poor, needy, and without clothes, the admiral generously provided for them out of the scanty revenue that had been collected for him, and he advanced the money for such as wished to return to Spain. In his generosity he made no distinction between those who had remained faithful to him and those who had rebelled against him. He treated them all with truly paternal and tender care. He embarked with his son and domestics on the ship sent to him by Mendez, and sent his brother with the others on board the other caravel. The ships sailed from San Domingo on September 12th, but now again Columbus had experiences of his usual ill luck from the weather, for a storm carried away his ship's mast, so that he was compelled to go with his party on board the other ship and send the disabled caravel back to port. The first part of the voyage was favorable. On October 18th the ship encountered furious storms, her mainmast was split into four pieces, the admiral was prostrated on his couch with a severe return of his gout, and it was only the Adelantado's energy and excellent skill that carried the ship through the dangers by which she was beset at every turn. Finally the ship, in a crippled condition, entered the port of San Lucar de Barrameda, on November 7th, 1504. But if his ship was bravely kept together and held from going to pieces, the health of the admiral was completely wrecked.

CHAPTER XIV.

> "Here is my journey's end, here is my birth,
> And very sea-mark of my utmost sail."
> —Shakespeare's "Othello."

> "At every little breath misfortune blows,
> 'Till left quite naked of their happiness,
> In the chill blast of winter they expire."
> —Young.

> A CASTILLA Y A LEON
> NUEVO MUNDO DIO COLON.
> —Epitaph of Columbus.

From the port of San Lucar de Barrameda the sick and enfeebled admiral had himself carried to Seville, where he hoped to find rest and repose after the disasters, misfortunes, and sufferings of his last voyage. He hoped soon to go from Seville to court; but misfortune followed him wherever he went, and every day and hour of his declining years. Seville was not then a congenial place for him; his friends, and even the learned and sympathetic Gaspard Gorricio, the Franciscan monk, were all absent. He was compelled to put up in a hotel; and as it was winter—the severest winter in the memory of men—his bodily sufferings from his old disease were intense. Confined to his bed, unable to move, he could only with great difficulty and pain use his pen, now so necessary for the promotion of his imperilled affairs and interests. Seville had become the centre of colonial business; the Admiralty of the Indies had become thoroughly organized as a marine and colonial administration, and was presided over by Juan de Fonseca, his implacable enemy. While he was confined to his bed by illness and sufferings his enemies were abroad. The late rebels who had conspired against his life were received at court and were plotting against him, and the documents relating to their misconduct had been carried back to San Domingo in the unmasted caravel. The sailors who returned with him now, including some who had opposed him, were still without their back pay; all these came to him in his own poverty to ask his pecuniary assistance, and for his aid in presenting their claims. If Columbus had suffered so intensely from his disease in the warm climates, to which he was accustomed, and in which he was constantly confined to his bed, unable to repose day or night from the agonizing spasms in his joints, what must now have been his sufferings in the severity of this unprecedented winter, especially when the excitement of discovery and adventure was withdrawn!

Great as were his physical sufferings, immensely greater were his mental agonies. While his few friends were absent from Seville, that city was filled with his enemies. Not the least of his humiliations was the fact that, while it was universally believed that his revenues were immense, and so they should have been, and his rank placed him under the necessity of maintaining a certain and a most expensive style of life, he was, from the frauds and injustice of his enemies and of the crown, suffering the pangs of actual poverty. Ovando had been ordered to restore to him and to his agents all his rights on the revenues and trade of Hispaniola, and also to examine his accounts and to ascertain all arrears due to him, and the damages sustained from his imprisonment by Bobadilla, the seizure of his house and other wrongs. The good and noble queen sent repeated orders in his behalf, but these were evaded, and the grossest injustice was now experienced by him. His personal demands on Ovando at San Domingo led to serious quarrels between them, and he could get from that insidious enemy only four thousand castellanos, when eleven or twelve thousand were due. He had been compelled to expend most of what his agents had collected in providing a ship to bring him home, and now, in a letter to his son, he states that ten million maravedis were due to him annually. Such was now his poverty that he was compelled to seek a loan where he could; he was living, in fact, on the kindness of his friends, and it is known several of these generously relieved his most pressing wants.

From his bed of suffering Columbus addressed repeated letters to the sovereigns, to his friends, to his son Diego, and others, urging the restitution of his rights and incomes, and strongly stating the grounds for their enforcement. He dwelt even more on the injustice done to his crew in the non-payment of their dues; and such were their delays and disappointments, and such their appeals to him, that he was compelled to aid them from the money he borrowed from others. The action of the king and queen in suspending his offices and dignities, his rights and privileges, and placing a governor in his stead, was the greatest of his wrongs, and against this he cried out from his bed of pain with persistent demand.

The maladministration of affairs in the Indies, the wrongs and injustices heaped upon the poor Indians, their almost entire annihilation, and that without their being brought to the Christian faith, agonized his soul. He addressed to their Majesties the most frequent and urgent letters and petitions, and again and again solicited through himself and others a reply from them, but all in vain. His enemies seemed alone to possess the ear of the court; and no man ever had such enemies. They boasted of the alleged and pretended failure of his last voyage; the pass he went to discover had no existence; the golden regions of Veragua had yielded no gold. The numerous rebels under Roldan and Porras, all now at large and unpunished, were so many accusers of the admiral. His son was at court, constantly importuning the sovereigns for a hearing and for justice; but Isabella was suffering from an incurable malady, and Ferdinand was known to be hostile to him and his just rights. The Bureau of the Indies, availing themselves of the fact that the papers relating to the Porras insurrection had been sent back to San Domingo in the dismasted ship, refused to act in the case, upon the pretext that there were no documents. Such protracted silence on the part of the sovereigns, such denials of justice at every turn, forced the admiral to attempt, at every risk, to go to court, and in person to importune the king and queen for justice.

Such was the nature of his disease and such the severity of the winter, that the admiral's life seemed imminently in danger. To attempt such a journey was regarded as sure to prove fatal to such an invalid. He resolved to make every sacrifice in order to reach the ear of the king, and for that purpose to be carried on a bier. When the discoverer of the new world applied to the cathedral chapter of Seville for the same bier that had served to bring the body of Cardinal Mendoza, he was required to give security for its return to the cathedral in good condition—so low was the credit of one who was then entitled to an income of ten million maravedis annually. Even when the security was given by Francisco Pinedo, it was found that the admiral's life would be most assuredly and fatally imperilled, and the visit to court had to be abandoned. In this severe disappointment he was compelled again to write long letters and appeals to express what he had intended to say in person at court. He could only write at night, owing to the malady in his hands. He pointed out in writing and in detail to his son the arguments and methods to be pursued in demanding justice for him. In one of his letters he writes, " The Indies are going to destruction ; the fire is at a thousand points ; I have had nothing, and I receive nothing of the revenue I own there ; no one will risk a claim for me in that country ; I live on loans."

In the midst of such wrongs and sufferings the heart of Columbus received a new grief in the accounts he received of the sinking health of his good and amiable friend, the gentle Isabella, his queen. Her life was in fact despaired of when he had landed at San Lucar, and death was advancing on this peerless queen with steady and rapid strides. This accounts in part, no doubt, for the silence with which the admiral's appeals were received at court, for the cold, calculating, selfish, and ungrateful Ferdinand was now in his own person the court. The generous and noble benefactress of Columbus was actually dead when he wrote to his son at court the heart-rending sentiments with which he heard the news of her approaching dissolution. His grief at her sad condition is known to have greatly aggravated his sufferings of mind and body. Informed of her death, then hourly expected, on December 3d, he had just written to his son, " May it please the Holy Trinity to restore our sovereign queen to health, for by her will everything be adjusted which is now in confusion." The noble and pious queen died on November 26th, 1504, at Medino del Campo, in the fifty-fourth year of her eventful and glorious life. In the midst of worldly grandeur and success she died a death accelerated by her sorrows—sorrows of a loving and tender soul ; sorrows of her maternal heart, which all the glories of earth could not heal. The death of her only son, Prince Juan ; then the death of her cherished daughter, the Princess Isabella, who had been to her also companion and bosom friend ; next the death of her grandson and heir-apparent, the Prince Miguel, and finally the evident development of mental infirmities in her daughter, the Princess Juana, and her domestic unhappiness with her husband, the Archduke Philip, had presented to the lips of the queen the full chalice of earthly afflictions. While her public life as a sovereign was crowned with unsurpassed success and glory, she wasted away and sickened under the misfortunes of her own home and household. A profound and incurable melancholy gradually subverted her fine constitution, intensified her physical sufferings, and carried her to the grave in the prime of her useful success and glory, and midway of a life that was generous, just, queenly, and Christian.

In keeping with the simplicity of her character and with the severely disciplined experiences of this noble woman was that passage in her will which reads, " Let my body be interred in the monastery of San Francisco, which is in the Alhambra of the city of Granada, in a low sepulchre, without any ornament except a plain stone, with the mortuary inscription cut on it. But I desire that if the king, my lord, should choose a sepulchre in a church or monastery in any other part or place of these my kingdoms, my body be transported thither, and buried beside the body of his Highness, so that the union we have enjoyed while living, and which, through the mercy of God, we hope our souls will experience in heaven, may be represented by our bodies in the earth." * Her will, the last and most solemn act of her life, exhibits the grandeur of the queen with the tenderest conjugal affection of the wife, the purest sentiments of the mother united with the affectionate love she always bore to her subjects, the enterprise of a strong and well-balanced character with the faith, piety, and humility of the true Christian, a noble exaltation of character with an unfaltering charity. Tarducci speaks of " her humility of heart" and " her sweetest piety and tenderest melancholy," of " her singular merits as queen, which not only made her most celebrated among all the women that have worn a crown, but place her on a level with the greatest monarchs recorded in history," and of " her right to have her name indissolubly joined to that of Christopher Columbus." †

Mr. Irving writes of Isabella as follows : " Such was one of

---

* King Ferdinand preferred in life that his body in death repose beside that of his peerless queen ; and the remains of both are deposited in the royal chapel of the Cathedral of Granada.

† Mr. Brownson's translation of Tarducci's "Columbus," vol. ii., pp. 351, 352.

several passages in the will of this admirable woman, which bespoke the chastened humility of her heart, and in which, as has been well observed, the affections of conjugal love were delicately entwined with piety, and with the most tender melancholy. She was one of the purest spirits that ever ruled over the destinies of a nation. Had she been spared, her benignant vigilance would have prevented many a scene of horror in the colonization of the new world, and might have softened the lot of its native inhabitants. As it is, her fair name will ever shine with celestial radiance in the dawning of its history." In glowing terms Prescott speaks of her exalted resignation in death, her graceful and benignant manners, her magnanimity, her piety, her strong and unswerving principles, her practical good sense, her activity in life and administration, her courage, her tender sensibility; and while he alludes to what he calls her bigotry, he excuses it on the plea that it was common to her country and age. He should have considered that bigotry, in its proper sense, was wholly inconsistent with the exalted virtues and splendid intellect which he himself attributes to Isabella. Bigotry is a relative quality, and it may be truly said that Isabella's religious character was free from bigotry as understood in any odious light.

While it would be quite a pleasant thing, and replete with useful advantages, to quote from numerous authors exalted tributes to the character of Isabella, our space compels us to adduce no further such pleasing testimony; but the language of the Count de Lorgues, tinged though it be with his usual enthusiasm, describes so beautifully and strikingly the ennobling relations and the contrasts between her and Columbus, that our readers will not regard the following passages as unwelcome or inappropriate.

"On being informed of her death, who shall tell the rending of heart and bitterness of grief he experienced? The father who loses his only daughter feels no keener anguish of heart. To paint this unutterable affliction it would be necessary to measure in its sublimity that attraction for each other of the two souls which Providence had predestined to elaborate the greatest work of the human race. By its immensity the grief of Columbus bordered on the infinite; its multiple suffering was as vast as the spirit that animated the body of that queen, which was stamped

with an indelible majesty. It was the rending of a superior
sympathy, rooted in tenderness of soul, fecundated with the
splendors of faith, and vivified in Christ, who was its principle,
its safeguard, and its immortal end.

" His only stay in this world was gone ; he had lost more than
a protectress, more than a sovereign—he had lost a friend. Yes,
the queen loved with a maternal tenderness and honored with a
respectful deference the man whom God had sent her to double
the known space of creation. Isabella re-found in Columbus her
own qualities—that is to say, her eminent virtues. She admired
in him especially that modesty of a hero, that simplicity of a
saint, and that artlessness of a child which the patriarch of the
ocean preserved throughout the vicissitudes of his unequalled
labors. An involuntary respect inclined the great and venerated
Isabella toward this old man, breathing grandeur, transpiring
the sublime, and beaming from this world with the impress of
immortality.

" Columbus always saw in the incomparable Isabella the type
of purity, of constancy, and of fidelity to her word ; the flower
of human graces and the poetry of humanity. To whom will he
henceforth recount the ravishments which the marvels of unknown regions produced in him ? Who now will undertake new
discoveries ? Who now will follow him in thought and thank
him for his distant fatigues ? Who will come to aid him ? to
realize in fine the chief object of his hopes—the deliverance of
the tomb of the Divine Saviour ? When he understood that his
loss was effected in the death of Isabella, he experienced a life-
lessness of heart. His desolation was as mute as the tomb ; his
unspeakable grief found no utterance. It is only known that his
physical sufferings were redoubled by it." *

Another joint tribute to Isabella and Columbus, from the
graceful pen of one of America's foremost women, is too beautiful to be omitted—" It was not money that Isabella put into
this scheme, even at a mortifying sacrifice, which secured its
success, but her confidence in Columbus personally, and what
we must call a wonderful enlightenment of mind and soul, by
which she took in at a glance all the favoring possibilities until

---

* Dr. Barry's translation of the Count de Lorgues' " Life of Columbus," pp. 517, 518.

they became probabilities; and these once grasped, all the chivalry of an exalted nature was pledged to their fulfilment. There was no withdrawing of confidence when once given. The sounding line of her womanly instinct, guided by the experiences of an extraordinary reign, had fathomed the sublime resources of Columbus and his motives, and no dastardly maligner could uncrown him for Isabella." *

These tributes to the noble character of Isabella would be incomplete if we omitted the following from the ever-faithful and devoted heart of the admiral: " A memorial for thee, my dear son Diego, of what is at present to be done. The principal thing is to commend affectionately and with great devotion the soul of the queen, our sovereign, to God. Her life was always catholic and prompt to all things in His holy service; for this reason we may rest assured that she is received into His glory and beyond the cares of this rough and weary world. The next thing is to apply yourself with zeal in everything and everywhere for the service of the king, our lord, and labor to make him forget his grief. His Highness is the head of Christendom. Think of the proverb which says, 'When the head suffers, all the members languish.' Therefore all good Christians ought to pray for his health, so that he may live long; and we, who are under greater obligations to serve him than others, ought to do it with more zeal and diligence." This generous appeal and prayer from Columbus for Ferdinand, at this juncture in the affairs of the former, go further to enhance our admiration of his character even than his tribute of gratitude to Isabella. " It is impossible," says Mr. Irving, " to read this mournful letter without being moved by the simply eloquent yet artless language in which Columbus expresses his tenderness for the memory of his benefactress, his weariness under the gathering cares and ills of life, and his persevering and enduring loyalty toward the sovereign who was so ungratefully neglecting him." †

While Isabella, on her death-bed, grieved over the wrongs and

---

* " Isabella of Castile, 1492-1892," by Eliza Allen Starr, p. 100.
† Irving's "Columbus," vol. ii., p. 467; De'Rebus, " Hisp, Mem.," lib. xxl.; Peter Martyr's " Op. Ep.," lib. xviii., cap. clxxiii.; Diego Clemencia's " Eulogy on the Catholic Queen;" Mr. Brownson's translation of Tarducci's " Life of Columbus," vol. ii., pp. 350-52.

misfortunes of her new subjects in the western world, and was indignant at the excesses and atrocities of Ovando, she with her dying breath exacted from King Ferdinand a promise that Ovando should be immediately removed from the office of governor, which he had disgraced and sullied with innocent blood. It throws light upon the character of Ferdinand that, in the face of such a promise, made, it might almost be said, sacramentally, to his expiring queen and wife, he actually continued Ovando in office for four years more, and with him continued without interference his infamous despotism over the Indians of Hispaniola. Ovando knew his superior : the governor poured the ill-gotten treasures of the new world into the lap of Ferdinand. How, then, could Ferdinand interfere with the administration of Ovando? Ovando thus became the superior of Ferdinand.

Columbus was fully alive to the peril in which his affairs stood now more than ever since the death of his friend and patroness, the queen. In addition to his son Diego, who had been representing him at court, he also sent thither his son Fernando, his brother Bartholomew, and his trusty friend Carvajal, to urge his suit before the king before his ever-vigilant enemies could complete their plans for his ruin. Knowing the character of Ferdinand, Columbus had instructed his friends at court to prudently keep his personal claims somewhat in the background, and to urge more immediately matters that would appeal to the sordid nature of Ferdinand. The king was thus given to understand that in Hispaniola there were great quantities of gold belonging to the crown, of which it was defrauded or delayed. He warned the king of the maladministration of the affairs of Hispaniola, of the dangers of further and worse troubles breaking out unless speedy measures were taken to give that country a good government ; and he urged and demanded of the king that he, the legitimate governor, should be sent back and restored to his prerogatives and offices in that island. He tendered his best and most faithful services to the king.

It was about this time that Columbus received from Pope Julius II. an intimation that the Holy Father was not satisfied at not having heard from the admiral, as his predecessors had heard, in relation to the interests of religion in Hispaniola. Columbus immediately wrote to the Pope a full account of his discoveries ;

but to avoid all danger of giving his enemies a new pretext for accusing him unjustly, he sent copies of this document to Ferdinand, to Archbishop Diego de Deza, the new Archbishop of Seville, his old friend and former defender in the famous Council of Salamanca. It also transpired that Columbus was now informed by some members of the Bureau at Seville that three bishoprics, one of which was to be an archbishopric, were to be established in Hispaniola. Not only had the king refrained from giving the legitimate governor and viceroy of Hispaniola notice of this important movement, but he also gave no answer to a demand from Columbus to be heard upon a question in which he was so deeply interested. What could be more significantly suspicious as to the motives of the king than this unjust silence, which was as discreditable to his motives as to his conduct toward Columbus? The ecclesiastics nominated for the newly created sees of Hispaniola were the Franciscan Father Garcia de Padilla, the Doctor Pedro de Deza, nephew of the Archbishop of Seville, and the Licentiate Alonzo Manza, a canon of Salamanca, whose nominations had been approved at Rome. The Holy See pursued a more just and enlightened course on this subject than King Ferdinand. Columbus managed to communicate his views on the subject to the Papal Nuncio. Though the nominations were approved the bulls were not expedited, nor did the bishops depart for their sees; for Columbus, with characteristic firmness and with zeal for the good of the Church, insisted on being heard on so important a subject. This led to further delay and investigation, which resulted in tracing the project for the erection of sees in Hispaniola to Ovando, who thus conceived the plan in the interests of his own speculative enterprises. It seemed rather strange that so sudden a need should have arisen for three bishops all at one time, especially since the natives had been annihilated rather than converted. Ovando concealed the obvious propriety of locating the archiepiscopal see at San Domingo as the principal city, for he did not desire to have in his capital so important a personage as an archbishop. So important a dignitary might overshadow his own office and importance; hence the metropolitan see was to be erected at Xaragua, a district distant over two hundred miles, almost destitute of inhabitants or dwellings, situated in the mountains, without a connecting road and without even an Indian village for the residence of the prelate—a see without a city or a flock. Well has the Count de Lorgues exclaimed, " Xaragua ! that dolorous image, that frightful memento, which Ovando ought never to have recalled, a place that was burnt after the massacre, a heap of ruins and of ashes given up to silence, to desertion, and to dismay !" One of the bishoprics was to be located at Conception, where there were about one hundred and fifty persons, and where beneath the cannons of the fort the pastor would have ample protection against the hostile attacks of his intended flock. The remaining see was to be erected at Larez, a newly projected city, founded by Ovando himself, where his interests would be greatly promoted by the advantages of having a resident bishop, where permanency and prosperity would thus be secured to his enterprise, and his prospective properties developed. In fact, the project seemed to assume the aspect of a speculation, and that, too, by an official of the government, and to be based upon the credit of the Church. Not satisfied with what he had done, Columbus, in the midst of his poverty, secured by the aid and credit of a few friends sufficient funds for sending his brother, Don Bartholomew Columbus, to Rome, where he communicated the admiral's views to the Pope, and where, in 1505, he published a history of the admiral's first voyage, together with a chart of his discoveries. It resulted that the admiral's remonstrances were heeded at Rome, though not at the Spanish court ; the bulls were not forwarded, notwithstanding the entreaties of the Spanish ambassador. The Count de Lorgues states that " before the Chief of the Church the confidential advice of Columbus prevailed over the assertions of the Spanish crown and the cunning of diplomacy."

An interesting visitor now called upon Columbus at Seville. This was Americus Vespucius, who had been called to court by the king in relation to marine affairs, and who desired now to improve the personal acquaintance of Columbus, to offer his services, and perhaps obtain a letter of introduction. It is true that Americus Vespucius had first appeared on the scenes of the new world as a companion of Alonzo de Ojeda, in an expedition to Terra Firma fitted out under Ferdinand's general license and aided by Juan de Fonseca, who had fraudulently given Ojeda a copy of one of the admiral's charts ; and though the expedition, in its conception and conduct on the part of Ojeda, was little better than a marauding adventure, still Columbus, not given to ungenerous or narrow conduct, knew well that Americus was not responsible for the conduct of Ojeda, that the expedition was licensed by the king and Fonseca, and his acquaintance with his visitor for several years had not unfavorably impressed him. He received Americus kindly, accepted his proffered services, and gave him a letter of introduction to his son Diego at court, in which he calls him "a very good man." He authorized his friends at court to accept the services of Americus, though he enjoins secrecy in this, as though it would injure any one to espouse the cause of the fallen admiral if it became known. Little did Columbus then imagine, when he gave this letter to Americus Vespucius, that he was destined, though not designedly on his part, to carry away from him the glory of giving his name to the new world. The history of this interesting question I have already given in a previous chapter.

Wearied at the refusal of the king to answer any of his repeated letters, the admiral now determined again to make the effort of going to court, in the hope that his presence might prove more efficacious. The most easy way for him to travel was on a mule "saddled and bridled," as the gait is quieter than that of a horse; but as it was forbidden by law to use mules in the saddle, he applied for and obtained the permission of the king to travel in that manner. Though the permit was obtained on February 23, he was not able to take the trip until May. In the mean time, he passed the Lenten season in Seville, and at his advanced age and with his infirm health he rigidly kept the fast, followed the strict observances of the Franciscans, and relaxed none of his austerities, though he was unable to leave his bed, and was spent with age, disease, and adversities. In May he started on his trip, mounted on a mule. He was taken ill at Salamanca, but finally, after much suffering, he reached Segovia, where the court was then held. Ferdinand received the man he had so much injured with politeness and even with apparent favor and pleasure, but the admiral's title of viceroy and the respect due to his rank had disappeared on the death of the queen. This certainly was significant; to the sanguine mind of Columbus it was conclusive. The king listened politely to his recital of his last voyage, of the mines of Veragua, of his shipwreck at Jamaica, his abandonment by Ovando, the revolt of

Porras, and his indignities received at the hands of Ovando. The king was polite but non-committal, and while he acknowledged the obligation of gratitude on the part of the crown, the cold and selfish Ferdinand found a way of terminating the interview without granting redress. To a reminder a few days afterward, which the king received from Columbus, he replied in a polite and cold manner, preserved a chilling courtesy and reserve, and significantly referred to the admiral's gout and rheumatism, with recommendations to take good care of himself, and even mentioned the appropriate medicines for him to take. Ferdinand had a significant nod by which he could always terminate an interview.

The courtesy under which Ferdinand endeavored to conceal his true sentiments could not deceive the discerning and anxious eye of Columbus. He read the king's heart, and his coldness made him feel more than ever the loss of his friend and queen, the noble Isabella. After his repeated letters to the king, with a constant representation at court in the persons of his sons, his brother Bartholomew, his faithful friends Diego Mendez, Alonzo Sanchez de Carvajal, and Geronimo, and the services of Americus Vespucius, and with the known friendship for him of Archbishop de Deza of Seville, who had formerly been the learned Dominican friar that defended his proposals before the Council of Salamanca, he had failed to gain justice from the king —what more than they had said in his behalf could the admiral now say? His venerable and dejected appearance, his eloquence in pleading the most just of causes, did not move the selfish Ferdinand. His friend De Deza had been promoted from the bishopric of Palencia to the archbishopric of Seville, while his enemy, Fonseca, had been transferred from the bishopric of Cordova and appointed to succeed De Deza as Bishop of Palencia. Columbus, ever thoughtful of every measure for gaining his cause, had sent his son on an embassy to Archbishop de Deza, and now, on the promotion of Fonseca, he had written to his son to present his congratulations to the new Bishop of Palencia, thus showing a superiority to all personal animosities as well as a desire to remove or smooth down all impediments to his attaining justice from the crown. This same prelate and official, Bishop Fonseca, was known to be the most influential and potent enemy the admiral had, the most implacable, and the one who had done him the greatest amount of injury.

After the death of Isabella there was a rumor that she had mentioned Columbus in her will, and he took fresh hope from this circumstance. The rumor was a false one, though it is the opinion of historians that she refrained from doing so not from any indifference to his just rights and claims, but from motives of delicacy ; for it was believed that such mention of him would not have aided his cause, while it might have stimulated the malice and machinations of his enemies. If she had in her will requested the king to have regard for the rights of the admiral, would the husband who had made a promise to his dying queen that, in charity for the poor persecuted natives of Hispaniola, he would remove Ovando, their persecutor, without delay, and had violated such a sacred promise—would such a husband have fulfilled a request relating to Columbus contained in her will ? He had already put his hand and seal, in conjunction with the queen, to a convention conceding to the admiral certain offices, titles, rights, revenues, and prerogatives, and he had again ratified the same, and when suspended had promised to restore them ; would any obligation have bound such a king against his interests ? The cause of Columbus did not go against him by default. He fully comprehended his rights, and there was never a moment, even during the perils of his shipwreck and exile on the savage coast of Jamaica, and up to the moment of his death, that he did not earnestly and resolutely demand their restitution. The learned and judicious Tarducci, referring to Isabella's unwillingness, from motives of delicacy, to formally impose her wishes in regard to Columbus on her husband by her will, concludes by saying, " But I have no doubt that, with her dying words to Ferdinand, she fulfilled the last duties of a tender friendship and of a loyal and just sovereign toward the discoverer of the new world." * Crippled in his hands by his unrelenting malady, he could only use them for conducting his important and voluminous correspondence in the dark and gloomy hours of the night, in which depressing hours his pen was busy with the protests and reclamations he unceasingly made for justice. It was just before he went to court mounted on a mule that the

---

* Mr. Brownson's translation of Tarducci's "Columbus," vol. ii., p. 355.

ships arrived from Hispaniola laden with gold for the king and many others, but with not a grain of gold for the sufferer. It was on this occasion that he wrote to his son at court, "Never was such injustice known ; 60,000 pesos left for me have disappeared." The treatment which Columbus received from the king was the common talk of Seville, outside of the circle of his enemies. Great and sincere was the sympathy felt and expressed for him and his wrongs. It is supposed that this sentiment and influence led Americus Vespucius to make a pilgrimage of sympathy to the great discoverer.

Discouraged as he was by the coldness and indifference of the king, Columbus never desisted from demanding his rights. Some days after his interview he addressed a letter to that end to the king, couched in language remarkable for its truthfulness, firmness, and candor, of which the first passage will convey an idea of its tone : " Most Potent King : God our Lord sent me hither miraculously to serve your Highness. I say miraculously, for I had presented my undertaking to the King of Portugal, who was more intent upon discoveries than any one else, and yet, in my case, his eyes, ears, and all his senses were so closed that in fourteen years I was unable to make him understand my meaning. I say miraculously also, because I received from three princes letters of invitation, which the queen (whom may God have in His glory) saw, and Dr. Villalano read. . . ." * This trenchant letter received a reply from Ferdinand at once wily and insincere ; the obligations of Spain to the admiral were admitted, but as his claims embraced so many different things, such as titles, government, pecuniary interests, accounts, indemnification, and other matters, it was necessary to submit them to the judgment of some discreet and able person. Columbus readily consented to this arbitration, and he suggested Father de Deza, a friend of himself and a favorite of the king ; but he expressly declined to arbitrate his restitution to offices, dignities, and titles, and the government of the Indies, for these he held under the signatures of his sovereigns already ; and more than that he could not get, as the signatures of the king and queen

---

* Mr. Brownson's translation of Tarducci's "Columbus," vol. ii., p. 357 ; " Colonial Documents," by Navarrete, pl. i., No. lviii. ; Barry's De Lorgues' "Columbus," p. 525 ; Irving's "Columbus," vol. ii., p. 472.

showed he was already entitled to them. The insincerity and want of good faith on the part of the king are manifest from the fact that he always defeated what he professed to be willing to agree to, by annexing in each case a condition which he knew Columbus would not and could not accept—the submission of his right to the government of the Indies. Of course the proposed arbitration fell through, as it was evidently the king's intention that it should. While the admiral repeatedly begged and urged his rights and claims, Ferdinand coolly smiled each time, and promised that he would consider them. This is not matter of inference, nor one resting on the common voice of history; but the statement of the royal perfidy rests upon the testimony of a distinguished and conscientious contemporary, the good and loyal Las Casas, who wrote, "But as to actions, the king not only showed him no signs of favor, but, on the contrary, placed every obstacle in the way; and at the same time was never wanting in complimentary expressions."

This venerable, aged, and enfeebled admiral and discoverer despaired of getting even a show of justice; he became disheartened. He thought he might secure something, now at least while he was alive, by offering, as he did in positive terms, to leave everything to the king's generosity, assuring him that he had no desire to become involved in lawsuits with his own sovereign. He only begged for some decision to be made promptly, that he might see the end of his disappointments and sufferings, and secure some repose to his declining years. The king replied now in somewhat explicit terms, but they were only words. He said he entertained no intention of depriving himself of the admiral's services; that he would give him full satisfaction; that he could never forget that he owed the possession of the Indies to him, and that he would not only give him what was his legal due, but would remunerate his great services from the estates of the crown. After such an explicit promise and pledge Columbus felt in duty and respect bound to believe the truth of his own sovereign, and to silently await his action.

The perfidy of Ferdinand was so glaring, that the sympathies of all honest Spaniards were with the subject and against the sovereign. If he had followed the court from city to city when he was a suppliant for recognition and for a chance to serve

Spain in a signal manner, he was now still more obliged to pursue King Ferdinand from place to place, petitioning for justice for signal services already rendered. It was not the question now of adopting Columbus's proposals for the discovery of a new world; it was a matter of rendering what he had promised and justly owed the discoverer. At every turn he received from the king nothing but cold smiles and courteous words. Was it not a shallow evasion of justice to refer the matter to the Junta de Descargos, a tribunal expressly appointed to carry into effect the will and discharge the obligations of the deceased queen, since the judges were appointed by the king, were his dependents, and as they could not, without open scandal, decide against Columbus, so they could not, without offending the king, decide against his known wishes? The king prevented a decision. This junta with equal evasion did nothing but inflict delay upon Columbus. How could it be alleged in extenuation of Ferdinand's injustice to Columbus, that the vastness of the concessions stipulated in his favor now exceeded all possible anticipations, since the Indies far exceeded in extent and wealth Spain itself, and it would be making a subject equal to a sovereign? The answer is too obvious, and is twofold: First, were not the dominions themselves out of which the concessions were to be satisfied proportionately increased, and was not the sovereign himself the gainer by the excess rather than the subject? Second, could dishonesty be resorted to in any event from a mere question of convenience? It was equivalent to saying, We owe him justly too much, therefore we will pay him nothing. Perhaps the king desired to consult his daughter, the Princess Juana. Then why repeat and renew his promises, and why deny justice on such a pretext? The very delay became a vital issue, since the life of Columbus was passing rapidly away. Conscience had no weight with Ferdinand; but why should he sully his name with such an infamy as this? The entire Indies, so far exceeding all anticipations, with all their gold and pearls and wealth, were not worth an immunity from payment purchased at the cost of such dishonor.

From Segovia, where the admiral had attended upon the pretended deliberations of the Junta de Descargos, and where the tactics of his enemies at Seville had been followed with the same cruelty, Columbus followed the court to Valladolid. At the latter place the venerable supplicant was again confined to his bed. Here, however, he wrote another urgent letter to the king, submitting all his rights to the king's generosity, only begging that his son Diego might be appointed to the government of the Indies. His days now but few, his aspirations seemed confined to securing for his son and family at least this recognition of his services. In his letter to the king he writes: "It is a matter that concerns my honor. Your Majesty may do as you think proper with all the rest; give or take, as may appear for your advantage, and I shall be satisfied. I believe that the worry caused by the delay of my suit is the main cause of my ill health."

Simultaneously with the above letter of Columbus to the king, he caused his son Diego to lay before the monarch a petition containing the same requests, and proposing that councillors be appointed by the king himself to assist him in the administration of Hispaniola with their advice. This simply elicited from the selfish and perfidious ruler the usual empty promises, which, as often broken as made, had now filled the measure of the admiral's sorrows and of the public disgust. Las Casas boldly asserts that the king's policy was to weary and harass the illustrious petitioner by delay into a renunciation of his just claims and the acceptance of Castilian titles and estates in commutation. This view is confirmed by the evidence of an offer from the king to Columbus of the fief of Carrion de los Condes and a pension. Columbus indignantly refused the unworthy offer. Surely it was not for this he had discovered the new world. Such was the dishonorable and unjust conduct of Ferdinand throughout, that he has laid himself open to the just suspicion of only waiting for the admiral's death to be relieved of importunity. The admiral himself has given utterance in the above-quoted letter to the king to the fact that his delays of justice had caused the present condition of his health. It cannot be denied that Ferdinand's injustice hastened and contributed to the death of Columbus. The latter now lost all hope. From his bed of sickness now, at Valladolid, he addressed to his good friend, Archbishop Diego de Deza, these stinging words: "It seems that his Highness does not think fit to fulfil the promises which I received from him and the queen (who is now in the bosom of glory), under the faith of their word and seal. To contend against his

will would be contending against the wind. I have done all that
I ought to have done, and leave the rest to God." The echo of
these indignant words of the great discoverer and benefactor of
Spain is repeated in our own time by the universal voice of history, as expressed by the following indignant passage from the
classic pen of our distinguished countryman, Mr. Irving: "The
cold and calculating Ferdinand beheld this illustrious man sinking under infirmity of body, heightened by that deferred hope
which maketh the heart sick. A little more delay, a little more
disappointment, and a little more infliction of ingratitude, and
this loyal and generous heart would cease to beat; he should
then be delivered from the just claims of a well-tried servant,
who, in ceasing to be useful, was considered by him to have
become importunate." *

The admiral entertained now the hope—it was his last hope—
that Ferdinand might be delaying in order to consult the new
Queen of Castile, the Infanta Juana, who succeeded her mother
in the government of that kingdom, hoping to find that she had
inherited the virtues and rectitude of her illustrious mother, and
that he would find in her that justice which had been denied him
by her father. The new queen arrived accompanied by her
royal consort, and was met at Laredo by Ferdinand and his
entire court. Columbus, as if inspired with the fire, energy,
ambition, and indomitable spirit of his stronger days, would have
gone in person to greet the new sovereign of Castile. A new
relapse of intense violence defeated this purpose. His brother,
Don Bartholomew, in his stead, presented his letter of congratulation, in which he gave the assurances of his best loyalty and
services, lamenting the disease which deprived him of the privilege of going in person, as he had intended, to receive the queen,
expressing the hope of yet rendering the crown most valuable
services, and expressing the same petition for the restoration of
his rights. Accorded an audience by the two sovereigns on May
7th, Don Bartholomew obtained a hearing. Ferdinand was
there; he was, of course, the master spirit of the occasion; the
royal answer was given in promises, and accorded with the perfidious conduct of the past—polite attentions and promises of
speedy action. This was the last public act of Columbus; it was

---

* Irving's "Columbus," vol. ii., p. 476.

the last insult Ferdinand had the privilege of heaping upon him. With the admiral, this last expression of his hope and confidence that he might yet accomplish some brilliant, extraordinary, and valuable enterprises for his sovereigns and his country, was the last flicker of the exhausted candle; the hope was dazzling, the offer was magnanimous; its cold and deceptive reception was perfidious! It was of Ferdinand!

It is interesting and instructive to recall the expressions of indignation which have been uttered by historians at the ingratitude experienced by Columbus from his king. Tarducci says: "The long years spent in running from one place to another to beg audience of kings, ministers, and grandees of the kingdom; the mockery and scorn with which he was received and repelled on every side; the struggles he underwent in support of his ideas; the fatigue, perils, and distress he suffered in carrying them out, and the grandeur of his achievements and the enthusiasm he had aroused on every side! And now, after enriching Spain with so many regions and such treasures as no human tongue ever told of, after changing by his discoveries the face of the known world, doubling the known space of the globe, he was now groaning in abandonment and contempt, in a wretched lodging-house, and had to beg for a loan of money to buy a cot to die on; and those who had ridiculed his undertaking were triumphing in wealth and ease, in power and honor!" *

The following eloquent though extravagantly expressed passage from the Count de Lorgues is no less appropriate in this place: "He saw disappearing indefinitely the deliverance of the Holy Sepulchre—the ardent desire of his whole life—at a time when everything seemed ready for its realization. Gold now abounded, and every new arrival promised for the next season greater riches; but there was nothing for Columbus! What must he now have felt in his heart? Still no complaint was heard from him. Confining in the depths of his loneliness the bitterness of his sorrows, he offered them to Him who had borne the cross. This calm in the height of affliction, does it not reveal something else besides virtue? Can we find in history an example similar to it? Philosophy is as incapable of inspiring as it is of explaining this sublime resignation. It was because the

---

* Mr. Brownson's translation of Tarducci's "Life of Columbus," vol. ii., p. 302.

messenger of salvation held the crucifix before his eyes. He remembered that our Divine Lord, coming to bring to poor humanity more than a world, and more than all the worlds—the Truth, the Way, and the Life—was calumniated, persecuted, bound with cords, scourged, given as a spectacle to the crowd, and delivered in death, notwithstanding His declared innocence. Like Him, the revealer of the globe remained silent; and, like Him, he pardoned his enemies." *

What could be more just than the following sentiments from Mr. Irving: " Attempts have been made in recent days by loyal Spanish writers to vindicate the conduct of Ferdinand toward Columbus. They were doubtless well intended, but they have been futile; nor is their failure to be regretted. To screen such injustice in so eminent a character from the reprobation of mankind is to deprive history of one of its most important uses. Let the ingratitude of Ferdinand stand recorded in its full extent, and endure throughout all time. The dark shadow which it casts upon his brilliant renown will be a lesson to all rulers, teaching them what is important to their own fame in their treatment of illustrious men." †

The voices of many other eminent historians, raised in unison with those whose language I have given, could here be quoted in proof that the verdict of mankind has been rendered in condemnation of the ungrateful, selfish, unstatesmanlike, disloyal, cruel, and deceptive treatment which Ferdinand extended to Columbus. In proportion as the king realized the grandeur of the services rendered by Columbus he should have honored and rewarded the benefactor. In proportion as the countries he discovered proved vast and almost unbounded, his gratitude to the discoverer should have increased. In proportion as the riches of the Indies poured into the lap of Spain and into the royal exchequer, so should have been increased the reward of the man who gave them to his country. The very grasping tenacity with which Ferdinand held on to all he had gained by Columbus, proves that he knew better than any one the value of his gains. When he promised titles, honors, dignities, estates, revenues, and jurisdictions to Columbus, all was conjectural and

---

* Dr. Barry's translation of De Lorgues' "Columbus," p. 531.
† Irving's "Life of Columbus," vol. ii., p. 483.

speculative; the reward was made conditional upon success; now that success was attained, the benefits were sordidly grasped and the promised rewards cruelly withheld. Could human perfidy, ingratitude, or baseness exceed this? Retributive justice is to be recognized as a feature in God's government of the world; and why should it not be? Events are so startling! The splendid possessions of Spain, which she got by the genius and services of Columbus, and for which she refused to compensate him even as she had promised, have been wrested from her grasp; and Cuba, the Queen of the Antilles, remains only as a mere souvenir of her former vast and opulent possessions. Who does not recognize the justice of the retribution? In the mean time, Columbus receives the homage of mankind.

When we contemplate the magnificent achievements of Columbus—his vast discoveries, his genius, his enterprise, his labors, his originality, the world-wide scope of his undertakings, from the discovery of a new world to the rescue of the Holy Land and the conversion of all nations to Christianity—it is hard to realize and humiliating to record the fate of such a man. Still more abhorrent to our sense of justice that such a benefactor of his country and of his kind should have died in neglect, poverty, distress, and injustice.

While Don Bartholomew, his brother, was making the last appeal for him in the presence of royalty, Christopher Columbus felt that his malady was growing alarming, and that his end was near. In the denial of all earthly rewards, this devout Christian now looked confidently yet humbly only for the rewards of heaven. Few death-beds recorded in history have been so reassuring, so dignified, so heroic as that of Columbus. As his disease became daily more alarming, he realized the approach of death. On May 19th he perceived that the end was at hand. Calling to his aid all the resources of grace and all the promised rewards of virtue, he heroically and calmly resigned himself to the inevitable. With a calmness that we have often seen him exercise in the most trying circumstances, he first determined to provide for his family and for his descendants by a proper disposition of his affairs in this world. His whole testamentary disposition was the work of different times and of different epochs of his life. His first will was made in 1498, and now he made a codicil to it before his approaching death. In 1502 he also made a will, which he confided to his friend, Father Gaspar Gorricio, a Carthusian monk. This will has never come to light, and is supposed to have been suppressed by the admiral's family shortly after his death for prudential reasons. These reasons are left to conjecture. When he made his first will in 1498 he was in the zenith of prosperity and glory, and in it he poured forth the sentiments of gratitude toward the Spanish sovereigns, much in keeping with his generous nature. But in 1502 his star was on the wane; he had already experienced the ingratitude of his king; and it is supposed that he omitted these expressions from the new will then made, for he was then smarting under the injustice done him in sending Aguado, Bobadilla, and Ovando in succession to Hispaniola, his imprisonment and chains, and his suspension from power; and it is conjectured that he spoke with bitterness even of the treatment he had received. In 1505 he made a codicil, dated August 25th, in which he firmly asserts that he " had made them [the king and queen] a present of the Indies, as a thing of his own, and claims the right to reject the line of division agreed upon between Spain and Portugal; and he asserts the correctness of his own line, which was established by the Pope—the papal line of demarcation. It is also said that on May 4th, probably in the paroxysms of intense suffering, he made an informal codicil in his own hand, and written on the blank page of a little breviary given to him by Pope Alexander VI. Mr. Irving states that Columbus made a codicil to his will about May 19th, 1506, the day before his death; but this is denied by the Count de Lorgues, and the fact is alluded to in a general way only by Tarducci, who simply says, " Sending for a notary, Columbus placed in his hands a codicil."

The general result of the testamentary disposition of Columbus may be stated thus: His son Diego is constituted his universal heir, and the entailed inheritance or mayorazgo, in the event of his death without male issue, was given to his brother, Don Fernando, and in the like case with him, it was given to his uncle, Don Bartholomew Columbus, descending always to the nearest male heir, and on failure of the male line it was to descend to the female nearest in lineage to the admiral. The inheritor of the estate was enjoined against alienating or diminishing it, but rather to increase its revenues, and he was also admonished promptly at all times to respond to every duty of service to the crown of Spain, and to promote the Christian faith. One tenth of the revenues of the estate enjoyed by Don Diego was to be devoted to the relief of the poor members of the family and others in need, but not until the estate had become productive; and from the bulk of the estate's revenues ample provision was made for Don Fernando and for Don Bartholomew. The will also provided for the erection of a chapel at the town of Conception, in the Vega, Hispaniola, after the estate had become sufficient for that and all other purposes, and that a hospital should be connected with it; and in such chapel masses should be said perpetually for the repose of the souls of himself, his ancestors, and his posterity. He provided for the poor of his lineage and family; for the maintenance and residence of one member of the Columbus family and his wife at Genoa; for the enlistment and equipment of an army for the recovery of the Holy Sepulchre; for the maintenance of the sovereignty of the Spanish sovereigns and their successors, and for the aid of the Church and of the Holy See in case of schism or other trouble. The provisions were munificent in proportion to the grand expectations which Columbus entertained as to the just revenues from his estates, properties, and offices in the new world. The will was substantially a renewal or confirmation of his will of 1497-98. So scrupulous was the illustrious testator in discharging every minute money obligation he had ever contracted, even those of gratitude, that he provided, among others, for the repayment of an assistance he had many years before received from a poor Jew of Lisbon, whom, on his not remembering his name, he described as living near the Jewry Gate.

Columbus received all the sacraments and rites of the Church devoutly from the hands of his friends, the Franciscans, for which he asked for the last time. His death occurred at Valladolid on the feast of the Ascension, May 20th, 1506. Such was the obscurity to which the neglect of his king had consigned the admiral that no notice of his death can be found in the contemporary chronicles of Valladolid. "It is hard to conceive," says Justin Winsor, "how the fame of a man, over whose acts in 1493 learned men cried for joy, and by whose deeds the adventurous spirit had been stirred in every seaport of Western Europe, should have so completely passed into oblivion." Even Peter Martyr, who wrote so much of the stirring events of his career, did not mention his death, although about the time of its occurrence he wrote five long and newsy letters from Valladolid. Montalboddo, who wrote an account of Columbus's early voyages, and revised it in 1507, had not even heard of his death. Madrignano, who translated the same work into Latin in 1508, had not heard of it. The *Cronicon de Valladolid*, extending from 1333 to 1539, though containing the most minute details of local interest, makes no mention of the death of Christopher Columbus for the year 1506.*

In the modest and austere chamber in which he died there were hanging, according to general tradition, upon the walls the chains which Columbus wore when he was brought back to Spain a prisoner, and by his express request his chains were buried with him. The chains, however, were not found among his relics at the times of their several removals. The illustrious patient wore in his last hours the brown habit of St. Francis. His two sons, some of his officers and friends, and the Franciscan Fathers attended the last moments of the expiring admiral, and gave him every consolation which religion alone affords in that supreme crisis. He addressed some edifying exhortations to those present. His mental faculties were clear to the last. He asked for the sacraments of the Church, and audibly joined in the prayers with which they were administered. He responded to the prayers for the dying as recited by the Franciscans. His last words were, "*In manus tuas, Domine, commendo spiritum meum*" ("Into Thy hands, O Lord, I commend my spirit!").

The body of Columbus was carried to the Cathedral Church of Valladolid, and there received the most modest obsequies; thence the Franciscans carried his remains and deposited them in the vault of their convent of Minors Observantines in the same city. Thus, as the Count de Lorgues observes, "Columbus, who first found an asylum among the Franciscans, received from them the last hospitality." The placing of his chains in his coffin, as related above, was not only in accordance with his own wishes, but was also in conformity with ancient custom, whereby in mediæval times the relics of saints and martyrs were accompanied with vials of their blood, the instruments of their torture, or images of them. Not only was his death unmentioned in con-

---

* Mr. Brownson's translation of Tarducci's "Columbus," vol. ii., p. 365.

temporary Spanish documents, but in following years he was mentioned as still living in works published in other countries of Europe.

At the court of Ferdinand his name was forgotten, only to be recalled once by the king with frigid ceremony, when on June 2d, 1506, he ordered the gold and other objects of the admiral to be sent to his son, Don Diego, without giving the least expression to any sentiment of regret, gratitude, or honor for his memory. But as the progress of discoveries in the great fields pointed out by Columbus revealed more and more every year the grandeur and vastness of his discoveries and services, an immense glory was accorded to his name, and Ferdinand was aroused by the expanding fame of his great achievements to make some tardy and reluctant concessions to public sentiment. He ordered the remains of the admiral to be removed with pomp and ceremony from the Franciscan convent at Valladolid to Seville, where a solemn service was performed at the cathedral, after which the Carthusians bore his remains beyond the Guadalquiver to their convent vaults in St. Mary of the Grottoes, and placed them in the chapel of St. Ann. This was done at the expense of the crown in the year 1513, while some have made the year 1509. Then it was that Ferdinand gave the admiral, according to a very doubtful tradition, whom he had so grossly wronged, an epitaph, written by himself,

"POR CASTILLA Y POR LEON
NUEVO MUNDO HALLO COLON." *

(" For Castile and Leon Columbus found a new world.") In 1526 the repose of his mortal remains was again disturbed, but only to receive by his side those of his son Diego, his heir and successor. On June 2d, 1537, the widow of Don Diego Columbus, Donna Maria de Toledo, obtained from Charles V. permission to remove the remains of Columbus and his son to San Domingo, in Hispaniola, the city he had founded, and to which he had given as a coat-of-arms the lion and the tower of Isabella, the cross and the key, the emblems of the Church; and now these venerated relics were deposited with great solemnity in a

---

* There is another rendering of this epitaph, which is followed by Mr. Irving, the Count de Lorgues, and others. It is given at the head of this chapter, and represents Columbus as giving rather than as finding a new world for Spain.

recess in the sanctuary of the cathedral, to the right of the main altar, according to the Count de Lorgues, but according to Tarducci, in the largest chapel of the cathedral. It is also said that the removal to San Domingo was in compliance with his own wish. But in 1795, nearly three centuries afterward, by the Treaty of Basle between France and Spain, Hispaniola became a possession of France, when Spain, desirous of always possessing the remains of Columbus, arranged for their removal to Havana, Cuba. Accordingly, on December 20th, 1795, the honored remains were disinterred with great pomp and with the most solemn obsequies in the presence of the clergy, the governor, and the assembled people; and after having been carried to the national vessel provided for that purpose were borne to Havana, and there again interred with grand funereal ceremonies and military honors near the great altar of the cathedral to the right of the sanctuary. The notables of the Church and of the State attended these magnificent and solemn ceremonies. It was now supposed at last that the admiral's remains were at rest. But in 1877 the world was startled by the announcement from San Domingo, that in excavating near the high altar of the cathedral of that city the casket containing the remains of Columbus was discovered still remaining there. The remains were authentically recognized in the presence of all the ecclesiastical, military, and civil authorities, and such was the intense interest felt in this strange yet grateful discovery, that immense numbers of the people turned out to contemplate the venerated remains. This singular state of things, on investigation, came to be explained. In this place were deposited not only the remains of Columbus, but also those of his son, Diego, and of his grandson, Luis, his two successors in the government of Hispaniola. In the many alterations and changes made from time to time in the great chapel of the Cathedral of San Domingo, the main altar was several times moved and its location changed; and though the three caskets containing the mortal remains of Columbus and of his son, Diego, and his grandson, Luis, had never been changed in location, yet the changes in the sanctuary and chancel left doubt as to the precise location of each. In 1877 Monsignor Rocco Cocchia, Bishop of Orope and Apostolic Delegate to San Domingo, while having the chapel repaired, discovered the casket, which on examination proved not to be the one containing the remains of either Don Diego Columbus or of Don Luis Columbus, but, to the astonishment of all, that of the admiral himself, which it was believed had been removed in 1795 to Havana. Though the dates showed clearly that the casket then found contained the remains of Christopher Columbus, the investigation was continued for the two caskets which contained the bones of the other two admirals, Don Diego and Don Luis, and on finding another casket, it was discovered on investigation to contain only the remains of Don Luis, for it was clearly inscribed with his name. It was thus made manifest that the remains of Christopher Columbus and of his grandson, Don Luis Columbus, remained in the Cathedral of San Domingo, and hence the remains removed in 1795 were clearly those of Don Diego Columbus, and not those of Christopher Columbus, as was intended and believed to have been the case. It was always reported and believed in San Domingo that the casket removed to Havana in 1795 was not that of Christopher Columbus. Visitors to San Domingo are to this day shown in the cathedral the casket claimed to contain the remains of the admiral. These visits are regulated by official rule, must be made after official permission obtained in the presence of three officials, and all present are required to make an entry of their visit and to sign it in a book kept for that purpose. After these preliminaries the glass casket is brought from a vault; it is rather small, being about three feet long, two feet high, and one and a half feet wide, and is crossed with two bands sealed with the State seal. Within the glass casket is an open zinc box containing the wasted bones of the illustrious deceased, and also a glass vase or jar containing the dust of disintegrated bones. At the time of the discovery of these relics a small silver plate was found with them, with an inscription, by which they were identified, and this is now suspended within the casket. Visitors are also shown where and how the remains were discovered in 1877. These details are disputed by the Academy of History at Madrid, and the remains of Columbus are claimed to be resting in the Cathedral of Havana; but the claim of San Domingo seems the stronger.

At the mouth of the river Ozema still stand the ruins of the old fort or castle, at the foot of a hill now called Santo Carlo, in which Columbus was imprisoned by Bobadilla. It is constructed of brick, and is in good preservation. But the race whom it was intended to keep in subjection have entirely disappeared, and even the Spanish settlement made about the fort in 1497 has almost wholly vanished. The once busy and bustling spectacles in which the loyal Ballester and the disloyal Roldan took an active part have been succeeded by dense forests of majestic trees. But the city of San Domingo now has a population of about fifteen thousand, and has interesting relics of Columbus, while the old Spanish town which grew up around the fort was destroyed by an earthquake on the morning of April 20th, 1564, during the celebration of mass. The ruins of the old Spanish church and convent are still visible. The destroyer, Time, has almost obliterated the traces of Columbus and his successors. Even the Spanish flag has been supplanted by that of France, and there is little left besides the island of Cuba of the great empires which Spain, by the genius of Columbus, founded in the new world; but in the midst of such mutations and decay, the fame of Columbus, the prisoner at Fort Conception, the admiral in chains, has electrified the world, and is to-day more glorified than when he entered the royal city of Barcelona, the discoverer of a new world returning in triumph.

The family of Columbus at the time of his death consisted of two sons, Diego and Fernando, the former of whom was his general heir and legatee, and the latter became his historian. Don Diego, after his father's death, continued to demand from King Ferdinand, as his illustrious father had done before him, the restitution of the offices, titles, and rights to which he had succeeded under the admiral's will, as well as by the stipulations of the sovereigns. For two years he sought justice in vain, and in 1508, on the return of Ferdinand from Naples, the young admiral frankly and firmly demanded of the king "why his Majesty would not grant to him as a favor that which was his right, and why he hesitated to confide in the fidelity of one who had been reared in his house." To this unanswerable appeal the unjust monarch replied that while he could confide in Don Diego personally, he could not venture to confide so great a trust to his children and successors. To this evasion the son of his father replied that neither justice nor reason could sanction his deprivation of a right on account of the possible sins of his children who were unborn, and might never come into existence.

Intent on vindicating the memory of his father and his own, and the rights of his descendants as his successors, Don Diego Columbus requested and obtained from King Ferdinand permission to institute a suit for the purpose before the Council of the Indies. This celebrated suit was commenced in 1508, was resisted with persistent ingratitude and sophistry by the king, and after lasting several years, was finally decided unanimously in favor of the young admiral and successor of Columbus. Even then the king delayed or declined to carry out the decision of the tribunal to which he consented, in favor of Don Diego. The latter, however, about this time gained another suit, for he married Donna Maria de Toledo, daughter of Fernando de Toledo, Grand Commander of Leon, and a niece of Don Fabrique de Toledo, the celebrated Duke of Alva, a brilliant general and favorite of the king. The bride's father and uncle were cousins germane to Ferdinand. It was a tribute to the glory shed by the great achievements of Columbus upon his family that his son was readily received into one of the proudest and most distinguished families of Spain. The most powerful family influence was now exerted on the king, and this proved more powerful and efficacious with him than the claims of justice. The importunity of Don Diego Columbus and his friends was now rewarded, but only in part. The king granted to him the dignities and powers bestowed upon Ovando, whom he recalled from Hispaniola. He persistently refused to the new governor the title of viceroy, which was always repugnant to him, even in the days of the admiral.

The administration of the second admiral was a succession of troubles and embarrassments, of old and new enmities and litigations, which partly ran through the reigns of Ferdinand and Charles V. Like his father, he died in the pursuit of justice denied. Don Luis Columbus was also compelled to seek his inherited rights by a suit against the crown, and obtained the title of captain-general; but by vexatious delays and denials of justice, a representative of the family of Columbus was compelled by compromise to commute all the concessions made to the admiral by Ferdinand and Isabella for the title of Duke of Veragua and Marquis of Jamaica, and a pension. The succession to the title and the pension passed into the collateral line, and finally in 1608 into the female branch of the family, and in the younger branch of the royal house of Bragança by marriage. The present representative of the admiral is the Duke of Veragua, who is said to bear a family resemblance to his distinguished ancestor. The present Duke of Veragua manifested a lively interest in the celebration of the four hundredth anniversary of the discovery of America, which he, accompanied by his family, attended as the guest of the American people. The blood of Isabella was similarly represented here by the Infanta Eulalie.

The remarkable character of Columbus is chiefly to be studied in his greatest enterprise, the discovery of America. In an age given, in an extraordinary manner, to maritime adventure and discoveries, he was the only man that conceived the idea of discovering a new world. In an age when gigantic strides had been made in extending the limits of the known earth and in discovering new portions of its surface, Columbus eclipsed all other discoverers by the unparalleled grandeur, importance, and value of his discoveries. In proportion as his work surpassed that of all others, so are his character and fitness, which achieved it, to be graded above others. The vastness and grandeur of his conceptions alone enabled him, of all men then living, to originate the great work which he proposed and achieved. His work was not the joint or combined result of the study or efforts of several minds; it was the sole achievement of his own genius. As Mr. Irving says, it was the offspring of his own mind. The world was against him. He had neither name nor fame, nor family influence, nor alliances, nor wealth to sustain him in the herculean task; but he stood alone and unsupported at the courts of Portugal and Spain, just as he stood alone at the gate of the Franciscan Convent of La Rabida. These facts show not only great originality of mind, thought, and study, but the long years of waiting, of disappointment, and of opposition which he encountered and overcame place him before us as a man of extraordinary will-power, perseverance, and courage. It is true that other qualities aided in this, but they were personal and characteristic traits and qualities of Christopher Columbus. His vivid and soaring imagination added greatly to the forces by which he carried his point, and it was the singular blending of the judgment and of the will with the contemplative and theoretical, the union of the real with the poetical, that enabled him to overcome all obstacles. While the Northmen, in the pursuit of their seafaring habits and roving tendencies, came upon portions of the Western Hemisphere, the event was not the result of geographical design or of study, and it had no effect at the time in revolutionizing the geography, the navigation, the commerce, the civilization of the world. Bold, brave, and indomitable as were the Norse discoverers of the tenth and succeeding centuries, and much as their achievements and spirit are to be admired and praised, the great achievement of Columbus presents itself in a different light to the historian and philosopher. There is no just or historic conflict between these two remarkable chapters in the history of the world. The first was the result of national traits and character, habits and tastes, based immediately upon accident rather than study or problems of science, and was transitory, leaving the world in such utter ignorance of the existence of the American continents that their discovery by Columbus was new, startling, scientific, and personal. To Columbus alone is due the grand result; all who participated in giving the undertaking assistance in ships, money, and men were his converts; and when the material means were provided, it was he in person, his genius and character dominating over unparalleled difficulties, that achieved the grand result. The first to conceive and announce an unseen and unknown world, and a route to it unknown and untried, he was the first to see, in his untiring vigils at night, the flickering light on the shore that was carried by a man of an unknown race—the beacon that revealed the new world to its illustrious discoverer.

Columbus was no ordinary man; he loomed up as a colossal figure among the men of his age. While ridiculed as a dreamer, a lunatic, he was the only man on earth that possessed the secrets of knowledge that revolutionized the world. He was a man of great and varied learning, though not of scholastic or scientific training, and he possessed the faculty of practically applying what he knew to the most valuable achievements and results. Having followed the sea from the age of fourteen, his knowledge of navigation, seamanship, and their kindred sciences was unequalled. His travels over seas and his visits to many lands made him acquainted with the earth's geography, and his pursuit as a map-maker in his days of poverty and delay gave to his profound study of the earth a detailed and practical direction, which made him one of the greatest of living cosmographers.

His travels also gave him an actual knowledge of men, and of various nations and languages, which prepared him to lead and rule over men. He was also a man of advanced and progressive learning, the result of study and his converse with books and men. He was a thorough student of the Scriptures, of both the Old and New Testaments, and had them ready at all times for the support of his views and theories. His "Collection of Prophecies on the Recovery of Jerusalem and the Discovery of the Indies" is a remarkable instance of devout and ingenious research and application, and it is interspersed with poetical effusions by the admiral of no mean character. He was familiar with the patristic theology and works of the Fathers of the Church; had studied the works of the Arabian Jews, and was quite conversant with and greatly influenced in his theories and opinions by the geographical writers of ancient and mediæval times. J. G. Kohl, a celebrated German traveler and scholar, said, "There was something visionary in Columbus's nature, yet when the time for action arrived he was never found wanting in decision and energy."

Columbus did much to enlighten the age in which he lived, to remove old and superstitious views of the earth, and to solve some of the most difficult problems of nature. With all the engrossing and harassing cares and solicitudes of his office and undertaking, he was a close and enthusiastic student of nature and of the phenomena of nature. His correspondence with Dr. Toscanelli, the learned cosmographer, and with Jayme Ferrer, the eminent lapidary, instances out of many of the varied learning of Columbus, and of his interest in and acquaintance with men of learning, and with the sciences in which they excelled. The services herein elsewhere recited as rendered by him to practical science are evidences of his scientific attainments. The blending of these solid accomplishments with a soaring imagination, a poetic cast of mind, and an intellect fruitful in theories, add a rare charm to the character of this remarkable man.

The administration of Columbus in new and unsettled lands and unexampled states of society was more difficult of success than the government of the most extensive and opulent empires of modern times. He knew how to accommodate himself to circumstances, however unusual or appalling, with rare sagacity. In the first contact of European civilization with the barbarism of the new world he had to exert powers of government, resort to measures of administration, and encounter stunning misfortunes and oppositions which are unexampled in history. He knew how to be stern in the administration of justice, and mild, generous, and forgiving whenever these were more efficacious than a resort to authority or physical strength, or were forced upon him by his situation. In his conflicts with the rebellious of his own people, he skilfully temporized when unable to cope in force with them, and he preferred to yield almost every point to save the very government, its viceroy, and its loyal subjects from annihilation. Had he met Roldan and his rebels in the open field, he would have been overpowered and his own valuable life have been sacrificed. He was humane, gentle, just, and affectionate to the natives of the countries he discovered, and was only severe toward them when their conduct stood in the way of his accomplishing his mission of founding the Spanish Empire in the new world. Some facts in his history would seem to countenance the charge that he favored and practised the enslavement of the Indians, but from this charge he has been exonerated by the most considerate and learned of historians. While he restricted the enslavement of the Indians to prisoners of war and implacable enemies of the Spanish dominion, he was even in this but the follower of the ideas and practices of his age and country, and of the education in which he was reared. Neither he nor any of his sons or brothers, the companions in his life-work, owned slaves. The learned and humane Las Casas, the friend and liberator of the Indians, himself excuses Columbus on this head, as if he erred, it was in common with the most learned scholars and theologians of Spain at that time. Mr. Irving, in allusion to the enslavement of prisoners of war or rebellious natives, says: "In so doing he sinned against the natural goodness of his character, and against the feelings which he had originally entertained and expressed toward this gentle and hospitable people ; but he was goaded on by the mercenary impatience of the crown, and by the sneers of his enemies at the unprofitable result of his enterprises. It is but justice to his character to observe that the enslavement of the Indians thus taken in battle was at first openly countenanced by the crown, and that when the question of right came to be discussed at the entreaty of the queen, several of the most eminent jurists and theologians advocated the practice, so that the question was finally settled in favor of the Indians solely by the humanity of Isabella." * Had the views and measures of Columbus been executed, had his earnest recommendations to the crown, so often repeated and urged, been followed, the first settlement of the new world would not have been attended by wars and enslavement, nor would the Spanish settlements have been composed of lustful conquerors or avaricious adventurers, but by peaceful colonists and by prudent and just rulers, jurists, and governors.

Columbus was a man in whom nature had been subdued and trained by study, meditation, prayer, and grace. Nature and humanity abounded in his character. His natural impulses were powerful, his sensibilities quick, the excitability of the man was intense, and his impressions were often suddenly received and strongly adhered to. Yet with all this natural manhood within him, he was conservative, reflective, judicious, just, politic, and prudent. His self-control was extraordinary. It was a rare and remarkable result of his self-culture, religious training, and conscientious self-inspection, that he brought under subjection and control a temper naturally violent. He was benevolent and generous. In the midst of the grossest ill-treatment, often repeated, he restrained his feelings and his conduct, he kept a fiery disposition subject to reason by the strong powers of his mind, and he knew how to practise, under the most appalling wrongs, forbearance, forgiveness, and benignity. He knew even how to supplicate when he was entitled to command; to pardon when he might have punished; to conciliate when he might have condemned. Revenge was utterly foreign to his nature, and repentance always opened his generous heart, even to the greatest criminals. If he understood the art of governing the unruly, the capricious, and the wicked within his jurisdiction, his conquest over himself was more extraordinary. In the most sudden emergencies he was calm, judicious, ready, and rich in expedients. Such, too, was the exuberance of his character that in the midst of the greatest calamities the slightest turn of the tide in his favor rekindled his hope, inspired his fancy, nerved his arm for new enterprises, and lifted him up even from the bed of suffering. When nearing his end, we have seen how a slight ray

---

* Irving's "Columbus," vol. ii., p. 490.

of hope seemed to restore him from the jaws of death to the brightest aspirations of his youth.

The magnanimity of Columbus was one of his most shining traits of character. This virtue he practised not only in forgiving the most lacerating injuries, in extending pardon to condemned and repentant criminals, in his ordinary dealings with men of the world and of business, in the pleasure with which he rewarded and praised the good deeds and the services of others, but also in the munificence of his charities, the generosity of his alms to the poor, his ardent affection, not only for his kindred, but also for his native country and his native city, and by his unbounded sympathy and support of the Church of which he was a devoted son. His magnanimous provisions out of the princely estates and revenues to which he was entitled, but which he never received, for the rescue of the Holy Sepulchre were in keeping with the grandeur of his soul and the expansiveness of his heart. No other single individual of all Christendom ever conceived so grand and munificent a plan of public benefaction. Not satisfied with his avowed intentions and efforts to carry this great scheme into effect during his lifetime, he made ample provision for it in his will. This trait of his character was also manifest in his relations with personal interests and with his methods of controlling and regulating the natural tendencies of men, especially in an adventurous age, toward self-aggrandizement. He has been accused of seeking through his great discovery the undue accumulation of wealth and estates. On the contrary, his demands never equalled his dues. Offices, dignities, titles, and estates he regarded as necessary to the support of his position before the world and in history, and so much was this the case that even in his days of pinching poverty he was compelled to keep up a state and dignity far beyond his actual means. Even when his fortunes were at their lowest ebb he insisted on all his rights, and would not commute them. All these things in a selfish and parsimonious man would seem grasping, but in Columbus they were merely the means by which he aspired to be generous, charitable, liberal, public-spirited, and munificent in his public and private benefactions. It would have been incongruous for a man of his pre-eminence to be content with rewards inadequate to the social, official, and public duties he had to perform. Is it just to accuse of a grasping disposition one who had designed to spend millions in restoring the Holy Land to Christendom, who provided not only for the poor of his own blood, but also for the relief of all the poor of his native city? Contrast if you will in this case the magnanimity of the subject with the sordid meanness of his own sovereign. In discovering new countries, he studied rather their availability for his country's good than any immediate gain or wealth to himself.

His loyalty was chivalrous, inexhaustible, and manly. While waiting on the action of his sovereigns to accept his proposals he went into the field to serve them in their wars. The first-fruits of all his achievements were generously laid at the feet of his king and queen, whose banner he was the first to raise in many distant lands and countries. His loyalty was not the fruit of royal favor, nor did it confine itself to periods of prosperity and public patronage, as is the case with politicians and public men of the modern school. No amount of wrongs, injustice, ingratitude, or neglect could wring from him a line or an expression of disloyalty. His admirable letters abound in the most devoted sentiments toward sovereign and country. This manly trait in the character of Columbus is forcibly portrayed in the following eloquent passage : " It is impossible to read the letter descriptive of his fourth and last voyage without the deepest sympathy, the occasional murmurings and half-suppressed complaints which are uttered in the course of this touching letter. These murmurings and complaints are wrung from the manly spirit of Columbus by sickness and sorrow ; and though reduced almost to the brink of despair by the injustice of the king, yet we find nothing harsh or disrespectful in his language to the sovereign. A curious contrast is presented to us. The gift of a world could not win the monarch to gratitude; the infliction of chains, as a recompense for that gift, could not provoke the subject to disloyalty. The same great heart which through twenty years of disappointment and chagrin gave him strength to beg and buffet his way to glory, still taught him to bear with majestic meekness the conversion of that glory to unmerited shame." *

With manly and robust virtues and traits of character there were united in Columbus many finer and more tender character-

---

.* R. H. Major's "Letters of Columbus," Hakluyt Society, London, 1847 ; " Memorials and Footprints of Columbus," by General James Grant Wilson, Bulletin Am. Geog. Soc., 1884, p. 168.

istics, such as would adorn the soul of the noblest woman and at
the same time refine that of the bravest man. Thus we observe
on all occasions in his conversations, letters, and actions a refined
sensibility, an exuberance of spirits, a chastened excitability,
quickness to receive immediate yet deep impressions, and a highly
poetic fancy. In keeping with these traits was his extraordinary
susceptibility to extreme paroxysms of grief; for we have on more
than one occasion, when his sense of wrong or misfortune or
injustice was greatest, seen him retire into his cabin at sea and
burst forth in copious tears, with heartrending sighs and groans;
or he would sink under his afflictions into a deep lethargy or rise
in heavenly vision, and receive thence most comfort, which he
recognized as coming from above; and again immediately thereafter he would appear upon the most active and stirring scenes
and events of human history, buoyant, gay, hopeful, confiding,
and generous. When Isabella received him with an outburst of
sympathy and gentleness, after he had been brought back to
Spain in chains, his heart was melted into grief and tenderness;
indignation gave way to softer emotions; sobs and tears in the
presence of the court relieved the wounded heart, and Columbus
again stood forth the noblest historic figure of his age. He was
always alive to impressions of joy or of grief, of friendship or of
anger, of pleasure or of indignation. There was a natural and
congenial friendship which bound together in unison the manly
soul of Columbus and the gentle and womanly heart of Isabella.

But in the character of Columbus religion made up the grand
staple of his manhood. His faith was childlike, yet intelligent,
aggressive, and heroic. Tender piety was conspicuous in his
every act, and his profound devotion sustained him in many a
crushing crisis. Such was his reliance upon divine Providence,
and such his gratitude to God for every success of his life, that
he seemed to hold perpetual converse with heaven. In all his
trials prayer was his chief consolation. His great discoveries
were always accompanied with public thanksgivings, and whenever he landed in a newly discovered country, he, first of all,
fell upon his knees to return thanks to God. His life of glory
and success was a perpetual *Te Deum!* In sorrow and affliction
the sad but appealing melody of the *Miserere* resounded in his
soul! How grand it was in mid-ocean, or when approaching
unknown and heathen lands, to hear resounding over the expanse

of waters the beautiful notes of the *Salve Regina* or other religious hymns at vesper time! Before starting out on the most perilous voyages he placed all under the protection and invocation of the Most Holy Trinity, and in the calendar of saints he had many patrons. To the Virgin Mother of God his devotion was as tender as that of a pious son. The names he gave to the islands and countries he discovered are but the records of his religious and devout emotions and grateful thanksgivings. To such a soul as his the gorgeous splendors of the Church and of her ritual were foretastes of the unspeakable glories and joys of heaven, of anthems sung by celestial choirs, of domes of majestic grandeur and endless vastness, of the beatific vision itself. Imaginative, theoretical, visionary, enthusiastic, and poetic as he was, his religious sentiments never lifted him beyond the human sympathies of real life, for he was charitable to the poor, sympathetic with the afflicted, affectionate to kindred, generous to the Church, and tender to his kind. Religion was depicted in his honest and sincere countenance, imparting to it a sombre expression of piety, an exalted dignity, a gentle benignity, a sober and sedate carriage, a trustful composure, and a reverential demeanor. In the midst of lewdness, lust, and infidelity he was continent and pure. His words were respectful, chaste, and considerate, and he never indulged in oaths, curses, irreverence, or levity. Such was the generosity of his nature that all the wrongs he suffered from men never embittered him against mankind. Such was his deep religious character and the fame of sanctity of his life, that some of his admirers have attributed miracles to him, and his earnest and sincere eulogist, the eloquent Count de Lorgues, and others have agitated the question of his canonization as a saint. Life was too short for such a man. Any one of the grand services I have mentioned as rendered by him to practical science was enough to immortalize his name. He cherished three great and exalted aspirations in addition to the many magnificent works he performed and services he rendered to his race—the discovery of the new world, the circumnavigation of the earth, and the redemption of the Holy Land from the hands of infidels and its restoration to Christendom. These were no visionary schemes. The last had been attempted with temporary but brilliant success by the combined Christian armies of Europe, under the sanction, appeals, and benedictions of the popes, leaving behind great moral effects. It has even now been partially accomplished for practical purposes by the opening of the accesses to Palestine and of the gates of Jerusalem to Christian pilgrims. An interesting fact attracts our notice here, the assignment of the holy places in Palestine to the guardianship of that seraphic order, the Franciscans—the very same who befriended Columbus in his earliest efforts to attempt the discovery of the new world, whose apostolic missionaries he introduced into America, to whom he was devotedly attached in life and in death, whose religious habit he wore in the streets of Seville, who attended him in his last moments, and interred his remains in their convent. This aspiration of the admiral may and certainly will be accomplished, under Providence, by the inevitable and evidently approaching dissolution of the Ottoman Empire, which now holds political jurisdiction over Judea.

The second grand aspiration of Columbus, the circumnavigation of the globe, under his leadership in revealing to mankind the geography and shape of the earth, and declaring it to be circumnavigable, and accomplishing in person a great part of the transit when it was unknown and perilous, has now become an affair of easy and familiar accomplishment, so that even a child now can start from New York or any other commercial city in the world, and make the tour of the earth in an almost incredibly small number of days.

The first great aspiration of Columbus was accomplished by himself, just as he had asserted that upon scientific data and principles it would be accomplished, and with unparalleled success. For as Cladera has so cogently expressed it, "His soul was superior to the age in which he lived. For him was reserved the great enterprise of traversing that sea which had given rise to so many fables, and of deciphering the mystery of his time." Not only did he accomplish this, but it was achieved by his personal and individual genius, by his energy and perseverance, his contempt of obstacles and opposition, and with means inadequate to so great an undertaking. Having discovered America in 1492, it was in the justice of God reserved for him also to be the discoverer of the continent. This last great achievement was executed by him in 1498; and here it is important to remark that for three years prior to this discovery of the continent by

Columbus, under the unjust sanctions and licenses given by King Ferdinand to private adventurers to sail to the countries discovered by Columbus, in violation of his rights, and although his enemy, Fonseca, at the head of the Indian Bureau, encouraged and stimulated such adventures, and even supplied copies of Columbus's map to them, not one of the bold and reckless mariners of his time was able to wrest this eminent distinction and well-merited glory from the admiral. He alone fully realized the vastness, the grandeur, and the value of his discovery, and of the pre-eminent dignities, offices, rights, estates, titles, revenues, and jurisdictions it conferred upon himself. The wily Ferdinand thought these latter were too great for any subject to possess, showing that while he, too, saw the vast empires and boundless wealth thus bestowed by a subject upon him and his successors, he was incapable of rewarding Columbus according to his merits or even in accordance with and in fulfilment of his promise. Of all men Columbus alone saw, with a vision peculiar to himself, the immensity of his achievement. It was the common and universal error of his age, in which he shared for want of time and means supplied for correcting it, as he would have done, that the countries he had discovered were the remotest parts of Asia. He had spent so many years of his life in the delays and opposition which beset him in high and low places, there was not afforded him sufficient time nor adequate means, even after the great discovery was accomplished, to continue his discoveries from the islands and the continents to the complete exploration of the earth and the perfect solution of the grand problems he had undertaken to unfold. Theoretically Columbus realized all in his mind and convictions, and yet his brightest fancies, his most soaring dreams, the most visionary flights of his fervid imagination never reached the knowledge of the full grandeur, the boundless development, the magnificent empires, the progress in arts and sciences, the political and constitutional liberty, the countless populations of civilized, enlightened, brave, and irrepressible nations, nor the financial, commercial, scientific, and political attainments that were to flow from the great discovery he had made. It was a rare sight to see one man alone struggling to solve those mighty problems now so familiar to us. Though the idea of the other ocean dawned upon his penetrating mind, yet little did he imagine then that the two oceans encircled continents wholly distinct and separate from the continents of the old world, equal to them in extent, more favored in their location, their natural resources and potential wealth, the richness of their soil, their inexhaustible mineral treasures, and destined in time to surpass them in arts and sciences, in civilization and constitutional government, in civil and religious liberty, the results of material development, and in the grandeur of their power and domains. Little did he then imagine that four hundred years thence, in 1892, mighty empires and republics, with their teeming millions possessing the magnificent world he had given mankind, would assemble in common with the other nations of the earth in this new world of his, and render, exultantly, an unequalled and an unprecedented homage to the name, to the genius, and to the unrivalled services of Christopher Columbus! Yet his enthusiastic spirit and his prophetic genius conceived an idea of future grandeur of the world he had disclosed to mankind. He realized them in extent and value, not in detail, as Asiatic, not as American. At times he seems to have seen all. To his intellect and heart may it be given, in other and better spheres, to see the discovery of these fair and majestic continents, as we see them now, crowned with all human development—the prophecy and the accomplishment!

NOTES.

I. Allusions having frequently been made in regard to supposed proceedings, instituted at Rome, for the canonization of Columbus, I have caused a direct inquiry to be made of the Sacred Congregation of Rites on this subject. The Right Rev. Monsignore O'Connell accordingly, at my request, addressed the following letter to His Eminence the Cardinal Secretary of the Congregation of Rites:

"YOUR EMINENCE: Mr. Richard H. Clarke, a distinguished American Catholic historical writer, is now, at the request of many Catholics, engaged in writing a defence of the life of Christopher Columbus, and begs me to inquire of the Sacred Congregation of Rites if the current report be true—to wit, that the Cause of Columbus was thrown out for the reason that, having abandoned his first lawful wife, he lived in concubinage with the second? Which, etc.
"D. J. O'CONNELL,
"*Rector of the American College, Via Umilta, 30.*"

To this letter His Eminence the Cardinal Secretary of the Sacred Congregation of Rites replied as follows:

"8 VIA S. APOLLINARE.

"The Sacred Congregation of Rites cannot treat of the Cause of Christopher Columbus till the diocesan processes be ended, and these have not thus far been begun."

Thus it is clear that the process for the canonization of Columbus has never been commenced, and consequently has never been decided.

II. The author announced in his prospectus that it was his intention to print the names of the subscribers in the work. But since that announcement the expression by the subscribers of a preference that this should not be done has reached us, and that preference is uniform. In deference, therefore, to the wishes of the subscribers themselves, I have concluded to omit the names.

INDEX.

Ælian, 61.
Affonso V., 35, 68.
Africa, 51-53, 57, 61.
African slavery, 402-405.
Aguado, Juan, 256, 321, 458-61, 480.
Alexander III., 18.
Alexander VI., 119, 222-25, 236.
Alfraganus, 60.
Aliaco, Cardinal, 63.
America, Name of, 394-402.
Anacaona, 315, 361, 544.
Antilla, 43, 44, 45, 65.
Antilles, 186.
Antipodes, 20.
Antonio, Nicolao, 103, 107.
Arana, Diego de, 112, 135, 146, 147, 161, 199, 245, 246.
Arana, Rodrigo de, 112.
Aranas, 101, 111, 112, 136, 146.
Aristotle, 44, 61.
Asia, 18, 57, 58, 59, 60, 61, 64, 65.
Astrolabe, 69.
Atlantic Ocean, 44, 60, 61, 65, 66, 160, 164.
Atlantis, 43, 61.
Augustine, St., 20.
Ave Maria, 191.
Ave Maris Stella, 170.
Azores, 43, 52, 60, 66.

Bahamas, 136.
Ballester, 368, 381, 411.
Bancroft, George, 21.
Barber family, 155.
Barrantes, 411.
Behaim, Martin, 69.
Behechio, 307.
Belloni, 129.
Belloy, Marquis de, 118.
Benedictines, 276.
Benjamin, Rabbi, 68.
Berardi, Juanato, 232.
Bethencourt, Jean de, 49.
Boabdil, 90, 94.
Bobadilla, 425-81.
Boggiasco, 25.
Boïl, Rev. B., 229, 249, 252, 271, 277, 300, 302, 313, 318.
Boyle, Father B., 272, 304.
Brandan, St., 45, 66.
Brazil, 241, 399.
Breviesca, the Jew, 344-46.
Bristol, 47.
Buldee, Raymond, 117.

Cabot, Sebastian, 167, 168, 215.
Cado, Fermin, 260, 263, 313.
Calvi, 25.
Cambalu, 59.
Canaries, 43, 44, 49, 60, 236.
Cancellieri, 104.
Cannibals, 237, 391.
Canonization, 124, 592, 596.
Caonabo, 242, 246, 247, 261, 263, 267, 305, 306-10.
Cape Bojador, 51, 52.
Cape Nun, 52.
Cape of Good Hope, 53, 57, 88.
Cape St. Vincent, 51, 66.
Cape Verde Islands, 50, 60.
Caribbean Islands, 237.
Caribs, 237, 241, 256.
Carillo, Diego, 319.
Carpini, 69.
Carvajal, 385-88.
Casseria, 25.
Catabanama, 546-50.
Carthaginians, 43, 45, 61.
Cathay, 41, 59, 64, 65.
Celer, Quintus Metellus, 62.
Centaurs, 263.
Chanca, Dr., 234, 248, 251, 257.
Charles V., 402.
Charles VIII., 297.
Chiavari, 25.
China, Northern, 64.
China, Southern, 59.
Church, The first, 259.
Cipango, 59, 65, 71, 171, 184, 187, 190.
Civezza, Marcellino, 116, 117, 145.
Clemencin, 94.
Cogoleto, 25.
Colmenar, Alvarez de, 118.
Colombo, Domenico, 25, 32, 42, 68.
Colombo family, 121, 122.
Colombos, Admirals, 29, 30, 32, 39, 45, 46.
Columbus, Bartholomew, 33, 88, 89, 110, 113, 124, 297, 298, 360-75, 501, 575.
Columbus, Christopher, birth, 24; birthplace, 24-51; portraits, 25; parents, 25; name, 26; baptism, 26; education, 26; trade, 27; his studies, 28; sailor, 29; early voyages, 29, 30; in Portugal, 32; Madeira, 33; first marriage, 36, 37; birth of son Diego, 38; death of first wife, 38; his hair turned gray, 39; voyage to Iceland, 38, 47; dates in his career, 39; voyages to Africa, 39, 48; draws maps, 42; at Lisbon, 42, 46, 56, 68, 88; his studies, 43-45; naval engagement, 46; Columbus and Prince Henry, 34-54; personal ap-

INDEX

pearance, 54; character, 54-56; broaches his ideas, 57; Toscanelli correspondence, 57-59; grounds of his proposals, 60-66; before John II.—his plan rejected, 71; treachery, 72; leaves Portugal, accusation refuted, 73-77; in Spain, 78; doubtful dates, 79; Convent of La Rabida, 79, 80; follows the court, 83; at Cordova, 82; Mendoza, Quintanella and Geraldini, 83; at court, 84; Council of Salamanca, 84-87; again follows the court, 87, 88; at Lisbon, 88; sends Bartholomew to England, 89; in Spain again, 89; summoned to Seville, 89; a soldier, 90; leaves the court, 92; at La Rabida, 92-94, 159; Juan Perez de Marchena, 92; summoned before Isabella, 93; at court, 94; negotiations, 94, 95; departure from court, 95; sent for and returns, 97; again at court, 97; terms accepted, 97, 98; ennobled, 98; Colon, 98; at Cordova, 100; Beatrix Enriquez de Arana, 101-57; second marriage, 101-57; question raised, 102; refuted, 100-57; thirty reasons sustaining second marriage, 111-27; his will, 145; first voyage, 158-77; at Palos, 159; sails from Palos, 162; discovers the magnetic point of no variations, 165-68; flight of birds, 172; sees a light on land, 174; land discovered, 175; the landing, 177-82; explorations, 184-95; desertion of Pinzon, 191; Cuba, 188; Hayti, 192; builds a fort at La Navidad, 199, 598; homeward voyage, 201; Pinzon's return, 202; in Portugal, 206; at Palos, 209; at Barcelona, 213; honors to Columbus, 217; anecdote of the egg, 217, 218; line of demarcation, 219-26; second expedition, 231; enmity of officials, 233; day of sailing, 235; discovers Caribbean Islands, 237; at Hispaniola, 242; sends Caribs to Spain, 256; mutiny, 260, 268; exploration of Hispaniola, 261; builds a fort, 263; distributes the army, 269; disaffection of Margarite and Boïl, 271; excommunication, 274; exploration of Cuba and Jamaica, 278-95; attack of lethargy, 296; return to Hispaniola, 297; sends Indians to Spain, 300; desertion of Boïl and Margarite, 304; rebellion of caciques suppressed, 305-11; Guamiquina, Indian name of Columbus, 309; capture of Caonabo, 309; conquest and tribute, 314; Aguado sent to Hispaniola, 321-25; returns to Spain, 325-32; accused at court, 326; gold discovered at Hayna, 326-29; arrival in Spain, 332; kindly received at court, 334; third voyage, 336-53; offered a principality, 337; establishes an entail by will, 338-40; delays, 341; insults, 344; discovers the continent, 349-59; theories on the shape of the earth, 356; at Hispaniola, 356-60, 376; Roldan's rebellion, 377-90, 411-15; slavery, 391-94, 402-405; Roldan and Ojeda, 411-15; rebellion of Moxica and Guevara, 416-19; despondency, 420, 421; hostility in Spain, 422-29; superseded by Bobadilla, 425-40; arrested and imprisoned by Bobadilla, 437-43; sent to Spain in chains, 441-43; sensation on his arrival, 443; his letter to the governess, 445; again at court, 447; 'the accusations, 448-55; infringements on his rights, 455-57; Bobadilla's administration, 457; Ovando in Hispaniola, 458-61; Columbus in Spain, 461-74; book of prophecies, 463-68; preparations for a fourth voyage, 468; Bank of St. George, 470; his signature, 471; fourth voyage, 475; Bobadilla and Roldan shipwrecked, 478-81; refused a shelter, 480; cruise in search of the inter-oceanic passage, 481-95; Veragua, 495-512; the hostile Quibian and Veraguans, 497-510; lethargy and vision, 510; departure from Veragua, 513; stranded on Jamaica coast, 516; *littera rarissima*, 518; revolt of Porras brothers, 525-29; delivered from exile, 539, 550; arrives at Hispaniola, 551; returns to Spain, 552; importunes the King, 554-73; end approaching, 575; his will, 575-77; death, 577; epitaph, 579; his remains, 578-81; his family, 582-84; character, 584-95.

Columbus, Diego, brother of Christopher, 42, 225, 226, 232, 234, 261, 298, 300, 319, 401, 431, 582, 583.
Columbus, Diego, son of Christopher, 38, 79, 113, 143, 159.
Columbus, Fernando, 48, 60, 66, 102, 113, 117, 121, 140, 141, 298.
Columbus, Luis, 583.
Continent discovered, 349-59.
Cordova, 82, 87, 100, 113, 114, 116, 123, 145.
Corêa, Pedro, 35, 66.
Cosmographiæ Introductio, 399.
Cuba, 188, 191, 278-95.
Cucarro, 25.

Dahlgren, Mrs. Admiral, 148.
Daly, Charles P., 25.
Dante, 63.
D'Arhues, 132.
Demarcation, Bull of, 219-26.
Desdemona, 137, 138, 148.
Deza, Diego de, 87, 91, 100.
Diaz, Bartholomew, 297.
Diaz, Bernal, 88.
Divina Commedia, 146.
Don, Title of, 159.
Dondero, A., 129, 142, 143.
Dragon's Mouth, 352.
Dublin Review, 27.
DuBois, Constance Goddard, 148.

Eleven thousand virgins, 240, 599.
Encomiendas, 391, 402.
England, 88, 89.
Enriquez, Beatrix, 101-57, 246, 274, 298.
Escobar, Rodrigo de, 161.
Europe, 61, 65.

Ferdinand and Isabella, 78, 81, 214, 227.
Ferdinand, King, 81, 89, 97, 100, 105, 229, 272, 554-73.
Fernandez, Garcia, 92, 96, 98.
Fiesco, Bartholomew, 523, 524, 533-35.
Finale, 25.
Fiske, John, v., 75, 224, 276, 393, 404.
Fonseca, Juan de, 228, 230, 233, 234, 412, 415.
Fort St. Thomas, 263, 264, 266.

INDEX. 599

France, 89, 92.
Funchal, 38, 40, 43.

Gama, Vasco de, 52.
Garcia, Alphonso, 116, 148.
Garcia, Gil, 234.
Genoa, 25-27, 67, 78.
Geraldini, 83, 100.
Gibraltar, 64.
Granada, 90, 91, 93.
Greenland, 17.
Grotius, Hugo, 62.
Guacanagari, 194-201, 236, 242-51, 306-12.
Guamiquina, 309.
Guatiquana, 307.
Guarionex, 308, 360-70.

Harrisse, 73.
Hayna Mines discovered, 326.
Hayti, 192, 193-201, 241.
Herrera, Antonio de, 118, 139.
Higuey, 545-50.
Hispaniola, 146, 192, 241, 266-70.
Homer, 25.
Humboldt, 108, 131, 133, 148.

Iceland, 15, 47.
India, 52, 61.
Indians, 178, 227, 265, 266, 364-66, 402-405, 541-50.
Indies, Council of, 227.
Innocent, Pope, IV., 69.
Inter Cetera, Bull of, 222.
Irving, Washington, 20, 107, 148, 223.
Isabella, 79, 83, 96, 97, 114, 115, 229, 258, 557-62.
Isabella, City of, 252-56, 259, 557-62.

Jamaica, 285, 291.
Japan, 59.
John II., 69, 70-72, 88, 89, 227, 230.
Julius II., 567.

Kenrick, Francis Patrick, 223.
Khan, Grand, 19, 56, 59, 186.
Khan, Kayuk, 18, 19.
Knight, Father A. G., 27, 105.

La Cosa, Juan de, 232.
Lactantius, 20.
Las Casas, Bishop Bartolomé, v., 27, 232, 393, 396, 401, 402-405.
Las Casas, Francesco, 232.
Lazzaroni, M. A., 118, 129, 141.
Ledesma, Pedro, 508, 537, 538.
Lisbon, 33, 40.
Lœtus, Pomponius, 215.
Longfellow, 63.
Lorgues, Roselly de, v., 21, 79, 133, 134, 139.
Louis, St., 18.
Lud, Walter, 398.
Luxan, Juan de, 264.

Machico, 35, 36, 43.
Madeira, 33, 50.
Maldonado, M., 234, 251.
Mandeville, Sir John, 64, 68.

Maney, Regina, 34, 76.
Mangi, 59, 65.
Manicatex, 311.
Maps: Ptolemy, 41; Marco Polo, 41; Mauro, 41.
Marchena, Antonio de, 231, 252, 259.
Marchena, Juan Perez de, 79, 94.
Margarite, Pedro, 232, 256, 264, 266, 271, 302, 313, 318.
Marine Pulmonate, 15, 19.
Marque, Diego, 238.
Marriage, Law of, 125, 129; at Common Law, 156.
Martyr, Peter, 216, 254.
Mayobanex, 372-76.
Mayorazgo, 120.
Medina Celi, 79, 100, 123.
Medina Sidonia, 79, 100, 123.
Mediterranean, 27, 28.
Mela, Pomponius, 17, 62.
Mendez, Diego, 501-12, 517, 522-30, 533-35, 539.
Mendoza, Cardinal, 83, 92-93, 100, 217.
Missionaries, 229.
Moniz, 27, 34.
Moniz, Philippa Moniz de Perestrello de Mello, 34, 37, 38, 39, 73, 77, 143, 144.
Moniz, Vasco Martius, 35, 36.
Monteno, Mariana, 27.
Moors, 45, 49, 87, 93.
Moquer, 161, 162.
Moya, Marchioness de, 93, 94, 96.

Napione, Galeani, 104, 149.
Navarrete, M. F. de, 105, 106, 119, 149.
Navidad, La, 199, 242-47.
Needle, Magnetic, 165-68.
Nepos, Cornelius, 62.
Nino, P. A., 161.
Northmen, vi., 17, 47.
Novus Mundus, 395-400.

Ojeda, Alonzo de, 231, 238, 255, 305, 306, 308, 411-15.
Olano, Sebastian de, 234.
Oneglia, 25.
Orinoco, 354.
Othello, 137, 148.
Ovando, 458-61, 531-33, 539, 540-50.
Oviedo, 139.
Ozema River, 326, 360.

Palestine, 69.
Palma y Freytas, 104, 121.
Palos, 93, 160-62.
Pane, Roman, 265.
Papal Power, 222-25.
Paria, 353.
Parillas, P. S. de, 143.
Pavia, University of, 26, 27.
Peñasola, 160.
Pereira, Gabriel, 34, 66.
Perestrello, 27, 34.
Peschel, 393.
Pinelo, Francisco, 228, 230.
Pinilla, 160.

INDEX.

Pinzons, 92, 160, 161, 163, 191-211, 318.
Pisa, Bernal Diaz de, 234, 260.
Plato, Dialogues of, 16, 43, 61.
Pliny, 62.
Polo, Marco, 18, 19, 41, 58, 59, 64, 65, 68.
Ponce de Leon, 232.
Popes, Temporal power of, 222-25.
Porras brothers, 525, 529, 535-39.
Porto Santo, 35, 66.
Portuguese voyages, 41, 42, 51-53, 56, 57, 68, 300.
Pradella, 25.
Prado, Prior of El, 79, 84.
Prescott, W. H., 21.
Prester John, 18, 56, 69.
Prince Henry the Navigator, 34, 50-53, 68.
Ptolemy, 17, 41, 47, 58, 60.
Pulci, 63.

Queen's Gardens, 288.
Quibian, 496-508.
Quinsai, 59.
Quintanella, 83, 94, 95, 96, 100.
Quintero, Cristoval, 161, 163.
Quinto, 25.

Rabida, Convent of, 79, 131.
Rascon, Gomez, 161.
Repartimientos, 408, 543.
Ringmann, 398.
Roldan, Bartholomew, 161, 163, 233, 367-71, 377-90, 406, 411-19, 478-81.
Romans, Marriage among the, 141.
Rubruquis, 69.
Ruiz, Sancho, 161.

Saint Dié, 397-400.
Salamanca, 84-87, 91.
Salve Regina, 170, 191, 237.
Sanchez, Alonzo, 218.
Sanchez, Roderigo, 161.
Saragosso Sea, 170.
San Salvador, 177.
Santa Fé, 93, 95, 97.
Santangel, Luis de, 94, 95, 96.
Savona, 25.

Seneca, 61, 62.
Sepulchre, Holy, 90, 99.
Serpent's Mouth, 351.
Seven Cities, 44, 66.
Seville, 89, 91.
Shakespeare, 139.
Shelford on Marriage, 127, 141.
Slavery, 391, 402-405.
Smith, J. Toulman, 62.
Soria, Juan de, 228, 230, 233.
Spain, 78, 140.
Spotorno, 105, 149.
St. Elmo, 237.
Strabo, 17, 61.
Swift v. Kelly, 129.
Talavera, 84, 87, 91, 94, 98.
Tarducci, 25.
Tennyson, 24, 25.
Terrarossa, 25.
Toledo, Maria de, 112.
Torquemada, 132.
Torres, Antonio, 297, 319.
Toscanelli, Dr. Paul, 19, 39, 42, 57, 65.
Trent, Council of, 126, 127, 128, 141.

Ursula, St., 240.

Vaz, Tristan, 35, 52.
Vega, Royal, 262, 266.
Venice, 67, 78.
Veragua, 437-514.
Vespucius, Americus, 232, 395-402, 564, 565.
Vincenti, Martin, 65.

Waldseemüller, 397.
Warner, Lord and Lady, 155.
Wheaton, 224.
Winsor, Justin, v., vi., 20, 66, 73, 98, 99, 168, 391, 394.

Xaragua, 543-45.

Yucatan, 482, 483.

Zarco, João Gonçalves, 35, 52.
Zuniga, 139.

THE END.

www.ingramcontent.com/pod-product-compliance
Lightning Source LLC
Chambersburg PA
CBHW021228300426
44111CB00007B/469